PSYCHOLOGY

PSYCHOLOGY

A Contemporary Introduction

Peter Scott &
Christopher Spencer

Open University and University of Sheffield

BLACKWELL
Publishers

Copyright © Blackwell Publishers Ltd, 1998

First published 1998

2 4 6 8 10 9 7 5 3 1

Blackwell Publishers Inc.
350 Main Street
Malden, Massachusetts 02148

Blackwell Publishers Ltd
108 Cowley Road
Oxford OX4 1JF
UK

Library of Congress Cataloging-in-Publication Data

Scott, Peter, 1946–
    Psychology : a contemporary introduction / Peter Scott and
 Christopher Spencer.
        p.   cm.
    Includes bibliographical references and index.
    ISBN 0-631-19234-4 (alk. paper). — ISBN 0-631-19235-2 (pbk. :
 alk. paper)
    1. Psychology.   I. Spencer, Christopher (Christopher P.)
 II. Title.
 BF121.S385   1988
 150—dc21   97-16961
                                                                       CIP

British Library Cataloguing in Publication Data

A CIP catalogue record for this book is available from the British Library.

Typeset in 10 on 13 pt Palatino
by Ace Filmsetting Ltd, Frome, Somerset
Printed in Great Britain by T.J. International, Padstow, Cornwall

This book is printed on acid-free paper.

Contents in Brief

Contents

Plates

Figures

Tables

Boxes

Contributors

Mark Blades, University of Sheffield (Chapters 2 and 15)
Jill Boucher, University of Sheffield (Chapter 2)
Richard Byrne, University of St Andrews (Chapter 4)
Nik Chmiel, University of Sheffield (Chapter 17)
Helen Cowie, Roehampton Institute, London (Chapter 3)
Alan Garnham, University of Sussex (Chapter 9)
Mike Harris, University of Birmingham (Chapter 6)
Rod Nicolson, University of Sheffield (Chapter 8)
Sheina Orbell, University of Sheffield (Chapter 11)
Alan J. Parkin, University of Sussex (Chapter 7)
Peter Scott, Open University (Chapters 1, 10 and 18)
Paschal Sheeran, University of Sheffield (Chapter 11)
Pauline Slade, University of Sheffield (Chapter 16)
Peter K. Smith, Goldsmith's College, London (Chapters 2 and 3)
Christopher Spencer, University of Sheffield (Chapters 1, 12, 13, 14 and 18)
Robin Stevens, University of Nottingham (Chapter 5)
Graham Turpin, University of Sheffield (Chapter 16)

Acknowledgements

The editors and publishers gratefully acknowledge the following for permission to reproduce copyright material:

Ablex Publishing Co. Inc., fig. 2.5; Academic Press Inc., figs. 7.7, 7.13, 7.16, 7.19 (a) (b), 15.7; Aldine de Gruyter, fig. 3.4; Allyn & Bacon figs. 5.4, 5.9, 5.10, 5.11, 5.17, 5.18, 5.25, 15.2; American Psychological Association figs. 2.9, 2.11, 15.1; Brooks/Cole Publishing Company figs. 5.8, 5.12, 5.13, 5.24; Cambridge University Press figs. 2.8, 2.13, 2.15, 7.10; W H Freeman & Co., fig. 3.3; HarperCollins Inc., fig. 7.1; Houghton Mifflin Company fig. 2.1; Macmillan Publishing Co. Inc., fig. 5.27; © Masson Editeur, Paris, 1981 fig. 8.7; Methuen/Reed Books Ltd, fig. 15.6; Oxford University Press, figs. 4.14, 6.10; McGraw-Hill Publishers Inc., figs. 6.8, 6.21, 6.30, 6.32, 6.35; Scientific American figs. 5.16 (© Albert Miller), 5.20 (© Ian Worpole), 8.6 (© Tom Prentiss), 5.22; Taylor & Francis fig. 8.3; Society for Research in Child Development, The University of Michigan, fig. 2.20; Worth Publishers, Inc., figs. 5.5 5.6, 5.14, 5.21, 5.23

The publishers apologize for any errors or omissions in the above list and would be grateful to be notified of any corrections that should be incorporated in the next edition or reprint of this book.

PART 1

Introduction

CHAPTER 1

Introduction to Psychology

Peter Scott and Christopher Spencer

CHAPTER AGENDA

- In this chapter we start to help you think about why you are reading this book and what you can expect to get out of it.

- We present a picture of a young and exciting discipline which does not so much aim to provide you with the right answers, but rather to help you to think more clearly about the right questions.

- We discuss psychology as a scientific discipline where theories should drive investigations, and where experiments provide evidence that can be used to look back and refine those theories.

- We briefly explain some of the terminology that psychologists use in their investigations.

- Some ethical considerations are introduced, and we emphasize the importance of maintaining a critical appraisal of the ethical stance of psychological research.

- Finally, through the structure of the book, we illustrate how the approaches of different sorts of psychologists might be viewed.

▓ Why are you Reading this Book? ▓

Welcome!

If you are reading this volume, it could be:

That you are skimming through in the bookshop, to find out what psychology is all about;
Or you have already decided to take a course in psychology, and you want an up-to-date guide;
Or, someone else has selected this as your course's set text;
Or, you are in a later year of a course, now studying the subject and its separate areas in some detail, and want to be reminded how it all fits together: surrounded by trees, and looking for the wood.

Whatever your purpose, we hope that we can serve your needs: we are not presuming that you have any prior knowledge of the subject; we aim to be as up-to-date as the publication process allows; we have written this as a stand-alone text, which can, none the less, with its apparatus (the teacher's guide, exercises, overheads and so on) form the focus of a taught course. We have our opinions about how the whole, diverse field that is contemporary psychology fits together; and where it at present has gaps; so we can offer the first-timer and the wood-seeker an overview, a plan, into which to fit your later-gained knowledge.

Some people will be taking a degree course in psychology; others will be including aspects of psychology as one component in their programme of study: psychology after all has implications for a wide range of other disciplines, from anthropology and sociology to engineering and architecture. And many professional courses have (or should have) a consideration of the relevant areas of psychology: you will realize the relevance for nurses and social workers, for police training and probation. There are textbooks in areas as diverse as archaeology, economics, literature and artificial intelligence which refer one back to the core understandings of human thought and behaviour. We hope therefore that, although we have constructed this book to integrate across its chapters, people will also be able to select those sections which are most closely associated with their interests beyond psychology.

This much can be said for most textbooks introducing psychology. What in particular are our aims in offering you this introduction?

Ours is an avowedly European-based text; it takes up a challenging stance on many issues; and should leave you with the feeling of an unfolding, continuing, and strongly evidence-based subject.

Let us explain:

North American research is a very dominant cultural influence in psychology. This is evident in all texts, including this one. However, we aim to emphasize European perspectives in the sense that, in some fields of the subject, the European research tradition has added distinct strands to this prevailing culture (which don't always make it into American texts). Thus, to give an example, you will find a particular emphasis on European research themes in our chapters on developmental and social psychology: such as theory of mind, social identity, non-verbal communication. In the same way, we have deliberately neglected many issues that are often seen as essentials in the North American basic texts and tried to avoid an encyclopaedic temptation – to focus, instead, at a useful level of detail on the issues we feel are the most important.

'Challenging stance' refers to the style of argument we believe is vital in approaching our discipline. Some texts obviously feel that any subject should be presented as simply and straightforwardly as possible: 'the causes of X are a, b and c'. Yet any researcher in the field will tell you that such statements are invariably both too bald and too definite. X may be generally associated with a; but this relationship can be modified by the presence or absence of factors b and c. And, we might add, we also suspect that this is only part of the story! Human behaviour is generally complex, multicausal and affected by biological, social, and cultural factors to some degree, generally with a good dash of random happenstance. For example, there are sociobiological factors which can start to explain why 'altruistic' behaviour occurs in our species; cultural prescriptions which may partly indicate rules for helping people; and social situational factors which demonstrably affect whether we actually do help someone who we understand to be in need. All of these could be put together into an inclusive predictor model: and yet it has been shown in studies of who helps in real-life emergencies, such as a big fire, that 'simply being there' at the scene of the action is as powerful an explanator as any of these other factors.

By 'evidence-based' we mean that understanding any aspect of psychology means understanding the range of theories that can be used to account for that aspect, and show how these have been derived from and then tested against a set of observations – the evidence. We discuss below how that evidence can be gathered from the complementary perspectives of different sorts of psychologist.

Most importantly, we want you to understand that life, human behaviour and feelings are complex and variable (you know that anyway!), and that as a consequence psychology should not be expected to offer very simple models.

▨ Aims and Approaches of the Book ▨

This introduction to psychology is unusual in that we start with the human lifespan: many texts tuck their consideration of human development somewhere in their middle sections; and worse still, would appear to think that the development of the individual ceases at adolescence!

In contrast, we believe that the whole lifespan, from infancy (and before) to old age, deserves full treatment; for, in a real sense, it provides the agenda for all else that is to follow in the text. In giving an account of how the individual develops, we necessarily have to call upon the biological, cognitive, social, environmental and health traditions within psychology; and we realize how they should interrelate. In sheer 'human interest' terms, we also feel that you would be keen to start with the developing child, and work your way into psychology (via adolescence, adulthood and old age). All the rest will then follow as you wish to find out more: what are the neurological developments which underlie the visible changes in the child's behaviour? How do the senses work, to give the child knowledge of what lies beyond?

From this, it is natural to lead you out into chapters on the cognitive world of the individual: learning, memory, reasoning and that tool of thought and communication, language.

These basic processes give the individual increasing mastery of the social world, via what we call 'social cognition'. This world has its own rules and roles, which link social identification and group processes. And all of this has a physical environmental, as well as a social environmental, context.

But up until now in the text, we will not have focused upon the development of differences between individuals: so the succeeding chapters redress that balance, considering first differences in personality and then in intelligence.

And finally, we come to applied areas in psychology: what of the individual in health and illness? And what of the individual's role in the world of work? Some texts have erected clear boundaries between the areas of disorders and health: we feel that it is a truer and more helpful approach to consider what these two have in common for a general introduction to psychology. (Were you to wish to study towards a postgraduate professional qualification in health or clinical psychology, then of course you would extend this treatment of the two areas very considerably.)

How Psychology Conducts Research

In a subject as diverse as psychology (where topics of study range in scale from the functioning of the nervous system to the social psychology of the crowd), you will hardly be surprised that we use a wide range of methods of research. What you may less expect is that, within topic areas, there can also be some considerable differences in methods used – for example, two developmental psychologists studying children's understanding: one might conduct their research by naturalistic, long-term observations of a single child in her or his everyday setting; whereas the second psychologist would devise a test situation in a laboratory. The working of the visual system, to take another example, might be tested by seeing under what circumstances we are susceptible to visual illusions; equally, one can use computer programs to model the information flow from retina to cortex that enables the viewer of sense data to interpret the world around them.

As you will discover, psychology uses this variety of research approaches to complement each other: data from one method may be most appropriate to ask one kind of question; while another question would demand a different method. In this section we will discuss some of the methodological terminology that you will encounter in this book.

QUANTITATIVE METHODS, in which one may count quantities and use statistical support to evaluate one's findings, have prevailed in many areas of the subject; but many psychologists have now seen the role of QUALITATIVE METHODS as giving insights into human experience and behaviour that a quantitative approach cannot give. Social psychology provides perhaps the clearest example of how recently this realization has come about. Until the 1990s, very few social-psychology journals would carry anything but quantitative research: social phenomena typically being studied 'from the outside' by observing behaviours, often in tightly controlled laboratory situations, and counting outcomes. Few such studies would find out what the participants (referred to formally as SUBJECTS) had thought about the test situation, let alone asked them to offer their own musings on life. Now a range of qualitative approaches, in which one can explore the quality of the experience of people, are highly regarded as scientifically useful – indeed as a

QUANTITATIVE METHODS

QUALITATIVE METHODS

SUBJECTS

5

valuable complement to the quantitative and statistical methods.

As we give a very brief introduction to some of the methods currently in use in psychology, see how each could be complemented by the others. See what research questions are best addressed by each; see whether the limitations of each can be patched over by a different method with its different strengths.

▒ Science in psychology ▒

When we describe psychology as a science we mean that it is based upon forms of EVIDENCE that can be inspected and questioned publicly. This public treatment of forms of evidence, which in psychology are most usually observations, is called EMPIRICAL. Of course, the collection of evidence in itself is not sufficient for a science – the purpose of working with evidence is to build and test theories. A THEORY is a coherent collection of principles which can be used to explain some phenomenon. Most theories in science tend to relate to the causes of things, but in psychology a substantial proportion of theories are also related to the mechanisms by which things work. Good theories are simple, elegant and economical with the mechanisms they propose to be involved with some phenomenon.

Most importantly a theory must make predictions that can themselves be tested with respect to evidence. These predictions are called HYPOTHESES. According to the philosopher Karl Popper (1934) an essential feature of scientific method is that theories should be FALSIFIABLE – that is, that theories should be capable of generating hypotheses that show them to be false. Popper's ideas about science and the debate about how it currently does, and ideally should, work are discussed further in chapter 9.

Experimental methods

An hypothesis is usually used to critically identify how some features of the phenomenon will vary according to the theory. These features are therefore called variables. Some of the variables in a situation will depend directly on how that situation is manipulated – called DEPENDENT VARIABLES. The variables that take some part in the manipulation are called INDEPENDENT VARIABLES. The most common type of situation that scientists seek to manipulate is called an experiment. In an experiment, one tries to manipulate a range of variables (independent) to observe how this effects the (typically one) dependent variable. An abstract description of empirical experimentation can be quite hard to follow, so let us continue introducing the terminology with a specific example.

Clever Hans was a horse famed for his intelligence.

Hans was clever in that his owner, a Mr von Osten, had taught him to respond to a wide variety of questions – in mathematics, history, geography, etc. Hans' responses were hoof taps – and so mostly the questions were of a true–false type, but his intelligent behaviour was striking. If you asked Hans to take 2 from 5 he would be able to tap his hoof 3 times. It took a few experiments before the psychologist Oskar Pfungst was able to reject his owner's theory (that Hans

Margin terms: EVIDENCE · EMPIRICAL EVIDENCE · THEORY · HYPOTHESES · FALSIFIABLE THEORY · DEPENDENT VARIABLES · INDEPENDENT VARIABLES

understood the *stimuli* – the questions, and could do mathematics!) in favour of a more economical theory.

In Pfungst's (1911) experiments, the *dependent variable* was the behaviour of the horse – hoof taps. The obvious first theory to test was that there was some deliberate manipulation of the horse's behaviour by the owner. An obvious hypothesis related to this theory would be that the owner was able in some way to directly cue the horse about the correct response. So Mr von Osten (an *independent variable*) was excluded from the experiment. Clever Hans remained clever.

This empirical manipulation was able to reject the simple fraud hypothesis – Mr von Osten was an honest man. Pfungst's next experiment involved blindfolding the horse – and suddenly Hans' clever behaviour was gone. Mr von Osten's theory too was rejected. Further careful study revealed that Hans was indeed clever, but not at mathematics or history, he actually seemed to be able to intelligently interpret very subtle and unconscious cues in the audience. The audience (who did know the right answer) behaved subtly differently, a nod, exhale of breath, or tense anticipation, when the right answer – in terms of hoof taps – was reached!

This more economical theory turns out to be consistent with a theory of learning called conditioning that you will find out more about in chapter 8 – Hans had been trained to associate a food reward with behaviour even his trainer didn't spot!

Experiments can be conducted in the laboratory or in the field. FIELD EXPERIMENTS are usually more naturalistic in that they are in less danger of distorting the evidence by taking the phenomenon out of its context. LABORATORY EXPERIMENTS are usually far from natural, but can make up for this in allowing the much more careful control of the different variables that might be involved in the phenomenon. The Russian researcher Pavlov (1927) whose work is discussed in chapter 8, was noted for his scrupulous control over independent variables – his animal work took place in temperature, light-controlled and even soundproofed lab conditions.

FIELD EXPERIMENTS

LABORATORY EXPERIMENTS

Self-report methods

Most psychological experimentation takes place with people rather than animals, and whilst the controlled experiment is just as valuable, people can be invited to add something about the quality of their experience via a SELF-REPORT of some kind: through an interview or survey, a test, introspection, think-aloud protocols, or even a diary study.

SELF-REPORT

Usually the most formal kind of self report is the TEST; this is normally highly quantitative in nature, as subjects' responses are tightly controlled. In chapter 15 we will examine in some detail the range of tests which are sometimes used as measures of relative intelligence – the intelligence quotient or IQ.

TEST

The most informal kind of self-report is called INTROSPECTION and the data that it produces is usually very qualitative. In introspection a subject is invited to speculate about their cognitive states and processes. Why not try this yourself –

INTROSPECTION

say a little about how you are reading this book . . . what do you think are the processes that happen in your head during reading?

As you will soon discover, with a little introspection comes the significant problem that most interesting cognitive states and processes are simply not available to this sort of conscious inspection – indeed the very act of thinking about them in this way may change them. Nor indeed are your introspections available to public inspection (which we offered above as one of the key features of a science), so one cannot verify or replicate any evidence that you offer from this source.

THINK-ALOUD PROTOCOL

A more useful source of data is called a THINK-ALOUD PROTOCOL, which can superficially seem similar to an introspection, but for which one may not speculate about process, (Ericsson and Simon 1993). Instead of thinking *how* you do something just say out loud *what* you are aware of thinking. So . . . look out of a convenient window and say out loud what you see. What you say (if you don't try to talk about how you are saying it!) quite possibly relates to what you are thinking at the time and can be used, in carefully managed situations, to reflect somewhat on the contents of your conscious mind. Protocol studies usually collect behaviour in an experimental or at least highly controlled setting, but one

DIARY STUDY

naturalistic complement to this is the DIARY STUDY. In this, subjects are asked to make their own recordings of their behaviour, feelings or whatever by keeping a log in a diary. In both cases, the data can be analysed in either qualitative or quantitative ways as appropriate – the researcher might seek to classify diary entries or protocol statements and then count them in some quantified method or to take some samples to illuminate a particular quality of the data.

Qualitative approaches can range from analyses of texts and conversations to focus groups and interviews. When you consider studies like the 'Robber's Cave' (Sherif and Sherif 1953) in chapter 12 you will see some of the richness of a quali-

OBSERVATIONAL APPROACH

tative OBSERVATIONAL APPROACH to human behaviour. The Sherifs' thorough and detailed accounts of the social dynamics of the interactions of a group of 12-year-old boys at an American summer camp provides extremely useful data to help us study issues such as leadership and group cohesion. This work is also an

CASE STUDY

example of a type of CASE STUDY, in which one particular example of a phenomenon is studied in great detail. Some very striking studies of this nature are the in-depth analyses of individuals suffering from amnesia that are reported in chapter 7. These detailed case studies of memory impairment involve batteries of quantitative tests and qualitative interviews.

The interview range of instruments is a very flexible set of tools in social research, but requires a great deal of skill on the part of the researcher to be used

STRUCTURED INTERVIEW

effectively. As a set of question-asking instruments it ranges on a continuum of structure and scale. A face-to-face set of questions posed to a subject is called an

OPEN-ENDED INTERVIEW

interview and can be fairly STRUCTURED or more OPEN-ENDED. A less personal version of the interview which is highly structured and usually intended for a larger

QUESTIONNAIRE

collection of subjects is called a QUESTIONNAIRE; whilst the least personal version,

SURVEY

usually an even more structured type of questionnaire, is referred to as a SURVEY.

Simulations in psychology

A final method in the psychologist's armoury, that stands in great contrast to the range of qualitative techniques just discussed, is that of simulation. As you will see, particularly in the cognitive Part 4, some psychologists are making increasing use of computer and statistical modelling techniques. These psychologists argue that while both qualitative exploratory data and quantitative empirical data can help refine a theory – one natural way to fully test any coherent theory is to build a working model of it! So in chapter 10 on language we find psychologists examining simulations as models that exhibit linguistic behaviour, and in chapter 8 (on learning) we can directly compare our learning to that of working models that actually appear to learn.

▨ Ethics in Psychological Research ▨

It is vital to remember that human participants in any psychological investigation, regardless of the methodology used, are more than simply subjects – they are people whose rights should be protected. Much of the time a reasonable application of common sense will help in discussing the ethics of any proposed study – does what is proposed properly protect the participant's psychological well-being, health, values and dignity? If any of these may be compromised by the proposed work, can the likely scientific benefit possibly justify this? These days (although it was not always so) professional psychologists invariably submit their proposed programme of investigation to some formal ethical approval – often embodied in some sort of ethics committee. This is not the end of the story of course and does not make the study ethical, but is a vital safeguard in any research setting. As you go through this text you might consider the ethical soundness of each study.

The current British Psychology Society 'Ethical Principles for Conducting Research with Human Participants' has a number of sections which are important for us to consider here, including Consent; Deception; Debriefing; Withdrawal; Confidentiality; Protection; Observation; and Advice.

Consent and withdrawal are quite complementary. A participant should CONSENT to the study and this includes being fully informed about the nature of the work. In the same way, they retain the right to their 'data', in that they should be able to WITHDRAW their consent at any time and have any data pertaining to them, not merely excluded from analysis, but destroyed. In some ways a subject is deceived when they are not fully informed about the nature of the experiment. However, because many investigations have a cognitive aspect that can be changed by conscious effort this restriction is often relaxed in favour of a full and effective debriefing. The subject must be DEBRIEFED after any session in which they could not be fully informed about the nature of the study before it commenced. Debriefing provides a useful yardstick in helping to evaluate the use of deception, in that any deception which would cause the participant to show

CONSENT

WITHDRAWAL

DEBRIEFING

unease or wish to withdraw after the debriefing is unacceptable.

CONFIDENTIALITY

It is important that the participant's CONFIDENTIALITY is protected in the storage and use of their data. Certainly any publication of data should be in such a way that no individual participant can be identified. The investigation should PRO-

PROTECTION

TECT the participant from any risk of physical or mental harm and, particularly in observation, should protect their privacy. Observational research, without a strong case for consent and debriefing etc., is only acceptable where participants might normally expect to be observed by strangers anyway, such as in clear view in public spaces.

ADVICE

Psychologists must be very cautious about giving ADVICE to participants in a study unless they are qualified to do so, but where an investigation gives rise to evidence of mental or physical problems, of which they may be unaware, there is some ethical obligation to ensure that qualified advice is given.

INTENTIONAL
DECEPTION

The role of INTENTIONAL DECEPTION in psychological research is probably the thorniest of these ethical issues. When you come to chapter 12 and studies of conformity like those of Asch (1956) and Milgram (1974), the role of deception is striking and it is important to ask how each would be viewed today. Both these researchers intentionally deceived subjects using confederates (other participants who appeared to be subjects, but were themselves part of the design). In Asch's case the confederates gave publicly wrong answers so that Asch could observe if the real subjects conformed to these clearly incorrect responses. This was certainly confusing to the real subject and for some of them a stressful experience. Very much more strikingly, in the Milgram studies, the confederates acted out a fellow subject in considerable distress – being 'the victim' of the real subject's apparent actions (a fake electric shock). It is clear from his reports that Milgram's subjects themselves suffered real stress during the experiment and their mental well-being was most clearly compromised. Both Asch and Milgram went to considerable pains to ensure that subjects were properly debriefed after the study, but the main defence of this sort of work is that the scientific gain outweighs the cost to the participant. On this, as with other studies that follow, we leave you to judge.

In animal research, this latter question – does the proposed scientific gain justify this investigation – is the principal point for discussion. Animal work is very important in the approach of biological psychologists for a number of reasons: some animals can provide genetic insights because they have a controllable genetic heritage and breed relatively rapidly; some animals' physiological and, in particular, neural function is very similar to that of humans; and even some animal social behaviours can be usefully compared to our own. When you read about genetics in chapter 4 you should know that much of this very basic understanding of ourselves derives from varieties of animal work. For instance, many fruit flies have been bred in psychology labs over the years so that researchers can rapidly interbreed them to explore certain genetic characteristics. When you come to neuroscience in chapter 5 you will see that much of our insight into the human brain relies upon basic biological investigations in animals. Similarly with some of the work in chapter 6 on perception – the electrodes used by researchers like Hubel and Wiesel (1959, 1979), to help us understand the basic mechanism of vision, were in the retinal cells of cats and monkeys. Biological psychologists argue that this basic research has led to significant advances, not just in our academic understanding of our bodies and brains but also in the practical treatment of human disorders and dysfunction. Now, we can hardly expect you to look critically at the empirical claims and theories of psychologists without also asking you to look critically at these methodological claims. As with the human ethical issues, you should be asking if this investigation could be done just as effectively in some other, possibly non-invasive way. And, whether the gain justifies the cost.

▨ The Structure of the Book ▨

To understand how we have chosen to structure this text, and to prepare you for each section, it is useful to look at the labels that psychologists use for themselves.

A number of labels are used to distinguish different sorts of psychologist under the broad umbrella of the discipline. The four key academic labels are usually: developmental psychologists; biological psychologists; cognitive psychologists; and social psychologists. Most typically, you will find these descriptions used for academics who work in a university setting. These will probably be people who have gained an undergraduate degree in psychology, who have gone on to some specialist postgraduate qualification (such as a Ph.D.), and then moved on to teaching and research in their speciality.

Beyond these core factions are a variety of other, more specialist groups, such as criminal psychologists, educational psychologists, clinical psychologists, and occupational psychologists. The criminal psychologist works closely with law enforcement and rehabilitation agencies. In a prison context, for example, a typical day might see her working with offenders on their rehabilitation programme. The educational psychologist is typically employed by an education authority to assist in the smooth running of the school system – a typical day, for instance, might see her working with children (and teachers!) with special needs. Clinical psychologists often work with people in a therapeutic role to assist them, and those around them, with psychological disorders. Occupational psychologists usually work in industries and as consultants to improve the experience and productivity of workers and the commercial process. Usually these applied workers are psychologists by virtue of their undergraduate training who have gone on to some relevant experience in their chosen field, and then returned to undertake a postgraduate qualification.

Psychologists use these names for themselves to distinguish their particular perspective on the discipline. Before each is described in detail in the coming sections it is worth a very quick sketch to illustrate some of the differences.

In Part 2 we look at the life-span with the perspective of researchers who tend to use the label 'developmental psychologists'. For them, the main puzzle is how people develop – changing through their life-span. One of the keys to that puzzle is the incredibly rapid changes that happen in the first few years of human life. A developmental psychologist might use an observational approach – perhaps sitting behind a screen or mirror in a lab, or even taking a more naturalistic field video which can be viewed and coded later. In a lab experiment they might set a range of children at different ages the same task to see at what age they succeed in order to make some inference about their developing abilities.

In Part 3 we focus on the physical side of human behaviour where an essential puzzle is the human brain. Through the eyes of the biological psychologist we see that humans are animals, adapted by evolutionary pressures and with the same basic biological engineering as an array of similar animals. An animal like the white rat is one of the keys to this puzzle, as it can have a known and controlled genetic history; can be managed in controlled and humane laboratory situations; and in its case quite complex but measurable behaviours can be manipulated alongside direct chemical and surgical interventions.

In Part 4 the cognitive psychologist views the mind itself – our cognition – as the essential puzzle for psychology. For the cognitivist, one key to the puzzle is that mind is a mechanism which you may not be able to directly inspect – but about which you can make inferences. So much of cognitive psychology is concerned with carefully controlled laboratory experiments in which subjects' reaction time in milliseconds, to different stimuli under different conditions, can throw light upon a proposed mechanism for thinking. Some cognitivists go further and use a simulation methodology to attempt to explicitly model some abstract theory of mind on a computer.

In Part 5 we see that the key puzzle for the social psychologist is how humans function in groups. The most important questions in psychology for the social researcher arise out of our relationships with others. The key methods used to unlock this puzzle are not unlike those of the developmental researcher: the carefully contrived lab experiment, this time with an observation of a group functioning under controlled conditions; and field observations of social interactions under various conditions, usually videotaped for later analysis. However, in addition, the social psychologist tends to use qualitative methods and instruments like surveys and questionnaires to more fully explore the richness of social behaviour.

From Part 6 onwards we move away from this simple labelled division which can be broadly associated with a methodological approach by focusing on two specific aspects of individual psychology.

Finally, Part 7 gives a very specialist account of two of the applied branches of the discipline. In very general terms 'health and clinical' approaches are usually associated with social and developmental methods; and 'occupational' approaches usually associated with more cognitive methods.

CHAPTER SUMMARY

1   Human behaviour is generally complex, multicausal and affected by biological, social and cultural factors to some degree.

2   Psychology is an 'evidence-based' discipline where theory is paramount. The scientific method requires that data is not merely collected for its own sake, but in the context of exploring and testing a coherent set of theoretical principles.

3   An important distinction in psychological research is that between qualitative and quantitative methods. Both approaches are useful in exploring and testing theories.

4   Psychologists have a wide range of instruments that they can use to refine or reject theories about cognition and behaviour. These range from carefully controlled, laboratory-based experiments to naturalistic, unstructured observations.

5   Psychologists are very careful to ensure that their work is always conducted within a clear ethical framework.

6   Within the umbrella of psychology are a diverse range of researchers including individuals who would broadly accept the labels: developmental, biological, cognitive, social, clinical, and occupational psychologists. Each sees psychology as a slightly different puzzle and so uses a slightly different set of keys to unlock it.

▨ Further Reading ▨

Robson, C. (1993; repr. 1995) *Real World Research*. Oxford: Blackwell.

>   An essential and very readable treatment of experimental methods (be sure to read the useful appendix on the British Psychological Society's ethical guidelines).

Bulmer, M. (ed.) (1982) *Social Research Ethics*. London: Macmillan.

>   An interesting collection of papers that runs the gamut of ethical issues bearing on human psychological research.

PART 2
Life-span Development

CHAPTER 2
Infancy and Childhood

Mark Blades, Jill Boucher and Peter Smith

CHAPTER AGENDA

- Development is a life-span process, from conception to death. We consider whether this process divides into distinct stages and examine the work of stage theorists such as Piaget (and, in the next chapter, Erikson and Levinson).

- We look at pre-natal development and consider what can go wrong as well as right in early development.

- We consider different aspects of development under several important headings: A section on cognitive development describes the research into children's thinking and reasoning, and how this changes with age, as well as the development of children's memory abilities.

- Social and emotional development is covered by examples of research into children's early attachment to their care giver; and the development and interrelationship of friendship, play, and aggression with peers, as well as sex and ethnic differences in behaviour.

- The development of language and communication is described with reference to the research into children's verbal and non-verbal skills, from children's earliest interaction with care givers to the development of vocabulary, grammar and communication skills.

▨ Introduction ▨

In this chapter, and the next, we will look at the 'stages of life': the ways in which we grow, develop and change through the life-span. Everyone is different – everyone has their own 'trajectory' or path through life – but there are significant common experiences for all of us. These can occur in several areas:

Physical development: from conception onwards we all acquire human form, are born, grow steadily through childhood, go through puberty, and later experience physical changes of ageing.

Social development: we all experience care giving, usually from parents, make friends, fall in love, and often become parents ourselves.

Thinking (or cognition) and language development: we all acquire basic knowledge about the world, about objects, and about people; acquire better memory strategies; and learn to speak at least one native language.

In this and the following chapter we will explore some of the main changes across the life-span, especially those which have interested psychologists; and look at some of the main issues and controversies which developmental psychologists have debated. We will start with one of these issues – whether development can usefully be thought of in terms of stages.

▤ Sequences and Stages in Development ▤

There's no denying that some aspects of development typically follow a certain order or SEQUENCE; for example, an infant cannot run before she can walk; and a child cannot talk in sentences before she can speak single words. Part of the job of a psychologist will be simply to document these changes. Although the main features of development will be clear to everyone, much more detailed descriptions of development can be put forward. In fact, some of the earliest investigators of child development did just this, often through 'baby diaries'. The famous biologist Charles Darwin, who formulated the theory of evolution, published an account of the early development of one of his own children in 1877. Here is a quotation from it:

> It was difficult to decide at how early an age anger was felt; on his eighth day he frowned and wrinkled the skin round his eyes before a crying fit, but this may have been due to pain or distress, and not to anger. When about ten weeks old, he was given some rather cold milk and he kept a slight frown on his forehead all the time that he was sucking, so that he looked like a grown-up person made cross from being compelled to do something which he did not like. When nearly four months old, and perhaps much earlier, there was no doubt, from the manner in which the blood gushed into his whole face and scalp, that he easily got into a violent passion. A small cause sufficed; thus, when a little over seven months old, he screamed with rage because a lemon slipped away and he could not seize it with his hands. When eleven months old, if a wrong plaything was given him, he would push it away and beat it: I presume that the beating was an instinctive sign of anger, like the snapping of the jaws by a young crocodile just out of the egg, and not that he imagined he could hurt the plaything. (Darwin 1877)

Much descriptive work was carried out in the 1920s and 1930s, in child welfare clinics and child study centres – many of which were set up in North America in this period. From such work, typical patterns of development in infancy and early childhood were clarified – when children made friends, what sorts of toys and games they played with, how soon they could learn about colours, shapes, numbers, and so forth. The typical pattern which is common to many children is referred to as NORMATIVE development. Psychologists are also interested in development which does not follow the normative pattern (for example, see Box 2.5 about children with autism).

NORMATIVE

However, psychologists generally want to go beyond description, to explanation. They want to find ways of understanding why people behave the way they do, and how and why certain persons develop in certain ways, and when. One powerful concept here has been that of stages in development.

Used in the psychological sense, a stage implies more than a sequence. A stage model of development implies that we can 'chunk up' the life span into a succession of stages, and that the change from one stage to another is (i) fairly rapid, and (ii) involves important changes. It is like travelling up stairs as opposed to a ramp. As an American psychologist called John Flavell has put it, a stage is 'an abrupt and synchronous metamorphosis'.

The word 'metamorphosis' may bring with it images of a caterpillar turning into a chrysalis; in fact, the sequence egg–caterpillar–chrysalis–butterfly/moth is an excellent example of a successful and useful stage model. The changes are rapid, and at a change point a host of structural/behavioural characteristics are altering in 'synchrony'. It therefore tells us a great deal to know which stage in the life-span a butterfly is at. But is this useful for human development? That continues to be a matter of controversy. Some people think that it is, others think not.

In favour of a stage model

Based on observation, description and experiment, psychologists have come up with several stage models for different areas of development. We will describe later in this chapter the model proposed by Jean Piaget, who delineated four main stages of cognitive development. The stage a child is in has implications for a wide range of cognitive functioning. In the next chapter we will look at a model put forward by Daniel Levinson. He described typical stages especially in the latter part of the life course, affecting social development, self-esteem and career. Chapter 14 refers to the stage model put forward by the Austrian founder of psychoanalysis, Sigmund Freud. He hypothesized five main stages of sexual growth during the life span, which he used to explain many aspects of development including neuroses. The clinician Eric Erikson built on Freud's model and generalized it to what he called 'psycho-social' stages. His eight stages are described in the next chapter (figure 3.5). Erikson's idea was that at each of these stages there are major characteristics – things which will normally be happening to a person – and what he called 'normative crises', meaning the particular challenges or difficulties faced at that stage in the life cycle. Erikson thought that if you overcame one normative crisis, you could move on confidently to the next stage; but that a failure to resolve a normative crisis would store up problems for later psychosocial development.

Against a stage model

Humans are not like caterpillars! Growth and change seem to be continuous, not discontinuous. Development of learning to speak, learning to count, learning social skills, are gradual, over years. Attempts to 'chunk up' the life-span are arbitrary – witness the fact that there are lots of stage models, but they all come up with different numbers of stages, happening at different times! Often, detailed stage models have come unstuck. As we'll see later, Piaget's model of development of thinking, while enormously influential from the 1950s to the 1970s, has been re-evaluated by more recent research.

A middle way?

The debate continues on the issue of stages, but there may be a middle ground. There are certainly two points where changes are relatively sudden: one is the moment of BIRTH, after being in the womb for nine months; and the other period of relatively rapid development is the time (spanning a year or so) of PUBERTY. (We use this latter period as the basis for division between this chapter and the next.) Beyond that, some aspects of development do seem to change together; for example, the first year or so of life sees changes in social and mental (cognitive) functioning which are largely achieved by 18 months and which may justify thinking about the period between birth and 18 months as a distinct stage of development. In other areas, stages may be more limited in scope. For example, they may describe one area of development but say nothing about others; or they may describe changes which are culture-bound to modern urban society (e.g. starting school, leaving full-time education, retiring) but not relevant to traditional, non-urban societies.

BIRTH

PUBERTY

▓ From Conception to Birth ▓

This period of about nine months constitutes a first stage in human development – itself divided into three smaller stages, illustrated in figure 2.1.

Germinal stage

The baby is conceived when a sperm cell from the father unites with an egg cell or ovum from the mother. The fertilized egg is called a ZYGOTE. The zygote starts dividing, and dividing again, with cells rapidly differentiating. After about a week, it starts to implant on to the wall of the mother's uterus. This is complete after two weeks, at which point it is called an EMBRYO.

ZYGOTE

EMBRYO

Embryonic stage

This lasts from about the third to the eighth week after conception. By the end of this time, although only an inch long, the embryo has the basic plan of a human body, with head, arms, legs, hands and feet. It connects to the PLACENTA, by means of the UMBILICAL CORD. The placenta is a special area on the wall of the uterus.

PLACENTA

UMBILICAL CORD

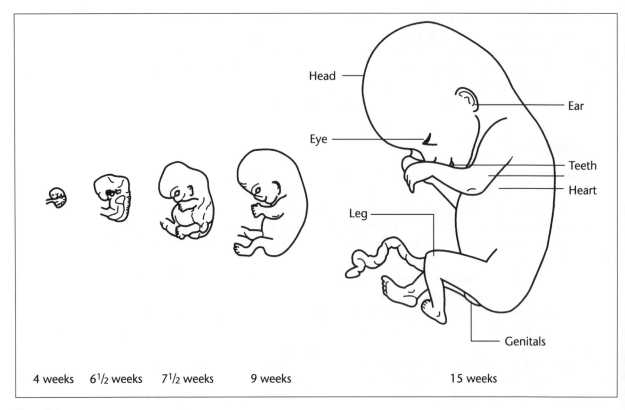

Labels on figure: Head, Eye, Ear, Teeth, Heart, Leg, Genitals

4 weeks   6¹/₂ weeks   7¹/₂ weeks   9 weeks   15 weeks

Figure 2.1
Development during the embryonic and foetal stages.
Seifert, K. Seifert and Hoffning, R., *Child and Adolescent Development* (3 ed.) (Houghton Mifflin Company, Boston, 1994), p. 108, fig. 4.3

AMNIOTIC SAC

Here, the blood supply from the mother meets that of the embryo and they intermingle through thousands of tiny blood vessels. By this means, the mother supplies oxygen and nutrients to the growing embryo. By the eighth week, the embryo is also safely cushioned in a kind of water bed – the AMNIOTIC SAC – which surrounds it and keeps it at a constant temperature.

Foetal stage

By now, the major structures of the body have differentiated, and bone cells develop, marking the stage of the foetus. Relatively small features develop – fingernails, eyelids, eyebrows; and cartilage in the bones is starting to harden. By the third month, the foetus is starting to move, and its heartbeat can be heard; and the movements become obvious to the mother by the fourth and fifth month. By the seventh month the foetus is able to breathe, cry, swallow, digest, and excrete – and has a realistic chance of surviving premature birth. The last two months of normal conception see a considerable increase in size and weight, with birth usually at nine months.

Pre-natal risks

CANALIZED

The process of pre-natal growth is 'CANALIZED' – that is to say, it is strongly predetermined. There are clear genetic instructions for the zygote to differentiate into the embryo, for the embryo to develop into the foetus, in ways broadly similar for every human being at this period. Pre-natal development is an example where nature (i.e. genetic instructions) – is very important. But nurture (i.e. the child's environment) is important too.

Things can obviously go wrong in development. Sometimes the abnormalities are genetic (for example, Box 2.1 describes the characteristics of Down's syndrome children, a condition arising from a chromosomal abnormality). Sometimes the causes are environmental. One class of environmental hazards are called TERATOGENS. Teratogen is an ancient Greek word meaning 'creating a monster' – a reference to the marked abnormalities that can sometimes occur in pre-natal development. This is especially so in the embryonic period – remember, this is when the basic ground plan of the body is being formed, with differentiation of major organs including arms and legs. Drugs and other harmful substances can reach the embryo through the mother's bloodstream, and if they do so in the embryonic period, some can cause gross body or limb abnormalities. For example, the drug thalidomide, prescribed to prevent recurrent miscarriages in the 1950s, led to babies being born with severe limb deformities – but only when the drug was taken during the first two months of pregnancy. Thalidomide is no longer prescribed in these cases. But other drugs such as cocaine, heavy consumption of alcohol during pregnancy, and heavy cigarette smoking, are among other RISK FACTORS for healthy pre-natal development. Other risk factors include poor maternal nutrition, and premature birth (before 36 weeks). A risk factor means that later problems are not inevitable, but they are more likely, especially if other risk factors or adverse circumstances are present.

TERATOGENS

RISK FACTORS

▨ The Newborn Infant: First Weeks ▨

At birth a baby may seem small, weak, and defenceless, but though a very young child is dependent on the support and attention of care givers to survive, the appearance of complete vulnerability belies the infant's capacity for survival.

Infant reflexes

Children are born with a number of REFLEXES (see table 2.1). A reflex means a particular pattern of behaviour which is triggered by a specific stimulus. Reflexes such as sucking and blinking are permanent; others (such as the Moro reflex and swimming reflexes) may last for a few months; and some (for example the rooting reflex) disappear within a few weeks. Most reflexes are important for survival – for example, the rooting and sucking reflexes guarantee that a newborn infant can find a source of nourishment. However, reflexes are not just mechanisms which contribute to a child's immediate survival, they are more complex parts of a child's overall development in the months before and after

REFLEXES

Box 2.1 Down's Syndrome

Plate 2.1 Down's syndrome child in a classroom
Source: Down's Syndrome Association.

Characteristics

Down's syndrome consists of a set of physical and psychological abnormalities present from birth. These almost always include:

- overall intellectual functioning in the moderate to severe range of general learning disability (mental retardation);

- particular difficulty taking in visual, auditory and other sensory information at speed, and slow reaction times;
- particularly poor memory for heard speech, leading to poor speech comprehension; also poor speech pronunciation;
- particularly poor number ability;

birth. Some reflexes may serve more than one purpose. For example, the stepping reflex may be an adaption to the womb, because a 'stepping' movement would allow a child to turn in the womb (Prechtl 1984), but the same reflex also provides the basis for later walking (Thelen, Fisher & Ridley-Johnson 1984).

Reflexes are not necessarily fixed sequences of behaviour, since infants can modify their responses. For example, the palmar reflex of a newborn child (see

- a flat appearance to the face, with a low bridge to the nose and high cheekbones; upward and outward slanting eyes with a conspicuous upper eyelid fold; floppy muscles, contributing to poor coordination and general torpidity.

Young children with Down's syndrome are usually sociable and friendly, though frustration and temper tantrums may occur. However, the rate of development of children with Down's syndrome slows down from infancy onwards, and adults commonly show a deterioration of mental abilities and sometimes difficult behaviour. The early decline in mental capacities is interesting in view of recent research which suggests that there may be links between Down's syndrome and Altzheimer's disease.

Causes

Down's syndrome is caused by a chromosomal abnormality. Normal people have 23 pairs of chromosomes in every cell, 46 in all. People with Down's syndrome have an extra chromosome no. 21, making a trio instead of a pair, and producing 47 chromosomes in all. For this reason, Down's syndrome is sometimes referred to as Trisomy 21.

The chromosomal abnormality usually originates in damage to the ovum prior to conception. Since a woman's ova are present from birth they are increasingly vulnerable to damage over time. This is why older mothers are more likely than younger mothers to have a Down's syndrome baby. Mothers aged 20 to 24 have a 1/9,000 chance of having an affected baby; whereas in mothers aged 45 or more the chances rise to 1/30 (Baird & Sadovnik 1988). However very young mothers also have an increased chance of having a Down's syndrome child, probably as a result of immaturity of the hormonal system. Paternal age is also associated with increased likelihood of having an affected baby .

Outlook

Down's syndrome babies are quite often born with heart and digestive tract abnormalities. They are also particularly susceptible to respiratory illnesses. Because of this, the life expectancy of people with Down's syndrome used to be very low (9 years, in 1932). Developments in the treatment of cardiac and respiratory disorders have raised the average life expectancy to middle adulthood, and a minority of people with Down's syndrome now live into their sixties.

The Down's syndrome child's level of spontaneous activity is low, and they need extra encouragement to explore, experiment and learn. Programmes designed to develop play and communication at an early age can be helpful (Cunningham & Sloper 1976). Because the Down's syndrome child's visual skills are better than their hearing and speech skills, they may find it easier to sign or even to read than to acquire intelligible speech.

Incidence

Down's syndrome occurs in approximately 1/800 live births.

Controversies to Explore

1. Should Down's syndrome children be educated in special schools or in mainstream schools with support?
2. Is development in children with Down's syndrome qualitatively different to normal development, or just slower and more limited overall?

the plate below) is a fixed sequence of fingers closing into a fist, but later the reflex becomes adapted to the shape of the object being grasped and later still such grasping movements come under an infant's voluntary control. Other reflexes also decline as a child develops voluntary control over her movements and is better able to adapt her behaviour to her environment.

Table 2.1 Infant reflexes

Name of reflex	Stimulation	Response	Age when response disappears
Rooting	stroking baby's cheek near mouth	baby will turn to side which is stroked	1 month
Walking	when baby held under arms so that her bare feet touch a surface	baby will lift each foot in turn to make 'steps' and if baby moved forward will give impression of 'walking'	2 months
Palmar	touching baby's palm with finger	baby will grasp adult's finger	4 months
Tonic neck	turning baby's head to one side when she is lying on her back	one arm will extend towards direction that head is turned and other arm will flex upwards	4 months
Swimming	when baby placed in water	baby will kick and paddle in motion like swimming	5 months
Moro	if baby's head drops slightly but suddenly	baby will extend her arms and legs and then bring them together as if 'embracing' something	6 months
Sucking	placing nipple or similar sized object in baby's mouth	baby will suck on object	permanent
Eye blink	bright light on baby's eyes	baby will blink	permanent

Temperament and personality

Arousal states

STATES

Young infants experience different levels of arousal (referred to as 'STATES') and these are described in table 2.2. Newborn babies spend a large proportion of their time asleep – up to a total of 17 in 24 hours (Parmelee, Schulz & Disbrow 1961), though periods of sleep can range from very short periods up to several hours at a time. There are two distinct sleep states: in quiet or 'non-rapid-eye-movement' (NREM) sleep a baby is comparatively peaceful with regular breathing and brainwave activity. But in active or 'rapid-eye-movement' (REM) sleep electrophysiological measures have shown that brain activity is similar to the waking state. Ruffwarg, Muzio and Dement (1966) suggested that REM sleep is necessary because it is one way that the central nervous system can stimulate itself and contribute to its own development. This is important, as babies spend

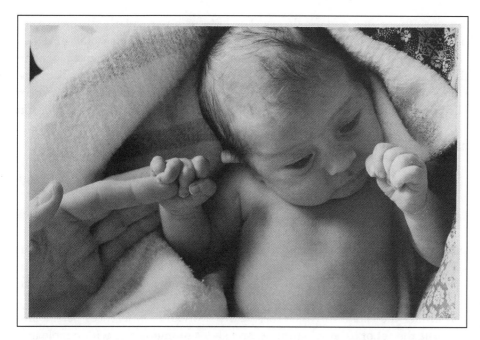

Plate 2.2 The palmar reflex
Source: Collections/Anthea Sieveking.

so much of their time in sleep states that external stimulation from the environment may be comparatively limited during the first few months. The pattern of different sleep states can also be detected in the womb (Hofer 1981), when of course there is little external stimulation.

Crying is a state which reflects a complex and important behaviour. Wolff (1966) identified different types of crying: a basic cry; an angry cry; a cry in

Table 2.2 Young infants' states of arousal

Name	Description
Quiet sleep	baby is comparatively motionless, breathing is regular; with eyelids closed and without any eye movements – this is the period of NREM sleep
Active sleep	baby has some movements and irregular breathing, some facial tensing; eyelids are closed but eyes may show REM; there may be sudden movements or sucking
Drowsiness	when baby is waking up or falling asleep; includes opening and closing of eyes; faster and more regular breathing than in quiet sleep and occasional smiling and face movements
Quiet alert	baby is relatively still and has regular breathing, and eyes are open and attentive
Active alert	baby is awake and exhibits body movements; irregular breathing; face may be tensed or relaxed
Crying	baby has much greater phsyical activity; increased respiration; face grimaces with distress; and often loud crying

response to teasing; and a pain cry. The latter is a particularly distinctive cry because the baby makes a long crying sound for three or four seconds and then remains quiet for another three or four seconds before inhaling and repeating the cry. The quiet period after the cry may give the impression that the baby has stopped breathing altogether, and it is this type of cry which is very effective for eliciting a rapid response from an adult. Adults (whether male or female, and whether parents or not) are good at distinguishing between different types of cries and identifying the needs of the infant (Frodi, Lamb, Leavitt & Donovan 1978; Zeskind 1980). Therefore, crying is an effective way for an infant to communicate with her care givers (see the section on communication and language below).

TEMPERAMENT

Very young babies differ from each other in TEMPERAMENT. Thomas and Chess (1977) divided babies into three categories: (1) easy children who are typically positive in mood, adaptable, and predictable; (2) difficult children who are typically negative in mood, active, irritable and unpredictable; and (3) slow-to-warm-up children who are quite inactive and moody, slow to adapt and resistant to change. There is considerable dispute in the literature on child development concerning the extent to which these early individual differences persist and underlie the set of habitual attitudes and styles of interacting with people and the world around us, which go to make up PERSONALITY. There is little doubt, however, that a very young baby's temperament influences the way others respond to her, and therefore the experiences she has of other people. Nor is there any doubt that, however much our innate temperamental traits may contribute to our personalities, fortuitous life experiences also affect our attitudes and interaction styles.

PERSONALITY

Sensation and perception

Taste and smell

Babies are born with a sense of taste, and newborn infants will indicate appropriate facial reactions to sweet and bitter tasting food. They prefer sweet tasting solutions and avoid tastes which they find unpleasant – for example anything which is too salty (Rosenstein & Oster 1988). Infants' early preferences reflect the importance of recognizing safe and nutritious foods (such as their mother's sweet tasting breast milk). Newborn infants also have some sensitivity to different odours and will screw up their faces or turn away from unpleasant smells.

PERCEPTION

Infants' PERCEPTION of smell may also help them identify care givers; for example, breast fed infants can recognize their own mother's underarm odour (Cernoch & Porter 1985).

Audition

Infants are quite sensitive to sounds, and children only a few days old will turn towards a sound, but their hearing is generally poorer than adults, and they have difficulty detecting sounds which only last for a short time (Clarkson,

Clifton, Swain & Perris 1989). None the less, newborn infants can distinguish their mother's voice, which they have heard while still in the womb, from the voice of a female stranger, and infants a few weeks old can also distinguish between similar speech sounds (like 'bah' and 'pah'), necessary precursors for language learning, as discussed later.

Vision

Visual perception is less well advanced in newborn children because the visual cortex continues to develop for several months after birth. Newborn infants have poor visual acuity (which is a measure of how well the lens of the eye focuses on the retina) and this means that compared to an adult, infants have a blurred image of the world (Courage & Adams 1990). Their ability to follow moving objects is also limited, and they can only track slowly moving objects with rather jerky eye movements (Aslin 1981). When very young infants look at a stationary object they tend to look mainly at the edges of the object (because the edges of an object against a background usually provide the area of greatest contrast), and it is only after about two months that infants scan objects more completely and thoroughly (Maurer & Salapatek 1976).

When we see two objects of the same size but one is close to us and one is far away, the object which is farther away makes a smaller image on the retina, but that does not mean that we think that the further object is actually smaller than the near one. Treating an object as the same size whatever its distance away, is called SIZE CONSTANCY. There is evidence that the visual system of newborn infants is similar to that of adults in making adjustments for the distance of objects, and that such young children do have size constancy (Slater, Mattock &

SIZE CONSTANCY

Box 2.2 Face Perception

Within the first hour of life babies have been found to spend more time looking at a schematic picture of a face than at a scrambled set of facial features, or at a blank but head-shaped oval (Goren et al. 1975). Each picture was slowly moved in an arc above the baby's face, and the baby's head and eye movements were recorded on video.

Maurer and Barrera (1981) showed that infants aged 2 months showed a similar preference for a realistic drawing of a face (but this time, the pictures were held static in front of them). However, Maurer and Barrera could not find any evidence that newborn children or infants up to the age of 2 months preferred the drawing of a face as opposed to the non-faces. It seems, therefore, that very young infants show a U-shaped

curve in their preferential responding to faces.

How can this be explained? Johnson and Morton suggest that babies are born 'knowing' what a schematic face looks like, and with a preference for looking at objects which move. This enables them to learn to recognize their own mother's face within the first week of life (Bushnell et al. 1989), which is important for bonding mother and child together.

However, this early ability is based on primitive visual mechanisms in the brain which are gradually superseded during the first two months of life. The dip in the U-shaped curve represents the phase when neither the primitive visual mechanisms nor the more advanced visual mechanisms are operating effectively.

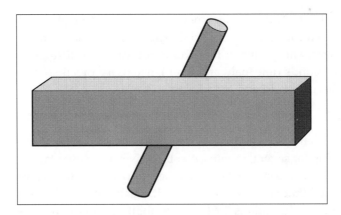

Figure 2.2 Materials used by Slater et al. (1990) to test infants' perceptions of occluded objects.
Slater, 'Newborn and older infant's perception of partly occluded objects' in *Infant Behaviour and Development*, 13, p. 41.

Brown 1990). In other words, it seems likely that very young infants, like adults, react to objects as three-dimensional forms in the world rather than simply as shapes on the retina. (See Box 2.2.)

None the less, there may be other aspects of a young child's view of the world which do differ significantly from an older child's or an adult's view. For example, Slater et al. (1990) showed 4-month-old infants and newborn infants a rod which was occluded by a block in front of it so that only the ends of the rod were visible. The 4-month-old infants reacted as if the rod was a single complete object, but the newborn infants reacted to the rod as if it were two separate rods (one on either side of the block); see figure 2.2.

In summary, research has shown that even newborn infants have sophisticated perceptual mechanisms (for size and shape constancy, for example) but there are other aspects of perception which may take time to develop as children gain experience of the constancies of the world (e.g. seeing complete objects).

▓ Cognitive Development ▓

Infants' learning abilities

If infants are to develop they must learn new abilities and new information from their experience in the world. Infants are capable of several forms of learning – the two most important are OPERANT and CLASSICAL CONDITIONING (see also chapter 8).

OPERANT CONDITIONING

CLASSICAL CONDITIONING

In operant conditioning, a behaviour which gains positive reinforcement is more likely to be repeated. For example, if the cord from a mobile hanging above a cot is attached to an infant's foot, an infant will rapidly learn that kicking her foot makes the mobile move, and she will increase foot kicking to achieve the desired movement (Shields & Rovee-Collier 1992). Operant conditioning may be present in newborn infants because researchers have shown that newborn infants' rate of sucking and head turning can be influenced by specific reinforcement (Jusczyk 1985; Papousek 1967).

In classical conditioning infants learn to associate one event with another. Blass et al. (1984) examined classical conditioning with the following procedure: while an infant was sucking a sweet liquid her head was stroked gently and this procedure was repeated several times. Then on a further occasion (when there was no liquid present) the infant's head was stroked and Blass et al. found that the infant would make sucking responses. In other words, the infant had learned to associate the stroking with the presence of the liquid.

Piaget's stage theory of cognitive development

Piaget proposed a description of development which included four stages – these are summarized in figure 2.3.

0–2 **years: Sensorimotor stage** – infants learn through their senses – i.e. by looking, touching and interacting with their environment they develop schemes (patterns of behaviour) which are the basis of their cognitive development in this stage.

2–7: **Preoperational stage** – Piaget thought that in this period young children's thinking was limited in several ways. In particular, they were 'pre-' logical – in other words, when they were faced with a logical problem they would not necessarily reason about that problem in the same way as an older child or adult. They might only focus on one aspect of the problem, and as a consequence will often reach an inappropriate conclusion.

7–11: **Concrete operational stage** – children's thinking is now more logical and they can approach many problems with effective reasoning skills, but their successful reasoning is limited to problems which are rooted in real-world activities and situations. Children in this period have difficulty if a problem is abstract.

after 11: **Formal operational stage** – adolescents can think and reason about hypothetical situations and solve abstract problems. They will approach problem tasks in a logical and ordered manner – to find the most appropriate solution. This the achievement of adult reasoning.

Figure 2.3 Main stages of Piaget's theory of development. (The ages given are only approximate, because different children might achieve each stage at slightly different ages.)

Sensorimotor period

The period from birth until about 18 months of age was referred to by Piaget as the SENSORIMOTOR STAGE of development (Piaget and Inhelder 1969). In describing the sensorimotor period Piaget tried to explain how an infant progressed from being a comparatively limited newborn to a thinking child, and Piaget was particularly interested in three aspects of a child's behaviour in this period – 'circular reactions'; 'deferred imitation'; and the 'object concept'.

SENSORIMOTOR STAGE

Piaget suggested that infants have 'SCHEMES'. These are consistent patterns of motor behaviour which are first based on reflexes – for example, the infant will have schemes for sucking or grasping. Piaget also suggested that in the first few months infants exhibit 'circular reactions' – by this term he meant that an infant

SCHEMES

has a natural tendency to repeat novel actions, and as she repeats schemes they become more elaborate. For example, when an infant attempts to grasp an object she may be able to grasp it immediately, and in Piaget's terms this would be an example of 'assimilating' the object, because the infant has taken the object into her existing scheme of grasping. But if, for instance, the object is too large for the infant to get hold of straight away, she may have to adapt her grasping scheme to hold it (say, by opening her fingers wider), and this adaptive behaviour is called 'accommodation' because the infant has altered an existing scheme in response to her environment. As an infant applies a scheme in an increasing number of different contexts the scheme will become more flexible and more elaborate.

Many of a young child's actions will be based on 'trial and error' responding. For example, if a child is shown an attractive toy which is placed on a cloth in front of her, but out of reach, she may try to grasp the toy directly. Such attempts will be unsuccessful, but in the course of trying to get hold of the toy she may accidentally grasp the cloth and in so doing pull the toy within reach. However, by the end of the sensorimotor period, a child will have advanced beyond trial and error responding, and without first trying to get hold of the toy directly will deliberately pull on the cloth to bring the toy closer before trying to grasp it. Such performance indicates that children are planning their actions before carrying them out. Planned actions imply that children have the ability to think about their behaviour, or to put it another way, that they can mentally run through the actions they intend to carry out. According to Piaget this is the main achievement of the sensorimotor stage, because children progress from acting directly on the world (using motor schemes) to thinking about the world (acting on their internal mental representation of the world).

Deferred imitation provides further evidence that children in the sensorimotor period have achieved an internal representation of the world. Piaget (1951) described an occasion when his own daughter, Jacqueline, at the age of 16 months, watched a little boy have a temper tantrum, and then the next day she also threw a tantrum. In the course of Jacqueline's tantrum she imitated the behaviour and actions of the boy she had witnessed the day before, and Piaget interpreted this as evidence that Jacqueline had retained a memory (i.e. a mental representation) of the boy's behaviour. Piaget believed that deferred imitation was only achieved towards the end of the sensorimotor period.

OBJECT PERMANENCE

Piaget also discussed 'OBJECT PERMANENCE' – the idea that objects which are no longer visible (for example, because they are placed in a container) still continue to exist even though they are out of sight. Adults usually take this belief for granted, but Piaget pointed out that young children may not realize that something which is out of sight still exists. He noticed that if a toy was placed within the reach of a young infant, but then the toy was covered with a cloth, the infant appeared to lose interest in the toy and did not attempt to reach for it. It was as if the infant believed that the toy had disappeared. Piaget found that children did not try to retrieve a covered toy until the middle of the sensorimotor period (about 8–12 months of age). He took this as the earliest evidence that children

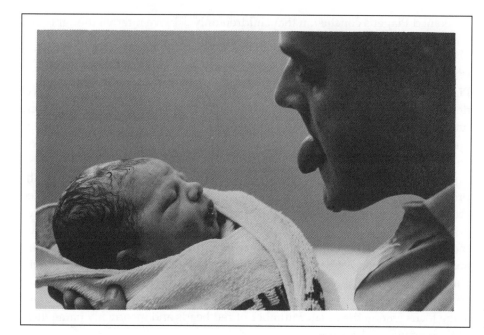

Plate 2.3 Baby imitating tongue protrusion
Source: Stephen Lovell-Davis.

were able to form a mental representation, because if infants searched for the hidden toy it implied that they had some memory or mental image of the object which they could no longer see.

There is no doubt that Piaget offered a pioneering and vivid description of infant development, but more recent researchers have shown that he underestimated the abilities of young children. Although Piaget claimed that imitation was a gradual development, Meltzoff and Moore (1983) found that children younger than one month could imitate facial gestures. There is some debate about what such facial imitation indicates about infants' early abilities, but other studies have demonstrated that 9-month-old children can remember and imitate a series of activities which they were shown a day before (Meltzoff 1988). The latter experiment is clear evidence for deferred imitation at an age much earlier than Piaget proposed.

Research since Piaget's original studies of object permanence have also produced results which indicate that young children have an earlier understanding of the permanence of objects than Piaget suggested. For example, Hood and Willatts (1986) dangled an object in front of 5-month-old infants and then switched off the light in the room. In the dark, the infant could not see the object, but she still reached out to grasp it. This result suggests that at the age of 5 months children have a memory (i.e. a representation) of the object which they saw before the light was switched off.

In summary, Piaget laid the groundwork for the investigation of infant cognition, but the interpretations he placed on the performance of children in the first two years of life may have underestimated infants' cognitive abilities. The more recent findings which stress the competence of even very young infants have weakened Piaget's conclusion that children only achieve internal thoughts and images towards the end of the sensorimotor period.

Piaget's preoperational stage

PREOPERATIONAL STAGE

Piaget called the period between about 2 and 7 years the PREOPERATIONAL STAGE of development. The name reflects Piaget's belief that children in this stage were unable to use various mental 'operations', and the lack of such operations led to failure in performing different cognitive tasks. Two examples of such tasks will be given as a way of illustrating some of the operations which Piaget described.

One task is the 'class-inclusion' problem. For example, children in the preoperational stage might be shown 20 wooden beads of which 16 are painted red and 4 are painted yellow. If children are then asked 'Are there more red beads or more wooden beads?', many children will answer by saying there are more red beads. This would be a failure to appreciate that the red beads are a subclass of the wooden beads and, according to Piaget, the failure is due to the children's difficulty in considering two aspects of the problem (the red beads and the wooden beads) at the same time. Rather, children in the preoperational stage focus just on the greater number of red beads and incorrectly name these as their answer to the question.

CONSERVATION TASK

A second example of a Piagetian task is the CONSERVATION TASK. Conservation refers to the fact that superficial changes in an object or group of objects does not necessarily alter the properties of those objects. For example, if a line of ten coins is repositioned so that the coins are placed in a circle rather than a line there are still ten coins – because they have been placed in different positions does not mean that the number of coins has changed. Similarly, if a litre of orange juice is poured from a jug into six cups there is still a litre of juice – because it has been divided between six cups does not mean that the quantity of liquid has changed. Piaget discovered that children in the preoperational period had difficulty realizing (for example) that the number of items in a group did not alter when the

Figure 2.4 Piaget's conservation of liquid task

A child is shown two glasses, A and B, with equal amounts of water in them. The child is asked to say whether there is the same amount of water in each glass. Children will usually say that there is the same amount in each glass.

Then the child watches as the contents of glass B are poured into C, a differently shaped glass. The child is asked again whether there is the same amount in each glass. Most children in the preoperational stage of reasoning will say that the glasses now have different amounts of liquid.

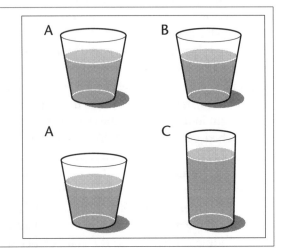

items were rearranged, or that the quantity of liquid did not change when it was poured into differently shaped containers (see figure 2.4).

Experiments like the one described in figure 2.4 have been replicated many times, and there is no doubt that young children often give incorrect answers to the questions posed in conservation tasks. Piaget explained children's failure in the following way – if, for example, in the liquid conservation task, a child said there was more liquid in the tall glass than in the small glass, Piaget said this was because the child was overinfluenced by the appearance of the liquid in the tall glass. Piaget suggested that children would often be incorrect because of the 'perceptual dominance' of the task – they would consider one aspect of the task (such as the height of the liquids) and think that the higher level indicated more liquid. In a similar way children in the preoperational stage tend to think there are more counters in a row which is spread out because the row appears longer.

Piaget argued that to succeed in a conservation task children need to overcome the appearance of objects. To do this they require certain operations (or logical reasoning). For example, in the liquid conservation task, if children have an operation for 'reversibility' they will be able to imagine the liquid they have seen poured into the tall glass being poured back into the small glass, and such reasoning may help them to realize that the quantity of liquid has not altered. Alternatively, if children are able to take more than one dimension of the task into consideration and they have an operation like 'compensation' they will realize that the higher level of liquid in the tall glass is compensated for by the narrower width of the glass. According to Piaget, children in the preoperational period lack such operations, and therefore they tend to fail conservation and other tasks which he invented.

Evaluation of the preoperational stage

Other researchers have argued that failure in Piagetian tasks may be less to do with children's reasoning and more to do with factors in the design of the tasks. One such factor is the language used by Piaget – for example, in the class-inclusion task, asking whether there are more red beads or more wooden beads is a strange and unusual question which may simply confuse young children. When other researchers have repeated the class- inclusion task but used language which has clarified which groups of objects are being compared, the performance of 'preoperational' children has improved (Donaldson 1978). In other words, it may be the language of the question rather than the logic of the task which made the original class-inclusion task difficult.

Donaldson argued that children may find Piagetian tasks difficult because they are often removed from any realistic context. For example, in the liquid conservation task children are shown two glasses and then see liquid transferred from one glass to a third glass, but they are given no reason for this change. Donaldson suggested that the arbitrary nature of the change may confuse children, because the task does not make 'human sense'. Some experimenters have carried out similar conservation tasks using Piaget's procedure, but they have embedded the task in a realistic context. For example, Light et al. (1979) showed preoperational children two small identical glasses with the same quantity of pasta shells in each, and then told the children that one glass had a broken and dangerous rim, and its contents needed to be transferred to a safer glass (which just happened to be a tall thin one). When asked whether the safe glass had more or less in it than the broken glass, many of the children were aware that the quantity of pasta had not changed. In other words, Light et al.'s procedure provided the children with a meaningful context, and in such a context preoperational children expected the quantity of pasta to remain the same.

In summary, Piaget established that children in the preoperational stage had difficulty performing certain tasks (like the class-inclusion and conservation tasks). He attributed the children's poor performance to a lack of mental 'operations', but more recent researchers (such as Donaldson 1978) have demonstrated that some of children's difficulties in typical Piagetian tasks may stem from the abstract and artificial nature of such tasks. Piaget emphasized limitations in the reasoning of preoperational children, but Donaldson emphasized such children's difficulties in interpreting the meaning of the tasks which Piaget asked them to solve. If children can solve conservation and other tasks at an age when Piaget assumed they were in the preoperational stage, it weakens his suggestion that this period is a distinct developmental stage characterized by children's lack of particular mental 'operations' such as reversibility and compensation.

Concrete operational stage

From about 7 to 11 years of age, children's thinking has developed so that their reasoning approximates to the reasoning of an adult. For example, children in this period no longer have difficulty in Piagetian tasks which require conservation or class inclusion. Children's processing capacity increases during this period, and they develop the use of memory encoding and retrieval strategies (Flavell et al. 1966; Kobasigawa 1974) and become more aware of their own capabilities and limitations (Kreutzer et al. 1975).

CONCRETE
OPERATIONAL STAGE

However, as Piaget emphasized by calling this period the CONCRETE OPERATIONAL STAGE, children's thinking still has some limitations. In particular, children may have difficulty reasoning in abstract tasks. For example, if children are told that Ann is taller than Barbara and that Barbara is taller than Clare, and asked to say who is the tallest, they may find it difficult to answer correctly. But if children are shown pairs of dolls (Ann and Barbara, and then Barbara and Clare) they will be able to work out which is the tallest. Children can perform the task with dolls because it is a 'concrete' task – i.e. one that is directly related to something in the real world. According to Piaget it is only in the following stage of cognitive development (formal operations) that children can reason hypothetically and solve abstract tasks (see chapter 3).

Vygotsky's description of cognitive development

In contrast to Piaget's focus on the way that children solved problems on their own, Vygotsky (1978) pointed out that it is rare for a child to act on her own. Vygotsky, a Russian, died in 1934, and his books were not translated into English until the 1960s and 1970s – only at that time did his ideas began to influence developmental psychology. Vygotsky argued that a child's learning and action takes place in well-structured social contexts, in which there are often adults or older children who can contribute to the child's performance.

To stress this point, Vygotsky described the ZONE OF PROXIMAL DEVELOPMENT (ZPD), which referred to those aspects of a child's performance which she would not be able to achieve on her own, but which she could achieve with support from another person. In other words, the ZPD referred to a child's potential to benefit from help or instruction. (See also the discussion in chapter 8, on the learning-theory aspect of Vygotsky's work.)

ZONE OF PROXIMAL DEVELOPMENT

Wood et al. (1978) asked children to construct a complicated wooden pyramid (rather like a three-dimensional jigsaw). The children were shown pictures which showed the sequence of construction, but children below the age of about 7 years were unable to build the pyramid on their own. Wood et al. asked mothers to help their children construct the pyramid, and they analysed the way that the mothers did this. After the help some of the children as young as 4 years were able to build the pyramid on their own. The children who learned least from the help had mothers who relied on showing or telling their children what to do. The children who learned most had mothers who encouraged their children to build as much as possible on their own, and only offered suggestions when the child had difficulty. The latter support left the child in control of the task and, most importantly, the mothers were offering support within their child's ZPD. Wood et al.'s study supports the ideas put forward by Vygotsky – that if children are given appropriate help they often have the potential to go beyond what they can achieve on their own.

The information-processing approach to cognitive development

Piaget's analysis of children's cognitive development was mainly in terms of general (and not too clearly defined) processes such as the 'operations' described above. More recent researchers have tried to be more precise in describing children's cognition in terms of information processing. Researchers who take an information-processing approach consider the way that children think about problems – the reasoning strategies they use, the previous experience and knowledge that they might employ in a problem-solving task and, importantly, any processing limitations that children may experience when thinking about a problem. For example, young children have less working memory capacity than an older child or adult – working memory is that part of memory which can be activated at one time (see chapter 7). Five-year-old children may only have a

Box 2.3   Brainerd's Analysis of Information-processing Limitations

Brainerd suggested several ways that failures in information processing could affect performance on a problem-solving task. As an example of a task consider an arithmetic problem like $(6 + 8 - 5) \times 7$:

1. Encoding failure. A child might not be able to encode all the information about the problem in working memory (e.g. she may only encode $6 + 8 - 5$).
2. Computational failure. A child may encode all the information about a problem, but may not have the rules for solving the problem (e.g. may not have learnt the procedures needed to perform multiplication).
3. Retrieval failure. A child may have learnt the procedures for multiplication and have these encoded in

long-term memory, but when thinking what these procedures are she may confuse these with other procedures and retrieve inappropriate ones from long-term memory (e.g. applies a rule for division rather than multiplication).

4. Storage failure. The information which the child has encoded in working memory decays before she can use it. For example, while calculating $6 + 8$ the child may forget the remaining part of the problem.
5. Work space constraint. The calculation in working memory may require more memory space than is available. For example, a child may be able to hold the original problem in working memory but not have enough space to hold the subtotals as she performs the different parts of the calculation.

working memory span of about 4 to 5 items, which means that they can only hold that many items of information in their working memory at one time: if a problem involves thinking about more than that number of items at the same time children may have difficulty. Working memory increases as children develop; a 9-year-old's may be 6 items, and adults have a span of about 7 items (Kail 1990).

An early example of this approach is Brainerd's (1983) analysis of Piaget's probability judgement task. Brainerd emphasized the role of working memory in children's ability to process information and suggested that there were at least five ways that limitations in working memory could influence children's performance (see Box 2.3). Brainerd analysed Piaget and Inhelder's (1951) probability judgement task in terms of an information-processing model. In the probability judgement task a child is shown two different sets of counters which are placed in an opaque bag. For example there might be seven red counters and three blue counters. After they are all placed in the bag one token is pulled out and before the child sees the counter she is asked to predict its likely colour. The counter is then replaced in the bag and a second counter pulled out and the child is asked again to suggest its colour (and so on for several trials). In this example the correct answer is always 'red' because there are always more red counters in the bag.

Piaget and Inhelder (1951) found that preoperational children were poor at the prediction task – such children do not consistently predict that a counter from the larger number is the most likely to be chosen from the bag. Many children answer red the first time they are asked but on subsequent trials they simply alternated their responses (blue, red, blue, red). Brainerd (1983) argued that if children were correct on the first trial they must have been able to encode the information about the problem and they must have had procedures (from long-term memory) for making comparisons between the two sets of counters. In other words, encoding and retrieval were unlikely to be the children's main problem. Brainerd suggested that children's difficulty, after the first trial, was that they remembered their own previous responses, and by retaining these in working memory they had insufficient space in which to make correct probability judgements in later trials. As children get older and the capacity of their working memory increases they can retain information about both the problem and their own previous responses without difficulty.

The improvement of children's information processing, and especially their working memory capacity, has been seen as a crucial factor in children's cognitive development.

Case (1985) suggested that the space in working memory does not actually change with age; rather, the available space is divided between operating space (which includes any current processing) and short-term storage space (which includes the information required for current processing). As children develop

Box 2.4 Memory Strategies

There are many strategies which can be applied to information which needs to be encoded in memory or retrieved from memory.

Encoding Information

Rehearsal: This means repeating information in working memory until it is retained well enough to be encoded in long-term memory. For example, given a list of words like dog, cat, car, house, book, pen, etc. it is useful to group (or 'chunk') items and then rehearse them – e.g. 'dog-cat', 'car-house', 'book-pen', etc. Young children rarely use rehearsal spontaneously (Flavell et al. 1966) and although by the age of 7 years children use rehearsal, it is still some years before children use the strategy as effectively as adults (Ornstein 1975).

Organization: Refers to grouping items so that it is easier to remember them. For example, Moely et al. (1969) showed 5- to 11-year-old children a mixture of pictures (of furniture, clothing, vehicles, etc.) and asked the children to learn the names of the objects on the pictures. The children were allowed to rearrange the pictures if they wanted to, but Moely et al. found that only the oldest participants chose to group the pictures into categories.

Elaboration: This strategy involves making associations to improve recall. Associations include mental imagery or verbal elaboration – to recall the words 'fish' and 'hat' a child could form an image of a hat with a fish in it, or the sentence 'the fish put her hat on'. Like other strategies, elaboration improves with age; one reason for this improvement is that older children have more knowledge than younger children and therefore greater scope for making more effective elaborations.

Retrieval Strategies

If information is already encoded in memory but cannot be retrieved immediately, it is possible to use a variety of retrieval strategies. For example, when trying to recall a name its is often useful to go through the alphabet because sometimes the letter which is the initial letter of the name triggers the rest of the name. Kreutzer et al. (1975) asked 5- and 10-year-olds how they might remember an event like receiving a puppy as a Christmas present. Half of the 5-year-olds were unable to suggest any retrieval strategies, but the 10-year-olds offered several different ones (e.g. recalling other presents received at the same time).

and gain more practice and experience of processing information they do so more efficiently and this leaves more space available for short-term storage (see chapter 7).

One way in which children become more effective at processing information is the development of memory strategies such as rehearsal, organization and elaboration (see Box 2.4). There is age-related improvement in memory strategies and this improvement is due to several factors. First, although children are rarely taught memory strategies explicitly, they may develop appropriate strategies as a result of schooling and the need for memorization in most educational contexts (Wagner 1978). Second, as children get older they realize more about their own memory abilities and the need to apply strategies effectively. Self-awareness of memory abilities is called METAMEMORY. Young children's metamemory is often poor – for example, 5-year-olds may overestimate their memory span by 50 per cent or more (Flavell et al. 1978). If children think their memory abilities are better than they actually are, they will not realize the need to apply strategies.

METAMEMORY

A third and important factor in memory development is knowledge – as children get older they learn more about the world and they can apply such knowledge in processing information. For example, the more knowledge a child has the more likely it is that she will be able to integrate new information with existing information and the more likely that she will be able to utilize knowledge in processing strategies (e.g. in the use of memory strategies like elaboration – see Box 2.4). Chi (1978) demonstrated the importance of knowledge by asking a group of 10-year-old children who were experienced chess players and a group of adults (with more limited knowledge of chess) to memorize chess layouts (with about 22 chess pieces in each). The 10-year-olds were more accurate than the adults at recalling the layouts – presumably because their greater knowledge of chess gave them more experience at recognizing patterns and grouping pieces on the board.

In summary, the information-processing approach has considered children's performance in terms of their processing abilities and limitations and this approach has often been able to identify the reasons why children of different ages have difficulty in tasks which require problem solving. Analysing children's performance with reference to their storage capacity or memory strategies (which can be identified and measured) has provided a more detailed analysis of children's cognitive development than Piaget's more descriptive and less precise concepts about children's mental 'operations'.

Although the information-processing approach has provided an important advance over Piaget's theories, both approaches are open to a common criticism. Piaget and most of the researchers in the information-processing tradition have carried out studies with children in what may be called 'laboratory' conditions. Most often, an individual child will be asked to perform a novel problem-solving task for a short period of time and the child's performance is than taken as a measure of her cognitive ability on that task. The use of laboratory tasks is essential when experimenters need to control all the variables which may be involved in performance, but such tasks are inevitably somewhat artificial and removed from the way that children learn and perform in more natural contexts.

Social and Emotional Development

Social attachments

Social attachment in infancy

We have seen how infants are equipped with abilities which help them get into social and communicative interactions with mothers and other care givers; and it is vitally important for them to do this. Although they can discriminate familiar adults from unfamiliar adults soon after birth, it is not until the latter part of the first year that an infant develops consistent ways of approaching and interacting with familiar care givers. An infant is likely to show ATTACHMENT BEHAVIOURS, or PROXIMITY-MAINTAINING BEHAVIOURS such as crying, vocalizing, clinging to the care giver, which by 7 to 9 months are directed preferentially to one or more persons.

ATTACHMENT BEHAVIOURS

PROXIMITY-MAINTAINING BEHAVIOURS

The development of attachment was described in detail by the English psychiatrist John Bowlby (1969). He viewed attachment as a behavioural system, designed to maintain appropriate proximity to the primary care giver (or ATTACHMENT FIGURE). Separation from the care giver 'activates' the attachment system in order to restore proximity. When the attachment system has achieved its goal – being in sufficiently close contact with the care giver – then attachment behaviours subside. The child no longer needs to cry or reach out to the care giver, and feels secure.

ATTACHMENT FIGURE

Bowlby also hypothesized that infants have a predisposition to explore the outside world. The need to explore and play which takes the child away from the primary care giver counteracts the need for proximity. Both parent and infant play an active part in this process and normally the attachment is reciprocal. The balance shifts when the child is distressed by some event or experience, when attachment behaviours are reactivated.

Secure and insecure attachments

Attachment theorists such as Ainsworth et al. (1978) and Main (1991) distinguish between SECURE and INSECURE ATTACHMENT. These patterns of attachment (which measure a relationship between an infant and a particular care giver) are measured by a procedure called the STRANGE SITUATION. This re-enacts in miniature a situation involving an infant being mildly stressed by being left with a stranger, and assessing response to the care giver on her or his return (Ainsworth et al. 1978). It is used with infants aged 1 to 3 years. A securely attached infant (labelled Type B) can use the attachment figure as a secure base from which to

SECURE ATTACHMENT

INSECURE ATTACHMENT

STRANGE SITUATION

explore, and when distressed, is reassured by the attachment figure. An insecurely attached infant does not use the attachment figure as a secure base so effectively, and in particular, when distressed, will show some ambivalence to (Type C) or avoidance of (Type A) the attachment figure, or may show a disorganized response (Type D).

A number of studies have suggested that (a) secure attachment follows from sensitive care giving, by an adult responsive to the infant's signals; and (b) secure attachment is predictive of later competence in the physical and social environment, including later peer relationships. However, the strength and generality of these relationships is still being debated (Bretherton & Waters 1985).

A major question is whether a measure such as the 'strange situation', developed in the USA, is valid in different cultures. Obviously there are cultural variations in patterns of child-rearing. Takahashi (1990) argues that the strange situation must be interpreted with caution when used across cultures. He found that Japanese infants were very distressed by being left alone in the strange situation because, in their culture, they are never left alone at 12 months. So fewer Japanese were categorized as Type B. In addition, there was no opportunity for them to show avoidance, and to score as Type A, since at reunion the mothers typically went straight to them and picked them up immediately. This meant that an unusually high number of Japanese infants were scored as Type C at 12 months, yet in other settings they did not appear to be insecurely attached.

Who can be a care giver?

MATERNAL DEPRIVATION HYPOTHESIS

In his earlier writings, Bowlby (1953) proposed a MATERNAL DEPRIVATION HYPOTHESIS – that between a critical period of around 6 months and 3 years the child needs continuous love and care from one person, the mother or a permanent mother-substitute. He went on to argue that significant separations between the child and his or her mother in the first three years of life would have a serious effect on the emotional and social development of the child. In his view, an absent mother cannot be sensitive since, through her absence, she is not available to meet the child's needs.

This emphasis on the unique importance of mothers as attachment figures now seems misplaced. It is widely accepted that attachment figures can include fathers, grandparents, older siblings, and familiar non-family adults such as nannies or child-minders. A more important argument against the maternal deprivation hypothesis (since Bowlby did admit the existence of mother-substitutes) is that a child can be attached to several such persons. Thus, care can be shared amongst a number of care givers, without adverse effects. Indeed, shared care giving is very common in most societies (Smith 1980), with father, grandmother, perhaps older siblings typically assisting in looking after infants and young children.

Are children at risk by daily separation from their parents?

Having proposed the maternal deprivation hypothesis, Bowlby expressed grave doubts about the advisability of mothers working outside the home before children had reached the age of 3. Attempts have been made to assess the risk to young children when they are cared for outside the home. Many research studies have compared children who are mainly cared for at home with children whose mothers place them in daycare while they go out to work. The conclusion reached in most earlier studies was that daycare need not have a bad effect on young children, provided it was of high quality (Belsky & Steinberg 1978; Rutter 1981). Children in daycare were just as securely attached to their parents as were those who stayed at home. Children of working mothers appeared to form an attachment to other care givers but to remain firmly attached to their own mothers.

Later studies elicited factors which were important, such as size of group being cared for, the training of the staff, the place where the daycare took place (Clarke-Stewart 1989). They noted that the amount of support which the mother had was an influential factor. There were also broad socio-cultural factors, such as poverty and deprivation, which had an impact on the quality of the relationship between parent and child.

This debate has been reopened in recent years, specifically regarding maternal employment and full-time daycare during the infant's first year. Belsky (1988) reviewed three studies which found that children, separated from their parents for more than 20 hours a week before they were one year old, were more likely to be anxiously attached to their mothers and showed more avoidance behaviour on reunion. Also, Baydar and Brooks-Gunn (1991), in a survey of over 1,000 children, found that maternal employment in the first year had detrimental effects on cognitive and behavioural development.

Other researchers dispute the conclusion that maternal employment during the first year need be a risk factor. They argue that the strange situation may be an inappropriate assessment, and that the quality of the daycare *vis-à-vis* home care is the overriding factor. In the UK, Melhuish et al. (1990) compared families using mothers, relatives, child-minders and nurseries for daycare. They found that attention, joint play, group activity, verbal and non-verbal vocalizations were most frequent in the home, least frequent in the nurseries. The nurseries did not provide interactional experiences as beneficial as those provided by other childcare environments, probably because of the lower adult–child ratio. But contrary to Belsky's worries, there were no differences in attachment to the mother. Also, the children in the nurseries showed more prosocial behaviour such as sharing, co-operation and empathy for others. Indeed, Clarke-Stewart (1991) found that children in high quality daycare centres tended to score higher on many developmental tasks than did home-care (family-reared) children, perhaps because of the range of peers and of educational opportunities in good daycare provision. In general, it is proving difficult to generalize about 'home' and 'daycare' environments when each kind of care can show enormous variation.

Later development of attachment

The proximity-maintaining phase of attachment ends at around 3 years. By then, children have developed an internal, abstract representation of attachment figures so that continual proximity is not necessary. These are called internal working models of relationships (Main et al. 1985). However there may be continuity in the quality of attachment to parents, even after infancy. Several studies have attempted to measure attachment quality in older children. Variants of the strange situation have been used with 3- to 6-year-olds (Main & Cassidy 1988), and a photographic test called the SEPARATION ANXIETY TEST with older children and adolescents (Wright et al. 1995). From studies like these it seems that children who have had a warm, satisfying experience of relationships are likely to see themselves as lovable, will expect others to like them and will place a value on close, intimate relationships with others. Those who have had a harsh experience of relationships, who have been rejected, who have not been comforted when in distress are likely to see themselves as unlovable, will have low expectations of relationships and will act in ways which are likely to elicit rejection.

SEPARATION
ANXIETY TEST

How children come to understand others

By about 9 to 12 months, infants can produce, and discriminate, a variety of emotional expressions; and begin to respond appropriately by interpreting the emotional expressions of others as a commentary on the situation. By 18 months (the completion of sensorimotor development), the infant has a well-developed sense of self and others, and is able to start responding appropriately to others as a result of their emotional state; for example, showing empathy and comforting someone in distress.

From about 18 months, we can start to see how children understand others by the way they talk about them (Bretherton et al. 1986). Use of words which label emotions (such as 'have fun', 'surprised', 'scared', 'yucky', 'sad'), while rare at 18 months, are common by 24 months. Interestingly, the use of these words for self and others goes very much in parallel. By 28 months, children are using language to comment on and explain their own feelings, for example:

Me fall down. Me cry.

and the feelings of others, for example:

You sad Mommy. What Daddy do?
Baby crying. Kiss. Make it better.

Wellman (1990) argues that by 2 years, children can be thought of as 'desire psychologists'. They can understand that other people have emotions and desires, and that a person's desire may lead them to a certain action. By 3 to 4 years, they can be considered 'belief-desire psychologists'. That is, they can un-

Plate 2.4 Child being helped
by father
Source: Collections/Sandra
Lousada.

derstand that someone's desire will interact with that person's belief about things, to result in a certain action.

How does the understanding of others come about? Paul Harris (1989) argues that there are three important precursors, or preconditions, for the child to be able to understand another person's mind. These are (1) self-awareness; (2) the capacity for pretence; and (3) being able to distinguish reality from pretence. He supposes that once a child is aware of his or her own emotional state, he or she can use the ability to pretend to project this emotional state on to in-animate beings (in pretend play), or on other people; and realize that the other person's imagined reality may differ from their own reality. As an example, take the child who said 'You sad Mommy. What Daddy do?' Perhaps this child has experienced sadness herself, and has experienced sadness because her Daddy was nasty to her. Her ability to imagine things in an 'as if' or pretend

Box 2.5 Autism

Characteristics

Children with autism usually have a normal physical appearance, but show the following abnormalities of behaviour (American Psychiatric Association 1994):

Impaired social interaction – they don't make friends or enjoy the company of others; they don't seek to share experiences, and lack emotional empathy

Impaired communication – spoken and written language, gesture and signing, and non-verbal communication are all affected. About 50 per cent of all individuals with autism never acquire useful language. Those who do, talk in a stilted, literal fashion on limited topics, breaking the unwritten rules

of conversation (language PRAGMATICS).

Impaired imagination and creativity – behaviour is inflexible and repetitive, including repetitive movements, speech-echoing, rituals and obsessions.

Additional problems are common: these include learning difficulties, clumsiness and hyperactivity. The common occurrence of dual or multiple handicaps is one of the reasons why children with autism are so different from each other. Another reason is, of course, that they have all have different personalities and life experiences. However, it is also possible that subtypes of autism exist.

Plate 2.5 Panorama of Edinburgh, a drawing by the remarkably gifted autistic boy, Stephen Wiltshire

mode enables her to suppose that Mummy too may be sad, because Daddy was nasty to her also.

Theories of mind

THEORY OF MIND

MIND READING

FALSE-BELIEF TASKS

Some psychologists think that it is useful to describe children as developing hypotheses about other persons' emotions, desires and beliefs. This is referred to as a THEORY OF MIND or skills in MIND READING. There is currently much debate about how theory of mind develops in children (Astington et al. 1988; Perner 1991; Wellman 1990). A crucial kind of study has used FALSE-BELIEF TASKS. Such tasks have been of particular interest, as they provide a test case for finding out whether children really understand the relationship between beliefs and behaviour.

A standard false-belief task involves someone looking for an object they have previously hidden. The child being tested has seen someone else move the object to a different place. So where does the child think the first person will look for the object? In the place they previously hid it, or in the place where the child

Causes

Autism is generally thought to result from some kind of damage or dysfunction within the brain. However, very little is known about the nature or location of any such damage/dysfunction. Many of the child psychologists who research into autism are particularly concerned to discover what it is which the autistic person's brain can't do (from birth or infancy onwards) which causes the impairments of social interaction, communication and creativity which are the hallmarks of autism. Current suggestions include impaired 'mind reading' skills and lack of a theory of mind (Baron-Cohen 1993); a basic difficulty in empathizing with other people (Hobson 1994), or that they have impaired mechanisms for controlling the stopping, starting and switching of behaviour (Harris 1993).

Outlook

There is no medical treatment for autism, although drugs and dietary changes may reduce some symptoms in some children. The large majority of people with autism will never be able to lead independent lives, remaining socially isolated and conspicuously 'odd'. However, young children with autism can benefit from various forms of play therapy designed to break down social withdrawal and encourage interaction. Older children may benefit from intervention based on learning-theory principles, and with appropriate support and education a small minority of very able children with autism may do well at school and even go on to lead independent lives.

Incidence

Severe forms of autism occur in about 1 in every 1,800 live births, although milder forms occur about four times as frequently as this. Boys are more likely to be affected than girls.

Controversies to explore

1. Is autism essentially a social disorder or a cognitive disorder? How meaningful is it to make this sort of distinction?
2. Should adolescents and young adults with autism, or other developmental disorders involving physical or mental handicaps, be helped to develop their sexuality?

now knows it is? The former answer is correct, but the child can only give this answer if she can realize that the first person has a 'false belief' about the object's location.

Wimmer and Perner (1983), in a study in Salzburg, Austria, told young children a story about a boy called Maxi who comes back with his mother from shopping. Mother lifts Maxi up to help him put the chocolate away in a blue cupboard. Then Maxi goes out to play. His mother later takes the chocolate out, and puts it back in a green cupboard. She leaves. Maxi returns. 'Where will Maxi look for the chocolate?' They found that 3-year-olds could not succeed on this task, and even many 4- and 5-year-olds failed. Those children who failed had not just forgotten the story, as most answered correctly the 'reality' question, 'Where is the chocolate really?' Subsequent studies using other false-belief tasks have found that children can sometimes succeed on such tasks at the age of 4 years, or just before (e.g. Lewis & Osborne 1990). Nevertheless, it is a consistent finding that most 3-year-olds fail false-belief tasks, and this indicates a major limitation in such children's cognitive abilities.

Autism is described in Box 2.5. Baron-Cohen et al. (1985) established that, compared to normal and to Down's syndrome children matched for mental age, children with autism had a specific disability on a standard false-belief task; very few could succeed at it. Baron-Cohen et al. argued that children with autism show a specific developmental delay in theory of mind. Such a discovery has important implications for interpreting some of the characteristic behaviours and difficulties associated with autism (Happé 1994).

Understanding emotions

Although young children can understand the more straightforward emotions such as anger, happiness or fear, some emotions are more complex and depend on one's behaviour in the light of the behaviour or expectations of others; for example, pride or shame or guilt. A child will feel pride when they have done something which gains someone else's approval, or shame if it gains their disapproval. Such approval or disapproval can be directly forthcoming from others, but older children can internalize such reactions in terms of social and cultural norms and obligations. Seven-year-olds, but not 5-year-olds, are able to describe situations which would bring about pride or shame. From about 7 years, they are also able to describe situations where they could experience mixed feelings – for example, feeling both angry and sad if their brother hit them.

In general, by 6 or 7 years children seem able to understand and manipulate emotions in a more complex way. It would appear that, as well as being able to understand that someone else can feel a different emotion (metarepresentation), they can begin to operate recursively on such understanding (Harris 1989). For example:

> Diana falls over and hurts herself. She knows that the other children will laugh if she shows how she feels. So she tries to hide how she feels.

What will Diana do, and why? Many 6-year-olds (but not 4-year-olds) are able to say that Diana will look happy, and explain why; for example 'she didn't want the other children to know that she's sad that she fell over'. This is an embedded sentence with a recursive structure of the form 'I may not want you to know how I feel'. Four year-olds can cope with 'I know how you feel', but only by 6 years does this further recursion seem to become possible. This marks another step forward in understanding emotion and in social-cognitive development generally.

Sex differences in development

Observations of 2- to 4-year-olds, at home and in nursery classes, show that boys tend to prefer transportation toys, blocks and activities involving gross motor activity such as throwing or kicking balls, or rough-and-tumbling; girls tend to prefer dolls, and dressing-up or domestic play. Many activities, however, do not show a sex preference at this age (Smith 1986).

In nursery school, children tend to select same-sex partners for play, and by the time children are getting into team games from about 6 or 7 years onward, sex segregation in the playground is much greater. Boys tend to prefer outdoor play and, later, team games; whereas girls prefer indoor, more sedentary activities, and often play in pairs. Boys more frequently engage in both play-fighting and in actual aggressive behaviour. Girls tend to be more empathic, and put more emphasis on intimacy and exclusiveness in their friendships (Lever 1978).

Even pre-school children have beliefs about what is most appropriate for one sex, or the other – SEX-ROLE STEREOTYPES (Kuhn et al. 1978). In a study of 5- and 8-year-old children in England, Ireland and the USA (Best et al. 1977), the majority of boys and girls agreed that females were soft-hearted whereas males were strong, aggressive, cruel and coarse. By 8 years of age children's stereotypes are very similar to those obtained with adults. Barry et al. (1957) made a survey of child-rearing in 110, mostly non-literate, societies. In more than 80 per cent of societies, girls more than boys were encouraged to be nurturant, whereas boys more than girls were subject to training for self-reliance and achievement. In many societies responsibility and obedience was also encouraged in girls more than boys.

SEX-ROLE STEREOTYPES

How parents bring up children is clearly one strong factor in sex differences – this is called the SOCIAL LEARNING THEORY (Bandura 1969). However, most psychologists accept that sex hormones also play a part. In normal foetal development male sex hormones perhaps predispose boys to become more physically active and interested in rough-and-tumble play. Children may also observe the behaviour of same-sex models, and imitate them; for example, boys might observe and imitate the behaviour of male figures in TV films in their playful and aggressive behaviour. Kohlberg (1969) argued that this growing sense of gender identity is crucial to sex-role identification. The process has been termed SELF-SOCIALIZATION by Maccoby and Jacklin (1974), since it does not depend directly on external reinforcement. A number of studies have found development of gender identity and constancy to correlate with the degree of sex-typed behaviour.

SOCIAL LEARNING THEORY

SELF-SOCIALIZATION

Development of peer relationships

By the age of 2 years, children are becoming very interested in peers – other children of about the same age. Most social interactions between under-2s are simple – looking at another child and smiling, showing a toy, or making a noise (Mueller & Brenner 1977). Infants have not yet learnt the skills of social interaction; whereas adults can 'scaffold' social interactions with infants, it usually takes young children some 2 or 3 years to become really competent at interacting socially with age-mates, knowing what are appropriate behaviours in certain situations, what behaviour to expect back, and waiting to take one's turn.

Early peer experience (say, in toddler groups or day nurseries) can help this

Box 2.6   Sibling Relationships (Dunn & Kendrick 1982)

Two psychologists at Cambridge University, Judy Dunn and Carol Kendrick, made observations in 40 homes where parents with one child aged about 2 years were expecting a second in a month or so. They made further visits when the second child was about 1 month old, and again at 8 months and at 14 months. Many first-born children showed signs of jealousy when the new sibling arrived. They had previously been the centre of attention from parents, but now the new brother or sister got more. Much of this jealousy and ambivalence was directed towards parents; but some showed ambivalence or hostility to the baby:

Child: Baby, baby (caressing her). Monster. Monster.
Mother: She's not a monster.
Child: Monster.

The great majority of the first-borns showed interest and affection towards the baby, being concerned if they cried. The sibling relationship was one in which considerable emotions may be aroused – both of love and of envy. This close and emotionally powerful relationship may be an optimal situation in which to learn how to understand others. Siblings seem to be learning how to frustrate, tease, placate, comfort or get their own way with their brother or sister. Dunn and Kendrick relate one incident in which 14-month-old Callum keeps trying to get some magnetic letters which his 3-year-old sister Laura is playing with on a tray. Laura repeatedly says 'no', but Callum won't stop. Finally, Laura picks up the tray with the letters and takes it to a high table that Callum can't reach. Callum is furious and starts to cry; he goes straight to a sofa where Laura's comfort objects, a rag doll and a pacifier, are lying. He takes the doll and holds it tight, looking at Laura! Laura now gets very upset, starts crying, and runs to take the doll. At an early age (14 months) Callum seems to have calculated how to annoy Laura so as to get his own back on her. These are interesting observations to compare with ideas about children's 'theory of mind', as well as the critique of Piaget's ideas about egocentrism.

along (Clarke-Stewart 1991). So can having siblings – brothers or sisters. Siblings are generally close enough in age to be important social partners for each other in the family. Older siblings can show great tolerance for younger ones, and can act as an important model for more competent behaviour. They can also show hostility and ambivalence; this has been observed in many different societies (Eibl-Eibesfeldt 1989). A study of the impact of siblings is shown in Box 2.6. Children can learn early social cognitive skills from older siblings; but also from adults and peers. Research on children without siblings shows that they do well on achievement and intelligence scores, and have no deficits in social adjustment (Falbo & Polit 1986).

The period from 2 to 4 years does see a great increase in the skills children have with peers. Mildred Parten (1932) observed 2- to 4-year-olds and described how they might be 'unoccupied', an 'onlooker' on other's activities, or, if engaged in an activity, they could be 'solitary', in 'parallel' activity with others or in 'associative' or 'cooperative' activity with others. In 'parallel' activity, children play near each other with the same materials, but do not interact much – playing independently at the same sandpit, for example. In 'associative' activity children interact together at an activity, doing similar things, perhaps each adding building blocks to the same tower. In 'cooperative' activity children interact together in complementary ways; for example, one child gets blocks out of a box and hands them to another child, who builds the tower. Solitary activity de-

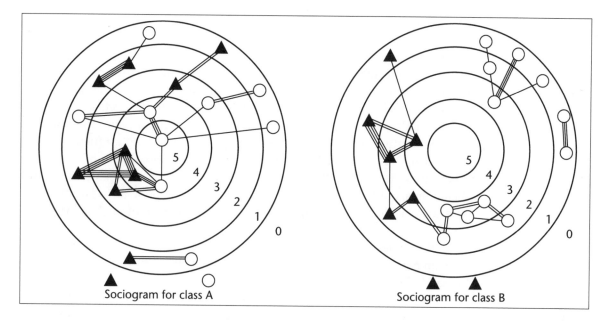

Sociogram for class A   Sociogram for class B

creases with age, associative and cooperative activity increase. Also, the size of playgroups increases consistently through this age period (Parten 1932; Hertz-Lazarowitz et al. 1981).

As children go through nursery and infant school, they start forming friendships. Young children think of friendships as playing with someone a lot; shared values and interests become more important later, and concepts of intimacy and commitment in adolescence (Bigelow & La Gaipa 1980).

In a group of children, some will be more popular than others; a few may lack friends entirely. The study of friendships in groups is called SOCIOMETRY. One way to do this is simply to watch who children play with, when they have a free

Figure 2.5 Sociograms of association networks in two classes of pre-school children: circles represent girls, triangles boys. Clark et al., *Journal of Child Psychiatry and Psychology*, 10, 1969 (Cambridge University Press).

SOCIOMETRY

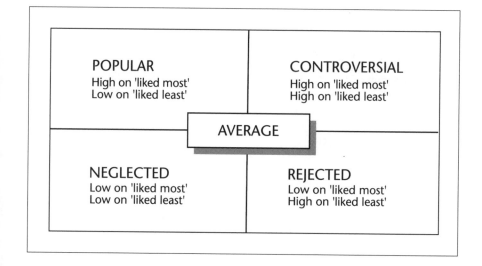

Figure 2.6 Five types of sociometric status. Based on material in Cole, Dodge and Coppotelli, *Developmental Psychology*, 18, 1982, pp. 557–70 (Copyright © 1982 American Psychological Association. Reprinted with permission).

SOCIOGRAM

choice – as they often do in nursery and infant school, or in school playgrounds. For example, the SOCIOGRAM in figure 2.5 comes from Clark et al. (1969), who observed nursery-school children. Each triangle represents a boy, each circle a girl; the number of lines joining two children represents the percentage of observations on which they were seen playing together. The concentric circles show the number of play partners a child has. In this class there is one very popular girl who links two large subgroups; one boy and one girl have no clear partners.

An alternative method is to ask each child 'Who are your best friends?', or to name their three best friends. Some investigators have also asked children to say whom they do not like (Coie et al. 1982). These researchers have not drawn sociograms, but have instead categorized children as 'popular', 'controversial', 'rejected', 'neglected' or 'average', according to whether they are high or low on positive and negative nominations (see figure 2.6).

SOCIOMETRIC
STATUS-TYPES

A lot of research has now been carried out using these SOCIOMETRIC STATUS-TYPES. In particular, there has been concern about children who are consistently 'rejected'. This has been found to be the most stable status-type between 8 and 11 years (Coie & Dodge 1983), and observations have confirmed that rejected children spend less time in cooperative play and social conversation, and more time arguing and fighting; they tend to play in smaller groups, and with younger or with less popular companions (Ladd 1983). They lack good skills for joining other children's play (Dodge et al. 1983).

The view that rejected children lack social skills has been developed by Dodge et al. (1986), and Crick and Dodge (1994). They suggest that the social skills of

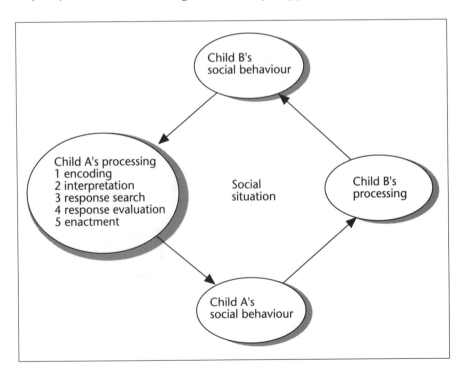

Figure 2.7 A model of social skills and social exchange in peer interaction.
Adapted from Dodge et al., 'Social Competence in Children' in *Monographs of the Society for Research in Child Development*, 51, 2, 1986 (Society for Research in Child Development).

peer interaction can be envisaged as an exchange model (see figure 2.7). The process of social interaction is broken down into a series of stages. Difficulties in social skills might occur at any one of these stages – for example, in interpreting another child's behaviour, or choosing how to respond.

What happens if children are rejected in school peer groups over a number of years? Reviews of a number of relevant studies (mostly in the USA) have shown that the number and quality of friendships children have, as well as degree of aggressiveness, predict dropping out of school early, and high rates of juvenile/ adult crime (Parker & Asher 1987). Whatever the difficulties of proof, many psychologists believe that social-skills training may be useful for those children who lack friends; this training is anyway usually directed to changing behaviours which are the correlates of peer rejection (such as high aggression, or high withdrawal).

Play in childhood

Although we have discussed aggressive behaviour between children, this is not usually very frequent; children spend a great deal of their free time playing together – or sometimes on their own. Piaget described stages of play, and this was elaborated by an Israeli psychologist, Sara Smilansky (1968). Both started with the kinds of simple mouthing and banging of objects during the sensorimotor period. From about 15 months onward, children start showing signs of PRETEND or SYMBOLIC PLAY. For example, they will start 'feeding' dolls, and putting them to sleep; or pretending that wooden blocks are cakes, for a tea party. These pretend games can develop – by the time children are 3 and 4 years – into elaborate role-play episodes, of mothers, fathers and babies, doctors and patients, heroes and monsters, and so forth, often influenced by books, TV programmes and films. Smilansky called this SOCIODRAMATIC PLAY. In addition she described CONSTRUCTIVE PLAY, in which children are using objects in non-pretend ways – for example, doing a jigsaw or pouring sand or water from one container to another. It seems likely that children are developing a lot of skills in these kinds of play, though exactly how important they are in the nursery school and infant school curriculum is still a matter of debate (Moyles 1994).

One kind of play was left out of Smilansky's scheme – ROUGH-AND-TUMBLE PLAY, where children chase and tackle each other, often smiling or laughing. This kind of play can be confused with aggressive fighting, because of their superficial similarity, but in fact most children are accomplished at telling them apart by at least 8 years of age (Costabile et al. 1991).

Aggression in childhood

Young children often engage in fighting, or in verbal taunts. Jersild and Markey (1935) described many kinds of conflict behaviour in nursery schools, such as taking or grabbing toys or objects held or used by another child; and making

PRETEND PLAY

SYMBOLIC PLAY

SOCIODRAMATIC PLAY

CONSTRUCTIVE PLAY

ROUGH-AND-TUMBLE PLAY

unfavourable remarks about someone such as 'you're no good at it' or 'I don't like you'. These tend to decline with age (Cummings et al. 1989). Some researchers distinguish *instrumental* and *hostile* aggression (based on whether the distress or harm is inferred to be the primary intent of the act); and *individual* and *group* aggression (depending on whether more than one child attacks another). An interesting distinction has been made between three types of aggression by Bjorkqvist et al. (1992). They describe *physical* aggression (hitting, kicking, etc.), *verbal* aggression (name-calling, taunting), and *indirect* aggression (telling nasty stories about someone, isolating someone socially). Of these, indirect aggression is done via a third party and is more difficult to detect. It does, however, become more common with age, and is more frequent in girls; physical aggression, by contrast, is more frequent in boys.

A certain amount of aggressive and assertive behaviour is normal. However, some children (often rejected by peers) show high levels of aggression, often of a hostile or harassing nature. If not dealt with at the time, children who show persistent high aggressiveness through the school years are at increased risk for later delinquency, anti-social and violent behaviour (Farrington 1990). Patterson et al. (1989) have suggested that certain key aspects of parenting are involved in this happening. Children who experience irritable and ineffective discipline at home, and poor parental monitoring of their activities, together with a lack of parental warmth, are particularly likely to become aggressive in peer groups and at school. Anti-social behaviour at school is likely to be linked to academic failure and peer rejection, they argue; and in adolescence, especially if parental monitoring is lax, these young people are likely to be involved in deviant and delinquent peer groups. Patterson et al.'s hypothesis is shown in figure 2.8. Interventions can focus on helping parents improve their child-management skills, for example via manuals and videotaped materials.

BULLYING refers to persistent aggressive behaviour directed towards a particular victim who cannot retaliate effectively. It can cause great distress to victims. Bullying is quite pervasive in many schools, and many victims keep quiet about it (Olweus 1993). However, schools can take action to reduce the problem, by

Figure 2.8 A developmental progression for antisocial behaviour. Paterson et al., 'A developmental perspective on antisocial behaviour', in *American Psychologist*, 44, 1989 (Copyright © 1989 American Psychological Association. Reprinted with permission).

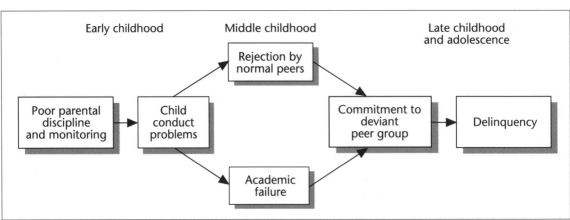

having definite policies on the issue, improving playground supervision, raising awareness through curricular activities, and working intensively with individuals and small groups who are affected (Smith & Sharp 1994).

Ethnic awareness, identity, preference and prejudice

As a child grows up he or she will become aware that people differ by ethnic origin. By 4 or 5 years children seem able to make basic discriminations, for example between black and white; and during the next few years more difficult ones, such as Anglo and Hispanic. By around 8 or 9 years, children understand that ethnic identity remains constant despite changes in age, or superficial attributes such as clothing.

Children often segregate by race, as well as by gender. A study of black and white kindergarten children in the USA (Finkelstein & Haskins 1983) found that 5-year-olds showed marked segregation by race, which increased during the year. However, neither black nor white children behaved differently to other-colour peers from same-colour peers. In older children too, segregation by race is noticeable, but less marked than segregation by sex.

Prejudice implies a negative evaluation of another person, on the basis of some general attribute (for example sex, race or disability), rather than their individual personality. Thus, racial prejudice means a negative evaluation of someone as a consequence of their being in a certain racial or ethnic group. Segregation in itself need not reflect prejudice, but it can make it difficult for children to overcome stereotypes by means of social interaction, and the experience of prejudice can be very damaging.

PREJUDICE can be measured by asking children to rate photos of children from different ethnic groups along scales of liking or evaluation (Aboud 1988); prejudice seems to increase from 4 to 7 years, mainly at the expense of minority ethnic groups. From 8 years on, white children tend to remain prejudiced against black or minority group children, while the latter show a more mixed pattern but often become more positive to their own group. Children also become able to think more flexibly about ethnic differences, and in terms of individuals rather than groups, so that their prejudice can be modified. Schools have been a focus for work to reduce racial prejudice in children. Cooperative group work, as well as a multiracial curriculum approach which emphasizes the diversity of racial and cultural beliefs and practices and gives them equal evaluation, may help in this process.

▓ Communication and Language ▓

The early development of communication

Communication is often represented as a linear process, in terms of sending messages from A to B (see figure 2.9a). However, human communication is a

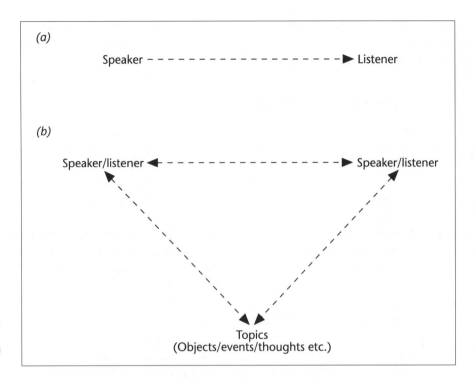

Figure 2.9 Models of communication. (a) shows the simplest form of linear model. (b) shows the 'communication triangle'.

two-way thing. It also involves referring to things in the world. It is therefore more appropriately represented in terms of a triangular relationship in which people share an understanding of things in the world, and exchange messages about these things. We will use the points of the triangle shown in figure 2.9b to consider early communicative development, focusing on how babies and their carers communicate together, and what they communicate about.

How babies and carers communicate

Babies and their carers use their faces, voices, body movements, and touch as their means of communicating. This kind of communicating without speech is called NON-VERBAL COMMUNICATION. Animals are totally reliant on non-verbal communication, and it may be tempting to think of it as a primitive method of communicating and something which humans later leave behind. This is far from the truth. We continue to use non-verbal communication throughout life, to supplement and to support speech (see chapter 12).

Babies' ability to communicate with their mothers is essential to their survival, and they are born with the basic means of doing this. Babies recognize their mothers' face from a very early age (see Box 2.2). They also recognize their mother's voice, having learned its distinctive sound while in the womb (DeCasper & Fifer 1980). Faces and voices also capture the very young baby's attention more than other sights and sounds. Babies are therefore well prepared not only to recognize primary care givers but also to watch facial expressions and listen to voices. By 10 weeks they can discriminate between facial expressions of hap-

NON-VERBAL
COMMUNICATION

Plate 2.6 Baby reaching out towards mother's face, showing recognition
Source: Collections/Sandra Lousada.

piness, anger and sadness, and by 6 months they can match up the emotional expression of faces and voices. They also respond to the parent's body movements and gestures, and by 4 to 5 months babies will look where another person is looking (Bakeman & Adamson 1982), and by the end of the first year they will look at something another person is pointing at (Butterworth 1991). These important skills are called, respectively, JOINT ATTENTION and SHARED REFERENCE.

JOINT ATTENTION

SHARED REFERENCE

In the section on the newborn infant we saw that very young babies have a number of differentiated cries. They also screw up their faces and use whole-body tension and movement to indicate distress. These involuntary signals are important to the newborn's survival in that they indicate that she has some immediate need. At around 6 weeks babies begin to smile, and they may vocalize and become more active when they see their mother's face and hear her voice (Brazelton et al. 1974). This is very rewarding, and reinforces the bond between mother and baby helping to ensure the baby's immediate well-being and ultimate survival. Later in the first year the baby's cries become more differentiated and the baby's range of expressive movement also increases as she gains

Plate 2.7 Three- to five-year-old child playing with straws
Source: Collections/Anthea Sieveking.

muscular control. For example, babies of 9 to 10 months raise their arms in a 'pick me up' gesture when they want to be fed, comforted, or played with; and early reaching for objects develops into an 'I want' gesture (Masur 1983) which later develops into communicative pointing (Butterworth, 1991). Conventional social gestures such as waving bye-bye or blowing kisses are often taught to infants in their second year.

Expressive vocalizations and gestural actions are learned in the course of routines centring around feeding, dressing, bathing and play. For this reason, the baby's early signalling system may be referred to as SENSORIMOTOR COMMUNICATION, emphasizing the fact that, like early cognitive development, communication in the first year and a half is rooted in action schemas and confined to perception and action in the here and now.

SENSORIMOTOR COMMUNICATION

Communicative interaction

From birth, babies involuntarily evoke conversation-like exchanges with others. For example, infant feeding consists of short bursts of sucking interspersed with pauses during which the baby gazes into her mother's face. The mother's natural response is to return the baby's gaze, smile, and to make some sound or movement acknowledging the baby's attentive look. The baby gazes back, returns to sucking, then pauses again. And so the earliest PROTOCONVERSATIONS begin. Two- to 3-month-old infants actually become upset if the mother fails to react to their vocalizations and movements. They are highly sensitive to the rhythms of speech, and during lap play may reflect these rhythms in their own body movements. This so-called INTERACTIONAL SYNCHRONY is another example of babies' readiness for communicative interaction (Condon & Sander 1974).

PROTOCONVERSATIONS

INTERACTIONAL
SYNCHRONY

To achieve the adult model of communication shown in figure 2.9b, babies have to learn that other people are persons like themselves, with shared perceptions, desires and emotions, and shared understanding of communication systems. The baby's innate capacity for imitation, referred to above, must entail that the baby's brain is so designed that she 'knows' that there are certain correspondences between herself and others. Similarly, her capacities for joint attention, shared reference, and perceiving emotions enable the baby to understand that she and another person can see the same thing, want the same thing, and have similar feelings about an object. It is probably not until the end of the second year, however, that the baby learns that other people have internal experiences which resemble hers (Wellman 1990). When the baby knows this she can use her communication not only to intentionally affect the actions of others, but also to affect their thoughts, beliefs, desires and knowledge.

Development of communication in early childhood

At some time in the first half of their second year most children begin to develop spoken language. Children must learn the sounds of their language, its vocabulary and its grammar.

Learning the sound system

Babies are innately gifted speech processors. As mentioned above, very young infants can discriminate between individual speech sounds such as 'bah' and 'pah'. They are also sensitive to the patterns of stress, intonation and rhythms used during speech, and use this sensitivity to discern the boundaries of syllables, words, phrases and sentences (Fernald & Simon 1984). However, despite this precocious ability to perceive and also to use simple intonation and stress patterns, the comprehension of complex intonational meaning is not achieved until adolescence: when the football results are read out on the radio adults can often guess from the announcer's intonation what the second score is going to be, but primary school children can't do this (Cruttenden 1974).

At around six months the first big step towards speech production is taken when the child begins to BABBLE. Babbling starts as the playful production of single consonant and vowel-like sounds, and develops into the production of repetitive syllable strings, such as 'da-da-da', 'goo-goo-goo'. All babies babble

BABBLE

Most English consonants begin to be acquired between 2 and 4 years of age. This diagram shows the order of emergence as found in a study which elicited pronunciations of words from 20 children, using photographs of familiar objects. The periods shown are averages, and the upper age-limit is based on a correct pronunciation by 90% of the children. The diagram also shows that some sounds were already being produced correctly by the majority of the children at age 2; and others were still not being said correctly at age 4.

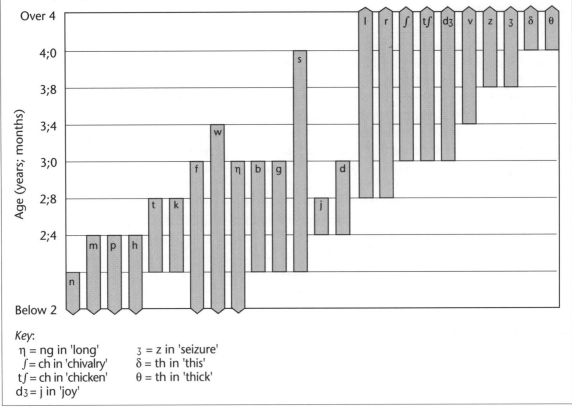

Key:
η = ng in 'long'
ʃ = ch in 'chivalry'
tʃ = ch in 'chicken'
dʒ = j in 'joy'

ʒ = z in 'seizure'
δ = th in 'this'
θ = th in 'thick'

Figure 2.10 The emergence of consonants. Crystal, *The Cambridge Encyclopedia of Language*, p. 240 (Cambridge University Press, 1987).

alike, regardless of their country of origin, and deaf children go through the early stages of babbling, though they do not reach the advanced stages of repetitive strings. This suggests that babbling is initially biologically determined, but subsequently maintained via the child's own auditory feedback (Locke 1993). Babble helps the baby to gain greater control of her speech mechanisms. However, it is important to remember that babble is not, from the baby's point of view, practice for speech. Babies babble because they enjoy it!

JARGON

Towards the end of the first year babbling turns into JARGON. This consists of syllable sequences which increasingly use the sound combinations, rhythms and intonation patterns of the language the child hears. Soon after this, the child's first words or word approximations appear. It is probably only at this stage that the child begins to associate the sounds she makes with objects and events. The sounds of English take four years or more to develop. Figure 2.10 shows the age at which English consonants typically emerge.

In the toddler who is developing speech the lack of a full sound system and

Table 2.3 Some typical child pronunciation errors in the second and third years

	Examples			
	Adult word	Child pronunciation	Age (yrs; mths)	Source
Substitution processes (replacement of a sound by another sound)				
Stopping (a fricative is replaced by a stop)	see	ti:	2; 9	Smith (1973)
Fronting (the place of articulation is fronted, with velar and palatal consonants being replaced by alveolars)	shoe goat	zu' dut	2; 0 2; 0	Velten (1943) Velten (1943)
Gliding ([w] or [i] is substituted for a liquid)	leg ready	jek wedi	2; 1 2; 1	I I
Assimilation processes (a sound becomes more similar to an adjacent sound)				
Voicing (consonants tend to be voiced preceding a vowel and devoiced at the end of a syllable)	paper pig	be:bə bik	2; 3 1; 5	Smith (1973) I
Consonant harmony (consonants tend to assimilate in words with the structure $C_1VC_2(X)$)	duck tickle tub	gʌk gigu bʌb	1; 7 2; 2 (no age given)	I Smith (1973) Menn (1975)
Progressive vowel assimilation (an unstressed vowel will assimilate to a preceding vowel)	bacon flower	bú:du fá:wü	2; 0 2; 0	Velten (1943) Velten (1943)

difficulty in making rapid transitions from one sound to another cause errors to occur. Children's speech-sound errors are quite consistent and lawful, and broadly similar for all normal children (Goodluck 1991). Some typical phonological errors and the rules which can produce them are shown in table 2.3.

Learning vocabulary

Babies start to show appropriate responses to individual words within their first year. Valentine (1942), for example, observed that his 6-month-old child regularly smiled in response to his name but not to other words. By the age of 14 to 15 months, healthy toddlers can understand approximately 50 words. However, it takes them a further 4 months to be able to produce that number of words (Benedict 1979). Comprehension continues to outrun production throughout life: there are many words which we can understand if someone uses them appropriately in context, but which we would not use with confidence ourselves.

The first words which babies use are usually names of people and pets, foods, body parts, clothes, but also some action words to do with feeding, bathing and playing, and words used socially or expressively, such as 'no', 'up', 'more', 'mine', 'bye-bye'. There is also early use of HOLOPHRASES, that is, two-word utterances which the child learns as if they were a single word, for example 'allgone', 'oh-dear', 'no-more'. Between the ages of 18 months and 6 years the average child learns around 14,000 words. This is an average of nearly 10 new words every day! (Templin 1957). New nouns and verbs are learned via a process referred to as FAST MAPPING, which enables a child to relate a novel object or action to a novel word via the formation of a new concept in as little as a single experience (Dollaghan 1985).

The child's first words are not always used with fully adult meanings. They may be used too narrowly (for example, using 'dog' to refer only to the family dog), or too broadly (using 'dog' to refer to cats as well as dogs). These types of errors are described as errors of UNDEREXTENSION and OVEREXTENSION, respectively. Children may also use words wrongly. This is called MISMATCHING. For example, one child on first seeing the sea shouted out excitedly 'big bah!' – a very understandable error if you are used to baths but not to the sea! Many children have their own words for familiar objects, or make up words which have no adult equivalent. Some highly abstract words, for example 'want' and 'know', are used by children as young as 2.0 (Bretherton et al. 1981). However, such words are learned and first used with limited meanings (e.g. 'Wanna biscuit'; 'Dunno'), their full adult meanings developing more gradually.

HOLOPHRASES

FAST MAPPING

UNDEREXTENSION

OVEREXTENSION

MISMATCHING

The development of grammar

Very little attention has been paid to children's comprehension of grammar. However, Macnamara (1972) has proposed that children at the first words stage begin to work out which words are nouns, verbs, etc. from their understanding of individual words and contexts. Within their third year children know (at an unconscious level) which words in their vocabularies are nouns, verbs, adjec-

Saying no

Several studies have been made of the expression of negation by young children.

1. The first negative words emerge in the second year – usually *no* or *not* as a one-word sentence.
2. The negative words combine with other words to make two-word sentences: *No sit, Gone no, Not there.* Several different meanings can be expressed at this stage – in particular, non-existence, e.g. *No car* (while looking for a toy); rejection, e.g. *no drink* (while pushing a drink away); and denial, e.g. *Not mine* (pointing to someone else's coat). (L. M. Bloom, 1970.)
3. During the third year, negative words come to be used within constructions, e.g. *You no do that, Mummy not got it.* At the same time, such verbs as *can't* and *won't* appear.
4. The negative words and endings come to be used more accurately: *not* replaces *no*, and *n't* is used with more verbs, e.g. *You've not got one, She isn't going.* 'Double' negatives for emphasis are a normal development, e.g. *Nobody don't like to go in.*
5. A few advanced negative constructions are not acquired until the early school years, e.g. the use of *some* vs *any* (cf. *I've not got any* rather than *I've got any*), or the use of *hardly* and *scarcely.*

Asking questions

One of the first topics to be studied by child language researchers was how children learn to ask questions. Three main stages have been proposed for English, and similar developments have been noted in several other languages:

1. The earliest stage makes use of intonation, e.g. *Daddy there?*, spoken with a high rising tone, in effect asks 'Is Daddy there?'
2. During the second year, children start to use question words. *What* and *Where* are usually the first to be acquired, with *why, how,* and *who* coming later. These questions become more complex as the third year approaches, e.g. *Where Daddy going?, What you doing in there?*
3. A major advance comes with the learning of the verb *to be*, and such auxiliary verbs as *have* and *do*. Children discover the apparently simple rule that turns statements into questions by changing the order of the Subject and Verb (e.g. *That is a car* → *Is that a car?*), and then learn that it is not so simple after all (e.g. it cannot be (*Went he to town?*, but *Did he go to town?*). Sentences that use question words pose particular problems: *Where is daddy going?* has in fact *two* forms indicating its status as a question – the word *where* and the inversion *is daddy*. Children often rely on the first alone, and for a while produce such sentences as *Where daddy is going?*. (After R. Brown et al., 1968.)

The complexity of question formation can be seen from the following selection of errors, all made by 2-year-olds:

Whose is that is?
What are you did?
What did you bought?
Is it's my car?
Don't he wanted it?

Despite this complexity, most of these difficulties are overcome before the age of 3.

Figure 2.11 The development of questions and of negation.
Crystal, *The Cambridge Encyclopedia of Language*, p. 243 (Cambridge University Press, 1987).

tives, articles and prepositions (Valian 1986), indicating that comprehension of some aspects of grammar is present from the age of about 2.0 onwards.

Towards the end of their second year, toddlers produce two-word utterances such as 'Mummy push', 'eat dinner'. At one time linguists claimed that children's two-word utterances could be shown to follow simple grammatical rules. However, none of the attempts to show that these utterances follow grammatical rules have proved successful, and it is now thought that they reflect knowledge of vocabulary rather than of grammar. In their third year, however, most children produce three- and four-word utterances which show the beginnings of grammatical structure, such as 'Daddy gone car', 'Go bye-byes now', 'Put on there'. Grammatical markers such as '-ing', '-ed', 's' are commonly omitted, as are words carrying relatively little information, such as 'the', 'and', 'is'. This gives the child's speech a TELEGRAMMATIC character. From about the age of 3.0 years, the telegrammatic character of the child's language reduces and longer sentences appear, initially formed by linking clauses with 'and' but soon incorporating other linking words such as 'so', 'then', 'cos'. Question forms ('What-?' 'Who-?' 'Why-' etc.) and grammatical ways of expressing negation develop in well-defined stages over the pre-school period (see figure 2.11).

TELEGRAMMATIC SPEECH

Through their fourth year, children learn the correct forms and usages of English verbs, including the regular past tense ending '-ed', as well as the use of auxiliaries such as 'do', 'does', 'is', 'was', 'are', 'has', etc. Here children make many typical errors, which are informative about processes underlying language learning. For example, during their third year, children rote learn irregular past participles of common verbs such as 'came', 'went', 'took' and use them correctly. In their fourth year, when they learn the past tense rule 'add *-ed*', they overuse this rule, producing errors such as 'go-ed' and 'taked', or sometimes hybrid errors, such as 'wented' or 'tooked', where both the regular and the irregular past tense forms are combined. These errors show that children do not learn language by simple imitation, but by a much more active process of inferring and applying rules.

LITERACY SKILLS

METALINGUISTIC

The acquisition of grammar continues well into the child's school years, increasingly influenced by the development of LITERACY SKILLS and METALINGUISTIC awareness.

How is spoken language learned?

All healthy children learn to speak in nearly adult ways by around 4.0. Given the complexity of language this is an amazing achievement, and the key question in the study of normal language development is 'How is this done?' Despite half a century or more of research, the answer to this question is still uncertain. The sheer speed at which children learn language, even in adverse circumstances, has led most linguists and psychologists to accept that language learning ability is an in-built faculty of the brain, a specialized ability developed by the processes of evolution. However, there is considerable controversy concerning what this in-built faculty does. Some theorists, notably Chomsky (1986), suggest that children are born with knowledge of Universal Grammar (UG). Other theorists suggest that children are born with general learning processes which enable them to learn language amongst other types of complex knowledge. These issues are discussed in greater depth in chapter 10.

UNIVERSAL GRAMMAR

Even if the brain is genetically programmed to learn language, some language input is needed for the in-built system to work on: this is obviously so, since English children learn to speak English, French children French, and so on. However, it is not enough for a child simply to listen passively to language. Bruner (1977) studied early language acquisition and concluded that for a child to learn language normally a Language Acquisition Support System (LASS) must be available. He suggested that this support system consists of highly familiar play or care routines, or FORMATS, within which mothers SCAFFOLD, or constructively support, each next step of their child's language development. Bruner's approach owes much to the work of Vygotsky, whose views on the role of social interaction in children's learning were outlined above.

LANGUAGE ACQUISITION SUPPORT SYSTEM

FORMATS

SCAFFOLD

One of the ways in which mothers and other adults, and also older children, help toddlers to learn language is by using what was once called Motherese, but which is now more usually referred to as CHILD-DIRECTED SPEECH (CDS). CDS usually consists of short, fluent, grammatically correct utterances, with enhanced intonation. The advantages of CDS for children are obvious. Instead of being told 'If you look downstream you might see a swan', the toddler in the pushchair is invited to 'Look! – see the big bird? He's in the water!' (with the voice and face dramatizing the exclamation and question marks). In the 1970s some researchers claimed that the existence of CDS seriously undermined the argument that language learning ability is innate. However, it appears that CDS is not necessary for normal language to develop, since it is not found in all societies (Snow 1986). Attention has therefore shifted to looking at the way CDS supplements innate mechanisms in the development of language. CDS has been found to stimulate language development, as does the RECASTING of ungrammatical utterances (e.g. 'Don't want none') into grammatical forms (e.g. 'Don't you want any?') (Nelson et al. 1984). Parents who use grammatical constructions just beyond the child's current range also help to develop their child's language.

CHILD-DIRECTED SPEECH

RECASTING

Finally, cognition has a role to play in children's language development. Cognitive and linguistic development normally proceed together, the one supporting the other. The child's first meaningful words are dependent on the prior development of concepts, and on the cognitive processes such as attention, memory, and categorization ability on which concept learning depends (McShane 1991). However, language is the main vehicle of human thought, and once a child has acquired language-for-thinking, her cognitive abilities are in turn greatly enhanced.

What infants and young children communicate about – the shared world

Whereas prelinguistic infants communicate mainly about their needs and desires, children from around the age of 2.0 use their developing speech and language in increasingly varied ways. They comment on things which interest them, they ask questions, they tell you things about themselves. From around the age of three they can recount events and tell stories, make up pretend-play dialogue, argue, joke and tease using language. As they move towards the school years they increasingly use language to remember, plan, reason and solve problems. Once in school, language becomes the main vehicle of learning for the normal child. The teacher instructs, explains, questions and responds using language. Friendships and group roles are influenced by language ability, the persuasive, articulate and verbally entertaining child often dominating those with less well-developed verbal skills.

The content of young children's communication reflects their developing knowledge of the world. This is acquired via individual and shared experiences. Children who have plenty of play materials (not necessarily expensive toys) at home, who have siblings and friends, who have an extended family, attend a crèche or a nursery, who are played with and read to, taken out and about, will, all other things being equal, have richer experiences and therefore more to talk about than children who, for example, are brought up in an institution, who come from very disadvantaged homes, or who have to spend long periods in hospital.

Communicative interaction

PRAGMATICS

The ability to use spoken language in communicative interaction involves learning the rules and conventions of language use, or PRAGMATICS (see chapter 10). Within their second year children can gain attention by establishing eye contact, by touching, and vocalizing (Wellman & Lempers 1977), and they will seek to share an experience with others by pointing. However, at this stage children's language is very limited, and they do not know how to hold another person's attention or how to provide the information the other person needs. Language at the two- to three-word level is therefore mainly used in responding to others, in detached comments or soliloquies rather than in initiating conversations, and children require a great deal of support from adults in order to maintain a coherent conversation of more than minimal length.

Between the ages of 3.0 and 5.0, however, children learn strategies for starting conversations ('Guess what we did? . . . '; 'Mummy, you know what? . . . '). They also know how to respond in ways which keep the conversation going, including clarifying and correcting errors, requesting clarification, and persisting in varied ways (Dunn & Shatz 1989). Children below the age of 3.6 to 4.0 know enough about people to adopt different ways of speaking to their playgroup teacher, to Granny, and to their best friend. However, it is not until their fifth year, when they have developed a theory of mind (see above), that they fully understand that other people may not know things which they themselves know, or that others may not be interested in things which they themselves are interested in, and learn to take other people's knowledge, beliefs and desires into account in conversation.

▨ **Whole Child Development** ▨

In preceding sections we have said something about the infant's and young child's early motor development, sensory development, and temperament, with more extended sections on the development of cognition, social and emotional behaviours, and communication and language. Within any section we have frequently referred to other sections, demonstrating that it is not possible in reality to treat the various aspects of development independently of each other. In reality, development of the human individual is not like a rainbow consisting of (more or less) distinct bands of colour. It is more like a tapestry in which all the different colours are interwoven to make a unique pattern. This can be clearly seen in the case of developmental disorders which might appear to be 'just' a sensory impairment (such as deafness), or 'just' a motor impairment (e.g. unusual clumsiness), or 'just' a speech difficulty (as in the case of cleft palate) (to take a few examples at random), but which will affect almost all aspects of a child's development. As psychologists we have to study the threads of development separately. However, in the end it is the interaction which makes us what we are.

CHAPTER SUMMARY

1   Developmental psychologists are interested in describing the typical sequences of development, whether physical, social, cognitive or language skills.

2   Some psychologists also favour more powerful stage models of development; there are arguments for and against such models.

3   One accepted stage is that of pre-natal development, divided into the substages of zygote, embryo and foetus. Pre-natal growth is strongly predetermined or canalized but can be disrupted by environmental hazards (teratogens). Genetic factors also influence development. Down's syndrome is an example of a chromosomal abnormality.

4   At birth, the infant already possesses reflexive abilities. Sleeping and crying are important infant states. Temperamental traits present from birth may influence personality in later life. Some perceptual abilities are present from birth: infants are interested in face-like stimuli and learn them rapidly.

5   The period from birth to about 18 months was characterized as the sensorimotor period, or stage, by Piaget. During this time infants develop schemes of motor behaviour, leading later to symbolic representations of the world around them. A particular achievement of this period is object permanence, the realization that objects continue to exist when out of sight. Recent work suggests very young infants may have greater competence than Piaget thought.

6   The period from about 2 to 7 years was labelled by Piaget as the preoperational stage. Piaget thought that at this stage children are still limited in their ability to reason logically; for example, they fail class-inclusion and conservation tasks. Other researchers have criticized Piaget in his task design and think that he underestimated children's abilities.

7   From 7 to 11 years, children enter what Piaget called the stage of concrete operational thought. While they still having difficulty with abstract tasks, in many ways their reasoning approximates that of adults.

8   Vygotsky emphasized the social context of learning with a more knowledgeable other, and described the zone of proximal development as the child's potential to benefit from this.

9   An alternative approach to cognitive development is the information-processing approach. This emphasizes developments in memory capabilities, such as working memory space, encoding and retrieval skills, memory strategies and metamemory.

10 By the end of the first year an infant has usually developed one or more social attachments to care givers. The 'strange situation' devised by Ainsworth is a measure of security of attachment in infancy.

11 Bowlby advocated a maternal deprivation hypothesis, arguing that a young child needed continuous care from one person between 6 months and 3 years of age. This hypothesis has been strongly criticized.

12 Beyond infancy, children are thought to develop internal working models of relationships which may show continuity with earlier experiences.

13 During the first few years, children start to understand others' emotional states, and later their desires and beliefs; this is referred to as a 'theory of mind'. The false-belief task is a standard test of some theory of mind abilities. Later, more complex emotions are understood, such as pride, shame or guilt.

14 Children with autism show characteristic deficits in social interaction, communication and imagination. One possible explanation is that they have a deficit in theory of mind abilities.

15 Sex differences are obvious from the pre-school period onwards. Hormonal factors, parental behaviour, and cultural norms and stereotypes may all influence sex differences.

16 Communication involves two people referring to things in the world. Infants are innately 'ready' to attend to faces and voices and to establish two-way non-verbal communication with care givers.

17 Infants can perceive speech sounds and intonation patterns very early, and respond to them. Speech starts with babbling and jargon, with first words appearing at about one year and vocabulary then increasing very rapidly. Children make typical errors of under- and overextension, and mismatching.

18 Sentences develop through holophrases (two-word utterances) to telegrammatic speech, and later whole sentences which may still show typical grammatical errors, through their fourth year.

19 Chomsky argued for the existence of innate knowledge of a Universal Grammar to explain the rapidity of language learning. Bruner placed more emphasis on the environment with his Language Acquisition Support System. Care givers may help language development through characteristics of child-directed speech, and recasting of ungrammatical utterances.

■ Further Work ■

1. What sorts of abilities do babies have in the first few months of life, and what abilities do they lack?

2. To what extent are Piaget's stages of children's development supported by recent empirical research?
3. In what ways are the development of communication and language related to developments in (a) cognition and (b) social interaction?
4. How important is attachment to a care giver in infancy?
5. What kinds of social and interactive behaviours are characteristic of the pre-school child?

Further Reading

Berk, L. E. (1993; 3rd edn) *Child Development*. Boston: Allyn and Bacon.

> Provides excellent and detailed coverage of all aspects of child development.

Dunn, J. (1988) *The Beginnings of Social Understanding*. Oxford: Blackwell.

> A readable account of research on how children begin to make sense of their social world.

Kail, R. (1990; 3rd edn) *The Development of Memory in Children*. New York: Freeman.

> Provides a very readable summary of the research into children's memory development, with well-chosen experimental examples.

Locke, J. (1993) *The Child's Path to Spoken Language*. Cambridge, Mass.: Harvard University Press.

> A very full but fascinating account of the development of communication and language.

Messer, D. J. (1994) *The Development of Communication: From Social Interaction to Language*. Chichester: John Wiley & Sons.

> A readable introduction to a complex area, and provides plenty of references which can be followed up for more technical and, especially, linguistic detail.

Smith, P. K. and Cowie, H. (1991; 2nd edn) *Understanding Children's Development*. Oxford: Blackwell.

> Chapters covering all the major issues related to child development.

Wood, D. (1988) *How Children Think and Learn*. Oxford: Blackwell.

> A clear introduction to child development, including a good introduction to the influence of Vygotsky's work.

PsyCLE MODULE: DEVELOPMENTAL PSYCHOLOGY

The first simulation presented in this module invites you to act as an experimenter using Piagetian conservation tasks with a small range of children. The background to this theory is presented in the section on Piaget's preoperational stage (see figure 2.3). Can you replicate Piaget's findings with the simulation?

The second simulation uses the same framework and models of children to present some aspects of the contemporary critique such as that presented by Donaldson (1978) and Light et al. (1979).

CHAPTER 3

Adolescence and Adulthood

Peter Smith and Helen Cowie

CHAPTER AGENDA

- In this chapter we focus on key issues in adult life.

- The process of change across the life-span is considered. We reflect on the adult in a social context and discuss the tensions between critical life events and stages in adult development.

- We begin with the transition from adolescence to adulthood, with reference to the interweaving of social context and biological factors in this process.

- We then explore several models of adult development, including Erikson's model of psychosocial development and Levinson's model of 'seasons' in a person's life. We also consider empirical studies by Gould and by Buhler. The use of biographical

and diary material in these studies is considered in the context of life-span development research.

- We also consider specific features of adult life including falling in love, choosing a partner, making the transition to parenting and other forms of care giving, dealing with losses through separation, divorce and death.

- We review studies of the role of grandparents in the family and the influences which they have across several generations.

- Finally, the ageing process is considered in the light of physical, intellectual and social changes in older people.

▦ Introduction ▦

Until recently, most textbooks on developmental psychology portrayed adulthood as a relatively stable period, coming after the turbulence of adolescence and culminating in a decline during old age. Yet adult life experiences, described in self-reports, literature and drama, seem to contradict this view. Some examples are shown in Box 3.1.

The accounts in Box 3.1, from adults of different ages, suggest that far from being static, adult life has the potential for unfolding in quite unexpected ways. Significant events, for example falling in love or bringing up a child, are often revisited and re-experienced from new perspectives at different points in a person's life. The establishment of a social role, typically through work, provides an arena for personal development and change. (This aspect of adult develop-

Box 3.1   Self-reports of Change in Adult Life

Here are some personal accounts by adults who were in the process of experiencing critical changes in their lives. You can consider these case studies in relation to various stage models in the text. To what extent do they confirm or disconfirm them?

(a)   'I was 32 in what I thought was a happy marriage with two young children when I discovered that my husband had been unfaithful to me. When I confronted him with it, he told me he was leaving as he could not stand the nagging! But all I wanted was his love. Anyway, he's gone now and I'm left with a pile of debts and two kids to bring up.'

(b)   'At the age of 39 my stable but rather dull life was turned upside down when I fell passionately in love with a man I met through work. My world was transformed. I discovered a depth of emotion which I had not thought possible. I had thought that only young people could feel this way.'

(c)   'At the age of 43, I was involved in a terrible accident which left me totally without the use of my hands. They were burnt so badly that only stumps remained. I could no longer work. I was depressed for months, even though everyone said I was lucky to be alive. I have not come to terms with my disfigurement. My wife and children have been incredibly understanding but I still don't feel a complete person.'

(d)   'When I was around 53 I realized that my job as a lecturer was no longer as satisfying to me as it had been but that my voluntary work with the Samaritans and other counselling agencies was opening up new avenues for me. I decided to train further as a counsellor. The course gave me the opportunity to reflect on my life and on the values by which I was living. This enabled me to take a very important decision which otherwise I would not have dared to do. I took early retirement and embarked on a new career as a freelance counsellor. My salary has plummeted but I have never been happier.'

(e)   'We became grandparents when I was 60 and my husband 63. My daughter, who is a hairdresser, loves her work and wanted to keep on working part-time while Jake was little, so we offered to look after him three days a week. Diane drops him off in the morning and we give him all our attention. We take him to the park on good days and play with him at home. We sing the old songs and nursery rhymes to him and tell him lots of stories. It's like having Diane all over again but we are more relaxed with Jake than we were with her and have more time for fun. He has brought such a lot of happiness into our lives and I can't imagine life without him now.'

(f)   'After Jan died I was very lonely and depressed. I thought that there was very little for me to live for. I am now 70 and have begun to study art at adult education classes. I never had time to draw and paint before; I was always too busy. Now I see things in a new way – shapes, colours, shadings. It's as if my eyes had been closed before. I have made new friends who share my interest. We often go on painting expeditions into the countryside and some of us now meet once a week in the local pub.'

ment is explored in chapter 17.) The concern of many adults to hand on knowledge and experience to the next generation is likely to involve them in the appraisal of life's values. Many adults report a compelling urge to find meaningfulness in their lives, particularly as they become older, and to take a reflective stance on significant issues. In this chapter we consider the impact on personal development of changes that can take place through adult life, such as falling in love, becoming a parent and later a grandparent, getting divorced, becoming older, and experiencing bereavement.

Psychologists have become aware of the need to know more about adult development for a number of reasons, shown in figure 3.1. The life-span development perspective, in contrast to traditional approaches, places emphasis on

Plates 3.1 (i) to (vi) James at different ages (i) as a baby; (ii) as an adolescent; (iii) as a parent; (iv) as a grandfather; (v) at his golden wedding anniversary; (vi) one week before his death at 79 years
Source: Helen Cowie.

LIFE CYCLE

change in the LIFE CYCLE. Paul Baltes (1973; 1987) has summarized distinctive features of the life-span perspective as shown in figure 3.2.

Baltes indicates a complex interweaving of critical life events (such as losing one's partner in a road accident), social context (such as being brought up in a very poor family), historical factors (such as living through the Second World War) and biological factors (such as being born with a physical impairment) which contribute to each person's unique development. How can we unravel these contributions and effects? Psychologists have used case studies, observational data, biographical accounts, interviews and questionnaires as sources of information

- Adults themselves report changes in their social and emotional growth throughout the life span.
- As society changes so its members are required to be more adaptable and flexible in their work attitude and experience; adults in our society can now expect to encounter change in career and family patterns.
- Adults in Western society live longer now than adults in earlier generations, and have higher expectations of the quality of their life; they are more likely to express dissatisfaction with a life pattern which remains stable and unchanging.
- There is an increasing interest in adults as learners throughout life, with changing needs and aspirations; specifically, courses designed for adult learners (for example, on counselling, social and health care) often feature aspects of life-span development in their content.
- Psychologists themselves have recognized the limitations of a developmental psychology which ignores the processes of change during adult life, and have identified a relatively new perspective, that of *life-span development*.

Figure 3.1 Reasons for interest in adult development

about the stages of adult development. These methods tend to be retrospective: participants are asked to recall their own life histories from the standpoint of the present. Since this perspective itself may change over time, the remembered material is not 'objective' evidence. But to the life-span theorist a person's subjective perspective on his or her life is a most important issue, and, by analysing sources of this kind drawn from adults of different ages (CROSS-SECTIONAL studies) or from the same adults at different points in their lives (LONGITUDINAL studies), researchers have been able to elicit some common themes which typically recur in adult development. We first look at adolescence and the transition to adult life.

CROSS-SECTIONAL STUDY

LONGITUDINAL STUDY

▨ Adolescence and the Transition from Child to Adult ▨

Adolescence – the teenage years – has been described as a period of turmoil, anxiety, 'storm and stress'. It is also a transition to independence, from child-

- Development is life-long: it does not stop after adolescence.
- Development is multi-dimensional, including social, emotional, cognitive aspects.
- Development takes different directions and paths, depending on the adult's circumstances, experiences and opportunities.
- Development is greatly influenced by the historical time in which the individual's existence takes place.
- Development also takes place in a social context.
- Development can be understood with reference to a number of disciplines such as psychology, sociology, anthropology and biology.

Figure 3.2 Characteristics of life-span perspectives
Source: Baltes.

71

Plate 3.2 The child in social context: James was orphaned during the First World War. He is seen here as a child on the left, with his brother, two aunts, an uncle and his grandfather
Source: Helen Cowie.

hood to adulthood. It brings with it the end of compulsory education, the right to vote, the right to marry. It is marked by the adolescent growth spurt and the onset of PUBERTY; and by an increase in ability for logical and conceptual thought. In this section we will look at these major aspects of adolescence.

PUBERTY

The adolescent growth spurt and puberty

Figure 3.3a shows typical curves for height attained at different ages by boys and girls, in the UK during the 1960s; while figure 3.3b shows curves for 'height velocity', or rate of change in height. After rapid growth in infancy, height increases steadily from early childhood to around 11 years for girls and 13 years for boys, and then accelerates for about a three-year period before levelling off towards adult height. This acceleration is called the 'adolescent growth spurt', and it is similar for weight as well as height. It can help account for the awkward feelings some adolescents experience, as their bodies change and shoot up rapidly.

HYPOTHALAMUS

The body of the adolescent is changing in other ways as well, as they become sexually mature. Triggered by the HYPOTHALAMUS, the body starts producing growth hormones and sex hormones. Besides growth in size, these result in the development of primary reproductive features – the ovaries, uterus, vagina and clitoris in the woman, the testicles, penis, prostate gland and seminal vesicles in the man – and in other features such as coarser facial and body hair in males,

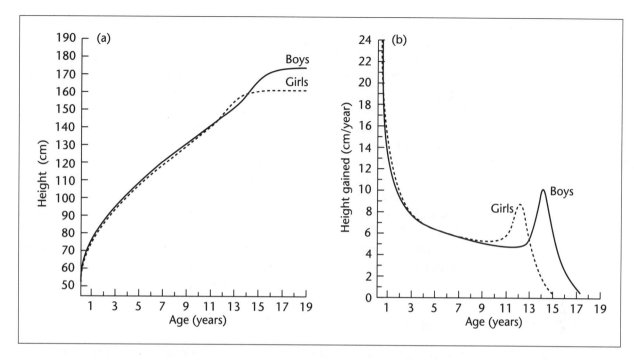

Figure 3.3 (a) Typical individual curves showing height attained by boys and girls; (b) Typical individual curves showing velocity of growth in height for boys and girls

breast development in females, and changes in body hair, skin texture, sweat gland activity and voice production.

The actual 'age of puberty' depends on the measure used, and also shows considerable individual variation. Nowadays, puberty often arrives at around 12 years for girls, 14 years for boys. Interestingly, in earlier times – in Europe at least – there is evidence for later onset of puberty. One study (Møller 1985) looked at when the voice change (breaking or deepening of the voice) occurred in Bach's choirboys in Leipzig during 1727 to 1747. From the records, it was clear that this usually occurred around 17 years, compared to 14 to 16 years nowadays. Historical analysis of age of beard growth – from portraits, letters and writings – suggest that this often started in the twenties, rather than around 17 years as today (Møller 1987). Analysis of age of MENARCHE in girls over the last 100 to 150 years in several European countries and the USA suggests a decrease of several years, from around 14 to 16 years in the nineteenth century, to around 13 years in the 1960s, a trend now levelling off (Roche 1979; Bullough 1981). Effects of poor diet during the period of the industrial revolution in these countries may help explain these long-term trends.

MENARCHE

There are marked individual differences, too, in reaching puberty; at 12 or 13 years, for example, one girl may show no sexual development and not have started periods, another may have been having periods for some time and have well-developed breasts and a more adult body shape. Psychologists have wondered whether early or late puberty has any psychological consequences. In general, early maturing boys tend to be more confident and popular; their increase in body size and strength can be an advantage in boys' peer groups, where sports and physical prowess is often a mark of status. Early maturing girls, however, do not have this advantage so much, and may initially feel awkward. Academically, there is some evidence that early maturers can score higher on school tests, though this finding is difficult to interpret – children from smaller families and higher social class groups tend to do better on school tests and also (perhaps because of better diet) reach puberty earlier.

A study in Sweden by Magnusson et al. (1985) showed that early maturation can have complex but long-lasting effects. These investigators followed the life histories of 466 girls from before puberty through to 25 years. They found that early maturing girls were more likely to be involved in taking alcohol and other drugs, and breaking social norms; however this was not true of all early maturers – only of those who associated with an older peer group. These effects were transient, since by 25 years there was no difference between the early and late maturers on these measures. But there was also a non-transient effect; early maturers engaged in sexual activity earlier, got married earlier, and by age 25 had more children and were less likely to have gone on to higher education.

Cognitive changes in adolescence

FORMAL OPERATIONAL THINKING

According to Piaget's stages of cognitive development (see chapter 2), by about 11 or 12 years of age children would be entering the stage of 'FORMAL OPERATIONAL THINKING'. This means that they would be able to think in abstract, logical and systematic ways. Piaget and his colleagues, including Barbel Inhelder, carried out studies to show this in schoolchildren. Two examples of formal operational tasks are given in figure 3.4.

---

(1)   A child is given some lengths of string, and different weights, to make a pendulum. S/he is asked what affects the time of swing – the actual weight, the length of the string, the amount the weight is pulled back before release, the push given to the weight? Before formal operational thinking, a child will not approach this task systematically. The sign of formal operational thought is the 'scientific' approach of holding all variables constant but one. For example, if you vary the weights while holding all else constant you can see whether weight has an effect; and so on for other variables such as length of string. The judgement about level of thinking is based not so much on what answer they get, but on how s/he reasons about the task.

(2)   How many words can you get from arrangements of the letters below?:

A   S   E   T   M

Well, you can get 'met' and 'meat' and 'set' – but maybe it would be best to do it systematically? Suppose you took words starting with 'm' and then looked at all the permutations of the following letters – this way, you would not miss any possible words (as long as you could recognize them!). This would be a mark of formal operational thinking.

Figure 3.4 Examples of formal operational thinking tasks

If you've tried the tasks in figure 3.4, you may think that you don't always use formal operational thinking! And you are probably right. Later work – for example in the UK by Shayer and Wylam (1978) – found that even by 15 and 16 years, schoolchildren are only using formal operational thinking a minority of the time; and Piaget (1972) admitted that formal operational thinking can be delayed, and not shown in many circumstances even by adults. However, it still may be true that it is only at around 11 or 12 years that children *start* to be capable of formal operational thinking.

Some writers, such as Elkind (1967), used Piaget's ideas to explain what were seen as typical adolescent preoccupations with how others viewed them, and their high degree of self-consciousness. The physical changes of adolescence might interact with the increased ability to think hypothetically and abstractly, to cause adolescents to think much more about how others might (hypothetically) be thinking about them. Also, this might explain the increased idealism and concern of many adolescents with moral and religious issues, as they start reasoning about what should be happening in the world, given certain belief systems or moral standards.

Identity in adolescence and Erikson's stages

Other life-span development theorists have proposed that the emergence of the sense of self and identity is a crucial development in the adolescent years. A key figure in this tradition is Erik Erikson, to whom 'a sense of identity means a sense of being at one with oneself as one grows and develops'. After all, in these years the young person is becoming sexually mature, and able to think in more abstract terms. In many societies, they are becoming able to marry, and to vote. And they have to decide what career to follow, and what religion or moral code to believe in. Erikson developed this further to describe identity formation as the 'normative crisis' of adolescence.

Erik Erikson (1902–94) was born in Germany of Danish parents. He moved to Vienna in 1927 and worked with Sigmund Freud's daughter Anna, before emigrating to the USA in 1933. In 1950 he published his first major work, *Childhood and Society*. In this book he proposed that the life-span could be described as a sequence of eight psychosocial stages of EGO DEVELOPMENT, three of which were concerned with adult life. He viewed the course of ego development as a process which goes on throughout life, and argued that certain aspects of human experience are characteristic of each stage (see figure 3.5). These stages were broader than those of Freud, less concerned with sexual development, and more open to cultural influences.

EGO DEVELOPMENT

Erikson thought that at each stage there was a 'normative crisis' in development – an aspect of development which should be dealt with successfully if healthy development was to continue (though each exists in some form at earlier and later stages). Progression from one stage to the next involves the individual in a shift of perspective, experienced as a developmental crisis which

	1	2	3	4	5	6	7	8
H old age								Integrity vs Despair, Disgust WISDOM
G maturity							Generativity vs Stagnation CARE	
F young adulthood						Intimacy vs Isolation LOVE		
E adolescence					Identity vs Role Confusion FIDELITY			
D school age				Industry vs Inferiority COMPETENCE				
C play age			Initiative vs Guilt PURPOSE					
B early childhood		Autonomy vs Shame, Doubt WILL						
A infancy	Trust vs Mistrust HOPE							

Figure 3.5 Erikson's stage model of development through the life span

TRUST

MISTRUST

HOPE

MORATORIUM

may be expressed through feelings of heightened vulnerability and emotional awareness. The shift to the next stage represents a fundamental turn in a new direction.

He also argued that development emerges from the interplay of opposites. For example, for the young child there is a polar contrast between TRUST and MISTRUST. Depending on how the infant resolved these two opposites, he or she could develop a quality of ego functioning which Erikson identified as HOPE, the capacity to view life with optimism. However, while Freud and the psychoanalysts thought that infancy and early childhood were the decisive periods for personality formation, Erikson did not agree. He had a more life-span perspective, but in so far as he saw one period as particularly influential, it was adolescence, with its normative crisis of identity versus role confusion.

His second major work, *Identity, Youth and Crisis*, was published in 1968. In this, he developed his ideas about adolescence. He argued that adolescence could be thought of as a period of 'psychosocial MORATORIUM' – a time in which society allowed or sanctioned young people to try out different beliefs, whether sexual, religious or political, without undue pressure. Also, one could try out different career aspirations. Each society, he argued, makes its own arrangements for young people to go through a period of psychological moratorium. During the middle ages, for example, a young man could have some years in a monastery to find a moratorium; in other periods, the army provided such a facility; richer adolescents in some historical periods would often go on a Grand Tour to broaden their horizons and extend their world view.

Erikson's theories were based on case studies and clinical experience rather than the more usual process of large samples and empirical study. In the area of identity development, James Marcia took Erikson's ideas further and put them in a testable form. He developed a SEMISTRUCTURED INTERVIEW to measure 'IDENTITY STATUS'. There are four identity statuses, shown in figure 3.6 together with typical statements illustrating them.

SEMISTRUCTURED INTERVIEW

IDENTITY STATUS

Marcia, following Erikson's writings, felt that young people would start in 'confusion' (or 'diffusion') about identity, and as they started to think about moral, political and religious issues and matters of identity in adolescence, might first move into 'foreclosure', adopting family or community values unquestioningly, before moving into 'moratorium', where they actively challenged conventional beliefs and worked through alternative ways of thinking and behaving, finally reaching 'achievement', where a clear identity had at last been reached.

Work by Marcia, Waterman and others has found some support for this sequence of changes (Waterman 1988). However, others feel there are strong limitations to this work (Cote & Levine 1988). First, despite his commitment to thinking cross-culturally (and innovative as his ideas were in his day), from current perspectives Erikson's work may be seen as culturally and historically limited. Is it true in all cultures that we should expect adolescents to 'rebel' against family or traditional values and 'experiment' with strange ideas? In many societies this would not be appropriate, or would just not be tolerated. And was the psychosocial moratorium a particular phenomenon of the late 1960s, when so many young people in western Europe and North America were, for a while, doing just this? And how final is identity achievement? With high levels of unemployment, and of divorce, many adults may also face challenges to a previously established identity (for an example, see Box 3.1(d)). Probably, identity formation is indeed a strong feature of adolescence and early adulthood, but beyond that, some of the implications and developments of Erikson's ideas are certainly questionable.

Confusion: 'Oh, I don't know . . . it doesn't really bother me.'
Foreclosure: 'No, not really, our family is pretty much in agreement on these things.'
Moratorium: 'Yes, I guess I'm going through that now. I just don't see how there can be a God and yet so much evil in the world . . .'
Achievement: 'Yeah, I even started worrying whether or not there was a God. I've pretty much resolved that now, though. The way it seems to me is . . .'

Figure 3.6 Marcia's four identity statuses, and typical responses to a question, 'Have you ever had any doubts about your religious beliefs?'

Parent–child and peer relationships in adolescence

By and large, parent–child relationships do seem to get a bit more distant and tense during adolescence. Indeed, it has been called a period of 'storm and stress'. Psychoanalysts such as Anna Freud stated that 'adolescence is by its nature an interruption of peaceful growth', and thought that it was characterized by mood swings and emotional outbursts due to the re-eruption of sexual urges after the psychoanalytic 'LATENCY PERIOD'. Subsequently, many writers were critical of this view. Often, adolescents have good relationships with parents, and disagreements may be over minor matters such as time of coming in at night or clothes worn, rather than really major issues (Coleman 1980). Rutter et al. (1976) reached a more balanced view in an article entitled 'Adolescent turmoil: Fact or fiction?' They looked at the experiences of 14- to 15-year-olds on the Isle of Wight, off southern England. There was some increase in signs of DEPRESSION and of conflict with parents, but these only characterized a minority of these adolescent children. The authors concluded that 'adolescent turmoil is a fact, not a fiction, but its psychiatric importance has probably been over-estimated in the past'.

Subsequent work has confirmed this assessment. Figure 3.7 shows measures of affective closeness between parents and children at three ages (10, 16 and 25 years), for two cohorts (whose adolescence was in 1941–55 or 1966–75), and for boys and girls, with mothers and fathers. These data, gathered from families in North America (Rossi & Rossi 1990), show that there is clearly a dip in affective closeness at 16 years, compared to either 10 or 25 years. In addition, the dip is more marked during the 1960s and 1970s than during the 1940s and 1950s (as we noted in the last section, the former cohort may have been a particularly non-conformist one in the adolescent years).

What causes this temporary distancing in adolescence? The possible explanations have been reviewed by Paikoff and Brooks-Gunn (1991). One factor may simply relate to the effects of puberty. Steinberg (1987) studied 204 families with 10- to 15-year-olds and found that, irrespective of when puberty occurred, it was associated with increased BEHAVIOURAL AUTONOMY, decreased emotional closeness towards parents, and increased conflict. Another factor may be the changes in thinking processes we have already reviewed, and thus in adolescents' expectations of parents and the attributions they make of their actions. Related to this may be changes in self-definition and self-image, and a need to establish a separate identity as Erikson supposed.

In addition, the peer group is thought to play a larger role in adolescence than in earlier childhood, and this might increase conflict with parents. Certainly, experimental studies of CONFORMITY in the face of peer pressure suggest that it peaks around 15 years (Berndt 1979). Anxieties about friendships are also very high at this age (Coleman 1980). Adolescents often associate in large gangs or 'crowds', and conformity of dress and interests is an important mark of belonging to a particular group. These groups will differ in outlook. Some

LATENCY PERIOD

DEPRESSION

BEHAVIOURAL
AUTONOMY

CONFORMITY

may value educational achievement, others sporting success, yet others rebelliousness or antisocial behaviour with respect to adult norms (Brown et al. 1994). In some instances, peer pressure or desire to belong to a particular group may lead to conflicts with parents over such matters as academic work, dress style, or sexual behaviour.

Delinquency and risk-taking in adolescence

Statistics in Western societies show clearly that there is a peak in criminal offences at adolescence. In the UK, Home Office statistics show a peak at 14 to 16 years of age, followed by 17 to 20 years. The great majority of these offences are for crimes such as house-breaking, shoplifting, car burglaries. Most are committed by young males, but there is a similar age trend for offences by females.

Arnett (1992: 339) hypothesizes that 'adolescents are over-represented statistically in virtually every category of reckless behavior'. In such behaviour, besides DELINQUENCY and crime, he includes driving at high speeds and while drunk; having sex without contraception; and illegal drug use. He explains this over-representation in terms of the usual cluster of influences at adolescence – hormonal changes associated with puberty; cognitive changes; and peer influences.

Arnett argues that this trend to reckless behaviour can be strongly influenced by socialization practices. In what he calls 'narrow socialization', typical of traditional societies, there are firm expectations and clear restrictions, and strong community pressures on young people. This reduces independence and creativity, and also reckless behaviour. By contrast, in what he calls 'broad socialization', typical of modern western societies, there are few restrictions on adolescents, which encourages self-expression and autonomy, but at the price of more reckless behaviour, including crime and delinquency.

As one example of reckless behaviour, we can consider various kinds of sexual intercourse. Adult attitudes to sexual intercourse among young people liberalized during the 1960s and 1970s. For

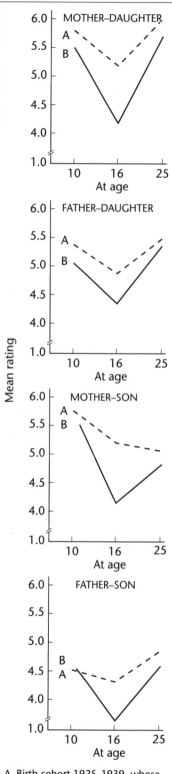

Figure 3.7 Measures of affective closeness between parents and children at three ages (10, 16 and 25 years), for two cohorts (adolescence in 1941–55 and 1966–75), and for boys and girls, with mothers and fathers.

Rossi, A. S. & P. H., *Of Human Bonding*, fig. 3.4 (Reprinted with permission from Rossi and Rossi, *Of Human Bonding: Parent–Child Relations across the Life Course*. [New York: Aldine de Gruyter] Copyright © 1990 Walter de Gruyter, Inc., New York).

A Birth cohort 1925–1939, whose adolescence was during 1941–1955 (aged 46–60 in 1985).

B Birth cohort 1950–1959, whose adolescence was during 1966–1975 (aged 26–35 in 1985).

Table 3.1 Percentage of respondents reporting experience of sexual intercourse

| | 17 years | | 19 years | |
	males	*females*	*males*	*females*
Schofield 1965	25	11	37	23
Farrell 1978	50	39	74	67
Breakwell 1992	54–66	55–66	71–84	76–85

Source From UK surveys by Schofield (1965), Farrell (1978), and Breakwell & Fife-Schaw (1992).

example, in the UK, comparison of data from the Schofield report of 1965 and the Farrell report of 1978 shows a marked increase in the proportion of 17- and 19-year-olds reporting sexual intercourse (see table 3.1). There are similar changes from North American data. This more liberal attitude to sex has continued into the 1990s. Breakwell and Fife-Schaw (1992) surveyed 2,171 young people aged 16 to 20 years.

Their figures for vaginal penetration are similar and perhaps higher than those of Farrell some 14 years earlier (table 3.1). Breakwell and Fife-Schaw also found that some 9 per cent of 17-year-old males reported having active anal penetration with a female, and 1 per cent with a male. These latter are high-risk activities for HIV transmission, and may even carry some risk when ordinary condoms are used (unfortunately the authors did not gather data on whether such precautions were taken).

HIV

▧ Development in the Adult Years ▧

We have seen how Erikson viewed the adolescent years as one of identity formation; and certainly it is a period of learning and adjustment while the young person typically leaves their birth family, acquires an occupational role, and often chooses a partner and thinks of having children. In Erikson's model (figure 3.5), with the period of YOUNG ADULTHOOD – usually in the twenties – comes the need to develop the capacity for intimacy, the ability to be committed to other people through friendship, sexual relationship and love, despite some sacrifice of one's own needs which this may entail. Where intimacy is not achieved the outcome is likely to be a growing sense of isolation and absorption with the self. By resolving the tension between these two opposites, the person develops the quality of love.

YOUNG ADULTHOOD

During Erikson's seventh stage – MATURITY – there emerges the need to be concerned to guide the next generation, whether through parenthood or through the process of passing on skills and knowledge to others. The polarities here are

MATURITY

GENERATIVITY and STAGNATION. The main issue at this stage is the giving of self without expectation of personal gain. Those adults who are unable to give in this unselfish way are, in Erikson's framework, likely to become increasingly preoccupied with their own concerns. The quality which emerges from the resolution of these two polarities is *care*.

In Erikson's final stage – old age – the individual encounters the polarities of *ego integrity* and *despair*. Ego integrity involves the calm acceptance of one's life as it has been lived and a recognition of its richness; by contrast, despair is the anguished regret for all that was not done or experienced and a terror of impending death. From the interplay and resolution of these opposites comes the quality of WISDOM.

Levinson: the seasons of a person's life

Daniel Levinson and his colleagues built on Erikson's work to make a more systematic investigation of the subjective experience of adult life (1978, 1990). Originally they studied a sample of 40 men; more recently they reported a comparable study of women's lives. Levinson's research methods incorporated biographical interviews, projective tests and interviews with participants' partners and colleagues; his aim was to tap both conscious and unconscious processes in adult life. Levinson aimed to discover answers to questions like 'What does it mean to be an adult?' and 'What are the key issues in adult life?'

Levinson's most distinctive concept, the life cycle, captures a sense of order and direction in human life:

> Many influences along the way shape the nature of the journey. They may produce alternative routes or detours along the way; they may speed up or slow down the timetable within certain limits; in extreme cases they may stop the developmental process altogether. But as long as the journey continues, it follows the basic sequence. (Levinson 1978: 6)

Levinson's concept of the life cycle incorporates the metaphor of SEASONS. He notes that this metaphor can take many forms – spring, summer, autumn, winter in the year; daybreak, noon, dusk and night within a single day; phases in a relationship. The metaphor recurs in poetry and song and is one which is meaningful to many people when contemplating the nature of the course of life.

On the basis of his empirical work, Levinson suggested that adult life can be viewed as a sequence of four overlapping developmental *eras* (see figure 3.8). The first era, that of childhood and adolescence, lasts from birth until around the age of 17. From the perspective of the life cycle as a whole, the attainments of the first era provide a base for the new kinds of development which will be required in the next era. The years from 17 to 22 form the early adult transition, a developmental period in which pre-adulthood draws to a close and the era of early adulthood approaches. Levinson saw this transition as a bridge between adolescence and adulthood, which was not fully a part of either. In the second era, early adulthood, the person begins to create a new life structure. Biologically the person is at the peak of his or her life cycle. This is the time to identify and pursue important aspirations, to find a place in society, to form close relationships, probably to establish a family, and to attain a more responsible position in the world of adults. It is a time of energy and creativity; at the same time there are great stresses. In Levinson's words:

> Early adulthood is the era in which we are most buffeted by our own passions and ambitions from within and by the demands of family, community and society from without. Under reasonably favorable conditions, the rewards of living in this era are enormous, but the costs often equal or even exceed the benefits. (Levinson 1990: 40).

Figure 3.8 Development eras in early and middle adulthood, based on Levinson's model

The mid-life transition from around 40 years to 45 years ends early adulthood

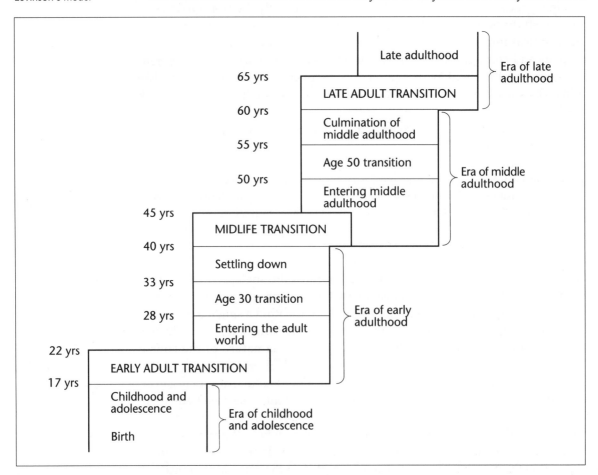

and marks the shift to middle adulthood. Research findings suggest that, at around this age, many people report the experience of a 'MIDLIFE CRISIS', a phenomenon which can take a whole range of forms.

MIDLIFE CRISIS

For example, Jo, a successful business executive who had risen to the top of her profession, had achieved most of her work goals and had a wide circle of friends, found that, in her late thirties, she became increasingly panic-stricken at the thought that her child-bearing years would soon be over. She experienced extreme feelings of regret over her deliberate decision not to have children. Other adults in this age group may feel trapped between the generations, with children growing up and leaving home on the one hand and ageing parents requiring extra support on the other. Earlier aspirations may not have been realized and a growing sense of discontent may develop. At this point, the adult may, uncharacteristically, embark on an intense affair or abruptly seek out a new career direction. The midlife crisis may be expressed in less dramatic ways but, nevertheless, it is a common experience to many adults at this point in the life span. (See also in Box 3.1.)

Levinson's research indicated that an important aspect of this transitional period is the move towards greater INDIVIDUATION – the process of becoming more reflective about one's own life, and becoming increasingly compassionate, accepting and more loving of self and others. The process of change, which begins during the midlife transition, continues throughout the third era, middle adulthood. Although the person's biological abilities are less during this era than they were, they are usually sufficient to permit the person to live an energetic and useful life, with responsibility and a concern for the next generation. This is a time when many adults become 'senior members' of their own world. This may be in the domain of work through responsibility or promotion, in the domain of voluntary or community work, or within the family. Levinson's studies suggested that, if some sense of recognition or of self-worth is not evident at this stage, the person's life becomes increasingly trivial and stagnant.

INDIVIDUATION

The late adult transition, usually between 60 and 65 years, links middle and late adulthood and is part of both. Levinson says very little about this transitional stage since his sample was not representative of this older age group. He tentatively described the fourth era – late adulthood – in the following way. Men and women who have been in employment will usually have retired by this age, but many continue to lead active lives and to remain physically fit. Levinson found that at this stage adults are likely to become even more inward looking; the prospect of death and separation from loved ones is an aspect of the broader individuation process of self-review and evaluation. (See also the final section in this chapter which deals with bereavement and loss.)

Other studies of life-span development

Some other studies seem to confirm the views of Erikson and Levinson that adult life goes through stages linked by transitional periods of crisis. Gould (1978), in a study of 524 men and women, found that mid-adulthood is just as full of 'storm and stress' as adolescence, and that the process of addressing developmental crises is a positive way of achieving personal growth. Gould noted a typical pattern in adult development:

1. tentativeness in early adulthood as the person forms significant relationships and searches for a personal identity;
2. a growing concern for adult roles and responsibilities in the early part of middle adulthood;
3. a period of questioning and re-evaluation in the later part of middle adulthood;
4. a move in late adulthood towards acceptance of life, greater tolerance of others; mellowing; a growing awareness and acceptance of the finiteness of life.

Similarly, Charlotte Bühler and her colleagues carried out a systematic analysis of over 400 biographies written by individuals from a range of backgrounds, including a subset of highly creative people. Bühler and Massarik (1968) proposed that there are five distinct stages of human development, three of which focus on adult life. Broadly, the analysis of these biographies revealed that between 25 and 50 years of age, individuals are typically engaged in the process of identifying goals in their personal and professional lives and working towards achieving them. Between 45 and 60 years, they are still active and energetic, despite some waning of physical powers, but there emerges a need to evaluate life and reflect on its meaning; in later stages, there was also a need to come to

EMPTY NEST

terms with changes such as retirement, the 'EMPTY NEST', significant losses of close partners and decreasing physical powers. Bühler and her colleagues found wide differences among adults in the age group of 65 years and over. Some people were very active – the highly creative subset in the sample, for example, continued to grow and develop in their work. Others in this age group adjusted to a more restricted range of activities. There are close similarities in the findings of Bühler and of Erikson. However, unlike Erikson, Bühler and her colleagues did not find open despair amongst their sample but rather a resignation to a sense that life was less fulfilling than before, and that it will end. Given that these were qualitative studies of relatively small samples of adults, you may like to discuss with a fellow student why this difference in the final stage of life was found.

The studies which we have reviewed here have in common a view that adult life goes through a series of phases, each stable to an extent, and each one distinctly different from stages which precede or follow it. Common concerns include: finding an identity; forming close, intimate relationships; establishing a career; caring for young; coming to terms with significant changes, including retirement and the fact that children grow up and leave home; searching for a meaning in life; and accepting that life will end.

In the next sections we explore some recurring themes of adult life: falling in love, choosing a partner, the transition to parenting and care giving, the transition to grandparenting, the process of ageing, and issues around grief, loss and death.

▨ Falling in Love ▨

Often, our expectations of falling in love have a strong romantic component (see Box 3.1(a, b)); and the novel, or 'romance', frequently expresses this. Emma, the heroine of Flaubert's novel *Madame Bovary*, described the passion which she had for Rodolphe, her lover, as 'a magic land where passion, ecstasy, deliriums would reign supreme'; her everyday existence with her husband, Charles, was, by contrast, 'a thing far off and tiny, glimpsed far below in the shadows cast by those high immensities' (Flaubert 1857, repr. 1981: 154).

Most people in our culture give romantic love as one of the most common reasons for being committed to a long-term relationship such as marriage or comparable partnership; not being in love with a partner would be grounds for separation or divorce. Romantic love is closely allied to sexual passion. But there are also aspects to love which involve affection, intimacy and commitment. The earlier stages of love are more likely to be expressed through sexual passion; over time, this gives way to a deeper affection between partners and a commitment which can endure even if the physical aspects of love become less important.

Sternberg (1988) has proposed a triangular theory of love, in which there are three key components – commitment, intimacy and passion (see figure 3.9). As the strength of each component varies, so the quality of the love is different. For example, romantic love of the type described by Flaubert is extremely passionate, physically intense and also intimate, but it lacks commitment between the

	Passion	Intimacy	Commitment
non-love	–	–	–
liking	–	x	–
infatuated love	x	–	–
empty love	–	–	x
romantic love	x	x	–
companionate love	–	x	x
fatuous love	x	–	x
consummate love	x	x	x
x = high – = low			

Figure 3.9
Sternberg's typology of love
Source: Sternberg 1988.

85

partners over a long period of time and in everyday settings. Emma Bovary's love for Rodolphe could only thrive in conditions of secrecy and private fantasy. By contrast, companionate love is characterized by strong degrees of intimacy and commitment, but is weaker in the intensity of passionate feelings. According to Sternberg, the most satisfying form of love is consummate love, which is strong in all three components.

Sternberg's analysis illustrates the many meanings of love, ranging from friendship and affection through to passion. Friendship usually involves trust, acceptance, respect, sharing confidences, offering mutual support and companionship, while romantic love involves, in addition, some quality of physical passion, emotional intensity and heightened awareness.

Sternberg's research has also shown that, in Western societies, satisfying marriages are characterized by mutual sharing of interests, emotions and experiences, with good communication at the heart of the relationship. In unsuccessful relationships, it is often the breakdown of communication which is the most salient difficulty.

However, the image of romantic love continues to exert a powerful influence on how many people develop love relationships. The men in Levinson's sample described a 'novice phase' during early adulthood when they experimented with love relationships, for example through impersonal sexual pleasure-seeking. The ideal was often the 'special woman' who would be lover, friend and helper. Levinson also found that many of the men in his sample had formed a 'Dream', and the special woman played her part in helping him to realize these aspirations and longings.

Some social scientists view romantic love more sceptically and consider relationships of the type described by the men in Levinson's sample as being yet another example of women taking a subordinate 'servicing' role towards men. From this perspective, the 'special women' were merely living out male stereotypes of earth mother, goddess, or nymph, and the relationships were based on an illusion.

Kitzinger (1987: 108), too, views the concept of romantic love with suspicion, and considers its dependence on 'individualism' and 'privatization' as something which contributes to the oppression of women in general and lesbians in particular. Rich (1980) proposed that a heterosexual preference was imposed on women by a variety of mechanisms, including rape, physical violence and the ideology of romantic love, and that these mechanisms reinforced male power. Feminist writers like Rich challenge the power of men by affirming the validity and stability of women's relationships with one another. Women's friendships with other women are, they claim, more likely to be satisfying than romantic relationships between couples, since they involve trust, acceptance, respect, the sharing of confidences, the offer of mutual support and companionship – qualities which are often absent in the relationships between men and women once the physical passion, emotional intensity and heightened awareness have waned. O'Connor (1992), for example, notes that friendships between women enable them to tolerate the contradiction between the ideal of a romantic relationship with a life partner and the more prosaic reality of many marriages.

Recently, Josselson (1996) has suggested a more flexible model for looking at intimate relationships and for analysing a range of ways in which societies and individuals think about love. From the stance of the COUNSELLING PSYCHOLOGIST, she brings to her research the wisdom and insight of her years of experience in helping adults in troubled relationships and an awareness of the existential pain which people experience when they are in this kind of difficulty. Josselson argues that how we think about love is central to our identity and to the quest for meaning in our lives. She has devised a method for asking people about their own 'lived experience', with the researcher deliberately in the role of 'interested other' rather than 'detached scientist'. Sixty-seven people in the age range 30 to 50 were invited to draw diagrams of their own relational 'space' at different points in their lives and to talk to the researcher about what their drawings meant to them. These accounts – visual and spoken – provide an opportunity to see the quality of a person's close relationships (which she calls 'the space between') and to chart the ways in which they changed across the life-span.

As a result of this research, Josselson identifies eight dimensions of the space between. The first four dimensions – *holding*, *attachment*, *passionate experience*, *eye-to-eye validation* – she considers as primary dimensions which emerge early in life. The second four dimensions appear later since they require cognitive maturation: *idealization* and *embeddedness* require the concept of self and the capacity to think about oneself in relation to others; *mutuality* and *tending* involve moving out of egocentrism into the world of others. Her thesis is that, although each of the eight dimensions is present in everyone's life, the balance and emphasis is unique to each person. Some might focus on caring; others on idealization; some might be enmeshed in early attachments; others free to explore new forms of living. In this open-ended model she begins to explore the complexity of adult relationships and the range of ways in which love may be experienced and shared with others.

COUNSELLING PSYCHOLOGIST

▨ Choosing a Partner ▨

The choice of life partner, whether same-sex or opposite sex, whether through mutual choice or arranged marriage, is widely viewed as an extremely important life task in which most adults are expected to engage. Romantic love is not everywhere viewed as the basis for a successful marriage, as is shown in societies where choice of marriage partner is arranged by parents or others in the kin group.

There are many reasons why people choose a particular other person as a partner. To some extent, we tend to choose someone similar to ourselves, in education, social class, and even in appearance (Rushton 1989). There are also typical sex differences – men tend to choose women who are slightly younger

Box 3.2 Couples in Violent Relationships

Goldner, Penn, Sheinberg and Walker (1990) combine a psychodynamic model of relationships with the feminist perspective which proposed that male violence towards a partner is symptomatic of male domination in society. Their participants were men and women who wanted to stay together despite the violence which occurred regularly between them. They came from every walk of life, including artists, professors, social workers, business people, unemployed people and mental patients. The researchers attempted to 'deconstruct the violent moment' by interviewing the couples soon after such an event, giving the participants the opportunity to reflect on their own motives and feelings at the time and to gain insight into the partner's perspective.

For the men, the violent act came across as a pseudo-solution to their own feelings of inadequacy, fear and dependency – feelings which they deemed to be 'unmasculine'. The women did not leave these relationships and they seemed to be caught in a contradiction about their own femininity. Many of the women had been reared in families in which they, as daughters, grew up in the belief that being loved depended on some form of self-abnegation. They tended to be the daughters of mothers who were themselves subjugated in their marriages. At the same time, they were also rebelling against this subjugation by engaging in confrontational behaviour with their partners, and they typically expressed a belief that the relationship, despite its violence, was a haven from the outside world. For example, Joe and Alice, a couple who stayed together and claimed to love one another despite the fact that Joe had broken two of Alice's ribs, described the special quality of their relationship:

JOE: Maybe at one level we argue like hell, which is really true, but at another level me and Alice accept one another a hundred per cent. She accepts my sensitivity and my weaknesses, unlike my mother, and she's given me free rein to develop according to my own way of developing.

ALICE: I don't know why there is a bond between him and me, and not between me and anyone else. I don't know why that's true, except he allowed me to see his weaknesses. Therefore I don't see him as a threat; even if he hits me I don't really see him as a threat. He allows himself to be vulnerable to me and I never had that role before, ever. That *set* our relationship. That formed the bond between us, and it's lasted to this day, damaged as it is. That hooked me. (Goldner et al. 1990: 59)

As the authors conclude, for couples like these, abuse and violence coexist with understanding and even friendship in a painful way. At the same time, the authors (and the participants in the study) recognized that they had severe problems. The violence within the relationships could be reduced, the authors suggested, where such couples were prepared to accept help in reflecting on key personal issues, for example in the course of counselling or family therapy. If they were given the opportunity to get in touch with their own feelings about themselves, about their partner and about their earlier experiences of intimacy within the family, then it was possible that they could change the quality of their relationships. This was likely to be a long and laborious process.

and physically attractive, while women tend to choose men who are slightly older and have good financial or career prospects (Buss 1994).

It is also useful to consider the choice of life partner in the context of early experience within the family. There is evidence (Main & Goldwyn 1984) that there are continuities between early experience and later adult relationships. The person's internal working model of relationships was described in chapter 2 in the section on ATTACHMENT THEORY. It is based on the first intimate relationships with primary care givers, and forms an expectation of the quality of relationships with others, including the self. Secure adults who value intimacy in relationships are more likely to be able to 'work through' any unhappiness from

ATTACHMENT THEORY

their childhood through the closeness of significant adult relationships, in particular with the life partner. However, repressed conflicts from childhood may resurface in close relationships. For example, the adult trapped in unresolved struggles with parents may find it difficult to cope with intimacy as an adult, in relationships with peers, and this may lead to problems in the choice and maintenance of long-term partnership. An example of a study on violence in relationships is given in Box 3.2.

Cultural factors also play an important part in the choice of life partner. An example of this comes from studies of gay and lesbian partnerships. The status of gay and lesbian relationships is evolving and public opinion is mixed, with the majority still not recognizing a homosexual relationship, however long-term, as a partnership equivalent to marriage. O'Connor notes that the emergence of 'lesbian' as a sexual identity appeared in the nineteenth century, and only gradually became established in public consciousness in the course of the twentieth century. The identity of lesbians continues to be stigmatized, and the fear of being labelled still places a constraint on women in their public demonstration of their feelings towards one another and in the extent to which they feel free to live openly with one another.

As Rivers (1996) points out, young people who 'come out' as gay, lesbian or bisexual have to contend with the possibility that parents and peers will reject them; they also face humiliation and bullying at school. In an ongoing longitudinal study of 140 such young people, Rivers found that most commonly they were called names, and ridiculed openly by others. They also faced physical attack: over 59 per cent reported regular beatings by peers. In a few cases, participants in this study reported being sexually assaulted or raped. Rivers (1996: 5) gives one young man's account:

> It [the bullying] started one morning after assembly. A boy in the same year group as me yelled the word 'poofter' and, like a fool, I looked round. From that moment on I was the subject of beatings, verbal abuse and so-called 'queer-bashing'. I received torrents of verbal abuse and I had things stolen from me not just by other boys, but also by girls. There was no way round it, I was punished for being gay.
>
> The injuries I received were numerous: I had my left arm broken (the bullies said that I was lucky it wasn't my right arm); I was held down while cigarettes were stubbed out on the back of my neck; and I was kicked repeatedly by both boys and girls even when a teacher was nearby. One teacher told me that my problems were my own fault because I refused to deny my sexuality. In retaliation I told him that G.A.Y. stood for 'Good As You'. I then got detention for insolence.

Despite such accounts of social rejection, there are a growing number of households in which gay or lesbian couples live together in a long-term relationship. The reasons which these adults give for entering into a long-term commitment are very similar to those given by heterosexual couples – they expect love, companionship, sexual compatibility and emotional security; these couples can also be concerned with child-rearing, whether through previous heterosexual relationships or through adoption.

▪ The Transition to Parenting and Care Giving ▪

The commitment of becoming a parent or care giver involves a radical change in the adult's perspective on life. To some life-span theorists (for example Erikson), the mutually fulfilling intimacy with a sexual partner is enhanced and deepened through the experience of caring for children.

In the very early stages of life it is usually the mother rather than the father who carries most of the responsibility for the care of the child, though other adults can, of course, take on this role. Research suggests that fathers can fulfil a parenting role just as much as mothers, for example in lone-parent father families; but that typically fathers do not play such a large part in child rearing and domestic tasks as do mothers (Lamb 1987). Even in egalitarian societies such as Sweden, mothers still do a larger share of childcare. Parke and Tinsley (1987) found that mothers and fathers use a very similar repertoire of behaviours when interacting with their new-born children – bouncing, talking, cuddling – and that the same sort of mutual pleasure in the interaction is commonly seen. But Parke and Tinsley also noted that fathers typically engage in a different set of behaviours from mothers when with older children. The father role includes more boisterous play activity and more games, in contrast to quieter interactions and routine care giving on the part of the mother. One explanation of these differences is that these are part of the sex-role differentiation for men and women in our culture. An alternative explanation could be that these represent biologically determined differences in the ways in which men and women interact with young children.

Recently there has been interest in alternative forms of parenting. A review of parenting by gay and lesbian couples is given in Box 3.3.

When we look at the child's attachments, it seems that in general infants prefer either the mother or the father to a stranger. However, where the child is frightened he or she is more likely to turn to the mother rather than the father (Lamb 1981). Lewis (1986) suggested that the more time mothers, fathers, or any care givers spend in care giving and becoming sensitively attuned to the baby's needs, then the stronger will be the child's attachment.

Type of attachment is also important (cf. chapter 2). Mothers of secure infants are likely to be rated as being 'more sensitive, responsive, accessible and cooperative during the first year than mothers of insecure infants' (Goldberg 1991: 395–6). Sensitive parenting involves the capacity to respond quickly to a child's needs; a secure attachment is then likely to develop. This forms the basis within the child for feelings of self-worth and self-confidence.

The mother's own experience of being mothered can, according to attachment theory, strongly influence her parenting style. Main and Goldwyn (1984) used

Box 3.3   Lesbian and Gay Parenting

The standard perception of parents is of a mother and father. The rearing of children by gay or lesbian carers is perceived by many as 'a risk'. The reasons given include: their sexual behaviour is deviant; they would corrupt children; they would supply inadequate role models.

The reality appears to be different from the myth, though the evidence is at times conflicting. Taylor (1993), for example, found no evidence that children reared in gay and lesbian families are more disturbed or have greater gender identity confusion than children reared in heterosexual families. Similarly, Falk (1994), in a review of the literature on lesbian mothers, concluded that there were many similarities and few differences between lesbians and heterosexual women; she found no confirmation of the stereotype that lesbian women are emotionally disturbed, lacking in self-esteem, or more prone to alcohol abuse or suicide than their heterosexual counterparts. However, the difficulties faced by these families are highlighted in a study by Lewis (1980). She interviewed the children of lesbian mothers and found that the younger children in particular expressed the need for secrecy, felt 'different' from their peers and

feared being ostracized by them; at the same time, they were proud of their mothers for challenging the norms of society and were able to appreciate the mothers' ability to stand up for what they believed in. The fact that their self-esteem remained high says much for the parenting skills of the mothers and the capacity of the children themselves to develop coping mechanisms for dealing with stigma.

Barrett and Robinson (1994), in their review of the impact of gay fathering on children, stress the need to take into account the fact that these children are likely to have experienced divorce in the family and to show the psychological distress that often accompanies it (see below, in this chapter). The few studies which have been carried out indicate that the children of gay fathers may be isolated and angry; they are also likely to need help in sorting out their feelings about homosexuality in general and about their own sexual orientation in particular. They are in little danger of being sexually abused; many adjust well to the family situation; their relationships with their fathers, although stormy at first, have the potential for high levels of honesty and openness.

the ADULT ATTACHMENT INTERVIEW to probe adults' memories of their own childhood experiences. Their work resulted in four major classifications (see figure 3.10). They found that adults who had a dismissive or enmeshed relationship with their parents, tended also to have an insecure attachment relationship to their own child. However, some mothers who had had very negative experiences with their own parents seemed to have come to terms with this, and ascribed rational reasons to it (for example, marital stress or overwork). These mothers would be classified as 'autonomous'; they were more likely to have secure infants themselves; perhaps they had succeeded in updating their own working models of attachment relationships; even, in retrospect, to the benefit of their relationships with their own children.

This research suggests that if adults have easily accessible memories of their relationship with their own parents and are able to talk openly about the positive and negative aspects of that relationship, then they are more likely to have a secure relationship with their own children. By contrast, if they find it difficult to get in touch with their feelings about their parents, or if they are still preoccupied with issues which were unresolved in their own childhood, then they are more likely to have an insecure attachment with their own children.

It is also useful for psychologists to understand the conditions which facilitate effective parenting and to consider what parents themselves report about the

ADULT
ATTACHMENT
INTERVIEW

AUTONOMOUS: Persons who could recall their own earlier attachment-related experiences objectively and openly, even if these were not favourable; these tended to be parents of securely attached children.

DISMISSIVE: Persons who dismissed attachment relationships as of little concern, value or influence; these tended to be parents of anxious/avoidant children.

ENMESHED/PREOCCUPIED: Persons who seemed preoccupied with dependence on their own parents and still actively struggled to please them; these tended to be parents of anxious/ambivalent children.

UNRESOLVED: Persons who had experienced a trauma, such as the early death of an attachment figure, and had not worked through the mourning process; these tended to be parents of children who showed an insecure disorganized pattern of behaviour in the Strange Situation.

Figure 3.10 Four major patterns of adult attachment
Adapted from Main et al. 1985.

experience. Oakley (1980) proposed that, contrary to the ideal of fulfilment through parenting, many women found it to be an extremely unsatisfying experience. Boulton (1983), in a study of white mothers of pre-school children, married, not in full-time employment, and living in London, found that while over half of the mothers in a UK sample were emotionally fulfilled through the experience of parenting, for a large minority parenting did not come naturally and the experience included feelings of boredom, depression and hostility to the child rather than the ideal of mutual fulfilment. She found in this study that working-class women were more likely than middle-class women to report that they found the tasks of childcare enjoyable. She concluded that motherhood should be seen in the context of the range of women's experiences, including social class, social relationships, whether in work or not, as well as personal characteristics.

Phoenix et al. (1991) are critical of the emphasis on maternal availability and sensitivity implied in some models of effective parenting. The caring relationship and maternal availability which is said to be necessary for the development of young children is offered at a price – the mothers' self-esteem, career aspirations and adult relationships. More recent studies (e.g. Small et al. 1994) paint a less gloomy picture but, nevertheless, indicate that 10 to 20 per cent of mothers are depressed in the first year after childbirth. The explanations offered by these participants suggested lack of social and emotional support, being exhausted or unwell, and having no time for themselves. While not denying that childbirth and parenting are normally the source of great emotional well-being and satisfaction, Small et al. argued that it is crucial for healthcare workers and other professionals to be aware of the contexts in which mothers are most at risk and in need of support.

The social context of parenting

It is essential for life-span theorists to look beyond the immediate family to the wider social context. Relevant here is information about the support that parents have in rearing their children, and which may have a powerful impact on their capacity to meet the needs of and be available to their children. In Western societies, it is usually expected that parents are responsible for the social and physical well-being of their children, irrespective of the wealth or poverty of the family. In fact, many parents share this responsibility with other adults in the extended family or in the community. Many families rely on the active participation of grandparents who can act as babysitters while the parents are at work (Smith 1991). (See also the section in this chapter, below, on grandparenting.) The grandparents' role is especially important in the case of lone-parent families where the incidence of poverty is more likely to be a significant factor. Many lone mothers live near their family of origin and the sharing of the parenting role is one way of alleviating the impact of poverty.

Other forms of back-up for parenting can come from the community, for example through nursery or playgroup provision or through child-minders. The importance of these social networks cannot be over-emphasized since the task of parenting is probably one of the most demanding which any adult will encounter.

The relationship between parents and their children is a developing and changing one throughout the life-span, and the multifaceted role of parent can, at different points in time, include teacher, moral guide, emotional supporter, social role model (Josselson 1996). It involves a shift away from the preoccupation of one partner with the other and, though for the most part child rearing is reported by parents themselves as a rewarding experience, the task is achieved at some cost. Not surprisingly, the experience of parenting can place strain on the relationship between the parents themselves.

Divorce and step-parenting

Divorce has become more common in modern Western societies; each year, between 1 and 2 per cent of marriages end (Richards 1994). Thus, by the time a child is 16, there is something like a one-in-four chance that he or she will have experienced parental separation and divorce. Partners who go through the experience of divorce usually suffer a period of emotional crisis. For many couples it is stressful or even traumatic; for only a minority is divorce reported as being without pain or distress (see Box 3.1(a)). What are the consequences of this for the child's development? As divorce has become more frequent in recent decades, several studies have been made in an attempt to answer this question.

Wallerstein and colleagues (1988), while not underplaying the trauma of divorce, argue that it is necessary to view divorce as 'a process of radically changing family dynamics' and to see it as part of a longer process which itself goes through phases. Family reactions will vary depending on the ages of the children and on the stage at which the separation itself stands. They described three phases in the divorce process. First is the acute phase, typically lasting about two years, in which the emotional and physical separation takes place. Second is a transitional phase, in which each parent experiences marked ups and downs while establishing separate lives. Third is a post-divorce phase, in which each parent has established a new lifestyle, either as a single parent or remarried. The impact on children varies through time as well; clearly longitudinal studies are vital to get any real understanding of the impact of divorce on children. Several such studies have been made in the USA.

Remarriage and the presence of a stepfather seems to improve matters for sons who may respond well to having a male figure to identify with; but the step-family situation may make matters worse for daughters, with the stepfather–stepdaughter relationship being a particularly difficult one. Step-parents are often seen as intruders by stepchildren, and find it difficult to strike a balance between discipline and disengagement. Ferri (1984) documented the difficulties facing stepfamilies in a study in London, but pointed out that many such families had successfully met the challenge. While remarriage can increase life satisfaction for the adults involved, forming strong relationships with stepchildren is often a gradual and difficult process.

Richards (1994), in a review of recent research into divorce, points out that children whose parents divorce show consistent behaviour differences from those whose parents remain together, and as adults they tend to have different life courses. They achieve on average a lower level academically; their self-esteem is lower and they have a higher incidence of conduct disorders; they seem to grow up more quickly; they are more likely to leave home early, to enter into sexual relationships early, to marry and bear children early. Their relationships with parents are more likely to be distant when they reach adulthood; they are more likely to be depressed.

These findings are based on averages and there is wide variation in the reactions of children to divorce, due to differences in quality of life, poverty, arrangements for access, feelings of the adults involved, and relationships among members of the reconstituted family itself. Material conditions play a part, as do legislation and the provision of social and emotional support for families in distress. Figure 3.11 shows a summary of some of the factors which may affect the impact of divorce on children, from Richards' review (1994). Herbert (1988) argues that children who report the most emotional damage are those whose parents were unable or unwilling to talk about the separation with them in a rational way; those who 'took sides' with one parent and continued to have a poor relationship with the other parent; and those who were unhappy with custody arrangements. Hetherington (1989) describes 'winners, losers and survivors' of parental divorce. Depending on circumstances, some children may continue to be damaged and insecure through to adulthood; others recover and 'survive'; yet others may develop particularly caring and competent ways of behaving as a result of coping with the experience.

Divorce-prone couples
Couples prone to divorce may have different styles of child rearing anyway.

Relationship with parents
The change from two parents to a single residential parent, and/or changes in contact and styles of parenting after separation.

Conflict
Conflict between parents can have negative consequences for children including lowered self-esteem.

Economic factors
A frequent decline in income, especially for mother-headed families, can damage life chances.

Life changes
Associated changes such as move of house or change of school are added stressors.

Relationship with wider kin
Loss of relationships in the wider kin network may deprive a child of social support.

Figure 3.11 Some processes affecting the impact of divorce on children
Adapted from Richards 1994.

Child neglect and abuse

Usually, parents love and care for their children. No parent is perfect, but most provide 'good enough' parenting. Some conflict between parents and their off-spring is inevitable, but generally such disagreements are kept within reasonable bounds.

In some cases, however, parents or other care givers may neglect a child, failing to give him or her the love, care and attention necessary for normal, healthy development. Even more drastically, some may subject a child or children to physical or sexual abuse. During the last twenty years, violence against children within the family has been identified as a major social problem. Abuse can result in severe injuries, long-lasting psychological trauma, and even death. Recently there have been graphic accounts of the experience of abuse by adult survivors, and in Britain children themselves have rung the telephone counselling service, ChildLine, in large numbers. The issue is firmly in the public arena.

Physical abuse has been defined as the intentional, non-accidental use of force on the part of the parent or other caretaker interacting with a child in his or her care aimed at hurting, injuring or destroying that child (Gil 1970). Sexual abuse has been defined as the involvement of dependent, sexually immature children and adolescents in sexual activities that they do not fully comprehend, to which they are unable to give informed consent or that violate the social taboos of family roles (Kempe 1980).

What leads a parent to abuse a child? Abusing parents have been found very often to have insecure attachment relationships with their children; this in turn may relate back to their own experiences of having been parented. Browne (1989) found that 70 per cent of maltreated infants had insecure attachments to their care givers, compared to only 26 per cent of infants with no record of maltreatment. Crittenden (1988) has examined the representations of relationships in abusing parents, using the idea of internal working models discussed earlier. She interviewed 124 mothers in Virginia, USA, many of whom had abused or maltreated their children, and gave them the SEPARATION ANXIETY TEST. She reported that adequate mothers generally had warm and secure relationships with both their children and their partner. By contrast, abusing mothers appeared to conceptualize relationships in terms of power struggles. They tended to be controlling and hostile with anxiously attached children, and to have angry and unstable adult relationships. Another group, of neglecting mothers, appeared to conceive of relationships as emotionally empty. They were unresponsive to their anxiously attached children, and were involved in stable but affectionless relationships with partners. These findings have implications for working with these families.

However, it is not only some parents who can be held responsible for child abuse. Belsky (1984) has advocated a model of parental functioning which distinguishes three main influences on the quality of parental functioning. In order of suggested importance, these are:

1. the personal psychological resources of the parent: this will include parental mental health, the quality of internal representations of relationships and their developmental history;
2. contextual sources of support: including the social network of support from partner, relatives and friends, and job conditions and financial circumstances;

SEPARATION
ANXIETY TEST

Figure 3.12 Belsky's process model of the determinants of parenting
Source: Smith & Cowie 1991.

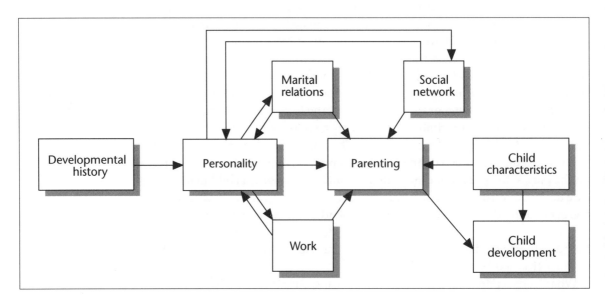

3. characteristics of the child: in particular easy or difficult temperament (see chapter 2).

Belsky's actual process model of factors influencing parenting is illustrated in figure 3.12. It clearly brings out the importance of a variety of factors, which in combination can make child abuse much more likely than the presence of any single factor alone. While useful for conceptualizing abuse and neglect in the family, the model is also useful more generally for understanding how variations in family functioning, satisfactory as well as unsatisfactory, may come about.

Feminist explanations of child sexual abuse have made connections between all forms of male violence within and outside families. Feminist perspectives, though they vary in emphasis, share the view that child sexual abuse is an abuse of male power. They stress the need to analyse the nature of power inequalities between men, women and children in society and to understand the nature of male sexuality in the social context. This takes the debate beyond the family to the wider social arena (Sarraga 1993).

▨ Another Transition: Becoming a Grandparent ▨

About 70 per cent of middle-aged and older people become grandparents. The average age of becoming a grandparent, in western societies, is approximately 50 years for women, and a couple of years older for men. Grandparenthood is thus an important part of the life cycle for most people, some 25 years or more. It is important, both as a personal experience and for its impact on others. For many, the role is very much a positive one. It is common for grandparents to report at least weekly contact with their grandchildren, and to have satisfying relationships with them (see Box 3.1(e)).

A few earlier studies on grandparenting were based mainly on impressions and case studies. Grandparents were sometimes portrayed as older people who were likely to be frail and cantankerous (as a function of their age), and to interfere in the raising of grandchildren, being inflexible, and variously either too lenient and indulgent, or too strict and old-fashioned in their views. There is some evidence that grandmothers in the 1950s were indeed stricter than mothers. Staples and Smith (1954) interviewed 87 grandmother–mother pairs, and found the grandmothers to have stricter and more authoritarian views than the mothers did.

These gaps between the views of grandparents and parents might have been especially large in the fifties, as a function of rapidly changing child-rearing opinions over the previous decades. Such differences in views may have lessened. Today's grandparents, at least the younger ones, will have had a much fuller education; also probably fewer live directly with the grandchild. Later evidence does not strongly support the notion of very strict grandparents (Neugarten & Weinstein 1964; Smith 1991). Recent research on grandparenthood reports on it in a predominantly positive light. Grandparents are seen as having quite frequent contacts of a positive nature with their grandchildren, and acting as important support agents in certain circumstances.

Grandparents can influence their grandchildren's behaviour both directly and indirectly (Tinsley & Parke 1984). Indirect influence is mediated by some other person or agency, without necessitating any direct interaction. For example, the parent–child interaction will be influenced by the way the parent has been brought up and the experiences of child rearing which the parent has had modelled by his or her parent, i.e. the grandparent. Such influences can of course be positive or negative. Huesmann et al. (1984) found that the severity of discipline received from parents when their subjects were 8 years old, predicted both to their subjects' levels of aggression at 30, and to their children's aggression at 8 years; that is, grandparents' disciplinary practices 22 years earlier, predicted the aggression of their grandchildren.

Grandparents can also continue to provide emotional and financial support for parents. We have ample evidence that the quality of parent–child interaction is affected by such factors as social support and economic circumstances (e.g. Brown & Harris 1978), so that grandparents can have a powerful indirect influence after separation.

The most obvious forms of grandparent influence are nevertheless direct, face-to-face ones, and have been documented by a number of researchers from Neugarten and Weinstein (1964) onwards. Perhaps the strongest case of direct influence is acting as a surrogate parent when the child is young (for example in a single-parent family, or teenage pregnancy, or as a care giver while both parents work). Radin et al. (1991) provide evidence that grandfathers can have a positive direct influence on the social and cognitive development of their grandchildren, in the context of young (1- to 2-year-old) grandchildren of teenage mothers.

Even if not acting as a surrogate parent, a grandparent who has contact with a grandchild can act as a companion and be an important part of the child's social network. Many grandparents enjoy conversations with grandchildren, asking them to run errands, giving them small gifts (Tyszkowa 1991). 'When we go fishing with Grandpa, we talk. We tell each other about ourselves.' 'With Grandma I can talk about my problems.' They can also act as a source of emotional support, as a 'buffer' in cases where a grandchild is in conflict with the parents, or where the parents are in conflict with each other. Just 'being there' can be important.

Several studies have suggested that grandparents may have a particularly important role to play when parents divorce. At a time of considerable uncertainty and distress for their grandchildren, a grandparent can be a source of continuity and support for them and for the parent(s) (Johnson 1985). Sometimes the paternal grandmother, for example, can maintain contacts with grandchildren when the father finds it difficult to do so. A recent issue has been that of custody and the rights of grandparents to have access to their grandchildren when their own son or daughter is the non-custodial parent. A considerable legal literature on this topic in the USA is reviewed by Thompson et al. (1989). In recent years, statutes granting grandparents legal standing to petition for legally enforceable visitation with their grandchildren, even over parental objections, have been passed in all 50 states of the USA.

In the USA there are now courses for grandparents. Strom and Strom (1989) offer an educational programme for grandparents to help strengthen families. The programme includes components on: sharing feelings and ideas with peers; listening to the views of younger people; learning about life-span development; improving family communication skills; and focusing self-evaluation. There are also 'foster grandparent' programmes. Werner (1991) describes how these give elders with low income the opportunity to provide companionship and caring for a variety of high-risk children and youths in return for a tax-exempt stipend. These take place in hospitals, residential institutions, daycare programmes, family shelters. The evaluation of these programmes appears to be positive.

▓ Characteristics of Ageing ▓

Ageing is a gradual but inevitable process, marked by physical, mental and social changes. In fact, some aspects of ageing start by the time people are in their twenties. By then we are already suffering a net loss of brain cells, and some

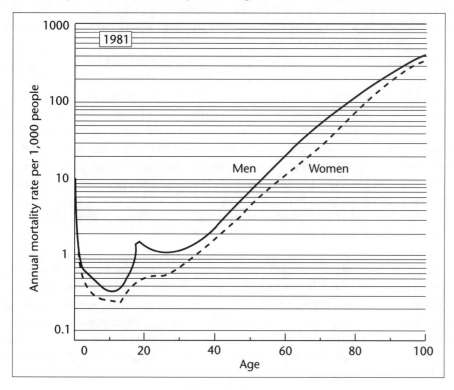

Figure 3.13 Mortality rates for men and women according to age, England and Wales, 1981

Box 3.4   Theories about Why Ageing Occurs

Different species of animals have markedly different life-spans, and some scientists believe that humans are 'pro-grammed' to live about 80 to 100 years. However, until this century, most people died of some accident or disease well before living a full life-span. This being so, it is argued that there was no need for natural selection to produce genes which brought about death by around 100 years. An alternative theory, called the 'disposable soma theory' (Kirkwood 1994), argues that natural selection has not acted to extend life unduly (and especially beyond the end of parenting), simply because accidents and diseases would have killed off many people by then; it would not have been worth the expenditure of biological resources to keep up the maintenance and repair of body cells and tissues for the relatively small chance (historically) that one would live into the sixties and seventies and beyond. On this theory, the body carries out only a limited amount of maintenance and repair of body and tissue cells (the 'soma'), and thus the amount of unrepaired tissue gradually accumulates.

measures of intelligence are beginning to decline. But in terms of the general view of ageing in western society, people over about 65 years of age are seen as 'older'. This is generally the age of retirement from work, and one which Levinson (figure 3.8) sees as the transition to later adulthood.

In the UK the average age of death is 78 for women and 72 for men. Figure 3.13 shows mortality rates for men and women from 1981 data for England and Wales. There is relatively high mortality in infancy, which falls off rapidly in childhood but peaks again (especially for men) with the RISK-TAKING behaviours of later adolescence; after another fall, mortality rates climb steadily from the forties onwards. While many people (especially women) live into their eighties, few live to be 100 years old.

RISK-TAKING

There are definite physical and physiological changes with increasing age, which may result from failing repair mechanisms. These include greying and loss of hair; coarsening and wrinkling of skin; loss of stature; changes in sleep patterns; weakening of eyesight; and increased susceptibility to certain medical problems such as rheumatism, and osteoporosis (thinning of the bones) leading to hip fractures. Another disease of old age is ALZHEIMER'S, the most common form of SENILE DEMENTIA, which is related to certain abnormalities in brain tissue. Dementia can also result from recurrent strokes or damage to small arteries of the brain. Dementia leads to memory loss and a general loss of coping skills, and can affect 5 per cent of people over 65 and more than a third of those in their late eighties and nineties (Rossor 1994).

ALZHEIMER'S

SENILE DEMENTIA

There are various theories as to why ageing occurs (see Box 3.4). Ageing is affected by both biological and environmental factors. In a rare abnormality known as Werner's syndrome (affecting around 1 person per 100,000), ageing is speeded up. In these persons there is no adolescent growth spurt, and early in adulthood there is greying of the hair, skin changes, osteoporosis, and other changes usually associated with the elderly. Life span is around 45 years. This syndrome clearly illustrates the importance of biological factors. But life-style and diet can be important too.

Plate 3.3 Jeanne
Calment held the
world's longevity
record, at an age of
over 120 years
Source: Popperfoto/©
Georges Gobel.

Leaf (1973) reported on some communities where many people live well beyond 100 years. In Georgia (in Asia), for example, some people have lived to be 130 or even 140 (see plate 3.3). While genetic factors cannot be ruled out, it is likely that a healthy diet and plenty of exercise, plus continuing active and productive work late into life, are important contributory factors to a long and healthy life span. Staying healthy appears to be an important part of enjoying one's later years. Unfortunately, older people are more susceptible to illnesses; but in those who stay healthy, the differences in physical functioning with younger persons are relatively few (Birren 1963).

Mental functioning is another area in which older people are thought to show declining powers. Indeed, on conventional IQ tests, the decline sets in during the thirties and forties, and the decline accentuates during the fifties and sixties. However, there are a number of problems in interpreting these data (Baltes & Schaie 1976).

First, IQ tests were devised to assess school achievement, and designed to show an increase in performance only up to age 16. They do not measure abilities particularly found in adults, let alone older adults. As it is, when broken down into components it is clear that the decline in intelligence scores is much less for 'general knowledge' items such as vocabulary tests or analogies, than it is for abstract tasks such as matrices (see chapter 15). And attempts to measure moral reasoning and wisdom – not found in conventional IQ tests – suggest that older adults may perform better than younger adults.

Second, there are likely to be 'cohort effects' which obscure the interpretation of these data. Intelligence test performance is influenced by schooling, and specifically by years in schooling. In Western societies, universal schooling up to around age 16 only came into being in many countries in the last 40 or 50 years, following the Second World War. People older than 60 or 70 at the present time will often have had shorter periods of schooling than those born later, and this is likely to have depressed their intelligence test scores quite independently of chronological age – it is an effect of the birth 'cohort' they are in.

Generally speaking, despite the above qualifications, there does appear to be some real deterioration in some mental abilities with age – sometimes gradual, sometimes fast. However, older people can still learn – a new language, new factual knowledge, new techniques; and they can compensate for difficulties (such as partial memory loss) by developing new skills. They may learn to use *aide-mémoires* (like brief reminder notes or tying a knot in one's handkerchief) or mnemonic techniques (for example, if a person has to remember to buy carrots, apples and tomatoes, they may remember the shopping list by noting the first letter of each word, in this case CAT). They may not be able to learn as fast as younger people, but their increased knowledge, experience and wisdom are important strengths (Baltes 1993).

Older people are also often seen as losing interest in social interaction. Metaphorically, the over-65s are seen as 'putting their feet up' by the fire or in front of the television, enjoying a well-earned retirement. Indeed a prominent theory, called 'disengagement theory' by Cumming and Henry (1961), held that old age involved a natural withdrawal from social activities and societal obligations. But in contrast to this, Neugarten et al. (1968) proposed an 'activity theory', that health and life satisfaction are maintained through continuing social activity and involvement, and that any decrease tends to be brought about by societal discrimination.

Research findings seem to favour activity theory over disengagement theory. For example, Dolen and Bearison (1982) looked at the lives of 122 generally healthy adults aged 65 to 89 years, living in New York. Neither social participation, nor scores on social cognition tasks, showed any pronounced decline with age. Nevertheless, social participation and social cognition scores did correlate significantly, indicating that those who remained socially active and involved also stayed cognitively alert and socially understanding. A study of elderly people in England aged 85 or over, by Grundy (1994), found that those who kept in

Plate 3.4 Nelson
Mandela, who took
office in his
seventies
Source: Camera Press/
Jan Kopec.

touch with family and friends had a lower risk of death (even allowing for differences in state of health). And social support generally provides a buffer against stress, including the age-related stresses of retirement and bereavement (see below).

To some extent, modern societies may discriminate against older people; for example by forcing retirement at an arbitrary age (such as 65) or by perpetuating, in the mass media and elsewhere, negative stereotypes of elderly people and the ageing process. Neugarten et al. (1968) labelled this 'ageism'. Birren (1969) proposed that, rather than use chronological age as a societal indicator, we might use 'functional age' – an individual's actual capacities, irrespective of chronological age. A consequence of this view would be that retirement age might be determined by say functional age, rather than by chronological age. So far, this view has not held sway widely; but in some domains, such as politics, quite elderly people have achieved or stayed in very influential positions. An acclaimed example is that of Nelson Mandela becoming President of the new South Africa at the age of 75 (plate 3.4). Not all elderly leaders are acclaimed, but the position does allow for the exercise of accumulated knowledge and wisdom more than many other societal roles.

■ Bereavement, Grief and Mourning ■

The death of a partner, parent, child, or a close friend can leave a person with intense feelings of loss; the process of coming to terms with this loss can be characterized by acute mental and physical pain. The experience of bereavement refers to the loss of a loved one. Grief is the emotional state of mind which occurs after such a significant loss. Emotional responses often include sadness and depression, but they can also be experienced as anger and guilt. Mourning refers to the culturally appropriate rituals and traditions which accompany such a loss.

Grief is a normal, healthy response to a bereavement yet, especially in Western societies, expressions of sadness in these circumstances can cause embarrassment. Adults who have suffered bereavement often comment that friends and neighbours drew away from them after the funeral and failed to offer them the companionship and support which they needed. Comments like 'It's six months since her mother died and she was, after all, 80 years old. Surely she should be over it by now!' are hurtful and display a lack of awareness of the need for a bereaved person to mourn.

Researchers in this area have identified distinct stages of grieving (for example, Kubler-Ross 1975), and although the stages do not necessarily occur independently of one another, and there are wide variations in individual response, the categories shown in figure 3.14 represent the most common patterns of response to traumatic loss. People need to work through grief in their own way, and it is important to be flexible in the interpretation of the stages. There are many factors which influence the nature of the grieving process. The closeness of the relationship with the person who is lost is, of course, highly significant. So too is the age of the person. The suddenness of the death is important. If there was no time to 'make peace' with the person before death, then it can take longer to recover from it, and the loss is more likely to be accompanied by prolonged feelings of anger and guilt. The amount of social support available to the bereaved person can play a key part in facilitating recovery. The rituals and ceremonies surrounding a death can be helpful.

If the bereaved person is not able to work through the process of grieving, they may suffer longer-term emotional damage. Some bereaved people report obsessional memories of the dead person; feelings of unreality; anger and moodiness; a reluctance to be in company; compulsive thoughts of regret, or even guilt over actions done during the life of the dead person; regret over unsaid words at the time of death. If these feelings, thoughts and memories continue over a longer period of time, it may be helpful for the person to seek out bereavement coun-

1. **Immobilisation**. The person is likely to feel numbed and overwhelmed. Thoughts and feelings will not be clear. There may even be denial at this stage.
2. **Awareness of the loss.** This is a reaction to the feeling of being numbed and frozen. There is a growing awareness of the loss with accompanying feelings of sadness, anger, guilt, regret.
3. **Depression.** This is the stage of accepting reality as it is – a reality which no longer contains a significant other.
4. **Letting go.** This is the stage of accepting reality as it is – a reality which no longer contains a significant other.
5. **Return to reality.** The bereaved person gradually returns to everyday activities and thinks less obsessively about the dead person. The person may try out new behaviours, new thoughts, even new life-styles.
6. **Search for meaning.** This can be a complex process which involves thinking about the finiteness of life, including one's one. These new meanings are acknowledged and internalized, and the person continues with their life. There is a renewed positive feeling about life.

Figure 3.14 Stages in the process of grieving

selling (Lendrum & Syme 1992). For the most part, however, people rely on their existing social networks and circle of friends to support them. Social support for the bereaved person can include practical help as well as words of condolence, and the reactions of grief usually lessen over time (see Box 3.1(f)).

Stages in Life

The concept of life stages or seasons recurs throughout history, and it has not disappeared from contemporary thinking about life-span development. As in the past, many adults still have expectations about the 'appropriateness' of the timing of certain key life events and crises. There is still a sense of 'rightness' and 'wrongness' in their occurrence, for example if a person in midlife decides to backpack round the world, or if a very young adolescent girl becomes pregnant, or if a child dies before a parent, or if a person in late adulthood becomes sexually involved with a much younger partner.

At the same time, stage theories face enormous difficulties in incorporating the great diversity of adult experience into a framework. There is controversy over whether the changes in adult life occur in stages, as Erikson, Levinson and others suggest, or whether adults follow any one of a range of possible developmental paths. It can be argued that many of the stages which adults would have traditionally been expected to pass through at certain ages are now, in contemporary Western society, becoming blurred. More people than in the past now marry, divorce and remarry. More women now delay the age at which they conceive their first child. Many adults return to education in later life. More men and women than ever before now embark on second or even third careers during their life-span. Adolescence and adulthood are characterized throughout by change and discontinuity as well as stability, and for any given individual it is not possible to make easy predictions as to the course of their development across the life-span.

CHAPTER SUMMARY

1 Development through adolescence and adulthood can show both stability and change, in only partially predictable ways.

2 Adolescence, often seen as a period of 'storm and stress', is marked by the biological changes associated with puberty. The age of reaching puberty shows historical variations, and individual variations which may have some psychological consequences. Adolescence also, according to Piaget's theory, marks the start of being able to use abstract, logical ways of thinking, which he calls 'formal operations'.

3 Erikson's stage model of psychosexual development marks out adolescence in terms of a 'normative crisis' of identity versus role confusion, and postulates a 'psychosocial moratorium' during which identity is developed – a scheme operationalized by Marcia but open to criticism as being historically and culturally biased.

4 Parent–child relationships appear to become less close during adolescence, and risk-taking and delinquency often increase, for reasons which may be related to biological, cognitive and social changes.

5 As well as Erikson, Levinson, Bühler and others described stage models for adult development, with Levinson describing the 'midlife crisis' in the forties.

6 Most adults experience falling in love. The romantic conception of love emphasizes passion, but this limited conception has been criticized by psychologists and by feminists. Sternberg's triangular theory

of love includes passion, intimacy and commitment. Choice of partner can be influenced by psychological considerations such as similarity, attractiveness and attachment security, as well as by cultural factors.

7 Becoming a parent is an important life transition, for many women and men. Parenting style is influenced by sex and by earlier attachment history, as well as social class, social support, and the wider social and cultural context. Gay and lesbian parents may experience difficulties but there is no evidence that children reared in such families are adversely affected.

8 Separation and divorce are painful experiences which often have negative consequences for children; such consequences can be ameliorated by taking the welfare of children into full consideration. Some children experience neglect and abuse from parents. Belsky's model of parenting provides a useful way of conceptualizing influences on parenting skills.

9 Becoming a grandparent is another important transition for many people. Grandparents can influence the development of their grandchildren in both indirect and direct ways.

10 Ageing is marked by physical and physiological changes, possibly related to decreased body maintenance and repair; and by psychological changes, influenced by the physical changes but also by increased experience, and social and cultural views of older people. Mental functioning shows some deterioration in old age, but there are some problems of interpretation of the data. 'Activity theory'

seems to have more support than 'disengagement theory' in understanding social changes in the elderly. 'Functional age' provides a possible alternative to chronological age in considering the role of older people in society.

11 Grief and mourning are normal, healthy responses to bereavement. There are distinct stages to grieving; social support and rituals can be helpful in the process.

Further Work

1. Is adolescence really a period of turmoil, and 'storm and stress'? If so, why is this?
2. How useful, and valid, are stage models of adult or life-span development? Can the different models be reconciled?
3. What makes a good parent? How useful is Belsky's model in considering this question, and what evidence is there for the model?
4. What distinctive contributions can grandparents make to their grandchildren's development?
5. Should ageing be seen as an inevitable process of intellectual decline and social withdrawal?
6. Is romantic love a necessary basis for a long-term relationship?
7. To what extent are people who are insecurely attached to their parents likely to have difficulties in maintaining intimate relationships?

Further Reading

Coleman, J. C. and Hendry, L. (1990) *The Nature of Adolescence*. London: Routledge.

> An excellent review of current work on adolescence.

Lewis, C. (1986) *Becoming a Father*. Milton Keynes: Open University Press.

> A very readable and scholarly account of research in the field of fathering.

Josselson, R. (1996) *The Space Between Us*. London: Sage.

> The task of charting intimate relationships across the life-span described from the standpoint of the counselling psychologist.

Kubler-Ross, E. (1975) *Death: The Final Stage of Growth*. Englewood Cliffs, NJ: Prentice-Hall.

> The classic study of the previously taboo topic – death and dying.

Lendrum, S. and Syme, G. (1992) *Gift of Tears*. London: Routledge.

> A moving account from a psychodynamic perspective from two practitioners with long experience in working with bereaved children and adults.

PART 3

Biological Psychology

CHAPTER 4
Evolution and Sociobiology

Richard Byrne

CHAPTER AGENDA

- It is fundamentally important to understand *why* the theory of evolution is accepted as correct, and *how* the mechanism of natural selection operates. From the starting point of evolution by natural selection, a range of other developments are explored in the rest of the chapter:

- A particular environment can be exploited in different ways. These survival strategies shape the body form and even the social behaviour of species that use them, sometimes causing unrelated species to 'converge' towards each other.

- Descent from common ancestors leaves a legacy of shared features that originated in the now-extinct common ancestor. Using a reliable phylogenetic taxonomy, it is now possible to reconstruct the evolutionary pathway and the characteristics,

even behavioural ones, of these ancestor species.

- Evidence from modern primates can be used to reconstruct human evolution. Most important for cognitive psychology, this includes the origins of various aspects of intelligence.

- The full extent of genetic influences on human social behaviour is only now being worked out, and the topic is still controversial. It is useful to approach it with a firm understanding of how genes can influence animals' social interactions – the subject of sociobiology. With humans, cultural influences interact with sociobiology in complex ways, but some particularly clear cases of genetic effects are explored: marriage patterns, infanticide and sexual competition.

▓ The Theory of Evolution ▓

Psychology gains important insights from viewing *Homo sapiens* as 'just another animal', from comparing ourselves with other species, and looking for the ancient origins of modern human behaviours. None of this could be done without the theory of evolution, one of the most revolutionary scientific advances of the nineteenth century. The story of its discovery illustrates its key elements, and is worth telling for its own sake. Perhaps the best starting point is a letter written between bouts of malaria on the island of Ternate in the Moluccas, now part of Indonesia:

> It occurred to me to ask the question, why do some animals die and some live? And the answer was clearly, that on the whole the best-fitted lived. From the effects of

disease the most healthy escaped; from enemies, the strongest, the swiftest, or the most cunning; from famine, the best hunters or those with the best digestion, and so on. Then I at once saw, that the ever-present variability of all living things would furnish the material from which, by the mere weeding out of the those less adapted to the actual conditions, the fittest alone would continue the race.

There suddenly flashed upon me the idea of the survival of the fittest. The more I thought over it, the more I became convinced that I had at last found the long-sought-for law of nature that solved the problem of the origin of species.

The ringing phrases 'origin of species' and 'survival of the fittest' are common-place today. Their writer was not Charles Darwin, but a professional collector of insects, Alfred Russell Wallace. He was writing *to* Darwin, to tell the famous naturalist about his brilliant idea. Darwin in fact had already had essentially the same idea many years earlier; he had written out the basic theory and deposited it in a safe, to be published after his death. Presumably he was conscious that the idea of species change (and the human kinship with apes that it leads to) would be controversial, but wanted eventually to be acknowledged as the discoverer of the theory. His feelings when he read Wallace's letter can be imagined. They announced their discovery jointly, and Darwin's famous book *The Origin of Species* followed shortly after, to immediate scientific acclaim.

Notice that the *problem* of 'the origin of species' was not a new one, since Wallace's letter mentions that the solution had been 'long-sought-for'. In fact, many people in the early nineteenth century, including Charles Darwin's father Erasmus, were convinced that species were not fixed but changed over huge spans of time – they 'evolved'. One reason for this conviction was that the idea of evolution enabled scientists to understand the origin of fossils, remains of non-living animals that were often found in the ground. If species change, fossils can be understood as the remains of species that had once existed, long ago, and had changed into the modern species over millennia.

But the *main* scientific problem that could potentially be solved, by the theory that species change in evolution, was the pattern of similarity of living things. Why are some animals very similar to each other, yet others utterly different? The fact that living things varied in this way, forming a hierarchical 'tree' of relative similarity, had long been known. Naturalists in the nineteenth century all used the system of classification that was devised by the Swedish botanist Linné. This classified all living things into groups on the basis of their similarity: the basic unit was the 'species', a group of interbreeding individuals; and closely similar species are grouped into 'genera'. The Latin names for a thing's genus and species form its scientific name even now, such as *Homo sapiens* or *Iris reticulata*. The Linnean system is hierarchical, with genera grouped into families, families into orders, and so on.

But when Linné was working (his system was published in 1758), belief in a single act of creation was unquestioned, so the similarities were seen as reflecting the thought processes of the Creator. By the nineteenth century, many people questioned this 'all at once' creation, and belief in evolution was quite

Plate 4.1 Evolution of marsupials

Plate 4.1 Evolution of marsupials

widespread. (This does not necessarily conflict with belief in God, as is sometimes imagined nowadays, but it certainly led to antagonism from some church-men.) The idea of evolution explained the old puzzle of why living species resemble each other to varying degrees. If species can change and split up over time, then the closest relatives – those that split most recently – would tend to be more similar to each other than ones that split apart aeons ago and have diverged greatly since. If all living things have evolved from a remote ancestor by splitting off at different points from each other, then the degree of similarity shows how recent was the split. The tree of life is a *family* tree, a tree of relatedness. The problem was, no plausible mechanism was known that could underwrite this process of evolution.

This was the big hurdle to overcome, as Darwin and Wallace well knew. Short of the absurd idea of a God idly tinkering for the fun of it, no one could think of a workable mechanism of species change. (In fact, almost as odd an idea as that *was* believed by those who accepted the views of the famous French biologist, Cuvier. He proposed that there had been seven creations; the one described in the Bible was the last one. Fossils are the remains of the other six!) Without a workable mechanism, whether one believed in evolution or single creation would be just a matter of personal preference. With the Darwin/Wallace hypothesis, scientists at last had a mechanism that could explain how species could change over time.

The mechanism, 'survival of the fittest', was a beautifully simply one. Death is not random, but is more likely to fall on individuals with inappropriate attributes for survival. This process quite *automatically* weeds out some individuals, those less 'well adapted to survive' – as Wallace's letter describes vividly. What is left to breed and so form the next generation, are those 'fitter' individuals with particular attributes, more useful ones in the natural world. Putting it slightly more precisely, individuals do not have to die young to produce the effect, but can be unfit simply by breeding less effectively. The term 'fitness' causes trouble: it has nothing to do with aerobic workouts. The definition of fitness in this special sense, DARWINIAN FITNESS, is the ability to reproduce successfully, to leave descendants. Any attribute that allows an individual to survive and reproduce confers Darwinian fitness. With our human perspective, we tend to think that dying young is a serious impediment to fitness: but it isn't, not if you have already had loads of offspring. Herrings find this an excellent strategy, and, to a lesser extent, so do rabbits.

DARWINIAN
FITNESS

This idea of the 'natural selection' of breeding was a plausible one: the wondrous evidence that artificial selection works was all around Victorian England, from Pekinese dogs to Aberdeen Angus cattle. Populations of plants and animals in different places may be subject to differential 'natural selection' to each other, since the attributes that give fitness will typically vary with the environment. In this way, isolated populations will sometimes grow apart – into new species that eventually become so different they cannot interbreed even when they meet. Seeing the apparent results of such a process in the Galapagos Islands may have inspired Darwin to make his discovery. Wallace, as an insect collector, had noticed that superficially uniform rainforests, like the Amazon basin, were divided into a mosaic of areas of similar species, but at the imaginary lines dividing these regions the species change is sudden; 'Wallace's line' across Indonesia is one such division between two adjacent areas inhabited by

Plate 4.2 Galapagos finches, a highly individuated species
Source: Mary Evans Picture Library.

almost entirely different animals. Modern understanding of climate change now allows these regions to be understood also as the result of speciation in 'islands' of relict forest at times of hot, dry world climate. (There is a current debate concerning whether new species can ever be formed in a huge interbreeding population, or whether only small, isolated populations – like island populations – can change fast enough to speciate. On the latter view, most of the time a species exists it will stay exactly the same, but these periods of stasis will be punctuated by quite brief bursts of rapid change when conditions are right. This is a technical point, but the opposite sides in the debate between GRADUALISM and PUNCTUATED EQUILIBRIUM get very heated, and commentators sometimes like to suggest that the whole idea of evolution by natural selection is in question. This is not so, and it is likely that both sides are partly correct: that often evolution occurs in rapid bursts between long, static intervals, but occasionally rather slow changes occur.)

Oddly, considering its rapid acceptance by scientists, Wallace and Darwin's statement of the theory of natural selection was flawed. The mechanism of inheritance, as wrongly understood at the time, was incompatible with natural selection. Darwin himself later came to realize the problem, and died believing that LAMARCKISM must be the correct explanation. Lamarckism is the idea that species can alter as a result of individuals gaining characters during their lifetime. Giraffes gained their long necks by many generations of hard stretching upwards, and so on. It is a delightful idea, but sadly quite wrong. The fact that

GRADUALISM

PUNCTUATED
EQUILIBRIUM

LAMARCKISM

acquired characters cannot be passed on is easy to check: by splitting a sample of animals into two, training up one half on a task (such as neck stretching) till they are much better at it than the control group, then breeding from both. Unfortunately for the theory, the offspring do not differ in ability: Lamarckism is incorrect.

The trouble with Darwin and Wallace's version of natural selection was all to do with the 'ever-present variability' that Wallace's letter mentions, and the way it is inherited. At the time they published, inheritance was believed to result in *blending*: tall man + short woman = medium-height children; fair-haired man + black-haired woman = brown-haired children, and so on. The trouble with blending is that each succeeding generation has *less* variation. Extremes diminish by blending with others, and in the end the population inexorably tends towards uniformity. This manifestly does not happen in nature. And from a theoretical angle, if variation collapses, natural selection has nothing left to work on.

At Darwin's death, a paper lay unread on his desk, the pages never cut: by a Central European monk, Gregor Mendel. He only published one paper on inheritance, and unluckily for him the man who would most have appreciated its immense significance did not read it. Mendel's work was rediscovered later, after others had independently reached the same conclusion: inheritance was PARTICULATE. Cross a tall and a short pea plant, and you did not get medium-sized progeny: only tall ones and short ones. The same applied to peas that were round or wrinkly, no offspring were ever half-wrinkly; and the same with yellow and green ones, offspring were yellow, or green, but not yellowish-green. There are mysteries to do with Mendel's work: for instance, he published breeding experiments on seven different characters of peas, and every time he described finding a neat one-quarter to three-quarters division of offspring for the character in question; the three-quarters of one type further divided up into one-third breeding true if crossed with itself, the rest not. This pattern is today called 'Mendelian inheritance' in commemoration. But in the messy, real world, there is often LINKAGE between the genetic basis of characters (now known to result from both genes lying on the same chromosome), giving less tidy results. Peas have only seven chromosomes, and every character Mendel investigated just happened to be on a different one. The odds of this happening are less than twenty-to-one against. Also, his numbers have since been shown to be 'too perfect'. A random process, like sorting the genetic material of one strain of peas with another, has a calculable variation in it: coins tossed twenty times rather seldom come up heads exactly ten times and tails exactly ten times. Mendel's data were apparently fabricated, by a man who knew much more about the structure of the data than he let on. Finally, it is strange that he give up his engaging hobby. Perhaps he was uncomfortably aware of the biological character that never, ever looks blended. Male crossed with female never, ever produces a blend! Hair-colour and height actually do give a simulation of blending, they are not obviously particulate; but *sex* is. Monks engaging in hobbies that involve breeding and sex may well find difficulties put in their way.

PARTICULATE INHERITANCE

LINKAGE

GENE

'Particles' is a clumsy term for the bits that carry the inherited characters: GENE is the modern term. A gene is any portion of chromosomal material that potentially serves as a unit of natural selection. (Note that this is *not* always how the word 'gene' is used. Since the discovery of the chemical basis of chromosomes, it has been realized that the smallest chemical unit that has an independent effect in the body is a protein, and that this is chemically built up by the instructions on a piece of DNA: this piece of DNA is called a CISTRON, and sometimes people use 'gene' interchangeably with cistron. Also, the building blocks of the protein, amino acids, are each built by the instructions on a triplet of bases along the DNA: this triple is called a CODON, and sometimes gene and codon are used interchangeably.) In this chapter, gene will be used only for a unit of inheritance.

CISTRON

CODON

Variation is maintained by the type of inheritance, but nevertheless those genes that do not confer any survival advantage will gradually die out in a population. Surely the total pool of variation must inevitably decrease, although very slowly, just because natural selection is operating? This is correct: under natural selection, especially under powerful selective pressures (that is, when there is high variation among individuals in the rate of die-off or failure to breed), variation inevitably gets 'used up' and declines. The reason that the whole system does not come to a grinding halt is that there is also a (rather slow) mechanism that produces new variation. It is called MUTATION, and the simplest way to look at it is as a matter of occasional copying errors. The genetic code along the DNA molecule in a chromosome is replicated every time a cell divides. Normally, this copying is very accurate, so that although genes keep getting mixed together during reproduction, and their frequencies vary because of natural selection, the same genes appear in each generation. But just occasionally, a copying error occurs. Most likely, this will destroy some important process in the body of the individual containing the new gene, which will die – and that's the last we'll hear of that! But very occasionally the new gene will do no harm, or even confer a benefit. Then it will survive to be copied itself, and the 'pool' of genetic variation will be increased.

MUTATION

With *particulate inheritance*, variation in characteristics is protected from rapidly diminishing, and variation is only 'used up' slowly with selection; with *random mutation*, the pool of genetic variation is gradually increased. Natural selection then works properly as a theory. Individuals that have the qualities that allow them to reproduce better (those with higher Darwinian fitness) are *selected* – meaning that they certainly don't die young and childless. But *all* individuals do die; the only thing that continues to the next generation is a set of genes. Preventing some individuals (made from thousands of genes) from breeding, and breeding from others (made from different sets of thousands of genes), is a very blunt instrument for 'selecting' certain sorts of animal: but it's the only one there is, and that's what animal selective breeding has to rely on. The same is true of natural selection: but here the process is *automatic*, not purpose-driven, which makes it even more desperately inefficient and slow. Dozens or hundreds

Plate 4.3 Langur monkeys, mother with infant
Source: Volker Sommer.

or thousands of lifetimes are needed to have much effect; so there is little chance in anyone's lifetime of studying evolution as it happens. But this very blunt instrument of non-random selection of individuals, working on entirely random variation, maintained by particulate inheritance of genes, can work powerful effects over very long time-scales.

▓ Socioecology: How Environment Influences Society ▓

If we now change perspective, and look at the process of natural selection from the environment's point of view, 'well-adapted' individuals are in a sense those which can successfully overcome problems the environment poses. Indeed, each individual species can be viewed as one 'solution' to a complex, multi-faceted problem of living in a particular way in a particular environment. Gazelles are selected for running speed, because the environment (in the form of cheetahs) poses a problem, solved only by fast-running animals; monkeys are perhaps selected for intelligence, because in the social groups they live in, there is a premium on smartness (remember, the 'environment' isn't just the physical world, it includes other animals, even members of your own species).

This idea of an environment setting up *possible solutions* that animals can fit in with (or die) is a powerful one. Over time, a species evolves to *fit* an environment (or becomes extinct); in a sense, the species fits into a slot defined by the environment. Ecologists call these slots NICHES; and they view an environment as composed of a set of niches, that can be filled by potential species. A niche in-

NICHES

CONSPECIFICS

cludes all the determinants of survival: food and water supply, safety from predators, competition with other species and with CONSPECIFICS.

This way of looking at environments as sets of niches emphasizes that a niche can be 'empty' if no species happens to currently exist which exploits the environment in that particular way. As a concrete example, American minks have become established in mainland Britain because they were kept in fur farms and escaped. At first, it was thought they would either cause havoc (that is, upset the existing ecology by changing the niche structure), or displace otters from their niche, exacerbating the existing, human-caused decline in otter numbers. Similarly drastic effects of introduced species are sadly common, most visibly on islands like Hawaii, New Zealand and Australia. In fact, Britain has been lucky in the mink case. Minks cannot displace otters from their niche, because they do not specialize in fish. They eat a wider diet, including many small birds and insects; and their colonization has not driven any of these birds or insects to extinction. Indeed, in most areas their effect has been unnoticed (although along the artificially tidy river banks of southern England minks have had a drastic effect on one prey species, the water vole). The niche for minks must have been there all along, but empty.

Also, a niche can be filled by more than one type of animal – and if the environmental 'problem' is the same, we must expect the various solutions to be alike in many ways. However, the process of natural selection will have different material to work on – a different set of current species – in different places, so the same niche may end up filled by unrelated animals, which have become more similar in form because they need to solve the same problems. This increase in similarity, in response to the same selection pressure, is called

CONVERGENT EVOLUTION

CONVERGENT EVOLUTION. A dramatic illustration of the power of niches in environments to mould, through natural selection, different material into similar form, is the convergence of Australian marsupials with placental mammals in the rest of the world. In Australia there are subterranean mammals that make tunnels, predatory nocturnal mammals with stripes or spots, long-tongued mammals that eat ants – and all of them are more closely related to kangaroos than to moles, cats or anteaters! But remember, natural selection is a continuous process driven mechanistically by differences in survival: it is limited by the genetic material available, and not able to cause a major 'jumps' to some completely different solution. Looking at the process from the outside, humans can sometimes imagine solutions that might be better, but these are usually simply unreachable from the genetic material of existing species. For instance, insectivorous birds would be able to catch more bugs if they could breathe smoke to stun thousands at once – but no bird has ever had genetic material that was remotely close to that needed to produce smoke-breathing. The animals we find living in a habitat will (inevitably) have been optimized by selection, but only

LOCAL OPTIMALITY

on a local scale. Only LOCAL OPTIMALITY is possible, by the planless mechanism of natural selection.

If species are optimized by natural selection to fit the niches that exist in their

Plate 4.4 Prairie dogs live in surprisingly organized communities
Source: Natural Science Photos/ © Beth Davidow.

environment, why should they continue to change? This was a serious issue in Darwin's day, since at that time it was not understood that environments might change over time, even without human interference. Darwin's description of evolution instead assumed that there *were* no particular optima, and that selection worked continually (at different rates in different species and habitats). It is likely that this was a major reason of concern for Bishop Wilberforce, in the great debate between evolutionists and churchmen. Wilberforce does not seem to have been a fundamentalist, opposed in principle to evolution; but he objected to the idea that God's creatures were imperfect, and if that's what evolution meant, he rejected it.

This problem no longer exists, because we understand that the environment is and has always been in flux. Partly, over very long time-scales, niches change as a result of the *pollution* created by the living creatures themselves: for instance, oxygen, a pollutant produced by blue-green algae early in the earth's history, gradually accumulated and made most habitats untenable for blue-green algae. This benefited a new group of creatures that managed to use oxygen constructively, recently including ourselves. Change also occurs by continental drift, properly called 'plate tectonics', in which parts of the earth's crust move about. Areas now in temperate or Arctic zones once lay on the equator and were then covered in moist forest; fossils record the change. Also, the world alters dramatically at rare intervals, when *mass extinctions* of large fractions of all living creatures occur. It seems most likely these extinctions are a result of comet collisions with earth, but this is not certain. After a mass extinction, many niches become vacant for the survivors, if there are any. Sixty-five million years ago (abbreviated 65Ma), the last of these big extinctions destroyed almost all of the dinosaurs, pterosaurs and icthyosaurs that dominated the planet, leaving a rather empty world for a

Plate 4.5 Primates are humanity's closest animal relatives
Source: Natural Science Photos/ © C. Dani.

group of small furry creatures who had previously kept out of the way, emerging in forests at night: the mammals.

All these forces for change mean that static environments are rare. Where they exist, little happens in terms of natural selection: it cannot, because species there are inevitably (locally) optimized. At 1,000 fathoms in tropical seas, there are still living creatures almost unchanged from 300Ma, called 'nautiluses'. The vast majority of their relatives, including ammonites and belemnites, died out in the greatest extinction event to date, one that destroyed over 95 per cent of living forms. Safe in the depths, little changed.

It is not simply body form that can be viewed as an adaptive 'solution' to an environmental 'problem': we can do the same for mental characteristics, and even social behaviour. Social behaviour, at first sight, is perhaps the *least* likely attribute of animals to show any effects due to environmental niches. 'Society' is commonly thought to be no more than the personal choices of the people that make it up, not an adaptation to survive in a particular environment. When scientists began to investigate animal societies, it soon became clear that, at least in insects, very elaborate and complex societies are sometimes found, and their organization is under genetic control. A gene *for* a particular social system, like any other gene, will be subject to natural selection. However, human society is crucially different to that of bees, wasps, termites and ants, in its extreme flexibility. In different parts of the world, or even in the same place, the same species has quite different social organizations. Insects' complex but highly constrained societies are certainly under genetical selection, whereas human's exuberantly variable ones are not – or so it was thought.

This assumption changed dramatically during the 1960s, mainly because of the work of John Crook. He began by studying a group of sparrow-like African birds, weavers, famous for their complex nest-making (Crook 1965). He noticed that he could predict the social system of a species just by knowing in what sort of habitat it was found. Some weavers live on grasslands: in these, males are bright-plumaged and females drab; they nest in colonies; they eat grass seeds; they pair to court and mate. But males do not help rear young; and males lose their bright plumage after breeding, becoming very like females. Other weavers live in forests: here, both sexes are similar in plumage, and the male looks the same all year; a pair nests alone, and the pair remain mated all year; both sexes help rear the young; and they eat insects. Crook suggested that *the environments determine the social systems*. For the first time, a society was seen as a direct result of niche occupation, a product of environmental constraints: to live in a certain way, in a certain habitat, a weaver must adopt a certain social organization.

Birds are evolutionarily remote from humans, and genetical constraints on their societies might have no relevance for ourselves: humans are primates. So Crook went on to test his idea with primates, checking for social patterns that correspond always with occupation of particular environments, and he found the same sort of correspondence (Crook & Gartlan 1966). For instance, all over the world there are small, nocturnal insectivorous primates – mouse lemurs in Madagascar, tarsiers in Indonesia, lorises in Asia, bushbabies in mainland Africa. In every case, individuals are solitary; but charting their occasional friendly associations shows that several females associate with a single male. Females' ranges overlap; whereas males form territories, make loud territorial calls, and drive out intruding males. Conversely, in open grassland primates have a quite different social system, whether they are hamadryas baboons, patas monkeys or geladas. They socialize in small units, consisting of several females with a single, leading male; sometimes there is another old male, or a much younger one, the father or son of the leader. These units regularly split off from much larger groups that associate in a friendly way. The large groups may sleep together, if safe sleeping sites are limited, or feed together at times of glut, but at times of scarcity the units will often go off alone. Sometimes, several of the 'one-male units' may choose to travel together, but these bands are variable in composition.

The underlying assumption of this approach, which is called SOCIOECOLOGY, is

SOCIOECOLOGY

Box 4.1 Hanuman Langurs

Plate 4.6 Langur monkey
with harem
Source: Natural Science
Photos/© S. G. Neginhal.

that a social system is a flexible thing, one that can change quite quickly over evolutionary time-scales. By contrast, bodily features like the digestive system, teeth and bones, are assumed to be 'fixed'. This enables correlations to be interpreted causally: if folivores always live in cohesive groups in small ranges, the diet can be assumed to cause the social pattern and daily movements, not the other way around. Although of course evolution modifies bodies too, the assumption of very different rates of change for society (compared to guts and bones) is often reasonable, and has been supported by the finding that some species of primate can change their social system to suit their ecology. One of the most striking examples of this is an Indian monkey, the Hanuman langur (see Box 4.1).

Socioecology has proved valuable in understanding the complex variation among animal societies, and its relationship to environmental needs. The extent to which ecological constraints apply to modern humans is still hotly debated, but the subject has made an interesting bridge between biology, economics and social psychology. There has been some enthusiasm for interpreting modern human behaviour as a relic of adaptations to a palaeolithic environment, and

Hanuman langurs are found in two different social organizations: (i) a small group of several females and one male, defending a territory against other groups, while those males without harems go around together in less favourable areas; and (ii) a large group with many males and females, ranging widely but not defending any particular area, so their range overlaps with that of other large groups.

In each case, the society can be understood as an adaptation to the ecology in which the animals live (Hladik 1975). Large groups are found in drier habitats, where the animals occur at low density, so are presumably an adaptation to semi-desert conditions. In Sri Lanka, Hanuman langurs even change their social organization back and forth each year, becoming territorial in the monsoon when there is much food, and aggregating into larger groups in the dry season! A territory is more efficient, because the holders have monopoly of the food in them; but a territory requires defence, so the area must be small enough to patrol regularly, and is not a feasible proposition if food is very sparse. These monkeys illustrate that socioecology does not imply that society is fixed by genetical evolution; instead society is seen as a product of the choices of individuals, which vary adaptively with conditions. Hanuman langurs are only unusual in that, instead of a range of rather similar social solutions occurring as the

environment varies, for them the two societies which emerge as optima in different environments are quite different.

Living in different social organizations has further implications for the monkeys. In the big groups with many males and females, males take little interest in babies; in small, one-male groups, males are attentive and helpful to babies. This makes sense as kin selection. In the one-male groups any babies *are* the male's kin, whereas paternity is uncertain in multi-male groups.

Occasionally, a group of excluded males makes an attack on a one-male group, trying to depose its leader. If they succeed, much fighting among the males follows, until only one is left. Infanticide follows: the new leader male then systematically kills baby monkeys in the group. This extraordinary behaviour, seemingly so at variance with the attentive and helpful behaviour usually shown by harem-leader males to babies, makes perfect sense as kin selection. Those babies killed are *not* related to the new leader, and by killing them the females will become sexually receptive all the sooner, so his chances of having offspring are increased. It is not suggested that langurs understand the genetical theory involved; the gene for switching to infanticidal behaviour briefly after taking over a group of females has become stable in langurs, since it increases inclusive fitness for males.

since the details of this former environment are not known there is much scope for speculation!

Are modern relations between men and women still reflecting adaptations to meat-exchange in hunter-gatherer societies, and are the minds that have to cope with the computer revolution really better adapted to monitoring social contracts in small kin groups (Cosmides & Tooby 1992)? Questions like these are currently generating considerable interest, and it is certainly reasonable that some aspects of the modern mind are primitive 'retentions' from earlier phases of evolution. However, there is a danger here of unfalsifiability: we can never know for sure what the precise ecological niche was during recent human evolution, let alone what the human mind was like then, so claims that specific modern features are retentions from those times will always be open to debate. Moreover, this debate misses the point of the socioecological approach, the assumption that social systems are relatively fluid and open to change. This points instead to the approach of looking for *current* ecological correlates of different social systems, among modern people.

Plate 4.7 Bushbaby: usually individuals are solitary
Source: Natural Science Photos/© R. P. B. Erasmus.

Crook himself has done just this, noting that one pattern of human marriage is virtually confined to a single physical environment, the very high altitude people of Central Asia, loosely called Tibet (Crook & Osmaston 1988). The marriage system of these Buddhist communities, persisting mainly in Indian Himalaya, involves a girl marrying all the brothers of a family (fraternal polyandry). Since the proportion of males to females at birth is 50:50 in humans, as in almost every mammal species, some girls do not marry; they remain in their brothers' household, and help look after the family. Female birth rate limits the population size, and although illegitimacy occurs among unmarried girls, the rate is low. The system has two important effects, ecologically: (i) land is not divided among offspring, so farms remain the same size, (ii) the population remains small. These effects are crucial to stability, since at 13,000 feet the pastures are not highly productive, and either an increased population or smaller farm sizes would be untenable. Interestingly, the people themselves concur with the socioecologist's explanations, and consider monogamy rather raffish and irresponsible!

Classification: the Human Place in Nature

Ever since the acceptance of Darwin and Wallace's revolutionary theory, people have regarded themselves as part of an evolutionary process that is still going on. Humans are related to animals by a shared descent in the distant past, and particularly to one particular order of animals – the PRIMATES. In fact, humans *are* a species of primate.

PRIMATES

Primates form an order of mammals that retain many PRIMITIVE features from the earliest mammals of 65Ma, when the primate order first originated. 'Primitive' is a technical term in evolution, and means that the feature is an ancient one, and so shared with quite distant relatives. The opposite is a DERIVED feature, whose possession is unique to the group of species descended from the single (originator) population. It does not imply 'poorly adapted', since any retained primitive feature must have had real evolutionary pay-off over millennia, or it would not be found now. Whereas some orders of mammals have striking derived features that make defining them simple (such as leathery wings, prehensile trunks, annually-shed horns or retractable claws), primates are less distinctive. The primitive five-fingered hand, for instance, is remarkably similar to that of a lizard.

PRIMITIVE

DERIVED FEATURE

The simplest defining feature of primates is the possession of *fingernails*, although some species do not have them on all fingers and toes. This might seem at first sight a trivial feature, but what fingernails give is the soft pads beneath, and soft pads have real importance because they allow a delicate but firm grip on objects. With pads on each finger, the five-fingered hand gives a superb grip – good for both holding eggs without breaking them, and wielding hammers. In the great apes and humans, this manipulative ability went one stage further, with much greater cortical representation of the hand, allowing independent control of every finger. Primates are *manipulative* specialists. Beyond this feature, primates show considerable variation across the various groups.

A modern classification scheme uses the possession of shared, derived features to define groups. (The approach is called phylogenetic or CLADISTIC TAXONOMY.) This means that each group in the taxonomy is descended from a single ancestor. By looking at the shared attributes of the modern species in a taxonomic group, a good idea of the attributes of the ancestor species can be obtained. This applies to all features, primitive and derived. In this way, a good phylogenetic taxonomy is a tool for reconstructing extinct species. It is popularly believed that excavating fossils is the main or only way of reconstructing the ancestors of living species; more often, the reverse is the case.

CLADISTIC TAXONOMY

Usually, a fossil is interpreted as ancestral to living forms, because of what the ancestor has already been deduced to look like (from cladistic taxonomy). Many fossils, indeed, probably gave rise to *no* living species, so identification of ancestors is liable to be fraught with error. The errors are nowhere more visible than in the claims of human fossil ancestors, whose interpretation changes annually!

The best modern taxonomies are based on molecular evidence of relatedness, because the large biological molecules are so complex they are inherently unlikely to have evolved more than once; misleading convergent evolution is less likely. The rates of molecular change can be estimated, which enables dates to be estimated for the divergence of each branch of the phylogenetic tree. These dates often have wide error margins, and are often controversial; part of the problem is that the rate of molecular change must be calibrated with the date of an ancestor species from the fossil record, and that operation suffers from the difficulty of accurate dating in many cases, as well as the difficulty of relating a fossil to its putative descendants.

Primate prehistory

The ancestral primates of 65Ma, the common ancestors of all modern primates, are believed to have looked a bit like modern tree shrews. However, that is not saying much, because tree shrews retain so many primitive features that it is probably true to say that the common ancestors of *most* modern mammal groups would have looked like tree shrews – though without fingernails, and with the forward-facing eyes and *binocular vision* found in almost every primate today, and therefore most likely in their earliest ancestors. Many predators have binocular vision (such as owls, lions, and hunting spiders), so it is likely that the earliest primates were nocturnal insect predators, and this niche selected for stereoscopic vision.

These early primates gave rise to two great branches of the primate order, the strepsirhines (lemurs and lorises) and the haplorhines (monkeys and apes). STREPSIRHINES retain many primitive features, and so seem 'less like us'. Many are *nocturnal*, and all have a *reflective tapetum* at the back of the retina, to maximize light absorption. They use smell a great deal and their noses have a *wet rhinarium* like a dog's. The other great branch, the HAPLORHINES, tend to use vision more than smell or sound; less reliant on smell, they lack the wet rhinarium. Most mammals are nocturnal and use their noses and ears far more than their eyes; haplorhines are unusual, because few are fully nocturnal, except for one small and apparently primitive group, the tarsiers.

Monkeys and apes, like birds, are largely daytime, *diurnal* animals, and in addition to their binocularity, they have good colour vision. Strepsirhines, like most mammals, are dichromats, with only limited colour resolution; haplorhines are generally trichromats. Most monkeys and apes eat fruit as well as leaves and insects, and the enhanced discrimination in the orange/green part of the spec-

STREPSIRHINES

HAPLORHINES

Plate 4.8 Chimpanzee using flexible stem as a fishing tool for arboreal ants
Source: Jennifer Byrne.

trum, given by the third set of cones in the retina of a trichromat, may have evolved for making fine differentiations about ripeness. Monkeys and apes are also *large-brained*, compared with either strepsirhines or any other groups of mammals.

Apes, whose line separated from that of the Old World monkeys about 30Ma, differ from monkeys in their means of locomotion: they swing (*brachiate*) through trees, and can hang beneath branches to eat; monkeys run along branches or the ground. Apes include the small-bodied gibbons, but the larger ones – the GREAT APES – are especially important for psychology, because they are our own closest animal relatives: the orangutan, gorilla, and two species of chimpanzee.

GREAT APES

In broad terms, this has long been accepted. But what is new and revolutionary in the molecular data is the finding that humans are actually more closely related to chimpanzees than chimpanzees are to gorillas! Using the best current estimates of the dates of divergence, the orangutan emerges as a rather distant

Plate 4.9 Great ape/male
Bonobo
Source: Natural Science Photos/
© David Lawson.

cousin at 16Ma, but humans and chimpanzees form a tight cluster, with the gorilla diverging at only 7.5Ma, and the human line finally parts from that of the two chimpanzees as recently as 6Ma. This pattern has been repeatedly confirmed, but the dates must still be seen as provisional; and their revision might well be in the direction of recency, to judge by the recent discovery of a hominid (i.e. human-line) fossil from 4.3Ma which showed several features previously thought unique to the chimpanzees.

▨ Discovering Evolutionary History ▨

COMPARATIVE
METHOD

Using the distribution of some bodily feature among living species to deduce at what point in evolution the feature was first seen, is an approach called the COMPARATIVE METHOD. Just the same logic can be applied to behavioural features. This opens the door to a new source of reliable evidence about the behaviour of extinct species, including our own ancestors, complementing fossil evidence. The fossil record can never show much about how human ancestors' minds worked in the past, what intellectual capabilities they possessed, or why they might have needed them. But the behaviour of living primates can tell us about the minds and behaviour of the ancient species that were the common ancestors of them and us. (The last few million years of human evolution are not amenable to this approach, since the only surviving species is *Homo sapiens*.) The approach works like this:

- speciation produces a branching pattern of related species;
- characteristics of living species, shared because of common descent from a single ancestor (i.e. derived features), are used to deduce the tree of their relatedness (a tree which shows evolutionary closeness is called a *cladogram*);
- the tree is used to work back, to predict the existence of various ancestor species;
- the appearance and behaviour of these ancestors are deduced by using *all* the shared similarities of the living species to which they gave rise.

In this way, we can in principle use the comparative study of living primates to reconstruct the behavioural capacities of a series of extinct species all of which are ancestral to humans. Crucial species to study include the two chimpanzee species (what we share with them is evidence of the common ancestor of 6Ma); the gorilla (what we, and chimpanzees, share with them tells us about the ancestor of 7.5Ma); the orangutan (taking us back to 16Ma); the monkeys (characters shared by all monkeys and apes tell us about the 40Ma ancestor); and the strepsirhines (characters shared by all primates tell us about the first primates of 65Ma).

To give one illustration of the power of this approach, we can apply it to recent studies of brain size and intelligence among primates, to ask 'How and when did human intelligence arise?' Intelligence is a concept which, as an American judge once said about pornography, 'I can't tell you what it looks like but I'd know it when I see it'. Human intelligence testing focuses on differences between individuals, but consider instead the question of how *typical*, average human intelligence evolved from ancestor species – which we presume were less intelligent. Human intelligence is multi-faceted and complex, a bundle of skills not a unitary trait; but the capacity to display intelligent behaviour must have evolved. Taking a common-sense definition of intelligence – 'efficiency and speed in solving problems, in extracting the essentials from a complex situation, and in reacting appropriately' – this is just the sort of thing that would pay an animal living in a complex world.

This leads to a problem: if intelligence is *always* desirable, why aren't all surviving animals smart? The answer probably lies in the high METABOLIC COSTS of the organ that supports intelligence, the brain. Brain tissue needs more meta-

METABOLIC COSTS

bolic energy than that of any other body part, and this demand is remorseless, day and night, whether the brain is 'in use' or not. If this energy supply fails for more than 4 minutes, the brain starts to decay irreparably. This is a very high price to pay, so there must be major selective advantages in big brains to those species that have evolved them. The actual investment in brain must be a compromise, between costs and benefits. Which species have specialized in brain enlargement?

The question is not straightforward because, on the whole, larger animals have larger brains. When brain and body weights of many mammals are plotted in logarithmic coordinates (a method called 'allometric scaling'), a linear relationship emerges, with a slope of 0.75. This is consistent with a limitation on metabolic cost, because the metabolic energy produced by the body increases at the 0.75 power of its total weight. However, it also means that absolute brain size is misleading as a measure of investment. Instead, we must ask which animals have *larger brains than expected* from the allometric relationship of brain/body: how much extra (metabolic) cost is a species prepared to accept? Among mammals, *relative brain size* is larger (Eisenberg 1981):

- in arboreal (tree-living) species;
- in species with more competition for their ecological niche;
- in species that have more overlap between generations, so spend more time with relatives before breeding.

These correlates make good sense, if intelligence is needed to cope with complexity. Arboreal species inhabit a three-dimensional world, and their locomotion (often involving potentially risky jumps or estimations of branch strength) is inherently more demanding than terrestrial locomotion. Species experiencing niche competition for food and other necessaries are meeting challenges never experienced by, for instance, island forms with few competitors. And companions are also competitors, with the special complication that association with them is beneficial for an individual of a social species. As we know in our technological world, an 'onboard computer' is necessary to deal effectively with rapidly changing and complex data; the metaphor of brain-as-computer makes sense.

When each order of mammals is compared in this way, some have conspicuously larger brains than others. The primates have the largest brains for their body sizes, double that of an average mammal; carnivores, pinnipeds (seals and sealions), and bats are also 'above average'. This shows that some groups of mammal are specialized for brain size – just as others are specialized for running fast (antelopes), or holding their breath (seals and sealions), primates are specialized for brains, which presumably means specialized for intelligence. When primates are divided into strepsirhines and haplorhines, it is only the latter – the monkeys and apes – that prove to be relatively large-brained, compared with the average mammal. But when the monkeys and the non-human

Plate 4.10 A chimpanzee deception
Source: David Bygott.

apes are themselves compared, no difference in relative brain size emerges. Only humans show extensive further specialization in brain enlargement, with brains three times that expected for an average monkey or ape (see Passingham 1982 for more details of this approach).

To some extent, evidence on primate intelligence supports this picture. Strepsirhine primates certainly do somewhat poorly on laboratory tests of learning speed and problem-solving skill, compared with that of monkeys and apes. However, laboratory problem-solving may be a poor measure of primate intelligence, since it is based on tests that differentiate among humans of different intelligence (in the same way that an IQ test standardized on one human group is not 'culture-fair' when used with another). Monkey and ape skills certainly seem much more obvious in the social arena: they use grooming to build up alliances and friendships with powerful individuals, who later pay them back in social support; consequently, social support is a strong determiner of success, and relationships damaged by conflict are 'repaired' by deliberate reconciliation; monkeys and apes employ deception in social manipulation, and sometimes their manoeuvrings are so complex as to have been termed 'political'. Strepsirhine primates do none of these things.

The prominence of intelligence in the social lives of monkeys and apes has led to the proposal that haplorhine specialization in intelligence can be explained as an evolutionary response to social complexity (Humphrey 1976; Jolly 1966): this is the so-called MACHIAVELLIAN INTELLIGENCE theory (Byrne & Whiten 1988). The idea is that living in social groups will set up a pressure to do better than other individuals in the group – while not disrupting group living, which has other advantages. This selects for the ability to manipulate, to deceive, and to cooperate – if it pays to do so; all of which need intelligence. The main alternative theory is that environmental complexity, particularly that of feeding on unpredictable fruits distributed over a wide range, was the challenge that selected for intelligence. One way of testing directly between these alternatives is to examine the size of the neocortex, since this is the part of the brain that chiefly varies among primates. In a rough-and-ready way, primate group size can be taken as an index of social complexity, and range size and the degree of frugivory as indices of feeding complexity. However, group size turns out to correlate with neocortical enlargement (Dunbar 1992). What is more, primate neocortical enlargement also correlates with the amount individuals of the species use deception in their social manoeuvres (Byrne 1993). Correlations do not prove causation, but the simplest explanation of the patterns of correlations is that the enlarged brains of monkeys and apes *allow* more complex social manipulation, which is *demanded* by living in larger groups.

However, in many ways the intelligence of great apes is qualitatively different to that of monkeys, and this does not match any difference of relative brain size. Great apes not only use deception, but also plan to deceive and show signs of understanding when they have been deceived. For instance, a chimpanzee, finding a prized food item while in the presence of a dominant individual, may inhibit its interest until the dominant has left, and thus not lose the food. The behaviour functions as deception, but the learning mechanism may be a simple, 'mindless' one: on a previous occasion, it may have gone straight for the food and been 'punished' by aggression and theft by the dominant individual. Simple learning would cause it to inhibit its immediate response next time. But suppose the apparently deceived chimpanzee leaves, but hides behind a tree and peeps out at what happens next. This would function to reveal the prized food, and now it is very difficult to imagine a plausible past history that might have allowed the trick to be learnt – without an understanding of deception. Yet exactly this has been observed in chimpanzees, and a range of cases of deception in other species of great ape are similarly hard to account for without invoking a rudimentary understanding of other individuals' minds (Byrne & Whiten 1991, 1992).

In the technical sphere too, great apes appear to understand more than monkeys. Chimpanzees in the wild not only learn to use tools, but also understand the simple mechanics of how the tools work. For instance, in many areas of Africa they use thin, flexible stems of grass or vines to 'fish' for termites inside the hard mounds in which termites normally live (see McGrew 1992 for details on how these habits vary in different populations). Monkeys in zoos, given tasks that can be solved for food reward by probing with a stick that is provided, learn to do so. However, if they are given a range of possible objects, they will try to

Plate 4.11 Capuchin monkey with tube task
Source: Elisabetta Visalberghi.

probe with sticks visibly too thick, too short or even a metal link chain. They seem to have no understanding of what properties a probing tool needs (Visalberghi & Limongelli 1994; Visalberghi & Trinca 1987). No similarly absurd errors are seen in young chimpanzees learning to fish for termites. Also, sometimes the termite mound is far from the source of probe; then chimpanzees make the tool, by stripping off projected leaves, in advance of reaching the termite site, showing that they work from a mental specification of what tool they need (Goodall 1986). Occasionally, evidence has even been obtained of great apes actively teaching their young, imitating the actions of others, or pretending an object is something else (Boesch 1991).

Humans share all these traits, but monkeys none of them. The capacity underlying all of them is sometimes called INSIGHT, or REPRESENTATIONAL UNDERSTANDING. The monkey/ape difference perhaps should not surprise: to the extent that the brain is an onboard computer, its power will depend on its *absolute* size (although the species' degree of investment will depend on its *relative* size, as explained above). Great apes happen to be large animals, compared to any monkeys, and so they possess much larger brains. (Alternatively, the difference may lie in some difference in their brain organization.) Certainly, the only strong evidence of understanding how things work (for instance, in choosing or modifying objects that meet precise criteria for tool use, in advance of the job), or what others think (for instance, in appreciating that they have been deceived, or planning deception without an opportunity of trial-and-error learning) come from great apes. Monkey achievements can always be accounted

INSIGHT

REPRESENTATIONAL
UNDERSTANDING

133

for as a result of very fast learning processes; some ape abilities suggest true representational understanding (Byrne 1995).

Putting these findings into a cladistic framework gives the following evolutionary history (see Byrne 1995 for details). Specialization for intelligence in human ancestry occurred in three discrete phases. The earliest primates were not intellectually different to other mammals, but the ancestors of the monkeys and apes (diverging at roughly 40Ma) had an enlarged neocortex, permitting much faster learning, particularly evident in the social sphere. This enlargement was dependent on a much heavier investment in brain tissue than that of a strepsirhine primate, committing most monkeys and apes to an energy-rich diet of fruit, rather than the more reliable source of leaves. A further investment in neocortical volume happened much more recently, specifically on the human line, somewhere in the last 6M years. It is tempting to relate this to another dietary switch to a more high-energy food, meat. However, in between these two jumps in brain size, another intellectual change took place, one that may not relate to brain size. This was specific to great apes, so it must have occurred at about 16Ma, and resulted in a representational understanding of how things work, and what other individuals may be thinking. Social complexity and competition within large social groups is strongly implicated as the cause of the first increase in relative brain size (i.e. the selective pressure to which it evolved as an adaptation). What triggered the qualitative shift in type of intelligence of great apes, and the further increase in relative brain size in hominids, is not yet known.

Sociobiology: Genetics for the Social Animal

Kin selection

One thing we can be very sure of is that every individual animal dies. Since only genes have the chance to 'survive' for many generations, not individuals, it makes just as much sense to talk of an individual's body as *a device constructed by genes to allow them to replicate*, as to talk of genes as the body's chemical instructions for making more bodies. An analogous point was once made by Samuel Butler, who observed that 'the chicken is the egg's device for making more eggs'.

This unfamiliar reversal of view is helpful for understanding how natural selection works in social animals. Expressed from this 'genetical' perspective, the Darwinian fitness of an individual becomes simply the chance of its passing its own genes to future generations. To find an individual's Darwinian fitness, we must work out how many copies of its genes are safely passed on to future generations. However, copies of *some* of an individual's genes are also inevitably found in its relatives. On average, about 50 per cent are shared with mother and father, with immediate offspring, and with any full siblings; 25 per cent are shared with grandchildren and grandparents, and with any half-siblings; 12.5 per cent are shared with cousins, and so on. The average proportion of genes that are shared is called the COEFFICIENT OF RELATEDNESS. (The exact proportion of genes an offspring gets from each parent cannot be known, since it is a matter of chance, but the 0.5 coefficient of relatedness gives the best guess.) This means that an individual's fitness does not just reside in its direct descendants, but is spread out over a whole lot of others. So, for instance, in genetical terms, a trait that results in two extra offspring of your full brother, is 'worth' the same as if it resulted in one extra of your own. This was first realized in the 1930s, originally by R. A. Fisher. One of those who followed Fisher's work, J. B. S. Haldane, once said that he'd 'gladly lay down his life for more than two brothers, more than four half-brothers or more than eight cousins!'

COEFFICIENT OF RELATEDNESS

The full implications of this for the evolution of social species (that is, species in which an animal may be *living* with its brothers, aunts and cousins) were only worked out by W. D. Hamilton in the 1960s. He began with the idea of 'spread out' fitness, defining the concept of the INCLUSIVE FITNESS of a trait, that takes account of all effects on relatives as well as the self. In genetical terms, the inclusive fitness of a trait is the sum of its effects on the reproduction of the individual itself, plus its effects (via the genes in common) on the reproduction of all of its relatives, each devalued by the appropriate coefficient of relatedness. Hamilton showed that one consequence of this is that, purely as a result of the automatic process of natural selection, animals will often act in ways that benefit other individuals more than themselves, sometimes even when there is a real cost involved. In other words, from the theory of natural selection, Hamilton predicted that ALTRUISTIC traits should evolve. Generosity, helpfulness, and self-sacrifice, all flow inexorably from a proper understanding of natural selection. Hamilton showed that this will happen in specific circumstances only, when the net benefit to the indirect side of the inclusive fitness equation outweighs the net cost to the direct side. Nature will not always seem 'red in tooth and claw'; Mr Nice Guy traits sometimes have a real selective advantage!

INCLUSIVE FITNESS

ALTRUISM

Immediately, this gave a way of explaining lots of puzzlingly altruistic behaviour that had already been observed in animals. Behavioural biologists had been concerned for many years about the problem that many animal traits appeared to disadvantage the possessor, but help others. A classic example is that of alarm calls: if one member of a bird flock or mammalian group sees a dangerous predator, it will often give a loud and distinctive call – helping to alert all the rest to the predator, but riskily drawing attention to itself. Hamilton's work showed that alarm-calling, as a genetic trait, *should* spread – provided the net benefit to all kin (alerting to the predator in time to avoid death), multiplied by the coefficients of relatedness in each case, outweighed the net cost to the self (increased risk from drawing the predator's attention). Use of inclusive fitness to explain apparent cases of altruism is called KIN SELECTION, but there is no new sort of process here: it follows automatically from a proper understanding of natural selection. The power of kin selection to account for

KIN SELECTION

Box 4.2 Kin Selection in the Ground Squirrel

Belding's ground squirrel is a diurnal social rodent living in meadows of the western USA. After mating in the spring, males wander off from the colony; females remain. Females, therefore, spend their whole lives surrounded by maternal kin. Adults behave very differently to young squirrels. Resident females cooperate with each other to defend their young. Males and immigrant females, however, actually kill and eat young squirrels, but not ones closely related to them. Cooperation among relatives, and conflict among non-relatives, is just what Hamilton's 'kin selection' theory predicts.

Kin selection affects animal communication, too. Ground squirrels give alarm calls if they sight a predator, like a coyote. Those who call are more likely to be eaten than silent ones. However, after an alarm has been given, the coyote or other predator is less likely to be successful in killing any ground squirrel. But alarm-calling is not automatic and unselective. Female ground squirrels are always more likely than males to give alarm calls, and they are more likely to call if close relatives are nearby. This is true even when the relatives are not their direct offspring (though that is the most usual case), but even if they are parents or non-descendant relatives. These findings match the specific predictions of kin selection. In addition, the fact that the reaction varies in the presence of different individuals (this is sometimes called an 'audience effect') shows that Belding's ground squirrels recognize individual identity and distinguish between kin and non-kin.

SOCIOBIOLOGY

animal (and perhaps human) behavioural choices has led to a whole new subject, SOCIOBIOLOGY.

But does this seriously mean that animals 'know' who their kin are, in any sense of the word? Not necessarily: provided the social system is predictably rigid in certain ways, they would not need to for the logic to apply. Pursuing the illustration of alarm-calling, in a society in which individuals are usually in earshot of several close relatives, a gene for alarm-calling would most likely spread – regardless of the caller's ignorance of its kinship. However, such an 'indiscriminate' alarm-calling gene would be outcompeted (that is, gradually replaced in the gene pool) by one that caused the individual possessing it to call *only* when kin were in earshot, and not otherwise. And in many species of animal, just that pattern has been found: animals do discriminate between different audiences, on the basis of their relatedness. A concrete illustration is given by the behaviour of the Belding's ground squirrel (see Box 4.2).

GROUP
SELECTION

Before Hamilton's work, many biologists would have explained friendly cooperation and altruism in a different way: as a consequence of GROUP SELECTION, the evolution of traits that have evolved for the good of the species or group, even though they disadvantage the individual. And indeed, a species whose genes caused every individual to help every species member would do very well as a species. Until, that is, a mutant gene cropped up that caused the individual to accept help but give none; individuals with that gene would do even better. Their descendants would spread rapidly and the 'selfish' genes would eventually outnumber the 'altruist' genes. That is to say, a population of individuals programmed genetically to behave as altruists to species members would be *unstable*: and given the very long time spans of evolution, it is highly likely that any species we see today is in a stable state. Thinking about which genetical 'strategy' is inherently stable, and would resist invasion by other strategies, is a good way of working out whether an explanation is consistent with natural selection (Maynard Smith & Price 1973). Strategies that cannot be invaded are called EVOLUTIONARY STABLE STRATEGIES (ESS). For instance, a population of individuals which give alarm calls only when the audience is made up of their own relatives is stable, because it cannot be invaded by genes coding for any different calling strategy, for example alarm-calling for the benefit of *any* other species member. The alarm-calling of Belding's ground squirrels (Box 4.2) is therefore an ESS. In every non-human case of cooperation and altruism that has been carefully studied, the results fit Hamilton's kin selection theory.

EVOLUTIONARY
STABLE STRATEGIES

The terminology can lead to confusion. Remember: genes are not *really* selfish or altruistic, or trying to help their possessors; ground squirrels' 'strategies' are not carefully thought out by the beasts. These words are human labels, for the superficial appearance of the actions of individual animals whose behaviour is partially governed by genes. Phrasing like 'a gene for helping brothers would spread' should never be taken too literally. This is a shorthand version of 'if a gene existed that, when it found itself in an individual that had a brother, predisposed that individual to be more likely to help the brother, all individuals having that gene would on average survive better than those that do not'. Sociobiologists use such phrasing to avoid the cumbersome longhand version, and hope that – since a gene is after all only a piece of a DNA molecule of some unspecified size, not an animate agent – this will not cause confusion. Their hopes are not always fulfilled.

Primates are evidently a prime candidate for kin selection to operate: many species live in social groups, the groups are semi-permanent (not like herds of antelope or deer that break up and reform continually), individuals are long-lived and often remain with many of their genetical relatives. Many primate behaviours that were formerly great puzzles to scientists can now be explained as kin selection. To give one very striking example, consider infanticide. This has been well-studied in the Hanuman langur (look back at Box 4.1), where it is now recognized that a male will kill infants, specifically in circumstances when it is most likely that the infants are unrelated to him. The deaths will result in the females resuming fertility, and so conceiving – with the male's own offspring – more quickly. Brutal as this sounds, such behaviour follows as a prediction of kin selection, and no other explanation makes sense. The deaths used to be put down to 'pathology'. Note that the sociobiological explanation does not imply rigid inflexible determination of behaviour by genes. In contrast, a male langur's behaviour is sensitively adjusted to the exact social organization and historical circumstances in which it finds itself. Once well-established as the harem-leader, a male in a one-male group is attentive and solicitous to infants, which are likely to be his own, and in multi-male groups, where paternity is uncertain, a male will take little interest in infants.

The extent to which kin selection applies to humans is controversial. Almost nobody would doubt that maternal love of a newborn baby has some genetical component, although in common talk 'the same blood' might be used instead of 'shared genes'. Conversely, few would claim that all of the most bizarre human propensities can be explained as genetical adaptations (a gene for sado-masochism?). Setting such extremes aside, it is perhaps fair to argue that the genetical influence of natural selection should be seen as a 'null hypothesis' when no good evidence is yet available, since natural selection is already amply validated and cannot help affecting humans to some extent. The onus should be on social scientists to provide evidence *against* its influence, in cases that can at first sight be accounted for as genetical selection. At present, social scientists are often so reluctant to consider genetical causation that they collect no evidence than can help us judge either way.

To pursue the illustration of infanticide, the possibility that child murder in humans has a genetical component should not be dismissed. Infanticide is not common in monkeys, but it occurs regularly in both chimpanzees and gorillas. The pattern is similar to that of langurs, in that the typical killing is of an unweaned baby, it occurs shortly after the mother has entered a new group, and is committed by a male or males unrelated to the baby. (Female chimpanzees and gorillas, understandably, are reluctant to change groups when they have babies under three years old.) This behaviour is normally explained as kin selection: a gene for infanticide will increase a male's inclusive fitness, as long as the infanticide is specific to babies under three years old belonging to females which have recently joined him. When two out of three species, in a group with a shared common ancestor, share a gene, one would expect the third to possess the same gene – in this case, the third is *Homo sapiens*! It is therefore unlikely to be entirely a coincidence that most cases of lethal child battering are carried out by stepfathers, to babies under three years old, of women who have only recently begun to live with the child's stepfather.

Yet it is only in very recent years that a few systematic attempts have been made to examine the coefficients of relatedness between murderer and victim. Perhaps the reluctance to even consider the possibility of genetical influence stems from the popular misconception that a trend based on the genes is irreversible, or even that it is in some way 'right'. This belief can be seen to be quite incoherent when the theoretical basis of natural selection is understood. The process is mechanistic and thus morally neutral. Rather than 'condoning' an undesirable phenomenon, a proper understanding of the underlying causes is most likely essential to its eradication. Genetical influences on adult organisms are not necessarily harder to counter than environmental ones, and to eliminate child murder all avenues should be investigated.

Equally, it is not the case that when a plausible sociobiological explanation can be constructed, no further work is necessary. Any such explanation is merely a hypothesis (albeit the null hypothesis in most cases), which needs to be tested against data. In the illustrative case of langur and ape infanticide, alternative hypotheses are implausible or fail to make correct predictions – this is not true in many other cases. The violently antagonistic feelings that the theory of sociobiology arouses in many people seems to stem from the belief that its proponents don't bother to test their hypotheses. Unfortunately, this complaint is not entirely unwarranted – and that is bad science. The big problem is that issues of genetically influenced behaviour are sensitive ones raising spectres of eugenics and genetic inferiority. Eugenics means improving the human race by selective breeding – and anyone who insists on marrying a healthy and intelligent person so that their children will be finer people is practising an individual form of eugenics. The real problem comes when the state intervenes. The closest that any modern nation comes to explicit eugenics is perhaps allowing mothers to abort foetuses with severe problems such as spina bifida, as is now done in Britain. However, earlier this century, the Nazis used eugenics as an excuse for their sterilization of the mentally handicapped, and their genocidal murder of Jews and Gypsies. Small wonder that eugenics is now shunned as a subject. However, our response should not be to suppress scientific understanding of the influence of genes on human behaviour, but to make sure that our understanding is a proper one – unlike the warped ideas of Hitler's collaborators. Examined as a science, Nazi beliefs about racial inferiority are sheer nonsense.

Reciprocal altruism

Finally, what is an evolutionary psychologist to make of cases of human behaviour that are altruistic in the sense that the agent *cannot* gain, or even loses, inclusive fitness? A few cases of this kind occur in non-humans also, and here they have been explained as RECIPROCAL ALTRUISM. In a long-lived social species, in which individuals recognize others and can remember their actions, there is a potential for mutual help over time. This has been most clearly shown in vampire bats. The probability, on any particular night, of a bat attaining a meal of blood is low; yet vampire bats have a finely balanced metabolism, and will starve to death if deprived of a meal for more than a couple of nights. In fact, unsuccessful bats are fed blood by their luckier neighbours at the roost, and they will reciprocate when they have in turn been lucky. This is true even if the donor is unrelated to the recipient, and after a donation, the recipient is reliably more likely than chance to return the favour on another night. Few such clear cases of reciprocal altruism have been identified, despite great interest in the issue; it seems most likely that reciprocal altruism is much more common between related individuals, when it cannot easily be distinguished from kin selection.

RECIPROCAL ALTRUISM

Reciprocal altruism depends for its stability on detection and rejection of cheating; this is facilitated by use of language and written records, so it is unsurprising that in most human societies people appear to rely heavily on reciprocal altruism. The great interest of members of some societies (for instance, the !Kung San) in strict fairness of debt repayment and exchange of presents is consistent with this interpretation. Clearly, in nation states at least, some altruistic actions go beyond possible interpretation in these terms: laying down one's life for Queen and Country, fighting a Holy War, or simply risking one's life to save an unknown child from mortal danger. Why should people be amenable to manipulation by societal norms (good or ill) to risk their lives in these ways? Human non-reciprocal altruism may perhaps be a by-product of a gene for 'docility'. Since so little of what we learn can be checked at source, a tendency to accept the statements of those in authority is advantageous in general, saving immense time and risk. In such a society, the genetical trait of DOCILITY is favoured; and altruistic actions beneficial to people in general can be inculcated, beyond the biological limits of kin selection or reciprocal altruism. However, general possession of this trait would allow the state to prosecute enterprises that endanger individuals, who themselves have no chance of benefit.

DOCILITY

The sociobiology of sex

Human sexual behaviour and marriage patterns are a prime candidate for sociobiological explanation. The two sexes invest different amounts in their young. In most animal species, the female invests more than the male in each offspring – bearing the cost of larger gametes, internal gestation, suckling, and often post-weaning care. All these differences apply to humans. Women's maximum reproductive potential is therefore much more limited than men's; even in quite extreme cases thirty children is beyond the bounds of possibility for a woman; whereas Eastern potentates with large harems have sired thousands, and the limit on male fecundity is largely a matter of opportunity. Given this situation, men would be expected to compete for fertilization opportunities, and to take chances of mating whenever they arise. Women would be expected to be more selective in their choice of mates, and in particular they might choose men on the basis of paternal care offered. Wherever males do offer care, they will be under selective pressure to protect against cuckoldry, and should show greater concern than females over mate fidelity. Are these sociobiological predictions borne out?

Examining both a broad sweep of anthropological evidence, and modern Western society, the answer is yes. The more promiscuous tendencies of men are shown in surveys of actual behaviour and of covert wishes; and the anthropological record is peppered with reference to the extramarital activities of men – though clearly their opportunities are restricted by the less promiscuous behaviour of women. A long evolutionary history of male competition over women is shown in a number of current human attributes. SEXUAL DIMORPHISM, with males larger than females or endowed with more dangerous weaponry, is characteristic of species in which males compete for females and mating is polygynous; this often goes with sex differences in life-span, the sex that invests less in body growth living longer. Whereas monogamous primates show no dimorphism, humans are moderately sexually dimorphic; also, men are more vulnerable to death from disease and senescence at every stage of their lives, and live less long than women. These body traits are consistent with a review of marriage practices in human societies. POLYGYNY is much commoner than monogamy, and POLYANDRY is very

SEXUAL DIMORPHISM

POLYGYNY

rare (effectively confined to the Himalayan people discussed earlier). This summary of what is accepted as permissible underestimates the amount of monogamy actually found, because in most polygynous societies few men are able in practice to support more than one wife.

Marriages often have the character of trafficking in women: *brideprice*, to purchase a wife from her male relatives, is widespread; where no price is paid, obligations are often incurred; even in our society, fathers 'give away' their daughters to approved husbands (note that *dowry* is not the opposite of brideprice, since it is not paid to female relatives of the husband, but remains with the couple). One sign of competition for women is seen in young men's drive for prestige and status, found in every society, and in the risk-taking that often goes with it. Studies of computer dating have confirmed women's much greater choosiness of partner for sex or marriage, and numerous studies have shown that their criteria of choice are different to men's. Men place more emphasis on physical attractiveness, whereas women are more concerned with other qualities, often especially those that denote or predict economic status or competitive success. Almost universally, husbands are older than wives. These findings are as expected from evolutionary theory: wealth and status index a man's ability to invest in the welfare of offspring, whereas youth is an excellent indicator of breeding potential in a woman. Human fathers do of course make considerable investment in their children, and as predicted they commonly take elaborate precautions against cuckoldry. Adultery laws are almost universally skewed such that when illicit intercourse takes place the 'offence' is to the husband (or male relatives of an unmarried woman); only in recent years in the West have men and women been treated alike in law. Male infidelity has seldom been seen as a crime, and homicide of cuckolds is frequently excepted from the legal category of murder. Often, 'paternity uncertainty' is explicitly given as the reason for this asymmetry.

Constraints on a woman's sexual behaviour are virtually universal, ranging from pressure to wear 'modest' clothing, through chaperoning and family vigilance over her virtue, threats to avenge her honour (which revenge may include her death as well as that of the male seducer), to the abhorrent practices of 'female circumcision' that are often clearly used to prevent intercourse by any but the husband. Investment is also commonly provided by others than parents, and the greatest single determinant is degree of 'kinship'. Systems of kinship are immensely variable, but in all cases the main correlate of kin closeness is genetic closeness. In some cases, kinship is weaker or absent down the male line, as might be expected where paternity is less than certain.

No other theory is in serious competition with sociobiology when it comes to explaining many of these human characteristics; certainly, the old view that culture is arbitrary and infinitely variable predicts none of these regularities. However, it should not be thought that *every* aspect of the panoply of human social customs and sexual traits can be predicted from evolutionary theory. In some ways, this is no different to the case with animal behaviour: predators slip and miss their prey, animals die before they can breed or influence their kin's breeding. And in general, not every act of every individual can be expected to be evolutionarily optimal, even on a local scale. Just the same must apply to human social behaviour. Beyond this, human social behaviour is influenced by our culture and our extensive information transmission by spoken word and written language in ways not well described by biology. This is not to say that traits can be partitioned into 'nature' vs 'culture', and each explained independently by the corresponding theory. The greater challenge is to come to terms with the messy reality, in which human biology and human culture interact with each other in subtle ways. (It is often useful as a shorthand to say that an attribute is 'innate' or 'learned', when what is meant is that the pattern of variance of the attibute is affected almost solely by genes or environment. But to see fully how any characteristic originates and develops, it will normally be necessary to tackle a complex interaction of genetic and environmental factors.) Sociobiology is often unpopular with social scientists, because it is imagined that successful analysis at the level of evolutionary biology and genetical theory precludes or eclipses other levels of analysis, for example those of social psychology, sociology or social anthropology. In reality, the notion that sociobiology makes other human sciences redundant is believed by few sociobiologists, and more often it is used as a 'man of straw' to attack. Given the pressing problems with which human society is now confronted, it is to be hoped that such attacks give way to more constructive sharing of methods and results.

CHAPTER SUMMARY

1 Evolution works as an automatic process of selection, in which the fundamental unit of evolutionary selection is the gene.

2 Variation among genes is preserved by the particulate nature of inheritance: genes do not blend. Variation among genes is created by mutation, and used up by strong natural selection.

3 Fitness is the ability to pass genes to subsequent generations. The environment determines which adaptations are successful.

4 Species are locally optimized within a particular environment. Species change ultimately depends on environmental changes – including pollution, plate movements or extraterrestrial influences.

5 Social behaviour as well as body form are indirectly shaped by environmental constraints, as a product of natural selection.

6 Shared, derived characteristics show which species descended from a common ancestor. The pattern of groups with a single common ancestor ('clades') is called a phylogenetic taxonomy.

7 Humans are primates. Primates as a whole retain many primitive features common to many vertebrate land animals.

8 The monkeys and apes (haplorhine primates) show neocortical enlargement above that expected from their body sizes, and they give evidence of intelligence, especially in the social domain, above that found in most other animals.

9 Both large brains and social intelligence may be explained as a consequence of selection for 'Machiavellian intelligence' to deal with the social complexity of living in large groups.

10 In contrast to monkeys (and most other animals) great ape intelligence has an insightful, representational quality. The origin of this monkey/ape difference is so far unexplained.

11 Humans are great apes, separated from the chimpanzees by under 6 million years of separate evolution.

12 Human customs are now increasingly understood as influenced by genetic effects, following the advances in understanding animal social behaviour as a product of natural selection.

13 Genetical relatedness is a major determinant of cooperation and altruism, and among non-relatives the scope for reciprocation and deterring cheating limits helpfulness. Traits do not evolve 'for the good of the species'.

14 Application of evolutionary principles enables better understanding of a number of consistent, puzzling regularities in human behaviour, from marriage partner choices to child murder.

▨ Further Work ▨

1. Why does the theory of natural selection depend on the fact that the material that encodes inherited traits is 'particulate'? Does the discrete coding of information in genes have other implications? (Hint: think about digital coding in information technology.)

2. What evidence would support, and what would refute, a claim that ecology could explain the origin of some particular social behaviour of a species?

3. Each of these three passages contains a number of misconceptions or half-truths. Identify each one; explain why it is wrong, misleading or incomplete; and say how the real explanation should run, assuming your audience doesn't know any technical terms.

    (a) Monkeys live in groups because they get frightened on their own. When any of the group sees a predator, it gives a cry of alarm; this is a result of evolution – groups whose members did not give alarms have died out.

    (b) Young male monkeys fight a lot because they are aggressive. Young females often try to help with looking after babies in the group; they do this by instinct, because babies look helpless and appealing to them.

    (c) Groups of monkeys in different areas eat different types of foods: originally, they had to experiment to find out what was edible, but once they found something, the habit could be passed on genetically.

4. If the human race were destroyed by a nuclear accident, how might evolution change a surviving species to exploit the human ecological niche?

5. In psychology, it is often found that errors and failures reveal the normal operation of a system. Human perversions, fetishes, homosexuality, adoption and use of contraception might be considered 'errors' from the point of view of

evolution: are the patterns we observe in these behaviours consistent with sociobiological understanding of normal human sexual behaviour?

6. Can cognitive psychology help to explain and measure the 'complexity' of a problem confronted by an animal? Would this apply equally to social problems?

▓ Further Reading ▓

Maynard Smith, J. (1975) *The Theory of Evolution*. Harmondsworth: Penguin.

> A lucid and intelligent account of evolution and the theory of natural selection, by one of the great pioneers of the modern approach.

Cronin, H. (1991) *The Ant and the Peacock*. Cambridge: Cambridge University Press.

> Explores the fascinating history of Darwinism, and the biological controversies it has generated.

Dawkins, R. (1989; 2nd edn) *The Selfish Gene*. Oxford: Oxford University Press.

> The implications of natural selection for animal social behaviour, including a sparklingly clear popular treatment of W. J. Hamilton's ideas and other important advances, are most accessible in this book. This is an ideal way to get clear the sometimes confusing concepts of kin selection and reciprocal altruism.

Slater, P. J. B. and Halliday, T. R. (1994) *Behaviour and Evolution*. Cambridge: Cambridge University Press.

> Explores particular topics on the evolution of behaviour at greater depth, including behaviour genetics, speciation, and the evolution of intelligence and social structure.

Dunbar, R. I. M. (1988) *Primate Social Systems*. London: Croom Helm

> The application of evolutionary theory to an individual's everyday decisions is called 'optimality theory' and has been applied with great success to the understanding of primate social behaviour.

Byrne, R. W. (1995) *The Thinking Ape: Evolutionary Origins of Intelligence*. Oxford: Oxford University Press.

> Pursues the approach of using evidence from living primates to understand the evolutionary origins of human cognition (including a treatment of social learning and imitation, theory of mind, and the origins of the large human brain).

Manning, A. and Dawkins, M. S. (1992; 4th edn) *An Introduction to Animal Behaviour*. London: Edward Arnold.

> Provides a more general, modern, ethologically based approach to animal behaviour.

Daly, M. and Wilson, M. (1983; 2nd edn) *Sex, Evolution and Behavior*. Belmont, Calif.: Wadsworth.

> A fascinating and thoughtful treatment of the evolutionary basis of human sexual behaviour, from which some of the examples in this chapter have been drawn.

CHAPTER 5

Neuroscience

Robin Stevens

CHAPTER AGENDA

- The focus of this chapter is on the relationship between brain and behaviour. The actions we perform, and the information that we take in and process, are dealt with by a complex mechanism. To properly understand mind and behaviour we need to understand the brain.

- To understand brain mechanisms we need to know what takes place at a microscopic level as well as how the brain is built, and how it allows us to see, learn, remember and so on. Neurones are the specialized cells of the nervous system that transmit and process information in ways that are well understood. You will learn how neurones function and signal to each other, and how psychoactive drugs affect these processes and thus alter brain functioning to help people who suffer from mild and serious mental disorders.

- A brain contains many subsystems for the processing of modality-specific sensory information and

for controlling muscles and glands. You will discover how some of these sensory and motor functions are mapped on brain structure, and how damage to this neural machinery leads to various sorts of neuropsychological deficits.

- The cause and treatment of disorders like schizophrenia and depression is controversial. However, the account given in this chapter will give you an insight into some strong psychobiological evidence on the development and treatment of these illnesses.

- An entirely brain-centred discussion of mind and behaviour is incomplete, since the brain works in tandem with hormonal mechanisms to regulate the body. To give you an insight into the importance of hormonal processes you will learn how the body responds to stress and how sex hormones affect body and brain development.

▨ Introduction ▨

The aim of this chapter is to provide an understanding of some of the fundamental principles of neuroscience, especially in relation to issues that are of interest to an audience of psychologists. But why should a psychologist be interested in the brain, since psychological processes or mental events presumably take place in minds; and what has the brain to do with mind? This problem of mind and brain has troubled philosophers for a long time. A dualist view of mind and brain is implicitly accepted by most lay-people and by many philosophers and scientists.

DUALISM

Well, what is DUALISM? This position was cogently argued for by the sixteenth-century philosopher René Descartes, who suggested that mind was an extra-corporeal entity (outside the body) that communicated with the body through the pineal gland. He chose the pineal gland because he thought it was the only singular structure in the brain, and it is located centrally in the brain. In his view there had to be a single point where mind influenced the brain and hence the body. According to Descartes the brain contained a reservoir of fluid that could be directed by the mind to flow through the nerves to exert an effect on muscles. Thus people were like robots controlled by a hydraulic system that was directed by the mind.

METAPHYSICAL
MIND

MONISTS

But if mind is not physical how can it influence the body? An alternative position is needed that allows us to explain mind, and most theorists, while accepting the importance of mind and consciousness, do not want to rely on a METAPHYSICAL MIND (mind as non-physical stuff). Maybe the dualists (those who argue for a mind–body split) are attacking the problem from an inappropriate premise. When Descartes argued for dualism he had no idea about the complexity of the brain nor any notion about how an information-handling mechanism might be naturally or artificially constructed. We are not so disadvantaged, and as we learn more about the wonders of the nervous system it is easier to accept that mind is a property of brain function. Those who believe that mind states and brain states are like two sides of a coin are called MONISTS. Although there are several variants of this mind–brain identity view, the most compelling is the suggestion that mind is an emergent property of brain function.

Modern dualists, such as the late Karl Popper (a philosopher) and John Eccles (a neuroscientist), accept the important role of the brain in controlling behaviour but remain unable to tell us how a non-physical mind can influence behaviour. But if brain states are equated with mind states, as in the mind–brain identity position, then there is no metaphysical problem to overcome. Mind can influence body because a mind state corresponds with a physical state, in the brain, that can have a physical influence on the body.

We shall assume that mental events are not just correlated with patterns of activity in the brain, but that neural states (states of the nervous system) are the basis of these mental events. Therefore it is necessary to learn how nerve

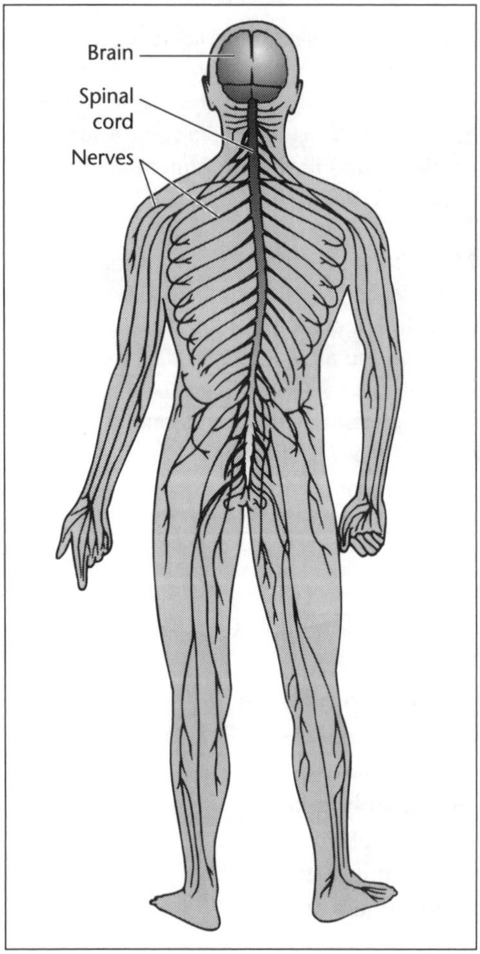

Brain

Spinal cord

Nerves

Figure 5.1 The human nervous system. The central nervous system consists of the brain and the spinal cord which passes down through the bones of the spinal column. The peripheral nervous system connects sensory organs, muscles and glands to the brain and spinal cord.

cells work; how they are constructed; how they transmit information; and how they communicate with one another. However, mental events are not easily reducible to what is happening in individual brain cells. We also need to know how nerve cells are assembled into clusters and networks that cooperate to support mental states. Thus the overall structure of the brain will be outlined.

Although an understanding of mind–brain events is desirable, what are the practical implications of studying the biological basis of mind? Neuroscience research on mental disorders like schizophrenia, depression and the dementias has revealed a biological basis for such disorders. It would be gratifying to say that this knowledge has gained us the means of curing all these illnesses, but the story here is patchy. There have been notable successes in the development of drugs for treating schizophrenia and depression, but the treatment of Alzheimer's disease, the most common form of dementia, remains an intractable problem. This is depressing since the disorder is related to brain ageing effects, and as people now live longer the number of cases will increase, causing serious social problems. However, there were predictions in the 1950s that the health services would be overwhelmed by people with disorders like schizophrenia and this failed to occur largely because of discovery of various psychoactive drugs. A treatment for dementias will come!

▓ The Cells of the Nervous System ▓

Nervous systems contain two types of cell, NEURONES (also called nerve cells) and NEUROGLIA, which literally means nerve glue and alludes to the role of these GLIAL CELLS, which provide a matrix that holds the neurones together. The neurones are the 'business cells' of the nervous system that convey and process information, while the glial cells provide the chemical support that is essential to maintain neural functioning. It is thought that the human brain contains about 10^{12} (10 trillion) neurones, of which 10^{10} (100 billion) are to be found within the cerebral cortex.

NEURONES

NEUROGLIA

GLIAL CELLS

Neurones

A neurone is a specialized cell that transmits information. There are two stages to this signalling process. One involves the transmission of information *within* the neurone and the other is the transmission of information *between* neurones. Most nerve cells transmit information externally by chemical means; therefore the neurone is a cell that is specialized to secrete neurotransmitter chemicals. It also transmits information internally over short or long distances and is physically differentiated for this purpose.

Although neurones come in many shapes and sizes the only real significance of this pertains to how many other neurones influence it, and the extent of its influence on other neurones. Like all cells, a neurone has a cell body (SOMA) that

SOMA

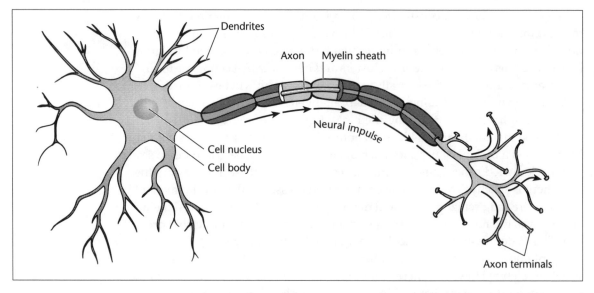

Dendrites

Axon   Myelin sheath

Neural impulse

Cell nucleus
Cell body

Axon terminals

Figure 5.2 A neurone.
A typical neurone is
shown here. It receives
inputs from other
neurones on its
dendrites and cell body;
outputs (action
potentials) travel away
from the cell body to
the axon terminals. The
myelin sheath that is
wrapped around the
neurone is made by
glial cells.

DENDRITES

AXON

TERMINAL OR
SYNAPTIC BOUTON

SYNAPTIC VESICLES

CISTERNA

NEUROTRANSMITTER

is enclosed by a complex membrane. This is about 7 nm thick (a nanometer – nm
– is one millionth part of a metre) and is composed of a double layer of lipids
(fats) in which are embedded various membrane proteins. Some of these provide special transport processes for essential substances that otherwise could
not pass through the cell membrane.

Neurones have some specialized features that support their role in information transmission. Attached to the cell body are many twig-like fibres called
DENDRITES (singular is dendron). Dendrites branch extensively and may stretch
over areas several times the diameter of the cell body. Inputs to the neurone take
place on the dendrites or the soma itself. Also attached to the cell body is a more
prominent fibre that is called an AXON. Axons can be short or may extend up to a
metre or more. They may also branch once or many times. At the end of an
axonal fibre there is a swelling that is the nerve TERMINAL OR SYNAPTIC BOUTON.
These butt on to the dendrites or cell bodies of other nerve cells.

Within each nerve terminal are several small (30–100 µm in diameter) spherical packets called SYNAPTIC VESICLES. The walls of these vesicles are stored in a
structure called the CISTERNA from which bits of vesicle membrane are pinched
off. The empty vesicles are then filled with a chemical that is specific to that
neurone, the NEUROTRANSMITTER that is secreted from the neurone to influence
other nerve cells.

Glial cells

There are about twice as many glial cells as neurones. Thus the bulk of the brain
is made up of glial cells. They physically support the neurones as well as helping to convey nutrients from the blood to the neurones. Glial cells also absorb
dead cells and other neural debris. Although central nervous system neurones

can grow and change after birth, they cannot divide to provide new cells. Thus when many neurones are lost, glial cells proliferate and generate scar tissue. Since mature neurones cannot regenerate, transplants of foetal neural tissue (which still can divide and proliferate) have been used in patients suffering from Parkinson's disease (see later discussion) – unfortunately without dramatic success.

Other types of glial cell, called OLIGODENDROCYTES, produce an insulating sheath that is tightly wrapped around the axons of many CNS neurones. These sheaths are made up of a fat-rich substance called MYELIN which accounts for the pink-white appearance of the white matter of the brain. The myelin sheathing is not continuous along the axon but is interrupted by bare portions of uncoated axon that are called NODES OF RANVIER. Axons that are wrapped in myelin conduct nerve impulses more rapidly and efficiently because the nerve impulse can 'jump' from one node of Ranvier to the next. The non-myelinated neurones are also covered by oligodendroglia, but the wrapping is loose and there is no myelin produced.

A similar function is performed by Schwann cells in the peripheral nervous system where most axons are myelinated. An important difference between Schwann cells and oligodendroglia is that only the former can guide axonal regrowth after damage. Thus unlike the neurones in the brain, those in the periphery can recover, if slowly, from serious damage.

▓ Anatomy of the Nervous System ▓

The nervous system has two major divisions, the CENTRAL NERVOUS SYSTEM (CNS) and the PERIPHERAL NERVOUS SYSTEMS (PNS). The CNS, in turn, is made up of the brain and the spinal cord, which are encased in bone (the skull and the spine respectively), whereas the PNS is outside this bony core.

The PNS is also divided into two parts, the SOMATIC nervous system and the AUTONOMIC nervous system (ANS). The former interacts with the outside world by conveying information from sensory receptors (in skin, muscles and joints) to the central nervous system and by sending motor signals to muscles and glands, while the latter helps regulate the internal environment. The axons of the peripheral nervous system combine to form nerves which are covered by tough

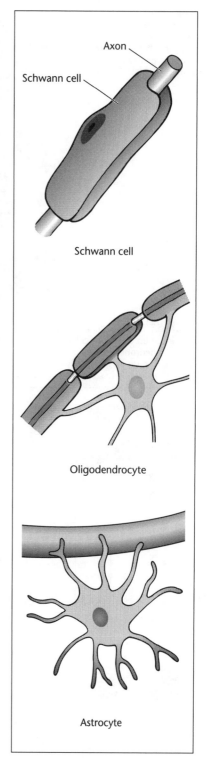

Axon

Schwann cell

Schwann cell

Oligodendrocyte

Astrocyte

Figure 5.3 Glial cells. Oligodendrocytes produce the myelin sheaths that surround and insulate the axons of many CNS neurones. Schwann cells do the same job for neurones in the periphery of the body. Astrocytes support CNS neurones and help form scar tissue when the brain or spinal cord is injured.

OLIGODENDROCYTES, NODES OF RANVIER, CENTRAL NERVOUS SYSTEM, PERIPHERAL NERVOUS SYSTEMS, SOMATIC, AUTONOMIC

Figure 5.4 A summary of the major divisions of the nervous system.
Pinel, J., *Biopsychology* (2 ed.) Copyright © 1993 Allyn & Bacon. Reprinted/adapted by permission.

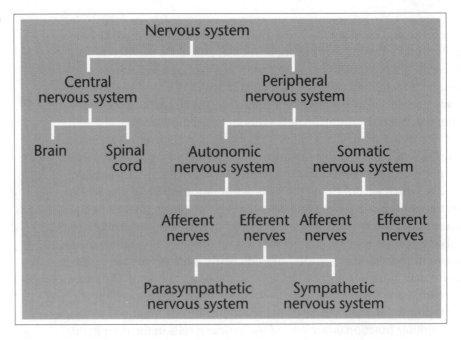

Figure 5.5 Spinal cord and peripheral neurones. The grey matter of the spinal cord contains the cell bodies of motor neurones and interneurones. The cell bodies of sensory neurones are located in the dorsal root ganglia that are attached to the spinal cord. Sensory neurones convey messages from receptors in the periphery to the CNS and motor neurones control muscles and glands. The interneurones lie entirely in the CNS and carry signals between other neurones.
Gray P., *Psychology* (2 ed.) fig. 6.2, p. 164 (Worth Publishers, New York, 1994. Reprinted with permission).

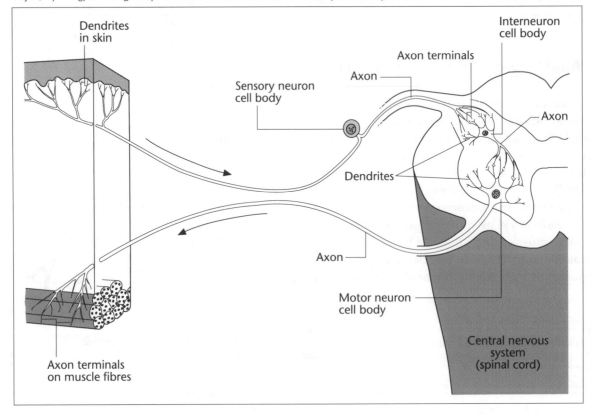

connective tissue. Peripheral nerves that contain only sensory neurones are called SENSORY nerves or afferent nerves. Those that contain motor neurones are MOTOR or efferent nerves.

Most of the nerves of the peripheral nervous system are attached to the spinal cord, but there are twelve that are connected directly to the brain. These are called CRANIAL nerves and they supply the head and neck region of the body. The optic nerve that transmits visual information from the eye to the brain is a cranial nerve, as is the 'oculomotor' nerve that commands the eye muscles that control gaze direction. Other cranial nerves send sound, smell and taste information to the brain.

The spinal cord division of the central nervous system conveys information to and from the brain. It is an extension of the brain stem (see below) that is encased by a tough membrane and lies in a continuous 'tube' – the spinal canal – that is formed by the vertebra that make up the back bone. Figure 5.5 shows a section through the spinal cord. Within the central grey area of the spinal cord are the cell bodies of the motor neurones of the peripheral nervous system as well as small 'interneurones' that allow for local communication within the cord. The white regions that surround the central grey area are formed by the myelinated axons of neurones that send information to and from the brain.

The Brain

The human brain is an unprepossessing structure of modest size, weighing about 1350 g. Although the brain is often talked about as a single structure, it is an amalgam of smaller interconnected organs. This can at least be partly seen in figure 5.6, which shows an external side view of the human brain. Dominating this view is the right cerebral hemisphere, but just beneath and to its rear lies the CEREBELLUM (which means 'little brain' in Latin). Another structure visible in the picture is the brain stem that appears to protrude from the hemisphere. The brain stem continues as the spinal cord.

When looked at from above (see figure 5.7), the brain is 'bilaterally symmetrical', with mirror image left and right halves. Functionally this symmetry is not always apparent since equivalent parts of the left brain and the right brain can have different roles. The left and right cerebral hemispheres, which together are named the CEREBRUM, dominate the external appearance of the brain. The cerebrum resembles a giant walnut because of the infoldings and deep clefts that occur. These clefts are called SULCI (singular is sulcus), and the ridges formed by adjacent clefts are called GYRI (singular is gyrus). Some of the more prominent clefts are used to divide the cerebral hemispheres into four lobes that are named according to the skull bones that cover them. The lobes are named FRONTAL, PARIETAL, TEMPORAL and OCCIPITAL.

Although from a surface view the brain looks uncomplicated, an examination of its underlying parts shows how elaborate it is. For the student fresh to this

SENSORY NERVE

MOTOR NERVE

CRANIAL NERVE

CEREBELLUM

CEREBRUM

SULCI

GYRI

FRONTAL, PARIETAL, TEMPORAL, OCCIPITAL LOBES

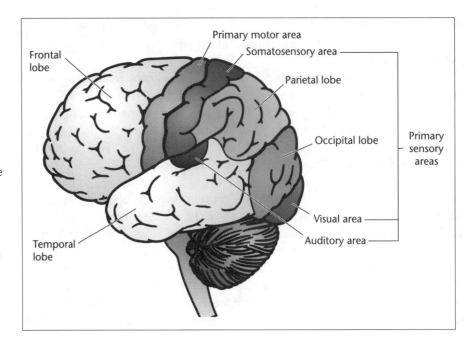

Figure 5.6 Cerebral cortex. The four major lobes of the left cerebral cortex can be seen here, as well as the primary cortical motor and sensory areas. About two-thirds of the surface of the cortex lies within the folds or sulci. Below the cerebral cortices is the highly convoluted cerebellum. Gray, P.,&*Psychology* (2 ed.) fig. 6.9, p. 174 (Worth Publishers, New York, 1994. Reprinted with permission).

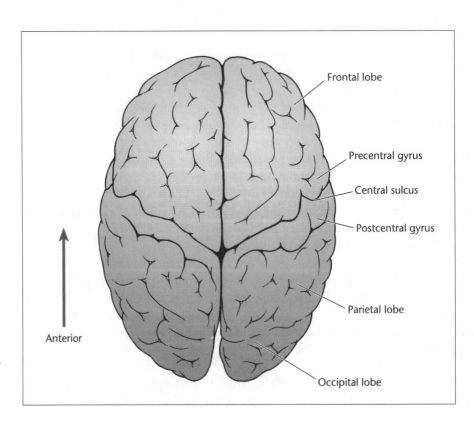

Figure 5.7 Cerebral hemispheres viewed from above. The longitudinal or midline fissure separates the two cerebral hemispheres.

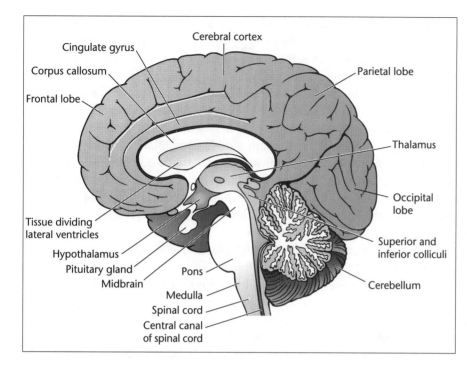

Figure 5.8 A midline sagittal section of the brain. This view of the brain shows that the convolutions of the cerebral cortex persist down the midline. The medulla and pons contain areas that help control important life-support processes including part of the sleep mechanism. Note the corpus callosum that contains millions of axons that allow each cerebral hemisphere to communicate to its partner. From *Biological Psychology*, by J. W. Kalat. Copyright © 1995, 1992, 1988, 1984, 1981 International Thomson Publishing Inc. By permission of Brooks/Cole Publishing Company, Pacific Grove, CA 93950.

topic matters are made worse because the early anatomists gave Latin or Greek names to different parts of the brain. For example, within the temporal lobes is a structure that looks like an almond and was therefore called the AMYGDALA, the Latin for almond.

    AMYGDALA

When the brain is cut in a vertical plane in a front to back direction a SAGITTAL SECTION is obtained, and a mid-sagittal section – taken between the eyes – is shown in figure 5.8. It shows parts of the brain stem, the midbrain and forebrain structures that are covered by the cerebral hemispheres. Towards the top of the brain stem is an enlarged portion termed the PONS. This area contains groups of neurones (called nuclei) that are involved in processes like sleep and arousal, motor control, and pain sensation and control. The MEDULLA, that sits below the pons, contains nuclei that help control body functions like heart beat, respiration and digestion.

    SAGITTAL SECTION

    PONS

    MEDULLA

Lying at the top of the brain stem is the diencephalon, a region that contains the THALAMUS and HYPOTHALAMUS. The thalamus is subdivided into several nuclei, that act as relays in the transmission of information to and from other brain regions. One of these is the lateral geniculate nucleus that receives visual information from the eye (via the optic nerve) and projects information to the optic region of the cerebral hemispheres.

    THALAMUS

    HYPOTHALAMUS

Just below the thalamus is a small group of nuclei called the hypothalamus. Despite its relatively small size this structure has been extensively investigated since it is involved in many important processes. The nuclei of the hypothalamus have been implicated in motivational processes such as hunger, thirst and sex,

PITUITARY GLAND

as well as the regulation of salt intake. They also play a role in emotion, sleep and reward. Because the hypothalamus plays a prominent part in many vegetative functions (basic processes that are essential to life) it has been described as the 'brain' of the autonomic nervous system, but it also exerts some of its effects via chemical messengers. It does so by directing the release of hormones from the PITUITARY GLAND that lies in a bony socket beneath the hypothalamus. Although there are neurones connecting the hypothalamus to the posterior part of the pituitary gland, there is a more important local capillary network joining the hypothalamus to the pituitary. Some neurones in the hypothalamus release (secrete) local hormones that enter this capillary bed. When these local hormones reach the pituitary gland they control the release of pituitary hormones into the general blood supply. The hypothalamic hormones are called releasing hormones. The hormones of the pituitary are targeted on many parts of the body, including the gonads and the adrenal glands, which play a role in stress.

CORPUS CALLOSUM

Another structure that is clearly visible in the midline sagittal section is the CORPUS CALLOSUM. This is a set of nerve fibre tracts that link the two hemispheres. It has a whitish appearance as axons making up the fibre tracts are covered with (fatty) myelin.

HIPPOCAMPUS

There are many important forebrain and midbrain structures that are hidden by the cerebral cortex. Some of these can be seen in figures 5.9 and 5.10. Lying in the temporal lobes are two structures, the HIPPOCAMPUS and the amygdala, that are major parts of the limbic system (a group of cortical and subcortical structures that are thought to act in an integrated fashion). Other components of the limbic system are parts of the thalamus, the hypothalamus, and the cingulate

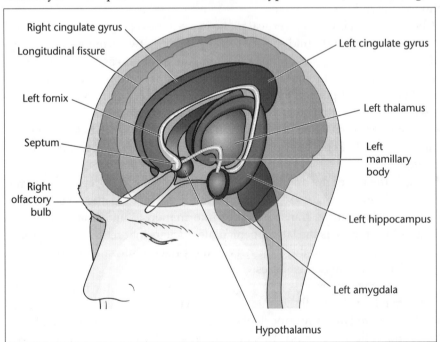

Figure 5.9 Limbic system. The parts of the limbic system lie within the depths of the forebrain. According to an early view these structures are serially connected and form what has been named Papez's circuit. Papez thought that the limbic system was the 'emotional centre' of the brain.
Pinel, J., *Biopsychology* (2 ed.) Copyright © 1993 Allyn & Bacon. Reprinted/adapted by permission.

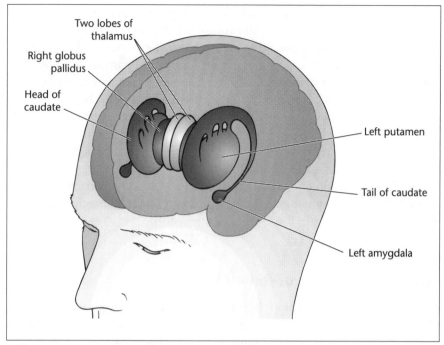

Figure 5.10 The basal ganglia. An alternative collective name for the globus pallidus, putamen and caudate nucleus is the corpus striatum (striped body), which comes from the appearance of these structures.

Pinel, J., *Biopsychology* (2 ed.) Copyright © 1993 Allyn & Bacon. Reprinted/adapted by permission.

Figure 5.11 The cerebral ventricles. The ventricles are an interconnected set of cavities in the depths of the brain that are filled with cerebro-spinal fluid.

Pinel, J., *Biopsychology* (2 ed.) Copyright © 1993 Allyn & Bacon. Reprinted/adapted by permission.

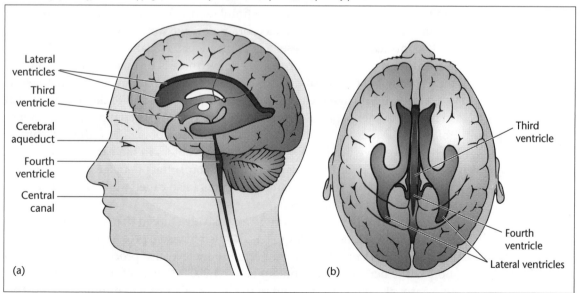

gyrus of the cerebral cortex. Although the limbic system has traditionally been associated with emotion, more recent proposals have implicated the whole system or parts of it in higher cognitive processes such as memory, learning and attention. A set of structures that have been collectively named the BASAL GANGLIA are located around the thalamus – these are the putamen and globus pallidus, and they are part of the motor control mechanisms of the brain.

Although it is not obvious from the appearance of a mature brain, in the early stages of development in the embryo the brain is a hollow structure at the front end of the NEURAL TUBE. Somewhat surprisingly, this neural tube is derived from the outer layer of cells – the ectoderm – of the developing embryo, the same layer that forms the skin and surface structures of the body. A consequence of this embryonic arrangement is that the adult brain retains characteristics of its original tubular structure in the form of cavities called VENTRICLES and the spinal canal.

Functions and mapping of cortical lobes

Outside the brain we find that each organ (or subpart of an organ) performs an identifiable function. Is this true of individual parts of the brain? A common approach taken in psychology is to divide mental processes into faculties such as memory, visual perception, motor skills, and language. Thus it is not surprising that there have been attempts to map or localize these psychological faculties onto different parts of the brain.

There is no doubt that localization of psychological functions to specific parts of the brain does occur, but its extent is still debated. Thus we find that there is a crude mapping of sensory and motor processing onto parts of the cerebrum. The evidence for this mapping comes from various sources. There is anatomical evidence, evidence from electrical stimulation of local brain regions, studies of people and animals with localized brain damage (often called lesion studies), and sophisticated techniques such as magnetic resonance imaging (MRI) and positron emission tomography (PET) scans (there is further discussion of these scans below). These are discussed in the section on mapping techniques below.

Sensory organs like the eyes and the ears are connected to the thalamus, that in turn sends nerve fibres to specific cortical regions. Thus the superior temporal gyrus that lies along the upper border of the temporal lobe is the first cortical region to receive input from the auditory receptors in the ears via the medial geniculate nuclei of the thalamus. If a person suffers damage to the auditory pathway or to the superior temporal gyrus (also called auditory cortex) they will suffer from partial or total deafness.

The visual system has been more extensively studied than any other sensory system. The amount of cortex that is devoted to visual processing is large: many regions that are not directly connected to the eye also process visual information. Optic nerves, which contain about 1,000,000 axons from neurones in the eye, meet at a point just in front of the hypothalamus and pituitary gland. This

Box 5.1 Methods for Investigating Brain and Behaviour

A major goal of the neurosciences is to find out what functions different areas of the brain support. To meet this need neuroscientists have developed some sophisticated (and expensive) methods, but much research still relies on classical techniques. Thus, simple tissue sectioning and staining is a mainstay of the discipline. This method provides basic anatomical information and is used to verify the placement of electrodes or the location of brain damage in animal or human brains. In this technique, the brain tissue is chemically treated to stop biodegradation of the cells, hardened and then cut into almost transparent sections. These are stained and mounted on glass microscope slides. The staining techniques can reveal cell bodies and cell fibres (axons).

Specialized staining techniques have been invented to trace the path of axons from their cell bodies to their terminals. In one of these, radioactively labelled amino acids are injected in the vicinity of the nerve terminals. The radio-labelled compounds are picked up by the neurones and transported back through the axons to the cell body. This retrograde transport can be followed by tracing the radioactivity in tissue slices. In another technique fluorescent dyes that attach to specific neurotransmitter molecules allow us to localize areas of the brain that are rich in such molecules.

These techniques are important but do not tell us what is happening in living brains. One way of doing this was developed by the Canadian neurosurgeon Wilder Penfield. He capitalized on the the insensitivity of the brain to pain by performing brain surgery under local anaesthetic in fully conscious patients. Such patients are able to describe what they experience as a tiny electrical stimulus is applied to the surface of their brains. This activates neurones in regions below the stimulating electrode and produces a neural state that can be interpreted by the brain. Depending on the location of the stimulus the patient will report an experience such as a sound, a memory, or a visual event. Alternatively there may be a motor effect like a twitch or limb movement.

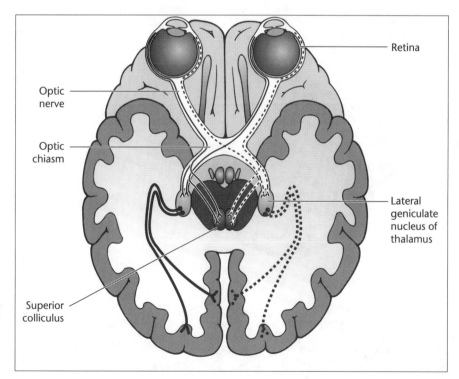

Optic nerve

Optic chiasm

Superior colliculus

Retina

Lateral geniculate nucleus of thalamus

Figure 5.12 Visual pathway. The optic nerves come together at the optic chiasm – located at the base of the brain and just in front of the pituitary gland – where half the axons cross to the other side of the brain. In the lateral geniculate nucleus the optic neurones synapse on other neurones that project axons to visual cortex.
From *Biological Psychology*, by J. W. Kalat. Copyright © 1995, 1992, 1988, 1984, 1981 International Thomson Publishing Inc. By permission of Brooks/Cole Publishing Company, Pacific Grove, CA 93950.

Box 5.2 The Topographic Organization of the Sensory and Motor Areas

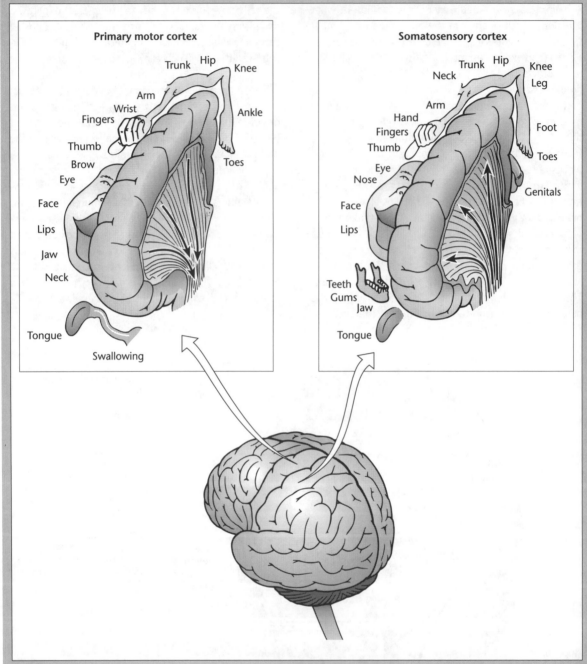

Figure 5.13 Organization of the primary sensory and motor areas. This shows how more cortical tissue is devoted to representing or controlling some body parts than others.

From *Biological Psychology*, by J. W. Kalat. Copyright © 1995, 1992, 1988, 1984, 1981 International Thomson Publishing Inc. By permission of Brooks/Cole Publishing Company, Pacific Grove, CA 93950.

The primary sensory and motor areas of cortex are organized such that adjacent neurones receive inputs from, or send outputs to, adjacent parts of the sensory or muscular tissue to which they are ultimately connected. Thus there is a mapping of the body surface onto the somatosensory and somatomotor cortex in the same way that the eye is mapped onto visual cortex, and this body mapping is termed a somatotopic representation. Although adjacent areas of the body are dealt with by adjacent parts of somatosensory cortex the mapping is not uniform, so the amount of cortical tissue involved is not proportional to the size of the body part being mapped. For instance, in somatosensory cortex the parts of the body that are more sensitive, for instance the lips, face, hands and fingers, are represented by large amounts of cortical tissue, whereas other regions like the back and thigh that are less sensitive are represented by much smaller amounts of tissue. Figure 5.13 shows the mapping of the body surface onto somatosensory cortex in the form of a distorted homunculus (little man).

There is a motor map of the different parts of the body on the precentral gyrus (see figure 5.13). The motor homunculus shows similar distortions to that seen in the sensory homunculus because of the need to exert finer control of the muscles in areas like the fingers, hands, face and mouth than for other parts like the thighs, arms and back.

It might seem that these sensory and motor maps are genetically programmed. This was the orthodoxy until research in the 1960s showed that early experience with unusual stimuli can significantly change the maps in young animals. More recently it has been shown that changes can take place even in adult animals. Recazone et al. (1992) trained adult owl monkeys by rewarding them with banana-flavoured food pellets to discriminate between two different vibrations applied to a particular spot on one finger. After extensive training they found that the part of somotosensory cortex that received inputs from the 'trained' spot of skin was two to three times larger than in animals that did not receive the specific training. The change was probably mediated by a reorganization in the patterns of connections in cortex.

junction is called the OPTIC CHIASM (means 'cross') where about half the nerve fibres from each eye cross to the other side of the brain. The optic nerves continue around the hypothalamic region to the lateral geniculate nuclei of the thalamus. These in turn project posteriorly to a region of cortex that has been given several names. This area is nowadays usually referred to as primary visual cortex, but it also referred to as striate (striped) cortex or 'Brodmann's area 17' (or just 17). The latter terminology is based on the work of a neuroanatomist called Brodmann who mapped the different parts of the cerebral cortices according to the layering and organization of the grey matter.   OPTIC CHIASM

A characteristic of the anatomical projection to visual cortex is that it provides a retinotopic mapping onto primary visual cortex. The retina is the inner layer of the eye. It contains light receptors and neurones that send information to the brain. Because of the optics of the eye the visual scene is represented spatially on the retina, with adjacent parts of the visual field being mapped on to adjacent portions of the retina. This spatial mapping is maintained in the projection from the eye to the thalamus and then to primary visual cortex.

As in the case of injury to the auditory system, if a person suffers from damage to any part of the visual system they will be partially or totally blind. However, in the case of partial blindness the person will frequently only show a neglect or blindness for a part of the visual field (termed a SCOTOMA). There is a 'filling in'   SCOTOMA process by the remaining intact visual processing system so the person only becomes aware of the blindness under special circumstances. This should not surprise us since even people with normal vision have a 'blind' area in their visual field. There are no visual receptors in the eye where the optic nerve emerges, but we are unaware of this deficit.

SOMATOSENSORY

The receptors that are present in our skin, muscles and joints contribute sensory input to the SOMATOSENSORY (body sensory) system. The information is passed through the afferent (sensory) axons of the spinal nerves and the cranial nerves of the peripheral nervous system to several nuclei in the thalamus. These in turn are connected to the somatosensory cortex (also called the postcentral gyrus) of the parietal lobe. This lies behind the prominent central fissure. Because the sensory fibres that convey somatosensory information cross from one side of the brain to the other within the brain stem, the sensory information from the left side of the body is dealt with by the cortex of the right hemisphere and vice versa. This crossing of nerve fibres from one side of the brain to the other is a common phenomenon that has been given the rather obscure name DECUSSATION.

DECUSSATION

SOMATOMOTOR

In parallel to the somatosensory system there is a SOMATOMOTOR system. The information flow in this system is in the reverse direction, from cerebral cortex to the muscles in the periphery. The primary motor cortex lies on the precentral gyrus, which is in front of the central sulcus (and somatosensory cortex). Electrical stimulation of different points on this gyrus in animals and awake human patients causes movement in some part of the body. The fibres that project from primary motor cortex cross over in the brain stem and then course down the white matter columns in the spinal cord, to terminate on neurones in the ventral horns of the spinal cord grey matter. Axons of the motor neurones in the spinal cord come together to form the peripheral motor nerves that innervate muscles.

Cerebellum and basal ganglia

Although the somatomotor system has a fundamental role in voluntary actions, it is just part of a complex neural motor control system. Other important areas include structures in the basal ganglia and the cerebellum. The cerebellum integrates rapid movements of the limbs without conscious monitoring – thus the movements once started are not modified by the use of sensory feedback. Patients with cerebellar damage have movements that are jerky, erratic and uncoordinated, they have to think out each part of a series of movements. Thus walking and reaching are not badly affected, since these actions are performed fairly slowly, but kicking and throwing are difficult actions for these patients. It is interesting that birds and monkeys have well-developed cerebellums, as both these groups need to make rapid, well coordinated movements in flying or leaping about in trees.

The basal ganglia lie either side of the thalamus. These motor centres have a complementary role to the cerebellum; they are involved in slower, deliberate movements like reaching or walking. Damage to the basal ganglia causes slowness of movement and difficulty in stopping one behaviour and starting another. An afflicted person can reach for an object accurately, but takes a long time to start the movement. Another characteristic of basal ganglia damage is a 'resting tremor', which is vibratory movements of arms or hands. These symptoms are characteristic of Parkinson's disease.

Evidence from studies on animals and human beings with brain damage shows that the planning of most complex behaviours, including movements, takes place in the frontal cortex that lies anterior to the precentral gyrus. This area is connected to primary motor cortex, which then directs and executes the desired movements. This frontal region is one of the so-called areas of ASSOCIATION COR-TEX. Such areas lie in the temporal, occipital and parietal lobes. Association cortex does not have direct sensory input or direct motor output but instead receives information from sensory cortical areas as well as other association areas.

ASSOCIATION CORTEX

Earlier in this section the issue of localization of function was raised. Further support for the localization position comes from patients with speech defects. Many of these patients are victims of cerebro-vascular accidents (strokes) and therefore the data derived from these cases can be inconclusive. The reason is that even when strokes occur in similar regions of the brain, the tissue death that follows from the loss of blood supply varies between patients. Nevertheless the speech deficits that were first recognized, named and localized in the nineteenth

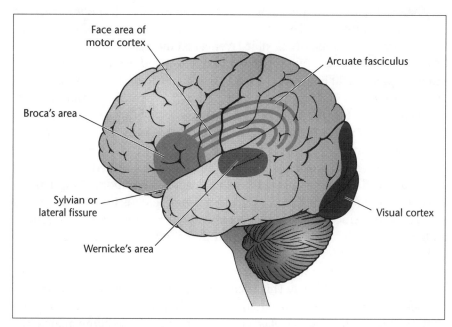

Figure 5.14 Language areas in the speech-dominant hemisphere. Damage to Broca's area, which lies close to the motor area controlling the face, causes a loss in the ability to produce grammatically complex sentences. Damage to Wernicke's area has little effect on speech production but leads to difficulties with understanding speech.
From *Biological Psychology*, by J. W. Kalat. Copyright © 1995, 1992, 1988, 1984, 1981 International Thomson Publishing Inc. By permission of Brooks/Cole Publishing Company, Pacific Grove, CA 93950.

century by Paul Broca and Carl Wernicke have stood the test of time. Modern brain-imaging techniques like CT scans and MRI in patients with speech defects have confirmed their proposals.

Broca suggested that the region at the base of, and just in front of, the precentral gyrus was responsible for organizing speech output. Thus people with BROCA'S APHASIA have slow and stilted speech – they have an expressive aphasia. In its pure form such patients have no difficulty in understanding the speech of other people. Another common speech defect occurs when someone has damage to the posterior portion of the superior temporal gyrus. Such patients are not deaf but they have difficulty in understanding speech and they produce fluent but meaningless speech. These may be related phenomena, since an inability to understand what words mean is likely to affect one's ability to produce meaningful utterances. This speech deficit is now called WERNICKE'S APHASIA.

Meninges and cerebro-spinal fluid

The brain and spinal cord are covered by protective sheaths or membranes. There are three layers of this connective tissue that are referred to as the MENINGES. Closely attached to the brain is the pia mater, which encloses the smaller blood vessels of the brain and spinal cord. Over this layer is the arachnoid membrane, separated from the pia mater by the subarachnoid space which is filled with cerebro-spinal fluid. The arachnoid membrane gets its name from the Greek *arachne*, meaning spider, because of the web-like threads filling the arachnoid space. Overlying the outer membrane is a tough but flexible layer called the dura mater.

CEREBRO-SPINAL FLUID is a plasma filtrate that is secreted from the capillaries of the choroid plexus that line the ventricles, and other cerebral blood vessels. The ventricles are the cavities found within the brain; these form a continuous system that also connects to the fluid compartment in which the brain floats. Cerebro-spinal fluid is continuously being manufactured and therefore must be continuously drained.

As will be clear from the above, the brain floats in a fluid-filled compartment – formed by the dura mater and skull – which confers an important mechanical protection to it The skull both encases the brain and defends it from knocks and blows. However, since neural tissue has a consistency somewhat like a thick porridge or jelly it would suffer continual damage from the small and large accelerations and decelerations that occur with head movements. (Imagine what happens to a plate of jelly when it is rapidly moved.) Nature's solution to this problem is a hydraulic buffer. This is created by the fluid-tight skull compartment enclosing the cerebro-spinal fluid in which the brain floats. Since fluids are incompressible but have some 'elasticity', the brain does not bump against the skull when the head undergoes moderate accelerations. However, when the skull suffers from large accelerations or decelerations, as arise in car accidents or in boxing, damage occurs. This arises when the brain impacts on the skull, thus bruising the neural tissue. In addition to this bruising there are shearing effects on blood vessels that lead to localized bleeding into the brain. Both effects frequently occur when boxers are punched on the head. Many professional boxers develop dementia pugilistica (punch drunkeness) and occasionally catastrophic damage occurs that can be life threatening.

Brain blood supply and the blood-brain barrier

The brain, which makes up about 2 per cent of a person's weight, uses about 20 per cent of total body oxygen and glucose. Thus, not surprisingly, about 15 per cent of the blood pumped by the heart goes to the brain. Because of this heavy demand, no neurone can be far from the capillaries that transport blood. The cerebral arteries supplying the cerebral cortices branch extensively on the surface of the brain and send many small penetrating vessels into the deep structures of the brain. In turn these vessels form extensive capillary networks. Although this vascular arrangement brings nutrients close to all cerebral neurones, the natural fluctuations in the composition of blood are still a problem. The mechanism that protects the nerve cells from these dangers involves the presence of a fluid compartment that surrounds the brain and nerve cells. This extracellular compartment is linked to the blood supply and is thus able to convey nutrients and chemicals to the nerve cells.

In addition to the chemical protection provided by the extracellular compartments that surround nerve cells there is the blood-brain barrier. This is partly maintained by a mechanical system formed by the tight junctions between the cells lining cerebral blood vessels. This physically prevents large molecules from penetrating the extracellular fluid compartment surrounding the nerve cells. In addition there are specialized transport mechanisms that only convey specific chemicals into brain cells. The blood-brain barrier helps protect the brain from toxic chemicals and infectious agents, but it also can hinder the passage of drugs or chemicals that would be valuable in treating functional disorders and infections.

Autonomic nervous system

The AUTONOMIC NERVOUS SYSTEM (ANS) is so called because it is self-governing, which means that a person has little conscious control over its operation. It receives information from and sends commands to the heart, intestines and other organs, and its role is to regulate vital bodily functions and to condition our bodies to cope effectively with the vagaries of life.

AUTONOMIC NERVOUS SYSTEM

The ANS has two separate systems that operate in tandem. One component is called the SYMPATHETIC SYSTEM and the other is the PARASYMPATHETIC SYSTEM ('para-' means besides or related to), and most organs innervated by the ANS receive both parts. The actions of the two are complementary such that heart beat increases because of sympathetic input and slows under the influence of the parasympathetic system.

SYMPATHETIC SYSTEM

PARASYMPATHETIC SYSTEM

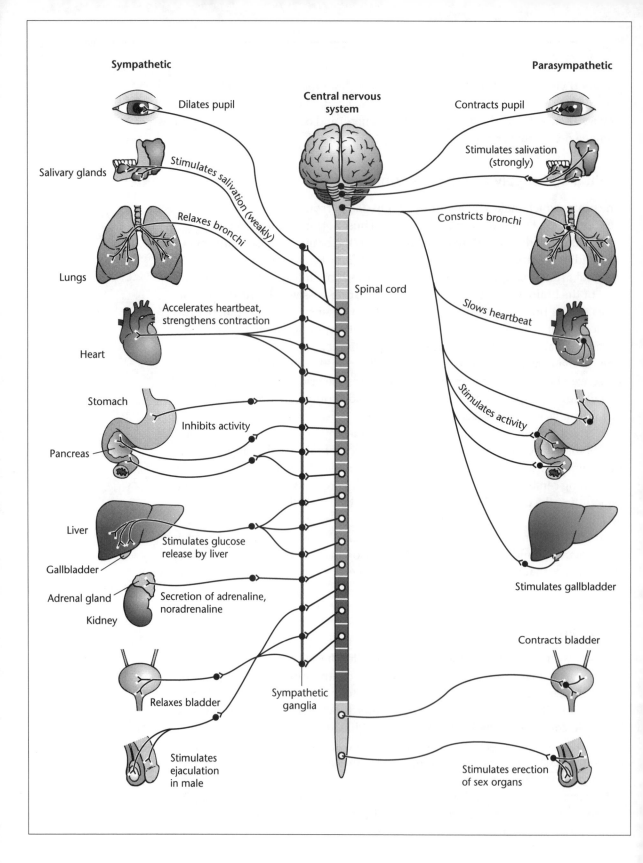

Figure 5.15 shows parts of the ANS as well as some of the structures and organs that it innervates. The sympathetic nervous system has a complex arrangement of GANGLIA (collections of neurone cell bodies). Running alongside the spinal cord is the linked chain of sympathetic ganglia. These receive axonal projections from the sympathetic motor neurones that are found in the grey matter of the spinal cord. Neurones extend from the sympathetic ganglia to various organs either directly or after being interrupted by further ganglia. All the synapses within the sympathetic ganglia release acetylcholine, but the target organs receive noradrenaline from the postganglion neurones. The sweat glands are an exception in that they are acetylcholinergically activated.

GANGLIA

The parasympathetic system is sometimes known as the cranio-sacral system because its nerves originate from some of the nuclei of the cranial nerves and the sacral part of the spinal cord. These neurones project long axons to ganglia located close to the target organs; shorter fibres then travel to the target organs. These neurones are all acetylcholinergic.

The sympathetic nervous system is often characterized as the 'fight–flight system'. When the body needs more energy, as happens if a person is confronted with novelty, or threat, the sympathetic system responds. This increases blood flow to skeletal muscles, and provides energy via the release of adrenaline from the adrenal glands, and increases cardiac capacity by increasing heart rate. The parasympathetic system promotes energy-conserving measures such as decreasing heart rate and facilitating digestive processes.

Transmission within neurones

The neurone is a cell that is specialized to transmit an electrical signal along itself, as well as to send a chemical signal to another cell (usually another neurone). All cells in the body are POLARIZED; that is, there is an electrical potential difference across the cell wall that is termed the membrane potential. Neurones have the additional property of being electrically excitable. Together these provide the basis for the action potential which is the signal that passes along a nerve cell.

POLARIZATION

To understand the membrane potential and the basis of the action potential you need to understand the functioning of the cell membrane.

Membrane potential and action potential

The cell membrane is selectively porous, thus it allows certain chemicals to enter or exit the cell while blocking the passage of others. The porosity occurs because

OPPOSITE
Figure 5.15 The autonomic nervous system. There are two complementary parts to the autonomic nervous system which monitors and controls the activity of visceral organs and glands. The sympathetic division promotes body arousal whereas the parasympathetic portion promotes body restoration, digestion and relaxation.
Gray, P., *Psychology* (2 ed.) fig. 6.4, p. 168 (Worth Publishers, New York, 1994. Reprinted with permission).

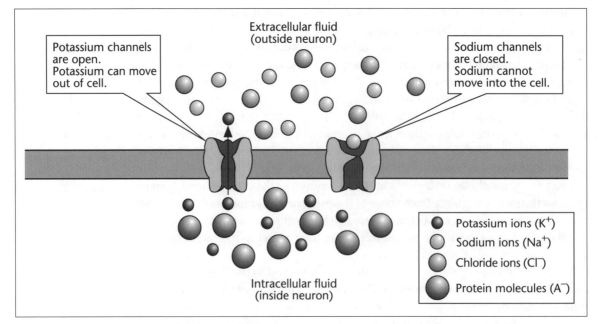

Figure 5.16 Cell membrane and the resting potential. The portion of a neuronal membrane that is shown here contains two selective channels. There are charged substances dissolved in the intracellular and extracellular fluids. Negatively charged protein molecules (A⁻) are found inside the cell, while potassium ions K⁺), sodium ions (NA⁺) and chloride ions (Cl⁻) are present both inside and outside the cell but in different concentrations. Because of the excess of positively charged ions outside the neurone the membrane has a resting potential across it of about 60mV, with the inside being negative with respect to the outside. Gray, P., *Psychology* (2 ed.) fig. 6.17, p. 183 (Worth Publishers, New York, 1994. Reprinted with permission).

there are protein molecules embedded in the membrane that act as channels for specific chemicals. These channels allow specific ions through under restricted conditions. Some channels are always open but others only open when electrically triggered.

Some of the chemicals dissolved in the fluid within the cell (intracellular) and bathing the cell (extracellular) are electrically charged. Soluble protein molecules that are negatively charged exist only in intracellular fluid. But other significant chemicals occur both inside and outside the cell and include: potassium ions (K⁺), which are more common inside the cell than outside; and sodium ions (Na⁺) and chloride ions (Cl⁻) that are more concentrated in the extracellular fluid than the intracellular fluid (see figure 5.16). Because the positive and negative charges across the cell membrane are not in balance, the inside of a neurone is maintained at about –60 mV compared to the outside, and it is this potential difference that provides the electrical energy that makes an action potential possible. There is a small leakage of potassium ions from within the cell, and an even smaller leakage of sodium ions into the cell through ungated selective ion channels. The direction of the flow is determined by the concentration gradients of the ions. If there were no restorative process then these two species of ion would tend towards a concentration equilibrium, and the basis for action potentials would be lost. To counter this leakage, there is an active pumping mechanism across the cell membrane that moves sodium ions out of the cell and potassium ions into the cell. This pump is aptly named the sodium–potassium pump. A large amount of the energy used within the brain supports it.

The action potential (signal) that passes along a neurone can be recorded using electrodes placed outside the cell and inserted into the cell. This signal is produced when a resting neurone (membrane potential of -60 mV) is depolarized by a brief current to a membrane potential of -45 mV. How this comes about naturally will be discussed later.

Figure 5.17 shows the trace of an action potential. This reflects the voltage changes that occur at a point on the axon of a nerve cell over a few milliseconds. The processes in the axon membrane that sustain the action potential are as follows. As mentioned earlier there are electrically gated sodium channels in the membrane. Some of these open when the membrane is depolarized by about 15 mV; this allows sodium ions to enter the cell, and further depolarizes it so

Figure 5.17 Propagation of an action potential. The action potential progresses along the axon as a series of localized inflows of sodium ions (NA$^+$) and outflows of potassium ions (K$^+$) through channels that open when stimulated by a local electrical current. The nerve impulse starts because the cell body becomes slightly less negative (because of EPSPs) and moves along the axon to the axon terminals (synaptic boutons). The small voltage effect opens sodium channels that allow sodium ions to rush into the cell as the initial phase of the action potential. This makes the interior of the neurone positive in just this location. Potassium channels are opened because of this local voltage shift and positively charged potassium ions rush out of the cell restoring the resting potential at this point of the membrane. The voltage changes are known as the action potential.
Scientific American, Sept. 1979, p. 60, 'The Neuron', Stevens C. author, courtesy Albert Miller/*Scientific American* 1979.

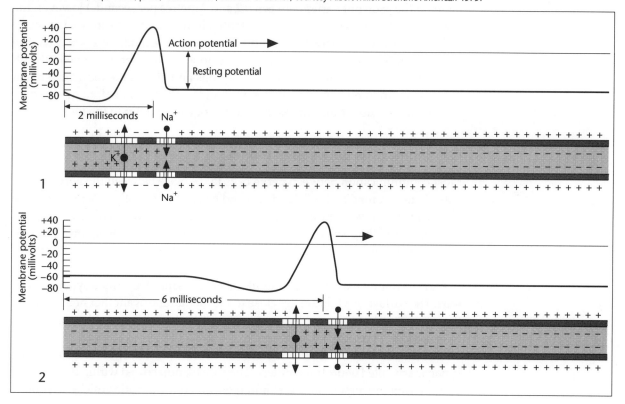

even more electrically gated sodium channels open. This cascade continues until the inside of the cell reaches about +30 mV. At this point the sodium channels close again. In non-myelinated axons there are electrically gated potassium channels that are slower to respond to depolarization than the sodium channels. When these open, positively charged potassium ions leave the cell, thus making the inside of the cell negative again. The recovery of the resting membrane potential takes about a millisecond longer in myelinated axons that lack the voltage-gated potassium channels. Although few sodium and potassium ions are involved in a single action potential, in constantly active neurones there is enough ion movement to keep the sodium–potassium pumps busy.

The action potential described above first occurs at the axon hillock which is the point where the axon leaves the cell body. Why does it then travel along the axon towards the axon terminal? The explanation is provided by the cable properties of the cell membrane. The cell membrane has a high electrical resistance but an electric current can travel along it. A small electric current flows along the membrane in front of the action potential, and thus is enough to cause the electrically gated sodium channels in the proximate region of the axon to open and so initiate the cascade of events that support the action potential.

In non-myelinated neurones the action potential has to be generated sequentially along the whole length of the axon, which will be a relatively slow process. The speed of transmission in such neurones is determined by the diameter of the axon but varies between 0.2 and 2 metres per second. However, the speed of transmission of the action potential in myelinated neurones is considerably faster: it varies between 12 and 120 metres per second. This is because the action potential can only be generated at the nodes of Ranvier. The myelin sheath prevents ion flows in the intermediate regions and allows the local currents in the axon membrane to traverse a longer length of the axon before dissipating. The action potential thus 'jumps' from one node of Ranvier to the next.

Communication between neurones

Most communication between nerve cells takes place between the nerve terminals of one neurone and the dendrites and cell body of another. Although there are two ways in which this communication can occur, we shall only consider chemical signalling since this is the most common form. The second type involves electrical contact between nerve cells and is beyond the scope of an introductory text.

Axon terminals expand into bulb-like structures that are termed synaptic boutons. The surface of a bouton lies close to the membrane of another neurone, and these 'contacts' are termed synapses. Thus the chemical signalling process is referred to as synaptic transmission.

The chemicals that allow one neurone to have an effect on another at the synapse are called neurotransmitters. They are manufactured within the synaptic bouton from precursor molecules and then stored in synaptic vesicles to protect

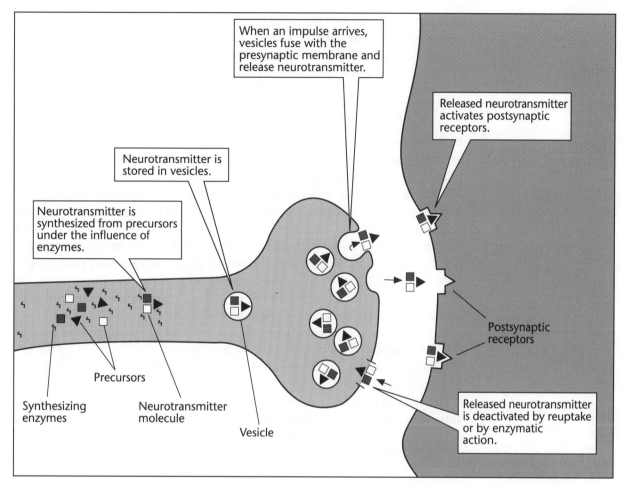

When an impulse arrives, vesicles fuse with the presynaptic membrane and release neurotransmitter.

Released neurotransmitter activates postsynaptic receptors.

Neurotransmitter is stored in vesicles.

Neurotransmitter is synthesized from precursors under the influence of enzymes.

Postsynaptic receptors

Precursors

Synthesizing enzymes

Neurotransmitter molecule

Vesicle

Released neurotransmitter is deactivated by reuptake or by enzymatic action.

Figure 5.18 Events at a synapse. The neurotransmitter chemical is made and stored in the synaptic bouton. The arrival of an action potential causes the release of the transmitter into the synaptic cleft, where it triggers an effect on the postsynaptic neurone by binding to a receptor site.
Pinel, J., *Biopsychology* (2 ed.) Copyright © 1993 Allyn & Bacon. Reprinted/adapted by permission.

them from degrading enzymes. The release of the transmitter molecules into the synaptic gap that separates the bouton from the next neurone occurs when an action potential reaches the axon terminal. This causes synaptic vesicles to merge with the neuronal membrane and empty their contents into the synaptic gap. Since this gap is so tiny the transmitter molecules rapidly diffuse and reach the postsynaptic membrane.

There are special channel proteins embedded in the postsynaptic membrane. These are in fact chemically gated channels where the chemical that unlocks the gate is a neurotransmitter molecule. When a transmitter molecules reaches the postsynaptic membrane and binds to a receptor site in the channel protein, the channel opens to allow ions to pass.

The transmitter molecules must be cleared from the postsynaptic receptor sites and the synaptic gap to allow further signals to be received by the postsynaptic neurone. There are two mechanisms that perform this task. One involves the presence of enzymes in the synaptic gap that deactivate the transmitter molecules. An alternative is the reabsorption of the transmitter molecules into the presynaptic bouton where they may be broken down or reused.

Postsynaptic events

Each neurone receives inputs via many synapses; some of these inputs are excitatory and others are inhibitory. The difference depends on whether the activated channel allows sodium or potassium ions to pass. When the channel is selectively permeable to sodium ions, the effect on the postsynaptic neurone will be excitatory, since sodium ions, which are more concentrated outside the cell, will move down their concentration gradient and enter the neurone. Since sodium ions are positively charged the inside of the neurone will become less negative. This event produces what has been termed an excitatory postsynaptic potential (EPSP). Unlike an action potential, which is an all-or-none event, an EPSP produces a local potential effect on the cell membrane which diminishes with distance from the point of origin and with time.

If the channel in the postsynaptic neurone allows potassium ions to pass, an inhibitory postsynaptic potential (IPSP) is produced. This is caused by the exit of potassium ions from the neurone which makes the inside of the cell even more negative.

Action potentials are initiated at the axon hillock when the axon membrane is sufficiently depolarized. This depolarization is dependent on the algebraic summation of all the EPSPs and IPSPs that have occurred in the recent past on the dendrites and cell body.

Neurotransmitters and psychoactive drugs

Because there are two types of postsynaptic potentials, one might think there would be two neurotransmitters. However, there are many chemicals that are known to act as neurotransmitters and more will be discovered. The transmitters we know of come in families that include acetylcholine, monoamines, amino acids and peptide. In addition to these neurotransmitters there are other chemicals called NEUROMODULATORS that alter the general sensitivity and responsivity of neurones.

NEUROMODULATORS

The same neurotransmitter substance can have an inhibitory action at one receptor site but an excitatory action at another. Moreover, there are differences in the speed of action of the same neurotransmitter at different receptor sites: some respond within milliseconds, whereas others give a slower response lasting from hundreds of milliseconds to minutes. These complexities are explained by some elaborate differences in the operation of the channel-opening mechanisms. This has led to the realization that there can be different receptor types for a specific neurotransmitter, and that there is a chance of designing psychoactive

Table 5.1 Classification of the monoamine transmitters

Monoamines	
Catecholamines	*Indoeamines*
Adrenaline	Aerotonin (5-HT)
Noradrenaline	
Dopamine	

drugs that are tailored to work at specific subtypes of a receptor.

As a prelude to considering how psychoactive drugs relate to neurotransmitters some principles about transmitter production and action need to be outlined.

Monoamine transmitters

There are four MONOAMINE TRANSMITTERS that share a similar structure. Two of them are also hormones that are produced by the adrenal glands (adrenaline and noradrenaline). Such shared functions do not seem to be unusual in the case of neurotransmitters. For example, several peptides that act as hormones outside the brain also perform as neurotransmitters in the brain (bombesin, cholecystokinin and somatostatin are instances). (See table 5.1.)

The neurones that release these transmitters contain the enzymes that are required to synthesize the transmitters from precursor substances. Two amino acids are the precursors for the monoamines – tyrosine in the case of all the catecholamines, and tryptophan in the case of serotonin. These two amino acids are readily available in our diets, but there have been suggestions from several people, including an American psychopharmacologist called Wurtman, that the constitution of our diets might alter the levels of these transmitters and affect mood and cognition.

There are several stages in the manufacture of the transmitter. Once synthesis is complete the molecules are packaged into synaptic vesicles. The production process is regulated via feedback mechanisms in the synaptic bouton. Sites on the synaptic bouton from which the transmitter is released are called presynaptic or AUTORECEPTORS. Thus when transmitter molecules are released into the synaptic gap, some engage the autoreceptor site which then modulates the activity within the synaptic bouton. In the case of noradrenaline the autoreceptor sites are named α_2-noradrenergic receptors.

Many transmitter substances are deactivated in the synaptic gap by enzymes that destroy the transmitter molecule. For example, figure 5.19 shows schematically how acetylcholine is broken down by the enzyme acetylcholinesterase.

However, to terminate their action on receptors the monoamines are taken

MONOAMINE
TRANSMITTERS

AUTORECEPTORS

Figure 5.19

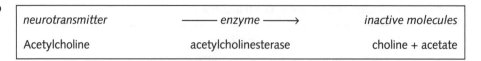

neurotransmitter	——— enzyme ———→	inactive molecules
Acetylcholine	acetylcholinesterase	choline + acetate

back into the synaptic bouton where they are either repackaged or degraded by enzymes. One such enzyme is monoamine oxidase, which plays a part in maintaining the transmitter at the correct concentration.

The distribution of neurotransmitters in the nervous system is not haphazard. There are specific anatomical regions where the neurones produce particular transmitters. Thus there is a region in the midbrain called the substantia nigra (black substance) that contains neurones that utilize dopamine. These neurones send axons to the corpus striatum, an area that was previously discussed in relationship to Parkinson's disease. It is not then surprising to find depressed dopamine activity in such patients. Other areas that are rich in particular neurotransmitters exist in the brain stem, where there are serotoninergic neurones and noradrenergic neurones. Moreover, since there are relationships between specific brain areas and psychological functions, we find that particular neurotransmitters are also implicated in these functions. Noradrenergic neurones are involved in the control of alertness and wakefulness; dopamine plays a role in motor control but has also been implicated in the serious mental disorder schizophrenia. Serotonin plays a part in the regulation of mood, in the control of eating, sleep and arousal, and in the regulation of pain.

Other neurotransmitters

Acetylcholine was the first substance to be widely recognized as a neurotransmitter. Unlike the monoamines it is usually an excitatory transmitter. It is present in the peripheral nervous system and in many parts of the brain including the hippocampus and the nucleus basalis of Meynert, both of which have been implicated in Alzheimer's disease. There have been unsuccessful attempts to treat patients with this form of dementia with drugs that increase acetylcholine activity. Acetylcholine is the transmitter that is released onto skeletal or voluntary muscles at a specialized synapse called the neuromuscular junction.

Glutamic acid (usually called glutamate), which is readily available from food, is found throughout the brain, and is probably its principal excitatory transmitter. Glutamate has been implicated in learning, a topic that is considered below. You may have heard of the 'Chinese Food Syndrome'; this is attributable to monosodium glutamate (MSG), which is used as a taste enhancer in oriental and other foods. When some people ingest a lot of MSG, it causes dizziness and numbness. Possibly MSG affects the amount of glutamate in the brain to cause these symptoms.

A neurotransmitter that is widespread in the brain and spinal cord is GABA (gamma-amino-butyric acid) that is derived from glutamic acid. It is an inhibitory transmitter that has an important role in making the brain stable. Because of the widespread connections that occur between neurones – neurones in cortex may have tens of thousands of synaptic inputs and may have thousands of synaptic terminals – excitatory activity must not overwhelm the brain. When it does, a person suffers from an epileptic seizure. GABA-secreting neurones keep neural activity in check. A group of minor tranquillizers called benzodiazepines produce their effect on GABA receptors. They do not act as classic false transmitters, since by themselves benzodiazepines can not open GABA channels. Instead, when they engage appropriate receptor sites on a GABA channel they make it easier for GABA itself to open the channel. Diazepam (Valium) and chlordiazepoxide (Librium) are benzodiazepines used to treat anxiety and promote sleep. Clearly nature did not create benzodiazepine receptor sites for the interest of neurochemists: the brain produces natural, or endogenous, anti-anxiety agents that probably allow us to cope with stress.

Figure 5.20 Ways in which drugs facilitate neurotransmitter effects.
Pinel, J., *Biopsychology* (2 ed.) Copyright © 1993 Allyn & Bacon. Reprinted/adapted by permission.

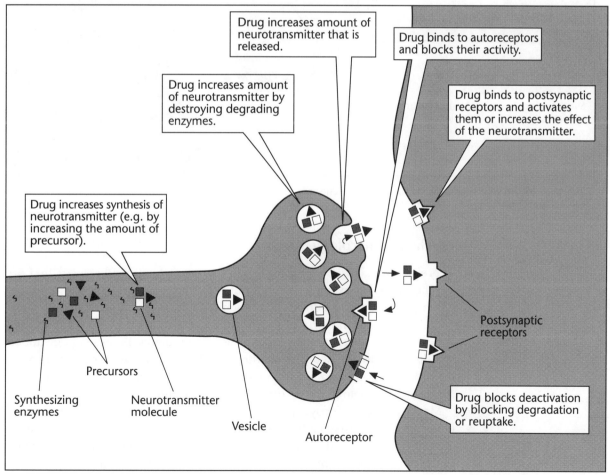

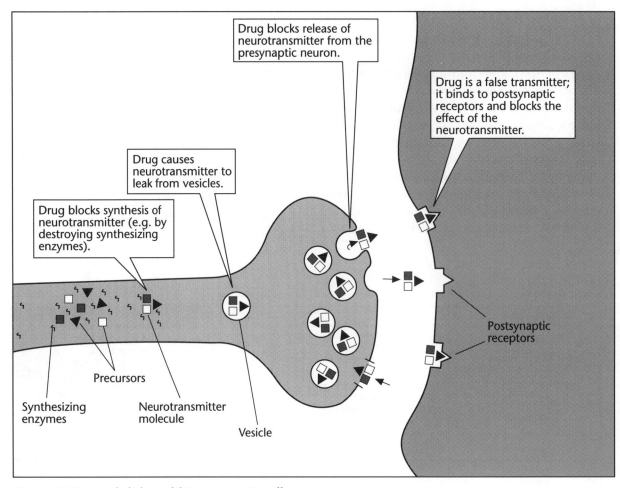

Figure 5.21 Ways in which drugs inhibit neurotransmitter effects.
Pinel, J., *Biopsychology* (2 ed.) Copyright © 1993 Allyn & Bacon. Reprinted/adapted by permission.

Psychopharmacology

There is a long history of people self-medicating with substances that are psychoactive. For example, alcohol not only makes us feel happy and relaxed when taken in modest doses, it can help people sleep and it relieves anxiety. Nicotine taken in the form of snuff or tobacco also helps people to relax; and coffee and tea, which contain caffeine, act as stimulants. Because of our understanding of how the neurotransmitters work it is possible to explain these effects. But more importantly we now have a principled approach to developing drugs that will help in the treatment of brain disorders.

Many, but not all, psychoactive drugs act on the synapse. Those that do, either facilitate postsynaptic events or they inhibit them. Drugs that facilitate are called AGONISTS, and those that block are ANTAGONISTS. There are various stages in the synaptic operation that can be influenced by these drugs.

AGONISTS

ANTAGONISTS

174

Availability of transmitter

One way of modifying synaptic events is to alter the availability of neurotransmitter substance within the synapse. If a drug increases the availability of a transmitter, then the drug is acting as an agonist; but if it reduces the amount of transmitter, then it is an antagonist. An example of the former situation is a substance called L-Dopa. This has significantly improved the condition of many patients suffering from Parkinson's disease. As noted earlier, there is reduced dopamine activity in the brains of these patients, and L-Dopa increases the level of dopamine. The reason is that L-Dopa is an intermediate compound in the synthesis of dopamine from the precursor substance tyrosine: Tyrosine–L-Dopa–Dopamine.

Thus patients receiving L-Dopa can synthesize more dopamine and this helps to overcome the symptoms. Why does the patient need to be treated with L-Dopa instead of tyrosine, which is readily available in the diet? The answer is that the enzyme that converts tyrosine to L-Dopa is incapable of producing more of this substance.

Another type of drug that increases the amount of neurotransmitter is the monoamine oxidase inhibitor (e.g. iproniazid). These drugs prevent the monoamine oxidase enzyme from destroying noradrenaline and serotonin within synaptic boutons, so there are more of these neurotransmitters to be contained in the synaptic vesicles. Patients take monoamine oxidase inhibitors as a treatment for severe depression.

Drugs that affect transmitter release and uptake

Facilitation of a transmitter's action would occur if a drug increased the release of the transmitter from the presynaptic membrane. Amphetamine has this effect on all catecholamine synapses, although it is more effective on noradrenergic neurones.

The opposite effect is demonstrated by botulinum toxin, produced by bacteria that grow in badly preserved food. This substance prevents the release of acetylcholine. Although the effects on the central nervous system of cholinergic blockade are profound, it also causes paralysis in skeletal muscles (acetylcholine acts at the neuromuscular junction). Breathing is dependent on such muscles so the effects can be fatal.

The illegal recreational drug cocaine is another agonist that acts within the synaptic gap. It retards the uptake of dopamine and noradrenaline by presynaptic boutons and consequently increases transmitter activity. Amphetamine has similar effects. Since both these are addictive drugs, and both are abused, the implication is that the monoamine transmitters are involved in brain reward mechanisms.

Receptor sites

A commonly used analogy for the relationship between a neurotransmitter and its receptor protein on the postsynaptic membrane is that of a key and a lock. The transmitter molecule has a three-dimensional shape that is able to fit into a site on the receptor molecule. When this occurs the receptor protein undergoes a change in shape that directly or indirectly opens an ion channel. Drugs can be made that are similar in shape to neurotransmitter molecules and these can act as false transmitters.

If the drug accurately mimics the true transmitter to open the ion channel it will be an agonist, since it facilitates the action of that neurotransmitter substance. Apomorphine is a dopamine agonist that acts in this way, but it is not used clinically to treat neurological disorders because it has unwelcome side-effects.

When a false transmitter molecule is able to couple with a receptor site, but not accurately enough to activate it, then it will behave as an antagonist. The reason is that this prior occupancy of the receptor site will block access for the real neurotransmitter. There are numerous examples of drugs that behave in this way, but a noteworthy one is chlorpromazine (Largactil) which is a dopamine antagonist that revolutionized the treatment of schizophrenia.

Synaptic changes and learning

Although we would like to know what happens in the brain when learning takes place, there is no simple answer – learning involves several levels of activity in the brain. However, a promising area of research is on the specific changes that take place in neurones during learning. Many studies have shown that a temporal lobe structure, the hippocampus, is involved in memory and learning (Squires 1992). The hippocampus is rich in neurones that use the neurotransmitter glutamate. There are at least three types of glutamate receptor that are named after drugs that stimulate them ('quisqualate receptor' after quisqualic acid, 'kainic receptor' after kainic acid, and 'NMDA' receptor after N-methyl-D-aspartate). The NMDA receptor has been of particular interest because of its role in the synaptic changes that may be responsible for learning in mammalian brains.

A fundamental type of learning involves the formation of a functional connection or association between stimuli. This is the basis of classical conditioning, for example; what is learned here is the association between a previously neutral stimulus like a tone and another stimulus like food. Initially the tone has no influence on behaviour, but after several pairings of the tone and food it does. After learning, the first stimulus develops predictive power so that salivation, the response to food, also occurs in response to the tone. If the two stimuli are represented in the brain by two distinct areas of neural activity then learning (association) could be a strengthening in the pathway between these two areas.

The neurones of the hippocampus have a plastic capability of the kind that

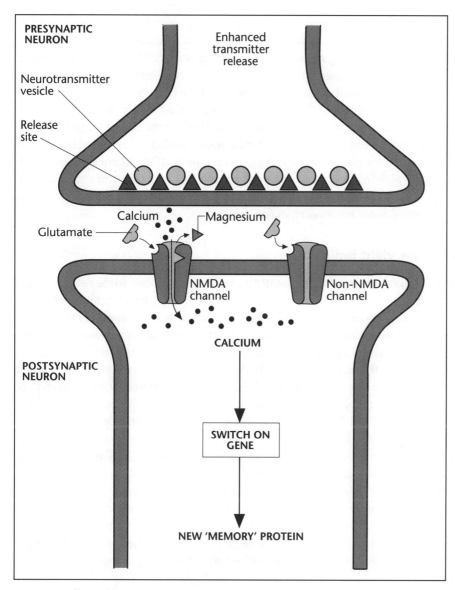

Figure 5.22 Effects of learning at a synapse. When some cells in brain areas like the hippocampus are strongly stimulated, so-called NMDA receptor sites are activated on the postsynaptic membrane. NMDA receptors have to be triggered by an electrical change *and* by the transmitter glutamate. The electrical change occurs when the postsynaptic cell is partly depolarized because non-NMDA channels allow sodium ions into the cell. The electrical effect removes magnesium ions which block the NMDA channels, so when glutamate binds to the receptor site the channel opens to let calcium enter the cell. Calcium indirectly causes a permanent change in the neurone by activating a gene site in the cell's nucleus.
Scientific American, Sept. 1992, p. 82, 'The Biological Basis of Learning and Individuality', Kandel, E. R. and Hawkins, R. D. authors, courtesy Ian Worpole/Scientific American 1992.

would be required for learning. Thus they can increase their responsiveness to a specific stimulus after this stimulus is paired with a different stimulus that consistently causes a strong response. This pairing is crucial in the development of the association. The associative mechanism involves NMDA receptors. These exist on the postsynaptic membrane, but they behave differently to the receptor channels so far discussed. They are voltage-gated as well as being chemically gated. Thus they will only open if glutamate binds to the receptor site when the postsynaptic membrane is already depolarized. In effect there must be convergent inputs on the postsynaptic cell to activate the NMDA channels. These channels allow calcium ions to enter the postsynaptic cell, and this produces structural changes (possibly increasing the number of non-NMDA glutamate channels) to make the cell more responsive in future.

Left brain, right brain

One aspect of the brain that frequently puzzles the newcomer to the neurosciences is its duplicate nature. Virtually all parts of the brain have a left and right component, including, most obviously, the cerebral cortices (cerebral hemispheres). For basic sensory and motor functions the two cerebral hemispheres are symmetric, in that each hemisphere processes sensory information from, or controls the muscles of, the other side of the body. However, this symmetry is lost when the association areas of the two hemispheres are considered, so we find in people that one hemisphere is dominant for language and the other hemisphere becomes specialized for non-verbal, visuo-spatial information processing.

Paul Broca (1861) and others in the nineteenth century recognized that people who suffer from left-hemisphere brain damage are more likely to show speech impairments (aphasias) than those with right brain damage. In the early 1900s a second aspect of lateralization was discovered by Leipmann. He found that apraxia, like aphasia, is almost always associated with left-hemisphere damage, despite its symptoms being bilateral (involving both sides of the body). Apraxic patients have difficulty carrying out movements when asked to do so, although they often can perform the movement when not thinking about what they are doing.

With this evidence that the left hemisphere plays a special role in language and voluntary movements, it is not surprising that people developed the idea of cerebral dominance. This view assumes that one hemisphere – usually the left – has a dominant role in the control of all complex behavioural and cognitive processes, and the other hemisphere has a minor role.

This concept of left-hemisphere dominance still pervades psychology, despite mounting evidence that the right hemisphere has special intellectual functions as well. The Russian psychologist Alexander Luria (1966) reported that people with right-hemisphere damage (mostly from war injuries) often have difficulty with tasks like reading maps, drawing geometric shapes, or recognizing faces. Brenda Milner (1974) and her colleagues in Montreal reported that patients with partial right-hemisphere surgical destruction had specific problems in recognizing or remembering pictures.

In the 1960s Roger Sperry and Michael Gazzaniga began to study people who had undergone a last resort treatment (pioneered by the neurosurgeons, Vogel and Bogen) for epilepsy in which the corpus callosum was entirely cut. These people are often referred to as having split brains, although this is not strictly true. Casual post-operative observation of these patients showed no marked effects, except that their epilepsy was eliminated or markedly reduced. These people showed no loss in measured IQ, ability to converse, or even in coordinating the two halves of their body in performing skilled tasks. Thus far Karl Lashley's jocular surmise that the corpus callosum's purpose 'must be mainly mechanical . . . i.e., to keep the hemispheres from sagging' seemed apt. But, Sperry and Gazzaniga, who were asked to evaluate the neuropsychological status of split-brain patients, showed that under special test conditions, where information was presented to just one hemisphere, these people behaved as if they had two separate minds with different abilities.

The foundation for the studies done on split-brain patients lies in the crossed sensory and motor connections of the brain. Thus the right hemisphere exerts motor control of the left half of the body, and similarly the right somatosensory areas receive sensory information from the left half of the body, and the reverse is true of the left hemisphere. For the visual system the situation is slightly more complicated (see figure 5.23 for an explanation), but just remember that information from the left visual field – the left-hand half of a person's field of view – goes first to the right hemisphere, and information from the right visual field goes to the left hemisphere. Providing a split-brain patient is presented with a picture or word in just one visual field, then this information will go to only one hemisphere. This of course means that the image must be flashed briefly in the appropriate visual field, otherwise the person could move her gaze to see the picture in the other visual field as well. Testing of these patients used the apparatus shown in figure 5.24. They were tested by presenting visual information in one hemisphere, or receiving tactile information in a single hemisphere by feeling an object with the opposite hand. The subjects could be asked to respond verbally or else to point to an object.

Not surprisingly these patients showed speech-dominant hemisphere effects. When shown common objects in the right visual field (to the left hemisphere) they described the objects as well as normal

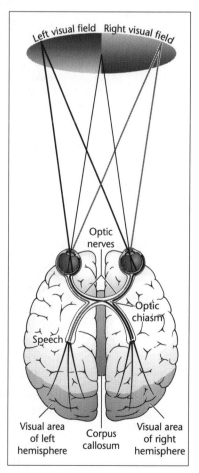

Figure 5.23 Visual input paths to each hemisphere in split-brain patients. Information in the left visual field goes only to the right half of the brain, and vice versa, because of the way axons in the optic nerve partly cross at the optic chiasm. Providing the visual information is presented briefly (about 150 msec) to one visual field, the person cannot change their gaze in time to receive the image in the other visual field.
Gray, P., *Psychology* (2 ed.) (Worth Publishers, New York, 1994. Reprinted with permission).

Figure 5.24 Testing arrangement used for split-brain subjects. Images can be presented briefly to either visual field using this apparatus. The person is asked to verbally identify the image or else to choose an unseen object, that matches the image, with one hand.
Gray, P., *Psychology* (2 ed.) (Worth Publishers, New York, 1994. Reprinted with permission).

people, but if shown an object in the left field (right hemisphere) they denied seeing anything or else made a guess. However, if the same subject was asked to feel the objects under the barrier with the left hand, then they reliably identified the object they had just denied seeing. Thus the left and right hemispheres were in disagreement.

A few split-brain patients show no spoken speech comprehension in the non-speech dominant hemisphere – they cannot perform the tasks just discussed since this hemisphere cannot understand the basic experimental instructions. Others have good understanding in this hemisphere – for instance, their non-dominant hemisphere can understand many written words, particularly concrete nouns, as well as spoken ones. This even extends to simple adjectives, so if presented with the written word 'sharp' in their right hemisphere they would be able to pick out with their left hand a sharp object like a knife or pencil from an unseen set of objects.

The right hemisphere does not have the verbal ability of the left but has it any special abilities? The evidence from these split-brain patients is that it has superior spatial abilities, thus these patients can solve spatial puzzles or draw geometric diagrams better with their left hand than their right.

There are many other issues regarding the split-brain procedure that are beyond the scope of this text. However, you may be wondering how a person lives with two apparently separate cerebral hemispheres in their head. Are the two ever in conflict, and how can coordinated actions take place? There is anecdotal evidence that conflict can occur but that the left hemisphere usually wins. For instance, one man described how while dressing in the morning his right hand was pulling his trousers on while his left hand was pulling them off (Gazzaniga 1970). Maybe the right hemisphere wanted to go back to bed? There is probably a lot of cross-cueing going on between the two hemispheres, with one hemisphere observing the behaviour that the other produces. For example, the left hemisphere may be able to report an emotional state (like sadness or anger) felt by the right because the latter has perceived something unpleasant and this has led to a frown.

Neuroscience and Mental Disorders

Because of the advances that have been made over several decades of neuroscience research there is now a better understanding of serious mental disorders. This research has usually been accompanied by improvements in patient treatment, but unfortunately, as in the case of Alzheimer's disease, this has not always been true. The mental disorders that have benefited from a neuroscience perspective include depression, manias, psychosomatic illnesses, anxiety disorders, sexual disorders, schizophrenia and dementia.

However, we shall only consider schizophrenia, depression and dementia.

Schizophrenia

Schizophrenics suffer from a disturbance in the form (but not the content) of their thoughts. It is common to find that they have disturbed speech, so they make grammatical errors and invent words, and their speech can deteriorate to the point where they are incoherent. Delusions can occur, so they might believe that thoughts are being inserted into their minds by some outside agency, or alternatively that their thoughts are being stolen. Their perception can be disturbed so that they hallucinate, and these hallucinations are more often auditory than visual. Some schizophrenics also make inappropriate responses to emotional events, such as failing to respond sadly or happily to events where these would be natural responses.

Although schizophrenia can occur at almost any age it is most frequently first seen in adolescence or early adulthood.

Many subcategories of schizophrenia can be found, but it is doubtful whether these divisions are of any theoretical value. Recently schizophrenics have been placed in one of two groups, 'reactive' and 'process' schizophrenia. The former can be considered an acute type of illness – like suffering from chickenpox, for instance – and the latter is a chronic (continuing) form of disorder.

Heritability and schizophrenia

A question that is frequently posed is whether a hereditary factor disposes a person to become schizophrenic. Although the evidence is not conclusive, there is a strong probability that this is so. Reviews of family studies show that other members of the family of a schizophrenic are more likely to suffer from the disorder than would be expected by chance. The incidence of schizophrenia in the population is about 1 per cent. But 5 per cent of the parents, 10 per cent of the siblings, and 14 per cent of the children of a schizophrenic are likely also to be sufferers.

Twin studies (examining differences and similarities in people who are twins) are often used when we wish to see whether genetic factors are involved in some characteristic. Several twin studies have been carried out on schizophrenics since 1930, and these show that the concordance ratio – the likelihood of one person having a particular characteristic when another person does – for non-identical (dizygotic) twins is between 10 and 15 per cent. The concordance ratio for identical (monozygotic) twins is about 50 to 60 per cent. Although these figures show that genetic transmission is likely to be involved in schizophrenia, the illness is not going to be caused just because of a genetic defect.

There have also been studies on the incidence of schizophrenia in the biological relatives and the adopting families of adoptees who develop schizophrenia (e.g. Kety et al. 1975). These studies are done to attempt to 'eliminate' the common environmental effects that are a problem with the family and twin studies. The conclusion we can draw from these studies is that schizophrenia is more likely to be seen in the biological relatives than in the adopting families. Therefore it is unlikely that it is the shared family environment that disposes members of the same family to develop schizophrenia.

There have been recent attempts to locate a 'schizophrenia gene'. Although there is some evidence favouring a defective gene on chromosome 5, a second candidate seems more likely: this is a gene on the X chromosome – which is of course one of the sex chromosomes, but since it is present in both men and women the expected frequency of schizophrenia is equal. But there is evidence (from Crow et al. 1989) that when there is paternal history of schizophrenia then schizophrenia is more likely to occur in children of the same sex. The genetic mechanisms that help explain this are complicated.

Physical changes in the brains of schizophrenics

It has been suggested that schizophrenia arises from a biochemical disorder in the brain. This disorder causes a toxic chemical to be produced, and this toxin creates the aberrant behaviour. An alternative possibility is that irregularities occur in the communication between specific nerve cells in the brains of schizophrenics so that these cells respond too readily to their neurotransmitter. This latter position is the favoured theory at present, at least for the reactive form of schizophrenia. I will elaborate the theory a little in discussing the treatment of schizophrenia.

Treatment for schizophrenia

During the 1950s the treatment of schizophrenia was revolutionized with the discovery of effective anti-schizophrenic drugs (these are often called neuroleptics). Chlorpromazine, which was mentioned in the discussion of dopamine antagonists, became the drug of choice. It belongs to a group of compounds called phenothiazines, and it, and the other neuroleptics, seems to work in schizophrenics because it blocks the action of the catecholamine neurotransmitters (noradrenaline and dopamine). This prevents the real transmitter from activating the recipient nerve cell; thus it seems that there may be too many neurotransmitter receptors or too much transmitter (of the catecholamine types) in the brains of schizophrenics. Additional evidence shows that dopamine is the catecholamine transmitter that is involved in schizophrenia. This includes the finding, based on post-mortem evidence, that there are more dopamine autoreceptors in the brains of some schizophrenics.

Two types of schizophrenia

Crow has for several years argued that there are two types of schizophrenia that seem to map on to the acute–chronic distinction made earlier. Type I schizophrenics are those with positive symptoms (for example, hallucinations and delusion). They respond well to treatment with neuroleptic drugs. The Type II schizophrenics have mainly negative symptoms (delusions, flattened emotions, poverty of speech, thought disorders and loss of drive). They are chronically hospitalized, they do not respond to drug treatment, and their prognosis is poor. About 30 per cent of schizophrenics are of the Type II variety. Until the first decades of this century, schizophrenia was known as dementia praecox (implying that the sufferer had cognitive impairments arising from neurological damage), so it is interesting to find the Type II form of the disorder is associated with brain damage.

Since Crow first put forward his theory there has been substantial evidence that a sub-population of schizophrenics have brain damage. This is not damage at the microscopic level as occurs in Type I schizophrenia, but damage on a scale that can be measured using brain-imaging techniques. The use of CT scans and MRI has enabled us to obtain information on the size of the ventricles in the brains of schizophrenics. These are larger than the ventricles found in control subjects who suffer from other psychiatric disorders, or those found in the brains of close relatives. If the ventricles are enlarged then there must be less brain tissue. Additional evidence that supports the argument that Type II schizophrenics have neurological damage is that they show symptoms that neurologists look for as indicants of brain damage. These signs include catatonia, high or low rates of blinking, deviation of eyes accompanied by speech arrest, bursts of jerky eye movements, and poor visual pursuit.

Although there is now sound neuroscientific evidence on what happens to the brains of schizophrenics, we still do not know what causes it. Many biologically based theories have been suggested. These include the possibility that it arises from a viral infection, since some schizophrenics have antibodies in their

Box 5.3   Imaging the Living Brain

Non-invasive techniques for obtaining pictures of the living brain have been developed recently. Some of these are improvements on older techniques such as the traditional X-ray, but aided by computer technology; others are novel. Computerized axial tomography (also called the CT scan or CAT scan) was the first of this new crop of imaging methods. Traditional X-rays of the brain cannot show any differences (contrasts) between different parts. One way of overcoming this problem is to increase the contrast by removing the cerebro-spinal fluid and replacing it with air – a painful and sometimes dangerous procedure – or by injecting a dye into the blood. CT scans have overtaken these practices. The patient's head is placed in the scanner, a large drum, and an X-ray beam is passed through the head and recorded by a detector on the opposite side. The beam is then rotated by one degree and the procedure is repeated. One hundred and eighty measurements are taken and the information is then processed by a computer to generate an image of a horizontal section through the brain. CT scans are in routine use in hospitals, but have also been used to research areas such as Alzheimer's disease and mental disorders.

Magnetic resonance imaging (MRI) is likely to supplant CT scans of the brain because of the superb images of the brain (and other parts of the body) that it produces. Also, unlike CT scans, alternative views of the brain, such as sagittal and coronal sections, can be provided. MRI uses the fact that atoms with an odd atomic weight (such as hydrogen) have an inherent rotation. A powerful magnetic field aligns the axes of rotation of these atoms. The body is then exposed to a radio frequency wave. When this is switched off, the atoms emit radio waves of their own. The MRI scanner measures these waves to produce an image.

Until recently the only way to obtain information on

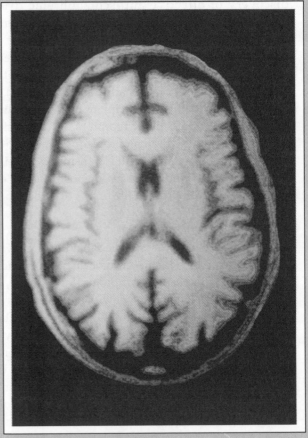

Plate 5.1 MRI scan of a normal brain
Source: Science Photo Library/Scott Camazine.

the dynamic activity within the brain was to record electrical activity from electrodes attached to the scalp. The electroencephalograph (EEG) records such activity and has been used to study brain activity during sleep and wakeful processes. A problem with the EEG is that it is not possible to obtain a picture of what brain areas might

cerebro-spinal fluid that indicate that they previously suffered from a viral infection of the brain (Torrey 1991). A related suggestion is that schizophrenia is a consequence of a viral infection that damages a developing foetus. This is supported by the finding that Finnish children whose mothers were pregnant during an outbreak of the Type A2 influenza virus in 1957 are more likely to suffer from schizophrenia. Moreover, the incidence of schizophrenia is higher in the children of those mothers who were in the second trimester of pregnancy. As

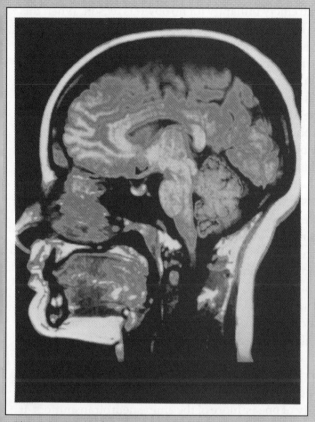

Plate 5.2 NMR (nuclear magnetic resonance) scan of an adult brain. Source: Science Photo Library/Petit Format.

ranged around the head measures radioactivity in different cerebral regions. A computer is then used to display an image reporting the relative amount of blood flowing to different parts of the brain. The rCBF method has been used to measure brain activity when people perform tasks like solving problems or listening to music (Andreasen 1988). Schizophrenic patients have been compared with normal subjects when solving problems (Berman et al. 1986). There were differences in the activity in the frontal cortex in the two groups during the task.

Positron-emission tomography (PET) is an alternative method for obtaining high-resolution images of brain activity. It uses the fact that when certain radioactive elements decay they emit an antimatter particle called a positron. This has the same mass as an electron but an opposite charge. When a positron collides with an electron they emit two gamma rays in exactly the opposite directions. The person who is being investigated receives an injection of glucose, or another chemical, such as a drug that binds to a specific neurotransmitter receptor site. These will be radioactively labelled. The person's head is then placed in the scanner. This contains a set of gamma-ray detectors that record the annihilation of proton-electron pairs. The location of the collision will be at a point half way between the two detectors. A computer calculates a map of relative positron activity and draws an image of the brain to reflect this. PET scans are used to diagnose brain disorders. They have also been used to trace how different parts of the brain become active during the first weeks and months of life. Chugani and Phelps (1986) found that the thalamus and brain stem were active by five weeks of age, whereas cerebral cortex and cerebellar cortex were relatively inactive at this age, but were more mature by three months.

be functioning during specific psychological activities. When an area of the brain becomes active it needs more nutrients and therefore its blood supply increases. Regional cerebral blood flow (rCBF) can be measured by having a person breathe air mixed with the radioactive isotope of the inert gas xenon. An array of sensors ar-

the brain undergoes major development during this phase of pregnancy, an infection that affects CNS development would be damaging at this time.

Mood disorders

These are sometimes called 'affective disorders' – the noun 'affect' refers to emotions or feelings. It is natural for each of us to be unhappy or to develop the 'blues' when sad events occur in our lives. When this unhappiness is severe it is called reactive depression because it occurs as a reaction to life events. However, some people become extremely unhappy for no obvious reason. When this unhappiness is accompanied by other symptoms such as feelings of apathy, lack of pleasure, disturbed sleep, self-reproach and suicidal tendencies, then the person has endogenous depression – implying the disorder is an inherent characteristic of the afflicted person.

There are two types of this severe form of depression. When the person only has depressive symptoms the disorder is called UNIPOLAR DEPRESSION. The lifetime incidence for this illness is about 6 per cent. It tends to first occur towards early middle age, and is twice as common in women than men.

UNIPOLAR DEPRESSION

The second type is called BIPOLAR DEPRESSION, or manic depression. This is so named because the sufferer alternates between periods of depression and mania. The symptoms of depression are as discussed above, but in the manic phase the individual is irritable, overactive, has grandiose ideas and plans, and shows extreme recklessness. Bipolar depression has an incidence of about 1 per cent, first occurs in late adolescence or early adult life, and is equally common in both sexes. People who suffer from either form of depression are likely to have recurrent episodes of disorder.

BIPOLAR DEPRESSION

Both these disorders probably have a biological basis. This hypothesis is based on evidence, in adoption and twin studies, for a hereditary factor, as well as evidence from the forms of effective treatment for the disorders – the only reliable and effective treatments are drugs or ECT (electro-convulsive therapy).

Although several explanations have been proposed for the endogenous depression, the favoured ones suggest that a person suffering either form of depression has an abnormality of one or more of the amine neurotransmitters. It was originally argued that there was under-activity in the brain mechanisms that involve amine transmitters (noradrenaline, serotonin, or even dopamine); this was proposed by Schildkraut and Kety, and Sulser. They reasoned that the drugs that are successful in the treatment of depression increase the effective levels of amine transmitters – they are agonists. These drugs belong to two groups, the monoamine oxidase inhibitors (MAOIs) and the tricyclics that are so called because the molecular structure of the drugs contains three rings. The MAOIs, such as iproniazid, phenelzine and tranylcypromine, prevent the destruction of the transmitter substance (see the previous section on psychopharmacology) and thus increase its availability; whereas the tricyclics (desipramine, imipramine and clomipramine are examples) block the mechanism that takes up the transmitter from the synaptic gap.

Although the MAOIs were originally popular they lost out to the tricyclics because clinical trials showed they were of limited value in severe depressive illness, and they have a side effect that has been named the 'cheese reaction'. This occurs because the monoamine oxidase enzyme is also present in the gut and liver. Here it destroys tyramine – a substance similar to the catecholamines – that is found in foods such as cheese, chocolate, wine and yeast extract (Marmite). If tyramine is present in too high a concentration it causes increased sympathetic nervous system activity. This can raise blood pressure and heart rate enough to produce intracranial bleeding or cardiovascular collapse.

The tricyclics are the most popular antidepressants. They are used to treat depression as well as to prevent relapse. The original tricyclics were considerably more potent in their effects on the catecholamine neurotransmitter, noradrenaline, and the indoleamine, serotonin (5-HT). Thus these two neurotransmitters have been viewed as the likely source of the transmitter problem in depression. In summary, this original view of the transmitter involvement in depression can be typified as the 'too little' hypothesis. But there is a problem for this position. Depressive patients taking one of the original MAOIs or tricyclic antidepressants had to wait weeks before their symptoms improved. Since the drugs should have had an immediate effect in facilitating the neurotransmitter action, something is amiss for the 'too little' theory.

Clearly these antidepressant drugs are acting differently in depressed patients than the original theory proposed. It is now thought depression may be a consequence of over-activity in these same neurotransmitter systems (Sulser & Sanders-Bush 1989). The reasoning here is that the long-term effect of a drug that acts on a synaptic system is unlikely to be the same as the immediate effect. Neurones are dynamic systems that have in-built regulatory processes that attempt to compensate for the effects of substances that interfere with normal neuronal functioning, and antidepressants seem to decrease, or 'down-regulate', the activity at monoamine synapses when administered on a long-term basis. The mechanisms that are involved in explaining the sustained effects of antidepressants are beyond the scope of this text. To conclude briefly, depression is now thought to arise from 'too much' instead of 'too little' transmitter.

One of the physical treatments for serious depression has gained some notoriety. This is electro-convulsive therapy (ECT), in which an electric current is applied to the brain of a patient to induce a convulsion. It is normally administered 6 to 12 times in a treatment lasting 1 to 2 weeks. Despite the obvious ethical problems with ECT, it may be the only way of treating depressed patients with psychotic symptoms (Paykel 1992). Such patients do not respond to drugs, and ECT has been shown in clinical trials to be an effective treatment in these cases. It is also superior to drugs in the severely depressed. Since ECT works more rapidly than the tricyclics it provides faster management of patients with suicidal tendencies. How ECT works is not known. It may act by altering the levels of amine transmitters in parts of the brain that control emotion.

The treatment of bipolar depression is a surprise – it is lithium. This is a common substance that belongs to the same chemical group as sodium and potassium. It is effective in the control of acute mania, and acts as a prophylactic against bipolar depression. Thus it stabilizes mood, and acts as a preventative against unipolar recurrent depressions. Like the other treatments of affective disorders, it has a slow onset. Patients who are treated with lithium carbonate need to be closely monitored as toxic effects can arise with doses of about one and a half times the clinically effective dose. It is not understood how lithium works. It may even be that its antimanic effects come about through a different mechanism to the antidepressant effects. Recent evidence indicates that it may inhibit a special class of ion channels in the postsynaptic membrane. As yet there is no clue as to what neurotransmitters may be involved.

▓ Hormones and Behaviour ▓

It would be wrong to think that the only biological processes that are important to understanding mind and behaviour involve the nervous system. There are endocrine or hormonal mechanisms that also affect behaviour. Hormones (chemical messengers) are produced by glands that secrete their contents into the blood supply, which then distributes the chemicals to all parts of the body. An advantage of this mechanism is that a hormone can have an effect on the whole of a large structure as well as being able to influence several target organs at once.

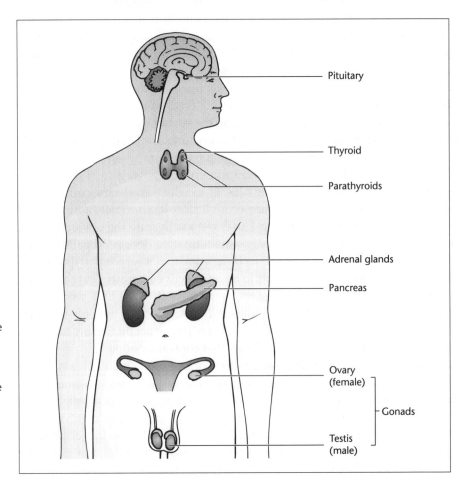

Figure 5.25 Location of some of the main endocrine glands. Some of the glands that secrete hormones into the blood supply are shown. Many of these glands are controlled by the pituitary gland that is in turn controlled by the hypothalamus.
Gray, P., *Psychology* (2 ed.) (Worth Publishers, New York, 1994. Reprinted with permission).

Hormone systems often act in combination with the nervous system. An example of this is found in the way that we respond to and cope with stress. The hormonal and nervous system responses have evolved to provide an immediate reaction to threat or danger (obvious stressors) and an intermediate response mechanism that backs up the initial coping response. In addition, there is a longer-term mechanism that deals with prolonged stress.

In an earlier section the autonomic nervous system was described, and it was pointed out that the sympathetic component of the ANS prepares the body for 'fight or flight' activities. Thus if a person is confronted with a dangerous situation, such as being in the path of a fast-approaching car or being threatened by an aggressive drunk, the sympathetic system increases heart rate and blood pressure, and switches the blood supply from the gut to the skeletal muscles. A further response also occurs, but has a slightly delayed effect because it involves the adrenal glands. These are located just above the kidneys and have two parts, an outer region called the adrenal cortex and an inner part named the adrenal medulla. The adrenal medulla resembles a sympathetic nervous system ganglion. It receives an acetylcholinergic input but it secretes two hormones, adrenaline and noradrenaline (both are catecholamines). These promote the release of glucose that is stored in muscle and liver as glycogen, as well as mimicking other effects of sympathetic activity. A common after-effect of this emergency response is that people feel their heart beating rapidly, as well as perspiring and feeling flushed.

The sympathetic response is evoked to deal with emergencies, but people are also confronted with prolonged or chronic stress. This can be in anticipation of some dreaded future event like an examination, or after an emergency that might be brief but shocking, such as witnessing a terrible accident. Post-traumatic stress disorder is now a recognized condition, and psychological counselling is available for people who suffer from this ailment. Possibly this counselling helps by modifying the chronic stress response – an example of a mind–body interaction effect. The psychophysiological mechanisms that allow people to cope with chronic stress involve the hormones produced by the cortex of the adrenal glands. Figure 5.27 shows pathways that determine the release of adrenal cortex hormones. The hypothalamus sends corticotrophin-releasing factor (a peptide) to the anterior pituitary gland. This then releases adrenocorticotrophic hormone (ACTH) into the blood supply, which conveys it to the adrenal cortex, which then releases hormones into the general circulation. The adrenal cortex produces several steroid hormones, but in response to stress the glucocorticoids (like cortisol) dominate. These help to release energy from bodily reserves to sustain the activity that helps cope with prolonged stressful events. However, this can be counter-productive, since in some emergencies people with elevated cortisol secretion are withdrawn and inactive for much of the time. Moreover, the extra energy of this coping response is provided at the expense of decreased immune system activity. When people experience stress over weeks or months they become vulnerable to various illnesses including cancer (Sklar & Anisman 1981).

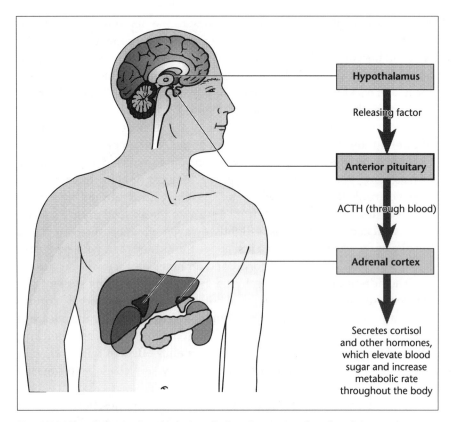

Figure 5.26 The pituitary–adrenal axis. Long lasting stress causes the adrenals to secrete cortisols that mobilize energy reserves as part of a coping response. The hypothalamus monitors the amount of circulating cortisol in a feed-back loop.
From *Biological Psychology*, by J. W. Kalat. Copyright © 1995, 1992, 1988, 1984, 1981 International Thomson Publishing Inc. By permission of Brooks/Cole Publishing Company, Pacific Grove, CA 93950.

Another area that shows how important hormones are to us is that of sexual behaviour. There are several classes of sex hormone, but we will consider only the sex steroids produced by the gonads (testes and ovaries). The oestrogens are more abundant in females while the androgens are more abundant in males. These hormones have two roles: one is to determine body structure both in the mature individual and during a critical period in development, and the other is to activate and influence behaviour.

Human beings have 23 pairs of chromosomes in their cells. Twenty-two of these are identical in women and men – the so-called autosomes. The other pair are the sex chromosomes, which are named X and Y. Women contain two X chromosomes and men have a Y to accompany a single X. Although the autosomes carry genes that control the development of male or female characteristics, these genes are sex-limited. This means their expression is dependent on the gene being activated by a sex hormone. For example, oestrogen activates the gene responsible for breast development in women, while beard growth is dependent on the presence of androgens.

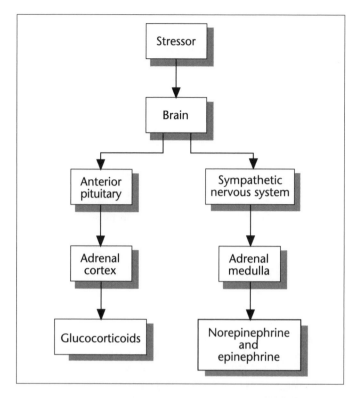

Figure 5.27 A two-part stress response. A short- to medium-term response to stress mediated by the sympathetic nervous system and the adrenal medulla hormones, adrenaline and noradrenaline. The coping response to prolonged stress involves the adrenal cortex.

Pinel, J., *Biopsychology* (2 ed.) Copyright © 1993 Allyn & Bacon. Reprinted/adapted by permission.

The embryo can develop either type of gonad, but when it contains a Y chromosome the primordial genital structure becomes a testis, while in its absence it forms an ovary, a phenomenon that has profound implications. Basically mammalian embryonic and foetal development produces structures that are characteristic of females, and metaphorically speaking the male fights to emerge. To achieve this the testis secretes androgens (developing ovaries are quiescent). One effect of the androgens is to cause the external genital structures to turn into typical male genitalia (with a scrotal sack and penis), instead of the labia of female genitals.

There are anomalous individuals who are insensitive to androgens. They have male chromosomes and develop testes (carried within the abdomen), but they none the less develop first as girls and then as women because the tissues that should become male genitals fail to respond.

The androgens secreted during development also cause changes within the brain. There are sexually differentiated areas in the brain, including the hypothalamus. The latter region controls copulatory behaviours and also provides the mechanism that ensures that women have menstrual cycles. If exposed to androgens during foetal development these brain areas switch from being characteristically female to programming male responses. These changes in the developing brain take place in about the third and fourth month of pregnancy.

Since the brains of men and women are modestly differentiated during foetal life, does this have any relevance to the development of homosexuality? There is

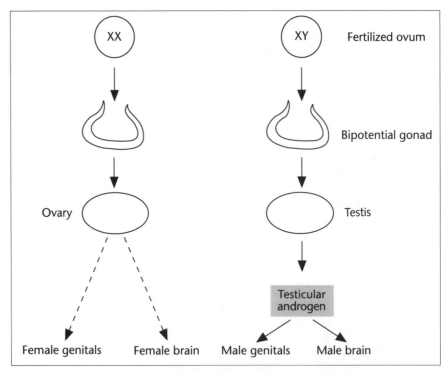

Figure 5.28 Summary of sexual differentiation. Female embryonic and foetal development takes place as a natural course unless the developing baby has a Y sex chromosome. The presence of a Y chromosome causes the bipotential primordial gonad to develop as a testis, that in turn releases androgens (testosterone). These circulate in the developing foetal blood supply to cause male genitals to develop and also to masculinize certain brain areas.

Gray, P., *Psychology* (2 ed.) (Worth Publishers, New York, 1994. Reprinted with permission, courtesy Macmillan College Publishing Co).

no definite conclusion about this, but LeVay (1991) found that one of the sexually differentiated (dimorphic) areas of the hypothalamus (the interstitial nucleus of the anterior hypothalamus) is smaller in homosexual males than in heterosexual males. As you might expect, this and related findings have aroused controversy. Some gays have welcomed a finding that may partly explain diverse sexualities, while others have criticized LeVay for daring to investigate biological factors in homosexuality.

To conclude this section, a controversial question: are there cognitive differences between women and men that come about because of sexual differentiation in neural mechanisms? There is evidence that women show superiority in several areas, including verbal fluency and perceptual and motor tasks, while men are better at spatial tasks and mathematical reasoning (Kimura 1993). It also seems that sex hormones may have some role in producing these differences – possibly by subtly altering neural connections in appropriate parts of the brain during foetal development. It should be noted that the sex differences in these skills are small, and that the distribution of abilities for the two sexes shows almost complete overlap.

CHAPTER SUMMARY

1 Psychological processes are founded on the workings of the brain. Most neuroscientists take the position that mind processes and brain processes have an identity and are like the two faces of a single coin.

2 Neurones (specialized cells of the brain) propagate signals (action potentials) along axons and communicate with each other at synapses by means of chemical messengers (neurotransmitters). Neurones are supported physically and functionally by glial cells.

3 Although there are many flavours of neurotransmitter, they have only two primary effects on recipient cells. These either become more likely to generate their own nerve action potentials or less likely to do so.

4 A functional view of the brain shows that sensory systems have a cortical component (a part of the cerebral hemisphere, such as visual cortex) that is connected to the sensory receptor via a synaptic relay in the thalamus. The motor system also has a cortical region where motor commands may be organized but various subcortical structures help guide movements.

5 There are specialized association areas in the cerebral hemispheres that allow us to talk and listen. Usually these are lateralized in the left hemisphere (speech-dominant), but the non-speech dominant hemisphere of split-brain patients frequently has some language understanding abilities.

6 Psychoactive drugs are classed as agonists (facilitators) or antagonists (blockers) of neurotransmission effects. The modes of action of both classes of drugs can be understood on the basis of how such drugs interact with the machinery for neurotransmitter production, release and regulation at the synapse.

7 There is strong evidence that the two main types of serious mental illness, schizophrenia and depression, occur because of brain dysfunction. In both cases there is supportive genetic evidence. Major advances in drug treatments have provided an insight into the cause and possible cure of these disorders.

8 Hormonal mechanisms and brain mechanisms operate in tandem in regulating many body processes such as in eating, drinking, sex and stress responses. Different hormonal mechanisms provide coping responses for short-term (acute) and long-term (chronic) stress. Sex hormones also sustain short-term and lifelong effects. If a developing foetus contains testes these secrete 'male' sex hormones that switch on specific genes that then cause male genitalia to develop and masculinize certain brain areas. A person's gender identity comes about partly because of their genital appearance and partly through brain organization.

Further Work

1. Does a knowledge of brain anatomy tell us anything about psychological processes and behaviour?
2. How is information transmitted within neurones and between neurones?
3. Because a patient with a specific type of brain damage shows a cognitive impairment, such as a speech or memory loss, is it reasonable to assume that the area that has been damaged supports that specific cognitive function?

4. What neurochemical mechanisms would you need to consider if you were asked to produce a new drug that blocked/facilitated the effect of a specific neurotransmitter?
5. Discuss the evidence that implicates a biological dysfunction as a cause for schizrenia.
6. How does the body respond to stress?
7. Is it reasonable to infer a biological-causal process for a mental disorder from evidence that a particular type of drug is an effective treatment for that disorder?

▨ Further Reading ▨

Carlson, N. R. (1994; 5th edn) *Physiology of Behavior*. Boston: Allyn and Bacon.

> If you read no other neuroscience, you should read Carlson's well balanced introduction – an excellent next step from this chapter.

Diamond, M. C., Scheibel, A. B. and Elson, L. M. (1985) *The Human Brain Coloring Book*. New York: Barnes and Noble.

> This vehicle for looking at the brain works very well and is also a great read.

Julien, R. M. (1995; 7th edn) *A Primer of Drug Action*. New York: Freeman.

> If you want to understand what the chemicals all do, then this is a very thorough primer.

Lickey, M. E. and Gordon, B. G. (1991) *Medicine and Mental Illness*. New York: Freeman.

> This treatment of mental illness from a biological perspective will nicely complement the analysis that you will encounter in chapter 16.

Scientific American Books (1993) *Mind and Brain*. New York: Freeman.

> Possibly not as enjoyable as the colouring book, but full of detailed and full-colour illustrations supporting some very thorough sections.

Spiegel, R. (1996) *Psychopharmacology: An Introduction*, Chichester: John Wiley.

> This is somewhat hard going for an introductory read – but well worth the attempt.

Springer S. and Deutsch, G. (1989; 3rd edn) *Left Brain, Right Brain*. New York: Freeman.

> If you are interested in the left brain/right brain discussion above, and a more thorough treatment of the split-brain studies, then this book will help.

CHAPTER 6
Perception
Mike Harris

▓ Introduction ▓

What is perception for? It seems obvious that, since perception provides our only contact with the external world, its role must be to provide a description of that world. What sort of description is required? It must obviously be reliable, since it provides the basis for all our interactions with the world. It must also go beyond a simple physical description of things and their relationships, for we need to know not just what things are, but what they are likely to do, how they might be useful, or whether they might be dangerous, for example. What is involved in providing such a description? That is what this chapter is about. It deals exclusively with vision and hearing because these are our major senses and provide the richest and most useful description of the world. But the basic approaches and methods described, and the general principles that emerge, apply just as well to touch, taste and smell.

Our conscious impressions suggest that perception is simple and direct. In vision, for example, the eyes seem to be windows through which we effortlessly observe events. But conscious impressions are based on the *results* of perception and provide no insight into the *processes* involved. It turns out that these processes are neither simple nor direct. To understand why, imagine the surface of a small lake, thrown into a complex, ever-changing pattern of waves and ripples by the activity of boats, ducks, rain and wind. Imagine that you cannot see or hear and that you have to locate and identify the objects on the lake by dipping your two index fingers into the water so that you can feel the ripples drifting past. This obviously difficult problem offers an almost exact analogy with hearing. The auditory world is really a more complex, three-dimensional lake, in which the movements of objects cause waves of air pressure, just like the ripples on the lake. Our only contact with these ripples is through a tiny membrane, the ear drum, in each ear. The ear drums act like our index fingers in the analogy, measuring the height of the ripples of air pressure as they arrive at each ear. The important point is that we have no direct contact with the objects in our auditory world, but can only sense their effects upon the auditory 'lake'. Yet we

Plate 6.1 The image as a pattern of ripples. The height of the surface at each point represents the amount of light at that point in a familiar black and white image.
Source: Mike Harris. Analysis performed on a Macintosh 8100/80AV computer using the public domain NIH Image program (developed at the US National Institute of Health and available on the Internet at http://rsb.info.nih.gov/nih-image/)

Plate 6.2 The image on which plate 6.1 is based (detail of Leonardo da Vinci's *Mona Lisa*). The square shows the region depicted in plate.
Source: Giraudon/Musée du Louvre.

locate and identify sound sources reliably and without apparent effort.

Vision, too, provides only indirect contact with external things. Light from the sun and other light sources fills the world, and some of it bounces off objects into our eyes, where it forms a pair of continuously changing images. Because images are familiar in our everyday lives and because they seem an excellent way to represent information, it is easy to believe that vision is somehow simpler and more direct than the analogy for hearing developed above. But this is a mistake, for images are really nothing more than patterns of ripples that seem direct only because our visual systems are very good at making sense of them.

This important point is illustrated by plate 6.1, which shows an image in a form that our visual systems are not designed to interpret. It is simply a map in which the height of the surface represents the total amount of light at each point in the image, rather like the water level in the lake analogy. It provides exactly the same information as plate 6.2, which is the conventional image on which it is based but, by preventing normal visual processing, plate 6.1 reveals the image

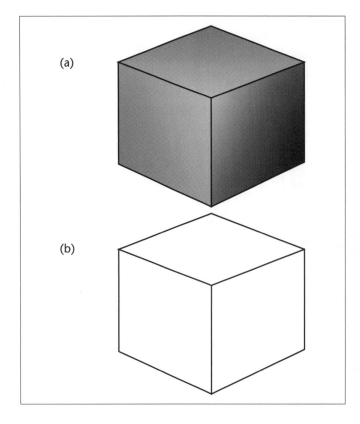

(a)

(b)

Figure 6.1 (a) A greyscale image of a cube. (b) A line drawing of the same cube: the lines represent only the edges of the cube.

for what it really is – a complex physical pattern of ripples.

Not only is an image indirect, it is also incomplete. Suppose we reduced an image like figure 6.1a to a more compact and useful description that someow captured its essential features. Such a process might result in something like figure 6.1b. This pattern is immediately recognizable as a cube – but does it really capture the essence of a cube? Some of the important elements of the cube are certainly present in figure 6.1b; edges of the cube show up as lines, its corners as junctions between lines, and its surfaces as distinct regions. But if we describe the image in its own terms, and then try to translate image features into the corresponding object features, lines into edges and so forth, we do not end up with a description of a cube. A cube consists of 6 square surfaces all joined at right-angled corners, but figure 6.1b contains neither squares nor right angles. An image is incomplete because it does not necessarily convey the characteristics that define the object that produced it.

Approaches to Perception

The stimuli directly available to our senses are not objects themselves but the effects of objects upon some physical medium such as light or air pressure. Our sense organs can measure these effects and, because the effects depend upon the underlying properties of the object, our perceptual systems can use the measurements to recover these underlying properties. An early stage in this process is, no doubt, to reduce the many millions of measurements to a more useful description that emphasizes the informative features of the image: the sort of process that would convert something like figure 6.1a into something like figure 6.1b. But the really fundamental question is whether or not any such description is sufficient to account for everything that we perceive. There are two quite different approaches to this question: the first characterizes perception as a process of active interpretation, the second as a process of passive description.

Perception as interpretation

The first approach, popularized most recently by Richard Gregory (1972), maintains that purely descriptive processes are not sufficient to account for perception. For vision, for example, it argues that, because an image is an incomplete representation of the world, a description of the image can only be the beginning of the perceptual process. Faced with a description like figure 6.1b, containing neither squares nor right angles, the perceiver must actively work out what object could have produced that description. This clearly requires some prior knowledge about cubes and this is thought to be used to build a PERCEPTUAL MODEL of the object that best accounts for the image. According to this approach, we consciously experience the perceptual model rather than the image. Because the role of the image is only to provide information, or CUES, that allow us to choose the appropriate model, this account is commonly termed the in direct approach to perception, emphasizing the tenuous link between the image and the final percept, and viewing the establishment of that link as a form of information processing. This usage of high-level knowledge (about

PERCEPTUAL
MODEL

CUES

Plate 6.3 An ambiguous figure. Salvador Dali, *The Slave Market with the Disappearing Bust of Voltaire*, 1940. Oil on canvas.
Source: Collection of the Salvador Dali Museum, St Petersburg, Florida. Copyright 1997 Salvador Dali Museum Inc.

TOP-DOWN
PROCESSING

objects) to make sense of low-level information (about images) is called TOP-DOWN PROCESSING.

AMBIGUOUS FIGURE

Plate 6.3 conveys something of the flavour of what is meant by a perceptual model and of why such models are thought to be important in perception. This is an example of an AMBIGUOUS FIGURE in which the central region of the picture can be seen either as an arch through which two nuns are walking, or as a bust of Voltaire. What changes here as our perception changes? Certainly the image does not change. According to the indirect approach, the same region of the image provides cues to two different, but equally plausible, models. We see the image as a nun's head or as Voltaire's eye because perception involves the building of a perceptual model, and the model determines our conscious experience.

Perception as description

The second approach maintains that there is no need for perceptual models and that descriptive processes alone are sufficient to account for perception. J. J. Gibson (1966), who developed this view, argued that it is misleading to think of the visual stimulus as providing an incomplete representation of the external world. Rather than considering a single image received by a passive, stationary observer, we should remember that the perceiver can take an active role in controlling the pattern of stimulation, moving round the world and sampling the world from different viewpoints. This means, in terms of the lake analogy, that we should not think of the fragmentary pattern of ripples arriving at a single point in space and time, but rather of the complete pattern of ripples over the whole surface of the lake. Gibson used the term OPTIC ARRAY to refer to the complete

OPTIC ARRAY

OPTIC FLOW

pattern of light available to a stationary observer, and the term OPTIC FLOW to describe the way that this pattern changes smoothly as the observer moves about. He argued that optic flow provides so much information that, in principle, it can account for everything we perceive. Thus, the squareness of a cube's surfaces may not show up simply as squareness in an individual image but it does show up as *something* in the visual input; perhaps, for example, as the characteristic way that the shape of a region in the image changes as we view the cube from different angles. According to Gibson, perception is concerned with the discovery and description of those aspects of the optic array or the optic flow that reliably signal the relevant properties of objects in the world. Such reliable aspects are called INVARIANTS, and the whole process is generally referred to as DIRECT PERCEPTION or, sometimes, ECOLOGICAL PERCEPTION. The directness emphasized here is not between the object and the image (squares do not necessarily show up as squares) but between the image and the percept; because invariants reliably signal object properties they can drive perception directly, without any need for internal perceptual models. The use of low-level information (stimulus invariants) to get at high-level information (the relevant properties of an object) is called BOTTOM-UP PROCESSING, though Gibson himself would not have used this term because he was not at all interested in the internal processes of perception.

INVARIANTS

DIRECT PERCEPTION

ECOLOGICAL
PERCEPTION

BOTTOM-UP
PROCESSING

A combined approach

The direct and indirect approaches are very different and it seems important to decide which is correct. However, although there are strong advocates of each view over the other, most perceptual scientists are content to allow both approaches to coexist. Such a compromise involves an initial Gibson-like descriptive stage providing input to a subsequent interpretive stage. According to this view, Gibson's invariants correspond to very powerful cues, allowing easy access to the appropriate knowledge. Despite the very different philosophies underpinning the two approaches, a compromise seems likely to prove correct in the end because perception is not just a single task but, like a service industry, contributes in many different ways to everyday life. Amongst other things, for example, vision is involved in object recognition, in guiding locomotion, in controlling the fine movements of hands and limbs, and in maintaining balance. Some of these tasks are obviously more difficult than others and its seems likely that some can be accomplished directly, as Gibson maintained, whilst others may require sophisticated internal knowledge and are thus better described by the indirect approach.

▧ Methods ▧

Although the route from the external world to the perceptual world is more complex than our conscious experience suggests, it is none the less much more direct and immediate than in any other area of psychology. Perception can be studied by a variety of routes and, though no one route can provide all the answers, a coherent story has begun to emerge from combination of different techniques.

Neurophysiology and functional anatomy

It is quite possible, using a microelectrode, to record the responses of individual sensory cells and, by studying how these responses depend on the pattern of physical stimulation, to build up a picture of what each type of cell does, and to ask questions about why it might be doing it. When coupled with anatomical studies of both the coarse and fine structure of perceptual pathways, we can build up a useful picture of the complex neural machinery that underpins perception

Figures 6.2 and 6.3 show the basic layout of the visual and auditory systems and are useful in keeping our anatomical bearings as we discuss specific processes in detail. Figure 6.4 and plate 6.4 show perhaps the greatest contribution of anatomy and neurophysiology to contemporary thinking about the visual system and, by extension, about perception in general. It has long been known that the visual cortex is RETINOTOPICALLY-MAPPED; that cells in adjacent regions of the

RETINOTOPIC MAP

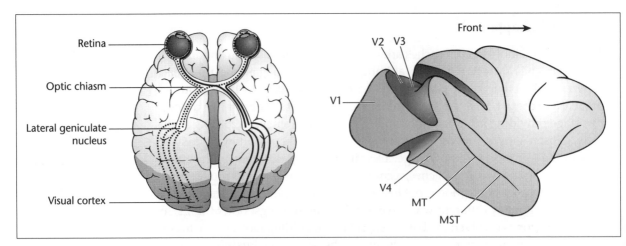

Figure 6.2 Gross anatomy of the primate visual system. The left panel is a top view of the neutral projection from the eye to the visual cortex. The right panel is a slightly exploded view of the cortex showing some of the main visual areas. MT = Media Temporal area, MST = Medial Superior Temporal area.

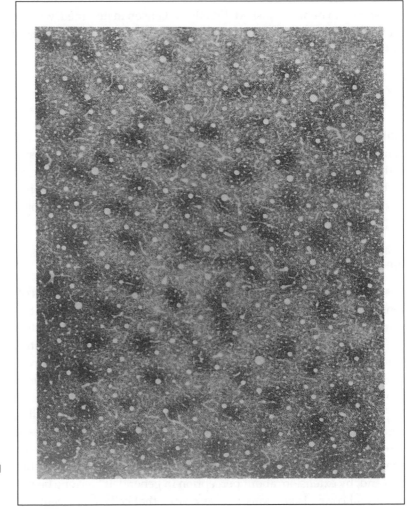

Plate 6.4 Cytochrome oxidase blobs across the surface of area V1 of the visual cortex
Source: Zeki 1993.

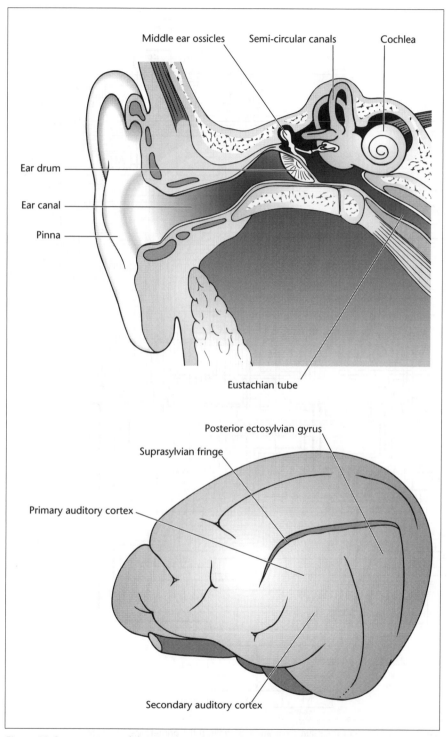

Middle ear ossicles Semi-circular canals Cochlea

Ear drum

Ear canal

Pinna

Eustachian tube

Posterior ectosylvian gyrus

Suprasylvian fringe

Primary auditory cortex

Secondary auditory cortex

Figure 6.3 Gross anatomy of the primate auditory system. The top panel shows the main features of the ear. The bottom panel shows some of the major auditory areas in the cortex. (Modified from Pickles 1982.)

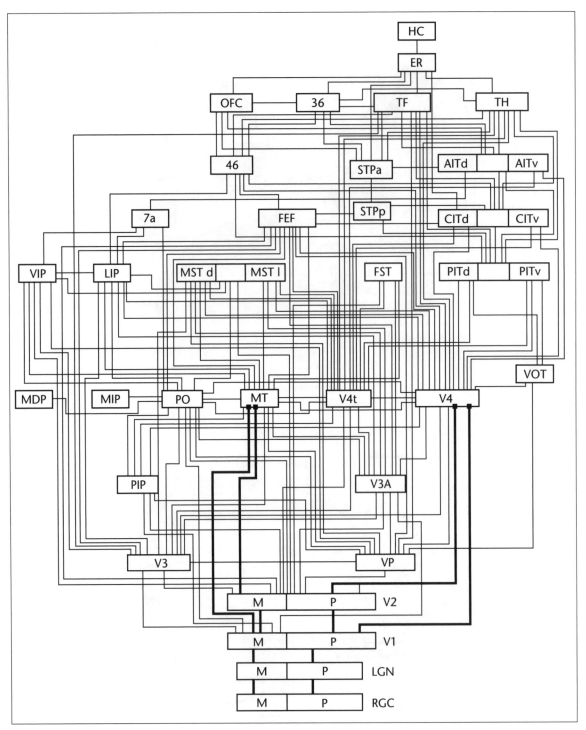

Figure 6.4 A schematic representation of some of the main areas and pathways in the primate visual system.
From Sekuler and Blake 1994.

retina project to cells in adjacent regions of the cortex so that, although there are systematic distortions, the retinal map is, by and large, preserved as a cortical map. In fact, there are many maps because (figure 6.2) there are many visual areas in the cortex and almost all of them are retinotopically-mapped. Recently, it has become increasingly clear that, superimposed upon the coarse anatomical map, there is a finer-grained structure. Each small region of a given map possesses the same intricate set of neural machinery for processing its own small region of the image. Different staining techniques reveal different anatomical structures, such as columns of cells, blobs, and stripes (plate 6.4) in the early stages of the visual cortex. Crucially, neurophysiological recordings suggest that each of these structures contains cells that are specialized to deal with just one aspect of the stimulus, its colour or movement for example. Figure 6.4 summarizes current thinking about the functional anatomy of the early stages of the visual system: it seems that different types of information about the stimulus are dealt with separately, projecting in different PROCESSING STREAMS to different specialized areas of the cortex.

PROCESSING STREAMS

Psychophysics

Whilst anatomy and neurophysiology tell us about the relationship between stimulus and neural response, psychophysics tells us about the relationship between stimulus and mental percept. The combination of these two approaches allows us to fill in the essential link between neural responses and conscious perception and thus to gain important insights into how the brain really works. Since it is not possible to gain direct access to another person's conscious experience, psychophysicists typically resort to indirect, but usually scientifically very rigorous, techniques. They may vary the intensity of a stimulus, for example, to discover under what circumstances it can reliably be detected. Or they may vary some aspect of the stimulus, such as its visual orientation or its auditory frequency, and ask the subject to discriminate it from, or match it to, some standard stimulus. We shall encounter several examples in the text of how psychophysical findings provide insights into perceptual processes.

Computer modelling

Science is essentially analytic, breaking complex phenomena down into small, understandable pieces. It has served the physical sciences well because, using mathematics, it is often possible not only to describe the individual pieces but also to predict how the pieces will interact when they are put back together. Even in relatively simple areas like physics, though, it is sometimes necessary to build computer simulations to see how complex systems perform. In psychology, there is no general language like mathematics to describe phenomena or their interactions, so a computer model is often the only way to see how a complex theory will perform. Such models simultaneously provide a way to put

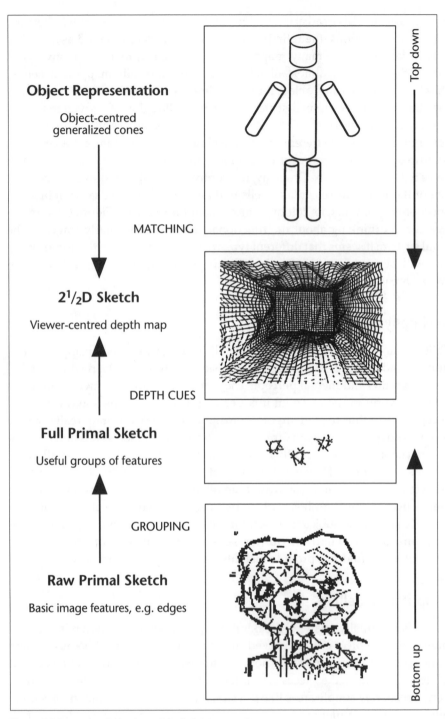

Object Representation

Object-centred
generalized cones

MATCHING

2$^{1}/_{2}$D Sketch

Viewer-centred depth map

DEPTH CUES

Full Primal Sketch

Useful groups of features

GROUPING

Raw Primal Sketch

Basic image features, e.g. edges

Top down

Bottom up

Figure 6.5 Summary of Marr's model of visual perception.

small ideas together and a rigorous test of whether the resulting system actually works. Some models simply test abstract ideas, with no concern about how the underlying processes are actually carried out, whilst others try to provide a plausible account of real neural processes.

One particular computer-based framework, that provided by David Marr, underpins much of the approach taken throughout this chapter. Figure 6.5 shows that Marr saw vision in particular (and, by extension, perception in general) as a series of stages. The first of these are descriptive and are designed to provide a rich and useful description of the available stimulus. The final stage is interpretive, and is concerned with how prior knowledge is matched with the description provided by the earlier stages. Marr's is thus a combined approach, concerned primarily with bottom-up processes, but also including the more top-down aspects of how knowledge is represented and used in the task of object recognition. It also attempts, at least in the early descriptive stages, to provide a neurally realistic account.

▨ Vision ▨

Descriptive processes

Almost all contemporary accounts of perception begin with the notion of features: those aspects of the available stimulus that capture important properties of the external world. In Marr's model (figure 6.5), the result of early descriptive processes is the Raw Primal Sketch, a list of such important image features as edges, each associated with a description of its relevant properties, such as position, orientation, colour and rate of movement. Just as the visual system does (figure 6.4), we shall begin by dealing separately with each of these properties.

Feature detection: the retina

Since we generally have no difficulty in making sense of black and white photographs, stationary, uncoloured images must provide enough information for us to recognize the objects that they depict. Which aspects of such images are important for this task, what do they tell us about the external world, and how might they be measured? We will consider these questions in some detail because a great deal of work has been done in this area, and it illustrates many general perceptual principles and approaches.

The first step is to measure the amount of light at each point in the image. This is accomplished by the RETINAL RECEPTORS, which line the retina as shown in figure 6.6. Each receptor produces a GRADED RECEPTOR POTENTIAL, a tiny voltage that is proportional to the amount of light striking it. Since receptors are very small and densely packed, the overall result, across all the receptors, is a very fine-grained map of the image. As a crude comparison, a good-quality computer

RETINAL RECEPTORS

GRADED RECEPTOR POTENTIAL

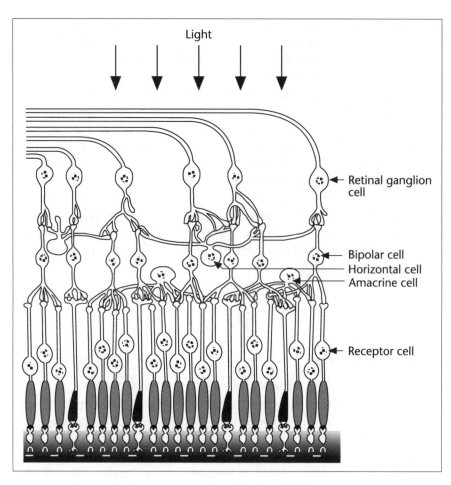

Light

Retinal ganglion cell

Bipolar cell
Horizontal cell
Amacrine cell

Receptor cell

Figure 6.6 A schematic cross-section through the retina.
(Modified from Frisby 1979.)

screen presents an image as a map made up of about one million points of light; the receptors in each retina produce a much smaller map containing over one hundred million points.

A fine-grained map of the image is a good place to start but, in this raw form, it represents a huge number of data, not all of which are important to the tasks of seeing. Returning to the lake analogy for a moment, the pattern of ripples is more important than, say, the overall height of the water. Similarly in the image, the way that the light changes from place to place is more important, for most purposes, than the overall amount of light. In fact, probably the most useful features of the image are its edges – the places where the amount of light changes fairly substantially from one position to the next. The lines in figure 6.1b correspond to the edges in figure 6.1a and confirm that we can easily recognize an object given only these important features.

To reduce our map of the image to a much simpler map of its edge features we just have to compare the amount of light at each point in the map with the amount of light in its immediate neighbourhood. We then ignore those places where a point and its surroundings are the same (no edge) and concentrate on those places where the point and its neighbourhood are different (a possible edge).

The neural circuitry of the retina is ideal for performing this type of comparison. As can be seen in figure 6.6, BIPOLAR CELLS typically collect together the responses from a few receptor cells, thus 'looking at' a small region of the image. HORIZONTAL CELLS typically collect the responses from a larger neighbourhood around this region. To make the proposed comparison we only need to subtract the response of each bipolar cell from that of its corresponding horizontal cell. This is achieved in the retina by inhibition (i.e. subtraction) between bipolar and horizontal cells. The process of comparison between the responses from neighbouring positions is generally called LATERAL INHIBITION and is found in almost all sensory systems. In general, then, sensory systems seem to have evolved to simplify their description of the stimulus by concentrating upon changes and ignoring uniform stimulation.

Lateral inhibition is most often studied, usually in cats or monkeys, by recording the responses of RETINAL GANGLION CELLS (figure 6.6) to small spots of light at different positions on the retina. Retinal ganglion cells carry the output of the retina, and are the first stage at which ACTION POTENTIALS or SPIKES, rather than graded potentials, are generated. There are, in fact, several different types of retinal ganglion cell but the type most relevant here are called P-cells. Figure 6.7 shows typical responses of an P-type retinal ganglion cell to various stimuli. There are several important properties to note:

> Even when unstimulated, retinal ganglion cells have a BACKGROUND FIRING RATE, so their response can either increase or decrease when stimulated.
>
> Each retinal ganglion cell responds to stimulation over a circular region of the retina, called the cell's RECEPTIVE FIELD and defined as the region of the retina where stimulation by light causes a change in the cell's response.
>
> The receptive field of a retinal ganglion cell is divided into two concentric, antagonistic parts, called the centre and SURROUND SUBREGIONS, which embody lateral inhibition.
>
> The centre and surround may be either ON-REGIONS or OFF-REGIONS. In an on-region, an increase in light causes an increase in the cell's response and a decrease in light causes a decrease in response. Conversely, in an off-region, an increase in light causes a decrease in response and a decrease in light causes an increase in response.
>
> In some cells there is a TRANSIENT RESPONSE, the cell responding only briefly when the light stimulation is turned on and off, though the responses of P-CELLS are characteristically fairly sustained.
>
> Cells are usually classified by the nature of the central subregion of their receptive fields and there are equal numbers of ON-CENTRE CELLS and OFF-CENTRE CELLS.

As can be seen in figure 6.7, uniform illumination of the whole receptive field of retinal ganglion cell produces, at best, a small change in response. This is

BIPOLAR CELLS

HORIZONTAL CELLS

LATERAL INHIBITION

RETINAL GANGLION CELLS

ACTION POTENTIALS

SPIKES

BACKGROUND FIRING RATE

RECEPTIVE FIELD

SURROUND SUBREGIONS

ON-REGIONS

OFF-REGIONS

TRANSIENT RESPONSE

P-CELLS

ON-CENTRE CELLS

OFF-CENTRE CELLS

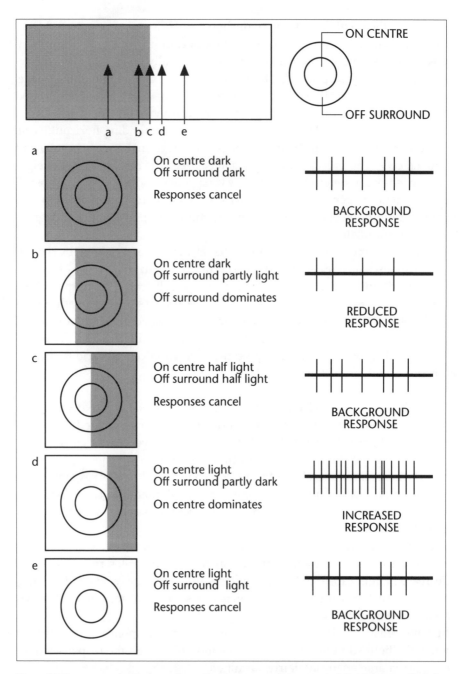

Figure 6.7 Responses of retinal ganglion cells. The top panel shows a dark/light edge on the left, and the receptive field of a typical retinal ganglion cell on the right. The responses of retinal ganglion cells with receptive fields centred on the points (a)–(e) are shown below. The left-hand side shows the pattern of illumination of the receptive field of each cell. The right-hand side shows the activity of the cell as a rate of action potentials.

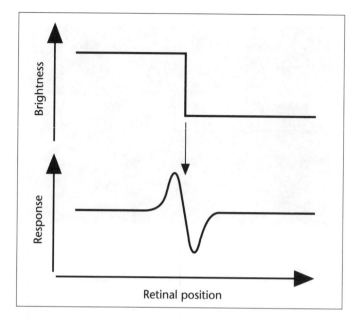

Figure 6.8 The pattern of response in an array of retinal ganglion cells to a light/dark edge. Most retinal ganglion cells respond only at the background rate. Those with receptive fields near the bright side of the edge respond above the background level; those with receptive fields near the dark side of the edge respond below the background rate. Note the cell with a receptive field directly under the edge responds only at the background edge (see cell (c) in figure 6.7).

because retinal ganglion cells perform exactly the type of comparison outlined above, changing their response from background levels only when the amount of light in the central subregion of the receptive field is different from that in its immediate neighbourhood. In effect, a retinal ganglion cell responds only if there is an edge somewhere within its receptive field. Figure 6.8 shows the pattern of response across a set of on-centre cells, each with its receptive field at a slightly different position on the retina. The response across a set of off-centre cells would simply be turned upside-down, positive where the on-centre response is negative and negative where the on-centre response is positive. Notice that the responses in only a few cells are needed to signal the presence of an edge feature

Figure 6.9, the Craik–O'Brien–Cornsweet illusion, provides an important psychophysical link between the biology of these retinal mechanisms and the psychology of perception. Although this stimulus is physically very different from a real dark/light edge, it is designed to produce the same pattern of response in retinal ganglion cells. This is because the abrupt change in light in the centre of the figure will produce a response but the shallow ramps on each side will not (because, so far as a retinal ganglion cell is concerned, a shallow ramp is much the same as uniform illumination). The crucial point is that two different stimuli that evoke the same retinal response produce the same conscious experience: figure 6.9 looks like a real dark/light edge. Thus, our conscious experience is better explained by the retinal description of the image than by the image itself. And our understanding of retinal processes provides a simple explanation of an otherwise puzzling illusion.

Figure 6.10 illustrates two further important aspects of how the retina describes image features. Here the top strip appears roughly uniform even though, physi-

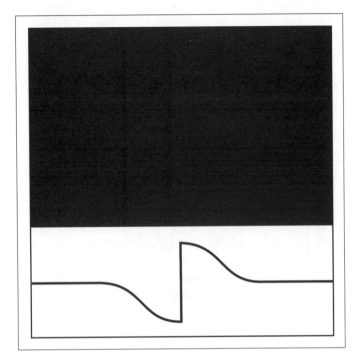

Figure 6.9 The Craik–O'Brien–Cornsweet illusion. This appears as a simple dark/light edge (it may help to screw up your eyes a little to blur the image). As the cross-section through the brightness at the bottom shows, both sides of the figure are physically the same. You can confirm this by covering the central strip of the figure with a pencil or narrow piece of paper; both sides of the figure will then look the same.

Figure 6.10 Lightness constancy and contrast. The top horizontal strip appears uniform in brightness but physically varies from dark on the left to bright on the right. The bottom horizontal strip appears lighter on the left than the right but is physically uniform. You can confirm this by covering the background region of the figure; the two strips will then appear as they really are.

Box 6.1 Perceptual Constancy

Perceptual constancy is such a good solution that we are generally unaware of the problem. Think about what happens to the image of, say, a door as it opens; the shape of the door's image changes dramatically and features like door handles and shadows may appear or disappear. Yet our immediate impression is of a simple event, rather than of a complex sequence in which re- gions of the image change shape and appear or disappear. Similarly we can recognize voices despite the distortion of a telephone, or distinguish the same tastes in the presence of different sauces or herbs. All of these are examples of perceptual constancy – cases where our perception remains stable despite gross changes in the physical pattern of stimulation at our sense organs.

cally, it is much lighter at one end than the other. This strip has been arranged so that it maintains a constant relationship with the varying background: in fact, it is always twice as bright as its immediate surroundings. This is an example of LIGHTNESS CONSTANCY: our conscious impression of lightness often remains the same even when the amount of light in the image varies dramatically. Conversely, the bottom strip in figure 6.10 appears lighter at one end than the other even though, physically, it is uniform throughout its length, This is an example of LIGHTNESS CONTRAST: things appear lighter against a dark backgound and darker against a light background. Lightness constancy and lightness contrast are two sides of the same coin, and both relate to the way that the retina works. Retinal ganglion cells compare the amount of light in a small region of the image with the amount of light in that region's immediate surroundings. They only change their response when these are different, so they will pick out the edges in figure 6.10. Moreover, the response depends upon the relationship between the region and its surroundings. Along the edges of the top strip, this relationship remains constant, so the responses, and our conscious impressions, remain constant (lightness constancy). Along the edges of the bottom strip, this relationship varies smoothly, so the responses, and our conscious impressions, vary accordingly (lightness contrast).

LIGHTNESS CONSTANCY

LIGHTNESS CONTRAST

The problem with VISUAL ILLUSIONS like those illustrated in figures 6.9 and 6.10 is that they emphasize how vision can sometimes go 'wrong' when presented with rather contrived stimuli. Lightness constancy and contrast are really very sensible solutions to a very difficult problem. In the real world, the overall amount of light in an image can vary over an unimaginable range, from deep twilight to bright sunlight. Simply turning on a light may increase the amount of light at each point in the image several hundred times, yet we are often unperturbed by such dramatic variations. Because retinal ganglion cells compare the amount of light in neighbouring regions of the image, they will not only pick out the edges but they will also filter out any overall changes in the amount of light. Thus, just a few cells into the visual pathway, the original image map has been transformed into a much more efficient and useful set of measurements; from a neural 'photograph' at the receptors, to a neural 'line drawing' at the retinal ganglion cells. The retina is a simple but very clever device.

VISUAL ILLUSIONS

Box 6.2 Perceived Lightness and Perceived Spatial Layout

Take a piece of white paper or thin card and fold it loosely in half. Stand it up like a tent on a flat surface in a position where the two sides of the tent are differently, but roughly uniformly, lit. Under these circumstances, the ridge of the tent produces a dark/light edge in the image which is correctly seen as a change in the angle of a uniformly reflective surface, rather than as a change in the reflectance of a flat surface. Now close one eye and keep your head perfectly still. This reduces the depth cues available and, with a little practice, you will be able to make the stimulus flip in apparent depth, so that the ridge of the tent is seen as a valley. When this happens, the lightness of the surface appears very unnatural; shimmering and, perhaps, seeming to be separate from the surface.

Since the physical shape and the pattern of light in the image have not changed at all, this illustrates that

the way that we see surface lightness depends on the way that we interpret the spatial layout of the external world. In particular, it indicates that there is more to the perception of lightness than the simple retinal processes described in the text. In order to make sense of the flat pattern of light in an image, the visual system must actually construct an internal three-dimensional model of the world. Moreover, in order to make sense of surface reflectance, the model must include some idea about the position and type of the light source(s). Under normal conditions, the visual system can generally find a consistent solution in which a particular combination of light source and surface reflectance make sense of the image. However, when we make the tent reverse in apparent depth, no such consistent solution is possible, and the resulting percept is, not surprisingly, unnatural.

Feature detection: the visual cortex

Retinal ganglion cells pick out edges. At the next stage of visual processing in the visual cortex, further measurements begin to refine the description of these important image features. The properties of cells in the STRIATE CORTEX, sometimes called the PRIMARY VISUAL CORTEX, AREA 17 or, in primates only, V1, were first revealed in studies of cats and monkeys by David Hubel and Torsten Wiesel. Figure 6.11 shows typical receptive fields of one type of cortical cell, called a SIMPLE CELL. Like those of retinal ganglion cells, simple-cell receptive fields typically consist of discrete, mutually inhibitory subregions, and each simple cell probably receives its input from several adjacent retinal ganglion cells. The most striking aspect of these receptive fields is that they are elongated, so that the cell will respond best to an edge with a particular orientation, and is thus ORIENTATION SELECTIVE. Hubel and Wiesel suggested that such cells might function as FEATURE DETECTORS and that the response of a simple cell might signal the presence of a line or edge at a particular orientation and at a particular position in the image. They further proposed that these features might be built up into a more elaborate description by a kind of NEURAL HIERARCHY. Thus the outputs of several simple cells were thought to be combined by a second type of cell, called a COMPLEX CELL, which is orientation selective but has a larger receptive field and might thus 'recognize' the relevant feature in a larger region of the image. Complex cells might then feed into a third type of HYPERCOMPLEX CELL, which has two preferred orientations and might thus serve to 'recognize' corners. Further, as yet undiscovered, types of cell might build these corners into shapes and the hierarchy would continue until specific cells would respond to, and thus 'recognize',

STRIATE CORTEX

PRIMARY VISUAL CORTEX

AREA 17

SIMPLE CELL

ORIENTATION SELECTIVE

FEATURE DETECTORS

NEURAL HIERARCHY

COMPLEX CELL

HYPERCOMPLEX CELL

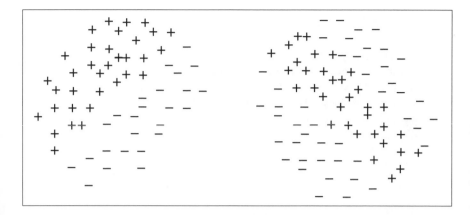

Figure 6.11 Receptive fields of typical simple cells in area V1 of the visual cortex. The receptive fields are typically elongated, having a distinct orientation, and are organized into separate on (+) and off (−) subregions.

the constellations of image features that correspond to specific objects in the world.

Although the basic notion of a DESCRIPTIVE HIERARCHY survives, with progressively more complex descriptions being built up from simple features in a bottom-up way, the idea that this might be achieved by a simple, 'hard-wired' neural hierarchy is no longer popular. ('Hard-wired' means permanently inbuilt.) It seems (figure 6.4) that the first cortical processes occur in parallel, rather than in series, and that complex cells, for example, receive input direct from retinal cells rather than via simple cells. More importantly, this kind of simple, rigid model could not provide a complete account of object recognition for at least two reasons. First, image features do not always correspond simply to object features; edges in the image may correspond to shadows, for example, rather than to object boundaries. Secondly, such a process can only produce a structural description of the image and, as we argued in the introduction, such a description does not necessarily provide an adequate basis for recognition.

Similarly, although edge features are still thought to be important, the idea that an individual simple cell could detect them has been considerably modified. A given simple cell will respond to a range of orientations and, by varying the intensity of the stimulus, the same level of reponse can be obtained to, say, a vertical edge as to one rotated through, say, 25 degrees. Thus, the response of this cell cannot unambiguously signal an edge with one particular orientation. Modern theories suggest that, instead of being detected by a single cell, orientation is measured by a set of cells, each optimally sensitive to a slightly different orientation. Further work by Hubel and Wiesel certainly suggests that the striate cortex is well-equipped to function in this way. Each small region of the retina projects to many tens of thousands of cells in the striate cortex, all in roughly the same place, and collectively called a HYPERCOLUMN. A hypercolumn is the first cortical stage of the intricate neural machinery for processing each small region of the image. The cells of each hypercolumn are organized anatomically into a series of columns, each perpendicular to the surface of the cortex. All the cells in any given column have receptive fields with roughly the same orientation, and

DESCRIPTIVE
HIERARCHY

HYPERCOLUMN

Box 6.3   The Tilt After Effect

Figure 6.12: Look briefly at the fixation point in the centre of the test stimulus and confirm that both patterns appear vertical. Then shift your gaze to the fixation bar in the centre of the adapt stimulus and allow your eyes to move up and down the bar for a minute or so. Finally, look back at the fixation point in the centre of the test stimulus. For a moment or two, the two stimuli should appear tilted in opposite directions away from the vertical.

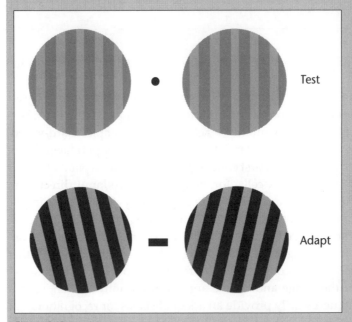

Test

Adapt

Figure 6.12

This simple after-effect provides quite powerful psychophysical evidence against the proposal that simple edge features are detected by individual cortical cells. Instead, it suggests that edge orientation is encoded by the pattern of response across a population of cells, each most sensitive to a slightly different otientation. Thus, for example, the orientation of an edge might be encoded by the identity of the cell responding most. Adapting to an oriented stimulus will then fatigue the most responsive cells, leading to a temporary distortion in the pattern of response and a corresponding temporary distortion of perceived orientation (see figure 6.13).

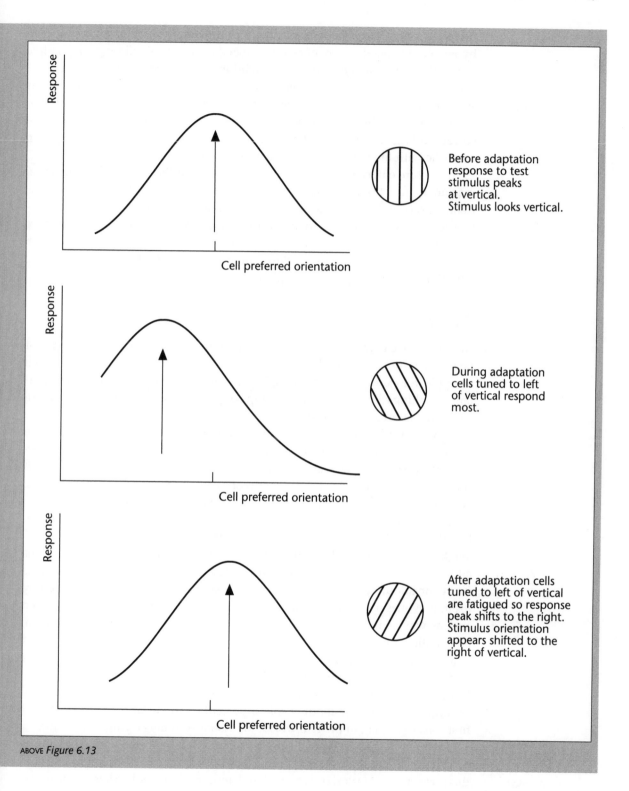

ABOVE *Figure 6.13*

preferred orientation changes gradually from column to column so that each hypercolumn contains a set of cells that together cover the full range of possible orientations. The suggestion that orientation is signalled by the pattern of response across these cells, rather than being detected by individual cells, is suported by perceptual phenomena such as the TILT AFTER EFFECT, elaborated in Box 6.3. Here the distortion in perceived orientation can easily be explained by a corresponding distortion in the pattern of response, but it is very difficult to reconcile with the notion of individual feature detectors.

TILT AFTER EFFECT

The picture emerging from this area is of a beautifully organized set of neural machinery, functioning to measure appropriate properties of the retinal image. Retinal processes emphasize edges and provide a description that is largely unaffected by gross variations in the overall amount of light. These beginnings are refined in the first stages of the visual cortex, where additional properties such as orientation are added to the description. Thus, the first elements of Marr's Raw Primal Sketch (figure 6.5) begin to emerge.

Colour

Although we can make sense of black and white images, the addition of colour helps in a variety of ways. It can help us to recognize specific objects or tell us if an apple, for example, is ripe enough to eat. In Nature it often plays an important signalling role, conveying that a type of plant is poisonous or that a particular animal is sexually mature.

WAVELENGTH

Conventionally, our conscious impression of colour is said to depend upon the WAVELENGTH of light. Visible light is a small section of a much broader spectrum of electromagnetic waves, varying from long wavelength radio and television waves to the very short wavelengths of cosmic rays and sub-atomic particles. What we see as light is just electromagnetic energy with wavelengths between about 400 nm and about 700 nm (a nanometer, or nm, is 1 millionth of a millimetre). Wavelengths a little longer than this (infrared) are felt as heat, while wavelengths a little shorter (ultraviolet) produce suntans. Ordinary sunlight contains all wavelengths in the visible range in roughly equal proportions, and is seen as white, uncoloured light. However, when a single wavelength is presented by itself, it evokes a strong sensation of colour: long wavelengths are seen as red and, as wavelength is progressively shortened, we see orange, yellow, green, blue, indigo and, finally, violet. Moreover, when single wavelengths are added together, the resulting mixtures evoke different colours: equal amounts of long (red) and medium (green) wavelengths produce white, for example. Single wavelengths and simple mixtures are actually rare in nature and, although these stimuli are important to understanding colour perception in the laboratory, we should first consider what, in the real world, the visual system is trying to describe.

SURFACE
REFLECTANCE

ALBEDO

When light strikes a typical surface, some of it is reflected and some of it is absorbed. Different surfaces reflect different proportions of the light and it is this SURFACE REFLECTANCE, or ALBEDO, that determines how light a surface appears.

Reflective surfaces appear light, whilst unreflective surfaces appear dark. The basis of colour perception is that a surface of a given overall reflectance will probably not reflect all wavelengths equally well. When white light strikes the surface, for example, the long and medium wavelengths may be absorbed and only the shorter wavelengths reflected. This reflected light would then contain mostly short wavelengths and the surface would appear blue. A second surface of the same overall reflectance might relect mainly medium wavelengths, and consequently be seen as green. Thus, by being able to distinguish between different wavelengths, the visual system can distinguish between surfaces that would look identical in a black and white photograph. In some ways, the conventional coupling of perceived colour and physical wavelength is misleading, because it emphasizes the messenger (light) rather than the message (the surface). Light wavelengths are only useful because they carry information about SPECTRAL REFLECTANCE: the extent to which a given surface reflects each visible wavelength.

SPECTRAL
REFLECTANCE

A surface appears coloured because it reflects some wavelengths more than others. In order to recover the underlying property of spectral reflectance from an image, the visual system must be equipped to do two things. First, it must be able to distinguish between different wavelengths and, secondly, it must be able to make comparisons between these different wavelengths. Experiments with single wavelengths and simple mixtures not only reveal that the human visual system is equipped to do both of these things, but they also provide important clues about the processes involved. Sir Isaac Newton (1704) was the first to isolate single wavelengths and to study the perception of simple mixtures. His work led to a set of rules for predicting the colours perceived when different wavelengths are added together, which can be summarized by the COLOUR CIRCLE shown in figure 6.14. This figure also refines colour into the two dimensions of HUE (which distinguishes, say, red from green) and SATURATION (which distinguishes, say, red from pink). The colour circle can be further refined by adding the final dimension of brightness to form the COLOUR SOLID, also shown in figure 6.14.

COLOUR CIRCLE

HUE

SATURATION

COLOUR SOLID

The most important finding from wavelength mixing experiments is that any colour can be produced by varying the proportions of just three suitable wavelengths, which are called primaries. This property is exploited by colour televisions, which produce the full range of colours by mixing together a red, green and blue picture in the appropriate amounts. There is no unique set of primaries but, in practice, they must include one long wavelength (seen as red), one medium wavelength (seen as green) and one short wavelength (seen as blue). The colour solid is no more than a useful convention based on the selection of three specific wavelengths as primaries and an extensive series of experiments in which human subjects adjusted the relative intensities of these particular primaries to make matches to all perceivable colours.

The finding that three primaries are needed, rather than, say, two or four, led Thomas Young (1801) and, later, Helmholtz (1866) to propose that the visual system contained three different mechanisms, each sensitive to a different range

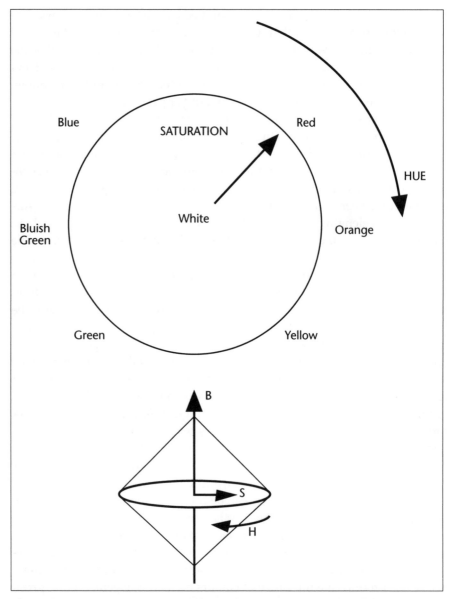

Figure 6.14 Top panel: a simple colour circle. As the wavelength of a monochromatic light is varied around the circumference of the circle, the perceived hue varies systematically as indicated. White light (containing equal amounts of all visible wavelengths) is represented at the centre of the circle. Moving from the centre to a point on the circumference progressively increases the perceived saturation of the colour (e.g. from white, through pink, to red). Complementary colours are arranged on opposite sides of the circumference. The circle can be used to predict the perceived hue and saturation produced by mixing together different monochromatic lights. Bottom panel: the colour circle can be extended to a colour solid by adding the extra dimension of brightness (B) to hue (H) and saturation (S). A narrower range of colours is perceivable at both high and low brightness.

Box 6.4 Colour Mixing

Artists and scientists often disagree on what happens when colours are mixed and on which colours may be regarded as primary colours. This is because there are two quite different ways to mix colours, each with its own rules, and scientists typically use one way while artists use the other.

Scientists typically work with monochromatic lights, mixing them together additively. For example, they may project two monochromatic lights, say one blue and the other yellow, onto a white screen. Under these circumstances, the screen reflects both lights into the eye and so the image contains the sum of the two lights (blue plus yellow). If the two lights are equally bright, this will be seen as white. In additive colour mixing, the stimulus becomes brighter as more colours are added.

Artists typically work with paints and pigments. These appear coloured because they absorb some wavelengths while reflecting others. For example, blue paint illuminated by white light will absorb most of the long (red) and medium (green) wavelengths, reflecting only the short (blue) wavelengths into the eye. Yellow paint absorbs most of the long and short wavelengths and reflects only the longish medium (yellow) wavelengths. Mixing two pigments together is subtractive because each pigment absorbs some of the wavelengths in the incident light and only those wavelengths that are not absorbed by either pigment are reflected into the eye. When blue and yellow paints are mixed, for example, almost everything is absorbed by one or other of the paints and only a few (medium) wavelengths are reflected,which are seen as green. In subtractive colour mixing, the stimulus becomes darker as more colours are added.

Figure 6.15

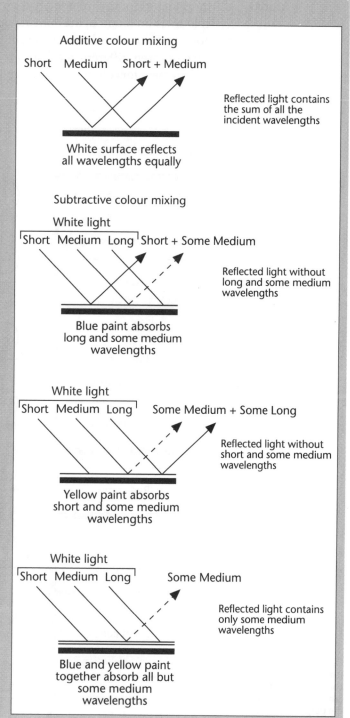

Additive colour mixing

Short   Medium   Short + Medium

Reflected light contains the sum of all the incident wavelengths

White surface reflects all wavelengths equally

Subtractive colour mixing

White light
Short Medium Long   Short + Some Medium

Reflected light without long and some medium wavelengths

Blue paint absorbs long and some medium wavelengths

White light
Short Medium Long   Some Medium + Some Long

Reflected light without short and some medium wavelengths

Yellow paint absorbs short and some medium wavelengths

White light
Short Medium Long   Some Medium

Reflected light contains only some medium wavelengths

Blue and yellow paint together absorb all but some medium wavelengths

TRICHROMATIC
THEORY of wavelengths. This is called the TRICHROMATIC THEORY of colour perception. Further support for trichromaticity is provided by the three common types of faulty colour vision found in the human population. Each type can be explained by the absence of, or a weakness in, one of the three proposed mechanisms. The existence of three different mechanisms provides the visual system with the first requirement for colour vision: the ability to discriminate between different bands

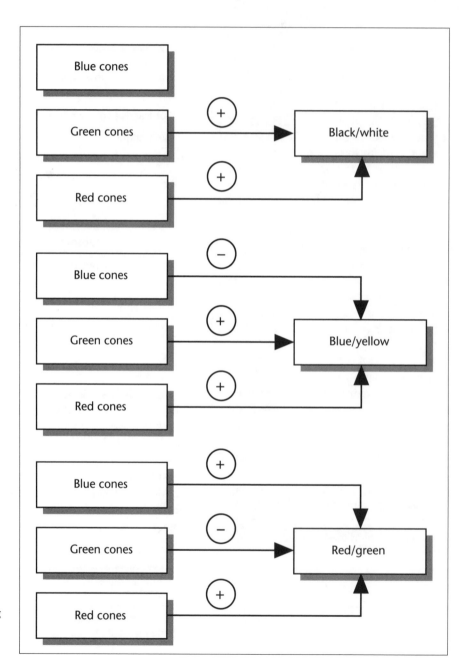

Figure 6.16 A schematic representation of how colour opponent channels are produced by combining the outputs of three different types of cone receptor.

of wavelengths. Incidentally, there is nothing magical about the number three; some animals are dichromats (two-colour mechanisms) whilst others are tetrachromats (four-colour mechanisms).

A second important finding from wavelength mixing experiments is not easily explained by the trichromatic theory and relates to the second requirement for colour vision. For every wavelength there is just one other wavelength that, when the two are mixed in equal proportions, produces a percept of white. These pairs of wavelengths are diametrically opposite each other on the colour circle and the colours with which they are associated are called COMPLEMENTARY COLOURS. Red/green, and blue/yellow are example pairs of complementary colours. Others can be found simply by looking at a coloured patch for a minute or so and then shifting your gaze to a piece of white or grey paper. This produces a COMPLEMENTARY AFTER IMAGE, showing the complement of the colour to which you have just adapted. Phenomena such as these led Ewald Hering (1964) to propose an OPPONENCY THEORY of colour vision, in which mechanisms sensitive to different wavelengths were wired up in an antagonistic fashion, as shown in figure 6.16. These opponent mechanisms would, in effect, meet the second requirement for colour vision: the ability to compare different bands of wavelengths.

Although trichromacy and opponency may seem like different accounts of colour perception, they are quite compatible with each other and actually address different stages of the same problem. Indeed, neurophysiological studies of the retina confirm the neural basis for both ideas. Retinal receptors fall into two general types: RODS, which function at low light levels and are responsible for night (SCOTOPIC) vision; and CONES, which function at high light levels and are responsible for day (PHOTOPIC) vision. In macaque monkeys, which perform identically to human observers in most colour tests and thus presumably have very similar colour systems, cones can be further subdivided into three types, differing in their sensitivities to wavelength. Figure 6.17 shows the SPECTRAL SENSITIVITIES of the three cone types, obtained by recording the responses of individual cones to each wavelength from the full visible range. These sensitivities are remarkably similar to those predicted by Young and Helmholtz, and it seems that the first stage of colour vision, at the receptor level, is indeed trichromatic.

Recordings from the very next stage of the visual pathway, the bipolar cells, provide direct evidence of opponent mechanisms of the type suggested by Hering. Some macaque bipolar cells typically show exactly the predicted pattern of positive and negative responses to different wavelengths. This pattern arises because the bipolar cell receives excitatory input from some combination of cone types and inhibitory input from a different combination. Thus, trichromacy at the receptor level has been used to produce opponency at the bipolar level: the visual system can discriminate between different bands of wavelengths using cones, and make comparisons between these bands using bipolars.

If the visual system were concerned only with measuring light, then these

COMPLEMENTARY COLOURS

COMPLEMENTARY COLOUR AFTER IMAGE

OPPONENCY THEORY

RODS

SCOTOPIC VISION

CONES

PHOTOPIC VISION

SPECTRAL SENSITIVITIES

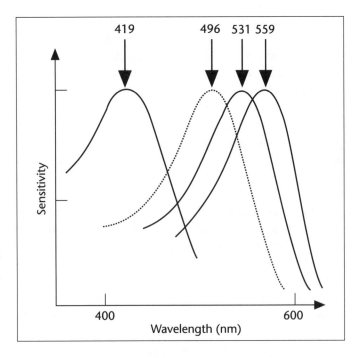

Figure 6.17 The sensitivities of different types of retinal receptor to different light wavelengths. The three types of cone are most sensitive at 419 (blue), 531 (green) and 559 (red) nm. Rods (dotted line) are most sensitive at 496 nm. Note that each type of receptor is sensitive to a wide range of wavelengths so that, at most wavelengths, all types will respond but at different levels.
(Modified from Barlow and Mollon 1982.)

processes would provide a good basis for colour vision. But the visual system is really concerned with using light to recover information about objects. The light reaching the eye from a surface depends not only upon the reflectance of the surface but also upon the light that strikes the surface. Thus, any change in the wavelength of the light striking the surface will produce a change in the wavelengths reaching the eye. This is a real potential problem because, although natural sunlight contains a roughly equal mixture of all wavelengths, many artificial lights do not, and the light in many natural settings, such as forests, has a strong preponderance of some wavelengths over others. Under these circumstances, our perception of colours should change. Yet, just as variations in the overall amount of light have little effect on perceived lightness (lightness constancy), so variations in the wavelength composition of the light source have little effect on perceived colour: we exhibit COLOUR CONSTANCY. According to Edwin Land's (1977) RETINEX THEORY, so called because it was originally thought to involve both the retina and the visual cortex, colour constancy is just an extension of lightness constancy. Lightness constancy works because comparisons of the amount of light in neighbouring image positions are unaffected by changes in the overall amount of light. The same trick will work if we perform these comparisons separately at different wavelengths. For example, a comparison of the amount of long wavelength light in neighbouring image positions will be unaffected by changes in the overall amount of long wavelength light. The equivalent is true for medium and short wavelengths. Since each separate comparison is unaffected by changes at its own wavelength, the pattern of response across the three comparisons will be unaffected by changes in the overall wavelength composi-

COLOUR
CONSTANCY

RETINEX THEORY

tion of the light. In other words, the pattern of response across three separate comparisons would provide a suitable basis for colour constancy.

Cells with the right sort of properties for retinex theory do exist in the LATERAL GENICULATE NUCLEUS (LGN), which is the stage of the visual pathway between the retina and the visual cortex (figure 6.2). These cells have double opponent receptive fields. For example, in some cells, long wavelength light produces an excitatory response in the CENTRE SUBREGION and an inhibitory response in the surround, whilst medium wavelength light produces an inhibitory response in the centre and an excitatory response in the surround. Such cells can do two things simultaneously; the comparison of the amount of light at neighbouring positions within specific bands of wavelengths, and the comparison of the responses at different bands of wavelengths. These are exactly the things needed for retinex theory

Colour processing is further refined in the visual cortex. Wavelength selective cells are clustered together within the hypercolumns of V1, forming what are called CYTOCHROME OXIDASE BLOBS (plate 6.4), because they can be revealed by selective staining with this chemical. These blobs seem to form a separate colour stream, projecting to a specific colour area in area V4 (figure 6.4). Individual cells in V4 respond only to a very narrow range of wavelengths, and adjacent cells prefer adjacent wavelengths. Perhaps most interestingly, these cells appear to be genuinely colour, rather than wavelength, selective. In an elegant series of experiments investigating colour constancy by drastically altering the wavelength composition of the light source, Semir Zeki (1980) found that the responses of individual cells of the macaque mirrored his own perception of surface colour rather than the physical composition of the light: whenever a surface looked, for example, red to Zeki, the monkey's cell would be responding. This is a rare and provocative example where the response of a single cell (albeit that of a monkey) can be directly related to a reliable conscious experience.

LATERAL GENICULATE NUCLEUS

CENTRE SUBREGION

CYTOCHROME OXIDASE BLOBS

Motion

The retinal image is in constant, often violent, motion as we move around the world, move our eyes, and as objects in the world move about. Making sense of the resulting confusion is a formidable task, but is well worthwhile. Things that move need to be checked and possibly dealt with, often quickly, and the importance that the visual system attaches to retinal motion is well illustrated by warning signs or advertisements that flash or move to grab our attention. The usefulness of motion is equally well demonstrated by a phenomenon called BIOLOGICAL MOTION, introduced by Gunnar Johannson. Small lights or reflective patches are attached to a person's shoulders, arms, hips and legs so that, when viewed in the dark, only a small set of bright points is visible. So long as the person remains stationary, the stimulus appears as a formless jumble but, as soon as the person moves, it is immediately and compellingly recognizable as a person walking, jumping, or generally moving about. So good is our ability to

BIOLOGICAL MOTION

make use of the resulting complex pattern of point motions that we can reliably distinguish gender, effortlessly make sense of two people dancing together, and even accurately estimate the weights of objects that the actors lift.

The description of retinal motion must begin with the ability to measure the speed and direction of individual features moving in the image. The human visual system seems to have two separate systems for achieving this (Braddick 1974). The first, long-range, or FEATURE-TRACKING, system seems to infer motion rather indirectly by tracking the changes in position of a given feature from one instant to the next. This system underpins our conscious impression of motion in films and TV, which essentially consist of a sequence of stationary pictures, rapidly presented one after another. The second, short-range, or MOTION-SENSING, system, appears to measure motion more directly by signalling changes in the image continuously over time. Neither system is yet fully understood but it is at least clear that the basic requirements are in place even at the retina. The P-type retinal ganglion cells, already described, function to emphasize abrupt spatial changes in the image. They are complemented by a second major type of retinal ganglion cell, called M-CELLS, which may function to signal abrupt temporal changes in the image. P-cells have small receptive fields and respond only to sharp spatial changes, but they typically give a SUSTAINED RESPONSE throughout the presentation of an appropriate stimulus. M-cells have larger receptive fields with rather weak inhibitory surrounds so that they respond to much broader spatial changes, but they typically respond in a transient fashion, only at the onset and offset of the stimulus. P-cells obtain their properties through lateral

FEATURE-TRACKING

MOTION-SENSING

M-CELLS

SUSTAINED
RESPONSE

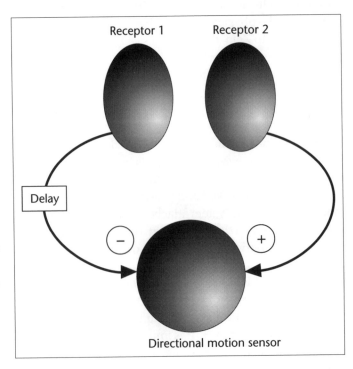

Figure 6.18 A simple detector that is selective for the direction of motion. Two receptors in adjacent positions are connected to the motion sensor, one via a delayed inhibitory link, the other by an immediate excitatory link. Motion to the left will stimulate Receptor 2 first and this will cause the motion sensor to respond. Motion to the right will stimulate Receptor 1 first, the delayed inhibition from Receptor 1 will arrive at the motion sensor at the same time as the immediate excitation from Receptor 2, the two inputs will cancel each other out, and the motion sensor will not respond.

inhibition, in effect comparing the amount at neighbouring positions and responding only when there is a difference across space. M-cells obtain their properties by DELAYED INHIBITION, in effect comparing the amount of light at successive times and responding only when there is a difference over time.

This segregation, beginning at the retina, of separate form and MOTION STREAMS (figure 6.4) appears to continue throughout the visual pathway up to the middle temporal area of the cortex, which contains many cells selective for different types of motion. In fact, most visual cortical cells prefer moving to stationary stimuli, and the motion stream is distinguished mainly because its cells are directionally selective, each cell responding best to one particular direction of retinal motion. One way to measure motion direction is to compare the responses in adjacent receptors using delayed inhibition, as illustrated in figure 6.18. Simple mechanisms like this are actually found in the retinas of relatively simple mammals like rabbits. In primates, direction selectivity does not emerge until cortical cells, where it may be based on the same principle, combining the responses, at successive times, of cells with receptive fields in adjacent regions of the image. However, to disentangle motion direction from other image attributes, such as brightness or orientation, requires at least one additional stage. Comparing (i.e. subtracting) the responses of cells tuned to opposite directions but which respond identically to changes in orientation, brightness and so forth, will simply cancel out the effects of these other stimulus attributes and leave a purely directional signal. The MOTION AFTER EFFECT, explained in Box 6.5, suggests that such a comparison is made within the human visual system, because adapting to motion in one direction upsets the normal balance of the comparison and produces perceived motion in the opposite direction.

Stereopsis

Images are flat, two-dimensional things and, since we perceive a solid, three-dimensional world, the visual system must somehow recover the depth that is lost in producing the image. In fact there are many ways of doing this and this section concentrates on just one type of measurement. Since we have two eyes, we have two images of the same scene. These images are slightly different, because they are taken from slightly different viewpoints, and the differences are caused by the different distances of objects in the world. The differences in the images are called disparities, and the recovery of depth information from disparity is called BINOCULAR STEREOPSIS (literally, solid vision).

Figure 6.20 shows how disparity is related to distance and demonstrates, in principle, how, by comparing the relative positions of corresponding features in the two images, we can measure disparity and thus directly recover relative distance. The first stage of the visual pathway at which information from the two eyes is combined and, consequently, where disparity might be measured, is cortical area V1. Here, many cells are binocularly driven, having a receptive field with similar properties in each of the eyes, so that appropriate stimulation

Box 6.5   The Motion After Effect

After looking at (and so adapting to) a consistently moving stimulus for a minute or so, stationary stimuli briefly appear to move in the opposite direction. For example, adapting to leftward motion produces an after effect of rightward motion. This phenomenon is often noticeable on a train journey when the train stops at a station. The station may appear to move backwards as a result of the motion after effect produced by consistent exposure through the window to forward motion.

This motion after effect is one of the oldest known

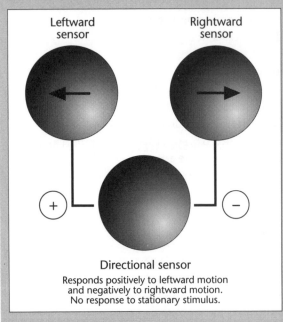

Leftward sensor

Rightward sensor

$+$ $-$

Directional sensor

Responds positively to leftward motion and negatively to rightward motion. No response to stationary stimulus.

Figure 6.19

perceptual phenomena. It suggests that motion direction is encoded by the balance of response in sensors tuned to opposite directions of motion. Horizontal direction, for example, would depend upon the balance of response in leftward and rightward motion sensors. During adaptation to leftward motion, say, the leftward sensor would become fatigued so that, after adaptation, a stationary stimulus would produce more response in the rightward sensor than the leftward sensor and, consequently, rightward motion would be perceived.

The strategy of encoding a stimulus dimension as the balance between opposing sensors illustrates a general sensory coding principle. It is also used, for example, in colour coding according to opponency theory. The strength of the strategy is that it removes the effects of other, irrelevant, stimulus attributes. A response in a leftward motion detector working by itself, for example, cannot encode stimulus direction because the response will almost certainly depend, among other things, upon the intensity of the stimulus: a bright rightward (inappropriate) stimulus might well produce the same level of response as a dim leftward (appropriate) stimulus. So the response of the leftward sensor is inherently ambiguous. By pairing opposing sensors, this problem is resolved because, providing both sensors respond identically to all attributes of the stimulus except direction, then both will be equally affected by any change in the irrelevant stimulus attributes and the difference in their response will reflect the stimulus direction. A dim leftward stimulus will excite both sensors weakly, for example, whereas a bright leftward stimulus will excite both sensors more strongly – but it will always excite the leftward sensor more than the rightward sensor.

of either eye will produce a response. Although the receptive fields in the two eyes always lie in roughly corresponding positions, there is some slight variation so that, for example, we might find a set of cells with receptive fields in the same position in the left eye but each with a receptive field in a slightly different position in the right eye. These cells are, in effect, disparity selective because each will respond best when a given feature in the two images exactly corresponds with the two receptive fields.

Unfortunately, to make use of disparity, the visual system must first work out which feature in one eye matches which feature in the other. The visual sustem is extremely good at solving this CORRESPONDENCE PROBLEM, as is demonstrated by

CORRESPONDENCE
PROBLEM

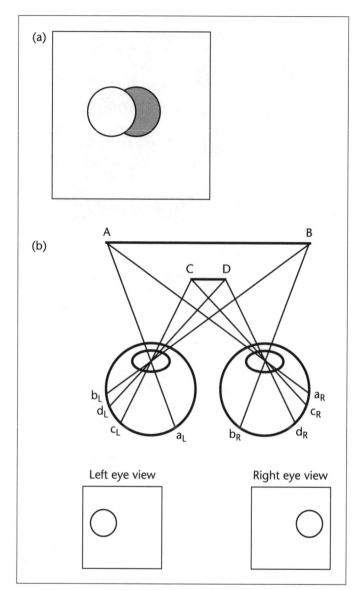

(a)

(b)

Left eye view

Right eye view

Figure 6.20 The geometry of retinal disparity. (a) A small circle lies in front of a square background (the grey area is its shadow). (b) As viewed from above, the edges of the square (AB) and the circle (CD) project images in both eyes. The circle will be offset to the left, relative to the square, in the left eye image, and offset to the right in the right eye image. As the circle is moved towards the square, its image will swing towards the centre of the square in both eyes. When there is no distance between the circle and the square, there will be no differences in the left and right images and, consequently, no retinal disparity.

the RANDOM DOT STEREOGRAM shown in figure 6.21. Here, each image contains many thousands of identical features yet, when one image is presented to the left eye and the other to the right, we can detect disparity and see a central square of dots standing out in depth from the background. Given that any one dot in the left image might correspond to any one of many thousands in the right, how does the visual system sort out the appropriate matches?

The correspondence problem is illustrated in a simple form in figure 6.22 (although the concepts it depicts are none the less not easy to grasp). Here there are just two objects but four possible matches, two of which correspond to seeing an object at the wrong position in the visual world. Notice, too that, in the bottom

RANDOM DOT
STEREOGRAM

Figure 6.21 A typical Random Dot Stereogram. A square of dots in the centre of the left image is slightly offset relative to the right image. When the images are viewed so that the left image is presented to the left eye and the right image to the right eye, this introduces a retinal disparity. Consequently, the central square appears to stand out in depth. You may be able to achieve this without special apparatus by crossing your eyes slightly to bring the images into the appropriate register in the two eyes.
Sekuler, R. & Blake, R., *Perception* (3 ed.) (McGraw-Hill, New York, 1994).

half of the figure, four different disparity selective cells will respond to the four possible matches, because each will have an appropriate stimulus in its two receptive fields. How does the visual system know which of these four cells to believe? Although the correspondence problem appears daunting, Marr and Poggio (1976) showed that it can be solved using just two simple assumptions about the world. First, we can see only one object at a time along any particular line of sight. Second, objects tend to be fairly smooth, so that abrupt changes in distance are fairly rare. These two assumptions can be built into a neurally plausible scheme, as is illustrated in the bottom half of figure 6.22. We simply connect disparity cells that represent the same line of sight by inhibitory links: these potential matches cannot coexist, so cells that signal them should compete with each other to decide a single winner. We also connect cells that represent the same (or similar) distances in neighbouring regions by excitatory links: these cells signal smoothly varying depth and so should cooperate with each other. Marr and Poggio were able to show, using a computer simulation, that this simple scheme could successfully extract relative distance from complex random dot stereograms. On first presentation, many cells respond, representing all the possible correspondence matches but, after a short time, the inhibitory and excitatory connections exert their influence so that the incorrect matches are killed off and only the cells signalling the correct solution continue to respond. This simulation provides an elegant example of a NEURAL NETWORK in which simple units are connected by exitatory and inhibitory links to produce a neurally plausible implementation of a well-principled theory.

NEURAL NETWORK

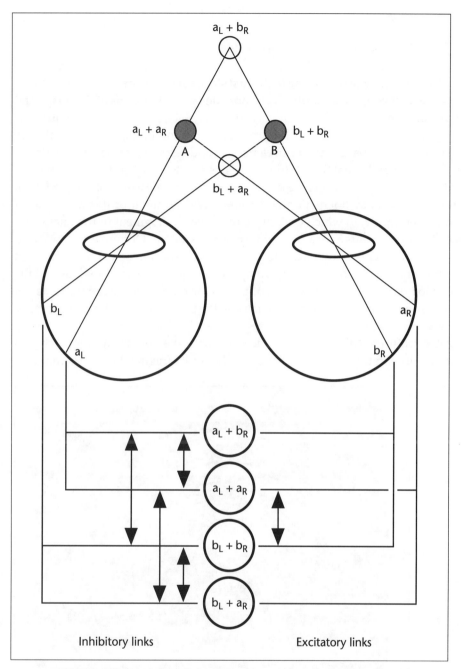

Figure 6.22 The Correspondence Problem. At the top of the figure, two dots (A and B) produce two images in each eye (a_L and b_L, a_R and b_R). To see the dots correctly, the visual system must correctly match the images, a_L with a_R and b_L with b_R. However, it is also possible to make the incorrect matches a_L with b_R and b_L with a_R. This would be equivalent to seeing the dots in the wrong places, as indicated by the open circles. These incorrect matches may seem easy to avoid when there are only two dot images in each eye – but a random dot stereogram projects many thousands of dot images to each eye and mismatches are then a considerable problem. The bottom of the figure represents four binocularly-driven cells, each with a receptive field in both eyes. All four cells will respond since each has an appropriate stimulus in both eyes. This is equivalent to making all the possible matches described above (each cell represents one possible match). The correct solution is found by (a) arranging inhibitory links between cells representing the same line of sight. Thus, for example, $b_L + a_R$ and $b_L + b_R$ inhibit each other because they fall on the same line of sight from the left eye. (b) arranging excitatory links between cells representing similar distances. Thus, in this simple example, only $a_L + a_R$ and $b_L + b_R$ excite each other.

▨ Integrative Processes in Vision ▨

Descriptive processes operating in the first stages of vision break down the stimulus in two ways. First, individual cells operate on small regions of the image and so break it down into tiny fragments. Secondly, each process measures just one aspect of the stimulus, so that luminance, colour and motion, for example, are represented in separate neural streams. The end result, according to Marr's notion of the Raw Primal Sketch (figure 6.5), is a description in which individual features of the object are represented together with measures of their relevant properties, such as orientation and colour. We can think of this as a kind of multilayer jigsaw, in which each piece represents a fragment of the image and each layer represents a separate propery, such as colour. Of course, jigsaws need solving, and there are two ways to go about this. We can look at the picture on the box and thus adopt a top-down approach by using our knowledge of the scene to help find and make sense of particular pieces. Or we can make useful progress with a bottom-up approach, using the physical properties of the pieces, such as their colour, to group them together and build larger-scale, more recognizable features. This section is concerned with the bottom-up approach and with the integrative processes that build the initial fragmentary measurements

Plate 6.5 Fraser's spiral. The dark/light 'barber's pole' lines are really concentric circles but appear to form a spiral.
Source: Frisby 1979.

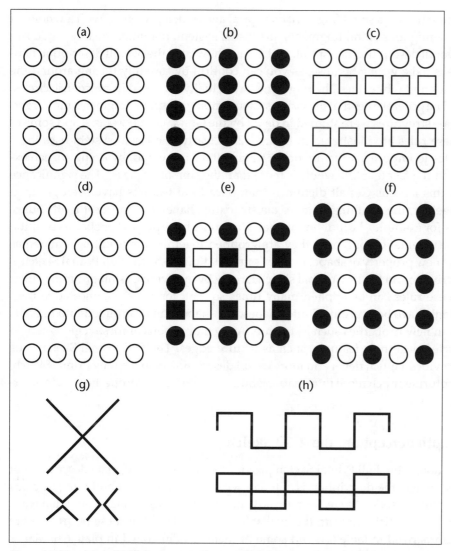

Figure 6.23 Examples of Gestalt grouping rules. (a) A 'neutral' stimulus may be organized into columns or rows. (b) Similarity of shading produces organization into columns. (c) Similarity of shape produces organization into rows. (d) Proximity produces organization into rows. (e) Similarity of shading can override similarity of shape. (f) Similarity of shading can override proximity. (g) Good continuation results in a percept of two crossing lines, rather than, for example, the alternative organizations shown below. (h) Closure means that the addition of a single line changes the organization from a line to a series of closed bricks.

into larger clusters, putting back together the information about colour, motion, and so forth.

Grouping processes: the Full Primal Sketch

The process of grouping the initial fragmentary measurements into larger-scale structures is revealed in plate 6.5, the Fraser spiral. Each section of the black and white lines is a small fragment of a spiral and, when presented with a whole set of contiguous spiral fragments, the visual system, not unreasonably, builds an overall description of a spiral. In this case, however, the overall description happens to be wrong because, as you can confirm by carefully tracing around the black and white lines, the fragments are actually arranged in concentric circles.

GESTALT
PSYCHOLOGISTS

The general rules that the visual system employs to group fragments into larger-scale structures were studied in detail by the GESTALT PSYCHOLOGISTS, and some of these rules are illustrated in figure 6.23. Clearly, the visual system uses these rules to impose a structure on its fragmentary input and, by doing so, can exploit the fact that 'the whole is more than the sum of its parts'. The significance of this famous Gestalt dictum is that, once local features have been grouped together, the resulting larger-scale structures have new and useful attributes. So, for example, the individual lines of a square have properties such as position and orientation but, once they are grouped together, the resulting square has the new property of shape. In Marr's model (figure 6.5), the Full Primal Sketch is derived from the raw primal sketch largely by applying Gestalt grouping rules. These rules can be applied many times so that, for example, once edge fragments have been grouped into shapes, the shapes can be grouped into regions, with new properties such as texture. And comparisons of these regions can, in turn, reveal new features, such as texture edges. The Full Primal Sketch thus provides a much richer and more useful description than the Raw Primal Sketch, capturing much more information about the underlying properties of the external world.

Depth perception: the 2½D Sketch

Although the Full Primal Sketch provides a rich and appropriate description of the image, the description is still flat, whereas both the real and our conscious worlds are solid. As we have already mentioned, there are many potential ways to recover distance from the available stimulus. Many of these DEPTH CUES are summarized in table 6.1, and some of them are illustrated in plate 6.6. Marr's notion of a 2½D Sketch (figure 6.5) recognizes the possibility of using these cues to add depth to the description of the available stimulus. The term '2½D' is intended to emphasize that the resulting description is a depth map of the world seen from one particular viewpoint: it is not fully 3D because it takes no account of hidden surfaces. A 3D description of a cube, for example, would specify the layout of all 6 of its surfaces, whereas the 2½D Sketch of a cube can only give the layout of the one, two or three surfaces that are currently visible.

DEPTH CUES

While relatively few depth cues are available directly from the Raw Primal Sketch, the Full Primal Sketch, with its explicit representation of such useful things as texture, provides an ideal basis for depth processing. Also, although there are many different routes to depth, they all start in the same 3D external world and they all end in the same 3D internal percept. Thus, one of the potential advantages of the 2½D Sketch lies in providing a common stage at which

Table 6.1 Depth Cues

Cue	Type	Explanation
Accommodation	Monocular, Physiological	The lens is adjusted to bring objects at different distances into focus.
Convergence	Binocular, Physiological	The eyes are rotated to bring the images of objects at different distances into register on each fovea.
Disparity	Binocular, Physiological	The two retinal images are slightly different because they are taken from slightly different positions. Stereopsis is the analysis of these differences, or disparities, to recover relative distance.
Shading	Monocular, Pictorial	The amount of light reflected into the eye from a surface depends on the angle from which it is viewed. Thus, curved surfaces, particularly, produce an image in which the brightness varies across the surface. Such variations in shading give clues about the changing angle of the surface, and are frequently used in pictures to give an impression of solidity.
Aerial perspective	Monocular, Pictorial	Light is scattered as it travels, so distant objects appear blurred. Short wavelengths (blue) are scattered more, so distant objects are seen through a bluish haze.
Height in visual field	Monocular, Pictorial, Linear perspective	Objects below the fixation plane (e.g. the floor) become higher in the image with distance. Objects above the fixation plane (e.g. clouds) become lower in the image with distance.
Texture gradient	Monocular, Pictorial, Linear perspective	Texture gradients become denser with increasing distance.
Converging lines	Monocular, Pictorial, Linear perspective	Parallel lines become closer together in the image with increasing distance.
Occlusion	Monocular, Pictorial	Distant objects are occluded in the image by nearer objects.
Motion Parallax	Monocular, Pictorial, Dynamic perspective	For a moving observer, the images of distant stationary objects move more slowly than those of nearby stationary objects.
Known size	Monocular, Pictorial, Cognitive	The known size of an object can be used to judge its distance. (For example, a large object that produces a small image must be far away.)

Plate 6.6 A picture making use of the depth cues listed in table 6.1
Source: Sekuler and Blake 1994.

information from different depth cues can be combined.

Marr himself proposed the 2½D Sketch as an essential stage in object recognition, where pre-stored 3D knowledge about objects could be compared and matched with a description of the current stimulus. As we shall see, this claim remains controversial but, whether or not it is true, it seems clear that the 2½D Sketch would be useful in a variety of other tasks that can, in principle, be accomplished independently of complete recognition. A depth map of the visible world could be used, for example, in guiding hand grasp and arm position when we pick up and manipulate an object. At a coarser level, it could help us to plan and carry out our movements about the world. As a final example, consider the important problem of estimating the size of an object. The size of the image that an object produces will clearly depend on viewing distance, with the image becoming smaller as the object gets further away. The fact that we show SIZE CONSTANCY, so that things do not appear to grow or shrink as we approach or leave them, clearly demonstrates that image size is interpreted in the context of perceived distance, perhaps making use of the kind of information available in the 2½D Sketch.

SIZE CONSTANCY

▓ Inferential Processes in Vision: Object Recognition ▓

The task of object recognition (literally, knowing again) requires us to match our description of the available stimulus with the appropriate, pre-stored knowledge about the object that originally produced the stimulus. We thus need a way to represent 3D object structure that is general enough to capture all recognizable objects and that can easily be matched with the kind of description provided by bottom-up processes. Rather than trying to represent complete objects,

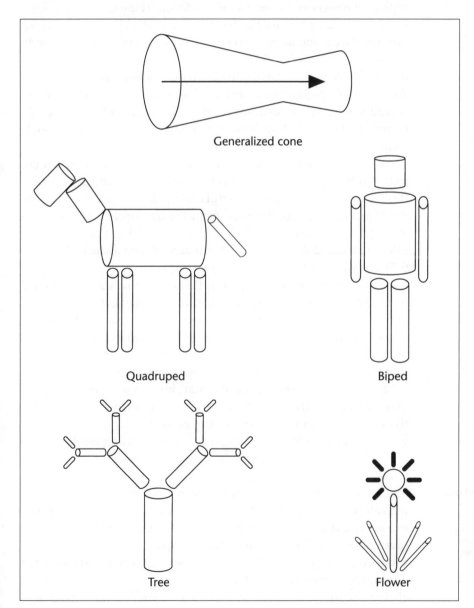

Figure 6.24 Marr's generalized cones consist of an axis (represented by the arrow in the top figure), a cross-section, and a function stating how this cross-section changes along the axis. Even in simplified form, they can easily be used to represent many objects.

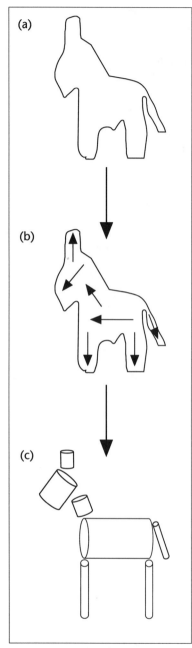

Figure 6.25 To match an image (a) to an object representation based on generalized cones, first segment the image into sections and assign an axis to each section (b), then use these axes to generate the appropriate generalized cones (c).
Source: Modified from Mann 1982

the most obvious approach to this problem is to try to identify a limited set of building blocks from which all objects can be constructed.

In Marr's scheme (figure 6.5), the basic building blocks are called GENERALIZED CONES. The essential features of a generalized cone, illustrated in figure 6.24, are an axis, a description of the cross-section, and a description of the way that this cross-section varies in size as we move along the axis. Figure 6.24 shows how, even when we simplify them to basic cylinders, different combinations of generalized cones allow us to describe many different objects. Moreover, we can represent objects at different levels of detail. At the coarsest level, for example, a human being can be thought of as a single cone. At the next level we could break it down into separate cones for head, body and limbs, and we could carry on adding detail until each component had been broken down into the smallest possible building blocks. Access to this description at any level would make the whole representation available so that, for example, if a fragmented view could be matched to a hand, we would immediately know about possible locations of arms, body and head.

Although particularly suited to natural things, just about all objects can be represented as collections of generalized cones, so the descriptive scheme seems powerful enough for the task. But how are the object descriptions accessed from the descriptions of the available stimulus? Marr suggests that the 2½D Sketch is first segmented into regions and that each region is then assigned an axis. As figure 6.25 shows, the resulting 'matchstick' figure is in the same general form as the pre-stored object descriptions and could thus be matched to the most appropriate one available. The precise shape of each generalized cone could then be investigated. Note that though figure 6.25 is necessarily two-dimensional, axes are assigned in the 2½D Sketch so that the same process would work even if the viewpoint were such that the donkey's legs were sticking out towards us.

Marr's scheme seems a plausible start but it has never been rigorously tested and there are important recent extensions and alternatives. Irving Biederman's (1987) theory of 'RECOGNITION BY COMPONENTS', for example, is based on a different kind of building block called a GEON. Geons are actually a specific subset of generalized cones and it is the logic behind them that makes them interesting. Biederman's account begins right back at the image by pointing out that certain of its features, termed NON-ACCIDENTAL PROPERTIES, convey reliable information about the 3D structure of the world. A straight line or a symmetrical region in an image, for example, are almost certainly produced by a straight edge or a symmetrical object in the external world. Biederman realized that even a small set of such simple dichotomies (straight/curved, symmetrical/asymmetrical) was enough

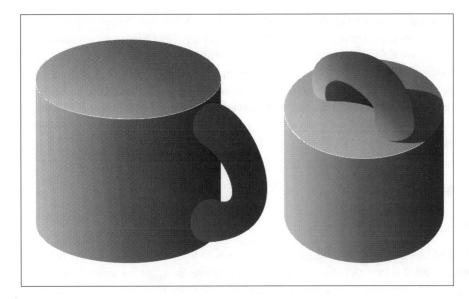

Figure 6.26 Simple objects built from geons. Two typical geons are shown, one with a curved cross-section and curved axis, the other with a curved cross-section and straight axis. Combining these geons in different ways leads to very different objects.

to form the basis of a powerful descriptive scheme. We can retain the essential cross-section and axis features of the generalized cone but, instead of providing detailed quantititive descriptions, using a limited vocabulary of qualitatively different types of geon based on simple dichotomies. One type, for example, might have a curved cross-section and a straight axis while a different type might have a curved cross-section and a curved axis. Using simple dichotomies in this way, Biederman proposes just a few different types of geon and argues that many thousands of different objects can be described as constellations of two or three geons. Figure 6.26 shows, for example, how two different objects can be represented by different combinations of the same two types of geon.

Biederman's scheme is atractive in a number of ways. It does not require detailed measurements of the stimulus, for example, but only simple decisions about whether things are straight or curved, symmetrical or asymmetrical, and so forth. Moreover, it does not require a 2½D Sketch because the types of decision needed can be made at the level of the Full Primal Sketch. This can be segmented into regions and each region can be assigned an axis, just as Marr proposed for the 2½D Sketch. Each piece can then be described directly in 'geon-language' (for example, straight, symmetrical cross-section, curved axis) so that, if Biederman's claims are correct, the description of just a few connected pieces allows direct access to the appropriate object description.

The main disadvantage of the scheme is that, while it would allow rapid recognition or classification of an object, it does not provide enough information for you to do anything about it. For example, one could not reach out and grasp the object because, having bypassed the 2½D Sketch, little is known about its 3D orientation. Perhaps, then, we should regard Biederman's scheme as a way to bring in knowledge about objects at an early stage of visual processing, so that this knowledge can be used, in a top-down way, to guide further descriptive processing. This would suggest a much more flexible interaction between bottom-up and top-down processing than the rather rigid hierarchy proposed by Marr (figure 6.5). It also highlights the reasonable possibility that the visual system uses different descriptions for different purposes. The 2½D Sketch may not be required, as Marr envisaged, primarily for visual object recognition because, if Biederman is correct, this can be achieved more directly from the 2D information provided by the Full Primal Sketch. Instead, the 2½D Sketch may be needed in rather different tasks like manipulation and locomotion.

▓ Hearing ▓

Descriptive processes

TYMPANIC
MEMBRANE

Sound has its physical origins in movements in the external world. Such movements cause waves of pressure variation that travel through the air and are picked up as variations in sound pressure level over time by the TYMPANIC MEMBRANE, or ear drum, in each of our ears (figures 6.3 and 6.28). Figure 6.27 shows two typical sound waveforms. Although such things as edges are obviously important features of an image, it is much more difficult to decide what might constitute

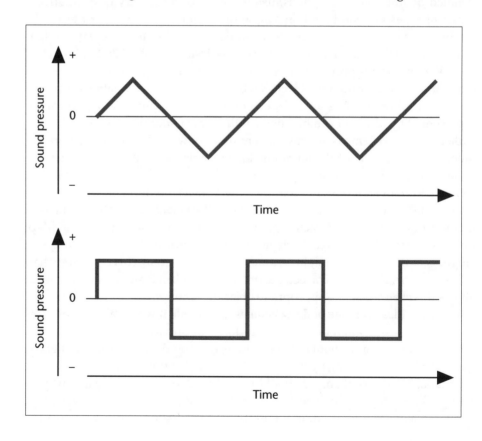

Figure 6.27 Two simple sound waveforms.

an important feature of an auditory waveform. However, the principles that govern descriptive processes in vision are general enough to apply to all sensory modalities, including hearing. Just as vision starts by measuring such basic properties of the image as the amount of colour and motion, hearing begins by measuring such basic properties of the auditory waveform as frequency and amplitude. And just as visual features are, in effect, changes in these basic properties, so auditory features are changes in the corresponding auditory measures.

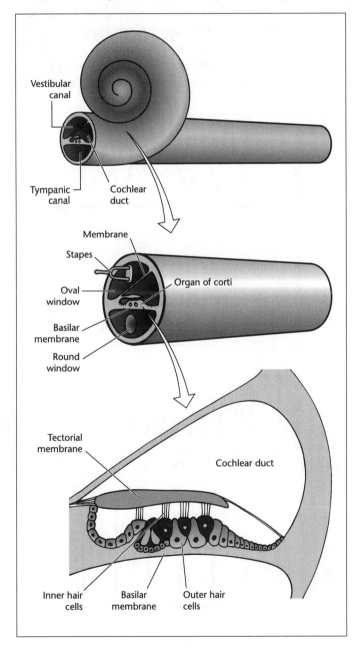

Figure 6.28 The anatomy of the cochlea.
Sekuler, R. & Blake, R., *Perception* (3 ed.) (McGraw-Hill, New York, 1994).

Pitch and timbre

The two waveforms shown in figure 6.27 might represent the stimuli produced by two hypothetical musical instruments, both playng the same note. Both stimuli are periodic, consisting of a series of identical cycles, and the perceived PITCH of such stimuli is determined largely by rate of repetition; higher rates of repetition, or frequencies, produce higher perceived pitch. The frequency of these two examples is the same, so both would have the same perceived pitch, but each would have a different sound quality, or TIMBRE, determined primarily by the different shapes of the two waveforms. Thus, for example, a violin sounds different from an oboe because of a difference in timbre. The description of both pitch and timbre begins at the BASILAR MEMBRANE, which forms part of the

PITCH

TIMBRE

BASILAR
MEMBRANE

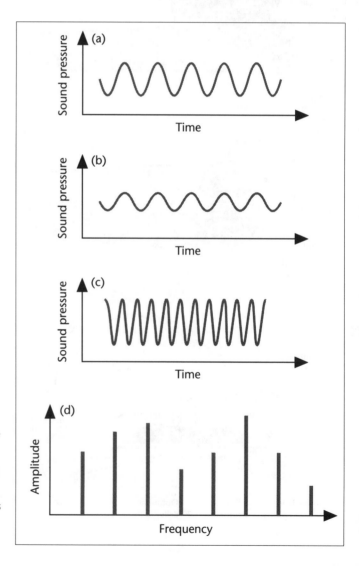

Figure 6.29 The Fourier series. (a)–(c) show simple harmonics or sinusoids. (b) has the same frequency as (a) but a smaller amplitude. (c) has the same amplitude as (a) but a higher frequency. All periodic waveforms are made up of such simple harmonics. The Fourier series (d) represents a periodic waveform by specifying the amplitude of each of its harmonics. The lowest frequency harmonic is called the fundamental frequency and, roughly speaking, determines a sound's perceived pitch. The overall pattern of harmonics determines a sound's perceived sound quality, or timbre.

COCHLEA, as shown in figure 6.28. To understand how this description works we must first introduce an alternative way to describe waveforms.

It is commonly known that musical sounds can be thought of as a series of HARMONICS. Harmonics are just a particularly simple type of waveform, illustrated in figure 6.29, sometimes called a PURE TONE or SINUSOID, which can vary in frequency and amplitude, but which always has exactly the same basic shape. The first harmonic of a PERIODIC WAVEFORM is just a pure tone with the same basic frequency as the original waveform. All the other possible harmonics have whole-number multiples of this FUNDAMENTAL FREQUENCY. For example, the first four possible harmonics of a waveform that repeats 100 times a second are 100, 200, 300 and 400 cycles per second, or hertz (Hz). As shown in figure 6.29, an alternative way to describe such periodic waveforms is simply to plot out the amplitude of each of its harmonics. The resulting harmonic spectrum is technically called a FOURIER SERIES. In fact, the same idea can be applied to any waveform, so that even non-repeating, or aperiodic, stimuli can be decribed in terms of their frequency content, although the spectrum of an aperiodic waveform is called a FOURIER TRANSFORM, rather than a series, and typically contains sinusoids of all frequencies, rather than a regular series of discrete harmonics.

There are thus two completely equivalent ways to describe the auditory stimulus (or, more generally, any waveform): we can think of it as a sound pressure waveform that varies over time or as a set of sinusoidal components of particular frequency and amplitude. Variations in the frequency of a periodic stimulus will change the fundamental frequency of the Fourier series and the perceived pitch. Variations in the shape of the waveform will change the relative amplitudes of the harmonics of the Fourier series and the perceived timbre. This basic logic is important because the description formed in the first stages of the auditory system is a kind of Fourier series.

Periodic sound pressure variations, such as pure tones, cause the ear drum to vibrate at the same frequency as the stimulus and these vibrations are transmitted by the tiny bones of the MIDDLE EAR to the OVAL WINDOW of the cochlea (figure 6.28). Here, each pulse of the vibration causes a pulse to travel along the basilar membrane, rather like the ripple produced in a slack rope by a flick of the wrist. The resulting TRAVELLING WAVE is illustrated in figure 6.30. Each point on the basilar membrane moves up and down as the pulse travels past, and this movement causes mechanical distortion of the HAIR CELLS that are arrayed along the membrane and which act as the auditory receptors. The distortion causes graded potentials in the hair cells which, in turn, may cause action potentials in the fibres of the AUDITORY NERVE that innervates the basilar membrane. The mechanical properties of the cochlea are such that the pulse changes in amplitude as it travels along the basilar membrane. High frequency sounds produce pulses that start large and become gradually smaller, whereas low frequencies produce pulses that start small and become gradually larger. Thus, the point on the basilar membrane at which the pulse is largest will depend crucially upon the frequency of the stimulus. Moreover, because the size of the pulse determines the amount

COCHLEA

HARMONICS

PURE TONE

SINUSOID

PERIODIC WAVEFORM

FUNDAMENTAL FREQUENCY

FOURIER SERIES

FOURIER TRANSFORM

MIDDLE EAR

OVAL WINDOW

TRAVELLING WAVE

HAIR CELLS

AUDITORY NERVE

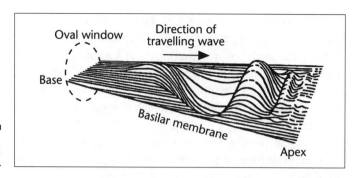

Figure 6.30 A travelling wave on the basilar membrane.
Sekuler, R. & Blake, R., *Perception* (3 ed.) (McGraw-Hill, New York, 1994).

of mechanical distortion and thus the size of the receptor potential in the hair cells, different sound frequencies produce action potentials in different fibres of the auditory nerve. In fact, recordings from these fibres show that each fibre responds only to a very narrow range of stimulus frequencies.

For periodic sounds, the mechanical distortion of the hair cells also occurs periodically, as the pulses produced by successive cycles travel down the basilar membrane. Thus, the activity in the auditory nerve fibres is also periodic, with a burst of action potentials for each cycle of the stimulus. This is termed PHASE LOCKING, referring to the fact that the action potentials in any given fibre tend to occur at the same position, or phase, on each cycle of the stimulus.

PHASE LOCKING

If we wanted to measure the frequency of a pure tone, then two aspects of the auditory response would potentially be useful. First, different frequencies produce maximum mechanical displacement at different positions on the basilar membrane and, since these different places are innervated by different nerve fibres, this produces activity in different nerve fibres. Activity in a given nerve fibre should thus reliably signal a specific stimulus frequency. This is called the PLACE THEORY OF PITCH PERCEPTION. Second, bursts of action potentials are synchronized with the stimulus so that, irrespective of the identity of the nerve fibre, the interval between bursts should reliably signal the duration of each cycle and, thus, the frequency of the stimulus. This is called the TIME THEORY OF PITCH PERCEPTION. These two theories are, to some extent, complementary. Place theory gives a rather poor account of the perceived pitch of pure tones at low frequencies, essentially because the position of the peak mechanical displacement of the basilar membrane does not change much at these frequencies. Conversely, time theory is limited at high frequencies because nerves cannot keep track of the individual cycles above about 5,000 Hz. However, pure tones are rare in nature and the real strength of the description provided by the basilar membrane becomes apparent only when we consider more complex sounds.

PLACE THEORY OF PITCH PERCEPTION

TIME THEORY OF PITCH PERCEPTION

When a mixture of two pure tones of reasonably different frequencies is presented simultaneuously, the basilar membrane breaks it down into its separate components because the resulting travelling wave has peaks at the two positions corresponding to the two frequencies. Moreover, at each of these positions, the basilar membrane moves up and down at the frequency of the corresponding component, so that the timing of the neural response at each

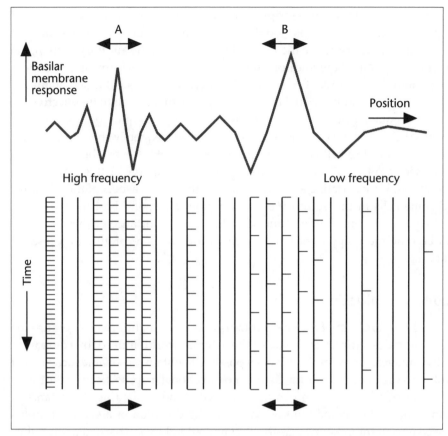

Figure 6.31 A schematic representation of how the basilar membrane works. A sound composed of two harmonics (A and B) produces a travelling wave on the basilar membrane with two distinct peaks (top panel). (A) corresponds to the higher-frequency harmonic, (B) to the lower-frequency harmonic. The bottom panel shows the pattern of action potentials in individual fibres of the auditory nerve. Each fibre innervates a different position on the basilar membrane. The harmonic structure of the stimulus is preserved in the identity of the fibres that are responding most. The temporal pattern of action potentials within these active fibres preserves the frequency of the corresponding harmonic.

position also preserves the frequency of an individual component. More generally, since any periodic waveform can be described as a Fourier series, the basilar membrane will, within its mechanical limits, break down any waveform into its harmonics, with the amplitude of each harmonic being represented by the amount of mechanical displacement at the appropriate position on the membrane and, hence, by the amount of neural activity associated with that position. Thus, the resulting pattern of response in the auditory nerve, illustrated schematically in figure 6.31, provides a description of the available stimulus that is very like a Fourier series. The identity of each harmonic is given either by the identity of the responding fibre or the temporal pattern of its response, whilst the amplitude of each component is given by the total amount of neural activity associated with that harmonic. This description, of course, captures not only the frequency of the stimulus but also the timbre of complex sounds.

In the visual system, the description of the image at the retina is based around simple features such as edges, and this description is refined in the first stage of the visual cortex to produce the Raw Primal Sketch. In the auditory system, the initial description of the auditory waveform at the cochlea seems to be more general and does not identify specific features. Much less is known about the auditory cortex than the visual cortex: many cells there seem to be selective for stimulus frequency but there is still some debate, for example, about whether or not these cells form a TONOTOPIC MAP, with preferred frequency changing systematically from cell to cell across the cortical surface. However, there is at least some evidence that auditory features do begin to emerge at this stage of the description. We can define a feature as a change in some aspect of the stimulus, and some cells in the auditory cortex do indeed respond best to changes in the frequency or amplitude of the stimulus. The importance of these features will become more apparent later, when we discuss interpretive processes in hearing.

TONOTOPIC MAP

Auditory localization

Locating the direction of a visual stimulus is fairly straightforward because the image provides a directional map of the external world. Indeed, by comparing the two images, for example, it is even possible to obtain reasonable measures of an object's distance. In hearing, there is no directional map, so locating the direction of a sound source is much more difficult, and measuring its distance is almost impossible. None the less, knowing the direction of a sound stimulus may be important in helping us to select and attend to one particular stimulus, such as one voice in a crowded room, a phenomenon rather quaintly called the COCKTAIL PARTY PHENOMENON.

COCKTAIL PARTY PHENOMENON

The two main sources of information about auditory direction rely upon BINAURAL COMPARISONS of the stimulus to the two ears. Sound waves travel relatively slowly so that, if a sound source is to the left, for example, the waveform will arrive at the left ear before the right. A measure of this INTERAURAL DELAY provides information about the direction of the source because it varies systematically with direction. This cue is useful where the sound source has clear 'landmarks', like onsets and offsets, or, if it is periodic, where the interaural delay is small in relation to the repetition period. But, for continuous high frequency stimuli where the delay is large in comparison to the repetition period, it is very difficult to work out which cycle in one ear should be matched with which in the other ear (an analogue of the correspondence problem described for stereopsis). Thus TIMING CUES are not very effective at high frequencies.

BINAURAL COMPARISONS

INTERAURAL DELAY

TIMING CUES

A second potential measure is provided by binaural comparisons of stimulus intensity. The head blocks sounds, casting an acoustic shadow so that, if a sound source is to the left, for example, the stimulus will be more intense in the left ear than the right and, in fact, the difference in intensity will vary sytematically with the direction of the source. This measure is useful at high frequencies but rather ineffective at low frequencies because the head does not block these sounds very well.

It is quite easy to show that the auditory system makes use of both timing and INTENSITY CUES in estimating auditory direction. If a tone is presented over stereo headphones with the signal louder in, say, the left ear than the right, the sound seems to come from the left of the head. If the stimulus to the left ear is then delayed slightly, thus providing a conflicting timing cue, the sound seems to come from a central direction. By varying the frequency of the stimulus and measuring the amount of one cue needed to balance the other, we can work out how effective each cue is at each frequency. As you might expect from the preceding description, the two cues complement each other nicely, with timing measures more effective and important at low frequencies and intensity cues more effective and important at high frequencies.

INTENSITY CUES

Unfortunately even both cues in combination are not sufficient completely to specify the direction of a sound source, because any given interaural difference in intensity and timing can be produced by a whole range of directions. For example, equal intensities and no interaural delay could result from a sound source directly in front, behind or, in fact, anywhere on an imaginary vertical plane passing through the centre of the head from back to front. These ambiguities can be resolved by head rotations or, in some species like cats and rabbits, by movement of the ears independently of the head. But the intricate shape of the external human ear, or PINNA, is also important in this role. The spiral-shaped folds of skin set up tiny echoes, and the delay between the orginal sound and the echo varies systematically with horizontal and vertical direction of the source. Although we do not hear these echoes consciously, they are important in locating sounds because, when the spirals are artificially distorted, our ability to locate sounds is systematically changed.

PINNA

▥ Integrative Processes in Hearing ▥

We have already seen that the waveform produced by even a simple sound source, such as a musical instrument, is complex and that the cochlea produces a description based on harmonic analysis that provides the information needed to ascribe pitch and timbre. How does the auditory system tackle the more difficult problem of sorting out the still more complex waveforms produced by several sound sources or instruments playing at once? We have already mentioned the cocktail party phenomenon, which indicates one solution to this problem: the auditory system appears able to separate out sounds coming from different directions. However, even when no directional information is available, as in a monophonic recording or radio broadcast, we are still able to recognize separate sound sources.

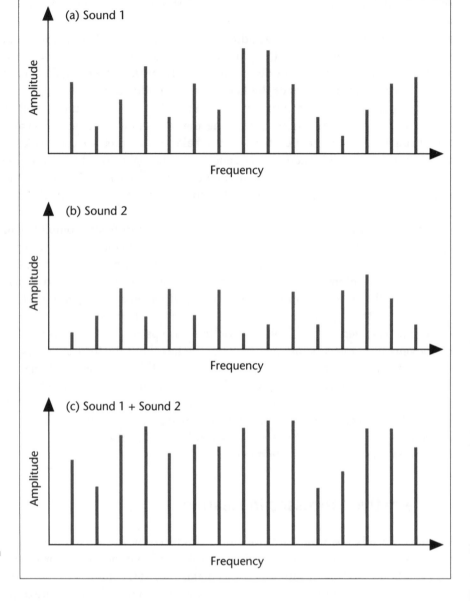

Figure 6.32 The problem of auditory segmentation. Two sounds (a) and (b) presented simultaneously simply add together to produce a new harmonic pattern (c). The cochlea is presented with this mixture and faces the problem of breaking it down into the original sounds.

Auditory segmentation

The general problem of auditory segmentation is illustrated in figure 6.32, which represents two musical instruments playing slightly different notes. Since the two sounds simply add together on the basilar membrane, how does the auditory system know that there are two sound sources, rather than one, and how does it decide which harmonic belongs with which sound? One solution to this problem is based on the fact that different musical instruments usually have

ENVELOPES different ENVELOPES: the sound produced by a piano, for example, rises quickly and then decays slowly, whilst the sound produced by an oboe is much more sustained and oscillates gently in both pitch and loudness. Each harmonic will have the same envelope as the overall sound so, in the pattern of activity on the basilar membrane, the set of harmonics associated with one instrument will follow a different time course from those associated with the other instrument. Thus, the two sounds could be segmented simply by grouping together the harmonics that follow similar time courses, and pitch and timbre could then be separately ascribed to each set. Indeed, one reason why the basilar membrane has evolved to perform a harmonic analysis may well be to allow this type of segmentation which, although we have described it in terms of musical instruments, is often required in the natural world.

▨ Inferential Processes in Hearing: Speech Recognition ▨

Speech recognition is a rather specialized and refined form of auditory recognition, although, reassuringly, it seems to follow the same general principles as visual recognition. Like vision, the first step is to define a set of building blocks from which all speech sounds can be constructed. Neither words nor syllables are suitable for this because there are just too many of them. Instead, the most obvious candidate is the basic speech sound called a PHONEME. The word 'good', for example, consists of the three phonemes: /g/oo/d/. Only about 50 phonemes are needed to describe all human languages and most languages make use of far fewer than this.

PHONEME

Phonemes, of course, are only useful if they can easily be recovered from the descriptions provided by bottom-up processes. At first, this appears a formidable task because many phonemes don't have an obvious, measurable, physical basis. Vowel sounds have a clearly perceivable pitch because they are periodic and so have a clear harmonic structure, consisting of discrete bands of frequencies called FORMANTS (figure 6.33). Another type of speech sound, called VOICED

FORMANTS

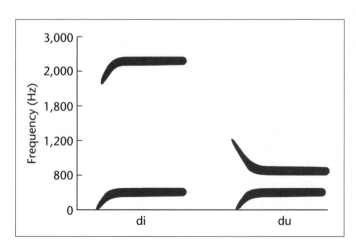

Figure 6.33 Two simple speech sounds (/di/ and /du/), each represented by two formants (bands of harmonics). The same sound (/d/) can be represented by very different patterns. Sekuler, R. & Blake, R., *Perception* (3 ed.) (McGraw-Hill, New York, 1994).

stops (/d/ and /g/, as in 'dog', for example), seems to involve changes in the frequency of these formants, called FORMANT TRANSITIONS. Unfortunately, these transitions depend crucially on their context so that, as shown in figure 6.33, the same phoneme /d/ can be signalled by very different transitions, depending on what it immediately precedes. Worse, when the succeeding sound is removed, the transitions by themselves do not sound like /d/ or, indeed, like any other speech sound.

Problems like this suggest that we cannot recover phonemes simply by describing the sound waveform, and led to early theories of speech recognition that were rather different in emphasis from those proposed in vision. The most extreme of these, called ANALYSIS BY SYNTHESIS, proposed that discrete phonemes did not exist directly in the speech waveform at all, but only indirectly in the commands that produced the waveform. A speaker would always issue the same motor commands to the speech apparatus when saying /d/, for example, but these commands would produce different movements of the tongue, say, depending on where it was at the end of the preceding phoneme, and where it was going for the beginning of the next phoneme. Thus, the sound waveform produced will depend crucially upon the context, and the only solution for the listener seems to be to sub-vocalize along with the speaker, testing hypotheses about what is being said to see if they produce configurations of the vocal tract that would, in turn, produce the speech waveform actually received. This is a very extreme form of top-down processing in which phonemes that can be extracted from the speech waveform act as cues to hypotheses that must then be actively tested. Such hypotheses cannot reasonably be based purely on the fragmentary physical evidence and so must also rely heavily on high-level knowledge about the meaning of the utterance and the grammar of the language.

The same speech sounds are, indeed, more easily understood in a meaningful, rather than a meaningless context, which does indicate the importance of high-level information in speech recognition. None the less, contemporary theories propose a more even balance between bottom-up and top-down processes, akin to that proposed for visual object recognition. The key to this change in emphasis is the realization that physical clues to phonemes are, in fact, present in the speech waveform, if only one knows what to look for. If we measure a few apparently abstract aspects of the speech waveform including, for example, rate of change of amplitude and frequency, then each phoneme produces a unique pattern of results (high rate of change in amplitude, medium rate of change of frequency, and so forth). This emphasis on patterns of description is reminiscent of what is thought to happen in vision. Moreover, the emphasis on changes, rather than fixed values, fits well with the general definition of 'features' and with the types of measure that cells in the auditory cortex seem to make.

Plate 6.7 The hidden figure of a dalmatian dog snuffling amongst leaves. At first, this picture should appear to you as a meaningless jumble of black and white blobs. With a little persistence, the dog will suddenly emerge.
Source: Original by R. C. James; from Lindsay and Norman 1977.

▓ Concluding Remarks ▓

Both vision and hearing seem to involve two rather different stages. The first begins with simple measurements and ends with a structured description of the available stimulus. The second involves inferential processes that use high-level knowledge to make sense of this description in terms of external objects. The distinction between the two stages is captured in plate 6.7, which contains the 'hidden figure' of a dalmatian dog snuffling among leaves. Descriptive processes can provide a rich description of the image in terms of blobs, shapes, textures, and so forth. But this description, no matter how sophisticated, makes no sense until inferential processes succeed in finding the right explanation of these things in terms of ears, nose, leaves, and so forth.

Biological and psychophysical approaches have begun to unravel the descriptive stage, providing glimpses of how the visual and auditory systems are structured, of how some of the neural processes work, and even of why they may work the way they do. The neural bases of the inferential stage are much less clear but, here, computer models, based for example on Marr's and Biederman's ideas, provide some insight into how knowledge might be represented and how it might be used. But such models also raise some very difficult questions. Both models 'know' about individual objects, but it is quite clear that much of our everyday perception is based upon sophisticated expectations involving interactions between many objects. When we first open the door to a new room, for example, we know why we are doing it and have useful, if often unconscious, expectations about the sort of objects that the room will contain and about how its occupants will be interacting with those objects and with each other. How is all this knowledge, which seems so essential to perception, obtained in the first place and how does it become structured to provide such useful expectations? It seems very unlikely that we are born with it, yet without it we cannot perceive and so cannot learn about the world. At the very least, we must surely have, or very rapidly acquire, the ability to build structured descriptions of the available stimulus in different sensory modalities, to classify them into types, to label them, to notice correlations between these types and with our own behaviour, and to recognize those combinations that can be associated with desirable states of affairs and those that cannot.

Equipped with basic rules like this, it seems plausible that we could form the first essential link between the internal and the external worlds so that, for example, a measurable feature of an image like an edge could come to stand for something in the external world like an object boundary. And once that essential link is forged, we would be on the way to developing the perceptual systems that we so often take for granted but which are so essential, for example, in warning us that a particular constellation of image features represents a child carrying a letter who may step out in front of our car as she crosses the road to reach a post box.

CHAPTER SUMMARY

1   The indirect approach to perception holds that the senses do not provide enough information to account for everything that we perceive, so that the process of perception requires prior knowledge about the world. The direct approach holds that the senses do provide enough information to account for everything that we perceive, and that prior knowledge is not required. It seems likely that some visual tasks (like object recognition) are indirect, whilst others (like visual navigation) are primarily direct.

2   There are several ways to study perception. Neu-rophysiology and anatomy tell us about the properties of nerves, while psychophysics tells us about how the nerves might be involved in performing specific perceptual tasks. Computer simulations provide a way to test the resulting theories about how nerves function and interact to accomplish perceptual tasks.

3   The initial stages of vision are descriptive. Cells in the retina and the early stages of the visual pathway provide a description of where edges are, and about the colour, motion and binocular disparity of each small region of the visual world.

4 The descriptions of each small region of the world are then put together by integrative processes, rather like solving a jigsaw puzzle, so that parts of the image that belong together are properly grouped together.

5 Though images are flat, information about distance can be recovered from depth cues. Some depth cues (e.g., binocular stereopsis) can be applied to the original description of the stimulus and may even help the integrative processes. Other depth cues (such as pictorial cues) can only be applied once the original description has been structured by integrative processes.

6 Visual object recognition involves the matching of a description of the visual stimulus to pre-stored knowledge about the structure of objects. There are several ways in which information about object structure might be stored, but all are based on some limited set of 'structural primitives' from which a wide range of objects can be built. Some schemes (e.g., Marr's generalized cones) allow a detailed model of the object's 3D form and position to be built up, which would be useful, for example, if it is important to be able to manipulate the object. Other schemes (e.g. Biederman's

geons) do not allow such a detailed description of 3D form but would be more efficient where it is more important simply to name an object or to mobilize general information about its properties. It is quite possible that the fundamental differences in the tasks that vision must accomplish would require several different types of object representation.

7 Like vision, the initial stages of hearing are descriptive. Cells in the cochlea and early stages of the auditory pathway provide a description of the pattern of sound frequencies present in the sound and of the directions from which they are coming. Again, like vision, this initial description needs to be structured by grouping together those parts of the sound that might come from the same source.

8 The processes of auditory object recognition (such as speech recognition) are less well understood than the equivalent visual processes. For example, it is less clear what properties an auditory 'structural primitive' should have. However, it is clear that, like vision, some auditory tasks require inferential processes and that these must depend upon a rich and flexible description of the auditory stimulus.

▨ Further Work ▨

1. Consider the variety of everyday tasks to which vision contributes. How is vision involved in these tasks? Which of them might be achieved by direct perception and which require indirect perception?
2. Would a complete description of a retinal image provide an adequate basis for perception?
3. What can be learned from the study of illusions and after effects?
4. Discuss some advantages of being able to see in colour.
5. Why do we have two ears?
6. Which perceptual problems are unique to each sensory modality, and which do all sensory modalities share?
7. What does the study of hearing tell us about the appreciation of symphonic music?

Further Reading

Bruce, V., Green, P. R. and Georgeson, M. A. (1996; 3rd edn) *Visual Perception: Physiology, Psychology and Ecology*. Hove and London: Lawrence Erlbaum.

> Recently revised and updated, this is a very good, readable book on vision, though the coverage is a little patchy. It provides a detailed and up-to-date account of descriptive processing in the early stages of the visual system, followed by a thorough introduction to Gibson's ecological approach.

Marr, D. C. (1982) *Vision: A Computational Investigation Into the Human Representation and Processing of Visual Information*. San Francisco: W. H. Freeman.

> An ideal introduction to vision for those who like a more formal approach.

Moore, B. C. J. (1982; 2nd edn) *An Introduction to the Psychology of Hearing*. London: Academic Press.

> Good, comprehensive and readable coverage of hearing for those who wish to know more about this relatively neglected sensory modality.

Sekuler, R. and Blake, R. (1994; 3rd edn) *Perception*. New York: McGraw-Hill.

Goldstein, E. B. (1989; 3rd edn) *Sensation and Perception*. Belmont, Calif.: Wadsworth Publishing Company.

> There are many general textbooks on perception. These are two of the best. They cover all the sensory modalities, though, like all others, they are strongest on vision. Both are well written and, consequently, very readable.

Zeki, S. (1993) *A Vision of the Brain*. Oxford: Blackwell Scientific Publications.

> A beautifully illustrated and written account of the initial stages of visual processing, written primarily from a biological, rather than a psychological, perspective.

PsyCLE MODULE: THE RETINA
PsyCLE MODULE: BASICS OF SOUND

The module on 'The Retina' is an ideal tutorial for the section on 'Feature detection: the retina'. It supports that discussion and figures 6.6 to 6.11 in the text. You can inspect the biology concerned and explore a simulation of a single retinal cell. The experiment which explores the receptive field of the cell was the inspiration for the work of Hubel and Wiesel on the primary visual cortex. The mathematical model of convolution which is presented as an explanation of this cell's function is discussed in detail in the Marr reading.

The module on the 'Basics of Sound' is designed to explain the basic terminology that is introduced in the section on hearing in the text (supporting figures 6.27 to 6.31) and providing a simple audible demonstration of pitch, harmonics, the fundamental frequency and the Fourier series.

PART 4

Cognitive Psychology

CHAPTER 7

Memory

Alan Parkin

CHAPTER AGENDA

- In this chapter we see that memory cannot be viewed as a single entity.

- We show that there is a fundamental distinction between the memory system supporting conscious mental activity and that representing our permanent store of knowledge.

- The modal model proposes a distinction between sensory memory, short-term store (STS) and long-term store (LTS).

- Memory operates by forming a code of the information to be remembered and the same stimulus can have different codes extracted from it.

- There are various lines of evidence supporting the distinction between STS and LTS, but that from human amnesia is the most compelling.

- Levels of processing has offered an alternative to the modal model, but it has run into problems, because it is a circular theory.

- Long-term store is not a single entity – it comprises episodic, semantic and procedural memory. We note that whilst the distinction between episodic

and semantic memory makes good intuitive sense, the evidence favouring it is not strong.

- An alternative to the systems approach is to examine memory in terms of how it is accessed. Explicit memory refers to memory associated with conscious recollection whereas implicit memory is associated with tests that do not require that conscious act.

- Retrieval is a reconstructive act.

- Some theories specify that recall and recognition are different components of retrieval, whereas experiments demonstrating encoding specificity suggest that recall and recognition are different aspects of the same underlying process.

- Context is a critical factor in memory performance.

- Forgetting is important and occurs either through storage or retrieval failure.

- Working memory is an expansion of the STS idea in which a single store is replaced with a central executive interacting with specialized slave systems.

▓ Introduction ▓

Most of us think of memory as the ability to recall things from the past – events that happened hours, days and months ago. However, being conscious is, itself, an act of memory. Consider hearing this statement: 'Tonight the weather will be clear but with a faint chance of a shower near dawn.' You hear it as a whole, as part of the present. However, to have understood that sentence you must have stored the first part of the sentence while dealing with the second part. Being conscious thus spans a small amount of time and, as such, must depend on memory.

The link between consciousness and memory is not new. In his *Principles of Psychology* William James (1890) called the memory system supporting consciousness PRIMARY MEMORY, distinguishing it from SECONDARY MEMORY which formed our permanent record of the past. James suggested that primary memory should be thought of as 'the rearward portion of the present space of time' rather than as the 'genuine past'. A property of primary memory was that its contents were highly accessible whereas retrieving from secondary memory required an effortful act.

Because of the advent of behaviourism James's ideas about memory, in which consciousness played a pivotal role, did not start to influence experimental psychology until the 1960s. However, the methodological principles used in this research were already well established. Hermann Ebbinghaus (1885) proposed that human memory could only be scientifically investigated if every step were taken to exclude the influence of extraneous factors on the outcome of experiments. A major contaminating factor could be the prior knowledge of subjects, and to solve this problem he suggested using nonsense syllables as target stimuli. These would be unknown to the subjects and thus any differences in the memory for these items under different conditions would represent a genuine property of memory.

Ebbinghaus conducted most of his research on himself. His basic technique involved repetition of a list of nonsense syllables until he could recall it

PRIMARY MEMORY

SECONDARY
MEMORY

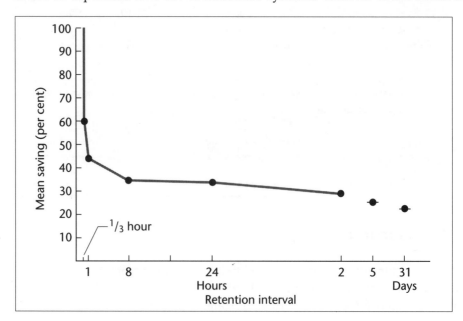

Figure 7.1 Forgetting rate, as measured by Ebbinghaus. From *The Psychology of Memory* by Alan D. Baddeley. Copyright © 1976 by Basic Books, Inc. Reprinted by permission of HarperCollins Publishers, Inc.

perfectly. In one experiment he examined rate of forgetting by testing how easily he could re-learn a list at different time intervals. Figure 7.1 shows the amount of savings in relearning after different retention intervals. At first forgetting is rather rapid but, after about eight hours, further forgetting occurs relatively slowly. This is one of a number of learning principles discovered by Ebbinghaus which remains true to the present day.

Not all psychologists are convinced that the Ebbinghaus approach is correct. They argue that using meaningless stimuli lacks any ecological validity – human beings do not, in their normal life, ever have to learn nonsense, so theories derived from experiments using this method have little or no value. An alternative approach, first put forward by Bartlett (1932), is that human memory can only be properly understood by investigating the learning of meaningful material. The problem with this approach is that it introduces many of the extraneous factors that Ebbinghaus tried to avoid. In particular, as Bartlett himself showed, subjects will tend to substitute their own general knowledge for information they are unable to recall. There are certainly occasions when the study of bias and distortion in memory are of major importance but, from the perspective of producing experimental evaluations of theories, the control offered by the Ebbinghaus tradition is still favoured by most investigators.

▧ The 'Multistore' Model of Memory ▧

The 1960s saw a massive growth in the use of computers and increased public awareness of how computers operated. Computers are essentially large databases that are operated on by a central processing unit. This unit represents the 'workspace' of the computer – the place where new information is input, existing information retrieved, and decisions involving the database executed. Psychologists were quick to see a similarity between this arrangement and the distinction between primary and secondary memory. Primary memory resembled the central processing unit and secondary memory represented the database. This led to Atkinson and Shiffrin's (1968) multistore model – this is often termed the 'modal model' because most psychologists accept the basic format.

The modal model characterizes memory as the flow of information between three interrelated stores. New information first enters SENSORY STORE. This is an extremely transient storage system which retains information about the pattern of sensory stimulation. Sensory storage of visual information is known as ICONIC MEMORY and its discovery arose from experiments by Sperling (1960). Subjects were presented with visual arrays comprising three rows of four random letters for very brief periods (e.g., 50 milliseconds). In the whole report condition they had to report as many letters as possible and, typically, subjects reported only four or five letters correctly. In the partial report condition a tone occurred after the display had terminated and this indicated which of the three rows should be reported. Performance in the partial report condition was almost perfect,

SENSORY STORE

ICONIC MEMORY

259

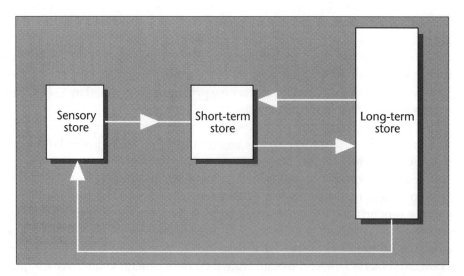

Figure 7.2 The multistore model of memory
From Atkinson & Shiffrin 1968 93.

providing the delay between end of the display and the tone did not exceed 500 milliseconds.

The fact that subjects could report the content of any row accurately suggested that they had more information about the array available than was indicated by the whole report condition. This partial report advantage was attributed to the operation of iconic memory, and the disappearance of this advantage at intervals greater than half a second indicated that storage in this memory system was extremely short lived. Although evidence such as this indicates the existence of iconic memory, its function remains less clear. Some people have argued that it serves no function whereas others have suggested that it is essential for the early stages of visual analysis.

ECHOIC MEMORY

The auditory equivalent to iconic memory is ECHOIC MEMORY. The need for a store of this nature is evident from the nature of various sounds we recognize. Phonemes in speech (basic units of sound), for example, are often only identifiable from the combination of perceptual cues that occur at different points in time. Many types of evidence point to the existence of this store but a particularly clear example is provided by Howell and Darwin (1977). They measured subjects' response times when judging whether two sounds were the same phoneme. On some trials the two phonemes were acoustically identical but on others there were slight acoustic differences. Same judgements were found to be faster for phonemes that were also acoustically similar, but only when the interval between the two phonemes was less than 800 milliseconds. People are therefore able to retain information about the detailed perceptual qualities of the stimulus but, like iconic memory, storage is very brief.

SHORT-TERM STORE

From sensory store, information passes to SHORT-TERM STORE (STS). This store was analogous to primary memory in that it represented the locus of conscious mental activity. The activities of STS were represented as various control processes which could be brought to bear on information according to requirements. STS had a limited capacity in that new information would displace existing information. Atkinson and Shiffrin stressed the importance of rehearsal in the transfer of information from STS into permanent storage – a structure which they termed LONG-TERM STORE (LTS). Rehearsal related to the natural human tendency to use repetition as a means of trying to remember something.

In addition they acknowledged the importance of ENCODING as a factor in memory functioning. Any memory system must store away information in terms of some form of code. Just as a telephone system translates your voice into an electromagnetic wave and then back into speech at the other end, human memory must convert information into a code and then convert this code back into a record of the information when recall is required. Understanding encoding is thus central to our explanation of how memory operates.

LONG-TERM STORE

ENCODING

Encoding differences

Investigations of encoding in human memory led to the view that STS and LTS might be distinguished by the type of code they used. Words are the predominant stimuli used in memory experiments. One reason for this is that words have three distinct encoding dimensions, that is, types of information that could serve as a basis for forming a code:

Orthographic – the visual pattern of letters comprising the word.
Phonological – the sound of the word.
Semantics – the meaning of the word.

A number of studies suggested that STS used phonological coding. Conrad (1964) explored the ability of people to repeat back, in the correct order, visually presented sequences of letters that were either phonologically confusable (e.g., CTVG) or non-confusable (e.g., XVSL). He found that phonologically confusable strings were more difficult to remember even when potential confounding influences of visual similarity were controlled for. This phonological confusability effect suggested that subjects used a phonological code in the immediate memory task.

Baddeley (1966a) showed that phonological confusability effects also occurred when subjects had to repeat back immediately sequences of similar sounding words (mad, map, man) compared with unrelated sequences (pen, dog, sky). However, confusability effects did not occur when semantically related word strings (huge, great, big) were used. In a subsequent experiment Baddeley (1966b) examined the effects of phonological and semantic confusability on delayed recall and found the reverse result: phonological confusability had no effect on recall but semantically confusable word strings were recalled worse than unrelated word strings.

These results suggested that STS and LTS might be distinguished by encoding differences, with STS being phonologically based and LTS semantically based. Although consistent with the data, this theory could not possibly be correct. If true it would predict that we would not immediately understand anything we saw, including the sentence you are currently reading. Furthermore, much of what we remember cannot be translated easily into a phonological code. People are, for example, very good at recognizing pictures of unfamiliar people they have seen for only seconds. This is not enough time to describe the face verbally and, even if it were, there is evidence that the description would have been irrelevant to subsequent recognition (Chance & Goldstein 1976).

Logic therefore leads us to reject the idea that STS could be based solely on phonological coding. However, we shall see in a later section that the phonological confusability effect has remained an important experimental finding.

The serial position curve

The STS/LTS distinction gained much support from experiments using the free recall task. This involves the sequential presentation of items, usually unrelated words, for about two seconds each. When the list is finished the subject recalls the items in any order. Recall is plotted as a function of each item's list position. The resulting serial position curve has a characteristic shape (see figure 7.3) and is divided into three portions: recency refers to the high level of recall for the last terminal items; primacy, enhanced recall of the first few items; and the asymptote describes low recall of middle list items. A number of theorists (such as Glanzer & Cunitz 1966) proposed that recency reflected the 'effortless' output of STS while recall of items from earlier list positions took place from LTS.

Serial position effects were not sufficient to support the STS/LTS distinction. More recent items might be just more strongly represented and this is why they were remembered more easily. To prove that the recency effect arose from a different store to that responsible for recalling the rest of the list, it was neces-

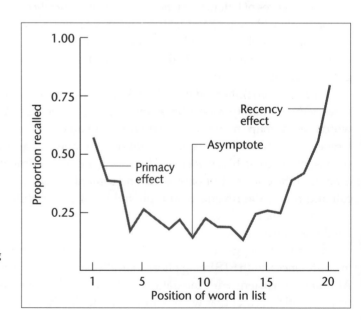

Figure 7.3 Typical finding of a free recall experiment, showing the three components of the serial position curve
Source: Adapted from Glanzer & Cunitz 1966.

sary to demonstrate functional double dissociation: if different parts of the curve reflect the operation of STS and LTS then one should, in principle, be able to show that those portions of the curve have different properties. This would be demonstrated by discovering variables that affect primacy and asymptote but not recency, and variables that achieve the opposite effect. If these conditions are met we can conclude that the serial position curve is the joint product of two stores, STS and LTS. Furthermore, the nature of the variables responsible for this functional double dissociation will give us important insights into the nature of the two memory stores.

Variables such as presentation rate, list length, and mental ability all affected primacy and asymptote portions of the curve, leaving the recency unaffected. Evidence for a selective effect on recency came from an experiment by Glanzer and Cunitz (1966). They compared the nature of the serial position curve under standard conditions with that obtained when subjects first counted backwards for either 15 or 30 seconds prior to recall. Figure 7.4 shows that the effect of this distraction was to obliterate the recency effect completely but leave the primary and asymptote portions of the curve unaffected. The data from delayed free recall supported the view that the STS had a limited capacity. Because the distracting task required the full capacity of STS, there was no option but to discard the last few items from the list, thus causing very poor recall.

If STS has a limited capacity it should be possible to measure it. If the recency effect arises from STS it is a simple step to argue that, if we can measure the recency effect, we can estimate the capacity of STS. Glanzer and Razel (1974) examined 21 free recall experiments and concluded that the average size of the recency effect was 2.2 words. However, this neat conclusion was undermined by their further experiments. First they tested free recall using proverbs (e.g.,

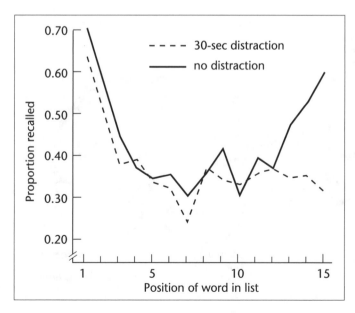

Figure 7.4 The serial position curve under conditions of no distraction and with 30 seconds distraction prior to recall

once bitten twice shy) rather than words and found that the recency effect was 2.2 proverbs! Using unfamiliar sentences as stimuli they found a recency effect of 1.5 sentences.

Glanzer and Razel's findings show that the recency effect cannot be measured in simple 'word units'. Instead, the amount of information contributing to the recency effect varies depending on what is being remembered. This illustrates a fundamental problem in attempting to measure human memory capacity. Artificial storage systems such as floppy discs, compact discs, and magnetic tapes, have measurable fixed capacities because information is fed into them in the form of basic information units such as 'bytes' of information. To measure human memory capacity we first need some similar method for reducing information into basic units. This may be possible in the future but, at present, our lack of a basic unit for measuring the size of different pieces of information put into memory precludes any attempt to measure memory capacity accurately.

Another problem was that the recency effect became more difficult to interpret than was initially thought. It was found, for example, that recency effects could be generated after quite long periods of distraction (see Parkin 1997). For this, and other reasons, additional sources of evidence are required if we are to accept the STS/LTS distinction.

By far the most compelling reason for accepting the STS/LTS distinction comes from studies of human AMNESIA. Damage to one of two specific brain regions, the temporal lobes or the diencephalon (see figure 7.5) can cause the amnesic syndrome. Patients with amnesia have immense difficulty remembering any new information (anterograde amnesia) and will often have problems recollecting events before the injury or illness that made them amnesic (retrograde amnesia). Perhaps the most well known amnesic patient is a person known as 'HM' (see Box 7.1).

AMNESIA

Figure 7.5 Two cross-sections of the human brain showing the major temporal lobe and diencephalic structures involved in memory

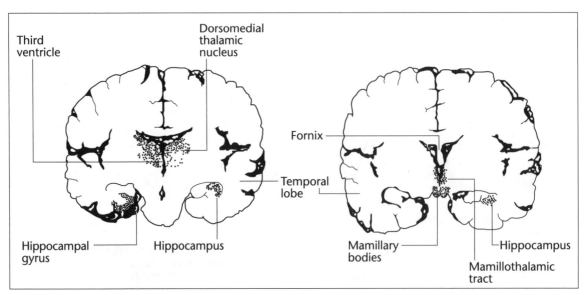

Box 7.1   The Case of HM

Perhaps the most well-known amnesic patient is a person known as 'HM'. In 1953 he was admitted to hospital suffering from intractable epileptic seizures, and it was agreed that the only remaining option for treatment was to remove the regions of the brain where the seizures arose. The operation involved TEMPORAL LOBECTOMY in which parts of both the left and right temporal lobe were surgically excised. In one important way the operation was a success, because HM's epileptic seizures were now controllable by drugs; but the operation also had a dramatic and, at the time, unexpected side effect – HM became AMNESIC.

HM is still alive at the time of writing this chapter but has remembered little of personal and public events that have occurred during the last 40 years (see Ogden & Corkin 1991). HM's father died in 1967 and his mother

in 1977, and he has lived in a nursing home since 1980. However, in 1986 he thought that he was still living with his mother and did not know if his father was still alive. He has learned only a handful of new words and prominent public events like the Vietnam War or the Watergate scandal mean little to him.

HM clearly has marked problems in long-term storage but what about short-term storage? This can easily be investigated using the DIGIT SPAN TASK. This tests the ability to repeat back a random series of numbers in the correct order immediately after seeing or hearing them, and it is regarded as a reliable test of STS . Normal subjects score an average of 7 plus or minus 2. HM's digit span has varied a little during the years but when last evaluated it was 7, therefore indicating normal STS. (See Parkin 1996.)

In figure 7.6 we can see the performance of a range of different amnesic patients on verbal and non-verbal memory span tasks and, in every case, performance of the group is well within normal range. This stands in marked contrast to their extremely poor ability on tests requiring the retention of information over

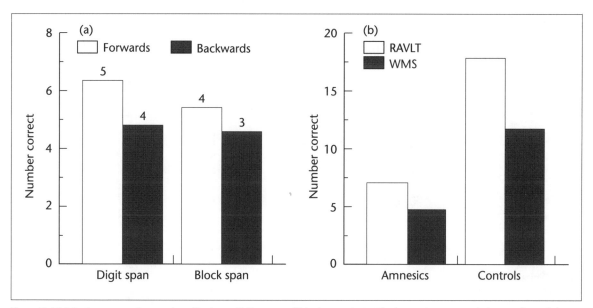

Figure 7.6 (a) Performance of amnesic patients on digit span and block span tests. Block span is a non-verbal equivalent of digit span. Forward span requires the subject to reproduce items in the same order as the experimenter. Backward span requires the subject to reproduce them in reverse order. The numbers indicate the minimum score within the normal range. (b) Performance of amnesic patients and controls on two tests of longer-term retention, the Rey Auditory Verbal Learning Test (RAVLT) and the Wechsler Memory Scale (WMS).

longer periods of time. With evidence like this there can be little doubt that short-term storage exists independently of the long-term storage that allows us to retain information over longer periods of time.

▧ Levels of Processing ▧

LEVELS OF
PROCESSING

Problems with developing the modal model led to an alternative approach to memory known as LEVELS OF PROCESSING (LOP) (Craik & Lockhart 1972). The LOP idea was that memory could be understood by examining the relationship between encoding and remembering. It was argued that encoding of a stimulus could occur at a number of different levels. These can be most easily understood thinking about how we remember words (i.e. orthographic, phonological or semantic) but can be applied to other forms of information.

Craik and Lockhart's approach centred on incidental learning – learning that occurs when a memory test is not expected. Incidental learning commonly uses orienting tasks in which subjects are required to make particular decisions about stimuli in order to bias the manner in which they encode the stimuli. Many experiments had shown that orienting tasks significantly affected remembering. Figure 7.7 shows data from Craik (1977): orthographic encoding produces poorest memory, then phonological encoding. Semantic encoding produces the greatest level of retention and, interestingly, performance is comparable with intentional learning.

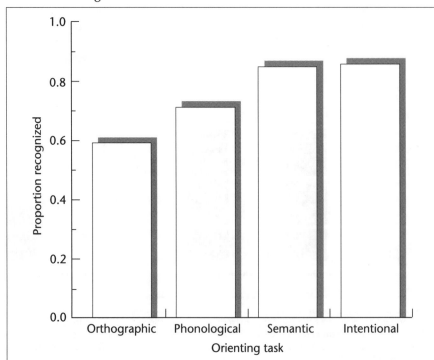

Figure 7.7 Typical effect of different levels of processing on memory performance. Craik, 'A level of analysis' view of memory in Pliner et al. (eds.), *Communication and Affect* vol. 2: Language and Thought (Academic Press, New York, 1977).

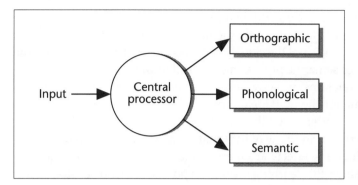

Figure 7.8 The levels of processing approach to memory. Processing of a stimulus is under the control of a central processor which can process the stimulus in one or more domains. Diagram shows the three domains relevant to word stimuli.

The results of incidental learning studies were explained by arguing that processing of a stimulus was under the control of a limited but flexible central processor. Retention depended on the activity of the central processor during learning – the 'deeper' the level the better the retention. Initially the LOP idea assumed a continuum between shallow physical analysis and deeper semantic analysis. However, this view was subsequently modified by Craik and Tulving (1975) who argued that different stimulus dimensions addressed different domains of processing (see figure 7.8).

Craik and Tulving confirmed the depth effect by showing, under a variety of conditions, that semantic orienting tasks always produced better retention than non-semantic tasks. However, they also made comparisons within the semantic domain and found that judging whether a word fitted the blank in a sentence (e.g., 'He met a _____ in the street': FRIEND) produced better retention than judging whether a target item belonged to a particular category ('Is the word a type of fish?': SHARK). Craik and Tulving explained this by suggesting that the sentence-frame task produced a more richly encoded or elaborated memory trace. Further experiments showed that this elaboration effect only occurred in the semantic domain, thus suggesting that the effect is dependent on the subject's ability to set up increasing numbers of semantic associations.

▨ Problems with Levels of Processing ▨

A major difficulty was the value of LOP as a theory – in particular the circularity inherent in the way LOP explained the relation between learning and retention: the demonstration that semantic processing typically produces better learning than non-semantic processing was explained by asserting that semantic process-ing is deeper. However, the assumption of deeper processing under semantic orienting instructions was itself assumed on the basis of better remembering.

In all their experiments semantic orienting tasks always took longer to per-form than non-semantic ones. From this Craik and Tulving reasoned that process-ing time might predict processing depth, with longer processing times indicating deeper processing and hence greater retention. To test this idea they devised a non-semantic task that took longer than a semantic task to perform. If processing time was a valid measure of depth, the non-semantic task should produce the best retention. This was not the case. Despite taking less time to perform, the normal superiority of semantic processing was still found.

Failure to find a relationship between processing time and retention was in some ways fortunate for the LOP idea. If processing time had predicted depth effects it would have undermined the whole idea that memory can be affected by qualitative differences in the way information is encoded. Instead, it could just be that orienting-task effects are merely one expression of the total-time hypothesis, which states that learning is simply a positive function of study time. Lack of a relation between processing time and memory means that the relationship between learning and memory is determined by more than just how long we spend attending to the stimulus.

Transfer-appropriate processing

Morris et al. (1977) pointed out that orienting tasks vary in the extent to which they place emphasis on the 'wordness' or lexical nature of the stimuli, but the retention tests always demand that the subjects remember words. Because semantic tasks always require attention to the stimuli as words, but non-semantic tasks do not (such as judging whether a word is in capital letters or not), Morris et al. argued that the semantic encoding advantage arose because the retention tests were biased towards the testing of semantic knowledge.

To prove their point they designed an experiment in which subjects first learned target words under either semantic or non-semantic orienting conditions. The semantic task was a sentence judgement task similar to that used by Craik and Tulving (1975) and the non-semantic task was a rhyming judgement, for example, rhymes with LEGAL? – REGAL. Two forms of retention test were used: indicate which of these words you saw in the orienting phase, and one in which subjects searched a list of words and indicated words that sounded similar to words used in the orienting phase. With standard recognition, the expected semantic advantage was found, but with the rhyming recognition test the non-semantic group performed best.

Morris et al. described their discovery as the principle of transfer-appropriate processing. Stated simply this asserts that the most appropriate learning strategy is the one that most closely addresses the information required at testing. This principle, which is rather difficult to dispute, rather deflated the LOP approach which, until then, had indicated that semantic processing was always superior to non-semantic processing.

It is easy to view the whole LOP idea as a blind alley in memory research. As a theory it proved largely untestable, although some progress was made concerning the circularity problem, and it failed to establish any absolute principles of learning. However, this rather dismissive view may not be justified. Until LOP appeared, memory theorists had paid little attention to the relation between perception and memory and to the idea that encoding processes could be flexible. Atkinson and Shiffrin (1968) had introduced the concept of 'control processes' into their version of STS, but this had not advanced beyond the study of rehearsal. LOP showed the enormous variation in encoding that could occur, and all theorizing about memory now takes account of this basic observation. Furthermore, LOP has provided the first substantial framework within which one can talk meaningfully of 'encoding deficits' as a reason for memory failure.

▧ Long-term Storage ▧

Consider these three questions:

- When did you last ride a bicycle?
- What is a bicycle?
- How do you ride a bicycle?

To answer the first question you will need to focus on your personal past and your answer will probably be accompanied by some image of you on a bicycle. Answering the second question is rather different: you will recall that a bicycle has two wheels, is propelled by pedals attached to a chain wheel, an so on. However, the answer does not require you to recall any personal events even though, on logical grounds, we must presume that your recollections derive from personal experience. Your answer to the third question is different again. Beyond stating that you sit on it, push off, start pedalling, and somehow stay upright, you will not be able to describe the acts of balancing and coordination that riding the bicycle entails – these kinds of memories are not consciously accessible and cannot be described; their existence is known only through the actions they give rise to.

Observations like these lead to the view that our permanent or long-term store (LTS) of memories is not a single entity but a composite of different kinds of memory each with its own properties.

Knowing how versus knowing that

Philosophers have long considered the nature of our permanent memories. One influential view, put forward by Ryle (1949), was that a fundamental distinction could be drawn between remembering based on 'knowing that' and remembering arising from 'knowing how'. Returning to our bicycle example, the answers to the first two questions would be of the former type: 'I know that I rode a bicycle yesterday', 'I know that a bicycle has two wheels'; whereas our answer to the final question would be of the second kind, 'I know how to ride a bicycle'.

If we assume that Ryle's distinction has psychological reality – i.e. that the memory system subdivides memories into 'that' and 'how' types – we are proposing that LTS has two fundamental components and that the subjective difference we have highlighted in contrasting our answers to the first two types of question is not functionally significant. Put another way, this dichotomy draws no distinction between recall associated with, or not associated with, some recollection of personal experience.

Episodic, semantic and procedural memory

EPISODIC MEMORY

SEMANTIC MEMORY

PROCEDURAL
MEMORY

Tulving (1989) has proposed that LTS has three distinct components: episodic, semantic and procedural memory. EPISODIC MEMORY is defined as an individual's autobiographical record of past experience. SEMANTIC MEMORY comprises our knowledge of language, rules and concepts. Episodic and semantic memory are similar, in that both forms of memory could be consciously accessed. Within this system, therefore, remembering the last time you rode a bicycle accesses a different memory store to that containing information about what a bicycle is. PROCEDURAL MEMORY is similar to the 'how' type of memory in that it is characterized as being consciously inaccessible. Within our example, procedural memory contains the information responsible for our bicycle riding skill.

It must be stressed that procedural memory is not just motor skill memory, because other forms of memory unrelated to motor skills also meet the definition of procedural. Figure 7.9 shows a visual puzzle which will take you some time to solve (providing you have not seen it elsewhere). Once you have solved it, close this book, wait a few moments, re-open and examine the puzzle again. You will find that the solution comes to you fairly instantly, showing that you have obviously learned something. However, in achieving these solutions you will not be aware of using any conscious knowledge in the process. Indeed, if you try to describe the knowledge you have about each puzzle you will be surprised at how superficial that knowledge is.

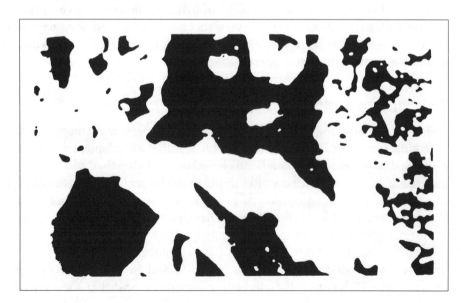

Figure 7.9 Can you make out the face?

Although episodic, semantic and procedural memories are held to be distinct, they are also interactive. All knowledge is initially derived from an experience but retention of that knowledge does not require the event itself to be retained. Remembering the meaning of a new word, for example, might not be possible without some episodic record confirming why that word means what it does. With time, however, the word's meaning will become part of semantic memory, making the episodic memory unnecessary. By not requiring the representation of knowledge to be linked to learning events an enormous saving in storage can be achieved, because memory for the events themselves can be discarded.

The episodic–semantic distinction makes a lot of intuitive sense. When remembering a fact or rule we are rarely also aware of the learning event in which we acquired that knowledge. The distinction also helped to clarify our thinking about what might be going on in a typical verbal learning experiment. In a test of free recall a subject listens to a list of words and, sometime later, attempts to remember them, but only half of the words are remembered. Within the episodic–semantic framework this can be seen as a failure of episodic memory. The subject has not forgotten the words completely, the subject has failed to remember that a given word was presented in a list at a particular time and place. For this reason accounts of verbal learning experiments often refer to the words subjects are asked to learn as 'word events' – the word serves as the focus for a specific learning event.

Procedural memory might also interact with episodic and semantic memory. Learning a skill like touch typing, for example, might at first rely on retaining some record of the keyboard layout that is needed when you are uncertain about where a particular letter key is. However, with repeated practice this record is no longer needed and can be discarded. However, not all procedural memory is facilitated in this way, because the acquisition of some skills occurs without any conscious mediation. A good example is the pursuit-rotor task in which the subject has to learn to keep a light beam on an irregular moving target. Subjects learn this task well, but it is difficult to see how conscious memory could be helping this occur – what is being learned, unlike touch typing, cannot be described in any way that could be entered into either episodic or semantic memory.

Experimental evidence for procedural memory

The most striking evidence for a separate procedural memory system comes from amnesic patients. Earlier we saw that amnesic patients could be regarded as having intact short-term storage but grossly impaired long-term storage. This latter point does, however, require clarification. Figure 7.10 shows the performance of HM and a group of control subjects on the the mirror drawing task. HM obviously learns the task even though he has no recollection of having done the task before. This type of residual learning ability has been shown in many other amnesic patients and in a variety of other procedural memory tasks such as perceptual learning (Parkin 1993; see Further Reading below). These data are

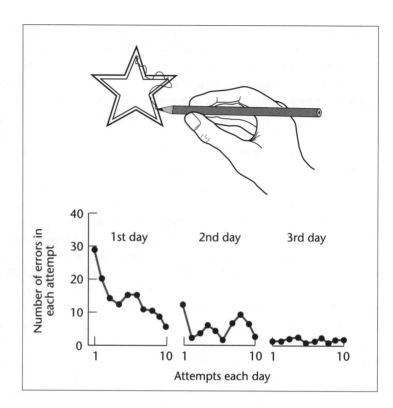

Figure 7.10 HM's performance on the mirror drawing task. This involves tracing between the lines of the star guided only by a mirror reflection. HM imporved greatly on the task despite being unable to remember doing it. Blakemore, *Mechanics of the Mind* (Cambridge University Press, 1977).

difficult to explain other than by suggesting that procedural memory is a separate system selectively preserved in amnesic patients.

Experimental evidence for episodic and semantic memory

At the centre of Tulving's theory is idea that the record of experience, episodic memory, exists separately from the knowledge gained from experience – semantic memory. Experimental evidence from normal subjects to support this distinction is, however, problematic because of the interdependence that must exist between these two systems. Once again it has been the evidence from amnesic patients that has been used as the primary basis for supporting separate episodic and semantic systems.

When you encounter an amnesic patient there are good grounds for assuming that you have met someone with an intact semantic memory but highly impaired episodic memory. Many amnesics have normal conversational skills and it can be a little while before you realize they have a memory impairment (this is usually revealed when the patient starts to ask the same questions over and over again). These anecdotal impressions can be reinforced by the typical psychometric profile of an amnesic subject which will show highly impaired memory performance on tests such as recalling an unfamiliar story in the presence of normal intellect as measured by standardized intelligence tests. HM, for exam-

Box 7.2   The Case of PZ

In trying to measure retrograde amnesia in an amnesic patient the experimenter is faced with a difficult problem. Everyone's experience is different and so, if a patient fails to retrieve a fact from their past, it may be because they never learned it in the first place. This point applies particularly to patients who become amnesic due to excess alcohol intake, because it is distinctly possible that their alcoholism interrupted their learning processes long before their condition became severe enough to be called amnesia. Recently, however, psychologists were presented with a unique case, that of PZ, which allowed a much clearer investigation of retrograde amnesia (Butters & Brandt 1985).

PZ was a science professor in a major American university. He had a severe drinking problem which eventually lead to Korsakoff's Syndrome – a neurological illness that has amnesia as its primary feature. However, in the years immediately preceding onset of amnesia, PZ wrote his autobiography. This, in combination with knowledge of his academic career, meant that researchers had reasonably accurate knowledge of what PZ did once remember about his life.

Figure 7.11 shows that, as expected, PZ showed very poor recall of events from most parts of his life except his early years – a finding consistent with impaired episodic memory. However, this figure also illustrates PZ's very poor definition of scientific terms current in his discipline at different times. Since we know that PZ was once familiar with these terms, and that this type of information would have been semantic rather than epi-

sodic in nature, we must conclude that his semantic memory is impaired as well.

If PZ has both an episodic and semantic impairment, it is simplest to conclude that episodic and semantic memory impairments might be two sides of the same deficit, i.e. expressions of a single damaged LTS. Other data from retrograde amnesia studies also point us in the same direction. We noted earlier that general tests of retrograde amnesia are difficult because the knowledge you are testing may never have been acquired by some subjects. A possible solution, however, is to examine the ability of patients to identify the faces of people who became famous in different decades. On the assumption that most people look at newspapers, films and television it can be assumed that people frequently in the news and entertainment would be familiar to most people – a fact we can confirm by testing faces on a wide range of normal subjects.

Figure 7.12 shows data from amnesic and control subjects on the 'Famous Faces Test' devised by Parkin et al. (1990). Performance in the amnesic group is poor and shows the familiar temporal gradient. On the assumption that the amnesic subjects once knew these faces, how might we explain this deficit? A deficit in episodic memory seems improbable. It is unlikely that any such identifications have an 'episodic' flavour, for, if you try to put names to some faces yourself, you will realize the identifications feel more like expressions of knowledge – the form of memory we would describe as semantic.

ple, has an IQ of 110 but forgets new information within minutes. However, is this kind of evidence sufficient to argue that semantic memory is preserved and must therefore be functionally separate from episodic memory?

As well suffering from an inability to learn new information, amnesic patients suffer a parallel loss of memories they acquired before their brain injury. This deficit, known as retrograde amnesia, exhibits a temporal gradient in that the deficit is more pronounced for memories acquired nearer the onset of amnesia. Thus an amnesic patient might talk clearly and accurately about his or her childhood and early adult life but be completely blank about the twenty years or so prior to developing amnesia (see Box 7.2).

For any intelligence to be 'general' it must assess only those aspects of knowledge and ability that one could reasonably expect most people to have acquired. To achieve this, IQ tests concentrate on aspects of knowledge acquired during

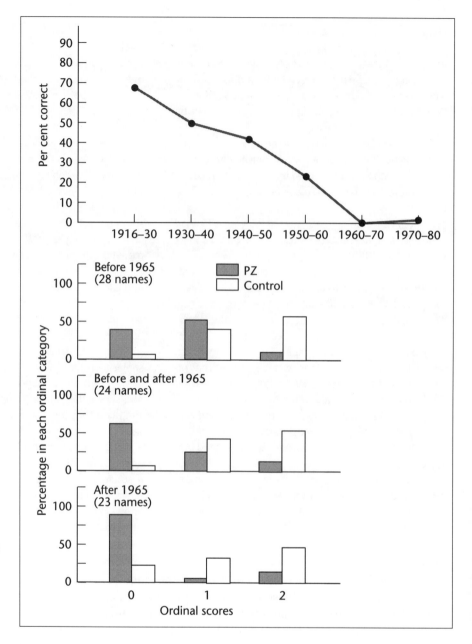

Figure 7.11 Above, PZ's retrograde amnesia regarding information in his published autobiography. Below, performance of PZ and control on identification of famous scientists. Scores 0, 1 and 2 represent an ordinal scaling of the adequacy of the two subjects' responses (0 least adequate, 2 most adequate)

the relatively early stages of life. Normal IQ might therefore be expected in an amnesic patient on the grounds that early memories, whatever their type, are preserved in amnesia and thus do not allow us to conclude that semantic memory is preserved in amnesic patients – this could only be achieved by showing that semantic memory acquired later in life was normal even though memory for episodes experienced at the same time was highly defective.

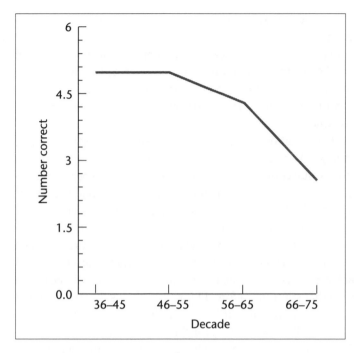

Figure 7.12 Ability of patients with amnesia to name pictures of people famous in different decades. Note how performance is much worse for more recently famous people. Normal subjects show similar performance on all decades.

▣ Explicit and Implicit Memory ▣

In the last few years an alternative approach to understanding the nature of LTS has been put forward. Unlike Tulving's approach, in which the emphasis is placed on defining the nature of different stores, this approach attempts to understand LTS by examining how it responds to different forms of memory test known as explicit and IMPLICIT MEMORY (Schacter 1987).

IMPLICIT MEMORY

A test of EXPLICIT MEMORY can be defined as one which requires the subject to recollect a previous learning event such as the presentation of a word list. Explicit memory can be tested using three different procedures:

EXPLICIT MEMORY

free recall: Subject attempts to remember the target information without any assistance from the experimenter.

cued recall: Subject attempts to remember the target information in the presence of some specific cue (e.g., an associate of the word they are trying to remember).

recognition: Subject is presented with a stimulus and must decide whether it is one that they were asked to remember. Recognition can be tested in either a yes–no procedure in which each item is judged individually, or by forced-choice in which one item from an array must be selected.

Implicit memory describes any memory task where memory for an event is tested without specific reference to that event. Implicit memory tasks therefore test memory indirectly, as opposed to explicit memory tasks, which address memory for the learning event directly.

The idea that memory for an experience can be expressed indirectly is not new and has been noted since the time of philosophers such as Descartes. Neurologists and psychologists in the nineteenth century were also well aware that memory for an event could be inferred from a patient's behaviour, even though they were consciously unable to recollect the experience.

This kind of anecdotal information has subsequently been confirmed using more sophisticated methodology. Verafaellie et al. (1991) investigated an amnesic patient known as TR and normal control subjects on a list-learning experiment. After 30 minutes a recognition test was given in which all the subjects had to identify the targets in a multiple choice test in which each target was embedded in a five item sequence. As well as measuring accuracy, any change in the subjects' skin conductance, known as the electrodermal response, was also measured as each test item appeared. An increase in skin conductance for a target relative to a previously unseen distractor is taken to indicate that the individual has, in some sense, a record of encountering that stimulus before. Figure 7.13 shows that the extent of this 'electrodermal recognition' was similar in TR and the controls. This contrasts markedly with TR's poor explicit recognition for the same items.

Tulving et al. (1982) asked subjects to learn a list of relatively infrequent words such as *toboggan*. Following a retention interval of either one hour or one week, subjects returned and undertook two types of memory test. The first was a yes–no recognition test examining subjects' explicit memory for the target stimuli. The second was not, ostensibly, related to the original learning event, and involved a task known as fragment completion. Subjects were presented with incomplete words, such as _O_B_G_N?, and asked to fill in the blanks to make

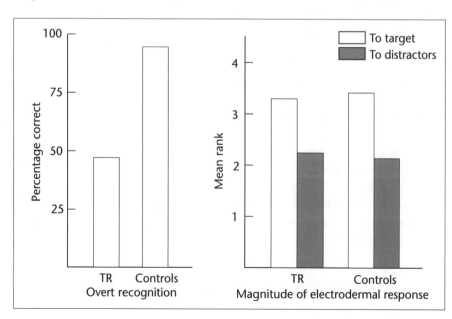

Figure 7.13 Performance of patient TR and controls on overt verbal cognition (*left*) and electrodermal recognition (*right*) in a list of learning tasks.
Verafaellie et al., 'Autonomic and behavioural evidence of implicit memory in amnesia' in *Brain and Cognition*, 15 (Academic Press 1991).

a word. In this task the solutions to half of the fragments were words from the target list, but subjects were not informed of this. Fragment completion therefore served as a test of implicit memory.

Subjects were more likely to complete fragments correctly when the solution corresponded to a target word – a phenomenon known as repetition priming. You may not find this result surprising – subjects might notice that some of the solutions are target words and that subjects simply use their explicit recollection to help them do the test. If correct, this would mean that repetition priming was just a form of explicit memory. However, an ingenious aspect of Tulving et al.'s study ruled out this simple interpretation. In the experiment each target word was tested for recognition and fragment completion and it was shown that the probability of correct fragment completion was no greater for target words that were recognized than target words that subjects failed to identify – repetition priming was therefore implicit memory.

▓ Retrieving Memories ▓

Under most conditions remembering seems such an effortless procedure that we fail to appreciate the complexity of what must be occurring. Our long-term store contains vast amounts of information and yet, in a split second, we can come up with a highly specific piece of information. The speed at which retrieval occurs belies an important fact – that retrieval is reconstructive.

GENERATION-RECOGNITION (GR) models of retrieval (e.g., Anderson & Bower 1972) attempt to model the reconstructive nature of retrieval. At the outset the system generates possible candidates for the memory that is being sought. These are then subjected to a recognition process which, if successful, results in that candidate being retrieved as a memory. These models assume a structure rather like semantic memory in which each item of information, such as a word, is represented by a node. When a subject learns a word, a 'tag' is set up to indicate that the word was part of the target list. When recall is attempted various candidates are generated and the corresponding nodes examined for markers which, if detected, result in recognition and hence retrieval. In recognition, access to the node was considered to be automatic and the recognition was dependent simply on detection of a marker.

GENERATION-
RECOGNITION

Under normal conditions free recall, cued recall and recognition behave in an orderly way. Free recall produces poorer retrieval than cued recall which, in turn, is inferior to recognition. Any model of retrieval must therefore account for this consistently observed relationship. GR models explain the natural ordering of these tasks on the grounds that, in free recall, the generation phase has less information to guide generation than that available when a cue is present. Recognition produces even better performance because the more error-prone generation stage is bypassed altogether and the subject simply has to detect evidence that the presented item is a target.

GR models were able to account for a number of other findings as well. A well-established finding is that words of high frequency in the language (e.g., *table*, *dog*) are easier to recall than low-frequency words (e.g., *barge*, *pine*), whereas the reverse occurs in recognition memory. Greater recall of high-frequency words can be attributed the greater probability of them being generated as candidates for recognition. Poorer recognition, in turn, arose because higher-frequency words might be expected to be associated with a greater number of occurrence markers, making it more difficult to decide whether that word was presented in a specific list.

The encoding specificity principle

GR was a good theory in that it gave rise to a testable prediction. According to the theory, recall of an item involves both successful generation and recognition, whereas recognition involves just the latter stage of the retrieval process. From this it follows that any recallable item must also be recognizable because recognition must have occurred at recall. This prediction was the subject of a series of experiments carried out by Endel Tulving and his colleagues (e.g., Tulving & Thomson 1973). The basic experiment consisted of four phases. In phase 1 subjects were presented with a target word along with a 'cue' word which they were asked to attend to but not try to remember. The target and cue word pairings were not closely associated with one another, e.g., *engine – black*. In phase 2 subjects were given another list of words, each of which was a strong associate of one of the target words in the learning list (e.g., *steam*). For each of these phase 2 words subjects had to generate several associations and, because of the list's construction, there was a high probability that subjects would produce target items from the list as associations (e.g., *steam – engine*). In the third phase of the experiment subjects were asked to indicate whether any of the words they had generated were target words from the list presented in phase 1. Finally, subjects were given the low-value cue words and asked to recall which items were paired with them during phase 1.

According to GR theory any target word recalled successfully in phase 4 should also have been recognized in phase 3: this follows on the assumption that the recognition process undertaken as part of cued recall in phase 4 is the same recognition process as carried out when only recognition was required in phase 3. The results contradicted this prediction in that words recalled in phase 4 were often not recognized in phase 3 – a phenomenon known as recognition failure.

On the basis of these recognition-failure results Tulving and Thomson (1973) put forward the ENCODING SPECIFICITY PRINCIPLE (ESP), which proposed that recall and recognition were different manifestations of a single retrieval system and that the retrieval of information depends critically on the degree of overlap between the features encoded in the memory trace and the features present in the retrieval environment (e.g., the information provided by a recognition probe or a cue). To explain their own data Tulving and Thomson proposed that the learn-

ENCODING
SPECIFICITY
PRINCIPLE

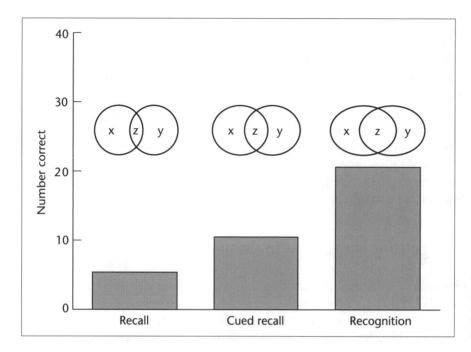

Figure 7.14 The typical relationship between recall and recognition according to the encoding specificity principle, where x = trace, y = retrieval environment, z = overlap

ing manipulation in phase 1 resulted in an encoding of the target word which emphasized its featural overlap with the low associative cue. When recognition was tested in phase 3 the target was presented in a retrieval environment specifying a different pattern of featural overlap to that encoded during learning (i.e. one emphasizing the target's relations with a strong association), with the result that insufficient overlap existed for a successful recognition response to occur. In contrast, the potentially more difficult cued recall task was in fact easier because the cues had a high degree of featural overlap with the target memory trace. Recall and recognition were thus independent of one another because they had differing featural overlap with the target as encoded.

The encoding specificity principle also accounted for the general relationship between recall, cued recall and recognition by arguing that, on average, recall tests provide a more impoverished retrieval environment than cued recall tasks which, in turn, provide less information about target memory than a recognition test (see figure 7.14). The essential proposal, therefore, is that the contrast between recognition and recall is not one involving qualitative differences in the underlying memory system. Rather it reflects the operation of a single retrieval system whose efficiency increases as the overlap between the memory trace and retrieval context increases.

Context

Encoding specificity experiments were important because they alerted theorists to the importance of CONTEXT in determining remembering. Context is a much   CONTEXT used and, according to some, much abused term which can be defined in a number of ways. One useful approach draws a distinction between intrinsic and extrinsic context. Intrinsic context refers to various features that are an integral part of a target stimulus. For a word, intrinsic context is the pattern of features encoded about that word at the time of learning (e.g., those features that associate *train* with *black*). Extrinsic context represents those features that are present when the target is encountered but are not, themselves, an integral part of the stimulus. Examples of this include the place and time where the stimulus was encountered plus other associations such as the experimenter's mannerisms. Returning to the encoding specificity results, it is clear that the results were obtained by manipulations of intrinsic context.

■ Forgetting – a Failure to Remember? ■

A commonly held view of forgetting is that it is entirely due to retrieval failure. The belief is that, for some reason, we store all our experiences away, and that forgetting arises because the mechanisms of retrieval fail to locate the memory we are searching for. From an evolutionary point of view it is difficult to imagine why we would develop a memory system like this. Even those of us with interesting lives doubtless have a surplus of mundane and routine experiences whose retention would serve no useful purpose. Why then does the idea of a permanent and total record of experience exist?

Partly the answer may lie in the work of Freud, whose concept of repression

Plate 7.1 Sigmund Freud
Source: Mary Evans Picture Library.

Plate 7.2 Awake cranial surgery. Stimulation of the cortex during such operations led Penfield to the erroneous view that all experiences are stored
Source: Science Photo Library/James King-Holmes.

emphasized that memories could be kept out of consciousness if they were unpleasant. There is certainly evidence that people with psychiatric difficulties can repress memories. A terrifying experience can result in hysterical amnesia where the person fails to remember a complete chunk of their life. More extreme are patients with fugue, whose adverse circumstances lead them to forget who they are. However, cases like this are rare, and it is difficult to explain all forgetting in terms of repressive mechanisms. Much of what we forget is what we want to remember, and so it is difficult to understand why we should repress it.

A second reason for believing in the permanence of memory came from the work of Penfield, who pioneered open-head brain surgery. In this procedure the brain of the patient is exposed and the surface stimulated to explore the function of that brain region (see plate 7.2). By carrying out this procedure Penfield noticed that many patients started to recall memories that were often extremely trivial experiences and, from this observation, suggested that he had contacted the permanent record of experience. We now know (Loftus & Loftus 1980) that Penfield's claims were not very accurate and that the phenomenon he reported was not reliable. However, even today, many people believe in the idea put forward by Penfield. This applies particularly to some practitioners of hypnosis, who claim, without any reliable evidence, that hypnosis can help people remember information they have forgotten. In fact, hypnosis merely increases the amount people recall; it does not increase accuracy (Parkin 1997).

Storage versus retrieval failure

If we dismiss failing to remember as the sole basis of forgetting we must entertain two distinct explanations. The first of these is storage failure, which can be defined as some inability of the memory system to produce a permanent memory trace of a given event. Storage failure might occur either because no transfer from STS to LTS was initiated, or because the permanent memory trace formed was lost for some reason. In contrast, forgetting due to retrieval failure has its origins in some inability to locate an existing memory trace.

Forgetting due to storage failure is most easily demonstrated in experiments where the normal biological processes of learning are interfered with in some way. Calev et al. (1989) examined the effects of the antidepressant drug 'imipramine' – a drug known to interfere with the biological processes responsible for memory. Patients given imipramine were compared with patients rendered

Plate 7.3 Electro-convulsive therapy
Source: Science Photo Library/ Will McIntyre.

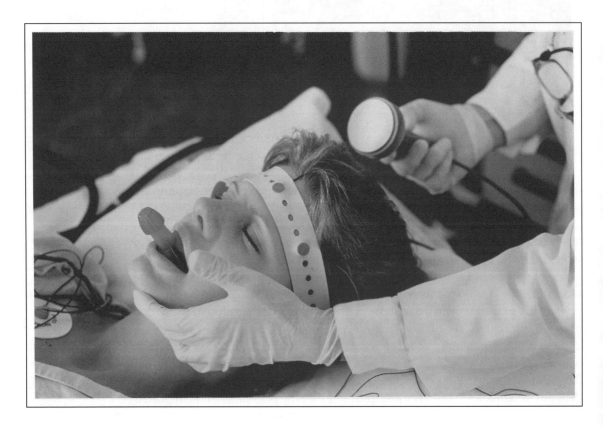

temporarily amnesic following electro-convulsive therapy (ECT) – a treatment for depression involving the administration of electric current to the temporal lobes. Imipramine subjects were as impaired as the ECT patients at learning new verbal and visual information. However, when asked to remember events from before their treatment, the imipramine group performed close to normal. The ECT group showed a pronounced inability to remember prior events, particularly in the period immediately before ECT treatment commenced.

The results obtained with imipramine can be found with other drugs as well (such as benzodiazepines, marijuana), and give us a clear indication that forgetting can be caused by a storage failure. However, although providing a strong case for this form of forgetting, these studies do not tell us much about the psychological factors that determine this storage failure under normal conditions. One idea might be to invoke the notion of intention. It is likely that if we try to learn something we are more likely to subsequently remember it. However, the reverse does not seem to hold. As La Bruyère observed, 'To endeavour to forget anyone is a certain way of thinking of nothing else.' Intention cannot be the only factor determining learning. Indeed, levels of processing research emphasized that incidental learning can be as effective as intentional learning, providing our processing of information occurs at a particular level. What constitutes the right level for remembering is undoubtedly complex. Intention can be a part, but the individual's past experience, current and future goals, and expertise also determine what aspects of experience are remembered.

Context effects

Experiments demonstrating the encoding specificity principle are good examples of how changes in intrinsic context between learning and test can affect memory. Light and Carter-Sobell (1970) also demonstrated how changes in the intrinsic context associated with a target could reduce recognition memory. Subjects studied simple sentences which biased subjects towards encoding one particular meaning of an ambiguous word (e.g., 'They were stuck in a traffic *jam*'). Retention testing involved subjects identifying the target words, which were again embedded in biasing sentences but, in half of these, the sentence was biased towards a different meaning to that used at encoding (e.g., 'They enjoyed eating the *jam*'). It was found that recognition of the targets was significantly reduced when the biasing context at learning was different to that at test.

Godden and Baddeley (1975) examined the effects of extrinsic context in two distinct environments: on land and underwater. It was found that free recall was better when the learning and test environments were the same than when they were different. However, Godden and Baddeley (1980) found no evidence of this context-dependent memory when a recognition test was used. Environmental context also appears to influence eyewitness accuracy. Smith and Vela (1992) staged an incident in which a confederate entered an introductory psychology class and announced that it was a fictitious person's birthday. He asked the class if 'she' was present and, when no one came forward he left. After varying intervals the subjects were given a recognition test for the confederate in either the same room or a different one. For those in the different room some were asked to try and reinstate mentally the original encounter with the confederate while others were left to their own devices. Correct identification of the confederate was significantly better in the same-context group compared with the different-context groups. In addition, those subjects in the different context asked to reinstate the original context did particularly poorly – an interesting finding given that mental reinstatement under other conditions is held to improve eyewitness memory (e.g. Malpass & Devine 1981).

Various psychoactive states, particularly ones involving alcohol, can result in state-dependent learning. Goodwin et al.'s (1969) subjects undertook recall and recognition tasks having either recently consumed a soft drink or a substantial amount of high-strength vodka. The next day they were required to perform the same tasks again either in the same state or a different state. A change in state (e.g., learn sober, test intoxicated) produced reliably lower recall performance, but there was no state-dependent effect on recognition. In a survey of state-dependent learning Eich (1980) noted that significant effects were only found when free recall was used. When either cued recall or recognition was used no state-dependent effects were found. This indicates that state dependent effects are not very large but, when they occur, they affect retrieval processes that operate without any external constraints.

▩ Working Memory ▩

In 1969 Warrington and Shallice reported the case of KF, a young man who suffered a closed-head injury after falling off his motor-bike. KF developed a number of deficits as a result of his brain damage but we shall concentrate on how this injury affected his memory span. Remarkably, KF had a reliable digit span of only 1! Normal people, you may recall, typically have a memory span of 7 plus or minus 2, so clearly something has gone badly wrong. So we have assumed that a single structure underlies short-term storage. We have variously called this primary memory, short-term store, or central processor, but all these concepts share the view that this memory is a single entity. Memory span has been taken as a basic measure of short-term storage so, in theory, KF should experience major memory difficulties. However, when asked to remember unrelated word pairs over a long time period KF performed normally.

One interpretation of this seemingly odd result might be that KF's short-term storage processes are impaired but that long-term storage is normal. However, this would be inconsistent with our assumption of an orderly transition from short-term to long-term storage. An alternative view, and one which we shall develop in this section, is that short-term storage does not rely on a single structure or process. Instead short-term storage involves a complex system in which different components carry out different tasks. From this perspective KF's deficit becomes easier to interpret because his memory span difficulties arise because a specific subcomponent of STS has been affected.

The working memory model

The idea that short-term storage involves a number of subsystems has been most actively developed by the work of Alan Baddeley and his colleagues (Baddeley & Hitch 1977; Baddeley 1992). It is termed WORKING MEMORY because the emphasis is on how the memory system is adapted to meet the needs of real-life conscious mental activities such as reading, thinking and mental arithmetic. Our starting point is Baddeley and Hitch's assumption that, if digit span reflects the capacity of STS and, in turn, if STS is a single structure, any task requiring the subject to retain a sequence of digits comparable to their memory span should make it extremely difficult for the subject to carry out any other task requiring STS capacity at the same time.

WORKING MEMORY

To test this idea it was necessary to devise a dual task paradigm in which the subject performs a primary task while carrying out, simultaneously, a secondary task. In one study subjects were given the primary task of learning lists of visually presented words while at the same time retaining either a sequence of three or six auditorally presented digits, or copying down pairs of digits as they were spoken.

If digit span does reflect maximum STS capacity we should expect subjects doing the list learning and retaining six digits at the same time to be quite impaired on the task because we are using up most of the available STS capacity. The additional load of six digits did generally reduce performance, but to nowhere near the extent one might expect if STS capacity was largely absorbed with digit span. Furthermore, the recency effect, which we have attributed to short-term storage processes, remained robust under the six-digit load.

Baddeley and his colleagues went on to explore the influence of secondary task performance on primary tasks involving other kinds of conscious processing. In one study subjects were asked to verify sentences of the kind 'Canaries have wings', 'Dogs have feathers'. Before each of these sentences was presented subjects were given a sequence of digits to remember which ranged from 0 to 8 numbers. The subjects had to repeat the sequence continually until they had verified the sentence in front of them. Even when subjects were keeping in mind seven or eight random digits they could still perform a reasoning task in two seconds with 95 per cent accuracy. It is extremely difficult to reconcile this and other similar results (e.g. Baddeley & Hitch 1977) with a unitary concept of STS in which digit span is assumed to be a measure of capacity because, if so, one would have expected verification performance to be severely disrupted when subjects were repeating seven or eight digits.

The articulatory loop

These experiments led to the view that the system responsible for memory span – as measured in the digit span task – was not the same as the memory system supporting all our conscious mental activity. Instead it seemed possible that the task of retaining short sequences of digits might, to a large extent, be carried out by a different system to that involved in tasks such as learning word lists and reasoning.

Using a variety of lines of evidence, Baddeley and Hitch (1977) suggested that the system underlying the retention of digits was speech-based, and they named it the articulatory loop. Earlier we discussed the phonological confusability effect – the finding that memory span is adversely affected if the items to be recalled have similar sounds (e.g., mad, man, mat). These data strongly suggest that the mechanism underlying memory span makes use of sound-based code, but it does not allow us to conclude that it is articulatory.

Evidence for the existence of an articulatory system underlying memory span came from an elegant series of experiments by Baddeley et al. (1975). The experiments were based on the observation that memory span for sequences of short words (e.g., *sum, wit*), is better than for long words (e.g., *aluminium, university*). Baddeley et al. examined whether this word-length effect depended on the number of syllables in short and long words or differences in the spoken duration of each word type. Baddeley et al. compared memory span for items that have equal numbers of syllables but relatively shorter or longer spoken durations (e.g., *wicket* versus *harpoon*). Memory span was lower for words with longer spoken durations, and they therefore concluded that the system underlying memory span was speech-based.

More evidence for an articulatory loop came from a second study where the word length effect was examined under conditions of articulatory suppression. In this secondary task the subject has to repeat a meaningless spoken sequence (e.g., 'the, the, the . . . ') while carrying out a primary task. Figure 7.15 shows that articulatory suppression causes the word length effect to disappear. Note in particular that performance on short words is reduced to the same level as long words. This is rather nice evidence that the advantage in recalling short words in a memory span task depends critically on the availability of an articulatory coding system. When this is not the case, as with articulatory suppression, short and long words are dependent on the same memory processes and are therefore recalled to the same degree.

These findings led to the first specific model of working memory. It identifies three components, the articulatory loop, a visuo-spatial scratch pad and a central executive (the latter two of which we will consider in due course). On the basis of experimental evidence the articulatory loop was characterized as a structure capable of holding and recycling a small amount of speech-based information. The articulatory loop was assumed to underlie subjects' ability to perform mental tasks relatively easily while simultaneously holding digits – the argu-

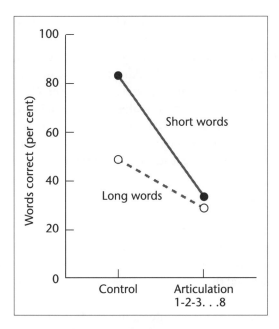

Figure 7.15 The influence of articulatory suppression on the word length effect.
Baddeley et al., 'Word Length and the structure of short term memory' in *Journal of Verbal Learning and Verbal Behaviour*, 14 (Academic Press, 1990).

ment being that part of all the digit load could be placed in the articulatory loop thus making little or no demand on other components of working memory. Similarly the phonological confusability effect (see above) arose because subjects unavoidably make use of the loop when carrying out memory span tasks.

With working memory model in mind we can reinterpret KF's poor memory span performance in terms of an impairment to the articulatory loop. This would explain why, despite poor memory span, he was able to show normal learning on other memory tasks – learning on these was not helped by the presence of an articulatory code. KF's case also raises another issue. If normal learning can occur with a defective articulatory loop, what is the loop for? So far we have only implicated the loop as a system involved in performing memory span tasks. However, memory span does not bear much similarity to the kinds of task we use our memory for in everyday life. As we noted earlier, the motivation of the working memory idea was to establish how memory was adapted in relation to mental tasks we routinely carry out.

The articulatory loop and reading development

An important characteristic of children with developmental dyslexia is that they have greatly reduced memory spans. This suggests a possible link between a failure to develop an effective articulatory loop and the presence of dyslexia. Shankweiler and Liberman (1976) found that superior readers showed a much greater phonological confusability effect than poorer readers. This result complemented an earlier study by Conrad (1971), who observed that phonological confusability effects only started to appear around the time children started to learn to read, suggesting that speech code might be essential for normal reading development.

The above evidence implicates the articulatory loop in language development, but what is its exact role? One possibility is that the articulatory loop is essential for encoding sequences of spoken sounds (phonemes) in the correct order. Consider a relatively simple word like *cat*. In order to read it aloud the visual input must be converted into a sequence of phonemes which are then blended in the correct order to produce the word. A poorly developed articulatory loop may make this task much more difficult and therefore lead to reading retardation.

The articulatory loop and fluent reading

A plausible case can be made for the role of the articulatory loop in reading and other aspects of reading development. However, what role does the articulatory loop play in fluent reading? When we read silently we still experience an inner voice and it has often been speculated that this inner speech has some functional significance.

Hardyck and Petrinovich (1970) carried out an interesting study involving students reading essays judged as either 'easy' or 'hard' in content. All subjects were wired up to apparatus which measured both throat muscle and forearm muscle activity. One group of subjects (normal group) simply read with the in-convenience of being attached to the apparatus. A second (feedback) group were told not to sub-vocalize and if they did a buzzer sounded. A third, control group read while maintaining their forearms at a particular level of flexion. Subsequently subjects answered questions on the essays. No effects were found when reading essay passages, but subjects forced to suppress vocalization remembered considerably less about the hard passages. These results suggest that the articulatory loop may be important in the reading of prose, particularly more complex material (see Baddeley 1992 for further research of this kind).

Visuo-spatial scratch pad

Baddeley (1986) has extended the concept of working memory with the addition of a second structure – the visuo-spatial scratch-pad (VSSP). Imagery is a prominent feature of our mental life and there is some reason to believe that it has a separate status from other, non-image-based mental processes. The idea behind the VSSP is that working memory has a specific component that provides a workspace within which a visual image can be stored and manipulated in order to carry out a particular task.

Evidence for a VSSP comes from dual-task studies such as that by Brooks (1968). Subjects were asked to keep in mind a letter F and then imagine an asterisk travelling around the F (see figure 7.16a). At each change of direction subjects had to indicate whether the asterisk was at an extreme or intermediate point of the F. Three modes of responding were used, vocal (yes–no), tapping – one

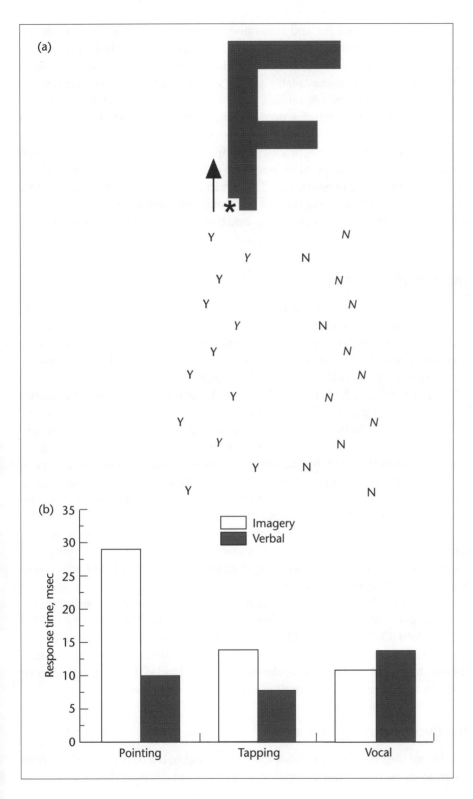

Figure 7.16 (a) Simple diagram used by Brooks (1968: 350–3) to study the scanning of mental images. (b) Response times in the different experimental conditions
Brooks. 'The suppression of visualisation by reading' in *Quarterly Journal of Experimental Psychology*, 19 (Academic Press 1968).

tap for yes, two taps for no, and a pointing response. In the latter, subjects had a visual array of spatially distributed Y and N symbols in front of them. As they imagined the asterisk moving, subjects had to indicate their response by pointing to the next Y or N location available as they worked their way down the array.

These three modes of responding were also used in a verbal task in which subjects had to work through a proverb and indicate whether or not each successive word was a noun. Figure 7.16b shows the results. For the verbal condition the three response modes produced comparable reaction times. For the visual condition, however, the pointing response produced far slower reaction times than the other two response modes. The fact that the pointing task only caused a significant delay when responding in the visual condition suggests strongly that subjects were retaining a spatial image and that this interfered with responding, which was also determined by spatial constraints.

The central executive

So far the components of working memory we have identified, the articulatory loop and visuo-spatial scratch pad, contribute to only a small percentage of our conscious mental activity. In terms of the model, the bulk of what we do is carried out by the central executive. Because it is the most complex it is perhaps unsurprising that it is also the least understood.

One approach to understanding the central executive can be described as the 'psychometric' approach. The basis of this idea is that the executive must, under a given set of conditions (e.g. reading comprehension), have a fixed capacity. Daneman and Carpenter (1980) have termed this the working memory span. They measured this span by presenting subjects with a sequence of sentences and asking them to retain the last word of each. Thus subjects might see or hear the sentences 'The sailor sold the parrot. The vicar opened the book.' After the sentences are presented subjects must recall the final words (*parrot*, *book*) and this constitutes a measure of working memory span. This measure was then correlated with each subject's score on a reading comprehension test. This correlation was highly significant indicating that reading comprehension was a positive function of working memory span.

The idea that the capacity of the central executive is related to reading ability gains support from other studies involving both adults (Baddeley et al. 1985) and children (Oakhill 1984; Oakhill et al. 1986). However, these studies measure working memory in purely quantitative, capacity-related terms – some account of how the executive actually works must be provided if the working memory model is to be a proper account of memory.

The dysexecutive syndrome

One recent idea has been to equate the functioning of the central executive with the processing operations associated with the frontal lobes. This research has

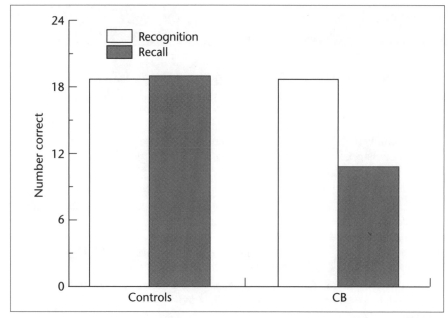

Figure 7.17 Comparison of recall and recognition abilities in control subjects and CB, a man with a frontal lobe lesion. Note that recognition memory is normal but that recall is badly impaired.
From Parkin et al., *Brain and Cognition*, 26: 23–42 (Academic Press).

been motivated by studying patients who have developed memory problems as a result of frontal lobe damage. The memory deficits these patients suffer are not as severe as those shown by amnesics such as HM, and they have been termed the dysexecutive syndrome (Baddeley 1997) on the grounds that their memory deficit reflects some impairment in the executive control of memory.

Earlier we saw that remembering is largely a reconstructive process in which we try to specify the nature of the information we are trying to retrieve. This activity can be viewed as a problem-solving activity which is most difficult when we test free recall because, under these conditions, no information is given about what we are trying to remember. Retrieval then gets progressively easier as we test cued recall and then recognition, because the problem-solving element is reduced. Frontal lobe damage consistently produces deficits in problem solving and so one would expect memory difficulties to be most pronounced on tests of recall. This is exactly what we find. Figure 7.17 shows the recall and recognition ability of a patient known as CB (Parkin et al. 1994), and you can see that he performs very poorly on recall despite normal recognition – this contrasts with a typical amnesic patient who would show impaired performance on both tasks.

CHAPTER SUMMARY

1 Human memory is divisible into three distinct stores, iconic memory, short-term store, and long-term store.

2 Levels of processing experiments emphasize that the nature of encoding determines learning. Learning will be most effective when encoding conditions resemble what is required at test.

3 Long-term store comprises procedural memory and declarative memory. The latter may also be divisible into episodic and semantic memory.

4 Explicit memory corresponds to memory of a specific past event. Implicit memory involves memory without conscious recollection of a past event.

5 Generation recognition models propose that retrieval involves two stages and that recognition is easier because the reconstructive component of retrieval is bypassed. Encoding specificity rejects this view and argues that both recall and recognition represent a single retrieval process.

6 Forgetting is not due solely to retrieval failure, but proving storage failure is difficult. Changes in context can lead to retrieval failure.

7 Working memory proposes that STS is not a single entity but one comprising three subsystems, a central executive, an articulatory loop, and a visuo-spatial scratch pad.

■ Further Work ■

1. What are the major reasons for proposing separate short-term and long-term stores?
2. What are the strengths and weaknesses of the levels of processing approach?
3. What are the subdivisions of long-term store?
4. Is the distinction between explicit and implicit memory a better way to explain the nature of long-term store?
5. What are similarities and differences between generation-recognition and encoding-specificity approaches to retrieval?
6. How does context influence forgetting?
7. Why does the working memory model propose three subsystems?

■ Further Reading ■

Baddeley, A. D. (1990) *Human Memory: Theory and Practice*. Hove: Erlbaum.

Alan Baddeley has produced an excellent primer of human memory in this text. It is very accessible and has a very clear view of the theoretical issues in memory research.

Neisser, U. (1982) *Memory Observed*. New York: Freeman.

This work by Neisser is now a classic.

Parkin, A. J. (1993) *Memory: Phenomena, Experiment and Theory*. Oxford: Blackwell.

Parkin, A. J. (1997) *Memory and Amnesia: An Introduction*, 2nd edn: Oxford: Blackwell.

To follow up on the amnesic research we have discussed – and the framework outlined in the chapter – both of these texts would be a good place to start.

PsyCLE MODULE: MEMORY

The focus in the text Boxes 7.1 and 7.2 on amnesia is echoed in this demonstration. You can run some of the simple tests that are used to explore the nature of the simulated amnesic's condition and compare your results with his. You should ask yourself – is the software amnesic like the real patients we discuss, HM and PZ?

CHAPTER 8
Learning and Skill

Rod Nicolson

CHAPTER AGENDA

- Learning is the fundamental human ability. It underpins all our skills – mental, physical and social. In this chapter we review the many aspects of learning, considering how such diverse approaches can be integrated into a more complete understanding.

- We look first at studies of animal learning and their implications for our study of human learning.

- We examine how we become expert at a task or skill – and ask what is automaticity and how we can develop it.

- What is the difference between natural learning and training – can we improve the ease of learning?

- Next, we look at the brain itself and how its structure becomes changed by learning, especially in infancy. How does this affect subsequent development?

- We consider how connectionism may provide us with a language for modelling low-level learning.

- Finally, we consider how it may be possible to account for the different views on learning within a coherent framework.

▓ Background ▓

In the first half of this century learning was at the very centre of scientific psychology. Studies of animal learning led to the development of a large theoretical edifice of learning theory which aimed at the complete explanation of behaviour, no less. The theories were immensely influential. Studies of rats and humans learning led to the development of a pedagogy of learning which promised, and delivered to a large extent, new methods of teaching children which were very much more efficient than previous approaches. Using a similar approach, the behaviourist B. F. Skinner provided amazing examples of how to train animals to acquire impressive skills, how to use the newly developed computers to further improve the effectiveness of learning, and even how to use the principles of REINFORCEMENT to create a modern utopia. But there was a wind of change blowing throughout the 1950s. Like the British Empire, the behaviourist enterprise was in terminal decline, to be replaced by the new 'information-processing theory', in which researchers drew an analogy between the way information is stored and processed in a library (or in a computer) and the way that an adult

REINFORCEMENT

294

might process information about the world – encoding, storing and retrieving information (see chapter 7 for more details). A serious drawback of the information-processing approach was that it had no method of representing learning, and the study of learning fell from mainstream psychology for three decades.

The history of learning became that of the various disciplines in which it was an important part – developmental psychology, motor skill, expertise and cognitive science. Because the different disciplines had different languages, different approaches, different preoccupations and different roles for learning, there has been no coherent attempt at an integrative *rapprochement* of these different aspects of learning. It is like the old Hindu tale, much loved by psychologists, of the four blindfolded men examining an elephant. One, feeling the trunk, said 'It's a snake'. Another, examining a leg said, 'It's a tree'. The third, examining the tail said 'It's a rope'. The fourth, examining the body, said 'It's a house'.

History does not relate the elephant's reaction. The task of this chapter is to attempt to draw for you the whole elephant. Why am I recounting this dull history? It is because learning has at last made a comeback. The demise of learning is one of the most extraordinary examples of the subjectivity of science, and the vagaries of scientific fashion. I believe that when introductory books on psychology are written in ten years' time, learning will be back in force, treated in an integrated fashion, and acknowledged again as the heart of psychology.

After experimenting with various formulations, it seems to me that the most appropriate method for attempting this resurrection is to present in turn the snake, the tree, the rope and the house, in the hope that juxtaposition will help reveal the complete elephant. This chapter will therefore outline in turn a succinct and partial summary of four major approaches to learning: starting with animals learning; then human adults learning; then human infants learning; then finally the brain learning. An advantage of this approach is that each section can be read as a self-contained and reasonably coherent unit, just as it is in the current literature. A disadvantage of the approach is that, once the parts are described, it is hard to perceive the whole. Consequently, at the outset, I shall start by giving a preview of my own biases in interpreting the literature. It is these biases that give my elephant its final form and colour.

What is learning?

To learn means to 'get knowledge of (subject) or skill in (art etc.) by study, experience, or being taught' (*Concise Oxford Dictionary*). That is not a bad everyday definition. Note the clear distinction between acquisition of knowledge (which overlaps very much with studies of memory – see chapter 7) and acquisition of skill. This distinction is known in cognitive science as the distinction between declarative knowledge ('knowledge that') and procedural knowledge ('knowledge how'). Whether or not it is an important distinction has been the focus of considerable debate to which I shall return later in the chapter. Psychologists tend to describe learning more broadly than dictionaries, with perhaps a standard early definition being that of Kimble (1961): 'learning is a relatively permanent change in behaviour potentiality that occurs as a result of reinforced practice.' This is actually a theory-bound definition. Even leaving aside the 'behaviour potentiality' borrowed from the behaviourists, the definition asserts that learning requires practice, it requires 'reinforcement', and that it is relatively permanent. We shall see later in the chapter that this definition is too narrow. One can learn instantaneously, without practice and without reinforcement. A more neutral definition is that given by Wingfield (1979), who suggests that learning is 'a relatively permanent change in behaviour or knowledge brought about by practice or experience'. Dropping the 'reinforced practice' does have some drawbacks. It would appear, for instance, that spraining one's ankle might qualify as learning under this rubric. Thorpe (1963) defines learning as 'the process which manifests itself by adaptive changes in individual behaviour as a result of experience.'

These are deep waters. Trying to start by defining learning means trying to describe the elephant before constructing it. Learning has many meanings and many facets. Let us start with the more important question – why learning?

What is learning for?

The influential cognitive scientist David Marr made a powerful point that one of the most useful things to know when trying to understand how something worked was to know what its function was – what it was for. '[T]rying to understand perception by studying only neurons is like trying to understand bird flight by studying only feathers: It just cannot be done. In order to understand bird flight we have to understand aerodynamics; only then do the structure of feathers and the different shapes of birds' wings make sense' (1982: 27).

So what is learning for? In evolutionary terms the general answer is obvious. Learning, in which an organism changes its behaviour in response to its experiences, is a potent source of evolutionary advantage. Even the invertebrate sea slug, aplysia, is capable of differentiated learning. An organism that learns will have a greater chance of transmitting its genes to the next generation than one that does not. So learning is a method of adapting to the environment.

It is now common to use the analogy of a computer as an aid to understanding the mind. As a result of experience, the mind/computer stores information, thereby improving the adaptability of its actions by the use of memory. It also uses the experience to improve the efficiency of its various control processes – attentional systems and the like. What has not been well enough appreciated, however, is that these learning processes, impressive though they are, are merely the tip of the adaptation iceberg. The theme running through this chapter is a powerful one. It is that the human brain is a uniquely designed 'learning machine'. The design is truly exquisite. Sculpted by evolutionary forces, and exploiting every available resource, the brain not only adapts to its environment, but adapts its environment to itself. As we shall see, however, unlike any machine, the brain changes not just its software, but also its hardware in order to optimize its adaptation. We have no analogy or metaphor to describe this extraordinary device. No wonder, then, that we have failed so far.

Cortical plasticity

This view of learning has important theoretical and applied implications. In order to motivate the considerable accommodation required by readers with existing knowledge of traditional approaches to cognitive psychology, I start by presenting a study (one of several) by Michael Merzenich and his colleagues which demonstrates the extraordinary plasticity of the primate brain.

Recanzone et al. (1993) trained an adult owl monkey to discriminate differences in sound frequency around a 2.5 kHz standard tone (the monkey had to indicate which of two tones was the higher). The monkey improved with practice (by a factor of about 8, over 100 sessions), and the improvement was specific to that frequency range. So far so good. This improvement with practice is as one would expect for most primates.

However, the experimenters had previously implanted electrodes into area A1 of the monkey's primary auditory cortex (the first cortical destination of the input from the ear). They were therefore able to map the receptive fields of each cell, by playing tones of various frequencies, and seeing which frequencies that cell responded to. The frequency map for an untrained monkey is shown in figure 8.1a. It can be seen that the auditory cortex is formed into reasonably consistent receptive areas, with increasing depth representing increasingly high frequencies. The three black areas represent those sensitive to 2.5 kHz. The 'contours' have been added to delineate the boundaries between the 1 to 2 kHz, 2 to 4 kHz, 4 to 8 kHz regions. Now consider figure 8.1b, the auditory fields for the trained monkey. Note that the overall relationship between depth and frequency remains, but that there have been considerable changes in organization. In par-

Figure 8.1 Cortical map: (a) untrained monkey; (b) trained monkey

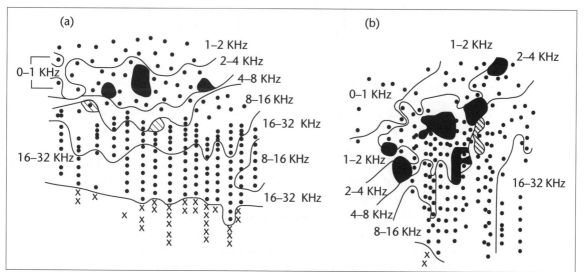

ticular, the critical area around 2.5 kHz has grown, colonizing the 1 to 2 kHz and 4 to 8 kHz areas especially. There are now six 2.5 kHz sites, at the expense of the other, less important frequencies.

CORTICAL
PLASTICITY

This is a staggering demonstration of CORTICAL PLASTICITY. (Plasticity means adaptability; cortical plasticity mean ability to change the cortex as a function of learning or damage.) Plasticity is generally considered to diminish to a very low level after the first few years of life, and yet this is an adult monkey, and the primary sensory cortex is generally considered to be among the least plastic of the cortical structures. Plasticity is much more likely in the association areas. Imagine now, that if the primary auditory cortex of an adult monkey can be so extensively modified by this auditory training, how much more could be achieved (and is achieved) in terms of the adaptation of a human baby's brain as a consequence of its early environment. (If the scientific background on this is not clear to you, you may need to turn back to chapters 5, 6 and 7 to refresh your memory.)

I shall return to this theme again and again in this chapter, and will focus on the development of the brain in the third section, below. However, most of the important insights into learning have been achieved without any knowledge of the neural events that underlie it. In the next section we consider studies of animal learning, followed by studies of human learning. I shall develop the theme that human learning has much in common with animal learning, but that the ability to learn to use symbolic constructs gives humans access to qualitatively different forms of learning.

▦ Animal Learning ▦

Considerable work was done on learning in Victorian England, with particular interest in Charles Darwin's views on adaptation and evolution. However, new agendas for the next 50 years' research on learning were set by work around the turn of the century by Ivan Pavlov in Russia and Edward Lee Thorndike in the USA.

Classical conditioning

Pavlov, who was originally interested in the digestive system, noticed (as would anyone who has prepared a meal for a dog) that as well as salivating when they ate food, dogs would salivate when they saw it, smelled it, or even when they saw the technician who brought it. He realized that this could be exploited to investigate the basic processes of learning. By implanting a cannula (tube) in the dog's throat, Pavlov was able to measure the amount of salivation and thus infer the degree of learning. A hungry dog is restrained on a stand (see figure 8.2) and every few minutes is given some dry meat powder, whose appearance is preceded by some arbitrary stimulus, such as the sound of a bell (or the illumination of a light). The dog salivates to the food, and after a few pairings of food and

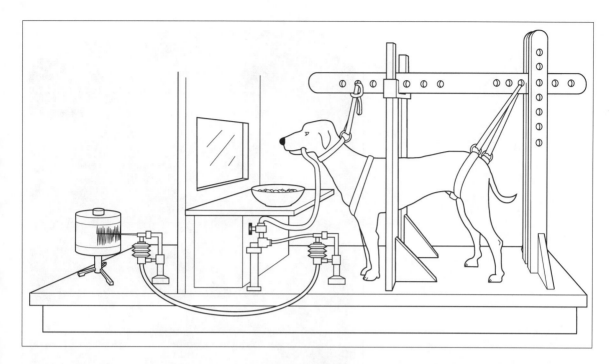

Figure 8.2 Pavlov's classical conditioning apparatus

bell, it will also salivate on hearing the bell. Indeed, after sufficient pairings, the dog will salivate to the bell whether or not the food is given. In Pavlov's terminology, the food is an Unconditional Stimulus (US), the salivation to food is an Unconditional Response (UR) (it always happens on presentation of the US), the bell is a Conditional Stimulus (CS) and the salivation to the bell is a Conditional Response (CR) (it only happens under certain conditions – specifically when the CS is paired with the US).

This process, known as CLASSICAL CONDITIONING, is a potent force in learning. It has been demonstrated in a number of animals, from aplysia (the sea slug) to humans, and for a number of responses (all unconditional ones, of course), from eye blinks to fear. It is clearly very adaptive for an organism, having had an unpleasant experience, to associate the stimulus with its consequences – the burnt child dreads the fire. One of the most impressive illustrations of classical conditioning (and one which caused grave difficulties for explanations in terms of temporal contiguity between stimulus and response) was that of taste aversion. Garcia and his colleagues (e.g. Garcia & Koelling 1966) gave a sucrose solution to thirsty rats. The rats drank it with relish. One day later they injected a lithium chloride (which makes the rat mildly ill). Subsequently, the rats avoided the sucrose solution, having been conditioned to re-evaluate it as unpleasant. Humans also show evidence of this phenomenon. If one eats a novel food and is then ill fairly soon afterwards (even for a demonstrably unrelated reason), one may well show an aversion to that food thereafter. It may well be that this effect lies at the root of the frustrating changes in food preference shown by babies and toddlers. Perhaps the saddest demonstration was that of the 11-month-old

CLASSICAL CONDITIONING

299

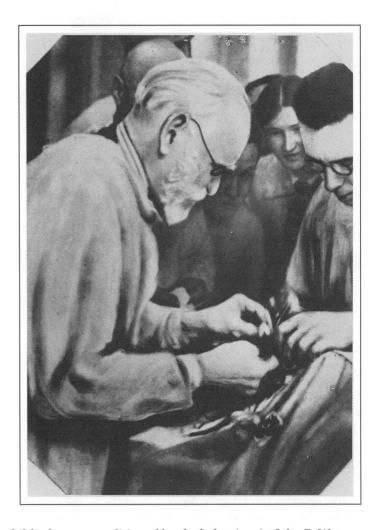

Plate 8.1 Pavlov operating on a dog
Source: Corbis/ Bettmann.

infant Albert – a child who was conditioned by the behaviourist John B. Watson (Watson & Rayner 1920) to be afraid of a white rat by pairing the appearance of the rat with a loud noise. Initially Albert reached out to touch the rat, but after two pairings of rat with a loud noise, Albert shrank from it, and his fear even generalized to a variety of furry items, animate and inanimate.

Pavlov believed that a 'conditioned reflex' between stimulus and response was created by classical conditioning, but subsequent research has shown that this belief was false. If a dog is satiated with food (and therefore would not have salivated if food was presented), then the dog will not salivate to the conditioned stimulus – say, the bell. The link cannot therefore be directly from CS to CR, but must be a CS–US link, i.e. stimulus to stimulus. Furthermore, more recent research has suggested that it is not so much *contiguity* between CS and US that counts (that is, the US occurs very shortly after the CS), but rather *contingency*, that is, the CS indicates that a US is more likely. Early evidence for this was derived by Rescorla (1968), who systematically varied the probability of presentation of the US (shock) following presentation of the CS. It turned out that the higher the probability of the US, the greater the conditioning, and no conditioning occurred at all when the pairings between CS and shock were random. Rescorla and Wagner (1972) put forward a formal model of conditioning which predicts that conditioning depends upon the discrepancy between expected and obtained reinforcement. If the reinforcement is as expected, no conditioning occurs, whereas if there is a discrepancy, then the strength of the link between CS and US is likely to be high.

Research on the underlying causes of classical conditioning is currently very active, focusing on how these links are caused, and, in particular, what brain structures are involved. We shall return to this issue towards the end of the chapter, but for the present it is worth noting that different structures and mechanisms may be involved for different types of conditioning.

The Law of Effect

Thorndike developed his insights from work with cats. He built 'puzzle boxes' in which the cat had to pull a lever (or press a panel, pull a rope, etc.) to open the door. Cats dislike confined spaces and make frantic efforts to escape. Thorndike noticed that the first time the cat was placed in the box, it scrabbled around frantically but aimlessly, eventually hitting on the right response by chance, and thus escaping. When placed in the box again, it would again frantically scrabble around, but this time it would hit on the right response faster. The next time it would be faster, and so on. This and related studies led Thorndike (1911) to formulate the LAW OF EFFECT, namely: 'If a stimulus S leads to a response R, which in turn leads to reinforcement, then the S–R connection is strengthened. If it leads to punishment, the S–R connection is weakened.' In the case of the puzzle box, the stimulus would be the entire puzzle box situation, the response would be the lever press, and the reinforcement is the escape from the box. Thorndike's idea was that the cat would have a lot of responses available – pushing with its paw, trying to squeeze through a gap, jumping up, scratching at a door, and so on. The cat would try first the response with the greatest 'strength' – presumably the one that had been most reinforced in the past (in different situations). The lever press would have little or no strength initially, being a novel response, and so would not be tried until the range of other responses had been exhausted. After each successful trial, the lever press would be reinforced, and thus get a bit stronger, and so it would move up through the hierarchy of responses, eventually becoming the first response to be tried. In this way, learning is incremental (little by little) rather than all-or-nothing.

LAW OF EFFECT

Incidentally, Thorndike's emphasis on trial-and-error, incremental learning set up a nice contrast with later work by the German Gestalt psychologist, Wolfgang Köhler. Köhler was interested in insightful learning, and performed a series of experiments which tested apes' problem-solving ability. For example, a banana was put just out of reach so that the ape had to use a stick, or join two

Plate 8.2 E. L. Thorndike
Source: Courtesy of National
Library of Medicine,
Washington DC.

sticks together, in order to reach it. Rather than scrabble around aimlessly, trying everything in the cage, the ape sat there without moving, and then got up,
picked up the stick, and used it to reach for the banana. Köhler argued that its
performance could only be described as insightful, with the characteristics that
the transition from pre-solution to solution is sudden and complete; performance based on insight is usually smooth and error free; a solution based on
insight is not forgotten; and the principle generalizes easily to other situations.
This led to the amusing idea (I believe it is attributable to Bertrand Russell) that
American animals rushed round randomly, trying anything and everything,
whereas the European animals thought their way through the problems, using
brainpower rather than mere energy to solve them! Of course, the real difference lay in the abilities of the animals and the complexity of the task. As we shall
see later, there are many forms of learning, and it is foolish to look for a single
principle that underlies them all.

Plate 8.3 Wolfgang Köhler
Source: Courtesy of National
Library of Medicine,
Washington DC.

Hull's theory of learning

Thorndike introduced a language for studying learning – positive reinforcement
(nice: presentation of food, water, sexual opportunity etc.), negative reinforcement (nasty: pain, loud noise, stress etc.), positive and negative reinforcers; and
punishment (presentation of a negative reinforcer (an aversive stimulus) in
order to reduce incidence of responding). Incidentally, Thorndike abandoned part
two of the Law of Effect in 1930, arguing instead that punishment *per se* led to no
reduction in connection strength. Other theorists developed this vocabulary, together with further techniques for investigating learning. Clark Hull developed a
formal, mathematical theory of learning based on a number of 'postulates' from
which he derived a series of equations describing learning. One postulate was
that if a stimulus S and a response R become linked through reinforced pairings,
then the 'habit strength' of the link increases each time the pairing is reinforced. A
further postulate stated that habit strength alone is not sufficient for an animal to

Box 8.1   B. F. Skinner: the psychologist who wished to change the world

Skinner pioneered a range of methods for training animals. The key idea was that of 'shaping' behaviour. For example, to train a pigeon to hop backwards around the cage, one would first reinforce the pigeon for any backward move, then when the pigeon had learned to circle backwards, one would then reinforce any backwards hop, and so on, slowly shaping the behaviour, a bit at a time, towards the required behaviour. Using these techniques Skinner was able to train animals to perform all sorts of tricks. One memorable demonstration was of pigeons playing table tennis, and another was where Skinner trained rats to demonstrate 'intelligent' behaviour, picking up a marble and dropping it down a tube to obtain reinforcement. These techniques are essentially those now used for training circus animals. Skinner has been criticized for his strict behaviourist approach, but it is important to note that he made it very clear that punishment was not an effective strategy, and that positive reinforcement was the key to behaviour modification. In order to change an unwanted behaviour, do not punish that behaviour, but reward the behaviour that one does want.

Skinner applied his approach to human learning, trying to account for human language learning, and pioneering the use of the computer for 'programmed learning'.

His suggestions for parents are as follows: (i) Decide the major personality characteristics you want your child to possess as an adult. Let's say you want her to be creative. (ii) Define these goals in behavioural terms: ask yourself 'What is she *doing* when she is being creative?' (iii) Reward behaviour that is in accordance with these goals as it occurs. (iv) Provide consistency by arranging the child's environment so that it also rewards the behaviour you consider important. Parents lacking this knowledge may achieve the opposite result to that intended:

> The mother may unwittingly promote the very behaviour she does not want. For example, when she is busy she is likely not to respond to a call made in a quiet tone of voice. She may answer the child only when it raises its voice. The average intensity of the child's vocal behavior therefore moves up to another level. . . . Eventually the mother gets used to this level and again rein-

make a response. It must also be in a state of 'drive' (a basic need of organism – hunger, thirst, sex, etc.) so that the response would reduce the drive. For instance, even though a rat has a high habit strength linking a bar press to receiving a food pellet, it will not display the behaviour unless it is hungry (has a 'hunger drive'). Hull's approach dominated learning theory in the 1940s, with his work cited by 70 per cent of all articles in the area of learning and motivation in that period, but disappeared from mainstream psychology very soon after his death in the 1950s. The main difficulty was that it was premature to try to construct a grand theory of learning when it was by no means clear whether there was any real understanding of what it was that was being learned. None the less, some such 'grand theory' has remained the elusive goal of theoretical psychologists ever since. As we shall see in this chapter, the 50 years of research after Hull have led to a very much better understanding of the various aspects of learning. Hull's approach has much in common with that of influential cognitive scientists such as John Anderson (1983), and it can also be linked to connectionist modelling techniques (see below). It may be that the time is now ripe for further attempts at the grand theory.

Reinforcement and instrumental conditioning

Where Clark Hull looked for general theoretical principles linking stimulus and response, the behaviourist B. F. Skinner, working around the same time, had a

forces only louder instances. This vicious circle brings about louder and louder instances. . . . The mother behaves, in fact, as if she has been given the task of teaching the child to be annoying. (1951: 29)

Finally, and most controversially, he advocated that behaviourist principles could be used to help create a new utopia, where everyone was happy and worked together. His books *Walden 2* (1948) and *Beyond Freedom and Dignity* (1971) contain much good sense and many insightful analyses, but even so they enraged many academics, who considered that Skinner, in attempting to systematize society, had thrown out most of what is good in society. An example of the scope of his approach is given below:

A culture is like the experimental space used in the study of behavior. It is a set of contingencies of reinforcement. . . . The technology of behaviour that emerges is ethically neutral, but when applied to the design of a culture, the survival of the culture functions as a value. . . . Physical and biological technologies have alleviated pestilence and famine and many painful, dangerous and exhausting features of daily life, and behavioral technology can begin to alleviate other kinds of ills.

. . . There are wonderful possibilities – and all the more wonderful because traditional approaches have been so ineffective. It is hard to imagine a world in which people live together without quarrelling, maintain themselves by producing the food, shelter and clothing they need, enjoy themselves and contribute to the enjoyment of others in art, music, literature and games, consume only a reasonable part of the resources of the world and add as little as possible to its pollution, bear no more children than can be raised decently, continue to explore the world around them and discover better ways of dealing with it, and come to know themselves accurately, and, therefore, manage themselves effectively. Yet all this is possible, and even the slightest sign of progress should bring a change which in traditional terms would be said to . . . promote a 'sense of freedom and dignity' by building a 'sense of confidence of worth'. In other words, it should abundantly reinforce those who have been induced by their culture to work for its survival. (1971: 178/209)

more applied approach. He developed a range of techniques for investigating learning quantitatively. It was he who invented the Skinner box – a box with a metal bar in which a rat was placed. In a typical experiment pressing the bar would lead to delivery of a food pellet. Bar presses were recorded automatically. A further invention was a pigeon Skinner box, where the pigeon pecked an illuminated key to obtain a food pellet. These tools allowed Skinner to investigate important aspects of learning, such as 'strength' of learning. This was measured by the number of presses the rat made when no food was given following the bar press (extinction). He also investigated the processes of 'partial reinforcement' – when the pellet was not given on every press, but only after every 10 presses (fixed ratio schedule) or every 5 minutes following a press (fixed interval schedule) or even after 5 minutes without making a press (omission schedule). An important distinction in Skinner's work, and that of Hull, was between primary reinforcement (food, drink, etc.) and secondary reinforcement (a stimulus which has become associated with primary reinforcement, such as the smell of food etc., and therefore acquires reinforcing characteristics in its own right). In our society, money is the archetypal generalized secondary reinforcer.

Skinner's ambition was to use the principles derived from the laboratory to materially improve our culture in a systematic fashion, as is outlined in Box 8.1. His ambitions were laudable, and provide an object lesson in the importance of long-term applied goals in psychological research. Even so, it is certainly the

Plate 8.4 B. F. Skinner
Source: Corbis/Bettmann.

case that, when taken too literally by those with a narrower view than Skinner, his 'behavioural science' approach seems horribly limited. A particularly clear example of this is the books of the 1940s child-rearing guru Dr Benjamin Spock, who, adopting behaviourist principles, advocated that an infant should be conditioned to wake up only at meal times (every four hours) and should be ignored if crying (one must not positively reinforce unwanted behaviour!). Emotional interaction appeared to be missing from Spock's books – there was no room for love, kindness and fun in his approach. As we shall see later, it may be precisely these qualities which allow the infant to develop cognitive skills, as well as emotional security. Perhaps the most extraordinary aspect of Skinner's work (and that of all the behaviourists) was their reluctance to use the idea of internal mental states in their theories, a failure that led them to underestimate the complexities of behaviour. Even so, there was much that was good in Skinner's approach. The challenge is to see how much of human learning he missed, so that a more complete model can be constructed.

We now turn to subsequent studies of human learning, starting with adult learning, since for obvious reasons most controlled studies of learning have been undertaken in the laboratory, with adult volunteers. As we shall see, there is good reason to think that there may be qualitative differences in learning between adults and young children.

▓ Adult Human Learning ▓

One of the most satisfying aspects of being human is that, with practice, one gets better at things. With more practice, one gets better still, and so on, almost indefinitely. This process of improvement with practice has been much studied by psychologists.

The Power Law of Practice

One of the clearest demonstrations of this continual improvement was provided by Crossman (1959), who studied the time taken by roll a cigar by cigar makers of different degrees of experience (figure 8.3).

Note that the scale is a log-log scale, and that for the first year at least, the graph is near linear – log cycle time (T) decreases linearly with the practice (P). In mathematics,

$$\log(T) = a - b \log(P), \text{ hence } T = aP^{-b}$$

where a and b are constants. This relationship is known as the POWER LAW OF PRACTICE (time decreases as a negative power of the practice), and has been shown to apply to a wide range of skills (Newell & Rosenbloom 1981); not just for motor skills such as cigar rolling, but also for cognitive skills such as solving geometry questions. But surely there's more to skill than just getting faster and faster! Let us turn now to studies of skill that make Crossman's seven years look like a mere apprenticeship.

POWER LAW OF PRACTICE

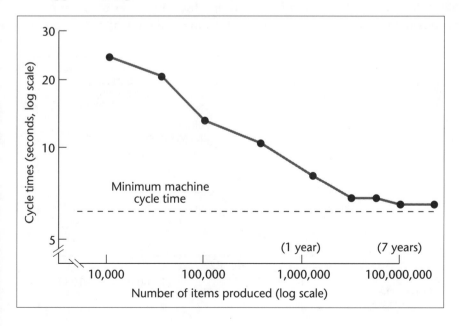

Figure 8.3 Continuous improvement in skill with practice.
Crossman, 'A theory of the acquisition of speed skill' in *Ergonomics*, 2 (Taylor & Francis, London, 1959).

Super-skills

We all know (either personally or through the television) people whose levels of skill at a particular task are quite extraordinary. In this section we consider what is the basis for this expertise, and whether anyone could, given the opportunity and the determination, acquire these levels of skill.

Ericsson (e.g. Ericsson & Charness 1994) has made extensive studies of the way in which world-class expertise develops. First he highlights the difference between different sorts of practice – play (an unstructured, enjoyable method of practice); DELIBERATE PRACTICE (in which individualized training is given on tasks selected by a qualified teacher); and work (which involves public performances, etc.). Following analyses of people acquiring a range of expertise (including music, sport and chess), Ericsson derived a diagram for the phases in acquiring expertise (figure 8.4).

In phase 1 (P1) practice takes the form of play. Most people never get beyond this stage, but those who are going to progress then typically are taught how to perform the skill better (phase P2). There is rapid improvement to begin with, but then diminishing returns set in, with each hour of practice leading to smaller and smaller amounts of progress. If the person wishes to proceed, it is then necessary to get a coach, an expert, to give further individual training (phase P3). It is rare to get to the final, expert, stage with much less than 1,000 hours of practice. This is often referred to as the 10-YEAR RULE, in that it is rare to achieve expert performance without at least 10 years' practice. To progress to world class one needs further specialist coaching from a champion coach!

These elite experts have almost certainly spent 10 years of essentially full-time preparation. They will have to adjust their life to optimize the opportunities for deliberate practice. They will practise around four hours per day, comprising four one-hour sessions followed by rest. Training will more often take place in

DELIBERATE PRACTICE

10-YEAR RULE

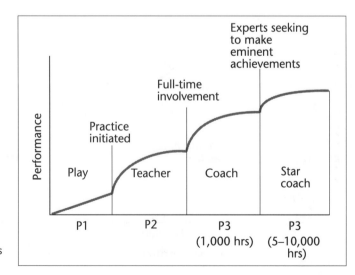

Figure 8.4 Four phases in acquiring expertise

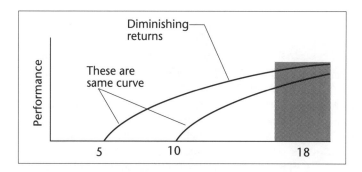

Figure 8.5 Starting age, and experience at age 18

the morning, and the expert will need lots of sleep and rest. Bearing in mind that, even with this terrifying dedication, most athletes and swimmers will never make it to the top, one has to wonder whether the effort would be worthwhile.

On the other hand, for skills like music, the lifelong enjoyment that it endows may well make it well worth the effort of persevering with one's piano lessons! Interestingly, music seems to be one of those skills where early exposure appears to be particularly beneficial. After all, Mozart was composing symphonies at the age of 4, and there have been many child prodigies at music. None the less, following a thorough survey of music learning and other forms of development of expertise, Ericsson and Charness (1994) concluded that there are, in fact, precious few, if any, genetic factors in true expertise. Instead they put forward the 'monotonic benefits assumption' – that expertise increases directly with the amount of deliberate practice. They attribute the advantage of starting young just to the fact that there is essentially a race to see who will be best in early adulthood. As can be seen from figure 8.5, if one starts at five years old, the benefits are still there at 18. The fruits of early starts and dedicated, deliberate training are shown most dramatically in the Japanese Suzuki music academy, where recruits start at 4 years old and perform superbly by 10 years (Suzuki 1981).

A probable exception to the monotonic benefits assumption is that dedicated practice in childhood may well lead to irreversible changes both in body and brain. There is no doubt that systematic gymnastic or athletics exercise before the age of 10 years or so may lead to anatomical improvements in muscular strength and lung capacity. More generally, vigorous physical activity stimulates the growth of bones and joints as well as muscles (Bailey & McCullough 1990). This is often very obvious in tennis players, where the racquet arm is very much more developed than the other. Interestingly, it appears that practice at young ages may be necessary for ballet dancers to achieve the maximal turnout at the hip needed (Miller et al. 1984), and that this extra 'flexibility' is actually achieved at the expense of flexibility in the opposite direction. There is also evidence that children may acquire 'perfect pitch', but only if given the appropriate training within the first few years of life (Takeuchi & Hulse 1993). We shall return to this important issue of brain plasticity below.

On the basis of these analyses, Ericsson concludes that anyone can become

Box 8.2 Multiple Intelligences?

All of us have strengths and weaknesses. We may be good at languages but bad at science, good at social interaction but bad at academic skills, good at sport but bad at music. To a large extent this may be attributable to early experiences. If at some time one has a passionate interest in something – whether it be dinosaurs, music, chess, football stickers or stamp collecting – one devotes exceptional time and effort to pursuing knowledge in that domain. Furthermore, the learning is fun. Compare this process of natural learning to that of school learning, where one is forced to acquire information for which one has no purpose and no motivation. My sons Ben and James collected football stickers and devoured the information upon them. They made up teams and played imaginary games with arcane rules. Soon they could tell me every player in the British Premier League (and their height, weight, transfer fee etc.). There were over 500 cards. Imagine what could have happened if they had devoted the same energy to, say, learning French. Similarly, if one enjoys a particular sport, and is perhaps a bit better at it than other sports, it is natural to spend more time on that sport, thus starting a cycle of increasing time, increasing ability, and increasing specialization.

There is nothing at all wrong with specialization (within reason). Many people's enjoyment of life derives from their hobby, and the British have a reputation for eccentric enthusiasm. Even so, one of the sadnesses in life is that skills and knowledge do not often transfer to other domains. There are extreme instances of this in the case of autism where individuals may show quite exceptional skills in very specific areas, while performing at very low levels indeed in most other areas. The artistic ability of Stephen Wiltshire (see chapter 2) is a real example, while the virtuoso performance in the film *Rain Man* of Dustin Hoffman as the autistic adult with extraordinary mnemonic abilities has great impact. Howard Gardner (1993) has proposed that in fact we have seven, really quite separate intelligences, namely: Linguistic Intelligence; Logico-mathematical Intelligence; Spatial Intelligence; Musical Intelligence; Bodily-kinaesthetic Intelligence (used in dancing, sport, etc.); Interpersonal Intelligence (social skills, etc.); and Intrapersonal Intelligence (self-knowledge). He based this separation on wide-ranging studies including the specific effects of brain lesions on different kinds of intelligence; distinctive patterns of development of the types of intelligence across the life span; evolutionary history; and evidence from exceptional individuals (including prodigies, savants and geniuses). He views cognition as modular, and attributes each of the types of intelligence to a different module. It must be said that as yet no hard evidence for the separate existence of these separate intelligences has been produced.

Consider your own skills. What are you good at? What are you bad at? How would you rate yourself on each of Gardner's seven types of intelligence? Does Gardner's analysis capture your own pattern of strengths and weaknesses?

expert at anything. All that is needed is to start at four years old, play for a few years, have two or three years of group teaching, four or five years of coaching, then maybe a few more years with a master coach! He suggests that the prodigies have shown some talent which has led their parents to get them deliberate practice at an early age, thereby giving them a lasting advantage in mind and body for their chosen skill (but not others). So, according to Ericsson, it is not so much in the genes as in the parents. Interestingly, Ericsson does concede that the steely determination needed to carry through this single-minded 10-year plus programme for expert skill may in fact be genetically determined.

In summary, according to Ericsson, the keys to development of expertise are the triumvirate of interest, aptitude and effort (deliberate practice). In his semi-satirical novel, *The Rise of the Meritocracy* (1958), Michael Young put forward the memorable equation:

MERIT = IQ + EFFORT

This equation appears to capture the basis for becoming expert. Or, in the famous slogan of triers the world over – No Pain, No Gain!

In some ways this is a comforting thought. The idea that anyone can succeed is very positive. The idea that such extraordinary dedication and coaching are needed is not. It is surely time we did a bit more than merely check performance levels, and get down to a careful analysis of what constitutes skilled performance, and how it is learned.

Characteristics of expert performance

The influential cognitive psychologist Donald Norman, whose textbooks inspired a generation of psychology students in the 1970s, attempted to capture the characteristics of expert performance across a range of tasks. Consider the task of learning to drive. As one starts off, everything seems difficult. It is difficult to change gear at all, then it is difficult both to change gear and watch for traffic, we don't like to be asked a question when changing gear, and so on. At first, driving itself is a challenge, and an event. Later on the processes involved – changing gear, watching the traffic, checking the car in front, anticipating likely hazards, and so on, become automatic to the extent that one can even go on 'auto pilot', not being aware of having driven for a minute or two. On the basis of this sort of analysis Norman (1982) characterized expertise as *smooth* – an expert performs with apparent ease, in an unhurried approach which is deceptively fast; *automatic* – an expert performs a task without having to think about it; *easy* – an expert needs to expend very little mental effort on the task and seems not to need to monitor his/her performance very carefully; and *routine* – for an expert the task just becomes routine – we just 'drive' in the same way as we just 'walk'. It is no longer remarkable in any way. We shall see shortly how these smooth, automatic skills develop.

Expertise in sport

Sports expertise has been studied quite extensively. The picture emerging both confirms and extends Norman's analysis, and tallies well with Ericsson's work. The consensus is that experts make adaptations specifically suited to the requirements of the domain. For sport, the main requirements usually include both speed and very fine motor movements. Even the best cricket players cannot make major corrections within the final 0.2 seconds before ball contact (McLeod 1987) – during which time a ball travelling at 60 mph will travel about a quarter of the cricket pitch! It is clear, therefore, that the batsman must pick up 'line and length' very quickly indeed. There is also clear evidence that increasing skill is associated with increasing perceptual abilities. For example, tennis professionals show a different pattern of eye movements while the opponent is serving, watching the racket arm more closely (Goulet et al. 1989), thereby allowing the earlier detection of the likely line – crucial for the 120 mph serves now typical of the professional game. Expert sports players also prepare their shots earlier, and have more control over the variability of their shot so as to optimize the timing – for some sports, timing precision of the order of 2 milliseconds is possible (e.g. Abernethy 1987; McLeod & Jenkins 1991).

Note the confirmation of Norman's analysis, namely that expert sports players appear to have more time available to play their shots, and thus appear to be less hurried. To some extent this will be caused by actual reorganization of their perceptual abilities (remember the owl monkey?). I am sure the visual cortex of the expert batsman will have specific adaptations for picking up the line and length of a cricket ball delivered at 60 mph from a height of 8 feet at a distance of 20 yards! Furthermore, the sports players are also able to appear unhurried because their extensive experience allows them to anticipate where their opponent is likely to play the ball, and their extensive practice means that they are able to integrate the various components of playing a shot smoothly and automatically. Whereas a novice waits to see where the ball lands, rushes across, then starts to prepare the stroke, the expert combines all three aspects in an integrated, effortless combined movement and stroke. We shall see later that this economy of effort through automatic pre-planning is the hallmark of skilled performance in both motor skills and cognitive skills. We start with an influential characterization of the stages in learning a skill.

The three stages of skill learning

My daughter Ellen has just learned to tie her shoe-laces. The stages she went through are nicely described by Paul Fitts' analysis of the three stages in learning a simple motor skill (Fitts & Posner 1967). The early or 'cognitive' stage involves initially understanding what the task is about and what to attend to, and then using one's general skills making the first efforts to carry it out. For shoe-laces this involves noting the initial and final arrangements, probably watching a parent do the operation, then using one's 'string handling' skills to attempt to do each operation in turn – picking up the shoe-laces in two hands, crossing them over and under, making a loop with one hand, taking the other lace round, and so on. The intermediate or 'associative' stage involves working out a method for actually doing the task. Here Ellen goes through all the stages herself, learning more efficient ways of moving from one stage to the next. Her performance is initially slow and error-prone, and the final bows are loose. None the less, the task is done. With further practice, her performance becomes faster and errors are eliminated. The late or 'autonomous' stage occurs after extensive practice and involves the escape from the need to attend consciously to the task – it has become automatic. At this stage one often loses conscious awareness of how the task is done. Do you end up pulling the right-hand lace with your left hand or right hand? The only way to find out is either to imagine it or do it! This three-stage analysis has proved a reasonable description of the acquisition of a wide range of skills. Fitts and Posner (1967) applied it to learning to fly and to learning telegraphy skills. When learning to fly the cognitive stage takes around 10 hours, but after that there are few major errors, and performance gets gradually quicker and more automatic.

John Anderson (1983) provided a major theoretical framework around this analysis of skill with his ACT* (Adaptive Control of Thought, pronounced 'A. C. T. star') architecture for cognition. He argued that the first stage requires the storing of the facts involved (declarative knowledge), and that the key to actually carrying out the task was to convert this declarative knowledge (knowledge that) to procedural knowledge (knowledge how). It is all very well to know that in order to change gear in a car with a manual transmission one has to depress the clutch, move the gear-stick to the appropriate slot, then release the clutch pedal, synchronizing the release with depression of the throttle. Learners spend weeks trying to acquire the knack of actually doing it. Early efforts require a careful, step at a time procedure, where one has to consciously attend to each step, then remember what the next step is, do that, and so on. Later efforts not only execute each step more efficiently but also combine the sequence of steps into a single, smooth operation. Anderson uses the evocative phrase 'knowledge compilation' for these processes. He uses the analogy of a computer, where tasks are normally expressed in a high-level language (such as Pascal or Basic). These computer languages are relatively close to the human language. Indeed, one might well express a command in Basic in the form

IF task = change_gear(3)
THEN depress_clutch: move_stick(3):engage_gear

where the various procedures were written to carry out the tasks as appropriate. The computer will have a compiler, whose task is to convert these commands into 'machine code' usable by the computer. Once a program is compiled it works much faster, but it is no longer possible to inspect the code easily. Anderson suggests that the process of knowledge compilation for skill is similar. Rather than the high-level instruction (e.g. 'draw an A'), this is compiled into an efficient 'motor program' which specifies the series of commands to the muscles needed to carry out the procedure. He suggests that there are two essentially separate memory stores, a declarative memory store which holds facts and semantic knowledge, and a procedural memory store which holds these compiled 'production rules'. As we have seen from studies of amnesia (chapter 7), there is considerable evidence to suggest that this is a plausible dissociation.

It is important to note that AUTOMATICITY wreaks havoc with the search for general laws of behaviour that apply to everyone. An early instance of this effect was the so-called cocktail party problem (Cherry 1953). How is it that, when

ACT*

AUTOMATICITY

Box 8.3   Controlled and Automatic Processing

Important theoretical work on the development of automaticity was carried out by Shiffrin and Schneider (1977). They used a variant of a target classification task invented by Sternberg (1966). A typical trial in the experimental setup is outlined in figure 8.6. At the start of each trial, the subject is presented with a set of possible targets (BZQL in the figure). After that a series of slides is presented with letters on. The subject's task is to make no response if the slide contains no target letters, but to press the button as fast as possible on seeing one of the targets. In this case the subject should press the button on seeing the Z on the fourth slide. It turns out that the

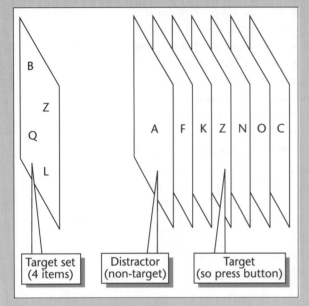

Figure 8.6 Shiffrin and Schneider's visual search paradigm

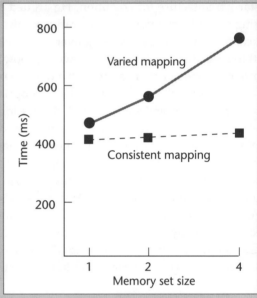

Figure 8.7 Automaticity only with consistent practice

holding a conversation in a crowded cocktail party (or the modern equivalent) that one can follow the conversation of the person one is speaking to? Furthermore, tests suggest that little or nothing is processed of the other conversations, but even so, if someone on the other side of the room mentions one's name, one automatically turns to attend to that conversation. The answer, almost certainly, is that through consistent practice over many years, one's own name has acquired a privileged 'automatic access and attention' status. It is therefore not necessary to attend to a conversation, there is a 'my name detector' module automatically scanning all auditory input for the target. No doubt everyone has their own automatic modules, again acquired through consistent practice. These 'home grown modules' are by far the most efficient method of processing information, and it is likely that almost all of our unconscious information processing is achieved by these individual, idiosyncratic methods.

This three-stage model for skill learning tallies quite well with one's intuitions, and it also fits in well with Norman's characterization of skilled performance.

more possible targets there are, the longer it takes to respond – Sternberg demonstrated that speed of response increased by a constant amount for each extra target. It is as though the subject mentally goes through the target set: 'Z; is it a B? No. Is it a Q? No. Is it an L? No. Is it a Z? Yes. Press the button'. There is no effect of target set size if the distractors are letters and the possible targets digits. Shiffrin and Schneider were interested to see whether this apparently automatic processing could be developed through training, and if so, how. They therefore introduced two training conditions. For one group of subjects they used *consistent mapping*. This was intended to be close to an ideal training method. Although the target set was changed for each trial, no item in a target set ever appeared later as a distractor. That is, the set of possible targets and the set of possible distractors were completely separate (cf. digits vs. letters). For the other group they used *varied mapping*. In this case there was no consistent relationship across trials between the set of targets and the set of distractors. For example, in varied mapping, Z might be a target on trial 6 and a distractor on trial 9, whereas for consistent mapping, if Z was a target on trial 6 it would never appear as a distractor. The results after hundreds of hours of practice are shown in figure 8.7. The varied mapping training had led to no improvement at all, and the slopes and times after training were essentially the same as the initial values. By contrast, the consistent mapping group were faster, specifically because they were not affected by the numbers of possible targets – they performed as though they automatically knew whether or not any stimulus was a target, as indeed they should after hundreds of hours.

Shiffrin and Schneider concluded that there are two qualitatively different types of processing: *controlled processing*, which requires attentional control, uses up working memory capacity and is often serial, and *automatic processing*, which, once learned in long-term memory, operates independently of the subject's control and uses no working memory resources. Controlled processing is relatively easy to set up, and is easy to modify and use in novel situations. It is used to facilitate long-term learning of all kinds (including automatization). Automatic processing doesn't require attention (though it may attract it if the training is appropriate – for instance, if we are trained to respond on hearing our name called, as are most children, then we will automatically hear our name and turn round even if we were not consciously attending to that conversation). Automatic processing is acquired through consistent mapping. Targets can acquire the ability to attract attention and initiate responses automatically, immediately and independent of other memory loads.

The idea of automaticity is at the heart of the development of expertise, and the idea of somehow downloading the necessary calculations to some low-level process independent of the need for conscious monitoring is clearly involved in the development of automaticity.

Learning complex skills

Most everyday skills, such as reading, or tennis, or car driving are complex, in that the complete skill depends upon a range of sub-skills. It is clear that for fluent performance of the complete skill the sub-skills should be automatized, but one important question is whether each sub-skill should be automatized individually, in isolation (which is easier), or whether all the sub-skills need to be automatized in the context of performing the complete skill. Shea and Morgan (1979) provided a clear answer to this issue. Essentially the answer is that it is important *not* to train the sub-skills purely in isolation. If this happens there is a danger that the automatic method that the subject develops for the sub-skill might require some resources that are needed for performance of one of the other sub-skills, and so, when one attempts to blend the sub-skills into the complete skill, there is interference between the sub-skills, preventing the complete skill from being performed efficiently. Therefore, in order to make sure that this interference will not arise, it is important to interleave sessions of the complete skill with automatization training on the sub-skills, so that the sub-skills are learned in a compatible fashion. This issue is known as that of 'part–whole' task training.

In summary, therefore, theoretical studies have suggested that we are able to automatize the components of *any* skill, as long as the training regime is appropriate. In particular, the training should be carefully designed such that it is consistent; the complete skill is interleaved with the individual components; and bad habits are not acquired. Automatization of the component skills allows more attentional resources to be deployed in the execution of the complete task, thereby allowing better and more adaptive performance.

Modules and automaticity

A really big issue from an evolutionary perspective is that an automatic skill is rather like an innately 'hard-wired' skill. The frog comes equipped with several important skills. If threatened, it jumps towards blue light (with any luck, a pool). If a fly comes within range, it catches it on its tongue with amazing dexterity. These skills are hard-wired – built into the genetic code. They are not modifiable. A frog does poorly in an environment with blue stickers, and will starve to death even when surrounded by dead flies unless some kind experimenter flicks them past the frog at an appropriate speed! By contrast, humans are able (by dint of considerable effort, and if the conditions are favourable) to 'grow their own' modules, specifically tailored to individual environments.

As Anderson (1983) notes: 'One thing that distinguishes us from other creatures is our ability to acquire complex skill. All distinctively human activities – such as mathematics, language, chess, computer programming, sculpture – are acquired skills . . . People become expert at activities for which there was no possibility of anticipation in our evolutionary history, and the essence of the human genius is just this plasticity.'

It is likely that all mammals (and probably most creatures) have some abilities for developing automaticity of various motor skills. The ability to develop the language skill opens up new worlds for development of expertise for humans, and it is to these higher level skills that we now turn.

Cognitive skills

So far our analysis has stressed the importance of fluency and automaticity in skill. Fortunately, sheer speed is only one part of the true expertise. For many skills, knowledge and problem-solving ability are perhaps more important than sheer speed. Problem-solving and reasoning skills are covered at length in chap-

Box 8.4   Expertise and Chess

One of the most carefully studied skills is that of chess. Chess lends itself to study because it is a formal cognitive game sufficiently complex to defy exhaustive analysis, sufficiently simple to be accessible to many players, and self-contained, in that it requires little or no knowledge of the world in order to play well. It takes years of practice to reach master level at chess, though many brilliant chess players have emerged as prodigies. The US player, Bobby Fischer, became US chess champion at 8 years old, and was for many years arguably the world's best player, but he was only briefly World Champion, largely because of a self-imposed exile when he was not allowed to create the conditions for chess matches which he felt he needed. The Hungarian player Judit Polgar, is the strongest female player ever, well able to match all but the top two or three grandmasters, and she was one of a trio of sisters, all coached carefully by their father, who reached world-class standards in their early teens. Expert chess players are truly expert. Saariluoma (1991) has confirmed under laboratory conditions that a chess grandmaster is able to maintain chess positions for 10 simultaneous chess games in memory (blindfolded) with virtually no errors.

An early method of studying chess was developed by de Groot (1965) who showed a chess position to the subject for a short time (typically 10 seconds), then swept off the pieces and asked the subject to replace them. De Groot tried this task with players of various abilities, from beginner to average player to good club standard to grandmaster. It turned out that the better the player, the better the recall. Interestingly, however, if the pieces were positioned at random on the board, then chess ability did not help – the chess masters' recall fell back to the same level as the beginners' (though subsequent research has tended to find some residual advantage for experts, even in random positions). From this, it appears that the chess masters do not have intrinsically better recall than the others, their recall is better because of their greater knowledge of the game and of the sorts of positions that come up.

The de Groot paradigm was used extensively by other researchers. Chase and Simon (1973) replicated the basic findings under a variety of conditions, and interpreted their findings as indicating that experts have better perceptual abilities in terms of ability to chunk positions, possibly through having stored thousands of chess positions. However, Chase and Ericsson (1981) suggest that it is more likely to be a better retrieval schema: 'Experts use their knowledge of a subject to develop abstract, highly specialized mechanisms for systematically encoding and retrieving meaningful patterns from LTM. This ability allows experts to anticipate the informational needs of a familiar task and store new information in a format that will facilitate its retrieval.'

Perhaps the most interesting demonstration, however, was by Chi (1978), who was investigating the developmental issue of why children's memories improved as they matured. Clearly children's knowledge increases as they mature, but it may be that they are also able to store memories more efficiently. If, in fact, the increase in knowledge holds the key, then good chess players should recall more than poor chess players, regardless of how old they are. Chi used four groups of chess players: good and poor, child and adult. It turned out that age was indeed irrelevant, all that counted in this task was level of skill.

ter 9, so in this chapter I shall mention only the role of knowledge in skilled performance.

Knowledge as an aid to information acquisition

The chess studies (see Box 8.4) have indicated the value of knowledge as a means of perceiving and remembering information. Other studies have confirmed that this advantage occurs for a wide range of situations. Voss and his colleagues have carried out a range of studies of this type. In one set of studies they divided their subjects into two groups, high baseball knowledge and low baseball knowledge, then had them read a newspaper description of a baseball match including passages like 'Beck, the Cougars' relief pitcher, was warming up in the bull pen . . . ' They then asked the subjects to recall the passage immediately afterwards, and then again after two weeks. It turned out that the high baseball knowledge group understood the passage better and more quickly, they recalled more and they forgot less!

In a related set of studies, Voss et al. (1983) investigated the effect of knowledge on problem-solving strategy and ability. They asked their subjects questions such as 'Assume you were the head of the Soviet Ministry of Agriculture and assume crop productivity had been low for several years. You now have the responsibility to increase crop production. How would you go about it?' They found that the non-experts tried to solve the problem straight away, and tended to generate a range of rather shallow solutions. By contrast, expert political scientists appeared to go through a two-stage process, where first they spent time deriving a good initial representation of the problem – marshalling the knowledge they needed to bring to bear on the problem ('hmm . . . This problem involves several ministries, plus the entire agricultural system, from its raw materials (fertilizer, seed), labour, etc., right to ability to deliver final product . . .')

They then tended to generate only a few well-argued, deeper, solutions which were: presented in depth with detailed support (the chain of support was three times as long as that for the non-experts); the solutions were more abstract, and considered the constraints, the objectives, and so on; and the solutions were more flexible – better able to cope with fluctuations in circumstances.

Summary on cognitive expertise

Glaser and Chi (1988) summarize the literature on cognitive expertise as follows: (i) Experts excel mainly in their own domains. Experts in mental calculations are not likely to be experts in medical diagnosis, etc. (ii) Experts perceive large, meaningful patterns in their domain. (iii) Experts are fast. (iv) Experts seem to use their long-term memory and short-term memory effectively. (v) Experts see and represent a problem in their domain at a deeper level. When asked to sort and analyse problems, they tend to deal with deep issues rather than superficial ones. (vi) Experts spend a great deal of time analysing a problem qualitatively, and tend to look at a problem from several angles before plunging into its solution. (vii) Experts have self-monitoring skills. They seem to be aware of their errors and are able to make 'online' corrections.

I would add to these a further three points: (viii) Experts use *knowledge* to keep track of information being processed. Their ability to *anticipate* decreases the effort needed; their ease of access means the effective working memory is greater; and the knowledge of which events are important helps *anchor* information in working memory. (ix) Experts use knowledge as an aid to *reconstruction*. Their knowledge of the events that are likely to have occurred aids their reconstruction of the original scenario; and their knowledge of the relative importance of the different components permits them to carry out a systematic top-down reconstruction. (x) Experts have the sub-skills for a task better *automatized.* Not only does this lead to faster performance, it also means that the task needs less effort, thereby leaving more spare capacity for further learning.

Ways of learning

So far, therefore, we have a reasonably consistent picture. If simple skills are practised extensively, they become more and more smooth and automatic, taking less and less conscious attention. A similar analysis applies for more complex skills, but here it is valuable to have an expert coach whose responsibility it is to make sure that the appropriate 'deliberate practice' is used. There does seem something rather unsatisfactory about this analysis. Apart from the cryptic reference to the need for expert coaching to achieve world-class performance, one might be forgiven for inferring that practice was the only method of acquiring such skills. It is important to correct this impression by noting the range of learning mechanisms that are available to us. Rather surprisingly, books on teaching give only a cursory analysis of the different forms of learning, and it is (to my knowledge at any rate) researchers interested in machine learning (the enterprise of building computer systems that learn, a branch of artificial intelligence) who have made the most systematic attempts to characterize the different forms of learning. Here I can provide no more than a brief listing of the major forms.

Let's start with natural forms of learning. Most of us learn all of the time just by staying alive and observing what happens. *Learning by observation* is therefore perhaps one of the most fundamental forms. We watch others doing things, and note good and bad ideas. We drive round a city and build up a map of its layout. We try on a new hat and watch other people's reactions. Indeed, the advent of the television arguably makes learning by observation the major form of learning for most people! For the more active adults (and certainly most children) *learning by doing* is the way to acquire (or refine) skills. It is no good talking a good game of football unless one can also play it. As we saw in the three-stage model for skill acquisition, one only proceduralizes skills by actually doing them, and then tuning the execution as appropriate. A powerful method of combining observation and doing is *learning by imitation*. As Skinner noticed, children quite frequently try to imitate the actions of their parents (indeed, there is good reason to believe that some imitative abilities are innate – see Meltzoff's studies in the following section). This triumvirate of natural learning methods provide a powerful toolkit for many forms of learning, and probably most animals have these capabilities to some extent.

Humans, because of our language capability, also have a fundamentally different mode of learning available, and that is some form of *learning by being told*. This can involve a mother (or friend) giving instructions or information, or (taking a more general interpretation) from reading a book. Clearly this normally involves some form of symbolic communication, quite different from the non-symbolic observation of a parent's actions.

There are, of course, a whole range of further methods of learning, and many methods will involve a combination of symbolic and non-symbolic methods. For instance, in the chess-playing examples, one may well be told or learn various rules (a queen is worth nine pawns, in the opening develop your pieces, in the middle-game try to dominate the open files, and so on). As we have seen, however, this information is only a part of the repertoire of pattern-based, subsymbolic knowledge needed for expert play. Many games such as chess (and disciplines such as mathematics) are 'scaffolded' by providing a lot of examples of good play or problem solving. Somehow we are able to *learn by examples*, extracting the gist of the technique from the examples given. There is no space here other than to touch the surface of this vast set of topics, and here I select just a few further examples of learning.

Learning via accommodation: the Socratic method

Piaget (see chapter 2) distinguished between two very different forms of learning: assimilation (where further knowledge is being added to an existing schema) and accommodation (where new schemas are being learned, or existing ones reorganized). It is accommodation that is the difficult mode to achieve, increasing as the learner gets older. Socrates, as described by his disciple Plato in *The Republic*, was a master of the art of getting people to accommodate. The basis of the Socratic method was as follows: (i) get the learner to make some statement that illustrates a misunderstanding; (ii) by a process of discussion and guidance, get the learner to derive a conclusion that is clearly incompatible with the first statement; (iii) draw the learner's attention to the incompatibility between the two statements. The learner should now be in a receptive frame of mind for accommodation; (iv) if the learner cannot see how to proceed, explain the reason behind the difficulty.

Note the wisdom behind this approach. One is always more receptive to a solution if one realizes that there is a problem that needs solving!

Learning by discovery

The power of the Socratic method is that in some sense it provides very high-quality learning, learning that we could not achieve by normal methods. Rather more recently, Seymour Papert (1980) provided an influential analysis of an alternative method for producing high-quality learning. He argued that learning by discovery led to much more lasting benefits than learning by being told, providing the telling example of how his exploratory play as a child with a mechanics set including gears led him to discover a series of important principles of physics, and provided him with the enthusiasm and the mental tools for a life of science. Papert also advocated learning by trial and error, making the very important point that most educationalists considered errors bad, and therefore discouraged experimentation. A much more valuable perspective is to consider an error as a half solution, providing an important pointer to the correct answer. Learning occurs following errors at least as often as following successes, and consequently one must never be afraid to be wrong. If more teachers took this approach, children would find learning much more fulfilling.

The zone of proximal development

The Socratic method is of course immensely difficult to achieve in practice (and, indeed, is very inefficient if an alternative method is available), and perhaps the closest educationally feasible approaches to this problem are those provided by Vygotsky (1934/1962) and Bruner (1981). As we have already noted in chapter 2, Vygotsky's insight was that there is a great difference at any stage in learning between what one can achieve unaided and by coaching. He suggested that at any moment there are some skills/knowledge which are attainable from the learner's current knowledge, and some which are not. He described the set of skills which are currently attainable (given coaching) as the ZONE OF PROXIMAL DEVELOPMENT (ZPD), and suggested that the art of effective teaching was to make sure that at all times the learner was presented with tasks within the ZPD – always give achievable challenges. Bruner introduced the notion of 'scaffolding': if a concept/skill is not within the ZPD, can we introduce some half-way house, some related skill which helps the learner climb towards the target skill? For a child learning to ride a bike, this scaffolding might take the form of stabilizers. In fact the stabilizers teach the child some of the wrong skills (they encourage the child to lean the wrong way), but the benefits in terms of confidence outweigh the disadvantages. Similar scaffolding is needed for acquisition of any complex skill. For instance, an expert reader will perceive a whole word at a time, but this does not mean that the 'whole word' method is the appropriate method of learning to read. The necessary scaffolding (which allows one to attack a word one has not learned already) is to learn the phonic 'letter by letter' blending approach (Adams 1990).

ZONE OF PROXIMAL DEVELOPMENT

Natural learning

Papert (1980) caused something of a revolution in educational theory when he confronted the issue of how to help children learn mathematics. His answer was very different from that of Ericsson. Consider skills in which we are all expert – skills like walking and speaking, seeing and listening – these in fact require a high degree of skill, and take a long time for children to learn. Children do get thousands of hours practice at talking and walking, but they are mostly self-taught. The world provides the learning environment! Papert advocated wholesale changes in education, putting forward the telling analogy of ski evolutif. Twenty years ago, beginning skiers were just given standard skis. Because the skis are long and cumbersome, it was necessary to teach the beginners a method of controlling them – the snowplough, and the snowplough turn. Once the skiers became more expert, they were then able to learn the parallel-turn method. To do this, they had to unlearn the snowplough turn, and learning to ski well was therefore a slow, expensive and frustrating business. The revolution occurred when it was noticed that children with short skis just seemed to learn the

Box 8.5   Dyslexia and Automaticity

Developmental dyslexia is defined as 'a disorder in children who, despite conventional classroom experience, fail to attain the language skills of reading, writing and spelling commensurate with their intellectual abilities'. In other words, children of average or above average ability, who for no obvious reason, write and spell very poorly. A typical estimate of the prevalence of dyslexia in Western school populations is 5 per cent, with roughly four times as many boys as girls being diagnosed. Dyslexia is therefore by far the most common of the development disorders. It has been assumed that the problems of children with dyslexia derive from impairment of some skill or cognitive component largely specific to the reading process, and the consensus view (e.g. Snowling 1987; Stanovich 1988) is that the deficits are attributable to some disorder of phonological processing (such as the ability to split words up into their constituent sounds). Training in phonological skills (such as knowing about rhymes, and ways of building up words from their sounds) is certainly one of the key requirements in helping dyslexic children learn to read better. One of the most frustrating aspects of dyslexia is that if appropriate support is given at an early age, the dyslexic children do seem to be able to learn to read reasonably well. However, the way dyslexia is currently defined in terms of reading deficit means that for a formal diagnosis it is necessary to wait until a child is at least 18 months behind in reading. This consigns a dyslexic child to at least 18 months of failure in initial schooling, a traumatic experience which cannot help but leave serious emotional scars.

In any scientific analysis it is important to distinguish between cause, symptom and treatment. Phonological processing difficulties are an important symptom of dyslexia, and phonological training is a valuable component of any remediation of the reading problems. However, it is possible that the phonological problems are not the underlying cause – they may be just one symptom of a deeper underlying cause. In a long-standing research programme, Angela Fawcett and I have

parallel turn naturally, without bothering with the snowplough. Ski evolutif, in which beginners were issued with short skis and taught parallel turns from the start, was born. Learning to ski is now simple and natural.

How do children learn to speak French? Papert asked. The best way is to live in France, to be immersed in the culture and the language. Surely the same thing would be true for mathematics. What we need is a 'Mathland', where mathematical principles are all around us. He designed the computer language Logo for children to use, together with a progammable 'turtle' which could be programmed to travel forwards, backwards, left and right, so that they could experiment, and learn from their mistakes. He reasoned that this would give children the 'natural' learning environment, so that they would discover mathematical ideas for themselves.

It is worth noting that many of our everyday skills, such as walking upright, talking and using our hands, are in fact truly most impressive. Although it is now possible for a computer program to hold its own even with the very best chess players, there are no robots that can walk as well as a three-year-old, never mind talk as well as a five-year-old. Furthermore, skills are relative. Only four centuries ago, scholars who were able to read and write were treated with reverence. For most children (though see Box 8.5 on developmental dyslexia) whose home provides a 'Book Land', learning to read becomes a pretty natural (though lengthy) process.

In fact, the results of Papert's approach have not been as promising as he had

been investigating the role of learning in dyslexia. Given the importance of automatization in acquisition of any skill, and its known importance in reading, it seemed possible that difficulties in skill automatization might be involved. We tested dyslexic and matched control children on motor skills – skills with no phonological component and therefore a key discriminator between the theories. Clear deficits were found, even when the dyslexic children just had to stand still without wobbling. Interestingly, the difficulties showed up primarily under dual-task conditions (for instance, when they had to count as well as balance), exactly as predicted by automatization deficit (Nicolson & Fawcett 1990).

Our subsequent research has focused on two issues: first, attempting to identify the cause(s) underlying the difficulties in automatization and phonological skill; and, second, attempting to develop a screening test which can establish which children are at risk of dyslexia when they first go to school, thereby giving them immediate access to the extra support needed to help them to read.

Research is still ongoing, but very promising results have been obtained. First, it appears that the underlying deficit may well be attributable, at least in part, to the cerebellum – the 'hind brain'. This structure is known to be involved in balance and motor skill and its automatization, and recent evidence suggests that it is also centrally involved in development of a range of linguistic skills. Our recent research (Fawcett & Nicolson 1996) indicates that many dyslexic children show the classic signs of cerebellar difficulty – problems in coordination and balance. Furthermore, using tests which are known to cause problems for dyslexic children, together with tests of motor skill, we have been able to develop the 'Dyslexia Early Screening Test', a simple 30-minute test which can be administered by a child's teacher when the child first starts school, and will indicate whether or not the child is at risk of dyslexia. This allows immediate support to be given (Fawcett et al. 1996).

hoped, but even so it is hard not to believe that there must be some way of combining the insights of Papert's approach with the systematic guidance offered by Ericsson's programme. It is at this stage that we turn to how children really do learn their first language. The answer turns out to be very much more impressive than was thought by Skinner or imagined by Chomsky.

▦ Learning from First Principles ▦

The three-stage model provides a valuable high-level account of the changes involved in adult skill acquisition. However, it's hard to believe that an infant learning to talk or to walk goes through a declarative stage: 'I see it now – I shift my weight forward, then just move each leg forward alternately. I'll worry about the stopping later . . .' Clearly some forms of learning by-pass the need for declarative mediation. My son James has just learned to whistle. One day he couldn't do it, the next he could (and now practises incessantly!). He doesn't know how or why he can whistle now but couldn't before. There seems to be no declarative knowledge involved. I can raise both eyebrows together. I can even raise my left eyebrow by itself. I can't raise my right eyebrow by itself. What's going on?

It is now time to return to the issue raised at the start of this chapter, the changes in brain structure as a result of learning and as a cause of learning. The human brain is remarkably able to adapt to its environment even in the womb. I argue

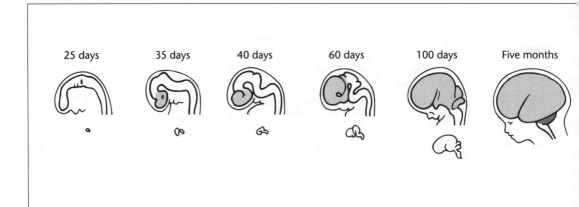

Figure 8.8 Ontogeny of the human brain from 25 days gestation until birth. Figures are enlarged for ages 25 to 100 days. *Scientific American*, Sept. 1979, p. 116, 'The Development of the Brain', Cowan, author, courtesy Tom Prentiss/Scientific American 1979.

that this adaptability or plasticity underpins the development of most of our most fundamental abilities, including those of perception and action, and that therefore an understanding of how the brain is formed, and how it adapts, is a prerequisite for understanding human learning.

Ontogeny of the brain

Before considering the human brain and learning, it is important to describe the near miracle by which the brain is formed. Much of this knowledge has been discovered within the past 15 years, and brain development is still an area of very active research. Figure 8.8 indicates the enormous growth in size of the brain during gestation. Note that it is about 5 months (22 weeks) before the mature brain structures are even recognizable. Neurons are typically formed in enormous numbers on the neural crest, and then have to 'migrate' to their destined position in the appropriate brain structure. It is estimated that there are 100 to 1,000 billion neurons in the brain, with a staggering 10 billion of them in the granular layer of the CEREBELLUM.

CEREBELLUM

Neuronal migration

The neurons migrate, guided by the radial glial cells, and miraculously end up in the appropriate layer of the appropriate brain structure. There is some evidence that subcortical structures such as the cerebellum are put together with some care (the cerebellum has two areas which send neurons), but in general it appears that the cells of the cerebral cortex are just thrown together haphazardly, with each neuron having a random position in the appropriate layer of the target structure.

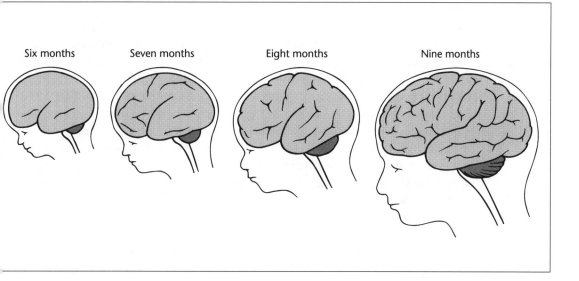

| Six months | Seven months | Eight months | Nine months |

Neuronal growth

Even when the neurons have been created and have migrated to an appropriate position their growth is very far from complete. First they grow prodigiously, with their axons snaking often quite considerable distances, even from one hemisphere to the other. At the same time 10,000 dendrites may sprout from a neuron's axon and will synapse with other cells.

Synaptic changes

It is easy to fall into the trap of thinking of neurons as analogous to electrical cables – they merely conduct signals passively from one part of the brain to another, and are not affected by doing so. In fact, it is better to imagine that every event in the brain will cause some changes in the neurons concerned (and, indeed, if no events occur to a neuron over a period, this may well lead to changes also). The main changes occur in terms of the connectivity of the synapses. One of the most dramatic forms of synaptic tuning (see chapter 5, figure 5.22, p.177) is by long-term potentiation (LTP). If a burst of stimulation is delivered to a neuron, then subsequently the effects of a single pulse to that neuron may become greatly enhanced, even for periods of months. It is as though that neuron has been sensitized (or potentiated), irreversibly, to stimulation. Of particular interest here is the so-called associative LTP, which is produced by the association in time between the firing of two sets of synapses. Kelso and Brown (1986) stimulated a weak input and a strong input to pyramidal cells in the hippocampus. If the two inputs were close together in time, then the weak input was strengthened (i.e., stimulation of it alone led to a larger response at the pyramidal cell). If the two inputs were not synchronized, there was no strengthening.

Thus, strengthening occurs only at the specific synapses active at the time of the strong input. LTP occurs via the conjunction of two events: activation of synapses and depolarization of the postsynaptic neuron. This was a particularly important finding because it provides the neural underpinning of the so-called HEBB RULE, after an influential book by Donald Hebb (1949; on which more below). Hebb argued that if cells in an organism followed a simple rule by which if two cells were activated at the same time the connection between them was strengthened, then it would be possible to create automatically a 'cell assembly' which might well be capable of quite sophisticated processing, including inter-sensory integration. There is now considerable evidence that LTP in the hippocampus occurs via the glutamate neurotransmitter system (see Carlson 1994, ch. 14 for an accessible overview of this technically demanding work).

Programmed cell death

A final stage of cell tuning takes place somewhat later. This phenomenon, known as programmed cell death or apoptosis, seems to occur after the first stage of learning takes place. Often large numbers of cells just die, peaceably, without the scar tissue and degeneration typical of damage to the brain. While the cause of this cell death is not yet understood, one plausible hypothesis is that cells which appear not to have much variability in their activation patterns (for instance, if they are either always inactive or always fully active) are clearly not contributing usefully to the brain's functioning, and therefore are sacrificed, thus leading to greater efficiency of the remaining cell assemblies.

Armed with this information about the many processes by which the brain develops, we are now in position to return to the question of how a child learns its first language.

Development of the human brain

If one compares the course of gestation of a human foetus with that of the other primates, it becomes clear that the human infant is born 'too soon'. The human brain at birth weighs around 0.3 kg, not much more than the chimpanzee brain at birth. The expected size for a human brain at birth, by comparison with brain/body analyses for other primates, would in fact be 0.86 kg. Furthermore, the human infant's brain keeps growing rapidly, topping 1 kg within 9 months of birth. Even though they spend 9 months developing in the womb, at birth human infants are completely helpless. Contrast this with a puppy, which after a 9-week gestation is born more competent than a human, and in less than a year has reached full size and reproductive capacity. These facts have led a number of theorists to suggest that the human baby is born 6 to 9 months ahead of its 'natural' time (Passingham 1973; Gould 1977). This theory is now reasonably well accepted, and one interesting speculation for the underlying cause of this adaptation is that it is a result of the hominids' evolution to an upright gait some 3 million years ago. Because of the much greater forces on the pelvis for an upright stance (the pelvis has to support the weight of the whole body), humans have a much solider pelvic structure than other primates. This means that the size of the pelvic birth canal is much reduced. While this was of little significance for small-brained early hominids, as the brain size of the hominids increased from *Australopithecus* to *Homo habilis* to *Homo erectus* to *Homo sapiens*, there reached a time when there was simply not enough room for the head of the foetus to pass safely through the pelvic birth canal. Naturally there would be considerable evolutionary pressure to find a suitable adaptation that did not result in death of mother and infant, and it is suggested (Gould 1977) that the birth of the human foetus 9 months too early is in fact just this adaptation.

Regardless of the reason for the adaptation, it has profound implications for human cognition. At birth the human infant is particularly helpless. Its brain is still in the process of being constructed. At the peak of brain development (around 30 weeks' gestation) neurons are formed at the rate of quarter of a million per minute (Cowan 1979), and similar rates of neuron creation continue after birth for several weeks. The infant nearly doubles the number of neurons in its striate cortex in the first two weeks of life, adding a further 50 million (Huttenlocher 1990). Not surprisingly, at birth the visual cortex is barely functional, though vision is possible via more primitive subcortical structures involving the superior colliculus. It takes two months for the visual cortex to become fully differentiated into the mature formation of six layers of different types of cell (Johnson 1990).

Early auditory/motor information and behaviour

As we have seen, the human visual cortex does not develop till after birth. After all, there is little point, given that there is no patterned light in the womb. Given the pressure on brain development in humans, it clearly makes more sense first to develop those modalities which do receive input in the womb. The foetus shows some spontaneous movement as early as 8 weeks, with 16 movement patterns available by 15 weeks, including somersaults and lateral rotations requiring organized limb and body control (Suzuki & Yamamuro 1985). Auditory processing occurs a little later, starting after 20 weeks or so. The womb is probably rather an interesting environment acoustically for the foetus. The mother's heartbeat will dominate, with the sound of blood rushing round in synchrony probably rather like the noise of the ocean – perhaps this is the reason for the soothing effect of the noise of the ocean waves. There will also be a range of other noises – digestive noises, bumps and thumps from walking etc., and patterned noise, heavily muffled from others speaking to the mother, and much less muffled from the mother speaking (via the throat). It turns out that the mother's voice should be easily discriminable above these other background noises (see figure 8.9). The specific speech sounds may well be muffled, but there seems no doubt that the prosody (the rhythms of speech) will be transmitted well to the foetus.

The ability of the foetus to hear speech has been clearly demonstrated empirically. If a loud noise is played next to the mother's stomach, the foetus will tend to clench its eyes. Indeed, an eye clench to an auditory noise after 25 weeks is the

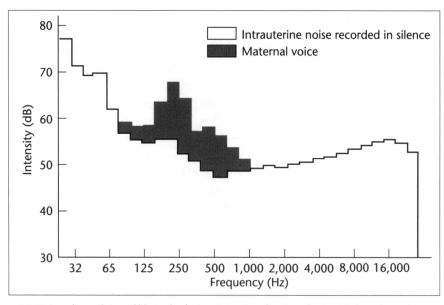

Figure 8.9 Maternal speech is audible to the foetus. Intensity of maternal voice (darkened areas) against other intrauterine noise. Note the large voice-to-noise ratio in the vicinity of 250 Hz, the fundamental frequency of most vocally typical women.

Querleu et al., 'Perception auditive et reactive foetale aux stimulations sonores' in *Journal de Gynecologie Obstetrique et Biologie de la Reproduction*, vol. 10, fig. 2–1 (© Masson Editeur, Paris, 1981).

earliest recorded facial expression for a foetus (Birnholz & Benacerraf 1983). Furthermore, following a study of heart-rate habituation, Lecanuet et al. (1989) claimed that foetuses in the final trimester of pregnancy were able to distingush between specific auditory stimuli (e.g., [babi] vs. [biba]). Heart rate slows following the first presentation of either stimulus, then returns to normal following repeated presentation of the same stimulus. If the other stimulus is presented, however, heart rate slowed again, for most subjects. Interestingly, the foetuses reliably produced leg movements as well as heart rate changes in response to the noise stimuli, further indicating the links between auditory input and motor output.

Perhaps the most famous study of learning in the womb is the so-called 'cat in the hat' study (DeCasper & Spence 1986). Mothers read a children's book to their foetus twice a day for the last 6 weeks of their pregnancy (one of the stories was Dr Seuss's *The Cat in the Hat*). Two days after birth the experimenters checked whether or not the infant had a story preference, using the sucking paradigm (the longer the infant sucks to get the story played, the greater the supposed preference for that story). It was found that the infant sucked more to get the story it had heard in the womb than a matched novel story, and they did so even if the stories were read by a stranger! No doubt the infant was responding more to the familiarity of the general prosodic pattern, rather than the specific words, but even so, this study indicates that auditory learning is possible, even before birth.

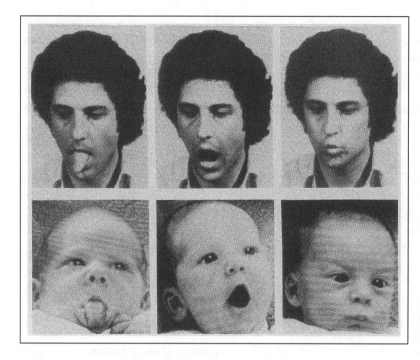

Plate 8.5 Stimulus faces of Andrew Meltzoff and a young mimic

Imitation in the neonate

Perhaps one of the most extraodinary and unexpected examples of infant competence was discovered by Andrew Meltzoff (e.g. Meltzoff & Moore 1977). Some neonate infants can imitate an adult's expression even at 45 minutes old (plate 8.5) even before seeing their own face! It is not at all clear how they do it, though not all do. After all, the visual cortex is not even developed at that stage. Neonates also show a clear preference for looking at their mother's face, in particular her eyes (even when she is speaking).

How does this multisensory ability come about – which facial muscles to instruct when they want to imitate another person's mouth movement. In the evocative words of Michael Studdert-Kennedy (cited by Locke 1993: 81) 'How does the light get into the muscle?' In an attempt to answer this question, we must consider the infant's need to coordinate eye, ear and muscle in order to learn to act. Here we follow the account of John Locke (1993), who writes elegantly of the link between facial movements and speech, suggesting that the neonate is 'speech-reading'. The account differs in every way from the strictures of Dr Benjamin Spock (see under 'Reinforcement and instrumental conditioning', above).

The infant shaping the mother

We have seen that humans begin to pay attention to and learn about the voice at a very early stage, even during the latter months of gestation. Locke suggests that, far from lying passively, waiting for its language centres to mature, from its earliest opportunity the infant seeks out the particular kinds of stimulation that it enjoys and that its brain may need in order to develop maximally. He notes that the human infant is more inclined to look at a pleasantly moving face than at one that is passive, and it prefers a voice that rises and falls to one with little tonal variation. Furthermore, Locke suggests that because the human infant is born helpless and completely dependent upon its mother, the human infant's major initial requirement is attachment to its mother, and it achieves this by paying especial attention to the mother's face and voice. The mother's natural tendency to inhibit and emit behaviours during 'on' and 'off' intervals in her infant's behaviour lead to rhythmic 'turn takings' including the use of voice. Locke suggests that, after a few months, infants usually begin to do their share to promote vocal rhythmicity, and so they therefore become increasingly inclined and able to imitate wordlike forms – this is the 'babbling' stage of speech development, where the infant may say 'bababa' repeatedly (see chapter 2).

Language and motor skill developing in step

Several researchers have highlighted the apparent correspondence between the stages in speech acquisition and those in other motor skills. The repetitive activities of babbling mirror the repetitive behaviour of the infant reaching for a rattle, and occur at roughly the same age. The change to variegated babbling (for example, the infant says 'bamabama' rather than 'bababa'), in which the infant begins to be able to emit varied output, mirrors the development of motor sequences, such as grasping. In particular, the sudden start of reduplicated babbling (around 6 months) happens at about the time of the sudden start of one-handed reaching, and at exactly the same time as the first evidence of a hand preference (Ramsay 1984). Furthermore, babbling also coincides with the onset of hand-banging behaviour (a further method of actively producing a sound). Locke and his colleagues (1995) speculate that the co-occurrence of these motor and speech milestones might be attributable to the initial development of the left hemisphere cortical control over the precisely timed muscular movements needed for reaching and speech; in particular, that the left hemisphere assumes control of speechlike activity, and that babbling represents the functional convergence of motor control and sensory feedback systems. As Michael Studdert-Kennedy (1991: 10) observes, 'language is not an object, or even a skill, that lies outside the child and somehow has to be acquired or internalized. Rather it is a mode of action into which the child grows because the mode is implicit in the human developmental system.'

Summary on infant development

The human is born around 6 months relatively too early. This adaptation allows/forces the brain to be very much more plastic than in other mammals. In particular, there is little or no need for any of the cerebral cortex to be hard-wired. There are primitive subcortical reflexes for rooting (finding and sucking the mother's nipple), for vision and for imitation that allow the neonate to survive, and also help to train up the still developing cerebral cortex. From the first moments there appears to be an extraordinary synergy between the senses, with ear, eye and muscles tuned to respond to the same stimuli. 'Plastic' is a poor word to describe the extraordinary adaptations of the brain. Neurons send out axons, axons sprout dendrites, dendrites synapse onto other neurons, pairs of synapses are strengthened or weakened by the Hebb rule as a consequence of their synchronized activity. Rather than a passive recipient of information, the infant actively seeks it out, adapting the environment, and, in particular, the mother to its requirements. As sub-skills are acquired, they become incorporated into higher-level skills (a process Piaget referred to as 'bricolage' – all our skills are pieced together from the building blocks we have available at the time). These developments occur before the appearance of any systematic declarative knowledge.

The challenge is to find some language for describing how these developments take place. CONNECTIONISM, which we next discuss, is the major formalism for the description of sub-symbolic learning.

CONNECTIONISM

▨ Connectionism ▨

So far we have seen the range of perspectives on learning, from animals to adults to infants, from descriptive to mathematical to stage models, from behaviourist to information-processing to neurophysiological frameworks. These different perspectives are difficult to integrate because they have few precepts in common. What is needed is a language for learning, a 'lingua franca' to facilitate communication between the different contributions.

A powerful method of scaffolding our own learning is by analogy – relating a new phenomenon to one that is already reasonably well understood. Perhaps the most evocative analogy was Sherrington's vision (1940) of how the brain might appear if its electrical activity could be visualized – 'an enchanted loom [in which] millions of flashing shuttles weave a dissolving pattern, though never an abiding one; a shifting harmony of subpatterns'. One of the more compelling analogies of the middle of this century was that of the telephone exchange – I remember my mother telling me that I must try to find connections between ideas so that I could connect up more and more of my neurons and so use the full capacity of my brain. Even 50 years ago, researchers were well aware of the need for 'brain-like' computation. The psychologist Donald Hebb (1949) made an important contribution in showing how assemblies of cells could learn to achieve quite complex tasks such as learning to recognize objects from any angle just by being trained with pictures of the objects continuously varying in viewpoint. This learning could be achieved by the simple method of association by the Hebb rule – if two cells are both active at the same time then the strength of connection between them increases. This insight, together with other cyber-

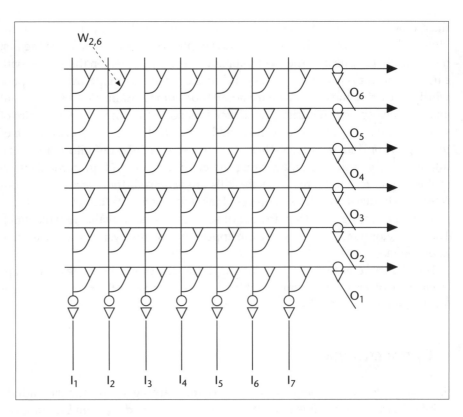

Figure 8.10 Connections in a two-layer neural network

ARTIFICIAL NEURAL
NETWORKS

netics work, led to a flourishing research field investigating brain-like learning. The basic assumption of these ARTIFICIAL NEURAL NETWORKS is that the network has a *structure* (comprising a set of 'nodes', with connections between them, with the connections differing in strength across the various pairs of nodes) and a *state* which varies over time (this is the set of 'activations' of the set of nodes).

The simple two-layer network shown in figure 8.10 has an input layer of 7 nodes and an output layer of 6 nodes, with all the nodes in the input layer connected to all the nodes in the output layer by connections which may be inhibitory or excitatory, and whose strength is determined by the history of inputs and outputs in the past. The analogy here is with neurons which are connected via dendrites to another layer of neurons. At any moment, the input nodes have an 'activation' varying continuously between 0 (completely off) and 1 (fully on), analogously to firing rate in a neuron (though scaled to the range 0 to 1 for mathematical convenience). The activation at each output node is then simply the weighted sum of the activations from the input nodes to which it is connected. If the 'weight' or 'connection strength' of a link is positive it is excitatory, if its weight is negative the link is inhibitory. If the weight is 0 there is effectively no link. While some may find the algebraic expressions here a little daunting, readers even with rudimentary mathematics should be able to see the simplicity of the idea. Algebraically the summation of the inputs can be expressed simply as follows (where the asterisks mean multiply):

$$O_1 = (I^1 * W_{1,1}) + (I_2 * W_{1,2}) + (I_3 * W_{1,3}) \tag{1}$$

where I_1, I_2 and I_3 are the activations of the input nodes, O_1, O_2 and O_3 are the activations of the output nodes, and $W_{1,2}$ is the weight for the connection from I_1 to O_2 etc. Consequently, if we know the input activations, assuming we know the connection strengths, we can calculate the output activations. So far, therefore, this looks like a reasonably plausible simulation of activation spreading through a real neural network, with activation summating across the various dendrites synapsing onto a given neuron. The power of the approach, however, derives from the fact that it is very easy to implement learning rules such as the Hebb rule in such a network. If node I_1 and node O_2 are simultaneously active, then the Hebb rule states that the strength of connection between them ($W_{1,2}$) should be incremented. Thus, using $\Delta(W_{i,j})$ to indicate the change in $W_{i,j}$:

$$\Delta(W_{i,j}) = \text{constant} * I_i * O_j \tag{2}$$

The crux of the technique is that it is then possible to 'train' the network to 'recognize' a pattern of inputs. The idea is that the connections start off with random weights, then there is a 'training phase' in which an 'input' is presented (by setting the activations of the appropriate nodes in the input layer to 1 (on) and the rest to 0 (off)), and the desired output node is also made active. After each training trial, the connection weights are changed appropriately (following the Hebb rule). After 100 input trials or so, we can then check the output of the network by inputting the pattern for one target input. The output should then be a close approximation to the desired output, with the activation of the desired output node close to 1.0, and the activation for the other output nodes close to 0. An important and generally desirable characteristic of this type of network is that it is robust – if there is a bit of 'noise' in the input, the output will still be close to 1.0. Another feature of this type of network is that, as the inputs vary continuously, the outputs will also vary continuously. Hebb suggested that this is the type of processing needed to learn to recognize a shape regardless of where it passes across the retina, and it is probably ideal for many types of learning.

Note that although the above simple Hebbian network is trained by being 'told' the right answer (the 'correct' output is associated with the input) it is not able to learn by trial and error. It turns out that much more powerful learning procedures are available if the network is allowed to generate its own output, and is then 'told' what the desired answer should have been. The simplest (and very powerful) trial and error learning method is the 'DELTA RULE'. In brief, the delta rule works by comparing the actual activation for each output unit (O_j) with the expected (correct) activation for that unit (E_j). The change on $W_{i,j}$ after that trial is then proportional to the difference between E_j and O_j. In fact the equation is:

DELTA RULE

333

$$\Delta(W_{i,j}) = \text{constant} * (E_j - O_j) * I_i \tag{3}$$

Note that this is the same equation as the Hebb rule (see above), except that we use the discrepancy between correct and actual output activation (the 'error') rather than the straight output activation. This has the interesting effect that if an output unit has the correct activation, then the weights for all connections to that unit are left unchanged. By contrast, the Hebb rule would keep changing them, almost certainly leading to errors on the next trial.

Despite this early success, little progress was made until the mid-1980s, when a general method was developed for training networks with three or more layers (with a three-layer net, the middle layer is known as a 'hidden' layer). The method is known as back propagation and is a relatively straightforward generalization of the delta rule for multi-layer nets. As with the delta rule, the error term for that unit is computed at each output unit, and this value is used to adjust the values of the connection weights from the previous layer. Next we move to the first hidden layer. Using these new values, one can then adjust the connection strengths in the previous hidden layer, and so on, working one's way backwards a layer at a time until the whole network is suitably adjusted. In this way, the error terms propagate backwards from output layer through hidden layer(s) to the input layer.

Back propagation has been criticized in terms of its neuroanatomical implausibility (e.g. Crick 1989), in that many areas of the brain do not have the rich forward and backward connections required to implement the algorithm (and it is not clear that the neural machinery would easily be able to implement the complex back propagation calculations). None the less, there is now increasing evidence that many brain regions that were thought to be purely feedforward (such as the early stages in visual processing) are now known to implement extensive feedback loops to 'earlier' stages. It may therefore be that, for some brain regions, an approximation to back propagation can be implemented. Knowing what we do about the extraordinary adaptability of the brain, I would speculate that if an algorithm *can* be implemented, then it (or a superior one!) *will* be implemented! We shall briefly return to issues of networks in the brain in the concluding section of this chapter.

Connectionism has been hailed as the major new paradigm for psychology (Schneider 1987) with applications ranging from visual pattern recognition to acquisition of syntax to models of brain function. Rumelhart (1989) claims that connectionist architectures have the following highly desirable attributes for any biological system: constraint satisfaction (finding problem solutions which are sensitive to the constraints operating in the specific situation); interactive processing (where a number of information sources need to be blended); rapid pattern-matching and content-addressable memory (a necessity for memory storage and retrieval); automatic generalization to new situations; graceful degradation (so that plausible solutions are obtained even when errors occur) and, last but most important, learning. In short, connectionist approaches are neurologically inspired; they avoid the fragility typical of purely symbolic learning; they have a variety of robust problem-solving and information storage methods; and they can evolve via interaction with the environment.

Connectionist techniques are being developed very rapidly, and new architectures are being constructed that promise to provide a range of different types of learning. Overall, the approach has been shown to have quite extraordinary power and generality. Connectionist models have been developed for all of the types of learning and expertise discussed in this chapter. Models have been created that learn skilled actions, that learn to pronounce written words, that learn to manipulate 'muscles' to control speech output, that learn to recognize objects, and that develop automatic processing. There is even a connectionist model of physics expertise.

Perhaps most intriguingly, networks have been developed that are able to reproduce many of the language-based skills that were previously thought to be the hallmark of symbolic thought. The most celebrated model of this type was the Rumelhart and McClelland (1986) model for learning the rules for constructing the past tense in English. This model, in which the learning was accomplished essentially by a simple 'feedforward' network (figure 8.10) using the delta rule, was trained on a corpus of word stem–past-tense pairs (coded in terms of the phonemic features). The authors presented the training corpus in a way intended to reflect the likely order of presentations to a young child, with 10 high-frequency words (which often have irregular past tenses) trained initially, and then 410 medium-frequency verbs. The model also showed two theoretically important characteristics. With some irregular verbs (such as *give*), the model first learned the correct past tense – gave. Later on, following presentation of many regular verbs, the link give–gived became stronger than that of give–gave, then eventually the link give–gave again became much the stronger. This pattern of over-regularization is known to occur in children, and had been considered a clear example of children applying rules. Second, the authors then presented 86 new low-frequency verbs (without giving the correct answer) to see how well the model performed on novel verbs. The model performed pretty well (though by no means perfectly), producing around 90 per cent correct phonemes. In some cases it 'predicted' the correct past tense for irregular verbs (e.g., weep–wept, presumably because sleep–slept had been in the training set). The point of crucial theoretical importance is that this model had no rules anywhere, nor did it incorporate any of the standard psycholinguistic distinctions of words into root, stem, affix, irregular verb, regular verb, and so on. This simulation of classic rule-based behaviour without any of the traditional symbolic structures posed a sharp challenge to psycholinguistic theory, and led to a heated debate in subsequent years.

Here, however, I wish to highlight the fact that the connectionist paradigm not only provides a tool for modelling psychological phenomena, but also a language for describing learning. Connectionist analyses have introduced and made concrete concepts such as supervised learning (where there is a 'trainer' avail-

HEBBIAN
LEARNING

able to indicate the error), self-organized learning (where there is no trainer available, but the network is none the less able to learn to classify patterns), learning by association, and learning by gradient descent (using, for instance, the delta rule for error-based learning). HEBBIAN LEARNING can be thought of as learning without feedback – the network is forced to give the correct response in the training phase. In most learning situations there is a significant opportunity for error. The child tries to say *ba* but says *da*, for instance. In such circumstances, it is reasonable to assume that the difference between the intended and the actual output is monitored (in this case, the child would hear its own output), and some attempt is made to modify the weights in view of this difference. Maybe it captures the idea of 'learning by doing', and learning by trial and error. Certainly the delta rule favours errors, since there is no learning whatsoever following a correct response.

It is also worth noting that connectionist work offers the opportunity to evaluate not just learning algorithms, but also learning architectures (Rumelhart 1989). Perhaps the two major issues confronting connectionist modelling are the two extremes: first, how to develop an architecture which takes into account the underlying brain structures and, second, how to develop connectionist systems which interface smoothly between the sub-symbolic learning at which they excel, and the planful, symbolic learning which characterizes adult cognition.

An ambitious framework for a neurologically plausible architecture is provided by Houk and Wise (1995). Their framework involves distributed modules linking the basal ganglia, cerebellum and cerebral cortex, and outlines how these might be implemented neurally, and how they might combine to control action. Despite their considerable promise, it is too early yet to evaluate such models. Research is moving rapidly. Other researchers attribute different functional requirements to these three structures. What is clear is that multidisciplinary research, informed by neuroscience, by connectionism, and by cognition, will be needed to continue to make progress.

▓ Discussion ▓

At the beginning of this chapter I stated the difficulties of understanding learning because it had been split into so many different approaches – it was like the Hindu story of the wise men and the elephant. My plan was to go through the different perspectives – the trunk, the tusks, the ears, the tail and the legs – trying to give a reasonable picture of the animal seen from each perspective. Finally, I have to try to integrate these views, to discover the whole animal. I hope you will forgive me if it seems still like a pantomime elephant, with rather uncoordinated limbs only sketchily joined together. This is probably the true picture at present! Let's see what can be done to integrate the visions.

Animal learning

Studies of conditioning revealed a number of common themes. Learning between stimulus and stimulus occurs by association between the two, probably more because of a contingency between the two than just a contiguity. In terms of our later analyses, this suggests that it is not just the Hebb rule (contiguity) between stimulus and response, but some higher-order form of learning, which attempts to identify those aspects of the environment which provide a greater opportunity for reinforcement. Studies of classical conditioning which reveal systematic differences between types of animal and types of stimulus may well be explicable in terms of the different brain regions and different neurotransmitter systems involved. It is not surprising, therefore, that despite the overall similarity of classical conditioning phenomena, they do appear to differ significantly when more detailed analyses are undertaken.

Hull's learning theory made explicit the clear link between number of reinforcements of an S–R pairing, and the increasing 'habit strength' between the two. What is the link between this and the three-stage learning process (declarative, procedural and autonomous stages) put forward by cognitive psychologists? Hull's increase in strength has much in common with studies of skill automatization (the autonomous stage), but because the behaviourists steadfastly investigated only the simplest situations, and foreswore assumptions about variables that were not observable, they never realized that automatization does not include only habit strength but also a change to a qualitatively different form of learning. Skinner's approach to behaviour modification by 'shaping' the behaviour by degrees to that required can be seen as a method of scaffolding the procedural stage of learning, where the organism has to learn how to carry out the target action.

Adult learning

Adults are able to learn, but their learning methods are but a shadow of those available to infants. Although there is some cortical plasticity (consider the Merzenich experiment which shows the enduring plasticity of auditory cortex), it is unlikely that much neuronal or synaptic growth is possible. Learning will typically involve the adjustment of synaptic strengths within networks, and will tend more to tuning and assimilation than restructuring. The three-stage learning model is appropriate, with declarative, goal-directed knowledge providing the key to learning.

Ericsson's assertion that deliberate practice is the most important aspect of acquisition of super-skills is no doubt valid, as is his suggestion that early learning is valuable in that it provides a greater time window for the development of expert performance. None the less, it seems likely that either genetic endowment or very early experience (even in the womb) may well provide a brain which is particularly well-suited to particular types of learning from the earliest of ages. We have already seen that very early experience is a prerequisite for the development of absolute pitch, and that the mother's language prosody tunes the foetus's auditory system to invariants of the mother tongue, at the expense of alternative languages. It seems very likely that early experience can be vital in setting up the appropriate connections between the senses. An important applied objective for learning in general, but especially for adult learning, is how to systematize coaching so that it can be achieved more effectively, more naturally, and more interestingly.

For adults, the three-stage learning model is appropriate, with declarative, goal-directed, knowledge providing the starting point to new learning. Mostly we learn initially by analogy with some knowledge or skill that we already have. The initial stages of learning will almost certainly involve controlled processing (see Box 8.3), where performance is completely under attentional control, and one sets oneself small subgoals, checks whether these have been attained, and makes changes as appropriate. Symbolic problem-solving processes, use of existing knowledge, and close, conscious attention therefore form the basis of much of adult learning.

Early learning

Brain development goes through several phases. First, neuronal creation and migration, under loose genetic control. Second, colonization – axonal and synaptic sprouting – under genetic and environmental control, with synaptic tuning occurring via versions of the Hebb rule. Third, consolidation, in which assemblies of neurons form themselves, largely under control of the environment, but also dependent upon structures that have already been formed. Neuronal pruning may also take place at this stage. Fourth, evolution – the assemblies develop and evolve by a process of bricolage, acquiring emergent properties. Skills develop and become automatic. Language emerges, providing the underpinning for a rich declarative store of knowledge, which leads to qualitative changes in expressive and analytical power of the brain. This leads to an important change in learning style, where the three-stage model of learning becomes appropriate, and the learner initially relies on declarative learning allied to a consciously controlled, goal-directed method of skill proceduralization (see under the 'Adult Human Learning' section above). The fifth, adult stage, is that of maturity. The major brain modules are already determined. It is still possible to learn, but most learning is by assimilation of further facts into the existing framework. Skills can still be automatized, but the process becomes increasingly difficult, owing to interference from previously learned skills.

Learning and the brain

Arguably the major objective of any living organism is to identify the regularities in the environment and to respond appropriately to those which are most salient to it. Even the simplest animals such as aplysia are able to learn by conti-guity, via synaptic strengthening mechanisms based on LONG-TERM POTENTIATION (and analogous to the Hebb rule). More complex animals show this ability to learn by long-term potentiation, but they are able to exploit much more subtle contingencies between stimulus and outcome than mere contiguity. These stud-ies therefore show clearly that pure Hebbian learning is an important aspect of low-level learning but it is by no means a sufficient explanation.

It seems therefore that some sort of error-dependent learning (analogous to delta-rule learning) must be involved even in low-level learning for mammals. It is likely that this type of learning is very important in early stages in skill acquisition. However, consider now the process of skill automatization. Follow-ing consistent practice, the need for attentional monitoring drops out, and the associations gain very great strength, to the extent that the link becomes auto-matic. This increase in association strength is in fact more like the Hebb rule than the delta rule (in that with the delta rule and its generalizations, there are no changes in connection strengths if performance is successful). It is very tempt-ing to speculate that the delta rule is needed in the early stages of learning, and that this is used to set up a 'consistent network' (such that the consistent connec-tions increase in strength towards some asymptotic value, as suggested both by the Rescorla–Wagner model (1972) of animal learning, and by studies of human skill automatization). It may well be that a network architecture in which new stages evolve by a process similar to what Piaget termed bricolage might pro-vide an appropriate architecture for these evolving requirements.

The 'mind as developing society' metaphor

The difficulty is finding a helpful analogy. The one I wish to suggest tentatively is that of colonization of a new world. Imagine, millennia ago, that an ancient race discovered a new island, teeming with life. The pattern of subsequent de-velopment would depend upon a number of predictable features. These would include primary features, such as mountains, rivers and the coastline; second-ary features, such as the fertility of the land, and natural gateways, ports etc.; and developmental features, such as proximity to natural lines of development from the initial place of landing. Clearly the key natural resources, such as food, fuel and shelter, would dominate in the early years, but as the settlements became better established, it is likely that other resources would become valued. Over the years, villages would develop, based on a complex and somewhat arbitrary pattern of colonization involving not just the natural features but also the history of the developments (with the early-established settlements domi-nating the economy) and even the particular preoccupations of the time. Local economies would be set up, largely self-sufficient but perhaps specializing in particular tasks (the charcoal burners in the woods, the fishers near the sea, the goldsmiths in the mountains, and so on). An increasingly complex web of vil-lages, resources and trade routes would be set up. In due course great paved highways would be built linking key settlements. The original pathways through the woods might well fall into disrepair. Once the pattern of development has been set, it is very hard to undo.

An important consequence of the 'mind as developing society' metaphor is that different minds will develop in different ways, depending upon their varying initial conditions and the varying external and internal environments that different minds experience. Consequently, a key requirement for understanding the mind is to understand more clearly the conditions from which the mind grows, and the methods with which it develops. It is very likely that the subsequent developments of a mind will tell us more about the environment in which it participates than the processes by which it is constructed. This view has led to the recent emergence of the 'dynamic systems' approach to human development (e.g. Kelso 1995; Thelen & Smith 1994) which attempts to characterize the dynamic changes that take place in development as a function of the existing organization of the brain, together with its preferred modes for self-organization.

▓ Conclusions ▓

It now behoves me to attempt to map out the stages in development of the mind, and the critical variables involved. There are three fundamental sources of all change in the mind of an organism. The first is the existing state of the organism; the second is input from the outside world; and the third is the consequence of action by the organism. In the womb, the inputs are via the umbilical cord, which brings blood and thus food and oxygen, together with state indicators such as hormonal secretions, etc., from the mother; from noises (both internal and external); and from touch (for instance, when the baby kicks the mother's stomach). Almost all learning in the womb must occur by association or by self-organizing learning. It is not unreasonable to assume that the baby is able to associate its internal environment with positive and negative states. The presence of a happy, relaxed state (and of a distressed one) will be transmitted via the blood. These states will auto-associate with the environmental stimuli then present (such as a slow even heartbeat, calm digestive noises, warm voice tones for happiness; rapid heartbeat, strident voice for stress) to predispose the foetus to prefer some physiological states and some environmental contexts. Furthermore, the auditory cortex will automatically self-organize itself to classify various prosodic features of the mother's speech into same and different categories, thereby giving an in-built advantage to the mother tongue. The motor activity is probably the only 'voluntary' activity available to the foetus (though one must consider the possibility of its actively attending to one modality rather than another). It seems likely that there is an in-built preference to explore, to kick out. The self-organizing components of the subcortical motor system (remember, the cortex is barely formed even at birth) will presumably auto-associate the input from the touch receptors on the foot with the corresponding proprioceptive information from the limbs, thus starting to build up the first maps of the internal world. Birth literally draws back the veils from the outside world. The world's finest learning machine, primed and ready, takes centre stage. In-built reflexes let the child root to find the mother's nipple. The combination of touch, sight, taste, smell, sucking sounds, muscular sensation and internal reinforcement combine to create a heady brew of multisensory information rarely equalled subsequently. The newly built cortex receives a volley of information that stimulates important connections between those areas of cortex and subcortical structures that receive input from the senses. From these input centres, neuronal axons grow, synapses form, then wither or flourish via the Hebb rule, forming an ever increasing network of villages. Pathways between like-minded villages become established, and villages group together into towns of specialists. Eventually, highways between towns become established. Confederations evolve for the efficient processing of important information – eye control, hand control, auditory processing, visual processing, and (later) hand–eye coordination. The mental world is in a constant state of dynamic change, with continual pressure to react faster, to process more efficiently, to deliver a better quality of product. Outdated structures decline and fall, and their workforce is recycled. An awesome blend of capitalism and socialism!

For adults, the situation is very different. The country has been settled, the major cities, institutions and communication networks are established. It is possible still to have significant changes in organization, as witnessed most starkly, following major damage to the brain, by the really quite exceptional abilities to recover, over time, considerable function. More routinely, similar changes seem to follow significant changes in life-style. None the less, the inertia of the system, in which modes of thinking and action become more and more strongly established, means that most developments are of an incremental nature, with new knowledge being assimilated into the existing structures, and new skills being developments of those that have already been learned.

The next few years will lead to quite extraordinary progress in understanding of the bases of brain ontogeny, of cellular learning, of developmental neuropsychology, and of connectionist modelling. These will lead to a much richer understanding of the processes in human learning, which will in turn lead to unprecedented opportunities to improve the quality of our education – for infants, for children and for adults. It remains to leave you with the words of Alexander Pope, 250 years ago.

'Tis education forms the common mind,
Just as the twig is bent, the tree's inclined.

CHAPTER SUMMARY

1 Learning is a method of adapting to the environment. The human brain modifies itself in the course of learning.

2 Animal learning theorists studied classical and instrumental conditioning. Skinner argued that it should be possible to develop a science of behaviour which would allow one to design a utopian culture.

3 Many examples of human learning can be explained in terms of a three-stage model, moving from the declarative stage to the procedural stage to the autonomous stage.

4 Acquiring true expertise typically takes at least ten years. Ericsson suggests that 'deliberate practice' holds the key to true expertise. Automaticity is an important aspect of skilled performance.

5 The processes by which an infant learns are probably much more powerful than those available later, in that the early experiences significantly affect the brain's effective modules.

6 Adults are able to more than compensate for their reduced brain plasticity by using their very large and well-organized repertoire of knowledge and skill.

7 Connectionism provides a formalism for modelling and explaining many of the processes occurring in sub-symbolic learning.

8 Analysis of learning is a multidisciplinary venture requiring contributions from every branch of psychology, cognitive science and neuroscience. It is likely that significant progress will be made in the next few years.

▪ Further Work ▪

1. What is the difference between classical and instrumental conditioning? Discuss how Skinner hoped to use the techniques of instrumental conditioning to develop a better society.

2. Exploration: Devise an experiment to see how effective instrumental conditioning can be for modifying people's behaviour. Try it out on a friend. Hint: you need to think of a reinforcer – you could smile encouragingly when they mentioned some type of topic, then use a shaping technique to tune the specificity.

3. Consider any skill that you have learned recently, or are trying to learn. Analyse the sub-skills and knowledge involved. How well is it described by the three-stage model?

4. What are the main differences in learning ability between children and adults? Which skills would an 8-year-old child find easier to learn than an adult?

5. Outline Ericsson's analysis of how expertise needs to be developed to reach world-class performance. Take any skill that you have practised a lot, and consider how well Ericsson's analysis holds.

6. What is long-term potentiation? In what ways may LTP be involved in human learning?

7. Why are some people better at tennis than others? Do you think there is such a thing as 'natural ability'? Justify your answer.

▨ **Further Reading** ▨

Eccles, J. C. (1989) *Evolution of the Brain: Creation of the Self*. London: Routledge.

> A wonderful book, providing the vision and wisdom of a Nobel Prize winner with the clarity and enthusiasm needed by good communicators. Taking a broad sweep of 2 million years, the book explains not only how our brain is organized, but also how it got to be that way.

Johnson, M. H. (ed.) (1993) *Brain Development and Cognition: A Reader*. Oxford: Blackwell.

> A series of chapters covering all aspects of developmental neuropsychology. Particularly relevant to the section on 'Learning from First Principles', above.

Carlson, N. R. (1994; 5th edn) *Physiology of Behaviour*. London: Allyn & Bacon.

> You should have discovered Carlson already in Chaper 5. A comprehensive and up-to-date text, packed full of information. Technically demanding for non-biologists, it provides an outstanding breadth of coverage. Advanced undergraduate/postgraduate level.

Anderson, J. R. (1995) *Learning and Memory: An Integrated Approach*. New York: John Wiley & Sons Ltd.

> This book, by one of the foremost researchers in the area, gives an unrivalled, detailed and coherent coverage of theory on learning and memory. Advanced undergraduate/postgraduate level, it is particularly strong on symbolic learning (less so on brain and learning), and it also gives a good overview of memory research.

Locke, J. (1993) *The Child's Path to Spoken Language*. Cambridge, Mass.: Harvard University Press.

> A comprehensive and very readable exposition of how humans learn to speak, from the womb to the first few words. It is outstanding in considering all aspects – perceptual, social, neural and cognitive.

Mackintosh, N. J. and Colman, A. M. (eds) (1995) *Learning and Skills*. Harlow, Essex: Longman.

> This book succeeds well in its aim of providing a set of tutorials on the key aspects of learning and skills. Chapters on animal learning, cognitive skill and motor skill are particularly relevant to the exposition here.

CHAPTER 9
Thinking and Reasoning
Alan Garnham

CHAPTER AGENDA

- This chapter begins by noting the central place of thinking and reasoning in our conception of ourselves as human beings. It then considers some examples of thinking in everyday life, to raise the question: What kinds of behaviour do psychologists wish to explain when they develop theories of thinking and reasoning?

- How do we think about the things in the world around us? The idea of a mental model (of part of the world), which can be changed without changing the world itself, is introduced, as the basis of one type of psychological theory of thinking and reasoning.

- How can reasoning be studied in the laboratory? Psychological work on deductive reasoning – reasoning from a set of facts to what definitely follows from them – is described, both as an example of the kind of reasoning that is easy to study in the laboratory and as an example of a type of reasoning that can be explained by a mental models theory.

- In one sense, deduction does not get us 'beyond the information given'. Yet much of our reasoning requires us to do just that. How do we do so? Induction (usually of general conclusions from specific pieces of evidence) and hypothesis testing (using specific pieces of evidence to see if general statements are true) are two types of reasoning that go beyond the constraints of pure deduction.

- Most people find mathematics difficult, so how do they reason when they have to take account of statistical considerations (such as the effect of environmental factors on health)? Psychologists believe that, under many circumstances, people are inclined to bypass mathematical calculation and use heuristic, 'rule-of-thumb' methods.

- Problem solving requires thinking and reasoning abilities. How do people solve problems? How do they apply their problem-solving abilities to playing games such as chess? What is the role of expertise in problem solving and game playing, and how is expertise acquired? These questions are considered at the end of the chapter.

▓ Introduction ▓

As a species we call ourselves *Homo sapiens*: we define ourselves by our ability to think. But how do we think? What are the mental mechanisms that underlie this ability? And are we good at thinking? By what standards might we make such a judgement?

Our thought processes, particularly those mediated by language, are considerably more complex than those of other animals – hence *Homo sapiens*. But compared with other psychological processes (perceptual processes, for example), thought is slow and error-prone. Perceptual processes must act quickly and accurately if we are to move around a changing three-dimensional world without sustaining injury or death. Large objects may move quickly, and we need to get out of their way. Thinking, on the other hand, although undoubtedly useful, is more of a luxury. And it can often be carried out at leisure, before we act (or afterwards, in a 'post mortem').

Thinking in everyday life is difficult to study and, as in other branches of psychology, psychologists have tried to bring thinking into the laboratory. Most of this chapter will consider laboratory research. But we will begin with two lines of research on reasoning that make a greater effort to make contact with everyday life. One of these lines of research – on people's mathematical reasoning when they are buying and selling – suggests that people are good at reasoning, at least of one specialized type. The other – which looks at people's ability to reason in the abstract about practical issues such as education – suggests that they are not so good. The rest of the chapter covers traditional areas of research in thinking and reasoning: deductive reasoning, inductive reasoning, hypothesis testing, statistical reasoning, problem solving, game playing and expertise. The research is presented in the framework of the MENTAL MODELS THEORY, which claims that we reason by forming models of parts of the world in our minds, and manipulating those models.

MENTAL MODELS
THEORY

▒ Reasoning in Everyday Life ▒

Street mathematics

In Brazil, as in many other countries, children sell goods in the street. They have to add up prices and calculate how much change should be given. They have to work out bargains, and to compete with one another for trade. Carraher et al. (1985) studied the arithmetical reasoning skills of Brazilian street vendors. They found that, although the children had little formal schooling, they solved complex arithmetical problems accurately, and performed better when working as street vendors than on analogous tasks, using the same numbers and operations, in a more formal setting. They also performed better than non-vendors with comparable education. What was interesting was the way the children solved the problems. They relied on invented procedures, rather than those they would have learned in school. For example, a child asked for the price of ten coconuts at 35 cruzeiros each, did not use the 'add 0' method of multiplying by ten, as she had undoubtedly been taught in school. She worked out the cost of three (105), added the cost of a further three twice (315), then added a further 35 (350). The children used different strategies in the street and in the formal situations. In the street they usually used *convenient groups* for their additions.

Plate 9.1 Brazilian child street vendors
Source: Andes Press Agency.

Attempts to use school-taught procedures usually interfered with, rather than helped, their problem-solving.

People making purchases in food stores show similar arithmetical dexterity. Lave (1988; Lave et al. 1984) either gave people verbal problems, asking them to imagine that they were in a store making decisions between products, or actually sent them to a food store, and asked them to describe their thoughts as they made real decisions. A typical problem was: 'Which is the best buy for sunflower seeds: package A, which costs 30 cents for 3 oz., or package B, which costs 44 cents for 4 oz.?' The difference between shoppers' arithmetic in the food store and on analogous problems in a paper-and-pencil task was remarkable. The subjects scored 98 per cent correct on the problems in the food store, but only 59 per cent correct in the formal setting.

When comparing prices of different brands with different amounts per pack, people only occasionally used the school-taught method of working out the price-per-unit for each brand. In the food store, they used two other strategies. In one, the *difference* strategy, they compared the difference in quantity with the difference in price, and assessed whether the one justified the other. When using the second, *ratio* strategy, they assessed whether the ratio of the prices was greater or less than the ratio of the quantities. For example, a 10 oz. tin of peanuts for 90 cents is clearly a better buy than a 4 oz. tin for 45 cents, because the larger tin is twice the price, but contains more than twice as many peanuts. In both contexts, the subjects were flexible in their strategies, and tended to choose one that fitted the problem. Their reluctance to use the unit price strategy in the food store perhaps reflects the fact that it can be difficult to work out and compare unit prices without pencil and paper. In fact, some people simply gave up when faced with the prospect of having to use unit prices!

Informal arguments

A different line of research has focused on a type of EVERYDAY REASONING that has fewer direct links with practical action: people's ability to develop convincing arguments about everyday issues (such as: Would providing more money for state schools significantly improve the quality of teaching and learning?). Perkins (e.g. 1989) argues that this kind of reasoning is based on SITUATION MODELLING – thinking about how things are and how things might be in the world. He suggests the errors result from situation models that are biased, or incomplete, or both. Completeness means consideration of all possible arguments about an issue. BIAS means considering mainly (or only) arguments on one side of the case.

Perkins assessed completeness and bias by counting the number of 'my-side' and 'other-side' arguments ('my-side' arguments are those that support subjects' initial judgements). He found that even students consistently produced sparse, one-sided arguments, and that unguided reasoning was poorer than reasoning guided by the experimenter. For example, when subjects were prompted, they could produce at least six arguments on each side. However, even graduate students produced on average only 3.3 arguments in favour of a position, and 1.3 objections, when left to their own devices. So, not only is everyday reasoning not very good, it does not improve much with education, maturation or life experience (see Perkins et al. 1991 for an overview of this work).

So, do people in everyday life approach important decisions in a biased manner, never see the true 'vexedness' of the problems, and make hasty decisions on the basis of simplistic situation models? The answer seems to be 'no', or at least 'not necessarily'. If someone perceives an issue as personally important, and recognizes that a decision may be difficult, they develop a more elaborate situation model than those typically produced for thinking about social issues in laboratory studies. Ironically, our view of reasoning can be distorted by studying *everyday* reasoning in the laboratory, just as it can be by the use of problems invented specifically for the laboratory. Nevertheless, Perkins et al. (1991) found that the ability to argue about personal and social issues correlated, suggesting that similar underlying reasoning mechanisms were being engaged.

Perkins and his colleagues also examined the effects of knowledge and general intelligence. They took judgements of the amount of time previously spent thinking about an issue as an index of knowledge about it, and found no evidence of a relation between quality of situation modelling and familiarity with

EVERYDAY
REASONING

SITUATION
MODELLING

BIAS

Box 9.1   The Capsize of the *Herald of Free Enterprise*

On the evening of the 6 March 1987, the roll-on roll-off car ferry the *Herald of Free Enterprise* left the Belgian port of Zeebrugge to sail across the English Channel. Shortly afterwards it capsized, and 180 people were drowned. This major disaster is just one of many that have occurred, at least in part, through faulty everyday reasoning. Like many disasters, the capsize of the *Herald of Free Enterprise* did not have a single cause: there were many contributory factors, such as the ship leaving harbour in a rush, and its having too much ballast on board, which made it low in the water. However, the accident would probably have been avoided if the bow doors had been shut, because they would largely have prevented the water from entering the ship. At the time the ship left Zeebrugge, the assistant bosun, whose job it was to close the bow doors, was asleep and he had not closed them. The captain of the ship, the chief officer and the bosun all made the plausible (inductive) assumption that the bow doors were shut, because in their past experience the doors had been shut under such circumstances. The bosun, in fact, admitted noticing that they were open, but it was not his job to close them so he assumed (again inductively) that the assistant bosun would do so, with terrible consequences.

an issue. By contrast, IQ did relate to how well-elaborated the situation models were, especially for students. However, the relation between IQ and number of arguments was stronger for my-side than for other-side arguments. Subjects with higher IQs use their intelligence to elaborate the case for their own point of view, rather than to explore issues more impartially.

Perkins distinguishes the kind of everyday reasoning that he studied from FORMAL REASONING. The prototypical type of formal reasoning is that needed for logic and mathematics. Perkins implies that, because many laboratory-based studies of reasoning have been inspired by ideas from logic, they are irrelevant to the study of everyday reasoning. This conclusion is, however, too strong. As we will see, people often perform badly, by logical standards, on these problems. And the way they perform suggests that they are applying their everyday reasoning skills to laboratory problems. Thus, laboratory studies can tell us much about how people reason in everyday life.

A clear indication that Perkins' conclusion is too strong is that the best-developed theory of reasoning inspired and tested by formal reasoning task – the mental models theory of Phil Johnson-Laird (1983; Johnson-Laird & Byrne, 1991) – is similar in many respect to Perkins' account based on situation modelling.

The notion that reasoning is based on the consideration of models of parts of the world as it is, was, will be or might be ('situations') can be traced back to the work of Kenneth Craik (1943). Craik pointed out that the advantage of such 'mental modelling' is that we can try out ideas, and see what follows from them, on a surrogate of reality, rather than risking the consequences on reality itself.

It may seem that this idea should underlie any sensible theory of how people reason. However, other accounts of thinking and reasoning are possible. The most important of these are based on the idea of formal RULES OF INFERENCE. The best known of these rules has the Latin name MODUS PONENS, and says that, no matter what statements P and Q stand for, if P is true and if it is also true that if

FORMAL REASONING

RULES OF INFERENCE

MODUS PONENS

P then Q, Q must be true as well. Thus, a theory of reasoning can be based on the idea that we encode what we know as sentences with certain formal structures, and we use a set of mentally encoded rules of inference to see what other sentences we can derive from them.

Deductive Reasoning

DEDUCTIVE REASONING is reasoning from facts that are known or supposed to be true, to other facts that necessarily follow from them. It is the type of reasoning that logicians have tried to formalize, and it has been studied extensively by psychologists.

DEDUCTIVE
REASONING

Three-term series problems

One kind of deductive reasoning problem that psychologists have studied is the THREE-TERM SERIES PROBLEM. A three-term series problem has two statements about three people or objects that can be ordered according to a relation such as height. For example:

THREE-TERM SERIES
PROBLEM

> Ann is taller than Barbara.
> Barbara is taller than Carol.

Three main theories have proposed to explain how people solve three-term series problems (and conclude that Ann is taller than Carol). The oldest, Ian Hunter's (1957) operational theory, focuses on the operations in short-term memory needed to integrate the information in the two premises. It is a forerunner of the mental models theory of deductive reasoning.

The second theory, the imagery theory, shares with the mental models theory the idea that the premises are integrated into a single array. The third theory (Clark 1969) identified two linguistic properties of three-term series problems that affect their difficulty. The first is whether the relational term in the conclusion matches the term in the premises, or whether the converse term is used (*short* instead of *long*, for example). The second is whether the marked (*short*) or unmarked (*long*) term of a pair was used. Johnson-Laird and Byrne (1991: 93) show that these ideas can be incorporated into a model-type theory as assumptions about how models of spatial arrays are built, and how information is preferentially read out of them.

Conditional reasoning

Much of our everyday reasoning is conditional in form. We argue that if so and so is true then something else must be. Johnson-Laird and Byrne (1991) argue that a conditional statement of the form 'if p then q' is initially encoded in two models. The first, which is represented schematically in the top line below, explicitly represents a situation in which both p and q are true.

[p] q

....

The square bracket means that there can be no other types of situation (and hence no other types of model) in which p is true. If another model in which p is true has to be constructed, q will have to be true in it as well. The second initial model of 'if p then q' (the dots), is called the *implicit* model, and it has no explicit content. It merely indicates that other types of situation are possible. This model theory of CONDITIONAL REASONING correctly predicts that the inference, 'if p then q', 'p', therefore 'q', is easy, because the additional premise 'p' means that there are no models in which p is not true. The explicit model represents the only type of situation consistent with both the premises, and hence 'q' must be true. The inference 'if p then q', 'not q', therefore 'not p', is harder, because it requires the fleshing out of the implicit model, which can represent situations of two kinds (in this, and subsequent diagrams, ¬p means not p).

CONDITIONAL
REASONING

¬p q

¬p ¬q

The premise '¬q' rules out the (original) explicit model and the first of the new models, leaving only the second, so it follows that '¬p'. The theory also explains Girotto's (1993) finding that this second inference is easier when the '¬q' premise is presented first. This premise forces the explicit representation of the possibility of ¬q, and hence helps subjects to avoid the most common error, which is to say that nothing follows.

Syllogistic reasoning

SYLLOGISMS

SYLLOGISTIC
REASONING

SYLLOGISMS are arguments with two premises, each of which must take one of four forms ('all A are B' (called A); 'some A are B' (I); 'no A are B' (E); 'some A are not B' (O)). One premise relates A and B, and the other relates B and C. The conclusion, which must also take one of the four forms just specified, relates A and C. In psychology, there is a long history of work on SYLLOGISTIC REASONING. One of the main findings is that syllogisms range from the very easy to the very difficult. For example, about 90 per cent of subjects validly conclude, 'all of the artists are chemists' from the premises:

All of the artists are beekeepers.
All of the beekeepers are chemists.

On the other hand, less than 10 per cent correctly conclude that 'some of the artists are not chemists' from (Johnson-Laird & Byrne 1991):

> All of the beekeepers are artists.
> None of the chemists are beekeepers.

The atmosphere hypothesis

In early work on syllogistic reasoning, subjects were asked to assess conclusions presented to them, rather than to generate their own conclusions. Although this task is somewhat easier, people still make many errors. In an attempt to account for such errors, Woodworth and Sells (1935) proposed the ATMOSPHERE HYPOTHESIS. This hypothesis is most simply stated as follows (Begg & Denny 1969):

1. Any negative premise (E or O) creates a negative atmosphere, in which negative conclusions tend to be accepted.
2. Any particular premise (I or O) creates a particular atmosphere, in which particular conclusions tend to be accepted.

Atmosphere makes no distinction between valid and invalid conclusions. The atmosphere hypothesis has considerable difficulty explaining the results of experiments in which subjects generate their own conclusions, since some conclusions that are consistent with the hypothesis are rarely, if ever, produced, whereas others are generated frequently.

Conversion

A syllogistic premise has been 'converted', if the two terms (A and B) are swapped around. For statements of type I and E, CONVERSION represents a valid inference. If 'some A are B', 'some B are A', and if 'no A are B', 'no B are A'. For statements of types A and O conversion is not valid. It has been suggested (Chapman & Chapman 1959) that some errors in syllogistic reasoning can be explained on the assumption that people illicitly convert one or both of the premises of an argument, and then argue from the converted premises. In some cases, the nature of the A and B may make it clear that conversion is invalid. For example, from 'all dogs are animals', one would not expect people to infer that 'all animals are dogs'. However, in other cases, the conversion may appear valid. For example, from 'all ticket holders may enter the exhibition' it may be reasonable to conclude that 'all the people who are allowed to enter the exhibition are ticket holders', or, to put it more naturally, 'only ticket holders are allowed to enter'. When people are asked to say what follows from individual syllogistic premises, conversion errors are common when they are not blocked by content (Newstead 1990).

ATMOSPHERE
HYPOTHESIS

CONVERSION

Table 9.1 Mental model representations of statements in the four moods of the syllogism according to Johnson-Laird and Byrne (1991)

All A are B		Some A are B	
[a]	b	a	b
[a]	b	a	b
....		....	

No A are B		Some A are not B	
[a]		a	
[a]		a	
	[b]	a	[b]
	[b]		[b]
....		....	

A model theory of syllogistic reasoning

The mental models theory of syllogistic reasoning claims that reasoning has three main stages:

1. Construct a representation of the first premise. Add information from the second premise.
2. Look for a conclusion interrelating the end terms (A and C).
3. Search for alternative representations of the premises that support different conclusions.

If there is a conclusion that holds for all possible representations, subjects should respond with that conclusion. If there is no such conclusion, they should respond, 'No valid conclusion.'

The mental models theory represents sets of things – the As, Bs and Cs of the premises – by representative members of those sets – with 'a' standing for a representative member of the set of As, 'b' of the set of Bs, and so on. The representations of the four types of premises proposed by Johnson-Laird and Byrne (1991, chapter 6), are shown in table 9.1.

To draw a conclusion from two premises, their mental models must first be combined, by identifying the b's in the models of the two premises. The subsequent procedure for deriving the conclusions is based on the idea that an argument is valid if there is no way that its premises can be true and its conclusion false.

With the partly implicit representation and the square bracket notation there are at most three relevantly different ways of combining two syllogistic premises. So, some syllogisms have one model, some have two models, and some have three models. An example of a three-model syllogism is:

Some B are A
No B are C

_____

so,   Some A are not C

The models of the premises are:

Some B are A		No B are C	
b	a	[b]	
b	a	[b]	
....			[c]
			[c]
		....	

The simplest way of combining these premises, by identifying the b's in the two models, is:

a	[b]	
a	[b]	
		[c]
		[c]
....		

This model suggests the conclusion that 'no A are C', or conversely 'no C are A'. However, there is no reason why one of the c's should not also be an a, though it cannot be a b, if the second premise is to remain true. So, there is a second model:

a	[b]	
a	[b]	
a		[c]
		[c]
....		

This model suggests the conclusions 'some A are C', 'some C are A', 'some A are not C', and 'some C are not A'. Only the last two of these four are compatible with the first model. However, it is possible that all the c's might be a's:

a	[b]	
a	[b]	
a		[c]
a		[c]
....		

In this model 'some C are not A' is not true, and 'some A are not C' remains as the only conclusion compatible with all three models. It is, therefore, the only valid conclusion.

The theory of mental models is intended to explain individual differences in ability to solve syllogisms, the relative difficulty of different types of syllogism, the kinds of mistakes people make in solving syllogisms, and the EFFECTS OF CONTENT and prior beliefs on syllogistic reasoning. Furthermore, not only is the mental models theory of syllogistic reasoning part of a more general theory of deductive reasoning, it is also part of a broader cognitive theory that accounts for other types of reasoning, and for the way representations of the world are derived from perception and language understanding.

The mental models theory identifies two major determinants of the difficulty of syllogisms. First, the number of models affects how easy it is to find a valid conclusion. Since mental models are constructed, manipulated and compared in working memory, and since working memory has a limited capacity that must be shared between storage and processing, the more models there are, the more difficult a syllogism will be. Many of the errors that occur on multi-model problems can be explained by assuming that subjects choose a conclusion that is compatible with one of the models, but not with the others. For example, for the three-model syllogism above, a common error is to claim that 'no A are C' or that 'no C are A', either of which is consistent with the first model. Conclusions that are compatible with none of the models, such as 'all A are C' are never drawn. Individual differences are be explained in terms of working memory capacity, which determines how many models a person can consider, and how easily operations can be performed on models.

Second, the positions of the A, B and C in the premises influence both the difficulty of a syllogism, and whether an A–C or a C–A conclusion is more likely to be drawn. The explanation of this effect is based on an idea taken from Ian Hunter's (1957) operational theory of three-term series problems. The more manipulations of the premises in working memory that are needed to create an integrated model, the harder a problem will be. In the three-model syllogism above, for example, the a's and b's had to be reversed before the b's could be put together.

There are four different layouts (called figures) for the A, B and C terms, and their difficulty increases as follows:

A – B	B – A	A – B	B – A
B – C	C – B	C – B	B – C

The effect of content

Like other kinds of reasoning, syllogistic inference is affected by content. Evans et al. (1983) asked people to assess the validity of a *single* conclusion. For example:

No addictive things are inexpensive.
Some cigarettes are inexpensive.

_____

so, Some cigarettes are not addictive.

They found an effect of the believability of the conclusion, especially when it was *invalid*. This result suggests that subjects accept believable conclusions uncritically, but are more likely to check the validity of unbelievable ones. Oakhill and Johnson-Laird (1985) showed that beliefs also affect performance when subjects draw conclusions for themselves. Furthermore, a series of experiments by Newstead et al. (1992), investigating in detail the earlier finding of Evans et al. (1983) that beliefs have a greater effect when the presented conclusion is invalid, have provided evidence that favours the mental models theory.

Beliefs could affect three aspects of the reasoning process, though the results discussed so far provide no information about where beliefs act. First, beliefs could distort the interpretation of, or representation of, the premises (as when premises are illicitly converted). Second, they could influence the deductive *process*: affecting, according to the mental models theory, which models of the premises are considered. Third, they could induce response biases: beliefs could be used to accept or reject conclusions presented for evaluation, without any reasoning taking place, or they could be use to filter conclusions derived by the deductive process. There is evidence that beliefs have their effect at all of these loci.

Oakhill et al. (1989) provided evidence for effects at the second and third of these loci. They found that, for one-model problems, performance was better when the conclusions were believable than when they were unbelievable. Since there are no other models to consider in this case, the obvious explanation is in terms of conclusion filtering. However, the results for multiple-model problems, especially ones with no valid conclusion, suggested that filtering is not the only locus of bias effects. For these problems, if a conclusion compatible with an initial model was believable, it was frequently produced in error; but if such a conclusion was unbelievable, subjects more often correctly concluded that there was no valid conclusion. For example, given the premises:

All of the Frenchmen are wine drinkers.
Some of the wine drinkers are gourmets.

many subjects draw the invalid, but highly plausible, conclusion:

Some of the Frenchmen are gourmets.

Although this conclusion is empirically *true*, it does not *validly* follow. By substituting 'Italians' for 'gourmets' the fallaciousness of the argument becomes apparent. These results support the idea that a believable conclusion curtails the examination of alternative models of the premises.

▓ Induction ▓

Deductive reasoning allows people to draw conclusions with certainty from facts they know to be true, or from suppositions that they make. It rearranges given information, without going beyond it. That is not to say deductive reasoning is easy, or that it cannot lead to unforeseen conclusions. However, not all reasoning is deductive – if it were, people would be hopelessly restricted in the conclusions they could draw. Often they need to go 'beyond the information given'. The price they pay is loss of the guarantee that the conclusion they have drawn follows from the premises. Non-deductive types of reasoning include *inductive* reasoning, *abductive* reasoning, reasoning by *analogy*, some kinds of *probabilistic* (or *statistical*) reasoning, and *practical* reasoning (including decision-making).

INDUCTION

In inductive reasoning, even if a person knows the premises are true, and knows that they have reasoned as they intended, they cannot be sure that their conclusion will be true. The conclusion of an INDUCTION is a *hypothesis*, which may have to be tested to see if it is correct (see below). Inductive reasoning is important both in everyday life and in academic, in particular scientific, investigation. In science, hypotheses *must* be subjected to formal experimental tests.

Abduction

In conditional reasoning, statements of the form 'p' and 'if p then q', support the conclusion 'q'. In most real cases of conditional reasoning, the statement 'if p then q' derives from knowledge of the world. Thus, 'p' provided an explanation for 'q'. For example, if someone knows that a blown fuse prevents an electrical appliance from working, and knows that the fuse in their hair dryer has blown, they can conclude that the hair dryer will not work, and they can explain the fact that it will not work by the fact that its fuse is blown.

ABDUCTION

Normally, however, people have to argue the other way round. Faced with a hair dryer that will not work, they have to find an explanation for its malfunction. They do not know the state of its fuse. The generation of an explanation for an event, from a theory of how the world works, is known as a specific induction, or an ABDUCTION. This form of argument is deductively invalid, because there could be other reasons for q other than p. Its plausibility depends, in large part, on the number and the likelihood of the alternative explanations.

Because abductions are not deductively valid, they need to be checked. It is necessary to look at the hair dryer's fuse to see if it is blown. They are, however, obviously useful, in that they generate possible explanations of events, and hence (at least potentially) allow us to control the world in which we live. If the fuse has blown it can be replaced. If it has not, another explanation for the malfunction of the hair dryer is needed, and abduction can provide one.

General inductions

A general induction occurs when, from observing that a series of objects or events have some property, it is concluded that all objects or events in the same class have that property. However, both in everyday life and in academic investigation, not all general beliefs or hypotheses are formed in this way. Some, for example, are produced by imaginative leaps, others by the use of analogy. Indeed, analogical reasoning is often crucial in the formation of scientific theories – many scientists mention the use of analogy when they describe their methods of working.

Some general inductions are purely descriptive, while some are explanatory. A further distinction is between inductions of general statements (on which we have focused so far) and inductions of concepts. The two are, however, intimately related (Johnson-Laird 1993). For example, the induction of the general statement that internal flights are late in the United States is directly related to the concept of a late internal flight, which might then be used in formulating a further (induced) general statement (e.g., late internal flights could be prevented by the building of more runways). As Johnson-Laird puts it, 'concepts are used to construct thoughts, which in turn are used to construct concepts, and on and on' (1983: 89).

Some philosophical considerations about induction

We have described induction as a process of generalization. However, the philosopher Francis Bacon (1561–1626), who first studied induction, recognized that there are two sides to induction: generalization and specialization, or the avoidance of over-generalization. No generalization can be expected to apply without restrictions, and over-generalization must be avoided. For example, too much watering may, in general, be bad for house plants, but there may be some such plants that are not adversely affected by it. It would, therefore, be misleading to claim without qualification that too much water was bad for house plants.

The procedure described by Bacon appears to describe neither the actual practice of research scientists nor the logical reconstruction of that practice that is presented in scientific treatises and research papers. Karl Popper (1959) argues that 'the logic of scientific discovery' is better characterized as *hypothetico-deductive* rather than inductive. This idea has influenced psychological research on HYPOTHESIS TESTING, particularly the work of Peter Wason described below.

Popper argues that hypotheses may be derived by induction or by any other process. They might pop into a scientist's head in the bath, for example. Furthermore, the genesis of a hypothesis has no (logical) bearing on its truth or usefulness. What is important in science is not inducing a hypothesis, but simply having one. Hypotheses are then tested by deducing specific consequences from them, and finding out whether those consequences are true. The testing of a general hypothesis can show it to be definitively false, but can never show it to be cer-

HYPOTHESIS TESTING

Plate 9.2 Montgolfier balloon
Source: Ann Ronan Picture
Library.

tainly true. Consider a general statement such as 'no machine can allow a person to fly in the air'. The flight of the Montgolfier balloon – a single instance – falsified this statement for good. But all the previous instances of failed attempts to fly did not show it to be true. According to Popper, falsifiability is the hallmark of a scientific hypothesis. However, it must be borne in mind that scientists rarely try to falsify their *own* theories. They try to falsify the theories of other (rival) scientists.

Johnson-Laird (1993, 1994) has proposed a theory of induction within the mental models framework. He defines an inductive inference as one in which the conclusion rules out more states of affairs than the premises. Thus, to perform an induction, a reasoner must mentally model the premises, eliminate some of the models that are consistent with them, and then formulate a description of the remaining models (the induced conclusion). On this view induction is a process that acts on and produces sets of models. It is not a process that acts on linguistic statements, though a description of the set of models produced by the process will almost always be formulated. In this respect, Johnson-Laird's theory has an advantage over the other main body of research on induction – the study of machine learning in artificial intelligence. There are a variety of forms of generalization based on linguistic considerations, but in Johnson-Laird's scheme they all arise via the same basic mechanism of eliminating a subset of models consistent with the premises.

Hypothesis Testing

Most of the psychological research on hypothesis testing has been inspired, directly or indirectly, by the work of Peter Wason, who invented three apparently simple problems – the selection task, the THOG problem, and the 2-4-6 task – for studying the way that people evaluate hypotheses. Wason was influenced by Popper's idea that hypotheses should be tested by the hypothetico-deductive method.

The selection task

The original, abstract, version of the selection task (Wason 1966) is as follows. The subject is shown one face of each of four cards, and told that each card has a letter on one side and a number on the other side. The subject is also presented with a general statement that may or may not apply to the cards: if a card has a vowel on one side, it has an even number on the other side. The cards are placed on the table in front of the subject with the following letters and numbers on the uppermost faces.

E	K	4	7
P	¬P	Q	¬Q

The task is to select those cards that must be turned over to find out if the rule is true. The four cards are referred to as the P, ¬P, Q and ¬Q cards, because a conditional statement is said to have the form 'if P then Q'. Thus, in the selection task, P becomes 'vowel' and Q 'even number'. The relevant contrasts are consonants (things that are not vowels, ¬P) and odd numbers (things that are not even numbers, ¬Q).

Before you read on you should decide which cards you think should be turned over. Most undergraduates select either just the P card (E), or the P and Q cards (E and 4). A few choose the ¬Q card (7) as well. All these choices are wrong. The

Table 9.2 Possible types of letters and numbers on the reverse of cards in the selection task, and their implications for the status of cards

card	type of number of letter on reverse and status of card			
P (E)	even number	confirming	odd number	falsifying
¬P (K)	even number	irrelevant	odd number	irrelevant
Q (4)	vowel	confirming	consonant	irrelevant
¬Q (7)	vowel	falsifying	consonant	irrelevant

correct answer is E and 7. To see why, remember that a hypothesis is not confirmed by specific instances that conform to it, but that it is falsified by instances that do not. Remember also that the subjects' task is to pick only those cards that *must* be turned over. Obviously, in this case, the rule could be tested by checking that each card satisfies it.

Table 9.2 summarizes the possible types of letter and number on the reverse of the four cards, together with their implications for the status of the card. Only cards that could potentially falsify the rule need be turned over.

Wason and Johnson-Laird (1972) showed that the typical level of performance among undergraduates, about 15 per cent correct selections, remained the same across a wide range of instructional variations. They proposed that the primary determinant of success in the selection task was *insight* into the logical structure of the task. Their *insight model* claimed that subjects can show three levels of insight. At the first level subjects focus on the possibility of confirming the rule, and choose only cards that might turn out to be confirming instances (P alone, the more obvious potentially confirming instance, or P and Q), at the second level they realize that FALSIFICATION is important, but they fail to see that confirmation is not. They therefore choose both cards that might be confirming instances and those that might be falsifying instances (P, Q and ¬Q), and at the third level, complete insight, they choose only cards that might turn out to be falsifying instances (P and ¬Q). The first and second levels of insight have often been taken to reflect a confirmatory bias. Such a bias would mean that when people are testing hypotheses, they tend to focus their attention on instances that conform to the hypothesis.

A different account of the poor performance in the selection task has been proposed by Jonathan Evans (Wason & Evans 1975; Evans & Lynch 1973). Evans's MATCHING BIAS MODEL claims that subjects chose cards in the selection task in two ways. The first is by correct logical reasoning, and leads to the selection of the P and ¬Q cards. In the abstract version of the selection task very few subjects select cards in this way. The second method is by looking at the items explicitly mentioned in the rule and choosing cards that match those items (the word *not* is discounted by this matching process, so 'not a vowel' matches a vowel). In the standard version of the task ('if vowel, then even number'), matching leads to the choice of the vowel (P) and the even number (Q). However, matching can

FALSIFICATION

MATCHING BIAS MODEL

lead to the choice of the P and ¬Q cards with some rules, thus increasing the number of correct choices. Evans found this result in a number of experiments. However, there was a stronger tendency to match the Q and ¬Q cards, than the P and ¬P cards, and more recently (1989) he has proposed a different ('if') heuristic (*if* focuses attention on the P card) to explain the rarity of ¬P choices with any rules.

It was soon established that performance on selection problems with more concrete rules was much better. For example, Wason and Shapiro (1971) presented subjects with the following rule: every time I go to Manchester, I go by car; and the cards:

Manchester	Leeds	Car	Train
P	¬P	Q	¬Q

each representing a particular journey. Over 60 per cent of the subjects correctly selected the Manchester (P) and Train (¬Q) cards only. Apparently, in this version of the task, they found it easier to see that if the Train card had Manchester on the back, the rule would be false.

In another concrete version of the task Johnson-Laird et al. (1972) made use of a rule formerly used in the British postal system. In the old two-tier system of postal charges, sealed envelopes cost 5d. (5 old British pence) to post, and unsealed envelopes (containing cards or other printed material) 4d. The rule used by Johnson-Laird et al. was: if a letter is sealed, then it has a 5d. stamp on it (there was also an Italian version). Again, this version of the task made it easier for subjects to see the potential relevance of the ¬Q card. If the envelope with the 4d. stamp on it is sealed, the rule has been broken.

Griggs and Cox (1982) explained effects of content in the selection task by the MEMORY CUEING HYPOTHESIS: familiar concrete content can remind a person of a similar problem that they have encountered in the past. However, the memory cueing hypothesis has recently been challenged by several authors. Cheng and Holyoak (1985; Cheng et al. 1986) have discovered an abstract version of the selection task (if one is to take action 'A' then one must first satisfy precondition 'P') on which subjects perform well. They have suggested that people use context-dependent rules of inference called PRAGMATIC REASONING SCHEMAS, such as a *permission schema*, to solve problems of this kind. Cheng and Holyoak claim that versions of the selection task which show thematic effects are ones that activate the permission schema (one of the few apparent counter-examples, the Wason and Shapiro study mentioned above, has proved difficult to replicate). Thus, Cheng and Holyoak can explain the findings that have traditionally been taken as evidence for memory cueing, but can also explain why subjects can succeed in versions of the selection task based on rules of which they may have had no direct experience, but which can be interpreted as giving permissions.

Cosmides (1989) presents a different view, based on the idea of SOCIAL

MEMORY CUEING HYPOTHESIS

PRAGMATIC REASONING SCHEMAS

SOCIAL CONTRACTS

361

CONTRACTS, which specify that, in social exchanges, if one takes a benefit one is expected to pay a cost. On this view, the potentially falsifying cards (those that might have P on one side and ¬Q on the other) correspond to possible cheaters who are trying to take the benefit of the contract (P) without paying the cost (¬Q). Thus, Cosmides obtained good performance with the rule: 'If a man eats cassava root, then he must have a tattoo on his face', which deliberately refers to an unfamiliar social context. Intriguing as this theory is, it is incorrect as it stands, since, as several authors have pointed out (Cheng and Holyoak, 1989; Manktelow and Over, 1990; Pollard, 1990), many of the best established facilitatory contexts do not involve costs and benefits that are socially exchanged. For example, in a drinking law problem ('If anyone is drinking beer, then that person must be over 18 years old'), being 18 is not a cost that people pay for being able to drink beer.

Like Cosmides, Manktelow and Over (1991) have shown that there are circumstances under which subjects regularly choose the ¬P and Q cards. With a genuinely permission-granting rule such as: If you tidy your room, then you may go out to play (said by parent to child), subjects select the P and ¬Q cards when checking whether the parent has broken the rule, but they select ¬P and Q when checking whether the child has. The reason for these choices is as follows. There are four ways in which a permission can be violated. The agent (or person who grants the permission) can be unfair or weak-willed, and the actor (or person to whom the permission is granted) can be self-denying or can cheat the agent. The first and third of these possibilities correspond to the combination of P (room tidied) and ¬Q (no playing). The second and fourth correspond to ¬P (room not tidied) and Q (playing). Manktelow and Over's instructions focus either on the case in which the agent behaves unfairly (where subjects need to be sure there are no cards with P on one side and ¬Q on the other – hence the choice of P and ¬Q), or on the case in which the actor cheats, which calls for a choice of ¬P and Q.

Gigerenzer and Hug (1992) present a revised version of Cosmides' social contract theory, which brings many of these results together. Empirically, they

SEARCH FOR
CHEATERS

showed that the instruction to SEARCH FOR CHEATERS, and not just the use of a social contract rule, was essential to produce facilitation. Theoretically, by shifting the focus to cheating rather than paying costs and taking benefits, they circumvent some of the problems of Cosmides' account. Furthermore, they distinguish between social contracts in which only one side can cheat (e.g. drinking rules, postal rules), and social contracts in which both sides can cheat (e.g. Manktelow and Over's room-tidying rule). Only the latter produce selection changes from P and ¬Q (when the the person laying down the rule cheats) to ¬P and Q (when the person to whom the rule is directed cheats).

Although the idea that people only succeed on the selection task when it causes them to engage in practical reasoning is an attractive one, it is not universally accepted. Johnson-Laird and Byrne (1991) argue that not all contents that produce facilitation invoke 'deontic' reasoning (i.e. reasoning pertaining to concepts of permissibility and obligatoriness). They explain facilitation in terms of a mental models theory of the selection task. On this account people encode explicitly

Plate 9.3 Georges de la Tour, *The Cheat with the Ace of Diamonds*, c.1620 Source: Giraudon/Musée du Louvre.

stated information into their models, but tend to leave other possibilities implicit. So, the rule in the abstract version of the WASON SELECTION TASK leads to an explicit model in which there is a card with a vowel on one side and an even number on the other, but not to an explicit model of the other possibilities (consonant/even number and consonant/odd number), nor to an explicit model of the disallowed combination (vowel/odd number). Johnson-Laird and Byrne propose that *any* manipulation that leads to these other models becoming explicitly represented will lead to facilitation.

WASON SELECTION TASK

The THOG problem

A second problem invented by Peter Wason is the THOG PROBLEM (Wason & Brooks 1979), which is about geometric figures with different shapes and colours, for example:

THOG PROBLEM

black square   black circle   white square   white circle

The person administering the THOG problem makes the following statement: I am thinking of one colour (black or white) and one shape (square or circle). Any figure that has either the colour I am thinking of, or the shape I am thinking of, but not both, is a THOG. Given that the black square is a THOG what, if anything, can you say about the other figures?

Again, before you read on, you should try and work through this problem. In the THOG problem the subject has to consider two possible rules. If the black square is a THOG, the rule could be either:

A THOG is either black or circular but not both.
A THOG is either white or square but not both.

After working out what rules the experimenter might have in mind, the subject has to work through the consequences of each possibility to see how it classifies the other figures (see table 9.3). The table shows that the two rules classify all three remaining figures in the same way. So, whichever rule the experimenter has chosen, the black circle and white square are not THOGs and the white circle is a THOG. Most undergraduate students get the THOG problem wrong. The most common answer is that the white circle is not a THOG and that the other two figures are THOGs, or that their status is indeterminate. Wason and Brooks called this error the 'intuitive error'. The white circle and black square share no features in common, so it is likely that they belong to different categories. The abstract nature of the problem, and the presence of disjunctions in the definitions contribute to the difficulties of the problem. However, subsequent research has identified some more specific problems that subjects have in attempting to solve THOG.

Some subjects confuse the two properties of the exemplar THOG (black and square) with the properties that the experimenter has in mind and, unless prompted, most subjects fail to construct the two possible definitions of a THOG (O'Brien et al. 1990). According to Newstead and Griggs (1992), both these difficulties arises from a failure by subjects to distinguish, in their thinking about the problem, between data (the figures) and hypotheses. This problem is com-

Table 9.3 Classification of the four figures in the THOG problem by the two possible rules that the experimenter might have in mind

	Figures			
Rule	black square	black circle	white square	white circle
black or circle	THOG (black)	non-THOG (both)	non-THOG (neither)	THOG (circle)
white or square	THOG (square)	non-THOG (neither)	non-THOG (both)	THOG (white)

pounded by the fact that each hypothesis about the definition (e.g. black and circle) can be interpreted as a description of a figure (e.g. the black circle). Newstead and Griggs' account explains why realistic scenarios are only useful if they help subjects to separate data and hypotheses (Girotto & Legrenzi 1993; Newstead & Griggs 1992). Newstead and Griggs presented subjects with a problem in which a person gives cards to each of four friends and keeps one for himself. He says he will buy a dinner for those friends who have a card with a same shape or same colour as his, but not both. Then he says, 'By this rule I must buy a dinner for Rob, can you work out who else I must buy one for?' In this scenario, the main character's card corresponds to the hypothesis, and the four friends' cards correspond to the data. Girotto and Legrenzi (1993) provided further evidence of the importance of separating hypothesis and data by showing that performance in the abstract THOG task was facilitated by giving another nonsense name (SARS) to the card corresponding to the colour and shape the experimenter has in mind.

The 2-4-6 problem

A third infuriating problem invented by Wason (1960) is the 2-4-6 PROBLEM. In the 2-4-6 problem the subject is told that the experimenter is thinking of a rule governing sequences of three numbers, and that the sequence 2-4-6 obeys the rule. The task is to discover the rule, by asking about other sequences of numbers. The rule is the very general one: any three numbers in ascending order. So, there are many specific rules all of whose instances are also instances of the experimenter's rule, for example: any three numbers ascending in twos, and any three even numbers in ascending order. Subjects are asked to note down the sequences they ask about and their reasons for doing so. Most subjects ask about sequences that conform to the rule that is their current hypothesis. Furthermore, subjects who announce a rule and are told that it is wrong often continue to produce sequences that conform to it. Wason described this effect as a 'failure to eliminate hypotheses'. Subsequently it has been seen as providing evidence for confirmation bias.

2-4-6 PROBLEM

▧ Statistical Reasoning ▧

People have great difficulty with arguments that depend on statistics or probability (psychology undergraduates learning about statistical hypothesis testing, for example). They also have problems with statistical arguments in everyday life. To take a simple example, many people fail to see that the fact that they have known smokers who have lived to ninety has no tendency to disprove the (statistical) connection between smoking and fatal diseases. A slightly more complex example from the same domain underlines this point. About ten times as many smokers as non-smokers die from lung cancer and about twice as many smokers as non-smokers die from heart disease. Nevertheless, giving up smoking reduces a person's chances of dying from heart disease more than it reduces their chances of dying from lung cancer, because the absolute number of people dying from heart disease is so much larger (in the UK, about 300,000 per year versus about 50,000 per year). As these examples show, STATISTICAL REASONING is often important in deciding how to conduct our everyday lives – whether or not to give up smoking. Our decisions do not, of course, depend on the statistical aspects of the problem alone, but on factors such as how much we value avoiding a premature, and possibly painful, death.

STATISTICAL REASONING

Psychological research on probability focuses on people's estimates of probabilities. These estimates are useful to the extent that they reflect probabilities in the real world. In addition, when the solution to a problem requires the combination of two or more pieces of probabilistic information, we can ask whether people make these combinations in the way the mathematical theory of probability says that they should. If they do not, errors in reasoning will ensue.

Tversky and Kahneman's heuristics

In fact, when people make probabilistic judgements about everyday situations they often make gross errors. To explain these errors, and intuitive statistical judgements in general, Tversky and Kahneman (e.g. 1974) proposed that people use heuristic methods (i.e. experimental, trial-and-error kinds of procedures) for assessing the probabilities of events or of properties that objects might have, and for making inferences from those probabilities. Tversky and Kahneman (1974) described three HEURISTICS: REPRESENTATIVENESS, AVAILABILITY and ANCHORING AND ADJUSTMENT.

HEURISTICS: REPRESENTATIVENESS, AVAILABILITY ANCHORING AND ADJUSTMENT

Representativeness

According to the representativeness heuristic, a person, thing or event will be judged to be a member of a class whose stereotypical members it closely resembles, regardless of other information. So, when people are given a description of someone, and asked whether they are an engineer or a lawyer, they base their judgement on whether the description is typical of what they think lawyers and engineers are like. In applying the representativeness heuristic, people therefore bypass the correct procedure, which takes into account the so-called *prior odds* of someone being a lawyer or an engineer (the *base rate* or relative frequency of those occupations in the relevant population).

The representativeness heuristic can lead to more serious errors of judgement, as the following problem illustrates (Tversky & Kahneman 1982):

> Linda is 31 years old, single, outspoken, and very bright. She majored in philosophy. As a student, she was deeply concerned with issues of discrimination and social justice, and also participated in anti-nuclear demonstrations. Which of the following statements about Linda is more probable? (1) She is a bank teller. (2) She is a bank teller who is active in the feminist movement.

Many undergraduates favoured the second statement. However, since every bank teller who is active in the feminist movement is also a bank teller, the first statement must be at least as probable as the second. Kahneman and Tversky call the error of selecting the second statement the CONJUNCTION FALLACY, since people fail to recognize that everything that is both A *and* B must also be A. The fallacy can be explained by representativeness. Linda is more representative of members of the feminist movement than she is of bank tellers. She is, therefore, more representative of bank tellers active in that movement than of bank tellers in general.

CONJUNCTION FALLACY

Considerations of representativeness can also explain the so-called *gambler's fallacy*, according to which a run of losses 'must be' followed by a run of wins to 'even things up': to make the current sequence of wins and losses more representative of the longer-term pattern. This argument is fallacious because, no matter how long a run of heads a fair coin has produced (for example), the probability of a head on the next toss remains one half.

Availability

According to the second heuristic, availability, the probability of an event, or of an item having a property, is judged by the ease with which instances can be brought to mind – their availability from memory. Availability tends, for example, to make people overestimate the frequency of highly publicized, but comparatively rare, events, such as dying in air crashes. It also explains why people think there are more words beginning with R than with R as the third letter, although the reverse is true. It is much easier to think of words from the letters they begin with – words beginning with R are more available than those with R in third place.

Anchoring and adjustment

Anchoring and adjustment is based on the idea that people often make estimates, of probabilities among other things, by taking an initial value, or anchor, and adjusting it. The anchor affects the final judgement because the adjustments are insufficient. Anchoring and adjustment can best be illustrated by a non-probabilistic example. High school students were asked to estimate, in five seconds, the values of the following products:

$1 \times 2 \times 3 \times 4 \times 5 \times 6 \times 7 \times 8$
$8 \times 7 \times 6 \times 5 \times 4 \times 3 \times 2 \times 1$

The mean estimates were 512 and 2,250, while the correct answer is 40,320. The different estimates for the two series are explained by the fact that, in typical left to right working, the anchor was larger for the second series. Insufficient adjustment explains why underestimates were obtained for both series.

The effect of an anchor on statistical judgements was demonstrated by asking people to estimate the percentage of African nations in the United Nations. Different groups of subjects were given arbitrarily chosen numbers, 10 per cent and

65 per cent, as a starting point. They were asked to say whether these numbers were over- or underestimates and to go on to give what they thought was the proper estimate. The mean estimates for these two groups were 25 per cent and 45 per cent.

Diagnosticity

The best science pits one hypothesis against another. To choose between hypotheses, *diagnostic* evidence is needed – evidence that is more likely given one hypothesis than the other. In determining the DIAGNOSTICITY of evidence, BASE RATES have to be taken into account. There may be more patients with chest infections who cough than patients with lung cancer who cough, but that may be because there are more patients with chest infections overall. The number of patients with the disease who do not cough has to be taken into account in deciding whether coughing is useful in distinguishing the two diseases.

DIAGNOSTICITY
BASE RATES

The idea that people tend to retain an initial (and in the real world, often favoured) hypothesis, together with the idea that people try to confirm rather than disconfirm hypotheses, has been used to explain the phenomenon of PSEUDODIAGNOSTICITY (Doherty et al. 1979; Beyth-Marom & Fischhoff 1983). Imagine that someone is trying to decide between buying a Ford and a Toyota and that their principal considerations are fuel economy and comfort. If they know that 90 per cent of Ford owners consider their cars economical on fuel, which of the following three pieces of information is most useful to them?

PSEUDODIAGNOSTICITY

1. information about how comfortable Ford owners find their cars
2. information about how economical on fuel Toyoto owners find their cars
3. information about how comfortable Toyota owners find their cars

Most subjects chose (1), though this choice is not so popular if the figure of 90 per cent is reduced to 50 per cent. If nine out of ten Ford owners are happy with fuel economy, Fords seem like good cars! But Toyotas might be even better than Fords on fuel economy, so although the 90 per cent seems to be providing diagnostic information, it is not. The information is only *pseudodiagnostic*. If only one other piece of information is allowed, (2) is the only one that, in conjunction with the original information, is diagnostic. Nevertheless, it is not clear that by choosing (1) people are really expecting to find out that Fords are comfortable, too, and hence attempting to confirm the hypothesis that Fords are good cars. If they are satisfied with the 90 per cent rating that Fords get on fuel economy, information about the comfort of Fords may be more useful in helping them decide, either positively or negatively, whether to buy a Ford.

Sample size – the law of large numbers

Kahneman and Tversky (1972) gave people the following problem:

A certain town is served by two hospitals. In the larger hospital about 45 babies are born each day and in the smaller hospital about 15 babies are born each day. As you know, about 50 per cent of all babies are boys. However, the exact percentage varies from day to day. Sometimes it may be higher than 50 per cent sometimes lower. For a period of one year, each hospital recorded the days on which more than 60 per cent of the babies born were boys. Which hospital do you think recorded more such days?

Most undergraduate subjects thought that the number of such days would be about the same in the two hospitals. Of the remainder, about equal numbers chose each of the two hospitals. The correct answer is that the smaller hospital will record more such days, because its 15 babies a day is a smaller sample, and the proportion of male babies in small samples is more variable. It will, of course, also record more days with over 60 per cent female babies. Tversky and Kahneman (1974) argue that this result, like the one in which prior odds were ignored, can be explained by assuming that subjects use the representativeness heuristic, rather than making correct statistical inferences.

Tversky and Kahneman (1971) argue that people, including research psychologists, follow what they call the 'law of small numbers'. That is to say, they take small samples to be more representative of populations than they are. For example, in the hospital problem, they expect the sample of babies born on a particular day in the small hospital to reflect the proportions in the general population of births more closely than it does. Similarly, people underestimate the likelihood of, say, a run of six heads in the tosses of a fair coin. They expect each small 'sample' of tosses to contain about half heads and half tails.

People do not wholly ignore sample size in their reasoning. For example, Nisbett et al. (1983) gave subjects information about some people from an unknown tribe, animals from an unknown species, or lumps of an unknown mineral. They were asked what proportion of the corresponding population they thought had that property. In some cases, such as a metal conducting electricity, subjects generalized to the whole population on the basis of one sample. However, with other properties, such as members of a tribe being obese, estimates of the proportion of the tribe who were obese increased as the number in the sample (all of whom were obese) increased. Where a property is seen as variable – in most countries some people are obese and some are not – the propensity to generalize is (correctly) tempered by sample size. However, Nisbett et al. found that this caution was not always evident in social judgements. People tend to make strong generalizations, even for social characteristics that are highly variable.

Correlation

As with other types of reasoning, reasoning about relations between variables is strongly influenced by real-world knowledge. Jennings et al. (1982) showed that people often expect to perceive correlations, and that their expectations are based

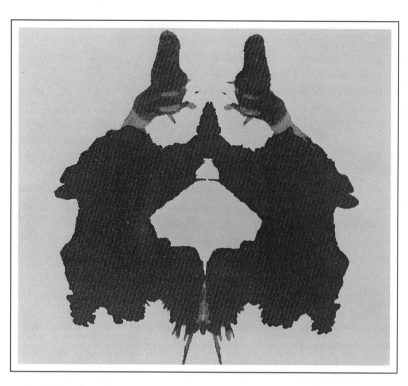

Plate 9.4 Rorschach ink blot

on how they think the world ought to be. For example, they predicted high correlations between students' self-ratings of intellectualism and students' self-ratings of ambitiousness. Indeed, even when presented with data that falsify this assumption, they may still perceive a correlation.

ILLUSORY
CORRELATION

This kind of ILLUSORY CORRELATION had earlier been demonstrated by Chapman and Chapman (1967), who presented subjects with clinical profiles of (fictional) psychiatric patients and figures of people allegedly drawn by them. The data did not, objectively, show a relation between suspiciousness and atypical eyes. However, the folklore of clinical diagnosis overrode the evidence! Chapman and Chapman suggest that these results help to explain why, despite being discredited, tests such as draw-a-person and the Rorschach ink-blot test continue to be used by clinicians. Tversky and Kahneman (1974) suggest that the phenomenon of illusory correlation can be explained by the availability heuristic. Although Chapman and Chapman's subjects did not know about the draw-a-person test, they knew that suspiciousness is readily expressed in the eyes, for example by failure to make direct eye contact. The availability of this everyday folklore is, according to Tversky and Kahneman, what accounts for the illusory correlation.

Problem Solving

According to the Gestalt psychologist Duncker (1945):

> A problem arises when a living organism has a goal, but does not know how this goal is to be reached.

In information-processing terms, this idea implies that a problem has three crucial elements:

1. a starting state;
2. a goal state;
3. a set of processes (usually called 'operators') that can transform one state into another.

The starting state is the state of the 'world' that poses the problem. The goal state is another state of the world in which the problem is solved. In chess, for example, the starting state is the board at the beginning of the game, and the goal (for either player) is any one of a number of winning positions. The processes are things that can be done to the world, in an attempt to move from the starting state to a goal state – in chess, the legal moves.

From a psychological point of view, the problems that are easiest to study are ones in which the starting state, the goal state and the processes can be clearly specified. These include most puzzle-book puzzles, mathematics and physics problems, and games on which psychological research has been carried out. However, many everyday problems are not well specified. People's ability to solve these problems is, therefore, at once more interesting and more difficult to study. Any one of the three elements of a problem may be poorly specified. Someone may feel unhappy, but not be sure what is causing the problem; they may know they have a problem, but not be clear what a solution to the problem would look like; and they may not know what they can do to get from where they are to where they want to be. However, a 'problem' in which all three elements are unclear is in danger of degenerating into a vague sense of unease!

Psychological research on problem solving is divided into research on puzzles (non-adversary problems), and research on game playing (adversary problems).

However, the importance of this distinction lies not so much in the methods used in the research, but in the fact that most research on puzzles has been carried out with novices – expert puzzle-book puzzle solvers are a comparatively rare breed – whereas much of the work on game playing has investigated the way that experts play games such as chess, and how their play differs from that of novices. Since about 1980 this divide has broken down in research on such topics as physics and mathematics problems, and problems of medical diagnosis. This work has focused, on the one hand, on individuals tackling problems

Box 9.2   Some Non-adversary Problems Studied by Psychologists

1. Eight Puzzle: eight movable numbers mixed up in a 3 × 3 matrix. Move them so that they are set out as illustrated below (or in some other specified configuration).

1	2	3
4	5	6
7	8	

2. Missionaries and Cannibals: transport three missionaries and three cannibals across a river, using a boat that can carry only 2 people, and that needs at least one person to get it across the river. There must never be more cannibals than missionaries on either bank, or the missionaries will get eaten.

3. Jug Problems: example – Three jugs, A, B, and C, can hold 8 litres, 5 litres and 3 litres respectively. A is initially full, B and C empty. Find a sequence of pourings that leaves 4 litres in A and 4 litres in B.

4. Tower of Hanoi (figure 9.1): three vertical pegs with 2 (or more) discs of decreasing size piled on one peg. Transfer all the discs to the third peg, moving only one disc at a time, and never placing a larger disc on top of a smaller one.

5. Cryptarithmetic Problems: example:

$$DONALD$$
$$+ \, GERALD$$
$$\overline{}$$
$$= ROBERT$$

Given D = 5 and that each letter stands for a different number between 0 and 9, find the numbers that make the sum correct.

6. Cord around the earth problem: a cord is wrapped around the equator so that it lies on the surface all the way around. It is then made one metre longer. If it is now the same distance above the earth's surface all the way around, how far above the surface is it?

7. A patient has an inoperable tumour. The tumour can be destroyed by radiation. Although weak radiation will not harm normal flesh, radiation strong enough to destroy the tumour will. How would you treat the patient?

8. How can you construct 4 equilateral triangles out of six matches so that each side of each triangle is equal in length to a match?

9. Estimate how much it cost the Prince Regent (later George IV of England) to build Brighton Pavilion (an ornate summer palace, built 1811).

Figure 9.1 The Tower of Hanoi

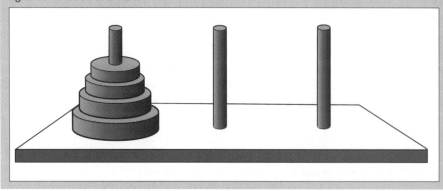

on their own and, on the other hand, on the use of domain-specific knowledge, and on differences between experts and novices.

For reasons that are largely historical, problem solving and reasoning have been treated as distinct research topics. Part of the explanation is that behaviourists, though they eschewed many aspects of the study of thinking, were for the most part happy to study the processes of trial and error that, according to Thorndike, enabled cats to escape from puzzle boxes. More recently an attempt has been made by Newell and Simon, and their colleagues (see especially Newell & Simon 1972) to assimilate other kinds of thinking and, in more ambitious recent versions, other aspects of cognition as well, to problem solving. In their earliest work, Newell and Simon studied theorem proving in the propositional calculus (Newell et al. 1957) and chess playing (Newell et al. 1963). Both theorem proving and chess playing can be thought of as types of problem solving, though theorem proving in propositional calculus sounds suspiciously like deductive reasoning! One of the most important ideas to emerge from this research was that of a *heuristic* procedure for solving problems, which has a good chance of finding a solution quickly, but which is not guaranteed to find one even if one exists. Heuristics are contrasted with ALGORITHMIC METHODS, which will always find a solution, if there is one, but which may be very slow.

ALGORITHMIC
METHODS

Ideas from the 'Logic Theory Machine' and the chess-playing computer programs were incorporated into the 'General Problem Solver'. This program attempted to generalize from the earlier programs and to establish the (heuristic) method of means–end analysis as a general method for solving problems. The ideas underlying this program were highly influential, even though the performance of working versions was not particularly impressive.

Plate 9.5 Garry Kasparov playing chess against a computer
Source: PA News/Neil Munns.

A further important development (Newell & Simon 1972) was the realization that heuristics could be expressed in a uniform way as sets of 'if...then' rules (if certain conditions hold, then perform a certain action – with the notion of action interpreted in a broad sense). Such rules are known as *production*s, and a problem solver or *production system* can, therefore, be built from a set of productions,

together with a CONFLICT-RESOLUTION STRATEGY for deciding what to do when the conditions for more than one production are satisfied.

Newell and Simon proposed that productions are stored in long-term memory, but that their use is *triggere*d by the contents of short-term memory, which are largely determined by the current focus of attention. A production is triggered when its conditions – the *if* part of the rule – are fulfilled. Limitations on short-term memory impose constraints both on how complex the conditions of an individual production can be, and on how many productions can be triggered at once. A further assumption is that the contents of short-term memory are open

THINK-ALOUD
PROTOCOLS

to conscious inspection. This assumption justifies the use of THINK-ALOUD PROTOCOLS, collected by asking people to 'say what is in their mind' as they solve problems.

Problem solving is thought of as a search through a space of possible solutions for an actual solution, and many cognitive processes other than problem solving can be characterized as search processes. Search techniques originally

PRODUCTION
SYSTEMS

developed for problem-solving applications in artificial intelligence research have subsequently been used in the simulation of a range of other cognitive abilities. The general applicability of PRODUCTION SYSTEMS suggests that Newell and Simon's

UNIFIED THEORY OF
COGNITION

views provide the basis for a UNIFIED THEORY OF COGNITION (Newell 1990).

How to solve puzzles

State–action representations

In puzzle-book problems, the starting state, the goal state, and the operators are usually described explicitly. The problem solver can, therefore, think about the problem, and more importantly, about ways of finding a solution to it, in the following way. At any moment, the world is in a particular state, and there are a number of ways in which the state of the world can be altered. A state of the world can be represented in a mental model of the relevant part of the world, and the actions can be represented as ways of getting from one state of the world to another. In any particular state of the world, more than one action is usually possible. The problem solver has to find a sequence of actions that lead from the starting state to one of the goal states – to choose the right action at each choice

STATE–ACTION TREE

point. The complete set of choices can be set out in a diagram called a STATE–ACTION TREE, in which the possible states of the world are represented together with the actions that lead from one state to another.

Figure 9.2 shows the first three levels of a state–action tree for the missionaries and cannibals problem (number 2 in Box 9.2). State–action trees rapidly become very large. For example, if there were three choices at each point, there

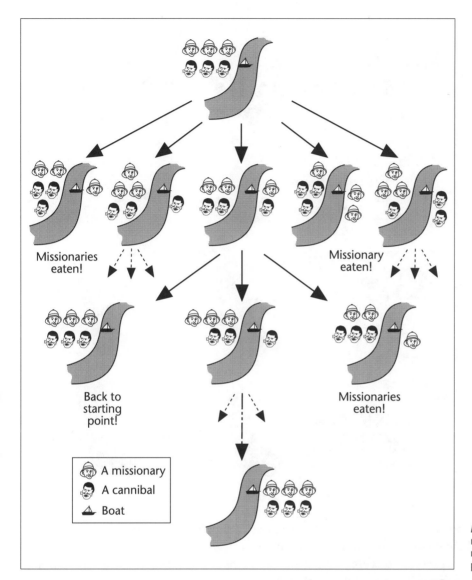

Figure 9.2 State–action representation of the missionaries and cannibals problem

would be three states on the line below the starting state and nine on the second. By the tenth line there would be nearly 60,000 states, and on the twentieth approaching 3,500 million! The missionaries and cannibals problem can be solved in eleven moves (requiring a twelve-level state–action tree, see figure 9.3). In chess, where the number of possibilities for each move is usually larger, and the number of moves in a game greater, the figures are even more astronomical.

People obviously do not solve problems by constructing state–action trees, and looking for solutions in them. They could neither represent enough distinct states (in chess, hugely more than there are neurons, or even atoms, in the brain), nor search through them to find a solution. However, problem solvers may well think in state–action terms – the state–action scheme is both a natural one and an

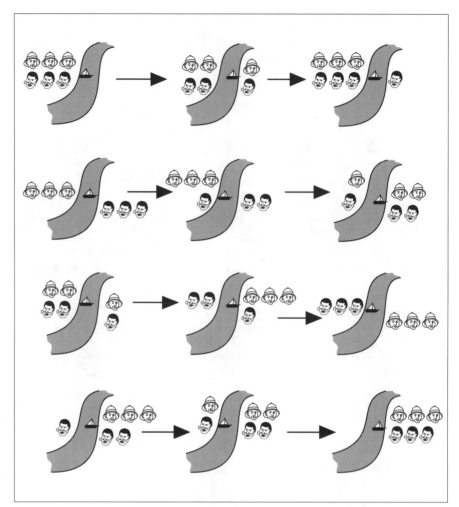

Figure 9.3 Solution to the missionaries and cannibals problem

appealing one. Even if a complete tree cannot be constructed, people may still have to search for solutions to problems.

If problem solvers think about problems in state–action terms, how do they set about finding solutions? A systematic search is a realistic possibility only for those problems that have small state–action trees. Systematic searches can either proceed *depth-first* or *breadth-first*. In a depth-first search, one sequence of moves is considered until a solution is found or until a point is reached where no further move can be made. In breadth-first search, every possibility at each level of the tree is inspected before moving on to the next level. Neither of these two basic schemes provides a plausible account of how people attempt to solve any but the simplest of problems. Hence the need for heuristic, rule-of-thumb, methods to select what one hopes is the best action. Many heuristic methods incorporate the following idea: people like to perform the action that gets them closest to the goal state.

Problem reduction

Given a problem in which the starting state, goal state, and operators are all well-specified, a state–action analysis is always possible. However, thinking about a problem in state–action terms is not necessarily the best way of thinking about it. A different technique, called PROBLEM REDUCTION, uses the method of 'divide and conquer' to reduce one large problem to several smaller ones. These problems are then further subdivided until the subproblems can be solved directly by the operators available.

PROBLEM REDUCTION

Not every problem can be usefully divided into simpler problems, but when a problem can be so divided, the problem-reduction method usually produces a more elegant solution than the state–action method. This is true, for example, with the Tower of Hanoi (number 4 in Box 9.2). A state–action analysis produces a sequence of movements of single discs that solves the problem. Of itself, it identifies no structure in that sequence, though someone using the method might see structure. The problem-reduction method is more insightful, and analyses the problem as shown in figure 9.4.

Empirical research on how naive subjects solve puzzles suggests that, although puzzles such as missionaries and cannibals are typically conceived in state–action terms, people's ability to look ahead through the search tree is severely limited. Indeed, one mathematical model of how people solve such puzzles

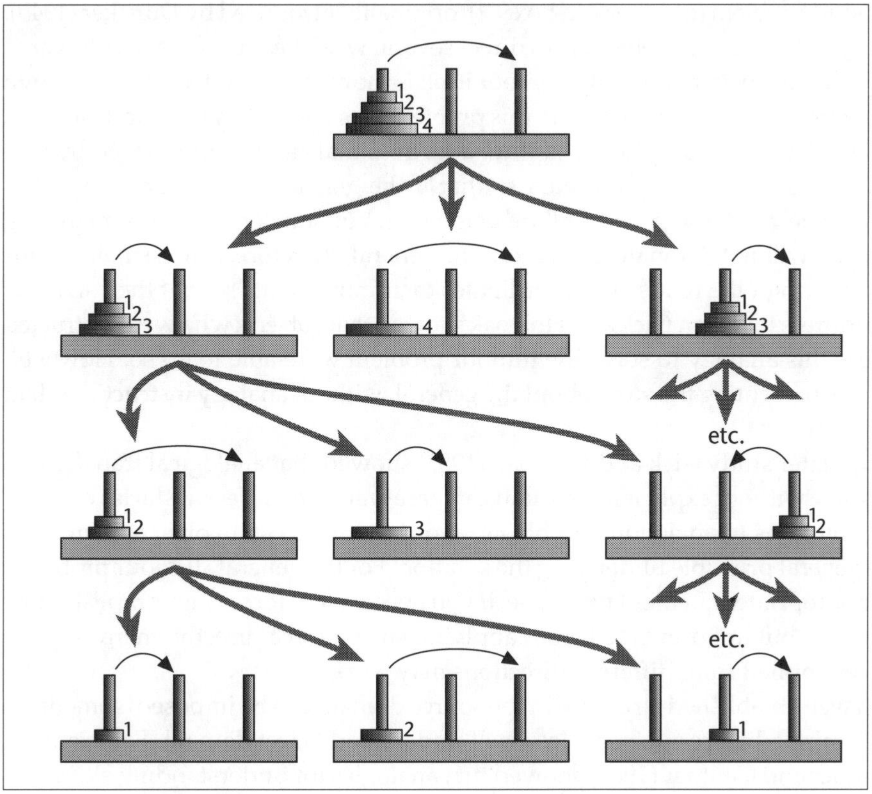

Figure 9.4 Problem-reduction representation of the Tower of Hanoi

(Jeffries et al. 1977) suggests that only the states reachable in one move are considered. The model also proposes that people hold (partial) information in long-term memory about states they have been in, and that they use this information to avoid repeatedly looping through sets of states. With problems that have a straightforward goal-reduction analysis, such as the Tower of Hanoi, people appear to impose this analysis on the problem, perhaps after a period of thinking about it in state–action terms (e.g. Egan & Greeno 1974).

Analogical problem solving

An alternative to searching for sequences of operators that solve a problem is to use the solution of another problem as a pattern. This method requires the establishment of a mapping between the domains from which the problems are drawn – the source (or base) domain and the target domain. There have been many claims about the importance and ubiquity of such ANALOGICAL MAPPINGS, both in everyday thinking and in high-level scientific thinking (in cognitive psychology the analogy between the mind and computer software is particularly important, for example). However, it has been relatively difficult to induce subjects in psychological experiments to make use of analogies to help them solve problems.

A favourite problem in the study of analogical reasoning is the 'inoperable tumour' problem (number 7 in Box 9.2), originally introduced by Duncker (1945). One solution to the problem is to direct several weak beams of the rays towards the tumour, so that only at the tumour itself is the combined effect strong enough to destroy tissue. An analogue to this problem was devised by Gick and Holyoak (1980). A general is trying to capture a fortress that can be approached by several roads. The roads are mined so that if the general's whole army marches down one road, the mines will be detonated, but smaller groups of marching soldiers will not detonate the mines. The general, therefore, sends small groups down each of the roads, and coordinates their movements so that they arrive at the fortress together. Gick and Holyoak showed that subjects who were instructed to use this analogy to solve the tumour problem were able to do so. However, simply presenting the story about the general, without analogy instructions, had no effect.

In a later study Gick and Holyoak (1983) showed that analogical transfer was possible without explicit instructions, if there were two different stories containing solutions to analogous problems, and if there was an explicit statement of the general principle underlying the solution. For the general/tumour problems an appropriate statement would be: if you need a large force to accomplish some purpose, but are prevented from applying such a force directly, many smaller forces applied from different directions may work just as well.

A well-established structure in the source domain can be imposed, sometimes with misleading results, on a less well-understood target domain. For example, Gentner and Gentner (1983) showed that analogies for understanding electricity

– based on water flowing in pipes, and on people teeming through turnstiles – produced different results when subjects had to reason about the operation of electric circuits. The effects of combining batteries in different ways were best understood on the water analogy. Separate batteries could be modelled by separate sources of water pressure, whereas the crowd analogy provides no satisfactory equivalent for batteries. Combinations of resistors were best understood on the turnstile analogy, in which the turnstiles themselves correspond to the resistors. The constricted pipes of the water-flow analogy do not model the properties of resistors so well.

Game Playing

In chess, the players take turns and each must take account of the likely moves of the other. Although each player is trying to win, the immediate problem is: which move shall I make now? To make a rational decision, players must evaluate the available moves. However, moves are not assessed in terms of the position they create immediately, but in terms of the positions that they will lead to a few moves ahead. Furthermore, most moves are not followed up. They are assumed to be worse that those that are.

Chess playing can be analysed using the state–action method. The states are board positions, and the actions are legal chess moves. The simplest method, conceptually, of choosing a move would be to consider all possible developments for a fixed number of moves. However, this technique is problematic for two main reasons. First, without a very powerful computer – which the top computer chess programmers have – it is not possible to look far enough ahead for the technique to produce good play: short-sightedness does not make for good chess. Supercomputers can play grandmaster level chess by following up each possibility for five moves on each side. Second, human chess players neither follow up every possibility, nor follow up possibilities for fixed numbers of moves. They follow developments through to so-called 'quiet positions', at which they hope to make a further in-depth assessment of the way they want the game to go.

The technique for mechanically choosing a move in a game of chess is known as MINIMAXINg. In the state–action representation of chess, the alternate layers correspond to moves by white and black. If a program views the chess from white's perspective, on its moves it will try to maximize its benefit. It must assume, however, that black will play rationally and, on its moves, try to maximize its own benefit. Since what is good for one player is bad for the other, anything that maximizes black's benefit minimizes white's. When white picks a move, it must therefore ensure that it MINImizes the MAXimum loss that black can inflict upon it – hence minimax.

MINIMAXING

▒ Expertise ▒

The principle of division of labour applies to thinking as well as to manual work. Indeed, there are many parallels between mental skills and other skills. For example, to reach a high degree of proficiency can take a long time – mental skills, like manual skills, can take many years to develop.

Expert performance

If certain kinds of problem solving are knowledge-based, having the right knowledge is crucial. However, people who are good at problem solving of this kind do not simply have additional factual knowledge. One way to find out what differentiates them from people who do not have the requisite knowledge is to compare experts and novices. Research of this kind was initially inspired by the work of de Groot (1965), who compared expert and novice chess players.

De Groot found that human chess players consider only a few developments of the game, unlike computer chess programs that may consider hundreds of thousands. From a psychological point of view, this finding is not surprising, given our knowledge about limitations on short-term memory. More surprising, perhaps, was de Groot's finding that excellent players (at the grandmaster level) do not follow up any more moves than good tournament players. They do, however, follow up better moves (as rated by other players), and they assess moves more quickly.

De Groot also studied short-term memory for chess positions. Players were shown board positions briefly and then asked to reconstruct them. Better players did so more accurately. In a more systematic study, Chase and Simon (1973) showed that highly skilled and less skilled players both performed poorly in remembering random configurations of chess pieces. They proposed that the difference between chess players of different levels was in the amount of information stored in long-term memory – in the form of board positions. They further proposed that moves are chosen on the basis of similarities between the current board position and positions stored in memory, and that searching ahead through possible developments is relatively unimportant. Chase and Simon suggested that a grandmaster might have 50,000 'chunks' of information in long-term memory, each encoding a significant grouping of pieces.

EXPERTISE This idea is consistent with the fact that EXPERTISE in chess is attained in large part by studying the games of other players. It also helps to explain why the attainment of grandmaster status requires about ten years of dedicated practice.

Experts know more than novices, but they do not simply have more information in long-term memory. Their knowledge is organized differently from that of novices, and it enables them to encode new information more efficiently. Research on textbook physics problem solving illustrates these ideas. Larkin (1979) showed that when physics students tried to solve problems, potentially relevant equations tended to come to mind one at a time, whereas professional physicists retrieved equations in related groups. More importantly, Larkin (1983) showed that novices' representations of a problem were *naive*, drawing on everyday concepts instead of the specialized concepts of physics. Indeed, the naive representations were often inappropriate and failed to lead to a solution to the problem. Naive representations are often based on superficial aspects of a problem. Chi et al. (1981) showed that, when asked to sort problems into groups, novices relied on such superficial features as whether the problem was about an inclined plane, whereas experts classified the problems according to the physical principles that were relevant to their solution.

Becoming an expert

The 'ten-year rule' suggests that about ten years of sustained practice is necessary to achieve world-class performance at a recognized skill. This idea is not inconsistent with the existence of innate abilities. It suggests, however, that having such an ability is, by itself, far from sufficient for skilled performance. Furthermore, as Howe (1990) points out, many reports of child prodigies are likely to be exaggerated, or to omit details of early training, thus creating the impression that the prodigious performance appeared 'from nowhere'. Howe argues that people such as H. G. Wells and Bernard Shaw have, for personal reasons,

Plate 9.6 Boy learning violin
Source Andes Press Agency.

exaggerated the poverty of their early years. Properly documented cases of child prodigies, for example the nineteenth-century British philosopher John Stuart Mill, almost always reveal parental encouragement, and sometimes extreme pressure, to do well.

Howe argues that, in addition to parental pressure, temperamental differences explain the acquisition of expertise. Those children who are prepared to stick at the tasks that they or their parents set are those most likely to succeed. The overwhelming importance of practice in skill acquisition is also stressed by Ericsson (e.g. 1990). Furthermore, since practice is specific to a particular skill, its effects do not transfer. Hence, a highly skilled pianist will not necessarily be skilled even on other musical instruments. Howe argues that the separability of skills

IDIOT SAVANTS

is further emphasized by the existence of so-called IDIOT SAVANTS. He also suggests a motivational explanation for the fact that moderate levels of different skills often go together. For example, a child who is motivated to do well in mathematics is likely to be motivated in English, too. On this view, there is no need to postulate an intrinsic link between the two abilities, such as general intelligence.

CHAPTER SUMMARY

1 People are good at reasoning about specific situations in everyday life, for example when they make decisions about buying and selling. They are not so successful at thinking in the abstract about issues such as education policy.

2 Deductive reasoning is reasoning from facts that one knows or supposes to be true, to other facts that follow with certainty from them. Except in the simplest cases, such as three-term series problems, people frequently make mistakes in deductive reasoning.

3 The mental models theory provides a detailed account of both the mental mechanisms underlying deductive reasoning and the way that mistakes arise (for example, from working memory overload). It also tries to account for other kinds of reasoning.

4 Unlike deductive reasoning, inductive reasoning goes 'beyond the information given' and can never

lead to certain conclusions. Inductions can be specific, for example when they provide explanations for things that happen (such as the failure of a hair dryer to work), or they can be general.

5 Since, the conclusions of inductive reasoning are uncertain, they can be thought of as hypotheses to be tested.

6 People are not very efficient at testing factual hypotheses, and fail badly on apparently simple tasks such as the selection task, the THOG problem and the 2-4-6 problem. They are much better at assessing whether situations conform or fail to conform to social rules granting permissions or imposing obligations.

7 Statistical reasoning is very difficult. People use heuristics (rules of thumb) such as representativeness, availability and anchoring and adjustment both to estimate probabilities and to make inferences from them.

8 Problems are often hard to solve because there are so many possible solutions. Two ways of thinking about how to find a solution are the state–action method and the problem-reduction method. The state–action method is more general, but must be supplemented by heuristic methods that attempt to home in on a solution.

9 An alternative method of attempting to solve a problem is by the use of analogy.

10 Experts, who make it their job to tackle difficult problems, bring a large amount of domain-specific background knowledge to bear on the problems they work on. In a complex domain, it takes about ten years to acquire this knowledge.

Further Work

1. Do the findings from psychological studies of everyday reasoning have implications for educational practice?
2. What can be learnt about how people normally reason from studying how they solve artificial problems such as syllogisms?
3. To what extent do studies of reasoning support the idea that people prefer not to think out solutions but to remember solutions to similar problems?
4. If people are so bad at abstract reasoning, how did they invent logic, science and mathematics?

Further Reading

Garnham, A. and Oakhill, J. (1994) *Thinking and Reasoning*. Oxford: Blackwell.

A much fuller discussion of the topics covered in this chapter.

Evans, J. St B. T., Newstead, S. E. and Byrne, R. M. J. (1993) *Human Reasoning: The Psychology of Deduction*. Hove, East Sussex: Lawrence Erlbaum Associates.

A more detailed account of research on deductive reasoning and hypothesis testing.

Kahney, H. (1993; 2nd edn) *Problem Solving: Current Issues*. Buckingham: Open University Press.

A readable introduction to problem solving.

CHAPTER 10

Language

Peter Scott

CHAPTER AGENDA

- This chapter aims to sketch out what human language is and how it works as a psychological mechanism. The first half of the chapter outlines some competence aspects of human language: those key descriptive features which capture what it is and does. The second half of the chapter focuses on performance aspects of language: how it works as a mechanism of the human mind.

- The first core competence to discuss is the relationship of language and thought. Is our language behaviour an expression of our thinking, or is our thought moulded by, or even created by, our use of language?

- Do animals other than humans have a system that we could call language? What features make human language different from, and similar to, animal communication systems?

- We look at how human language varies among different human societies and consider the features that all human languages share.

- We note that language can be studied at a number of different levels. At a low level, you are here, 'reading' just a bunch of marks on paper, and when you listen to a conversation you hear a stream of sound. At a higher level, you can pick out characters (or sounds) that go together to make up identifiable words. Then you can identify clumps of words that belong together to make phrases, sentences, paragraphs, even stories.

- In the performance part of the chapter, we focus upon the sentence level within this analysis and pick out two sets of models to examine in some detail. Both of these kinds of models aim to help us to understand how natural language might actually work as a mental mechanism. The first set of models emphasize the role of language syntax, the second set emphasize the role of semantics.

- Finally, we raise some important issues beyond the simple models presented. Language works because it is a cooperative act. We adhere to, or deliberately break, a set of maxims that are essential to make our communication work.

▒ Introduction ▒

Human language is amazing. It is one of the first things one would point to as evidence of human intelligence. From a cultural point of view it enables us to pass complex knowledge about the world down through generations directly, rather than indirectly via our genes. Once one human has learned a simple rule, like 'if you want to avoid detection by an animal with a keen sense of smell then you should stay down-wind', or complex behaviours, like 'if you take these seeds and plant them, water them and protect them over a few months they will grow into something tasty', they can communicate this rule to their language community directly and ensure that it is passed directly into subsequent generations. Communicating knowledge through generations via other means does happen. For instance, as we saw in chapter 4, evolution is itself a powerful communication mechanism, in passing genes on through future generations, but this sort of genetic communication of information is a very slow medium.

For humans, language is an essential part of the social act of communication. Social communication also involves non-verbal communication like proxemics, eye-gaze, paralinguistics, accent and appearance (for the detail on these see chapter 12). The clothes you are wearing, the way you stand, all these things communicate things about you to other humans. But few of these things are deliberately manipulated (do you know what information someone may take from your accent, or the colour of your clothes?) In language we can control (to some extent) the message we transmit.

In this chapter we first attempt to characterize what language is and what is its relationship with thinking; and then look at the possibility of language in other places in the animal kingdom. We will also seek to consider features which are universal across all languages and cultures. Finally, we will explore some models of language that seek to explain this powerful feature of human cognition.

What is Language?

Natural language (NL) is a productive but regular system of communication. Its productivity means that it can be creatively used to generate sentences that have never before been generated. This also means that it can produce an infinite number of sentences. Language is regular in that sentences evidence a clear structure by which they can be judged. Infinite power does not mean infinite variety, for only certain sentences are permitted. Because of these features, a key assumption behind the study of language is that it is a rule-governed behaviour. We do not refer here to the prescriptive rules of style by which many cultures seek to bind their language learners ('do not split infinitives', 'don't say ain't, say isn't') but rather to descriptive rules about what languages do and do not.

Competence versus performance

The process of scientific discovery seems to move from descriptive types of theories (e.g. the Gas Laws – this is what gases do) towards explanatory types of theories (e.g. molecular laws – molecules bang into each other). It seems plausible that we need to have a firmly established description of what appears to be going on before we can move on to compare different mechanisms that might explain how it goes on. So in NL research we also tend to start with formal theories in which we try to describe the nature of language. These descriptive formal theories tend to arise from linguistics. In examining a descriptive theory, a linguist can judge the quality of that theory by how well it describes what a language does and does not appear do. For a psychologist, a theory must explain how some sort of psychological mechanism actually does it. So you find psychologists examining the work of linguists (and more recently computer scientists), looking for features of their work that could be psychologically real – i.e. features which could be supported by some psychological mechanism.

COMPETENCE

PERFORMANCE

The linguist Noam Chomsky described these different sorts of theories as competence and performance theories. COMPETENCE is the abstract knowledge about the phenomenon – in this case language – the description of what it is and does. PERFORMANCE is the actual use of language and how it works. It might be easier to understand the distinction if you think of them as Description versus Explanation, or perhaps Theory versus Mechanism. To understand the progress we have made in trying to understand language you must understand that some theories primarily address competence issues whilst some primarily address performance issues. In the sections that follow we will try first to establish some of the basic competences of language before going on to look at models which have been proposed for both language competences and its performance.

Language is diverse

Natural language consists of a finite number of constituents which can be used in an infinite number of ways. In English there are:

- 26 letters in the alphabet,
- 40 or so phonemes (basic units of sound),
- 100,000 words – changing all the time.

Most linguists will tell you that there are some 4,000 to 5,000 languages in use in the world at the moment, although estimates can vary from between 3,000 and 10,000. They are difficult to count because more are being discovered all the time. In the same way, there is some argument about whether some are 'dead' languages or just 'dialects' of other languages.

No human culture has ever been discovered without a spoken means of communication that we can readily recognize as a language (many do not have a non-spoken form, such as writing). Furthermore, it is possible to translate from any human language to any other. The difficulty of this translation is attested to by the enormous translation budgets of political organizations like the United Nations and the European Union, but that these organizations can function at all is a testament to the commonality of a human language system. It is worth noting here that despite this diversity, much of the research that we shall discuss below arises from work in a very few languages, particularly English. And it is a major assumption of this work that its findings are true of other languages as well.

▨ Language and Thought ▨

'We only know just what we have meant to say after we have said it.'

Joseph Joubert (1754–1824)

One critical question that we must ask is: what is the relationship between thought and language?

Linguistic determinism and relativity

The hypothesis that language determines thought (linguistic determinism), and that different languages will therefore encode different thoughts (linguistic relativity), is primarily associated with Benjamin Whorf (1940; see Carroll 1956), but is also associated with the earlier work of his teacher Edward Sapir (Sapir 1921), and so is usually referred to as the SAPIR–WHORF HYPOTHESIS. There are, however, a number of different versions of this hypothesis. The 'stronger' versions focus on linguistic determinism, the 'weaker' on linguistic relativity.

SAPIR–WHORF HYPOTHESIS

The most extreme version of the LINGUISTIC DETERMINISM hypothesis is that not just language but more specifically 'speech' determines thought. This was most clearly expressed in the work of behaviourists like Watson (1924) and Skinner (1957). As we have seen elsewhere, behaviourists thought it most unsatisfactory to theorize about such intangibles as 'thought' and 'mind'. They sought to ground all psychological phenomena in observable behaviour.

LINGUISTIC DETERMINISM

> The behaviourist advances the view that what psychologists have hitherto called thought is in short nothing but talking to ourselves. (Watson 1924: 238)

They therefore theorized that the overt behaviour of speech must be the origin and controller of the covert behaviour we experience as thought. Someone who can think covertly without speaking overtly must have learnt to hide all of the muscular and motor activities of 'normal' speech. A less extreme version of this view is that it is the symbolic behaviour of language which is internalized as thought, if not speech activity itself. This sort of view is that expressed in the work of the Soviet psychologist Vygotsky who described thinking as some form of 'inner speech':

> thought is not merely expressed in words; it comes into existence through them. (Vygotsky 1934: 125)

For both of these 'strong' versions of the hypothesis there are a number of clear objections. There is plenty of developmental evidence to indicate that children understand language well before they themselves can produce it. There are clear cases of children who have serious language handicaps who patently can still think and act intelligently. There are ample cases of deaf people with no apparent learnt language system who still appear to think. The most striking and oft-cited argument against all aspects of the behaviourist view of language behaviour was produced by Noam Chomsky (1959). Chomsky convincingly demonstrated that a description of language in terms of the observable behaviour of language was hopelessly inadequate, and failed to account for the most interesting features of language, such as its creativity.

The 'weakest' version of the Sapir–Whorf hypothesis would be that while language may not determine thought it must at least influence it. This is referred to as LINGUISTIC RELATIVITY. This would most clearly be seen in the different thoughts that must arise from the world's very different languages.

LINGUISTIC
RELATIVITY

Do our words affect our perception?

The most frequently cited example offered by Whorf in support of relativity is the word 'snow'. In English we have essentially one word for it, while Eskimos have several, perhaps a dozen (Pullum 1991). In Aztec the word which covers snow also encompasses a variety of associated 'cold things' like ice. Does this mean that the Eskimo, English and Aztec speakers somehow 'see' snow differently from each other? At one level snow clearly 'means' something rather different to someone surrounded by the stuff regularly as the Eskimo, or rarely as the Aztec. The importance of phenomena to you will naturally be reflected in your vocabulary. Indeed, English speakers like sport skiers have brought so many extra words for snow into the language (like 'powder') that we are probably not that far off the Eskimo total. But does your vocabulary shape the thoughts you can have about the snow or vice versa?

> He had read somewhere that . . . they would distinguish between thin snow and thick snow, light snow and heavy snow, sludgy snow, brittle snow, snow that came in flurries, snow that came in drifts, snow that came in on the bottom of your neighbour's boots all over your nice clean igloo floor, the snows of winter, the snows of spring, the snows you remember from your childhood that were so much better than any of your modern snow . . . and snow that despite all of your efforts to train them, the huskies have pissed on. (Douglas Adams 1984: 13)

Linguistic relativity and colour words

Most work at the lexical level has been done on colour. The world's languages can have very different ways of representing colour. In a cross-linguistic survey Berlin and Kay (1969) found that all languages seem to have a small set of 'basic' colour terms and that these terms are arranged in a clear hierarchy. All languages have at least two identifiable colour terms. This hierarchy should be read from left to right. If the language concerned has only two colour terms these will

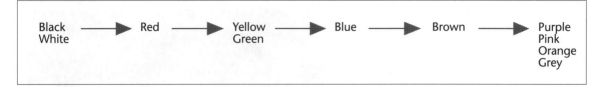

distinguish between black (and darker colours) and white (and lighter colours). If only three colour terms are used then these will be black, white and red. If four, then it will be these three plus yellow or green. If five then it includes both yellow and green, and so on.

English uses all of these terms, whilst the Dani people of New Guinea use only the first two for distinguishing between darker and lighter colours. A very striking feature of a universal hierarchy of this sort is that its universality is a good indication that all humans must at some basic level 'understand' their perception of colour in the same way. In a very well-known set of studies Elanor Rosch (1974) investigated the colour perception of Dani and English speakers and found no difference in the Dani perception of colour and that of her US subjects. However, there has been a recent critique of the technique used by Rosch, and some work by Kay and Kempton (1984) indicating that our perception of colour is indeed somewhat dependent on the words we have for them.

Is language unique to humans?

Many animals use signs and signals to communicate with others. Some of these behaviours are very complex, such as in courtship rituals, and some are simple, as when a dog barks, pants, snarls and bares its teeth. While this communication may be very effective, what parts of this behaviour are communication-like-language and which not? When a traffic light turns red we may consider it to be communicating 'stop' to us, but would be unlikely to accuse it of having a language system. Some animals clearly use signals in the wild which communicate effectively. Amongst the primates Cheyney and Seyfarth (1982, 1985) reported that vervet monkeys in Africa used clearly distinct calls to warn of different threats. Guard monkeys would 'chutter' to indicate a snake threat, causing other monkeys to look around them at ground level. They would make a 'kraup' noise to indicate an aerial threat such as an eagle, causing others to scan the sky. Or they would 'chirp' to warn of animals like leopards, causing the troop to take to the trees. Even in the insect kingdom, we can find very effective communicative signals. The honey-bee dance is a very impressive communicative system. The tail-waggling dance is a common example: the bee moves in a straight line (in the direction of the food), waggling its abdomen, and circles back to the start of its line, usually alternately turning to the left and to the right. Other bees in the hive can extract from this performance the precise location of the food source.

So how can we start to compare these communication systems with what in humans we call language? Charles Hockett (1960) proposed a set of 13 features

Plate 10.1 Vervet monkeys on guard
Source: Natural Science Photos/© Pete Oxford

by which human spoken language could be contrasted with animal communication systems. These features are characteristics of spoken human language which animal communications do not all share. Here we list five of the features which he identified:

1. *Discreteness of Units*. Language has units such as words that are clearly separate from each other. When a dog barks the vocalizations are quite discrete.
2. *Semanticity of Units*. Linguistic units used are designed to convey meaning by being associated with something in the world. A dog 'panting' is not a 'signal' according to Hockett, as the response is a biological one to lose heat rather than a communicative act about being hot. On the other hand, a dog's barking is a signal that may have a communicative function, but it is not easy to relate to some specific thing in the world. What does any individual bark mean? 'I am unhappy, excited, lonely, angry, afraid . . . '?
3. *Arbitrariness of Units*. The units themselves are not directly related to that thing. When we use a word like 'elephant' the word, its shape, sound and so on have no direct relationship to a large grey mammal with a trunk. When a

Plate 10.2 Lassie (with Roddie McDowall). In the script, Lassie's bark carried a great deal of meaning
Source: Kobal Collection/MGM

dog bares its teeth and snarls the signal is not arbitrary as it is directly related to a threat to use the teeth in biting.

4. *Displacement.* The units in language can be used in the absence of the thing which they refer to. We can talk about elephants and snakes without any being nearby in space or time, but it would be hard to interpret a dog snarling as relating to some aggression it felt yesterday.

5. *Productivity.* The human language system can combine its units in infinitely different ways to produce new utterances. The range of potentially meaningful signs that a dog can produce is quite limited.

Interestingly, Cheyney and Seyfarth's monkeys did respond very intelligently to the signals made, in that they were observed to respond quickly to signals issued by adults, but to double-check first any signals made by juvenile monkeys before responding. Their signals also seem discrete and arbitrary, although the warnings would not be very effective if they were displaced!

Measured by this set of features the bee dance is one of the more sophisticated animal communication systems that we know of. It is reliably semantically related to a source of food, it can productively indicate any location of a source of food, and is certainly displaced from it. However, the dance is not arbitrary in a number of respects: the speed of the dance is directly related to distance from the food source; and the orientation of the dance to the direction of the food source. Neither are the units really discrete, in that the dance is continuous with a number of distinct features.

The ape studies

Failing to find a natural communication system that appears to be a language in the human sense, some researchers have tried to teach linguistic behaviour to animals. The most striking attempts are in the primate world, our nearest neighbours in a genetic sense. The earliest projects sought to get apes to speak, and failed miserably. No other animals, including our close relatives like chimpanzees, have the palate or basic vocal machinery to reproduce the same sounds that humans use for language. Indeed even the impressive mimicry of birds like parrots and mina birds is made without the machinery we use. The mina uses a sophisticated double-valved whistle that enables it to modulate two tones independently and thereby fool us into detecting discrete words in the warbling stream.

If they don't have the vocal machinery to speak, perhaps they still have the mental machinery to use some other symbolic medium for language. Basically, there have been two sorts of attempts to teach apes such a system: one has involved the use of sign language; the other has been to invent a new 'written' form of language for the apes to manipulate.

The best-known sign language study involved the female chimp Washoe (Gardner & Gardner 1969, 1975), who was taught the American Sign Language AMESLAN. Her training began in 1966 when she was just under a year old and in about four years she had acquired over 130 signs. Under 'double-blind' conditions (controlling for an experimenter knowing what she was supposed to be saying) she did 72 per cent accurate signing. In addition she was observed to produce some of the signs as short sequences which resembled the early stages in human language development, for example 'time drink', 'good me'. Another famous chimp, Lucy (Fouts & Mellgren 1976), is credited with putting words together to describe a new concept, for which she had no sign. Confronted with a watermelon, Lucy produced these two sequences to describe this new food, 'fruit drink' and 'candy drink'.

However, given the mass of signs generated by these apes, the anecdotes of a few sequences which would be judged by us as grammatical is pretty unconvincing. Even if the symbols they had learned were being generated at random – and they are clearly not as they are meaningfully associated with the world perceived by the chimp – we would expect some proportion of 'interesting'

Plate 10.3 Ape studies/ psychologist using sign language to communicate with a chimpanzee
Source: Magnum/Paul Fusco

sequences. Terrace (1980) trained the chimp Nim Chimpsky (a jest at the expense of Noam Chomsky) and was very critical of the paucity of syntax that Nim developed. He noted that Nim's best 'mean length of utterance' (MLU) was about 1.5 (basically one or two words per 'sentence'). Experiments which sought to provide apes with a new symbolic language more suited to their manipulative skills found very similar results. Sarah (Premack & Premack 1972) used plastic symbols which she placed on a magnetic board. Sarah was capable of complex problem solving including conditionals (such as if–then, same/different). But again there was very poor evidence of syntactic development or convincing word ordering. The most obvious critique of this research offered by critics like Chomsky is that apes having the ability to use language and not using that ability is rather like having the ability to fly and not doing it! In summary, then, it is evident that apes can learn to associate symbols with meanings, but there is little good evidence to suggest that this is a linguistic ability *per se*.

▓ Language Universals and Primitives ▓

In attempting to find the key features of human languages linguists have sought to characterize all of the languages of the world. From these classifications they hope to find features which are universal to all human languages. We have already noted a few of these. We have noted that colour words present a universal hierarchy to humans. And Hockett's list of features was explicitly designed to characterize things which are true of all human languages.

Another characterization is to look at the favourite word order in languages.

The simplest forms in most languages are described by linguists as SAAD sentences (meaning SIMPLE AFFIRMATIVE ACTIVE DECLARATIVES). 'Simple' in this linguistic jargon is fairly self-evident and contrasts with complex sentences that can have many simple sentences combined together. Any sentences containing words like 'and' and 'or' are complex because these little words help us to combine simple sentences together. 'Affirmative' means that the sentence is saying that something is true, contrasting with a 'negative'. For example, the affirmative 'Jack loves Jill' is assumed to be linguistically simpler than its negative counterpart 'Jack does not love Jill'. 'Active' is a linguistic form in which somone/thing is doing something. This can be contrasted with the 'passive' in which the thing is being done to them. So, for example, the active 'Jack loves Jill' is considered simpler than its passive counterpart 'Jill is loved by Jack'. 'Declarative' refers to the sentence making a declaration about something as compared to, for example, an 'interrogative' which questions something. So the declarative 'Jack loves Jill' is considered simpler than an interrogative like 'Does Jack love Jill?'

Linguists look at these SAAD sentences to see how those languages treat the order of the Subject (S), the Object (O) and the Verb (V). Essentially, the subject of the sentence is the 'doer' of some action, the object is the 'done-to' of the action, and the verb is usually the action itself. So in an example sentence:

the man bit the dog

The chunk with 'the man' is considered to be the logical subject, the verb is 'bit', and the logical object is 'the dog'. Languages such as English and French are described as SVO languages because the most common or favourite order (a.k.a. canonical order) for simple sentences is Subject–Verb–Object. Languages like Japanese and Korean are more typically SOV. So while in English one may typically say

I am English

the Japanese equivalent would be

I Japanese am (*Watahi wa nihonjin desu*)

In a large survey Ultan (1969) classified the world's languages using the 6 possible word orderings (see table 10.1). It is important to note that, while object-first languages are clearly so rare that they are closer to 0 per cent than 1 per cent, a few of each have been found. A small group of Amazonian languages, for exam-

Table 10.1

SOV 44%	VOS 2%
SVO 35%	OVS 0%
VSO 19%	OSV 0%

ple, appear to favour an OVS structure. Also, it is quite difficult to be entirely sure of the 'favourite' order for 'simple' sentences. While SOV seems to be the most common simple order in Japanese, OSV is also quite a common Japanese construction.

The most important thing to note from this survey is that the subject almost always precedes the object in the vast majority of the world's languages.

There are a number of other syntactic universals which accompany these findings. Many different lexical categories are tied to the canonical order. For example, where English in SVO has prepositions that come before nouns – we say '. . . in Japan' – SOV languages like Japanese treat these as postpositions – they say 'Japan in' (*Nihon ni*).

All languages permit one utterance to be embedded into another, and embedding to the right is acceptable in all languages. For example,

(John said (Frank thinks (I'm a fool)))

Plate 10.4 Yoda in *The Empire Strikes Back* is made to sound alien as an OSV speaker ('sick I have become', 'your father he is'). Source: Kobal Collection/ Lucas Film/20th Century Fox.

Many languages, like Japanese, can also left embed. However, all languages have a low limit to centre embedding.

(the man (who the woman (who I like) married) keeps bees)

Think about it. It is all right, but quite hard to work out.

TOPICALIZATION

All languages show a feature referred to as TOPICALIZATION, in which certain sorts of phrases which are 'normally' expected to be buried deep within an utterance may be brought to the front (and made more topical).

For example, while the sentence is 'normally' expected to be:

I find that suggestion totally revolting.

its topicalized form becomes:

That suggestion I find totally revolting.

Even Japanese does this in exactly the same way, despite its radically different SOV structure.

Many of the sorts of explanations for the above universals are framed in terms of the universal function of language to communicate, associated with general limitations on memory and the capacities of the cognitive system (see e.g. Clark & Clark 1977). So embedding functions to more effectively express a complex relationship between each of the utterances that are merged together. And the limit on centre embedding is probably related to short-term memory storage problems. Topicalization is possibly related to a universal function of bringing an important topic to the front and thereby into greater focus.

Pidgins and creoles

The obvious question to ask in seeking universals of language is if there is in the world a language that is more 'primitive' than any of the others. The answer seems to be that there is no 'natural' human language that seems to be missing any of the major linguistic features we find in all human languages. However, there are some non-natural languages which are more primitive. These languages

PIDGINS

are the 'created' trading languages known as PIDGINS. When two or more cultures settle down together for some reason such as in trade with each other – often, for example, in the encounter of colonial and native cultures – then it is common for an 'artificially' stripped-down version of the dominant tongue to take on features and vocabulary from the other language or languages and become an established means of communication.

Much is lost in the artificial pidgin language. For instance, pidgins don't have subordinate clauses – the result of the embedding we saw was a natural universal above. So the relative clause 'this is the man who I love' and the complement clause 'I think that I love him' are very much harder to express. Indeed many things become unwieldy in the pidgin. For example, it seems very hard to do things like 'displacement' (speaking of something removed, as discussed above).

The anthropologist Margaret Mead in New Guinea in the 1920s extensively studied the language Tok Pisin (literally, 'talk pidgin'). The following is a Tok Pisin extract from a court transcript of that time which illustrates the difficulty of expressing complex ideas in the language:

> Now me sell em along one fellow man, he man belong one fellow sister belong me fellow, all right. This fellow man he sell him along one fellow man, he belong Patusi, he like marry him one fello pickaninny marry belong em. He no pickaninny tru belong em, thats all, he help em papa belong this fellow marry. All right . . .

This excerpt is attempting to convey some relatively complex concepts and would be hard to understand even for practised pidgin speakers. But, according to Mead (cited in Slobin 1979: 72), the translation would run as follows:

> Now I gave the pig to a man who is my sister's husband. This man gave the pig to a man in Patusi who wanted to marry a daughter of his. She was not his own daughter, but he worked with her father . . .

The English translation is clearer to us because it can use a number of linguistic devices which we use readily, but which appear to be unavailable to the pidgin speaker.

A very striking feature is what happens when the pidgin language becomes the native language of the speech community as the 'mother tongue' of the children. As soon as a pidgin is learned as a native tongue it changes! It soon acquires the full range of linguistic devices missing from the primitive pidgin, including inflections, pronouns, subordinate clauses, and so forth. This new language is described as a CREOLE. If we look at the uses of 'all right' and 'thats all' in the above pidgin court transcript we can see that they may be acting as primitive clause-boundary markers.

CREOLE

Slobin relates this example of the same language discussed above, Tok Pisin, from the 1970s.

> na pik ia ol ikilim bipo ia bia ikampa olsem draipela ston

Which translates as:

> and (the) pig *(ia)*
>   they had-killed-it before
>   *(ia)* would turn into a big stone

In the story told here the speaker has embedded one utterance into another. The marker 'ia' is a new constituent of the language that seems to be marking the embedded clause's start and end. We have shown it here with an *(ia)* indicating the subordinate clause. It seems, then, that the new creole language is not just a reflection of adult ideas of language as in the pidgin, but a much more sophisticated product of children's own internal 'theory' of natural language.

▨ Understanding the Levels of Language ▨

Consider this imaginary conversational segment between two speakers, A and B.

The phone has just rung at A's end. A picks it up and speaks immediately.

A.1: Hello. (*0.5 sec. pause*) 826561. (*0.3 sec. pause*)
B.1: Is Frank there? (*3 sec. pause*) He is in today? (*0.1 sec. pause*)
A.2: Sorry. I'll see.

Now this is a very small chunk of conversation with a very few short words, but let us look at some of the levels upon which A and B have been communicating.

At the Dialogue level: A and B have engaged in turn-taking without interrupting each other and with very small gaps between their turns. They have identified some shared information about the identity of an individual referred to by B as 'Frank'. A has identified the goal of B as being to speak to this individual. And there has been a rapid repair of a minor hitch as A appeared momentarily confused about B's goal.

At the Utterance level: Neither of B's questions are answered. Both indeed are treated by A as notification from B that B wishes to speak with Frank. Both utterances by B in the extract are treated as questions, but only the first is in a standard interrogative form. The second form is declarative, formed as a declaration about 'he' being 'in'. But it is marked in the transcript with a question-mark to show that intonation and stress are being used by B to flag this as a question.

At the Word level: The string '826561' as A's second utterance is not treated like any other word, but recognized as a number and therefore subject to a different set of rules.

Neither A nor B seems to have any trouble understanding what the word 'there' and 'he' refers to in the real world, but they will cheerfully use these words in other utterances to refer to very different things.

At the Physical level: All of this interchange is just a stream of sound. If you were to look at a sound graph (audiogram) of all this you would find it hard to pick out the speech from all the other noises at each end – the sound of A's dog barking and the traffic in the street. However, any human listening could identify the speech signals from the extraneous sounds, even if they do not speak the language concerned. Only an English speaker, though, would be able to tell confidently where the boundaries of each word lie. There are no gaps between the words to help out.

To begin to examine language one must look through all of these layers to identify the key concepts. Let us start from the bottom level and work back up.

▨ Levels of Terminology in Language ▨

Sounds

Phonetics is the description of physical aspects of speech sounds; for example, the part of 'spit' and 'pit' written 'p' are physically different and are produced differently. Therefore they are phonetically different. Phonology: phonemes are classes of phonetically different sounds which are functionally equivalent. The 'p' in 'spit' and 'pit' is phonologically the same. Spelling is related to the phonological level.

Words

Morphology refers to the shape or structure of words. For example, the word 'lifted' is made up of the morpheme 'lift' and the past tense morpheme '-ed'. The lexicon contains the meaning of morphemes – the lexical entry for 'lift' might be defined in terms of meaning primitives that might be written 'propel' and 'up'.

Sentences

Syntax is the constituent structure of sentences and phrases: for instance, the sentence 'the cat ate it' is made up of a subject noun-phrase 'the cat' and a verb-phrase 'ate it'. Semantics concerns the literal meaning of sentences and phrases: the meaning of 'the cat ate it' is the meaning of the verb-phrase 'ate it' predicated of the meaning of the subject 'the cat'. These meanings in turn stem from the lexical entries for 'the', 'cat', 'eat' and 'it'.

Context

Pragmatics: not all of the meaning of sentences stems from literal meaning or semantics. Part depends on the context and what the speaker and hearer know. For example, part of the meaning of 'the cat ate it' depends on what there is in the world and in the minds of the speaker and listeners for 'it' to refer to.

▨ Models of Language ▨

The big question for psychologists is what is the machinery in our minds which supports language? How does the language processor in the head work? Figure 10.2 shows Winograd's simple box model of how the human language processing system may work. The comprehension of language, listening and reading,

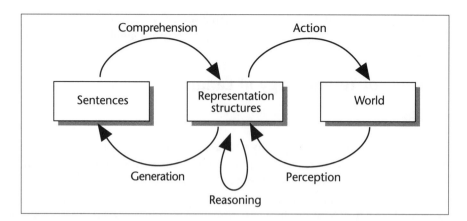

Figure 10.2 A model of sentence processing
Source Winograd 1985.

means that utterances are stored in some sort of representation system. Language generation, speaking and writing, are produced from that representation system. The representation needs some form of internal processing which is shown here as a loop called 'reasoning'. And one must not forget that there are other (extra- or non-linguistic) processes in our interaction with the world that may affect the representation system, such as when we act upon the world or perceive it.

The central box is what we would normally describe as 'cognition'. Winograd's point here is to focus on representation as the key aspect of cognition to help us understand how we deal with language.

▓ The Syntax versus Semantics Debate ▓

Many researchers artificially set in opposition the syntactic-driven and semantic-driven models. In fact, it is clear that both are combined in our language-understanding machinery. The question is only about how.

In natural speech people don't speak very rigidly syntactically.

I umm . . . should your . . . you really . . . I mean, if . . .

And at times we can effectively communicate without it.

Skid. Crash. Hospital.

But, we can and do regularly use rigid syntactic structures, especially in writing and reading, and when other cues, like paralinguistics, are unavailable. Most new words are learned when they appear in well-defined syntactic roles. And syntax is clearly very important to meaning.

(a) She drank it.
(b) It drank her.

Box 10.1 ELIZA

ELIZA (named after the G. B. Shaw heroine Eliza Doolittle) was a computer conversationalist produced by Joseph Weizenbaum in 1966. Weizenbaum showed that with very simple 'pattern-matching' techniques one could simulate a relatively natural conversational interaction.

The best known version of this program is one in which the computer is acting the role of a Rogerian 'non-directive therapist' in a psychotherapeutic setting. In the following conversation the human is the client in therapy typing in responses to the computer-program therapist.

Client:	Men are all alike.
ELIZA:	In what way?
Client:	They're always bugging us about something or other.
ELIZA:	Can you think of a specific example?
Client:	Well, my boyfriend made me come here.
ELIZA:	Your boyfriend made you come here.
Client:	He says I'm depressed much of the time.
ELIZA:	I am sorry to hear you are depressed.
Client:	It's true. I am unhappy.
ELIZA:	Do you think that coming here will help you not to be unhappy?
Client:	I need some help, that much seems certain.
ELIZA:	What would it mean to you if you got some help?
Client:	Perhaps I could learn to get along with my mother.
ELIZA:	Tell me more about your family.

This is a good choice of conversationalist. A non-directive therapist is often simplistically characterized as encouraging the client to talk, and so the 'echoing' back of clients responses, as a request for clarification, is expected.

In fact, ELIZA very simply responds to key words & simple patterns in the client's input. She has rules mapping these patterns onto plausible reply patterns. For example,

I AM X → WHY ARE YOU X?

So this sort of interaction is possible:

Client:	*I am* unhappy.
ELIZA:	*Why are you* unhappy?

She also has simple echoing exchange rules to turn 'You are' into 'I am' and 'Me' into 'You', etc., in the echoed segment. For instance,

I am sure <u>you are</u> against <u>me</u>.
Why are you sure <u>I am</u> against <u>you</u>?

It is interesting to note that in the transcript above ELIZA can also support a very small element of context. For example, she can store interesting keywords for return to later if stuck. For example,

You mentioned your mother . . .

If really stuck and with no keywords to throw back at you, she will resort to encouraging phrases like 'TELL ME MORE'. Unfortunately, ELIZA can only act plausibly if you 'play the game'. It is very easy to make her say stupid things:

Client:	I am you are.
ELIZA:	Why are you I am?
Client:	Nee zlooff***y.
ELIZA:	Tell me more.

ELIZA cannot respond intelligently to these nonsense inputs because she doesn't know anything about what makes good (or bad) language. She can never fool an intelligent 'client' for very long. Much more sophisticated pattern-matching systems have been built that incorporate techniques to try to fool the user into attributing intelligence to the computer system. Alas, programs of this kind tell us much more about how people readily attribute intelligence to almost anything on the flimsiest of evidence (known as the anthropomorphic fallacy) than they do about language. To be fair, Weizenbaum himself has never proposed ELIZA as a psychologically real model of language and indeed was apparently horrified at how seriously his paper was taken by the scientific community (Weizenbaum 1976).

Both sentences are sensible English, but they both mean very different things. Chomsky noted that people are actually excellent intuitive linguists. Consider the following two sentences that contain the same words. (Note that, conventionally, linguists mark with an asterisk utterances which we would consider in some way illegitimate.)

(1) The sexy fish ate a wombat
(2) Fish a wombat sexy ate the.*

Most English speakers would rate (1) as legitimate English and (2) as illegitimate English, even if they had no formal language training and did not even understand the meaning of the words. Noam Chomsky's famous example is:

Colourless green ideas sleep furiously

Chomsky shows that even where the words and their meanings may be absurd (what does it mean to sleep furiously, how can a thing be both colourless and green?) the mere fact that we can ask such questions shows that we are able to impose a structure on these utterances. A pattern-matcher like ELIZA (a computerized conversationalist – see Box 10.1) is incapable of doing this while people intuitively 'know' the rules of grammar (even if they don't 'know' they know them).

The models of language that we are going to explore are not all exclusive, but rather provide us with insights into the structure of syntax and semantics in human communication.

▒ The Structure of Natural Language ▒

This section examines the concept of language as symbolic, novel and structured. We look at some attempts to provide useful models of these features and explore how they might work in systems that actually try to understand language.

Language without structure

Maybe the language that we see in people is just a large collection of fixed patterns of behaviour that they can reproduce as a response when the stimulus is right. These rules might be learned in a very simple behaviourist way that invokes almost none of Winograd's proposed representation and reasoning. They could be of the form 'If you say X then I should say Y'. One can imagine a developmental scenario where the 2-year-old learns the rule:

IF mummy says 'what is your name?' THEN I should say 'Peter'.

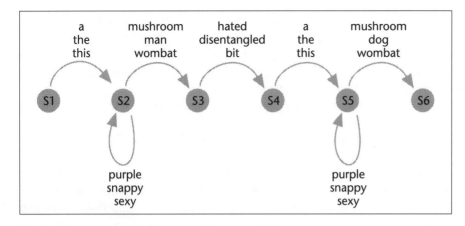

Figure 10.3 A finite state machine for a set of simple English

This is the sort of learning mechanism proposed by the behaviourist theorists, and models of this sort have indeed been constructed, but have been found to be seriously limited (see ELIZA, Box 10.1).

A key problem, that we have already noted, is that it is not possible to capture the infinitely different sentences that humans are capable of producing and comprehending with a finite number of input–output patterns. The human language-understanding machinery must (within a finite machine – the human brain) capture that infinite power. Theoretical linguists point to a simple mathematical machine, the finite state transition network (also known as the FINITE STATE MACHINE) as the simplest demonstration of a model that can theoretically do just this.

FINITE STATE MACHINE

In figure 10.3 we can see a simple mechanical device that can guarantee to produce a legitimate sentence in English. It is drawn as a state-transition diagram, were you start at state S1 and cross the arcs until you reach state S6. Each time you make a transition across an arc with a word on it you add a word to the

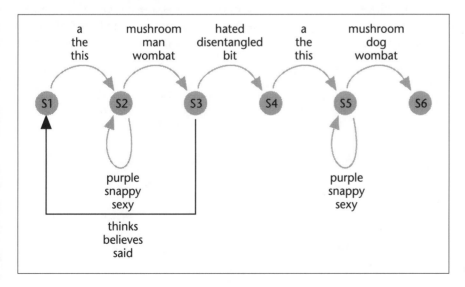

Figure 10.4 A more complex finite state machine

output language string. Now even though it only appears to have 6 states, because we have added in a loop on states S2 and S5, it can produce an infinite number of sentences. Most of these sentences would be hard to read, and might repeat some words, but should be, in principle, understandable. This is easier to see if we add some more arcs (figure 10.4).

This machine could produce embedded sentences like:

a man said the wombat hated this mushroom

Now while it is entirely possible to imagine growing a machine like this with arcs and nodes galore, pretty soon it becomes unwieldy, and impossible to work with. Furthermore it is missing out on a great deal of the natural structure that one can immediately see within it. Some words always appear together in an interchangeable cluster, and some sequences of words also always appear together.

▨ The Structure of Language – Syntax ▨

LEXICAL CATEGORY

PHRASAL
CATEGORIES

Note that all of the words on each transition in figure 10.5 share much in common. Linguists consider words that can appear interchangeable in the same places in a sentence as sharing the same word class, or in the jargon, LEXICAL CATEGORY (or part of speech). The basic categories shown in the example here are determiner (shortened Det here, also known as 'article'), adjective (shortened Adj here), noun and verb. The next thing to note here is that having clumped words together into categories one could look at the sequences of transitions that tend to appear together and aggregate these into categories also. These aggregates are called PHRASAL CATEGORIES, because they are classes of words collected in phrases. The phrases are named after the word that is considered to be the most important lexical category – called the head of the phrase. The Det–Adj–Noun sequences are called noun-phrases as the noun is the head. The collection of

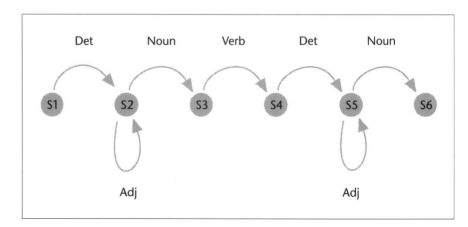

Figure 10.5 A machine with lexical categories

Sentence	→	Noun phrase, verb phrase
Noun phrase	→	Determiner, (adjective)*, noun
Verb phrase	→	Verb, (noun phrase)
A Dictionary		
Determiner	→	a / the / this
Noun	→	Mushroom / man / wombat
Adjective	→	purple / snappy / sexy
Verb	→	hated / disentangled / bit

Figure 10.6 A very simple phrase structure grammar

verb plus following noun-phrase is called a verb-phrase. We could continue to work with the machine model, and some theorists do, but these regularities are just as easy to read in another (equivalent) form, as rules.

A PHRASE STRUCTURE GRAMMAR (PSG) is a set of rules of the form

$$X \rightarrow Y, Z.$$

where X, Y and Z are language constituents, and the rule reads that the constituent X may be rewritten as the constituent Y followed by Z. In this terminology we will call any size 'chunk' of language a constituent of that language. The list of rules in figure 10.6 covers the basic machine we have been discussing so far. The parentheses mean that a constituent is optional, the star that the constituent may be repeated, and the slash that the constituent is an alternative.

The PSG rules are a 'GENERATIVE GRAMMAR'. This has nothing to do with the production of utterances! It means that the grammar can be viewed as way of generating *all and only* those sentences that are legitimate in the language in question.

One important feature of these sorts of rules is that they are easy to read, and it is easy to read important structural information from them. How the rules show the structure of any sentence can be readily seen via a PARSE TREE. Parse trees are usually drawn as upside-down trees where each branch represents one rewritten constituent in each rule. So for a simple sentence that is rewritten as a

PHRASE STRUCTURE GRAMMAR

GENERATIVE GRAMMAR

PARSE TREE

Figure 10.7 A parse tree for 'They are eating apples.'

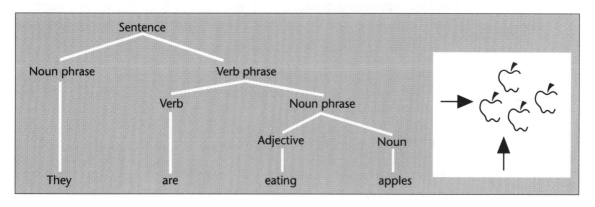

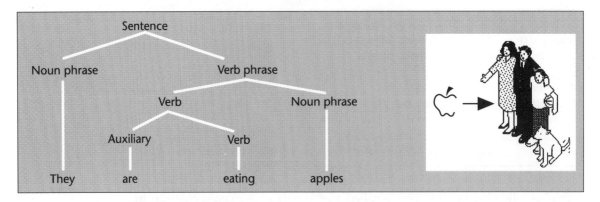

Figure 10.8 An alternative parse tree for 'They are eating apples.'

noun-phrase followed by a verb-phrase we have two branches at the top. The leaves of the tree, near the bottom, are the words of the sentence themselves. In figure 10.7 we see an example of this.

The example sentence we have chosen is ambiguous. As shown by this parse, it could be read as indicating some apples whose type is 'eating' (as opposed to, say, decorative or poisonous apples). Alternatively, it could be read as pointing to some 'they' who are currently 'eating' things called 'apples'. This alternative parse is shown in figure 10.8.

The most famous generative grammarian is Noam Chomsky, who has dominated the field for many years, and still does!

As Chomsky explains, like the machines we have discussed, the PSGs share the important property that infinite sets of sentences can be handled by finite rules. Similarly they can cope with features of language like the simple embedding of one utterance into another.

We have noted that many sentences in a language are simple. And indeed, as we saw above, it is possible to characterize languages by their favourite order for simple affirmative active declarative sentences (SAAD). Unfortunately, much linguistic behaviour is significantly more complex than these simple SAAD forms. Indeed, much of our linguistic behaviour appears as though we are deliberately jumbling up these simple utterances by moving constituents of the sentence around! This is described by linguists as MOVEMENT. Movement is where a consituent appears to belong somewhere in a sentence, but actually turns up somewhere else! Recall the example of topicalization given above. The (relatively) simple sentence:

MOVEMENT

I find that suggestion totally revolting.

can be 'topicalized' to become:

That suggestion I find totally revolting.

In this movement, the constituent 'that suggestion' seems to naturally belong after 'find' but appears to have been moved to the front of the sentence. Alas, while PSGs can handle some embedding, they are technically incapable of handling movement.

In his theory of TRANSFORMATIONAL GRAMMAR, Chomsky (1965) proposed a set of rules, which he called transformations, that could be added to PSGs to cope with the movement of constituents. In his theory he suggested that the most basic sentences, essentially SAADs, were transformed into more complex sentences by a sequence of one or more of these transformations. Chomsky's work has generated a substantial body of research which has tried to test the psychological reality of the sort of mechanisms he proposed. However, most researchers now argue that transformations are, in principle, too complex as a theoretical mechanism to account for human language. Chomsky (1986) has recently refined his theories in the search for a UNIVERSAL GRAMMAR that can account for all human languages in a single, much simpler, system.

TRANSFORMATIONAL GRAMMAR

UNIVERSAL GRAMMAR

▓ Semantics ▓

'When I use a word,' Humpty Dumpty said in a rather scornful tone, 'it means what I choose it to mean – neither more nor less.'

Lewis Carroll, *Through the Looking-Glass*

How many meanings can you think of for the word 'mean':

1. I mean to be there tomorrow. (intend)
2. He's one mean bastard. (nasty)
3. The mean miserly fellow. (canny)
4. No mean measures please. (small)
5. Those clouds mean thunder. (signify)
6. The red light means stop. (order)

In (1) 'mean' is used to express an intention to do something. In (2) its connotation is 'nasty' or 'unkind', while in (3) it is more to do with what the Scots would call 'canny'. In (4) it is used to refer to a small thing. In both (5) and (6) it used as a 'sign' of something, but with different connotations. Clouds mean thunder in that they are a sign or indication of some correlation between the two. The red light is a demand that you stop, an order to do so. So the word 'mean' means all of these things. (What does the second occurrence in the last sentence mean?)

Linguists usually begin their analysis of meaning with reference to the meaning related to logic proposed by Frege in 1892. Frege proposed that we distinguish between SENSE and REFERENCE in meaning. A word's sense is its definition in terms of other words. The sort of definition that one might look up in a dictionary and that we were exploring with the word 'mean' above. The word 'go' has over 50 different meanings, or senses. A word's reference on the other hand is its definition in terms of a specific context. One sense of the word 'president'

SENSE REFERENCE

Box 10.2 An Informal Experiment – Word Semantics

The Task:

Consider this story: The plane banked left just before landing, but then the pilot lost control. The strip on the field runs for only the barest of yards, and the plane just twisted out of the turn before shooting into the ground.

- Can you understand the story?
- Do you know the meaning of each individual word?
- Is the meaning of any word ambiguous?

According to Johnson-Laird (1983) every single 'content word' (i.e. not words like 'the' and 'of') in this story is ambiguous.

For example, what senses of the noun 'plane' can you think of? Here are a few:

- The plane landed on the runway.
- Imagine a sphere divided by a plane.

- The carpenter smoothed the wood with a plane.
- All the trees fell apart from the plane at the end.

It is clear from this demonstration that a few common meanings are readily available for words But even the relatively rare uses make sense, when used in the appropriate semantic context. We have restricted you to the spelling here, but had the story been read to you the ambiguity increases manyfold as you have to consider words that sound the same as plane. 'The rain in Spain falls mainly on the plain.' 'Try another piece of this plain cake.'

INTENSION
EXTENSION
PRINCIPLE OF
COMPOSITIONALITY

includes the figurehead role of various organizations and governments. But with particular reference to the President of the USA, at any one time its reference has been the individual known as Nixon, Reagan, Clinton, etc. Sense and reference are also sometimes referred to as INTENSION and EXTENSION respectively. Frege then proposed the PRINCIPLE OF COMPOSITIONALITY which states that

> The intension of a sentence can be built up compositionally from the intensions of its constituents in a way that depends on their grammatical combination.

So, in this simple model, one can combine the basic meanings of all of the words involved in an utterance to determine the meaning of the whole. As we will see, this turns out to be a rather simple model. But the relationship that it presents between syntax and semantics is a nice and straightforward one. Under the logic model, the sentence is a logical proposition making some sort of assertion, with regard to truth and falsity, about the world. In figure 10.9 we have shown how the logical semantic structure of a sentence (b) could be directly related to the syntactic structure of the sentence (a).

In a SAAD sentence of this sort the first noun-phrase is the logical subject of the proposition. The verb-phrase is called the logical predicate of the proposition and may consist of just an action for verbs which take no logical object (as in 'the dog swam'), or one object as in this case; or two objects (as in 'the policeman gave the man a flower'), or even linguistic complements or adverbs. This statement is making the assertion that 'some specific dog bit some specific man' whose meaning is, at least in part, related to its truth or falsity.

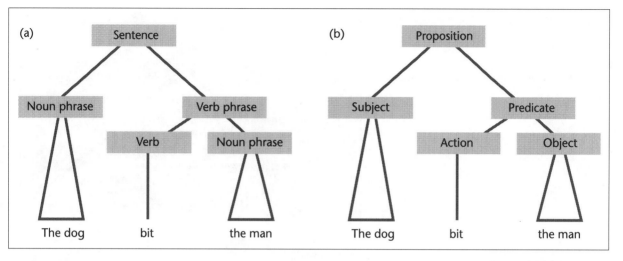

Figure 10.9 (a) A syntactic structure for a simple sentence; (b) a semantic structure for a simple sentence

Semantic grammars

The task of applying semantics to language understanding has been best pursued by those who seek to extend the sense and reference meanings of words and phrases into a grammar that could then directly deliver the meaning of any sentence. This work is described as SEMANTIC GRAMMAR. Some of these researchers have argued that semantics is even more important to our understanding of language than syntax.

SEMANTIC GRAMMAR

Consider these two sentences:

1. Mary hit the woman with the long hair.
2. Mary hit the woman with the long stick.

Both sentences are syntactically ambiguous in exactly the same way, but a different meaning is preferred by human parsers. Indeed, the other meaning may take some thinking about. The ambiguity here is about who has the stick/hair. The preferred reading of sentence (1) is to attribute the hair to 'the woman', while (2) tends to attribute the stick to 'Mary'. People tend to see 'the long hair' as a distinguishing feature of Mary's victim, while the stick is attributed to Mary because she is seen as hitting the woman using it as an instrument. It appears from examples like these that people are making semantic predictions about the sentence as they go along. In seeking to construct something meaningful we rarely see any alternatives.

This suggests that people use the input words of the sentence to activate the relevant semantic concepts in their memory – which then predict meaningful further information to look for. In this case, the act of hitting can have an instrument and 'the long stick' is a very suitable candidate. It is important to note that the parser may have to do a great deal of inferential work here to determine the attributes of 'stick' that make it good for hitting and which make 'hair' less good.

409

Plate 10.5 Humpty Dumpty in *Through the Looking-Glass*
Source: Macmillan Children's Books.

CASE GRAMMAR

The classical work on semantic grammars is that of CASE GRAMMAR. A case grammar seeks to determine the semantic roles of the noun-phrases in respect to the semantics of the verb. Fillmore (1968) set out a case grammar based upon 6 basic cases: these were agentive, objective, instrumental, dative, factitive and locative. Quirk (1985) has refined this model. This sort of scheme is much more complex than the logical subject and objects offered above. If we just consider the first three of these cases we can see that the agent is the doer of the action (determined primarily by the verb), the object is the done-to of the action, and the instrument is the done-with.

The cop saw the robber with the binoculars.

In this sentence, the cop is the agent, the robber is the object and the binoculars are the instrument. As we saw above, with our 'hair and stick' example, it is not always trivially easy to assign these case roles.

Semantic primitives and conceptual dependency

Roger Schank has classified a small set of primitive conceptual acts around which he focuses his own version of case grammar. He calls his semantic grammar –

using the notation above – CONCEPTUAL DEPENDENCY (CD). The reasoning behind this name is that CDs aim to represent the key concepts in language and seek to capture the dependencies between them. He has a graphic representation for showing how these case roles relate together. In the example in figure 10.10 we see how one might graphically represent the sentence 'The man took a book'. The basic semantic of the sentence connects together the main action of the sentence (the 'take') with the actor (the 'man'). To indicate the importance of this to the meaning of the sentence Schank's notation uses a double arrow to join them, with the actor to the left and the action to the right. He also places flags above the arrow to indicate important features of the relationship – here he notes that the 'take' happened in the past, 'took'. The sentence also tells us that the object of the action was a book. Again this is shown graphically with a marked arrow connecting the case role to the action.

CONCEPTUAL
DEPENDENCY

past   object
man ⟺ take ⟵ book

Figure 10.10 A basic semantic representation
Source after Schank 1981.

Schank notes that a case-grammar approach expects one to make simple inferences about the cases which depend upon the action. In this case he would say that we can say that it is implicit in the meaning of 'take' that the object has a direction with a 'from' and a 'to'. If the man took a book then it came from somewhere (X, an unknown place) to the man (see figure 10.11).

past   object   direction   to → man
man ⟺ take ⟵ book ⟵   from ← X

Figure 10.11 An extended semantic representation

Schank notes that many actions which are syntactically very different look very similar when represented semantically. The sentences 'the man took a book'

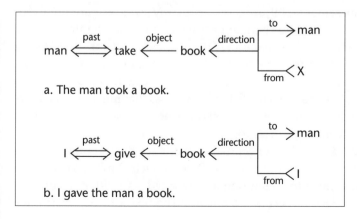

past   object   direction   to → man
man ⟺ take ⟵ book ⟵   from ← X

a. The man took a book.

past   object   direction   to → man
I ⟺ give ⟵ book ⟵   from ← I

b. I gave the man a book.

Figure 10.12 Comparing two different semantic acts

CD	Means	Examples
1 atrans	**A**bstract **TRANS**fer (possession)	Give, take, receive, sell, buy
2 ptrans	**P**lace **TRANS**fer (location)	go, walk, move, fall
3 mtrans	**M**ental **TRANS**fer	read, forget, teach, promise
4 ingest	to take inside	eat, drink, breathe
5 propel	apply force	hit, kick, push
6 mbuild	**M**ental **BUILD**	realize, wonder
7 grasp	elaborates acts like	hold, snatch
8 move	move a body part, involved in e.g.	push, kick
9 speak	elaborates verbs like	say, tell, shout
10 attend	elaborates sensory inputs like	listen, look
11 expel	to send out (esp. of body)	puff, spit, sneeze

Figure 10.13 Eleven semantic primitives (after Schank 1982)

and 'I gave the man a book' are syntactically very different, but as you can see from figure 10.12 the graphic semantic representations share many similarities.

Schank argues that there are many verbs with a semantics related to the 'transfer of possession' – words like steal, sell, own, bring, catch, want . . . – and that all share these similarities. Schank would class the 'take' act above as some sort of Abstract TRANSfer, or ATRANS for short, as it is the transfer of an abstract thing – possession.

Acts 7–11 are labelled 'instrumental acts' by Schank as they are used to qualify the 6 primitive acts (i.e. they explain how the act took place). So the verb 'to see' can be considered as basically an mtrans in that it involves the mental transfer of information from the world to someone's mind, but it clearly also generally involves the ATTENDing of that person's eyes to the visual stimulus. In the same way 'to kick' is clearly a PROPEL of something towards something else, but it also involves the a body-part MOVE (i.e. with a 'foot'). A representation of a sentence may often consist of a number of these acts combined, with 1–6 as the more fundamental ones, modified by the rest.

Further modifications of the CD may well be required to represent the variety of other aspects of the information contained in a sentence. This information may refer to simple syntactic details such as the tense and time of an act. It may also include complex semantic information: about any *states* that are involved, for example, that 'kill' is a state-changing act which turns alive into dead; or whether any of the roles involved have any *features* mentioned, for example, the noun-phrase 'John's dog' refers to a 'dog' which has the feature of being possessed by 'John'; or if any *causal* links are necessarily implied, for example, that X happened 'because' of Y; and so on. Schank proposes that much of this information, particularly the semantic implications of an act, can be embedded in the semantic primitive dictionary entries for each verb-as-an-act.

Figure 10.14 shows a complex conceptual dependency diagram for a simple sentence. The sentence is deceptively simple, 'Mary punched John.' Yet as soon as Schank's CD parser finds the definition for 'punched' as a PROPEL concept, this rich set of dependencies becomes available. The object of the punch, for

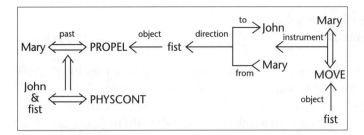

Figure 10.14 A complex conceptual dependency: 'Mary punched John.'

example, is highly likely to be a 'fist'. Furthermore, the act has an instrument which is itself a MOVE of a body part whose agent is Mary and whose object is the fist. The triple arrows beneath the PROPEL act indicate a 'causal connection' depending on a 'punch', which is inherent in the meaning of this punch – that John and the fist will come into physical contact.

The most striking feature here is that it shows how much inference Schank is arguing that a language understander can make automatically. All of this comes with the semantic dictionary definition of 'punch'.

Memory in Language Understanding

Organizing inferences

The early CD work of the group led by Schank went on to explore inferences and memory structures. One of their first systems was called MARGIE (Memory Analysis Response Generation and Inference in English). The MARGIE system included a semantic parser which made an attempt to render an English-language sentence into the semantic notation of conceptual dependency, as above. The system then added even more knowledge to the CD representation based on plausible inferences about the motivations and effects that are often attached to primitive acts like 'to hit'.

So for example the sentence,

Bill kissed Mary because she hit John.

could be represented as a set of PROPELs and MOVEs and it could have a number of plausible (causal) inferences attached to it, such as :

1.   Mary's hitting John caused John to be hurt.
2.   John's being hurt pleased Bill.
3.   Bill's pleasure was caused by Mary's action.
4.   Bill feels positive emotion towards Mary.
5.   This causes him to kiss her.

Other possible inferences might include:

6. John may fall to the ground.
7. John may become afraid.

Unfortunately, with this approach it is very difficult to know where the chain of inferences may reasonably be extended and how far you can go. The essential difficulty is that this approach is vulnerable to an INFERENTIAL EXPLOSION. That is, that it cannot easily tell when to *stop making inferences* to add to the initial parse. Subsequent work attempted to contain this explosion by providing an explicit story context which can inform the system about the range of inferences that are reasonable in certain types of situations.

Scripts

Consider the following short story:

Story 1: Zoe walked to Pizza Hut. She had a deep pan vegetarian. Then went to the cinema.

Adults easily make the inferences necessary to answer questions, such as:

What sort of place is 'Pizza Hut'?
What did Zoe eat?
Who took Zoe's order?
What other events most probably took place?

and so on.

Schank has argued that people can do this because we have knowledge in memory relating to STEREOTYPE situations. Schank called this knowledge a SCRIPT. Here is a much- simplified account of a stereotypical trip to a restaurant:

A Restaurant Script:
Event 1. Actor goes to Restaurant
Event 2. Actor goes from Door to a Seat
Event 3. Actor asks Waiting-Person for Food
Event 4. Actor eats Food
Event 5. Actor gives Money to the Waiting-Person
Event 6. Actor leaves Restaurant

This sequence of general events is represented in memory and when a specific story is to be understood the script is activated and used to guide the understanding of the story. Consider our example story above:

A Story:
Event A. Zoe walked to Pizza Hut

Event B. She had a deep pan vegetarian
Event C. Then went to the cinema

If the script is a memory structure helping us to understand the story then we can make the reasonable inferences. For example: if Zoe is the Actor who goes into the restaurant, then she should be the Actor who leaves (note that Event C does not explicitly say who left); that 'had' in Story Event B is actually a form of eating; and that she pays for it before leaving.

Understanding Ambiguity

Many jokes work via syntactic ambiguity like this classic Groucho Marx gag:

Time flies like an arrow.
Fruit flies like a banana.

This gag relies on a phenomenon known as 'priming' in which an early stimulus affects your perception of a later stimulus. It also introduces the effect of garden pathing, in which your analysis of a sentence is 'led up the garden path' before turning out to be wrong. The 'time' gag acts like a garden path because you are led to impose the same syntactic structure on the second sentence (primed to the syntax), only to find out that, while legitimate, this syntactic structure requires a meaning that is comically absurd.

The classic garden-path sentence is harder to read because the parse you are led to (up the garden path) is not merely absurd, but illegitimate.

The horse raced past the barn fell.
The cotton clothing is usually made of grows in Alabama.

These are legitimate, but may take some reading. To help you get them right we can try to semantically prime the correct syntactic interpretation, by putting some appropriate contextual material first.

The horse that walked past the barn was fine, but the horse that raced past the barn fell.
The cotton that those sheets are usually made of comes from Egypt, but the cotton clothing is usually made of grows in Alabama.

Language as an Act

One perspective on semantics is to note that the meaning of an utterance is often what it does (Austin 1962). For instance, an utterance may act as a statement or assertion, it may describe, warn, remark, comment, command, order, request, criticize, apologize, censure, approve, welcome, promise, and so on. Consider the sentence:

You will go home tomorrow.

Now logically we can see that this has the truth conditions:

For addressee A on day D this is true if and only if A goes home on day D+1.

But the sentence meaning actually depends on what act was intended by the speaker.

In the following we show different ways that the sentence could be flagged as a different sort of act. And how this might match a suitable response:

Act	*Response*
John asserted that ...	How do you know that ... ?
John asked if ...	Yes.
John predicted that ...	That's what you think!
John told me to ...	Okay.

If you are told to go home tomorrow then you can comply or not. If you are asked if it is true that you are going you can inform the questioner. If the speaker makes a prediction or an assertion you may wish to know the basis of the statement, and so on.

Speech acts

SPEECH ACTS

According to Austin an important part of meaning resides in SPEECH ACTS and the intentions of the parties involved in them. In the jargon, the speaker issues a locutionary act, which has illocutionary force and may also be a perlocutionary

LOCUTION

act. The LOCUTION is the utterance itself. The ILLOCUTION is the intention of the speaker transmitted to the listener. The PERLOCUTION is the effect of the locution

ILLOCUTION

beyond any intention by the speaker.

PERLOCUTION

For example,

- The locution 'Jill is coming' is said by Fred to Jack.
- This acts as an illocution whose force is in this case 'a warning'. (You do not see her, but she is coming, be aware of this.)
- The perlocution may be that Jack becomes afraid. (Fred did not intend to frighten Jack, but Jack is afraid of Jill and so the warning has this extra effect.)

Interestingly, in some speech acts, the utterance itself becomes the act. For example, 'I hereby name this ship . . . ' by its utterance causes the ship to be named.

Plate 10.6 Cartoon
signification
Source: Brian Melville

When the referee says 'You are out' your becoming out happened because she said so. This is particularly true of promises; for example, 'I promise to wash the dishes'.

John Searle (1969) refined this basic analysis to look for the rules governing recognition and production of illocutionary acts. He noted that while some acts were clearly direct others were distinctly indirect. Consider the following utterances:

1. Can you pass the salt?
2. Would you mind not making so much noise?
3. You are standing on my foot.
4. The door is open.

Listeners clearly need to go some way beyond the literal speech act to determine the real act which is the speaker's intent. Acts 1 and 2 here are literally 'request-for-information' acts, while 3 and 4 are literally 'informing' acts. But they are all usually issued as 'requests-for-action'.

In order to understand indirect speech acts one must model the beliefs, knowledge and intentions of both speaker and hearer(s).

Communication as cooperativity

Grice (1975) has noted that communication is a social and cooperative activity which works because we obey some communicative rules. He described these rules as the cooperative principle. The principle consists of a set of maxims. Here are four of them:

The maxim of *Quantity*: Be informative, but not more than necessary.
The maxim of *Quality*: Don't lie or say what you don't have enough evidence for.

The maxim of *Relation*: Be relevant.

The maxim of *Manner*: Be perspicuous (clear).

Communication works because we hold to these maxims – or flout them deliberately.

If we say 'Oh, that is just great', but in a context where our speaker cannot believe that we are being truthful (breaking the maxim of quality), then we may be producing an indirect speech act of 'sarcasm'. It is important to note that these maxims are not merely 'conventions'. They are a competence requirement of successful communication.

CHAPTER SUMMARY

1 Human language is a productive but regular system of communication which appears to be governed by rules.

2 We can look at language from two perspectives. The first seeks to establish competence rules for language – which describe what languages are; what they can and cannot do. The second perspective seeks to establish performance rules for how language works: as a mechanism, in practice.

3 Language is a diverse, social activity.

4 In the debate about the relationship between language and thought the strong version of this relationship is described as linguistic determinism. This asserts that our language determines our thinking. The weaker version of this relationship is called linguistic relativity, which asserts that our language influences our thoughts. There is little compelling evidence for either version.

5 Many animal species have very sophisticated communication systems. None of these systems seems to approach the sophistication of human language. While there is still some debate about how much of the human language system can be taught to primates, it seems as though the answer is 'not much'.

6 Linguists have outlined a number of universal features that all human languages seem to share, such as a favourite or canonical order in which the subject precedes the object.

7 While there seem to be no natural primitive languages, there are artifical ones called pidgins. These are primitive in the sense of missing features such as the ability to embed one utterance into another to express a complex proposition. Linguists have observed that when a pidgin becomes a creole language (the mother tongue of the children of pidgin speakers), these missing features suddenly appear.

8 We can look at language at a number of different levels: as sound, via phonetics and phonology; as words, via morphology and the lexicon; as sentences, via syntax and semantics; and in its use in some specific context, via pragmatics.

9 Much contemporary research has focused upon exploring models of a cognitive mechanism for language which may be psychologically real.

10 A model which presupposes no linguistic structure, such as a set of simple input–output patterns, cannot account for the richness of language behaviour we observe.

11 At the sentence level, models are often distinguished by the emphasis they place upon the role of syntax or semantics in the representation and processing of language.

12 In the syntactic tradition, the simplest theoretical model which could account for the productivity and regularity of language is the finite state machine. The machine can be used to illustrate that certain words seem to clump together in categories and that certain categories seem to clump together into phrases. Regularities like these are used by some linguists to argue that language has an inherent phrasal structure.

13 This simple mechanical device can be presented in a more readable form as a set of rules. A set of rules for language is referred to as a grammar. A set of rules that illustrate that language can be seen as lexical categories stuctured into phrasal categories is called a phrase structure grammar.

14 Unfortunately, a phrase structure grammar cannot itself capture one vital feature of language which is called 'movement'. Chomsky proposed a 'transformational grammar' to address this problem.

15 Logic provides a simple model for meaning, through the composition of word senses and references into propositions that can be tested in the world as true or false.

16 Some theoreticians have developed radical alternatives to syntactic grammars, which use the idea of semantic cases. One of the most well developed case grammars is Schank's conceptual dependency theory, which proposes a set of semantic primitives for language.

17 Schank's computer implementations of his theory also elegantly demonstrate the importance of memory and inference in human natural language understanding.

18 Another semantic theoretical perspective on language notes that our communication is an act, which we perform for some specific purposes. It functions in a cooperative setting and is governed by a set of rules that are much more than mere conventions.

▧ Further Work ▧

1. Use 3 of Fillmore's basic cases to work out the case interpretations of the following sentences. The first one is filled in for you. Note that the sense of the verb 'to break' here is 'to physically damage' (cf. Mary is broke; Mary broke her promise; Mary broke the bank at Monte Carlo).
    1) Mary broke the window.
    2) Mary broke the window with the hammer.
    3) The hammer broke the window.
    4) The window broke.

TO BREAK	AGENT	OBJECT	INSTRUMENT
1	Mary	Window	Unknown
2			
3			
4			

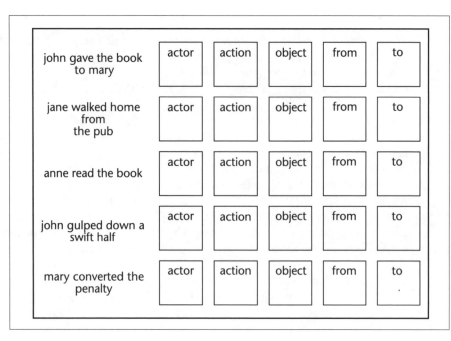

Figure 10.15

2. Using Schank's conceptual dependency primitives and cases fill in roles for each sentence (fig. 10.15). Sketch out Schank's graphical CD diagrams for any two of these.

3. Consider ambiguity. In the text we introduced the phrase 'time flies like an arrow' and showed how it could mislead your analysis of a very similar phrase. The analysis of the similar phrase was not wrong, merely absurd. Write down as many different interpretations of the 'time' sentence (however absurd) as you can think of. The one that was intended might read 'Time moves as quickly as an arrow moves.'

4. Above, we introduced Yoda from the film Star Wars as an example of that extremely rare class of OSV speakers. However, when you look closer at the corpus of his speech from the films you may note that much of the time (particularly at tricky bits in the plot exposition) he sticks to the English favourite of SVO – to assist the English-speaking film-goer! Perhaps it is better to consider him as an SVO speaker who really likes to topicalize a lot?

   A corpus is just a collection. Linguists dearly love to collect and categorize large chunks of language. Collect your own small corpus for analysis. What proportion of the data is in the canonical order? Can you pick out examples of topicalization, of left and centre embedding? Can you draw some phrase structure trees for the simpler sentences?

   NB: beware of newspapers! Journalists are masters of multiply embedded sentences that can run on for paragraphs.

5. Compare and contrast syntactic and semantic approaches to understanding natural language.

6. What is the role of inference in natural language understanding? How might a

structure in memory, such as a script, assist with this role?

7. The key to understanding language is to see it in context – as a social act. Discuss.

Further Reading

Crystal, D. (1987) *The Cambridge Encyclopedia of Language*. Cambridge: Cambridge University Press.

Crystal, D. (1992) *An Encyclopedic Dictionary of Language and Languages*. Oxford: Blackwell.

Crystal, D. (1995) *The Cambridge Encyclopedia of the English Language*. Cambridge: Cambridge University Press.

> An excellent series of large format books based upon a dictionary or encyclopaedia view of language research. They are wonderful collections to just dip into for a gem.

Pinker, S. (1994) *The Language Instinct: The New Science of Language and Mind*. London: Allen Lane.

> Certainly the best essay on language in recent years and very readable.

Osherson, D. N. (1995; 2nd edn) *Invitation to Cognitive Science*, vol.1: *Language*. London: Bradford Books.

> A very advanced view of how linguists and psychologists are coming together to view language through cognitive science presented in this excellent collection.

PsyCLE MODULE: LANGUAGE

The two sections in this software directly echo the discussion in the text. The first part of the module helps you to think about the section 'Is language unique to humans?' by asking you to classify some animals according to Hockett's features. The second section allows you to explore a simple recursive transition network model and discusses its limitations (see figures 10.3 and 10.5).

PART 5

Social Psychology

CHAPTER 11

Social Cognition: Self, Attitudes and Attributions

Paschal Sheeran and Sheina Orbell

CHAPTER AGENDA

Following this chapter, you should be able to:

- Understand the scope of social cognition and the implications of this approach for how we think about people;

- Identify and apply a coding scheme for systematically categorizing people's self-concepts – the ways that people typically describe themselves;

- Outline the importance of cultural factors, feedback from other people and social comparisons in shaping people's views of themselves;

- Understand the role of the self-concept in interpreting information and guiding behaviour;

- Define the major conceptions of attitudes and describe how these ideas can be used to understand how and why people's attitudes differ;

- Describe some of the techniques for measuring attitudes;

- Outline the variety of devices that people use to protect and maintain their attitudes;

- Understand the major theories concerning when and if there is a relationship between attitudes and behaviour;

- Identify factors which are likely to be responsible for successfully persuading people to change their attitudes;

- Understand when people are likely to believe a person behaved in a particular way because of the type of person they are or because of situational constraints;

- Compare, contrast and critically evaluate models of causal attribution;

- Apply theories of social cognition to people's self-concepts, attitudes and explanations of events in the 'real world'.

▓ Introduction: the Social Thinker ▓

When people are asked why they want to pursue a course in psychology, one of the reasons most often given tends to be along the lines of wanting to understand what makes us see the world the way we do. How we make sense of ourselves, other people and situations is the concern of SOCIAL COGNITION. Social cognition is the study of the ways that people think about their experiences of themselves and others.

SOCIAL COGNITION

Social cognition tries to acknowledge the importance of both cognitive and social processes in our everyday understandings. Social psychology has always been cognitive, even during the 1950s, when experimental psychology was dominated by 'learning theory' (Fiske & Taylor 1992; see chapter 8). Cognition is important because identifying, recognizing and assigning value to objects in our environment allows us to make the world meaningful. This involves processes of receiving, selecting, transforming, and organizing information such that we can construct for ourselves versions of reality in the form of attitudes, beliefs and attributions (cognitions).

Social worlds are important because our cognitions invariably originate from, and are concerned about, our experiences of ourselves, other people and our environment. Consider, for example, the importance of a shared physical environment even for the language we use to characterize physical objects. Inuit people have several different terms for describing types of snow – because attending to, recognizing and remembering different types of snow is useful, and is learned and reinforced by social interactions in that culture. There is, of course, another more immediate sense in which cognition is social in origin. Our genetic endowment and early socialization are likely to have only a marginal role in explaining our current thinking about ourselves and others. This is because our recent experiences and the beliefs we have derived from them, the people we are with and the situation we are in at any particular moment provide the context for what we attend to, remember and talk about at that time. Our social context will determine what is most important to us, or appropriate to express at any given moment. Describing and theorizing how this is achieved is a principal concern of social cognition.

Social worlds do not just have a role in explaining the context of our cognition, they also strongly determine the content of cognition. Imagine how dull a party would be if everyone agreed not to talk about themselves, other people and even imaginary characters in books or films! The psychological constructs such as attitudes and attributions which are discussed in this chapter invariably refer to our experiences of being in the world with others. The profound disorientation experienced by people isolated from others (e.g., Byrd 1938), moreover, shows how individuals' experiences are normally intimately tied to the experiences of others. This underlines a final point about the social nature of cognition, namely that cognition is socially shared. While every person's experience inevi-

Plate 11.1 Homeless person
Source: Collections/
Select.

tably differs from that of everyone else, and therefore how they think about themselves and others will inevitably differ, it would be foolish to ignore the enormous commonalities in experience which derive from being born into and belonging to social groups. Cultures based on geographical location, religious beliefs and political and social ideologies provide shared information and hence shared meanings for individuals to construct their own versions of reality.

▨ Perceiving the Self ▨

What do we think about most often? The answer, almost inevitably, is ourselves. However, the self is not just important to us or frequently thought about. It is also unique in social cognition because it is *reflexive* – our perception of any other object in the world involves the subject and object being different; only with respect to the self do the subject and object of perception refer to the same concept.

Distinguishing between the self as subject, agent or knower (the 'I') and the self as object or known (the 'Me') is the starting point for most social-psychological theories about the self. Historically, research has been mainly concerned with the self as an object of perception (THE SELF-CONCEPT) and has addressed questions such as how we can describe the variety of different ways that people see themselves, and why people hold the views of themselves they do. More recently, studies have examined the self as a subject of perception, and examined the implications of our self-views for how we process information about the world and how we regulate our behaviour. Each of these three questions are examined in turn below.

THE SELF-CONCEPT

The nature of the self-concept

Rosenberg (1979) provides a useful definition of the domain of the self-concept: the totality of the person's thought and feelings having reference to him/herself as an object. You will get an idea of this totality and of the variety of different ways people view themselves if you begin by trying to describe yourself. Take a few minutes to write your answer to the question 'Who am I?', using twenty words or phrases.

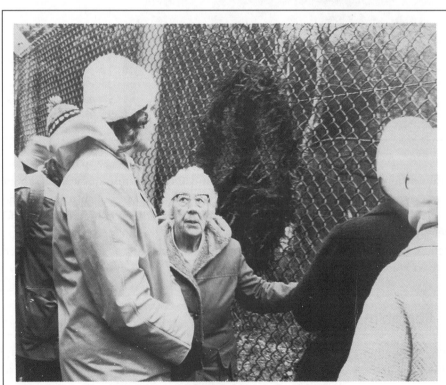

Plate 11.2 Greenham Common women, an anti-nuclear protest group
Source: Sheina Orbell.

Table 11.1 Gordon's (1968) system for classifying responses to the 'twenty statements test' (answers to the question 'Who am I?' using 20 words or phrases)

A. Ascribed Characteristics
    1. Sex *(e.g., a woman, girl)*
    2. Age *(e.g., 19 years old, first year)*
    3. Name *(e.g., Phil T. White, Theoborzanes Smith)*
    4. Racial or national heritage *(e.g., Irish, Asian [not current citizenship])*
    5. Religious categorisation *(e.g., Jewish, Protestant [definite group mentioned])*
B. Roles and Memberships
    6. Kinship roles *(e.g., a daughter, married, a father)*
    7. Occupational role *(e.g., a dentist, ratchatcher, part time ...)*
    8. Student role *(e.g., a psychology student, passed first year)*
    9. Political affiliation *(e.g., Labour party supporter [definite group mentioned])*
    10. Social status *(e.g., working class, rich family)*
    11. Territoriality, citizenship *(e.g., English [current citizenship])*
    12. Membership in actual interacting group *(e.g., member of a debating or sports club)*
C. Abstract identifications
    13. Existential, individuating *(e.g., an individual, indefinable [denial of categories])*
    14. Abstract category *(e.g., a human being, a voter)*
    15. Ideological and belief references *(e.g., a liberal, a vegetarian, Christian)*
D. Interests and Activities
    16. Judgements, tastes and likes *(e.g., Heavy Metal, Picasso's paintings)*
    17. Intellectual concerns *(e.g., interested in philosophy, literature, etc.)*
    18. Artistic activities *(e.g., singer, dancer, painter)*
    19. Other activities *(e.g., football player, hiker, trainspotter)*
E. Material references
    20. Possessions, resources *(e.g., rented flat, financially secure)*
    21. Physical, body image *(e.g., sexy, tall, unhealthy)*
F. Major Senses of Self
    22. Competence *(e.g., talented, skilful, make mistakes)*
    23. Self-determination *(e.g. ambitious, lazy, need deadlines)*
    24. Unity, integration *(e.g., confused, at one with myself, 'together')*
    25. Moral worth *(e.g., responsible, reliable, dishonest)*
G. Personal Characteristics
    26. Interpersonal style *(e.g., friendly, shy, hard to get to know [typical actions])*
    27. Psychic style, personality *(e.g., moody, optimistic [typical thoughts and feelings])*
H. External References
    28. Judgements imputed to others *(e.g., popular, disliked by teachers [others' impressions])*
    29. Immediate situation references *(e.g., tired, hungry, dark outside)*
    30. Uncodable responses *(e.g., Eat the rich, Donald Duck)*

If you look at what you've written, it is likely that you will have begun by mentioning your age, sex, and perhaps your race. You might have mentioned that you are currently studying psychology or, perhaps, that you are a member of a tennis club. So far, you have probably not given too much away. You have listed only social identity elements – groups or social categories to which you belong. While these social identity elements express what you surely are, they may not express what you feel you truly are (Rosenberg 1979). To express what you truly are you will probably have mentioned your likes and dislikes, the ways you typically think, feel and act, or your moral and political beliefs.

Social psychologists have collected self-descriptions from large numbers of people using the technique you have just used. The 'Who Am I?' test (also known as the 'twenty statements test') was developed by Kuhn and McParland (1954) as a method for determining the content of self-concepts. If you look at your answer and consider that there are more than 17,000 adjectives that you potentially could have used to describe yourself (Allport & Odbert 1936), as well as all the nouns that could refer to social identity elements or your likes and dislikes, then the need for a comprehensive system for analysing the content of self-concepts becomes apparent.

ASCRIBED CHARACTERISTICS

ROLES AND MEMBERSHIPS

ABSTRACT IDENTIFICATIONS

Perhaps the most widely used system for analysing responses to the 'Who Am I?' test is that devised by Gordon (1968). He outlines 30 categories of responses under eight broad headings (see table 11.1). ASCRIBED CHARACTERISTICS and ROLES AND MEMBERSHIPS both refer to social identity elements, though they are elements of different kinds. Whereas ascribed characteristics refer to categories that are assigned to a person at birth (e.g. sex and age), roles and memberships involve groups that a person has had at least some choice about joining (e.g. a political party or sports club). While ascribed characteristics are usually inescapable, roles and memberships can be changed. The third heading, ABSTRACT IDENTIFICATIONS, involves self-descriptions that are too abstract or general to constitute social identity elements (e.g. a human being).

BODY-IMAGE

While a person's membership of social categories constitutes an important aspect of his/her self-concept, the person's connection to objects outside the self and the sense of having a physical reality must also be considered. The 'interests and activities' heading refers to the wide variety of judgements, tastes and concerns a person might see themselves as having, as well as the artistic and other activities with which the person is involved. 'Material references' involve references to possessions such as a car or a famous person's autograph as well as perceptions of one's own body. This latter category is also known as the person's BODY-IMAGE and may involve relatively neutral descriptions of one's height or weight, or evaluative judgements of one's appearance such as 'attractive', 'athletic', etc.

The next heading, 'major senses of self', is intended to represent the person's view of him/herself with respect to issues of adaptation, goal attainment, integration and maintenance. These are considered by Parsons (1959) to be the major problems faced by any type of system, social or biological. In terms of the person's self-concept, these issues are reflected in self-descriptions which involve concerns about competence, self-determination, integration and moral worth, respectively. The final substantive heading is 'personal characteristics', which refer to the way a person typically acts towards others (their interper-

Plate 11.3 Footballer after scoring a goal
Source: Colorsport.

sonal style) and to how they typically feel or act (their psychic styles, or what we mean by the term 'personality' in everyday language). These two categories are likely to represent a good deal of what a person feels they truly are. Responses to these categories represent our accumulated knowledge of ourselves as participants in our social world. Answers in this category are usually single adjectives such as 'kind', 'friendly', 'brave', etc.

While Gordon's scheme for classifying responses to the 'Who Am I?' test probably captures most people's descriptions of themselves at a particular moment, not all of our views of ourselves may refer to the present or even to how we 'really' see ourselves. People also have views of themselves in the past (for instance, 'Me when I was at school') and views about how they would like to see themselves. Higgins (1987) distinguishes between the IDEAL SELF ('Me as I would like to be') and the OUGHT SELF ('Me as I think I should or ought to be'). Similarly, Markus and Nurius (1986) discuss POSSIBLE SELVES – views about what the self

IDEAL SELF

OUGHT SELF

POSSIBLE SELVES

Box 11.1   Self-Esteem: Why Do I Love Me?

Global self-esteem – the overall positive or negative direction of the self-concept – has been the most widely, and often exclusively, researched aspect of the self in social psychology. Most researchers would agree that our desire to protect or enhance a favourable view of ourselves is perhaps the most powerful motive governing our social behaviour. The importance of the self-esteem motive may be due to a basic need (high self-esteem is innately satisfying) or because high self-esteem is associated with pleasurable experiences in childhood (Rosenberg 1979). The 'terror management theory of self-esteem' (Solomon et al. 1991) suggests that self-esteem arose in our evolutionary past as an aid to survival – if we were preoccupied with developing and maintaining a positive view of self then we could manage the terror of knowing that we are mortal!

While the importance of self-esteem is uncontested, there are a number of views about what self-esteem is and how it should be measured. Perhaps the earliest formulation is that of William James (1890) who suggested that self-esteem be defined as the person's aspirations divided by their achievements. Modern theorists have also defined self-esteem in this way, where self-esteem involves comparison between elements of the current and ideal self (e.g. Moretti & Higgins 1987). Other researchers define self-esteem in terms of self-acceptance and feelings of self-worth (e.g. Rogers 1960). The Rosenberg (1965) 'self-esteem scale' was designed to measure this conception of self-esteem. This scale consists of ten statements including 'I feel worthless as a person', 'I feel that I am on an equal plane with others'. Participants are asked to use a tick to show whether they strongly agree, agree, disagree or strongly disagree with each statement (see Box 11.2).

Self-esteem can be distinguished from a person's self-confidence or *self-efficacy*. Self-efficacy refers to the person's perceptions of their ability to do things successfully or make things happen in accordance with their inner wishes (e.g., 'I am confident that I will get a First Class mark in my exam'). While self-esteem and self-efficacy are related, they are not identical concepts – a person can have high self-esteem and have low self-efficacy in a variety of domains. Bandura (1992) has reviewed evidence suggesting that high self-efficacy leads to greater effort and persistence and makes action more likely.

might be like in the future. Possible selves may represent realistic goals, unobtainable dreams or selves that one is afraid of becoming (e.g. a knitter or pipe-smoker).

The content of our self-concepts, then, may vary along dimensions such as 'past–present–future', 'actual–possible', and 'real–ideal'. Two other dimensions, or ways of describing, the content of one's self-concept must also be considered – *importance* and *direction*. Direction refers to how positively or negatively a particular element of the self-concept is viewed by the person. For example, a social identity element such as 'old' or a psychic style element such as 'angry' might be evaluated positively or negatively by different people. Direction can refer not only to elements or contents of the self but also to the self-concept considered as a whole. The overall direction of the self-concept is usually termed SELF-ESTEEM (see Box 11.1). People may also differ in the extent to which different elements are considered important. For one person, taking part in sport is extremely important, whereas for another person, their ambition to be a clinical psychologist dominates their view of themselves. Typically, there is a strong association between those self-concept elements which we consider important and those elements upon which we positively evaluate ourselves, and vice versa (Pelham & Swann 1989).

SELF-ESTEEM

Self-concept formation and change

One of the great paradoxes of research on the self-concept concerns evidence that, on the one hand, our views of ourselves are stable and resistant to change (Swann 1985) and, on the other hand, our views of ourselves can vary dramatically depending upon the situation in which we find ourselves (McGuire & McGuire 1988). What factors has research suggested are influential in determining the content of our views of ourselves?

One obvious factor influencing our social identity elements are major life transitions such as losing one's job or having a baby. Similarly, mood appears to influence which aspects of the self are salient and how positively or negatively elements of the self are viewed (Brown & Taylor 1986). Several other influences can also be suggested, however. These include culture, social-structural position, feedback from significant others and social comparisons (Rosenberg & Pearlin 1978).

Culture

Unfortunately, cross-cultural studies of the self-concept are still quite rare in social psychology. Papers by Triandis (1989) and Markus and Kitayama (1991), however, have drawn attention to differences between the ways people from more individualistic cultures (such as Western countries) and people from more collectivist cultures (Asian countries, for example) typically describe themselves.

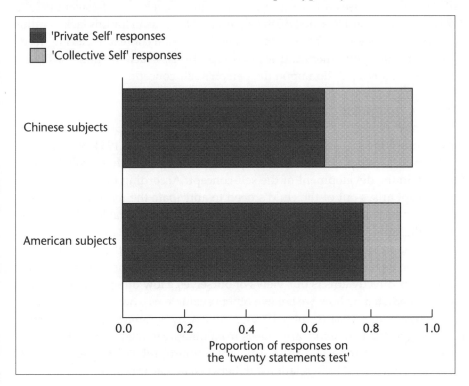

Figure 11.1 Proportion of 'private self' and 'collective self' responses on the 'twenty statements test' by Chinese and American subjects
Source: adapted from Trafimow et al. 1991.

In collectivist cultures the self-concept is generally described in terms of in-groups, relationships with others and the requirements of the specific situational context. The ideal self is concerned with belonging to the group, with being flexible and with adjusting to the social context. In contrast, people from individualistic cultures typically describe their self-concepts in terms of autonomy, separateness from social context and internal attributes. The person's ideal self is concerned with 'being oneself' and validating one's internal attributes. In an empirical study, Trafimow et al. (1991) divided responses to the 'twenty statements test' from American and Chinese students into two categories: responses representing social identity elements (the collective self) and responses representing personal characteristics and major senses of self (the private self). As figure 11.1 shows, Chinese respondents gave more collective self-descriptions and fewer private self-descriptions than American respondents.

Social-structural position

Social-structural position refers to a person's standing in the social hierarchy, including variables such as one's sex, age, ethnicity and social class. Again, these broad features of the social world have been relatively neglected in studies in this area. Where sex, race, and so forth have been examined, research has concentrated on their influence upon one dimension of the self-concept only – self-esteem. Reviews of literature have found virtually no evidence to suggest that men and women, people of different ages or ethnic backgrounds, or people of different social classes differ significantly in their levels of self-esteem (Wylie 1979). Rosenberg and Pearlin (1978) suggest that the reason for this lack of influence relates to factors in the person's immediate social context, including feedback from significant others and social comparisons, which mediate the effects of social-structural position upon the person's self-concept.

Feedback from significant others

We all know how good it can feel to receive praise from people we admire and how painful criticism can be. 'Symbolic interactionism' (Mead 1934; Stryker 1982) is a theoretical perspective which is explicitly concerned with the role of social feedback in the development of the self-concept. According to this theory, the self-concept arises out of the child's need to anticipate the reactions of significant others such as a parent towards him/her. This involves taking the perspective of the other person towards the self – seeing the self as an object. This 'objectification' of the self represents the beginning of our self-conception.

Symbolic interactionists do not suggest that verbal and non-verbal feedback from others directly affects our views of ourselves. How others actually evaluate us is mediated by how we believe others evaluate us – our REFLECTED APPRAISALS or LOOKING-GLASS SELF (Cooley 1902). A review by Shrauger and Schoeneman (1979) suggested that actual appraisals from others are related to reflected appraisals and that reflected appraisals are strongly related to people's self-concepts. They found little relationship between actual appraisals and people's

REFLECTED
APPRAISALS

LOOKING-GLASS
SELF

self-concepts, supporting the view that reflected appraisals mediate their influence.

Not everyone influences how we see ourselves, however. People we care about and those whose views we trust are most influential (Rosenberg 1979). Mead (1934) suggests that we develop a global view about how we are seen by others, which he termed the GENERALIZED OTHER. This 'internal audience' may sustain our self-concepts even in the face of explicit criticism in particular situations. We also generally develop relationships with others who confirm or verify our views of ourselves (Swann 1985). Indeed, it is relatively rare to obtain explicitly negative feedback from others since such criticism is contrary to the rules of most social interactions (Blumberg 1972).

GENERALIZED OTHER

Social comparisons

Festinger (1954) proposed that when we do not have objective evidence relevant to our opinions or abilities (such as an exam result) we compare ourselves with other people in order to determine our standing in that domain. The questions of when we make comparisons, what we compare, and why, as well as with whom comparisons are made, are the concern of SOCIAL COMPARISON THEORY.

SOCIAL COMPARISON THEORY

The impact of social comparison upon self-esteem was demonstrated in a classic experiment by Morse and Gergen (1970). Participants responded to an advertisement for a part-time job as a research assistant in a Psychology Department. Upon arriving for interview the participant was left alone in a waiting room and asked to fill in some forms including the first half of a self-esteem scale. When the secretary came to collect the completed questionnaire another interview candidate also entered the room. For half of the participants the new candidate was a 'Mr Clean'. He appeared confident and was wearing a suit and carrying a briefcase. The other half were exposed to a 'Mr Dirty', whose appearance was bedraggled and who seemed 'dazed by the whole procedure'. After one and a half minutes, the secretary returned with more forms including the second half of the self-esteem scale. Consistent with social comparison theory, participants who were exposed to 'Mr Dirty' reported higher self-esteem scores on their second form, whereas participants exposed to 'Mr Clean' showed lower self-esteem scores. Some limits to this effect were observed, however. Participants with very inconsistent views of themselves were strongly influenced by the other candidate, while people with consistent self-concepts showed little change between the two halves of the self-esteem scale.

Social comparisons with other individuals (interpersonal comparisons) do not invariably affect our view of ourselves, of course. Factors such as how close we are to the other person, how well the person is performing and how important the performance domain is to us can combine to determine our response. For example, when someone close is performing very well in a domain that is not relevant to you (for example, suppose you do not play tennis yourself, but you see your friend win a tennis tournament), you can BIRG – bask in (their) reflected glory! We do not make comparisons only with other individuals, we also

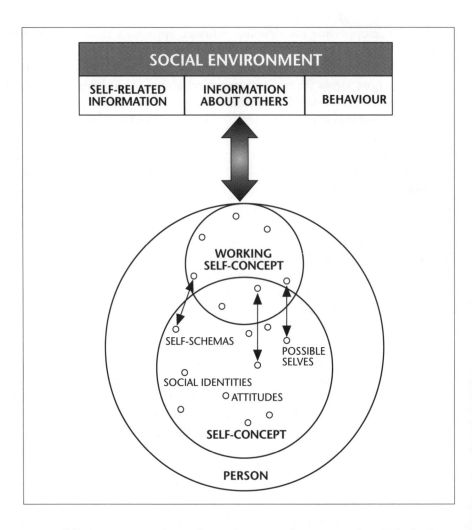

Figure 11.2 The working self-concept
Source: adapted from Markus & Wurf 1987.

compare different aspects of ourselves – for example, our actual and ideal selves, or our past and present selves. Sheeran et al. (1995), for example, have shown that comparisons with the past self are very salient for job-losers and are strongly correlated with depression. Social identity theory draws attention to another level of social comparison, comparisons between my group and other groups (INTERGROUP COMPARISONS, see chapter 12).

INTERGROUP
COMPARISONS

The working self-concept, self-schemas and self-efficacy

While culture, social feedback and social comparisons may each influence the content of our views of ourselves, we also need to be able to consider how these sources of stability and change affect the self-concept – we need to understand why we have the multifaceted and dynamic views of ourselves we do. One useful suggestion draws upon the notions of working and long-term memory in cognitive psychology (see chapter 7). According to Markus and Wurf (1987), the self is a particularly well-elaborated, complex and active cognitive structure. It contains a huge variety of possible views of ourselves including possible selves, social identity elements, etc. At any particular moment, however, only a subset of this universe is active – those representations of the self that are invoked by the requirements of the situation which may have been stored in memory during experiences in similar situations. This temporary structure is called the WORK-ING SELF-CONCEPT – the configuration of self-views made salient by ongoing social events (see figure 11.2).

WORKING
SELF-CONCEPT

Kunda et al. (1993) have shown how variable the content of the working self-concept can be. They asked one half of a sample of students 'Are you happy with your social life?', while the other half were asked 'Are you unhappy with your social life?'. Both groups were requested to list examples of past behaviours, thoughts and feelings that came to mind as they tried to answer the question and both groups also rated themselves on a scale ranging from −5 ('extremely unhappy with my social life') to +5 ('extremely happy with my social life'). Even though there was no reason to suppose that the two groups actually differed in their feelings about the their social life, figure 11.3 shows that subjects who were asked if they were unhappy with their social life rated their happiness lower than subjects who were asked if they were happy with their social life!

This finding can be explained by the notion of a working self-concept. Subjects who were asked if they were unhappy were scanning their memories for evidence of unhappy experiences in their social life. Subjects who were asked if they were happy, on the other hand, were searching for memories of happiness in their social life. The results of subjects' thought listings support this interpretation. Subjects who were asked if they were unhappy with their social life listed more unhappy thoughts than subjects who were asked if they were happy with their social life. In this instance, the questions subjects were asked altered the content of their working self-concepts.

There have been only a very small number of studies which have investigated the working self-concept, but this construct does seem to offer a useful account of how ongoing interactions with environments interact with attentional and memorial processes to produce dynamic changes in our views of ourselves in real time. If the working self-concept helps account for the malleability of the

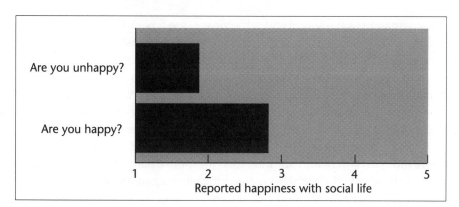

Figure 11.3 Self-rating of happiness by subjects asked whether they were happy with their social life
Source: adapted from Kunda et al. 1993.

self, how can we account for self-concept stability from this perspective?

According to Markus, self-concept stability arises from two sources. First, the universe of self-representations of which the working self-concept is a subset is relatively stable – there are limits to the variety of self-views that we can sample because of the limits of our individual experience. This is not to say that we do not develop new representations of ourselves – only that acquiring entirely new self-descriptions is not very common because of our investment in more established views of ourselves.

The second source of stability relates to the importance dimension of elements of the self-concept. Some elements reflect areas of enduring importance, investment and concern to us that are likely to be invoked in many different social situations. These elements are called SELF-SCHEMAS: 'cognitive generalizations about the self derived from past experience that organize and guide the processing of self-related information contained in the individual's social experiences', as Markus (1977) puts it.

SELF-SCHEMAS

Self-schemas are 'chronically accessible', meaning that they are easily recruited to the working self-concept and therefore readily available for information processing. Markus and Wurf (1987) have reviewed the extensive evidence concerning the impact of self-schemas upon attention and memory for self-related and social information. SCHEMATICS are usually defined in experiments as people who rate themselves highly in a particular domain and who see that domain as important to them (e.g., 'masculine' schematics would see traits such as 'dominant' and 'aggressive' as both very descriptive of them and very important to them: Markus et al. 1985). Relative to ASCHEMATICS (people who do not possess a self-schema in a particular domain), 'schematics' tend to:

SCHEMATICS

ASCHEMATICS

- display greater attention for schema-related information;
- process schema-related information more efficiently (i.e. more quickly, confidently and consistently);
- show greater recognition and recall for schema-related information;
- resist information that is counter to the self-schema when they are given false feedback by an experimenter.

Self-schemas, possible selves and self-efficacy (see Box 11.1) each have important implications for how we regulate our actions. Kendzierski (1990) has shown that 'exercise schematics' (people who rate exercise-related words as descriptive of, and important to, them) are more likely to engage in future exercise than aschematics. Markus and Ruvulo (1992) asked participants to write essays about themselves in the future, either describing themselves as very successful ('successful' possible self) or describing themselves as unsuccessful ('failure' possible self). On a subsequent task participants who had invoked a successful possible self were more persistent and accurate than the failure possible self group and a control group who had simply been made to feel in a good mood.

How we organize and regulate our actions is one of the most complex issues in social cognition and has been approached from a wide variety of perspectives. One of the most important approaches comes from attitude theory. The impact of attitudes upon behaviour is one of the issues considered in the next section.

■ Social Attitudes ■

We rarely simply give and receive information about our social world. Our talk and actions are overwhelmingly evaluative. We judge continuously – liking, raving about, disagreeing with and despising what we see around us. Our evaluations of people, objects and issues – the positive or negative feelings we experience when we think about or encounter them – are our attitudes. Our attitudes constitute the 'interests and activities' element of our self-concept (see table 11.1), and manufacturers, advertisers, politicians, artists and writers all want to us to hold attitudes that favour them and their products.

The nature of attitudes: three views

The term 'social attitude' was introduced by Thomas and Znaniecki (1918) in order to explain differences in the everyday behaviours of Polish farmers living in Poland and the USA. Early views of attitudes (e.g. Rosenberg & Hovland 1960) asserted that an attitude had three components: a behavioural component (how we tend to act towards the entity), a cognitive component (what thoughts we have about the entity) and an evaluative component (how we feel about the entity) (see figure 11.4, panel 1). One difficulty with this three-component view is that very few studies have actually measured all three of these components. Most measures of attitude, as we shall see, examine only the evaluative component.

A second problem for the three-component model of attitudes is that it seems

Figure 11.4, panel 1 The three-component model of attitudes
Source: adapted from Hovland & Rosenberg 1960.

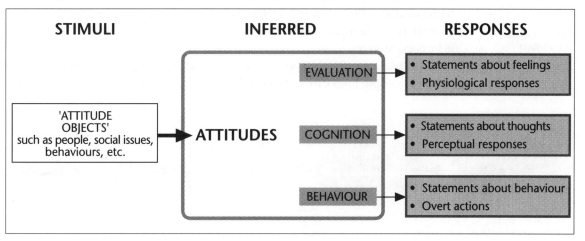

439

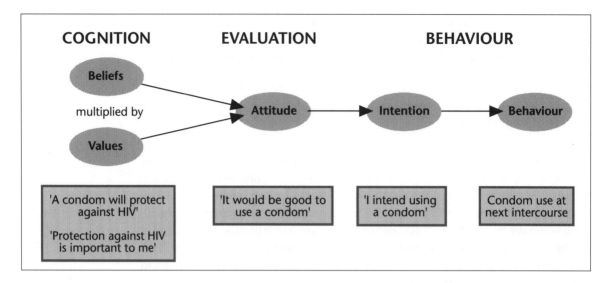

COGNITION   EVALUATION   BEHAVIOUR

Beliefs

multiplied by   Attitude → Intention → Behaviour

Values

'A condom will protect against HIV'

'Protection against HIV is important to me'

'It would be good to use a condom'

'I intend using a condom'

Condom use at next intercourse

Figure 11.4, panel 2 The expectancy–value model of attitudes Source: adapted from Fishbein & Ajzen 1975.

BELIEF

BEHAVIOURAL INTENTION

EXPECTANCY– VALUE MODEL

Figure 11.4, panel 3 The attitude accessibility model Source: adapted from Fazio 1985.

to assume that the behavioural, cognitive and affective components will invariably be consistent. However, this consistency is rarely perfect. I may be extremely fond of ice-cream (evaluation) but also believe that it is fattening (cognition) and therefore refrain from buying it hourly (behaviour).

Fishbein and Ajzen (1975) suggest that is useful to use the term attitude to refer only to the person's overall evaluation of the entity, and reserve the terms BELIEF for the cognitive component and BEHAVIOURAL INTENTION for the tendency to act towards the entity in a particular way. Their EXPECTANCY–VALUE MODEL is a uni-dimensional, or one-component, view of attitudes (see figure 11.4, panel 2). Attitude refers to the overall evaluation of the entity (e.g., 'It would be good to use a condom'). The person's attitude derives from beliefs about the entity and the values associated with those beliefs. Beliefs are the person's opinions, knowledge or thoughts about the entity. More formally, beliefs refer to the person's expectations that the entity possesses certain characteristics (e.g., 'A condom is likely to protect against HIV infection'). Values refer to desired end states of being or doing (Rokeach 1973). Here values are the person's evaluations of the characteristics associated with the entity (e.g., 'Protection against HIV infection is important to me').

The expectancy–value model provides a useful basis for understanding why different people hold different attitudes towards the same entity – people may

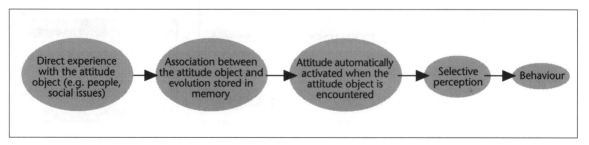

Direct experience with the attitude object (e.g. people, social issues) → Association between the attitude object and evolution stored in memory → Attitude automatically activated when the attitude object is encountered → Selective perception → Behaviour

Table 11.2 Selected beliefs and evaluations of characteristics of using the contraceptive pill by pill users and non-users (adapted from Werner & Middlestadt 1979)

	BELIEFS		EVALUATIONS	
	Users	Non-Users	Users	Non-Users
Increase in my sexual pleasure	1.27	0.10*	2.70	2.32
Taking a chemical substance that hasn't been proven completely safe	1.30	2.23*	−1.77	−2.06
Increased risk of blood clotting	0.77	1.74*	−2.43	−2.55
Regulation of my menstrual cycle	2.37	1.87	2.33	1.58*
Having more responsibility for contraception than my partner	2.07	1.97	−0.53	−1.61*

* indicates a significant difference between the scores for pill users and non-users. *Beliefs* were measured by questions about whether using the contraceptive pill would have these consequences. Answers ranged from the pill would 'completely achieve' the consequence (score +3) to 'completely prevent' that consequence (score −3). *Evaluations* were measured by questions about whether these consequences of using the contraceptive pill would have good or bad consequences. Answers ranged from 'good' (score +3) to 'bad' (score −3).

differ in their beliefs about how likely it is that the entity possesses particular characteristics and/or differ about how much they value the characteristics associated with the entity. For example, Werner and Middlestadt (1979) examined 14 beliefs and values of users and non-users of the contraceptive pill. Users of the pill had stronger beliefs about the safety of the pill and about how pleasurable they are to use. Users of the pill also valued regulation of menstruation and taking sole responsibility for contraception more highly (see table 11.2).

Another approach which stresses the evaluative component of attitudes is Fazio's (1990) ATTITUDE ACCESSIBILITY MODEL. According to Fazio, an attitude is a learned association between an entity and its evaluation which is stored in memory. For example, if one watched opera on TV many times and disliked the experience each time, a strong association between opera and negative evaluation would be stored in memory. The strength of the association between the entity and the positive or negative evaluation can vary for different people and for different entities. The stronger the association, however, the more *accessible* one's attitude – the more readily available it is for interpreting incoming information. The time a person takes to respond positively or negatively to a particular entity (the response latency) is the most commonly used method of measuring attitude accessibility (see Box 11.2 on methods of measuring attitudes).

The accessibility of an attitude seems to depend largely upon how much direct experience the person has with the entity. Even very simple experiences such as reviewing past behaviours one has performed that are relevant to one's attitude (Fazio 1987), or repeatedly expressing one's attitude (Fazio et al. 1982),

ATTITUDE
ACCESSIBILITY
MODEL

Box 11.2 Attitude Measurement: Not Just Marking an 'x' for Brand X

Since we cannot directly observe someone's attitudes, we must infer the person's evaluations of people, objects and issues on the basis of what they tell us. A person can 'tell' us their attitude in words or through their physiological responses.

The most commonly used method is to ask someone to report their attitudes either in speech or writing. Open-ended interviews can provide a rich picture of a person's attitudes. Unfortunately, such interviews are very time-consuming if one wants a large sample, and comparing the responses of different groups (e.g. women versus men) can be difficult. Attitudes researchers have therefore developed more structured methods of inferring attitudes called *scales*. Attitude scales usually contain a variety of statements relevant to the attitude issue. A person must choose one or more statements that best sum up how they feel. Because the different statements can be given different values (say −2 to +2), it is easy to then compare people's attitudes.

The oldest type of attitude scale is the *Thurstone scale* (Thurstone 1928). To construct a Thurstone scale about 100 attitude statements must be generated and about 100 judges must rate the statements as pro- or anti- the relevant person, object or issue. From the 100 original statements, approximately 20 are selected which must cover the entire range of opinion on the matter *and* do so in such a manner that the distance between each statement is the same in the overall view of the judges. Not surprisingly, the Thurstone scale is rarely used today because it is so difficult and laborious to construct.

A brief Thurstone scale

Judges' rating (+2 to −2)

+2	Nuclear power stations should be dismantled now
+1	Nuclear power stations should be phased out
0	Nuclear power stations need to be investigated
−1	Nuclear power stations should be expanded
−2	Nuclear power stations should replace all other power stations

The *semantic different scale* (Osgood et al. 1957), on the other hand, is easy to construct and use. This scale is based on the assumption that concepts have different meanings for people and that these meanings can be measured by asking people to rate the concept on a series of bipolar scales (adjectives or phrases with opposite meanings). Osgood et al. suggest that there are three meaning dimensions common to all concepts: evaluation (e.g. how good or bad); potency (e.g. how strong or weak); and activity (e.g. how active or passive). The person's attitude is inferred on the basis of the sum or average of his/her ratings provided the ratings for the entire sample are *reliable*. A scale will be reliable if all the items on the scale relate to the overall scores on the scale, i.e., if every item makes a contribution to the total score. This is determined by including only those items in the final scale which have a correlation coefficient of $r = 0.20$ with the total score.

A brief semantic differential scale

Nuclear power stations are . . .

good	+3	+2	+1	0	−1	−2	−3	bad
harmful	−3	−2	−1	0	+1	+2	+3	beneficial
safe	+3	+2	+1	0	−1	−2	−3	dangerous
trustworthy	+3	+2	+1	0	−1	−2	−3	untrustworthy
undesirable	−3	−2	−1	0	+1	+2	+3	desirable

A Likert scale (Likert 1932) is also quite easy to construct and use. Like the Thurstone scale a larger number of attitude statements are first generated but, rather than judges' rating the statements, respondents themselves are asked to indicate how strongly they agree or disagree with each statement. Again every item on the scale must contribute to the total score on the scale – the scale must be reli-

can make an attitude more accessible. Highly accessible attitudes are thought to be activated automatically when we encounter the relevant entity because the strong association in memory instantly comes to mind. This in turn leads to perception of the attitude object in terms of one's attitude and to behaviour in line with one's attitude (see figure 11.4, panel 3).

able – so items with correlations less than r = 0.20 are excluded from the final scale. The sum or average of the person's agreements or disagreements is used to infer their attitude.

A brief Likert scale

Nuclear power stations should be dismantled now
Strongly Agree/Agree/Disagree/Strongly Disagree

Nuclear power is a cost-effective energy source
Strongly Agree/Agree/Disagree/Strongly Disagree

Nuclear power stations are dangerous
Strongly Agree/Agree/Disagree/Strongly Disagree

Nuclear power is the only way to meet future economic needs
Strongly Agree/Agree/Disagree/Strongly Disagree

Nuclear power stations create waste that endangers the environment
Strongly Agree/Agree/Disagree/Strongly Disagree

The expectancy-value model of attitudes uses both Likert and semantic differential scales. Most studies use semantic differential scales to measure the affective component (attitudes) and Likert scales to measure beliefs and evaluations (see table 11.2).

The affective component of attitudes has also been measured using physiological responses. One such indicator is the *galvanic skin response* (GSR). The GSR measures the electrical resistance of the skin which changes when people are emotionally aroused. In one experiment, changes in GSR accruing from white subjects being touched by black and white experimenters were used to infer racial attitudes (Porier & Lott 1967). Unfortunately, the GSR measures the intensity or extremity of a person's emotional reaction rather than the positive or negative *direction* of their response. The *facial electromyogram* (EMG) does not have this difficulty. The EMG uses electrodes to measure the activity of the smiling and frowning facial muscles. The EMG represents a useful method of accurately inferring people's attitudes. People cannot easily give a *socially desirable* answer, i.e. an answer that may not reflect the person's attitudes but one which the person thinks would be socially acceptable (e.g. anti-racist views).

Socially desirable answers are a significant problem for attitude researchers and, unfortunately, it is rarely possible to use the EMG on a large sample. Another method which has been used to obtain an accurate view of someone's attitudes is through the *bogus pipeline* procedure. This technique uses a mock lie-detector. Respondents are convinced by the experimenter that the machine can detect when someone is not being truthful – for example, by asking respondents to deliberately lie about their age when the person's age is known to the experimenter. The false answer is then shown in faked output to respondents to convince them that the machine is accurate. This method was used by Biglan et al. (1990) to try to ensure that the attitudes towards safer sex and drug use obtained in the study were accurate.

A final method that is less time-consuming and laborious than the bogus pipeline and which can be used in conjunction with attitude scales is employment of a social desirability scale. Social desirability scales typically contain items such as 'I have never eaten a whole bar of chocolate in one go' – items that almost everyone would admit were true if they were being honest. If people answer a series of such questions in a manner that suggests that they have never committed even a minor indiscretion then it is inferred that the person is trying to give socially acceptable answers. This consideration is then taken into account when inferring the person's attitude.

One of the most useful aspects of Fazio's attitude accessibility model is that it can help us to understand why two people who express the same attitude, for example on a questionnaire, might show inconsistent attitudes or behaviour a short time later. In an experiment on attitudes towards US presidential candidates, Fazio and Williams (1986) examined not just how positively or negatively the candidates were evaluated but also how accessible were respondents' attitudes towards the candidates. When respondents were asked three months later about how well they thought the candidates had performed in two television debates, those with highly accessible attitudes were more likely to judge the candidates in line with their original attitude than respondents with less accessible attitudes. Respondents with highly accessible attitudes were also more likely to vote for candidates in line with their original attitudes.

Fazio and Williams's study illustrates two functions of attitudes that have been extensively researched in social cognition: namely, that our attitudes influence what we attend to and remember and also how we behave. Attitudes may serve as important guides for our information processing and for directing our actions.

Attitude functions I: attitudes direct information-processing

Studies by Jamieson and Zanna (1989) illustrate how useful attitudes can be, especially when people are under time pressure and are unable to weigh up all the evidence available. These researchers used mock juries to examine the effects of attitudes towards the death penalty and positive discrimination on verdicts on these issues. In one condition the jurors had time to examine the evidence, and in a second condition the jurors had just three minutes to reach their decision. Consistent with the view that attitudes provide useful shorthand for examining information and making decisions, they found that jurors' initial attitudes were strongly related to their verdict when they had a time limit for their decision-making.

DISSONANCE THEORY (Festinger 1957) suggests that people are motivated to attend to and prefer information that is consistent with their current attitudes rather than information that is inconsistent (dissonant). Because a person wants to believe their attitudes are 'right', inconsistent information is perceived as undermining the person's attitudes and intentions and thereby produces tension (dissonance). Such dissonance is intrinsically aversive; the person will try to reduce the tension experienced by avoiding the dissonant information and/or seeking out information that is consistent with their attitude.

Accumulated evidence suggests that people try to maintain or protect their attitudes and that attitudes consequently serve a variety of cognitive or information-processing functions. Our attentional, interpretive and memory systems appear to be far from neutral when it comes to processing information that is relevant to our attitudes towards people, objects and issues. This selectivity about attitude-relevant information has been demonstrated in several ways, elaborated below.

Selective exposure – seeking attitude-consistent information that is not already there

Frey and Rosch (1984) asked respondents to decide whether or not a manager's contract should be extended on the basis of a written description of their ability. Half of the respondents completed the task under a reversible condition (they

DISSONANCE
THEORY

could change their decision later), and half could not later change their decision. After making their judgements, respondents were given the opportunity to receive additional information about the manager. The information was presented in a manner that made it clear whether the information was positive or negative.

Consistent with the selective exposure hypothesis, respondents sought positive information about the candidate when they had a positive attitude towards extending the contract and negative information when they had a negative attitude. Seeking consistent information was particularly pronounced under the irreversible condition, which suggests that a degree of commitment to one's attitude is important in producing selective exposure effects. Subsequent research suggests that people will seek out dissonant information when their attitudes are particularly strong (and dissonant information can be integrated or argued against), or when their attitudes are particularly weak (and people feel it might be better to have the 'right' attitude and change it now rather than later).

Selective attention – seeking attitude-consistent information that is there

Sweeney and Gruber (1984) neatly demonstrated the ways people attend to information that supports their attitude and ignore information that is inconsistent with their attitude in the context of the Watergate scandal. US President Richard Nixon was investigated for illegal activities and was forced to resign in 1973. People who had voted for Nixon's opponent in the presidential election were found to eagerly follow media coverage of the investigation. People who had voted for Nixon, on the other hand, avoided news about the investigation whenever they could. A great deal of evidence suggests that we spend more time looking at attitude-consistent than attitude inconsistent information (Broch & Balloun 1967), though we do appear to attend to non-supportive arguments if those arguments can be easily refuted (Kleinhesselink & Edwards 1975).

Selective interpretation – seeking attitude-consistent information when information is ambiguous

People also protect their attitudes by interpreting information in a manner that is consistent with them. For example, people's attitudes towards the Arab–Israeli conflict influenced their judgements of how fair they thought coverage of the conflict was ('it's fair if I agree with the coverage!'). Similarly, in judging the behaviour of a TV character, respondents with racist attitudes interpreted the character's ambiguously racist remarks as an accurate portrayal of reality, while respondents with anti-racist attitudes interpreted the remarks as a satire on bigotry (Vidmar & Rokeach 1974).

Selective judgement – using information to draw conclusions that are consistent with one's attitude

A variety of social cognition theories (e.g. ASSIMILATION-CONTRAST THEORY – Sherif & Hovland 1961; and ACCENTUATION THEORY – Eiser & Stroebe 1972) suggest that

ASSIMILATION-CONTRAST THEORY

445

our attitudes provide a standard against which we judge other people's attitudes. According to assimilation-contrast theory, when other people hold attitudes similar to our own we tend to exaggerate the similarity between our own and the other person's attitude position (see greater similarity than might actually be true – assimilation). When our attitudes differ, on the other hand, we tend to exaggerate the difference between our own and another person's attitude (contrast).

Selective recall – better recall for attitude-consistent information

Levine and Murphy (1943) conducted a classic experiment on attitude-congruent recall in which pro-communists and anti-communists read and tried to recall both pro- and anti- messages. While this study showed evidence of better recall for supporting arguments, several disconfirming studies followed. A review of these studies (Roberts 1985) found a small but statistically significant effect of attitude on memory. In line with other research on the information-processing consequences of attitudes, Judd and Kulik (1980) draw attention to the significance of strongly held attitudes in accounting for this weak relationship. They suggest that attitudes improve recall for statements that are strongly agreed with or strongly disagreed with compared with statements about which people feel relatively neutral.

Attitude functions II: attitudes guide behaviour

The cognitive consequences or knowledge function of attitudes has preoccupied research on attitudes somewhat less than the behavioural consequences of attitudes. The field of attitude–behaviour relations has a long history, which, Fazio (1990) suggests, has had three phases, each characterized by a slightly different focal question:

1. Are attitudes related to behaviour?
2. When are attitudes related to behaviour?
3. How are attitudes related to behaviour?

The three-component model of attitudes and, to a lesser extent, the expectancy–value model assumed a good deal of consistency between attitudes and behaviour. Early reviews of research addressing the question of whether attitudes and behaviour are related found evidence of only weak associations between attitudes and behaviour (Wicker 1969). Ajzen and Fishbein (1977) suggested that methodological difficulties might be responsible for the poor relationships obtained. Their work ushered in the second phase of research by making the search for conditions under which attitudes were predictive of behaviour the topic for empirical research.

Ajzen and Fishbein identified differences between the questions used to measure of attitude and the questions used to measure behaviour as the major difficulty with previous research. Very general measures of attitude (e.g. 'I agree with my Church's teachings') were being used to predict quite specific behaviours (e.g. church attendance). Ajzen and Fishbein suggested that general measures of attitude should be used to predict aggregates of behaviour (multiple behaviours or multiple observations of a behaviour). They compiled a list of 100 religious behaviours and devised four general 'attitude towards religion' scales. The average correlation between attitudes and specific behaviours (such as church attendance) was very small ($r = 0.14$), while the average correlation between attitudes and aggregates of behaviours was much bigger ($r = 0.63$) (Fishbein & Ajzen 1974).

Specific behaviours could only be predicted from attitudes if attitudes and behaviour were measured at the same level of specificity. Fishbein and Ajzen suggested four elements of specificity:

- the action – what behaviour is to be performed (e.g. voting)
- the target – towards what target the behaviour is directed (e.g. what candidate)
- the context – in what context the behaviour is to be performed (e.g. local election)
- the time – when the behaviour is to be performed (e.g. next Spring)

Davidson and Jaccard (1975) showed how specificity led to improved prediction in the context of contraceptive use. They found that a general measure of attitudes towards contraceptive use correlated $r = 0.08$ with use of the contraceptive pill over two years, while a specific measure correlated $r = 0.57$.

Fishbein and Ajzen recognized that specificity was not the only difficulty with research on attitude–behaviour relations. For example, we may not behave in accordance with our attitudes because of social pressures in the particular situation. Drawing upon the expectancy–value model of attitudes they developed an account of attitude–behaviour relationships which they termed the theory of reasoned action (Fishbein & Ajzen 1975) (see figure 11.5).

According to the theory, a person's intention to perform a behaviour is the immediate predictor of action. The person's intention is predicted by their attitude towards the behaviour and by their SUBJECTIVE NORM regarding the behaviour – their perceptions of social approval for their performing the behaviour (e.g., 'Most people who are important to me think that I should use a condom the next time I have sex'). Attitudes towards a behaviour are determined by the beliefs about the consequences of the behaviour multiplied by evaluations of those consequences. The subjective norm component is determined by beliefs about whether specific others would approve of the person performing the behaviour (NORMATIVE BELIEFS – e.g., 'My closest friend thinks that I should use a condom the next time I have sex'). Since other people are not all equally important in determining how much social approval the person feels, each normative belief must be multiplied by the MOTIVATION TO COMPLY with that person or group

SUBJECTIVE NORM

NORMATIVE BELIEFS

MOTIVATION TO COMPLY

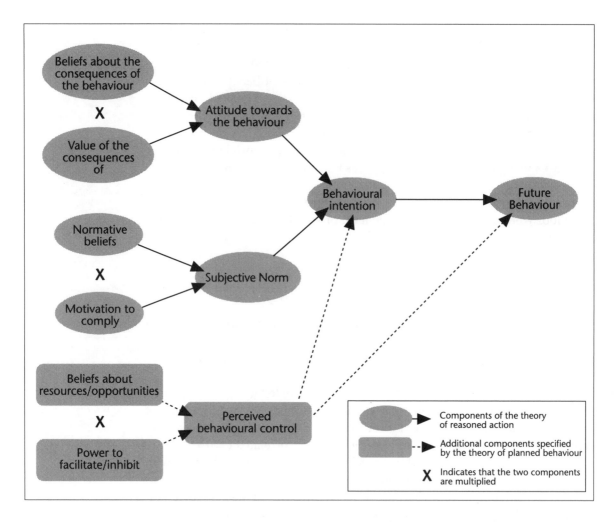

Figure 11.5 The theory of reasoned action (Fishbein & Ajzen 1975), and Ajzen's 1991 revised model, the theory of planned behaviour

(e.g., 'I generally want to do what my closest friend thinks I should do').

Studies have shown that the theory of reasoned action is successful in predicting a variety of behaviours, including blood donation, voting, contraceptive use, purchase of consumer goods, alcohol and drug use, and exercise and diet. Reviewing 87 studies, Sheppard, Hartwick and Warshaw (1988) found that the average correlation between intention and behaviour was large (r = 0.53), as was the average correlation between the combination of attitude + subjective norm and intention (r = 0.66). Bentler and Speckart (1979), however, pointed to an oversight in the theory of reasoned action, namely that past behaviour is a good predictor of future behaviour. In a study of alcohol and drug use, they found that people's past behaviour had a direct effect upon their future behaviour. According to Bentler and Speckart, the theory of reasoned action neglected the role of HABIT in explaining people's behaviour.

HABIT

Further criticism of the theory came from Liska (1984), who suggested that this account of attitude–behaviour relations was unsuitable for understanding not just habits but also behaviours that required resources, skills, particular opportunities or the cooperation of others. Responding to critics, Ajzen (1985) suggested that while the theory of reasoned action was able to explain volitional behaviours – behaviours over which the person has a good deal of control – a new component was needed to explain less volitional behaviours. Ajzen (1985) termed his modification of the theory of reasoned action the THEORY OF PLANNED BEHAVIOUR (see figure 11.5). The new component was PERCEIVED BEHAVIOURAL CONTROL, which referred to the person's perceptions of how easy or difficult it would be for them to perform the behaviour. Perceived behavioural control, according to Ajzen (1991) takes account of past behaviour and situational and resource factors, and can have direct or indirect effects (through intention) upon behaviour.

THEORY OF
PLANNED
BEHAVIOUR

PERCEIVED
BEHAVIOURAL
CONTROL

Initial tests of the theory of planned behaviour have been supportive. Madden et al. (1992), for example, found that for a behaviour that presented few obstacles (e.g. taking vitamin supplements) the theory of planned behaviour and the theory of reasoned action performed equally well. For a behaviour that required a good deal of perceived behavioural control (e.g., getting a good night's sleep), on the other hand, the theory of planned behaviour was better able to predict the outcome than the theory of reasoned action. While the theory of reasoned action and the theory of planned behaviour seem to offer successful accounts of the relationship between attitudes, norms, intentions and behaviour, critics suggest that these models ignore many other determinants of behaviour. Important among these are feelings of moral obligation or PERSONAL NORMS (Spencer & Budd 1985) and SELF-IDENTITY. Sparks and Shepherd (1993), for example, found that one's identity as a 'green consumer' was just as important as attitude in predicting the purchase of vegetables.

PERSONAL NORMS

SELF-IDENTITY

Fazio (1990) is also critical of the theory of reasoned action and the theory of planned behaviour on the grounds that they offer an overly rational or deliberative view of attitude–behaviour relations. According to Fazio, these models assume that people have the time and inclination to assess their performance of a behaviour in some depth. He points out that people may not have this opportunity and draws attention to the importance of attitude accessibility in determining whether attitudes guide behaviour (see Fazio & Williams 1986 mentioned above). According to Fazio's model, it is only by considering the accessibility of attitudes in working memory that we can understand how attitudes guide behaviour.

Attitude change: persuasive communications

Expectancy–value theory and Fazio's attitude accessibility model both offer accounts of how a person's attitudes are formed. Expectancy–value theory stresses the importance of socially learned beliefs about the attitude object, while the accessibility model stresses the learned association in memory between the person's feelings and the attitude object. While the question of how attitudes are formed has received relatively little attention, how attitudes change has been the subject of a great deal of research. This question has usually been examined in terms of people's responses to messages that attempt to 'change their minds' – PERSUASIVE COMMUNICATIONS. Social-psychological studies of persuasion examine what factors determine whether a message which is known to differ from participants' initial attitudes is successful in changing those attitudes.

PERSUASIVE
COMMUNICATIONS

The process model of persuasion

McGuire (1985) offers an account of the cognitive processes involved in attitude change. The PROCESS MODEL OF PERSUASION suggests that the effect of a persuasive communication is determined by a five-stage process: (i) attention; (ii) comprehension; (iii) yielding; (iv) retention, and (v) behaviour. Thus, for example, a message designed to promote positive attitudes to recycling waste will produce attitude change if, and only if, the message is attended to, the message is understood, the arguments contained in the message are accepted, the message is remembered, and there is an opportunity to change one's attitude and act upon it. According to McGuire, the recipient of a persuasive communication must go through each of these stages for attitude change to be successful. Moreover, recipients must have successfully completed the previous stage before they can go on to the next stage.

PROCESS MODEL OF
PERSUASION

Two factors are thought to be largely responsible for whether a message is attended to and understood. The first is motivation. People can easily ignore a message, if they so desire. That is, there may be other motives operating at the time which compete with the motive to attend to the persuasive communication. Indeed, the general lack of success of mass-media campaigns in producing attitude change is indicative of the fact that the majority of people do not pay them much attention (Hovland et al. 1953). Motivation is also important in determining message comprehension, since greater motivation will produce greater efforts at understanding. Ability is also an important factor, however. A person must have the opportunity to attend to the message and be capable of understanding (perhaps complex) arguments.

The factors which determine whether the recipients of a persuasive communication accept the message have preoccupied researchers since the Second World War, when social psychologists first attempted to understand wartime propaganda. Research on acceptance has been plagued by contradictory findings, however. For example, an expert, trustworthy or attractive source has produced attitude change in some situations but not in others. Similarly, presenting both sides rather than one side of an argument is sometimes successful and some-

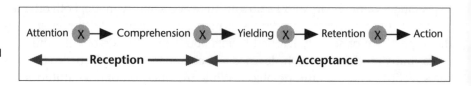

Figure 11.6 The process model of persuasion
Source: McGuire 1986.

times not. A theory which was developed to try to account for these contradictory findings was the elaboration-likelihood model of persuasion (Petty & Caccioppo 1986).

Elaboration-likelihood model

According to the ELABORATION-LIKELIHOOD MODEL OF PERSUASION (ELM), acceptance of a message can be achieved by two routes, the CENTRAL and PERIPHERAL routes to persuasion (see figure 11.7). Which route acceptance takes depends upon how likely it is that the recipient elaborates the message, that is, the extent to which the person thinks about and evaluates the arguments contained in the message. Motivation and ability will determine the extent to which a communication is elaborated. If the person cannot, or will not, think carefully about the message, then acceptance of the message depends upon peripheral aspects of the message rather than the arguments the message contains.

ELABORATION-LIKELIHOOD MODEL OF PERSUASION

CENTRAL

PERIPHERAL

Examples of peripheral aspects of the message which might lead to its acceptance include the expertise of the person who made the communication or that person's attractiveness. We are much more likely to agree with someone we believe is an expert on the particular issue than someone we think has little relevant expertise. Our beliefs about the person's competence (relevant accomplishments and status) and trustworthiness will be important in our deciding whether the person is indeed someone 'who knows'. We are also likely to agree with someone we think is attractive. Advertisers use this peripheral cue to persuasion a great deal, bombarding us with images of beautiful people. A study by Suzanne Pollack (1983) cleverly demonstrated the influence of attractiveness of the source of a communication. She showed two groups of women the same article advocating financial support for the arts. One group also saw a colour photo of an attractive man who had supposedly written the article. The other group saw only a blurred photocopy of the man's photograph. Despite the fact that the same article was read by both groups, those women for whom the attractiveness of the source of the message was a peripheral cue were more persuaded than those women for whom attractiveness was not salient.

Recipients of a message may also think about or elaborate the arguments contained in a message. This is the central route to persuasion in the ELM. Acceptance of an elaborated message is thought to depend upon two factors: (i) the extent of elaboration and (ii) the favourableness of the thoughts generated by the arguments contained in the communication (see figure 11.7). The extent of elaboration refers to how much opportunity the recipient of the message has to reflect upon the arguments. The favourableness of the thoughts refers to the number of agreements with the message a recipient generates when they are asked to write down what they were thinking while attending to the message. Recipients may, of course, generate unfavourable thoughts or arguments counter to those contained in the message, or indeed thoughts irrelevant to the message (e.g., 'that researcher has an awful haircut!').

If a message contains strong arguments, and recipients have the opportunity

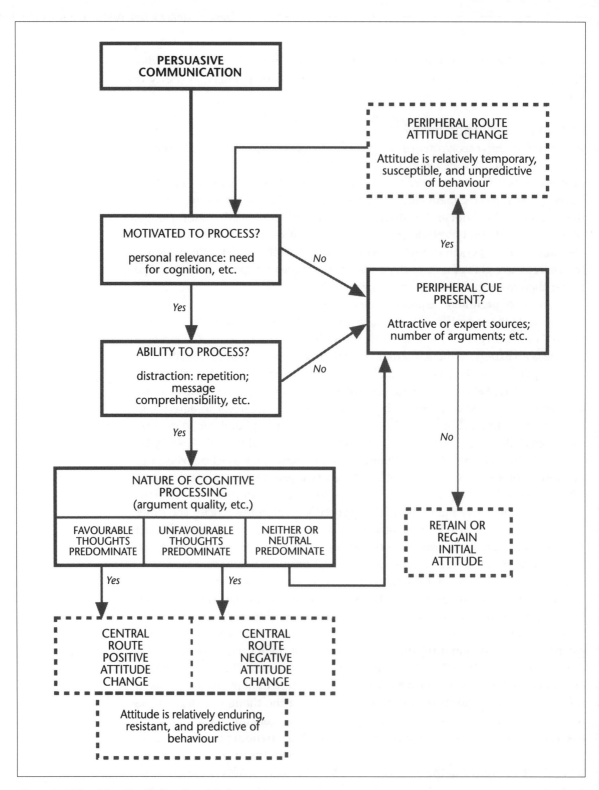

Figure 11.7 The elaboration likelihood model of persuasion
Source: adapted from Petty & Caccioppo 1986.

to process those arguments, then attitude change in the direction of the persuasive communication should occur. If a message contains strong arguments but recipients do not have the opportunity to process the arguments, then attitude change is unlikely. Extensive elaboration, in other words, enhances the persuasive impact of strong arguments. Having an opportunity to scrutinize arguments will have the opposite effect when the message contains weak arguments, however. Weak arguments will persuade the recipient if they are not elaborated. But if weak arguments are elaborated a boomerang effect can occur – the person may become even more opposed to the side of the argument which the message is advocating!

Petty et al. (1976) examined the effect of extent of elaboration and favourableness of thoughts in a study which tried to alter attitudes towards university fees. Extent of elaboration was manipulated by having one group of message recipients complete a task which would distract them from scrutinizing the arguments contained in the message (low elaboration group) while another group was not distracted (high elaboration group). Half of each of the two groups heard strong arguments (arguments which participants in another study rated as persuasive) and half heard weak arguments (unconvincing arguments according to the participants in the other study). The results for the four groups, low elaboration/strong arguments, low elaboration/weak arguments, high elaboration/strong arguments, and high elaboration/weak arguments are presented in figure 11.8. The results supported the predictions of the ELM that people are most persuaded by strong arguments when they have an opportunity to scrutinize them, while they are least persuaded when they can scrutinize weak arguments.

One question which must be asked about the ELM is: what determines whether a persuasive message goes through the central or peripheral route? In other words, what factors are involved in determining whether peripheral cues or elaboration are employed in response to a message? Petty and Cacioppo (1986) suggest that people who have a tendency to engage in and enjoy thinking,

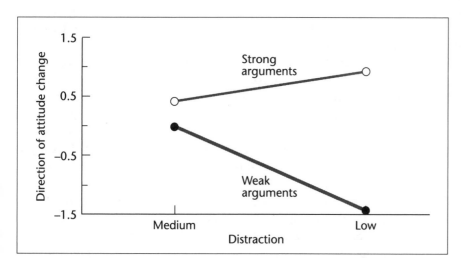

Figure 11.8 Effects of argument quality and distraction on attitude change
Source: adapted from Petty & Cacioppo 1986.

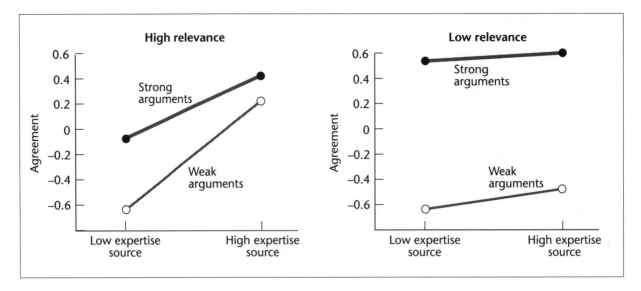

Figure 11.9 Impact of personal relevance on people's use of argument strength as against source expertise in determining agreement with a persuasive communication
Source: copyright data from Petty & Cacioppo 1986: 154.

NEED FOR
COGNITION

people with a high NEED FOR COGNITION, are more likely to elaborate the arguments contained in a message, while those who are not interested in the effort of analysis are more likely to use peripheral cues. They also suggest that when a message has personal relevance this greatly enhances the likelihood of elaborating the message and is more effective than using peripheral cues. In a study designed to examine the effect of personal relevance on whether a message goes through the central or peripheral route, students were divided into groups and listened to a speech favouring a plan for more examinations at university. Some groups heard strong arguments while others heard weak arguments (argument quality). Some groups heard the arguments delivered by an expert (a professor of education) and other groups heard a non-expert (a second-level pupil). Varying the expertise was designed to manipulate the peripheral cue of expertise of the source. The key variable in this study was personal involvement. This was manipulated by having the speaker advocate the introduction of more exams in the students' own university (high personal relevance) or advocate the introduction of more exams at another institution (low personal relevance).

There were clear effects for the impact of personal relevance on whether participants scrutinized the arguments or relied on the expert's opinion (see figure 11.9). When participants thought the plan would not affect them personally, they responded favourably to the expert and unfavourably to the non-expert, regardless of the content of the message. When the plan might be instituted at their own university, however, participants attended to the quality of the arguments. These groups were persuaded only by strong arguments and they rejected weak ones regardless of who espoused them.

The ELM has been quite successful in bringing together a large number of seemingly contradictory findings, and research with this model is ongoing. While the role of personal relevance and elaboration versus peripheral cues in message processing has been extensively researched, one key question remains un-

Plate 11.4 Market researcher
Source: Collections/Brian Shuel.

answered. This concerns argument quality: what makes a 'strong' argument and what constitutes a 'weak' argument? Petty and Caccioppo (1986) acknowledge that the ELM has not yet addressed this question, but instead relies upon groups of people rating a large number of arguments as either persuasive (strong) or not persuasive (weak) so that these arguments can then be used in the main experiments. How we can define the quality of arguments remains a key issue which will need to be addressed in future studies.

We noted earlier that if we believe the source of a message is trustworthy, then this can act as a peripheral cue in persuasion. However, what if the source of the message is a scientist who is paid by the nuclear power industry and that the message is trying to persuade us to allow a nuclear power station in our locality? Are we likely to think that this scientist is trustworthy or are we likely to think that this person is just doing their job? In the next section we examine this kind of question – how do we decide whether a person behaved as they did because of the type of person they are or whether it was because of situational circumstances? How we decide what characteristics are true of a person, and what information we use in deciding why someone behaved as they did, are the central concerns of attribution theory.

▓ Attribution Theory ▓

Attribution theory is concerned with how people explain the events and behaviours they see around them. An attribution is a person's belief about the cause of an event or behaviour. Several models of attribution have been proposed. We will examine three such accounts of the way people think about and attribute causes: the models of Heider (1948), Jones and Davis (1965) and Kelley (1967).

Heider's (1948) model

Fritz Heider's 1948 book *The Psychology of Interpersonal Relations* drew attention to the parallels between visual perception and the ways we understand each other. He pointed out that even though we move about, and the image that something we are looking at casts on our retinas constantly changes, we do not see the object constantly changing (the phenomenon of object constancy – see chapter 6). In much the same way, when we perceive someone we know quite well, we generally see an enduring personality behind the wide variety of behaviours that the person performs. What we see are characteristics of the person that give rise to the changing behaviours, rather than a meaningless variety of behaviours. According to Heider, the characteristics of the person which give rise to behaviour are TRAITS or DISPOSITIONS – enduring tendencies to respond in particular ways, such as kind, generous, brave, etc.

TRAITS

DISPOSITIONS

We always have difficulty, however, in making decisions about the nature of someone's personality or dispositions on the basis of their behaviour. This is because we have to interpret the person's behaviour in the light of the situation. Often we have to acknowledge that the person's behaviour is being determined by the situation rather than their dispositions. Thus, for example, I may believe that my friend is an extroverted and very talkative person, but I do not change my views of those dispositions or believe that my friend has changed when I see her quietly taking notes during a lecture. I recognize that her behaviour is in this instance governed by the social rules of the lecture situation. If she was similarly quiet at a party, then I would, perhaps, change my view.

Heider's pioneering contribution to attribution theory consists in his drawing a distinction between the internal or dispositional causes of a person's behaviour and external causation, namely, the demands of the situation in which the person finds him/herself. The attribution models of Jones and Davis (1965) and Kelley (1967) both attempt to formalize and extend Heider's (1948) work.

Jones and Davis's (1965) correspondent inference theory

Jones and Davis (1965) start from the position that a person's action can have many effects, and that it is only those effects and the action that gave rise to them that we can observe. Their model is concerned with how we reason from

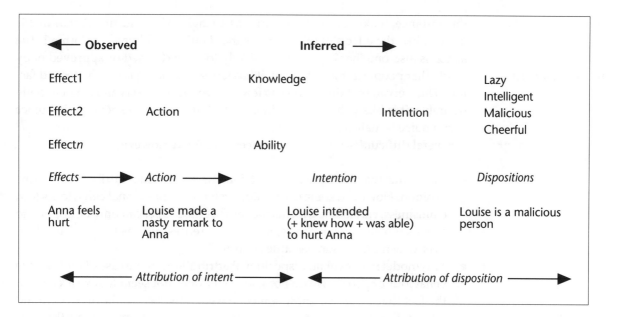

← Observed		Inferred →	
Effect1		Knowledge	Lazy
			Intelligent
Effect2	Action	Intention	Malicious
			Cheerful
Effect*n*	Ability		
Effects →	*Action* →	*Intention*	*Dispositions*
Anna feels hurt	Louise made a nasty remark to Anna	Louise intended (+ knew how + was able) to hurt Anna	Louise is a malicious person
← Attribution of intent →		← Attribution of disposition →	

Figure 11.10
Schematization of correspondent inference theory
Source: Jones & Davis 1965.

observing a behaviour and its effects, to inferring the intention of the person who performed the behaviour, and inferring the disposition that gave rise to the person's intention. In the example given in figure 11.10, then, how do we reason from seeing that Anna feels hurt (an effect), and seeing that Louise made a nasty remark to Anna (the action), to deciding that Louise intended to hurt Anna (the intention), and that Louise is a malicious person (the disposition)? 'Correspondent inference theory' (CIT) is concerned with whether a person's disposition corresponds with the person's action and its effects (i.e., were Louise's remark and Anna's hurt the result of Louise being a malicious person?).

According to Jones and Davis, this involves a two-stage process: the first involves an ATTRIBUTION OF INTENT and the second involves ATTRIBUTION OF A DISPOSITION. In order to attribute intention to Louise (the actor or person who performed the behaviour), the observer must believe that Louise knew the effects that her action would have (the knowledge condition) and that Louise was able to successfully perform the action (the ability condition). Thus, if Louise had no idea that her remark would hurt Anna, or if Louise did not have information with which she could hurt Anna or was incapable of making a hurtful remark, then no inference of a hurtful intention could be made.

If the knowledge and ability conditions are satisfied, however, and it is inferred that Louise intended to hurt Anna, then the process of determining whether Louise has a disposition which gave rise to the intention begins. Two factors are thought to mainly influence whether a dispositional attribution is made. The first concerns the number of NON-COMMON EFFECTS the action had. In order to determine the non-common effects of an action, the observer must think about what alternative courses of action were available to Louise and must decide if the action she actually performed had a small number of very specific effects. In

ATTRIBUTION OF INTENT

ATTRIBUTION OF A DISPOSITION

NON-COMMON EFFECTS

457

this instance, making a nasty remark has a single effect (hurting Anna) that is quite unlike the effects of other actions that Louise could have performed. The action is also one that is probably unlikely to be performed or approved of by most other people in that situation, it has low SOCIAL DESIRABILITY (the second factor). Thus, given that the action has few non-common effects and is not socially desirable, it is likely that a dispositional attribution or correspondent inference (that Louise is malicious) is made.

Several difficulties with CIT have been identified, however:

- CIT claims that attribution of intention always precedes attribution of a disposition. However, some dispositions refer to unintentional behaviours (e.g. clumsiness, carelessness). This means that the model can only be applied to actions which involve choice, not to occurrences such as laughter and fear, over which the person has little control.
- This model may explain dispositional attributions in the case of undesirable behaviour of people we do not know. CIT does not seem to take account of the fact that when we know someone well, however, we have background information about the person which we may rely on more than the non-common effects or social desirability of a particular action they have performed.

In 1976, Jones and McGillis acknowledged that CIT does not capture how people usually make attributions, but should be considered a 'rational baseline model' against which to compare actual attributions.

Kelley's (1967) ANOVA model

While Jones and Davis (1965) were concerned with the questions of how we infer both intent and dispositions, the key question for Kelley (1967) was 'what type of information does the person use in order to make a causal attribution?' Kelley viewed the person as a 'naive scientist' who weighed up evidence in deciding how to explain events and behaviours. In order to explain, for example, why Clare argued with her father, Kelley suggests that we need three types of information:

Distinctiveness information – information about the stimulus, in this case the father. If Clare argues only with her father, then the stimulus is highly distinctive. If Clare argues with everyone, then the stimulus has low distinctiveness.

Consensus information – information about the person, in this case Clare. If a lot of people argue with Clare's father, then there is high consensus for Clare's arguing. However, if Clare is the only person who argues with her father, then there is low consensus for Clare's behaviour.

Consistency information – information about the circumstances, in this case the

Table 11.3 Kelley's (1967) ANOVA model levels of distinctiveness, consensus and consistency information, leading to stimulus, person or circumstance attributions

Attribution to the:	Distinctiveness	Consensus	Consistency
Stimulus	High	High	High
Person	Low	Low	High
Circumstance	High	Low	Low

time and place of the argument. If Clare always argues with her father, i.e., argues with him in many different situations, then the circumstance has high consistency. If Clare only argued with her father on this particular occasion, then this circumstance has low consistency.

According to Kelley we combine information about the stimulus, the person and the circumstance in a manner that is similar to a rather complex statistical procedure called ANOVA. That is, combinations of different levels of distinctiveness, consensus and consistency lead us to make a causal attribution. That attribution may be to the stimulus (the father), the person (Clare), or the circumstance. Table 11.3 presents the general rules for combining the three types of information in making these different causal attributions. You may find it helpful to write out the types of information that would lead one to assign the causal role to the father, or Clare, or the circumstance, in our example.

McArthur (1972) conducted one of the first experimental tests of Kelley's model. She presented statements such as 'John laughed at the comedian' to participants, and also provided combinations of consistency, consensus and distinctiveness information. Her results were supportive of the ANOVA model, though she found that consensus information was not used as much as information about distinctiveness and consistency. A study by Beattie and Anderson (1995) tried to replicate aspects of McArthur's study using a more open-ended methodology. Respondents were asked what type of information they would like to know in order to make a causal attribution (instead of being providing with pre-packaged consistency, consensus and distinctiveness information). When simple declarative sentences such as 'John laughed at the comedian' were employed, participants did spontaneously seek out consistency, consensus and distinctiveness information as Kelley's model would suggest. However, when the focal issues were a rape or an argument in a restaurant, these types of information were asked for less and were much less likely to be asked for in the participants' first three questions.

On the basis of their findings, Beattie and Anderson suggest that consistency, consensus and distinctiveness information are not always asked for (and are therefore not always used) in ordinary situations. They point out that using pre-packaged information in experiments (such as McArthur 1972) may have over-estimated the importance of these types of information in making causal attributions. It is also the case that consistency, consensus and distinctiveness information is not always available for us to use in order to explain an event. Kelley acknowledges this point by saying that where such information is not available, we use our general knowledge about causes (called 'causal schemas') in order to make an attribution. Fiedler (1982) is critical of the notion of causal schemas, however, arguing that while such an idea is intuitively plausible, nobody has successfully demonstrated their existence and functioning. A more fruitful avenue in recent research has been to examine the idea that people have stable ways of explaining the positive and negative events in their lives. We examine this notion of EXPLANATORY STYLE below, and describe applications of this approach to the areas of mental and physical health.

EXPLANATORY STYLE

Kelley's ANOVA model has attracted a great deal of criticism for being overly rational and deliberative, and for ignoring the importance of culture and self-esteem in the attribution process (Hewstone 1989). The errors and biases people often make in attributing causes to events and behaviours seem to depart quite radically from the logical and statistical procedures that the ANOVA model proposes. There is a great deal of evidence which suggests that we are infrequently inclined, or indeed able, to handle the complex procedures which both Kelley's and Jones and Davis's models suggest we employ in our causal explanations. It is perhaps best, therefore, to think of these accounts as normative models – models of how people ought to use information. The biases in the attribution process which we outline below are descriptive models which tell us what people actually do.

Errors and biases in the attribution process

Studies of how people usually make attributions suggest that we often seem biased in the ways we explain events. While error refers to a mistake which can be reliably established, this term should not properly be used in the context of attribution theory. Error has, however, come to be used to describe some phenomena even though the term *bias* (the under- or over-use of otherwise correct procedure) is more accurate.

FUNDAMENTAL
ATTRIBUTION ERROR

The FUNDAMENTAL ATTRIBUTION ERROR refers to the tendency to overestimate the impact of dispositional factors and to underestimate the impact of situational factors in making attributions. The fundamental attribution error may be responsible for findings showing that we tend to attribute road accidents to drivers rather than to the vehicle or road conditions or that some people attribute unemployment to the person rather than to economic factors such as recession or government policy. Ross et al. (1977) also demonstrated this phenomenon in a laboratory study which divided a sample into the roles of quiz show questioners and contestants and instructed questioners to ask difficult questions. Despite the fact that questioners had the distinct advantage of being able to ask questions about their own special areas of interest, Ross et al. showed that observers of the quiz and contestants both thought that questioners were more knolwedgeable than contestants (in fact, contestants and hosts would at some point have to swap roles to determine who was more knowledgeable!). Culture may have an important role in explaining the fundamental attribution error: more individualistic societies are likely to see dispositions as causes, while collectivist societies may see situations as more influential. Miller (1984), for example, showed that American subjects were more likely to attribute a behaviour to a person's dispositions compared to Indian subjects' attributions for the same behaviour. The English language is also an important factor – we have many more terms to describe a person's dispositions (e.g. kind, brave, etc.) than we have to describe different types of situations (Brown & Fish 1983).

ACTOR–OBSERVER DIFFERENCE refers to a tendency for actors to attribute their behaviour to the situation and for observers to attribute the actor's behaviour to dispositions. Nisbett et al., for example, asked male students to write essays about their girlfriends and their choice of course. The same students also wrote essays about their best friend's girlfriend and choice of course. Analysis of the essays suggested that while external factors were important in determining the student's own choices, the best friends' behaviour was explained by the type of person they were (dispositional attributions). The most plausible explanation of actor–observer differences concerns the different foci of attention of actors and observers. For the actor, the situation is salient so the attribution is made to the situation. For the observer, however, the actor is salient and s/he attributes the cause to the actor. **ACTOR–OBSERVER DIFFERENCE**

The FALSE CONSENSUS EFFECT refers to the tendency to use our own attitudes and behaviour as the basis for deciding consensus for that behaviour – to overestimate the number of people who share our beliefs and habits. Ross et al. (1977) demonstrated false consensus by asking people would they agree to walk around college wearing a sandwich board which said 'Eat at Joe's'. Respondents also had to estimate how many people would agree with their choice. Both those who agreed and those who disagreed thought that more than 60% of people would agree with their choice. The false consensus effect would seem to advantage self-esteem by implying that the person's own attitudes are good attitudes to hold and are therefore widely shared ('lots of people agree with me!'). Self-esteem can also be raised by underestimating the number of people who share a personal characteristic. This seems to be particularly true for skills and abilities which show FALSE UNIQUENESS ('my opinions are common but my talents are rare!') **FALSE CONSENSUS EFFECT**

FALSE UNIQUENESS

The SELF-SERVING BIAS refers to a tendency to attribute one's success to internal factors ('I worked hard for that exam') and one's failure to external factors ('that lecturer always asks really tough questions'). The self-serving bias means that we can avoid blame for negative events and accept credit for positive events thereby increasing our self-esteem. A particularly interesting example of the self-serving bias, called SELF-HANDICAPPING, involves making an attribution before one has performed a behaviour. For example, a student may claim that they haven't done any work for an exam so that they avoid being thought of as not very **SELF-SERVING BIAS**

SELF-HANDICAPPING

Plate 11.5 Students reading exam results
Source: Tony Stone Images/ Penny Tweedie.

intelligent if they fail. On the other hand, if the student succeeds in the exam, then, of course, it is because the student is very very intelligent!

The self-serving bias does not operate only with respect to our own personal behaviour, however. We can also be self-serving regarding the groups to which we belong. Taylor and Jaggi (1974), for example, asked Hindu office workers to make attributions about desirable or undesirable behaviours performed by Hindus and Muslims in a series of stories. When the behaviour was desirable, far more internal attributions were made for Hindus' behaviours than for Muslims' behaviours. When the behaviour was undesirable, on the other hand, more internal attributions were made for Muslims than for Hindus.

▥ Conclusion ▥

In this chapter, we have looked at that area of psychology where social and cognitive psychologists coincide in the laboratory – social cognition! We have emphasized the social origins, social contents and socially shared nature of cognitive processes, such as attention and memory, and we have introduced three key areas of social cognition research.

We began by considering the nature of, and processes involved in, 'perceiving the self'. We attempted to classify the wide variety of ways that people can describe themselves, and examined the influence of culture, feedback from other people and social comparisons upon these self-descriptions. Using the notion of the working self-concept, we tried to explain the paradox that all of us have both one self and many selves, that our views of ourselves are both stable and at the same time constantly changing in response to ongoing events. We also looked at self-esteem – the judgements and feelings we have about ourselves. The importance of maintaining or bolstering a favourable view of ourselves can be seen throughout this chapter: from the particulars of how we describe ourselves, through the ways that we protect our attitudes from inconsistent information, to the manner in which our explanations for our own and other people's behaviour are often self-serving.

Our attitudes towards people, objects, social issues, and behaviours are components of how we see ourselves. We pointed out that different theorists place different emphasis upon whether attitudes should be defined in terms of the thoughts (cognition), feelings (affect) or action tendencies (behaviour) we have regarding the object. We emphasized the role of attitudes in explaining what we attend to, and remember, in our everyday interactions. We also examined 'if and when' our attitudes guide our behaviour, and drew attention to concepts such as 'subjective norm' and 'perceived behavioural control' which are important for understanding why we don't always do what we say we will do! Finally, we examined the sorts of factors that explain when our attitudes change and how attitude change can occur through peripheral or central routes.

Our talk about ourselves, other people and the events we witness is also characterized by our need to explain why things happen – to make attributions about the causes of events and behaviours. We began by acknowledging that a person's behaviour could be caused either by a characteristic of the person such as bravery or by the circumstances in which a person found him/herself. We also examined the sorts of information people use to arrive at different types of explanation. We identified the difficulty involved in developing a formal model of how people make attribution – our explanations are not affected solely by the information we have available, they are also influenced by the culture we live in, what seems to be most salient to us at the time, and by our need for self-esteem.

Research in social cognition does not have a neat conclusion. We have seen that there are many different accounts of the self, different theories which define attitudes in different ways, and several models of attribution and attributional biases. When we are dealing with phenomena as complex and multifaceted as the self, attitudes and attributions, we have to acknowledge that research and debate is not over! We suggested at the beginning of this chapter one of the reasons people most often give for wanting to pursue a course in psychology is to understand what makes us see the world the way we do. The theories and empirical studies of social cognition outlined here do not represent the final word on these issues. The final words should be questions that you ask yourself: To what extent are my views of myself explained by research on the self-concept? Can the notions of belief and value explain why my friend and I have different attitudes? Does that TV advertisement employ factors outlined in theories of persuasion? What information did that person use to arrive at that explanation? What study would I do to support my ideas about a particular aspect of social cognition?

CHAPTER SUMMARY

1   Social cognition is the study of the ways that people think about their experiences of themselves and others in their social worlds. Cognitive processes determine how we identify, recognize and assign values to objects and people in our social world. Many of the cognitions we hold are shared with other people. This is because we live in social groups defined by culture, geographical location, religion, or political and social ideologies. Within these social groups we share information with each other and construct shared interpretations of reality. This can be demonstrated by examining the use of particular words by different cultural groups and the different meanings different groups attach to them.

2   The study of the self as object (the 'me') concerns the way we view ourselves. The study of the self-concept shows that the content of our self-concept is multi-faceted. We view ourselves in terms of ascribed characteristics (sex, age), roles and memberships (father), abstract identifications (human), interests and activities, material possessions, body image, major senses of self, and personal characteristics. We also hold views of ourselves as we 'ought' to be, as we would 'ideally like to be', as well as how we are.

3   The formation of the content of the self-concept has been explained by two principal processes. Symbolic interactionism suggests that our beliefs about how others evaluate us determine the content of our own self-beliefs. Social comparison theory suggests that in the absence of objective information about ourselves, we form our self-views by comparing ourselves with others whom we see as similar in some respects.

4   The self-concept with its many elements is stored in memory. When we encounter feedback from other people, or opportunities to compare ourselves with others, particular aspects of our self-concept are made salient and become active in working memory. As a result, the way in which we see ourselves can vary widely with context. The concept of self-schemas refers to important elements of our self-concept which are easily retrieved into working memory and guide our behaviour. We attend more to schema-related information, process this information more efficiently, recognize and recall it more quickly, and resist information that is counter to it. Self-schemas therefore give rise to relatively stable self-conceptions.

5   Attitudes refer to our evaluative judgements about our social world. The expectancy value model of attitudes suggests that attitudes derive from a person's beliefs about an entity and the values associated with those beliefs. According to the attitude accessibility model an attitude is a learned association between an entity and its evaluation which is stored in memory.

6   Attitudes have two important functions. First, they direct our information processing. We attend more to information which is consistent with our own attitudes. Second, attitudes guide behaviour. Attitudes which specify the behaviour to be performed, its target, context, and time frame, are more likely to be related to subsequent behaviour. The theory of reasoned action proposes that behaviour is immediately determined by intention. Intention in turn is determined by a combination of attitude towards the object and subjective norm.

7 Attribution theory is concerned with how people explain the events and behaviours they see around them. When we view someone's behaviour, we may attribute it to their enduring personality (internal causes) or to external causation (the situation in which they find themselves). This distinction has been extended in various ways. According to correspondent inference theory, the attribution of intention to internal causes depends upon the observer believing that the actor both had knowledge of the effects of her actions and was able to successfully perform the action. If these conditions are satisfied, and the behaviour is also undesirable and has common effects, then we may attribute cause to the person's disposition. The main difficulty with the theory is that when we know someone well we have background information which we may rely on more to make our judgements than the factors specified by the theory.

8 The ANOVA model of attributions is concerned with the types of information a person uses to make causal attributions. According to this model, we need three types of information: distinctiveness information, consensus information and consistency information. These types of information may not always be used, however; and it has been suggested that we may have stable ways of explaining the positive and negative events in our lives.

9 Four principal types of bias exist in the ways in which we explain events. The fundamental attribution error concerns our tendency to overestimate dispositional factors and underestimate situational factors when making attributions. We also possess a tendency to attribute own own behaviour to the situation and others' behaviour to their dispositions (the actor–observer difference), and to assume that other people share our beliefs and habits (the false consensus effect).

■ Further Work ■

1. To what extent can the self-concept be viewed as a product of our social environment? What theories and evidence suggest that it can, and what theories that it cannot?

2. Test your self-concept by completing the 'twenty statements test'. Write down twenty statements about yourself in the order they come into your mind. Then using table 11.1 decide what category each of your statements falls into. What did you learn about yourself?

3. Attitudes guide behaviour. Discuss.

4. Using Box 11.2, devise a Likert scale, with ten items, to measure students' attitudes towards ecstasy use.

5. What factors might lead a person to believe someone behaved in a certain way because of the type of person they are or because of situational constraints?

▒ **Further Reading** ▒

Eiser, J. R. (1986) *Social Psychology*. Cambridge: Cambridge University Press.

> A social-psychology text which provides a thorough overview of issues in attitude theory, and particularly the attitude–behaviour relation.

Hewstone, M. (1989) *Causal Attribution*. Oxford: Blackwell.

> Gives a detailed overview of research on attribution theory.

Fiske, S. and Taylor, S. (1992; 2nd edn) *Social Cognition*. New York: McGraw-Hill.

> Good coverage of self-concept and schema theory.

PsyCLE MODULE: ATTRIBUTION THEORY

This module supports the section on attribution theory – by first illustrating the principles with examples that you are invited to complete, and then asking you to explore Kelley's framework by making attributions about scenes that you are asked to imagine.

CHAPTER 12

Social Group Processes

– from the Dyad to the Small Group to the Crowd

Christopher Spencer

CHAPTER AGENDA

- Communication and relationships between two people are the first focus of the chapter: can we analyse what makes these work in terms of the whole range of channels of communication, non-verbal as well as verbal?

- We next look at the small group as its own world in miniature; and ask how groups form, persist, change and dissolve. What attracts an individual to a particular group?

- How is the group structured? Can we predict what leadership styles will lead to the group achieving its goals?

- What pressure to conform can the group exercise over its members? We will see that, on occasions, the group can become so focused on a powerful leader or aim that it cuts itself off from outside reality.

- Yet there are often free-thinking minorities within the group: how can they have an effect on the group's decisions?

- We next show how broader social phenomena, such as stereotyping and prejudice, can have their origins in the most minimal of interactions between groups who feel themselves to be distinct. We examine some classic experiments of social psychology which have shown the process in action; and which have suggested ways of ameliorating the situation.

- Finally, we ask: are we right to accept the popular view of the crowd as primitive, suggestible, and potentially dangerous? Or can we offer a more sophisticated view of the crowd?

Introduction

The last chapter described the social origins of the self, focusing on how that self develops as the individual grows in their social understanding. As we shall see in this chapter, the self also is powerfully shaped by SOCIAL INTERACTIONS, and GROUP MEMBERSHIP and identification.

Consider how you might describe yourself to a stranger: after a few vain

SOCIAL INTERACTION

GROUP MEMBERSHIP

467

attempts at physical description, most likely you would say that you were a student, at X College, studying psychology, whose home town was Y.

Notice what you would be doing here: 'self' is being described in terms of others, of the groups, activities, places that you feel best characterize you. What you have done is both complex and selective. Your list of self-descriptions is both diverse – you have included in the list some very different types of 'memberships' – and yet it is also selective: there are many other 'groups' you could have included, but which had lower relevance to your self-identity: perhaps 'commuter on the 97 bus', and 'user of the student canteen' would be examples of such lesser 'group identities'.

In this chapter, we shall see how these group memberships shape not only long-term self-concepts but also immediate behaviour, both within the group and between groups.

We spend much of our lives in groups, both the formal, organized groups of, for example, our workplace; and the informal ones which characterize our leisure. In the same way as an individual has a developmental history and recognizable personal characteristics, so we can examine groups' histories, and distinctive characteristics. Research on these topics will be the focus of the section below entitled 'The Small Group as the World'. In this section, we shall ask: How do groups form, persist, change, dissolve? Why are individuals attracted to particular groups and not others? Does this process reflect individual needs, and how might these mesh with those of other group members? Are individuals attracted to each other in any predictable way? (There are plenty of popular beliefs about this: how well do they stand up to empirical tests?) How do ROLES AND SPECIALISMS develop within the group: leaders, experts, and those whose role seems to be more social- than task-related. Could we predict which group member would be most effective in each role?

ROLES AND
SPECIALISMS

CONFORMITY AND
COMPLIANCE

We shall also look at the topic of CONFORMITY AND COMPLIANCE to the group (a subject once overstated within social psychology), and discover that contemporary psychology offers an account of a much more subtle interplay of forces between what the individual brings to the group and what it has on offer to her/him. There are spectacular cases, of course, where groups or individuals *do* exert overwhelming influence, or obtain obedience of a worrying level: but these are exceptional, and we can indicate the unusual circumstances under which, for instance, an important decision-making group suffers the phenomenon labelled 'groupthink' (discussed below), coming to unwise group decisions it later cannot explain. Another way we can show that early social psychology oversimplified its discussions of social influence processes is by realizing how it neglected the subtle power of *minorities* within the group: influence can be as much a matter of information exchange as it is of power.

The next section will confront the paradox that not only are society and its groups the source of much of our information, support and pleasure; they can also be shown to be the origin of our prejudices and stereotypes about others, leading at their worst to hostility, war and genocide. What has social psychol-

Plate 12.1 Crowding on to the London underground
Source: Katz Pictures.

ogy to say about the conditions which bring these about? Quite surprisingly, instead of treating these as the products of disturbed people or situations, we will find the discipline seeing them as predictable extensions of normal relations between groups. One of the most memorable lines of research in social psychology has been that which has sought the minimal conditions for producing INTERGROUP AWARENESS AND HOSTILITY: this has involved the experimental creation and (of course) elimination of prejudice between newly created groups.

STEREOTYPES, we shall argue, are importantly similar to all other categorizations, by which, as work in cognitive psychology shows, the individual simplifies and imposes order and meaning upon the complexity of the world. However, they also incorporate as a central feature, the – often negative – judgemental factor which gives occasion for concern. What then can be done? What effects might we predict affirmative action and legislation might have?

Another set of public concerns we shall examine, in the final section of the chapter, are to do with *crowds*. Under some circumstances, peoples' behaviour when in a large crowd becomes less ruly, more given to violence. Why might this be? Nineteenth-century thinking characterized the crowd as animal-like, but, while this reminds us that crowds are not just small groups grown large, it does not amount to an explanation of the forms of behaviour we may show in a crowd: these are not so random as to be unpredictable.

The chapter thus expands in scale, from within-group processes to interactions between groups, and finally to the scale of the crowd.

And it is thus appropriate that, before all of this, the chapter's first section, 'Communicating and Relating to Others', should be at the smallest scale of

INTERGROUP
AWARENESS AND
HOSTILITY

STEREOTYPES

social behaviour: encounters between two individuals. Here, we will examine the interplay of verbal and non-verbal channels in our communication with the other person.

▨ Communicating and Relating to Others ▨

Encounters and continuing interactions with other people are the stuff of social psychology; and this first section of the chapter asks: how do these interactions work? Later sections will in effect be concerned with the outcomes of these interactions – compliance, decisions, conflict, and so on. Here, we are concerned with the basic processes of social interaction. To simplify things, we will take as our baseline situation, two individuals meeting – the DYAD (see Argyle 1971 for an extended introduction to this area). Only later will we worry whether adding some more individuals (or indeed many) alters the working of the processes that operate in dyads.

DYAD

In both new and continuing social interactions, we can usefully consider the dyad's 'work' as being information sending and gathering. In addition to any direct, verbally given, information ('that seat is taken'), dyadic encounters involve: IMPRESSION REGULATION – control over the output from oneself to the other; and ATTENTION TO THE OTHER – interpreting their output. (Here we extend the consideration of chapter 11.)

IMPRESSION
REGULATION

ATTENTION TO THE
OTHER

For the two individuals are working towards a SHARED DEFINITION OF THE SITUATION: what is the nature of the encounter? This is the meta-level issue they must resolve for a working encounter, both parties tacitly agreeing on the type of social situation they are in; what SCRIPTS, rules and expectations govern such a type; and which roles within the situation each is playing. A mismatch between the two participants in any of these elements may lead to misunderstandings of information sent, or even a complete breakdown of the situation.

SHARED DEFINITION
OF THE SITUATION

SCRIPTS

At the detailed-process level, the dyad has the task of managing the smooth running of the conversation. Two people have, simultaneously, to monitor own and other's output, to predict, understand, mesh, adapt, so as not to speak at the same time, but anticipate the other's drift, to the point that switches between turns are accomplished smoothly, and the two participants contribute to a joint endeavour. We are all, since early childhood, such frequent players of such situations that it is difficult for us to stand back and realize what a skilled process we are involved in. Only in some breakdown situations – where our usual social scripts and expectations do not hold good in another culture, for example – do we have occasion to realize.

Impression regulation and management

Schlenker et al. (1992) have said: 'As social psychology has matured as a discipline, it has increasingly endorsed a more dynamic, purposeful, and strategic

Plate 12.2 An initial encounter between two people, with its many sorts of interactions
Source: Cefn Newsham.

view of human behaviour.' We should see interpersonal communication as inherently instrumental: it is aimed at achieving the personal agendas of the participants. And central to this is the control of information about self and other.

Early symbolic interactionalists (Cooley 1902; Mead 1934) argued that the individual imagined him/herself in the position of the other, observing them; and adjusted own behaviour accordingly. Goffman (1959) extended this: he offers the extended metaphor of social life as a stage performance, with individuals selecting the roles and scripts to be played.

While one might presume that self-glorification was a main motivator here, recent research (see the summary by Schlenker et al. 1992) indicates that other motives are also powerful: for example, SELF-CONSISTENCY – validating the self by confirming one's beliefs about the self; and SELF-AUTHENTICATION – trying to learn the truth about oneself by carrying out limited social experiments. People may wish for such information, even if it is not self-enhancing.

Recently, this DRAMATURGICAL APPROACH (from Goffman's metaphor of the stage) has been used to explain behaviour in social situations as diverse as: helping, aggression, eating patterns, face-work in industry, and criminal behaviour.

As individuals are constructing these desired social identities for themselves, they are often collaborating with the other person within an agreed definition of the situation, in mutually supportive roles. Here, as Goffman's insightful descriptions of shop assistants and of hotel staff indicate, the dyad (or team) may well be playing in front of an audience who are not 'in' on the situation; or, to

SELF-CONSISTENCY

SELF-AUTHENTICATION

DRAMATURGICAL APPROACH

put it another way, whose role as customer is defined as not breaching the home-team's performance.

Channels of communication

Language, discussed in chapter 10, has such a richness and range of possibilities for communicating feelings, ideas, requests and all other parts of social exchange, that during much of psychology's early history, it was the only channel given serious consideration.

Then in the 1960s, social psychology 'rediscovered' the other ways individuals communicate; and, with missionary zeal, set about overstating their importance!

What are these other 'channels'? You know them well and use them every day.

Imagine that you have come for an interview: consider what cues are available to you about the situation and how well you are doing in it. Politeness and interviewer technique may limit the strictly verbal feedback you receive; yet even from the outset, you perhaps felt at ease because:

the interview room was informal – this is the *physical context*

that impression was reinforced by the interviewer's *physical appearance*

PROXEMICS   the interviewer sat close to you – PROXEMICS

having welcomed you with a handshake – *bodily contact*

(s)he continued smiling as you talked – *facial expressions*

GAZE PATTERN   and kept looking at you – GAZE PATTERN

reinforcing what you said both by nods and 'aha's – *gestures* + NON-VERBAL

NON-VERBAL VOCAL   VOCAL TONE;
TONE

you even had a feeling that, as you shifted position in your chair, the interviewer did so too – an aspect of posture noted by psychologists as POSTURAL

POSTURAL ECHO   ECHO.

All the time, whether you were fully aware or not of these channels, you would

VERBAL CHANNEL   be cross-checking between them and what was being said: the VERBAL CHANNEL.

We can ask:

- Are these all kinds of language? (Think back to chapter 10's definition.)
- Are some more attended to than others?
- Are some more specialized than others?
- If they appear to conflict in their messages, which will be given credence?
- Are they universals, or do cultures each have their own patterns?
- What part do these channels play in the smooth running of a conversation?

Let us consider these issues as we review the channels.

Physical settings and the messages they send will receive our attention in chapter 13, on psychology and the environment.

Physical appearance: the individual's physique, their facial appearance, hair, clothes, are all used by us as indicators of that individual's personality and social background – i.e. longer-term information about the individual. Some of these aspects are open to manipulation by the individual, so as to change the perceiver's impression of them. There is a whole psychology of self-presentation, and, equally, psychology is needed to give an account of the perception rules that govern our interpretation of appearance.

Proxemics: the general rule is, the closer the two choose to be, the greater intimacy and friendliness is implied. Hence, in a new encounter, there must be an initial 'negotiation' between the two people about the agreed level of friendliness, using proximity as one way of communicating these feelings. Rules governing our expectancies for distance have been elucidated by Hall (1966):

Intimate distance	Up to 0.5 metres apart
Normal personal distance	0.5 to 1.25 metres
Social distance	1.25 to 4 metres
Public distance	4 metres and further apart

You can already begin to imagine the kinds of relationships typically operating at these distances, from lovers and very close friends (note the metaphor), through everyday friends, to casual and formal encounters, finally to public occasions, such as a public meeting.

Consider, however, that Hall's observations were mainly USA based, and that although such zones probably exist in all cultures, they may translate into different actual distances in different cultures from the ones tabulated above: Watson and Graves (1966) observed much closer distances in Arab societies. Does this matter? It could well prove disastrous, if in an interaction between an Arab and a Canadian ambassador, each read the other's proxemic cues as if their own. The Arab might wrongly read coolness into the Western comfortable one metre, and attempt to reduce the distance, whereupon his behaviour is seen by the Canadian as inappropriately intimate for everyday converse. Argyle (1988) has developed what he calls 'cultural sensitivity training packages' òo meet just such differences in social expectancies.

Bodily contact: from our earliest years with our parents, to intimate contacts in adulthood, the communicative power of touch can dominate other channels. Formal use is made of various contacts in greetings – handshakes, patting, etc., according to cultural practices. Touching can variously convey sympathy, uncertainty, superiority, guidance, playfulness, aggression. (Questions for you to consider: How do we realize which of these is being conveyed? What role has the context to play? And other concurrently available information?) Jones and Yarborough (1985) conducted the classic observations on our patterns and understandings of these various functions of touch.

Facial expression: this is the non-verbal channel that has highest expressive power. Studies of attention patterns during interaction show that indeed the face is most closely monitored by the other.

Its signals can indicate the current state of the individual – the whole range of emotions – and can also provide feedback to the speaker of how the listener is receiving and comprehending the message. Facial signals range from the completely automatic (because under autonomic nervous system control), such as blushing and blanching; through reactions such as smiling and grimacing, which can be partly shaped by expressive intentions; through to stylized and fully controlled facial gestures, used, for example, to amuse. Correspondingly, we find that there is a continuum of universality. There are those expressions, such as smiling to indicate pleasure, which appear in all cultures, are thus recognizable when members of two cultures meet, and whose innateness seems to be confirmed by the fact that they are used by the congenitally blind. At the other end of the continuum are those expressions which can lead to cross-cultural misunderstandings, usually not because the physical expression itself is unfamiliar, but because the cultures differ in the significance that can be attached to it. The apparent 'inscrutability' of the other in some such encounters is one manifestation; but so also is the appearance of insincerity, over-effusiveness, etc.

From your own experience, consider an incident of cross-cultural misunderstanding: its origins, course and resolution. How could we be trained in greater sensitivity? Think also how such incidents can occur between two individuals from the same culture.

Gaze pattern: the very pattern of looking at the other can have communicative value, from clinically significant continued gaze-aversion, through the predominantly averted pattern we label shyness, to patterns of frequent gaze associated with confidence, near-constant gaze 'staring' (usually read as aggressive or hostile), to the prolonged and mutual gaze of lovers. Within the mid-range, amount of gaze is read as a measure of friendliness, openness and interest.

Patterns of looking, on top of this, have a key role in ensuring the smooth running of a conversation. Clearly, we do not have to have visual contact with the other speaker: consider the mechanisms at work in an effective telephone conversation. But research has shown, when mutual vision is available, it is used to permit smooth turn-taking, anticipating the ending of the other's utterances by monitoring their gaze. Early work by Kendon (1967) first showed how speakers characteristically look away as they start to speak, and look back as they end a sequence. This may be caused by the speaker's internal needs to structure thoughts and present them in words, but we can show that it is received by the other as a TURN SWITCH SIGNAL. (Again, we should see non-verbal operating in context: clearly the listener is mainly tracking verbal output, anticipating ends of turns by the logical structure of the utterance. Occasionally, the speaker may even offer an overt structure, giving such a meta-communication as: 'My final word is this . . .', though these may not be foolproof!)

TURN SWITCH SIGNAL

Gestures: hands, together with head, shoulders, etc., can (unintentionally) trans-

Box 12.1   Gazing in Triads: How Three People Manage not to Speak at Once

Social psychologists studying how we interact have often started, and finished, with perhaps the easiest case: the dyad. Even here, as we have seen, using the range of available channels to ensure smooth communication, turn-taking, and switches between the two speakers has proved to be a highly skilled process.

Linguists have tended to stress the role of syntax: all speakers in a conversation are monitoring the logical structure of each others' sentences so as to know when to get in themselves; psychologists suggest that they are also monitoring the non-verbals.

How then do three (or more) individuals mesh their conversations? In dyads, there can be no misunderstanding who the next speaker can be; in triads this is not so.

Akko Kalma (1992) has studied such triadic communications, paying particular attention to their gaze patterns. During the course of conversation, people tend to gaze and look away during their speech, balancing the needs to gain feedback from others, and to avoid disturbance as their thoughts are being formulated. Towards the end of their utterance, the speaker gives an extended gaze which is picked up by the listeners as heralding a point at which to come into the conversation.

In the triad, unlike the dyad, there then arises the question to whom is this sustained turn-signalling gaze directed? From his analysis of hours of taped conversations, Kalma has shown that in effect the speaker is choosing which person will next speak by the direction of this gaze.

Using a panel of four video cameras (one for each person, and one for the triad as a whole) Kalma studied the detailed behaviour of 23 separate groups, and recorded 3,775 speaker switches in total. On only one occasion was prolonged gaze not followed by the speaker yielding the floor; and in the majority of cases the gaze stimulates its receiver to take the floor.

Furthermore, this confident use of the prolonged gaze pattern is particularly characteristic of those who are seen (by observers) as having most influence in the group.

mit information about emotional state: for example, a nervous state may 'leak out' from fidgeting with objects.

More importantly, gestures can replace or supplement spoken language:

1. as the components of FORMAL SIGN LANGUAGES, where each specific gesture has its agreed definition;

    FORMAL SIGN
    LANGUAGES

2. as illustrators of speech, amplifying, extending statements. We may be aware of using these, but often they have such a spontaneous character that we may be observed using them even when talking on the telephone.

Whereas sign languages, to be effective, have to operate in as rule-governed a way as spoken language, spontaneous gestures show considerable individual differences: and are also notably varied between cultures. Morris and his colleagues (1979) have, for example, been able to produce an atlas of gestures for Europe, showing local variants of meaning. Some indeed are strikingly discrepant in adjacent areas – the innocent greetings of one area being perceived as the direst insult in another.

Posture and postural echo: the whole body can also be seen as communicative, indicative of mood, affect and behavioural intention. Experimental evidence shows that people take up different postures with those they like than those they dislike: more open with the liked. Status and power are also clearly indi-

Plate 12.3 Gesturing while
on the telephone, an
ingrained habit
Source: Roger Scruton.

cated by posture: videos of interactions shown to a panel of judges usually receive high agreement.

Posture can reflect three levels of information: situational-cultural norms for a particular behaviour setting (contrast the norms for religious service and a university tutorial). Within these general expectancies, we then get the variations just discussed, indicating liking, etc. (here, we could contrast ease of posture in a tutorial with a popular teacher, against a less popular one). The finest detail information will be nested within these other two levels, indicating moment by moment changes in the relationship; as, for instance, interest waxes and wanes, social strategies are tried, etc. (for instance, within your favourite tutorial group, your tutor at last realizes how much you have been bluffing up until now).

One indicator at this micro-level of the degree of concord between speakers can be postural congruence: each mirrors the other's posture. (Tutor leans forward, student does too, very shortly afterwards; student relaxes, legs crossed, tutor follows suit. Neither will probably be aware of this 'dance'.)

Non-verbal vocal: we attend not just to the words of the speaker, but also to the intonation, phrasing, patterns of pauses, etc., for these too convey information: on emotional state, confidence, expertise, sincerity. The cadences both support and emphasize sentence meanings; and are used as part of that monitoring process which allows one to have smooth switches of speaker. Speech is also processed by the listener for speech errors (which are much more common than we consciously realize: try transcribing exactly a tape-recording of yourself in conversation): these may be used to ascertain the speaker's confidence or excitement levels. And, the 'standing' characteristics of the voice, including accent and tone of voice, can be shown to evince strong stereotypical expectations which could frame all else said by the speaker. Accent may be used by the listener to infer not only the regional origins of the speaker, but also their social class, likely attitudes and interests, and even their intellectual level. Similarly, tone of voice may be used by the listener as one clue to the speaker's personality. Imagine yourself as the producer of a play for radio, and see how you would make use of these stereotypical assumptions when choosing your cast. (Note: we are not here saying that these listener judgements are necessarily accurate.)

Channels together: in general, as participants, we expect the non-verbal channels (NVCs) to be carrying messages which are consistent one with the other, and which are supportive of what we are hearing on the verbal channel. Yet all the time we are monitoring the other for inconsistencies, for these too have meaning. Is the speaker less than sincere? Or more nervous than the words alone would indicate?

Deception may leak out via such inconsistencies: individuals do not have complete control over all channels if they wish to deceive, as we can show experimentally. Video subjects who have been instructed to make some claims which were true and others which were not, demonstrate on the screen some subtle differences between 'true' and 'false'. These may take some initial pointing out; arms tend to be more closely held together, and feet more restless during the false claims. Not major differences, but consistent. Your next research question is this: how would you devise an experiment to see whether these subtleties affect naive observers' impressions of the other and what they are saying?

How indeed do we handle cases of discrepant information? Supposing that the words spoken seemed friendly, but non-verbal channels signalled neutral or even hostile feelings in the speaker, which would be more attended to? It is possible to study this experimentally: an actor can generate a series of video clips in which the same message is delivered with a variety of non-verbal styles; each viewer only sees one clip of each message, and rates the speaker on it. By comparing scores for each clip, one can then assess the impact of discrepancies between channels. Early attempts to adduce from such studies exact weightings for verbal and for NVCs were misguided, as situational and topic factors intervene, as does the degree of discrepancy; but with any more than a very small discrepancy, the NVC is taken as more informative.

We also use information from the various channels to balance each other. Argyle and Dean (1965) were early in recognizing this, and suggested an 'EQUI-LIBRIUM MODEL'. You will recall in the brief review of each channel above that many of them carry information on the friendliness of the other – gaze and distance being prime examples. Now, a dyad may 'agree' on its preferred level of intimacy, yet be somewhat constrained by circumstances in how this is expressed. For example, you are engaging in a friendly chat with a colleague while walking together into the lift. As you are now closer together, your amount of eye gaze will drop, to compensate for the changed proximity. Argyle and Dean demonstrated this effect by having dyads converse from chairs fixed at close, medium and further distances; and found a corresponding increase in gaze as distance increased. Their idea of equilibrium seeking is now generally accepted.

In this section of the chapter, we have taken the dyad, the smallest social situation, an encounter and then a conversation between two people, to illustrate in some detail how the mechanics of all social interactions work. Just as we have discussed the 'work' of the dyad, so you can now begin to think of the work of the small group in similar terms. Remember the stages we went through with the dyad: initially, there had to evolve a shared definition of the situation. (Is it primarily formal, task-related, or more relaxed and sociable?) Next, social skills, both verbally and non-verbally based, come into play, to manage the smooth running of the interaction.

▦ The Small Group as the World ▦

Source of social pressure, versus purveyor of social reality?

The social psychology of small groups mainly used to stress their power to change and shape the individual's behaviour: main textbook headings might typically be – 'compliance', 'conformity' and 'obedience'. Undoubtedly, our thoughts and actions are shaped by social forces: the mere presence of another in the room is sufficient to change, for example, our work pattern; and finding oneself in a minority on a committee or a jury is hardly a neutral experience.

However, one must also see that the group provides the individual with elements of identity, as well as more immediate social rewards – such as CONSEN-SUAL VALIDATION for one's views, and satisfaction of one's needs for sociability.

To exaggerate this, we could label the traditional approach 'individual in the group', a faceless, identityless individual; in contrast, SOCIAL IDENTITY THEORY (Tajfel 1981) looks at the group in the individual: groups are not just aggregates of unrelated individuals; rather, the very membership of a group offers identity to its members, especially, as we shall see below, when their group has a context of other, possibly competing, groups.

EQUILIBRIUM MODEL

CONSENSUAL
VALIDATION

SOCIAL IDENTITY
THEORY

Plate 12.4 Jury in
discussion: a scene from
Twelve Angry Men
Source: Kobal Collection.

Belonging to a group (of whatever size and distribution) is largely a psychological
state which is quite distinct from that of being a unique and separate individual,
and it confers social identity, or a shared/collective representation of who one is
and how one should behave. (Hogg & Abrams 1988)

A pioneer of REDUCTIONIST PSYCHOLOGY, Allport (1924), argued that there was
'no psychology of groups which is not essentially and entirely a psychology of
individuals'. Yet other early writers talked of the group as an organism in itself:
McDougall (1908) even talks of the group mind, which is internalized by each
member.

REDUCTIONIST
PSYCHOLOGY

What is the evidence? Is there anything distinctly 'social' about individual
behaviour in the presence of others?

Social facilitation/inhibition

Before we even look at behaviour in a group, consider the effect of performing
a task with just one other individual in view. For our experiment, let us take a
task with some measurable output – typing would be a good example, where
we could take speed and accuracy as our measures. We establish how an individual typist performs when alone; then introduce into the room a stranger,

Plate 12.5 Two people typing: work rates
Source: Cefn Newsham.

CO-ACTOR

and see how the output changes. (Our stranger could either be sitting in quietly, as audience; or you could have them also typing: a CO-ACTOR.) What happens?

For some typists, the mere presence of another person improves their work rate; yet for others, their error rate increases and their overall efficiency declines. This puzzled the early social psychologists, who at first had only noted the performance improvements, and thus had labelled the phenomenon SOCIAL FACILITATION. (Typical tasks which showed these improvements included a sprint cyclist's personal best circuit time being improved still further when a second cyclist was present; or, rather splendidly, an entirely satiated chicken starting eating all over again when a second chicken was added to its pen: see for example Triplett 1898.) Zajonc (1965), however, was able to bring order out of chaos, by noting that one saw the improvements with the highly skilled typists, and the decrements with the beginners. His explanation drew on the theories of psychological drive then current, arguing thus: the presence of audience or co-actor is arousing. Arousal, however caused, leads the individual to make their most likely response; this, for the skilled person, is a correct response, but for the unskilled, it is an error.

SOCIAL
FACILITATION

You might also feel that a more social-level explanation could be given; and that performers would vary in terms of the amount they were apprehensive of being evaluated by the other: you could indeed demonstrate this within your study by, on one occasion having the audience be an expert typist, on another, a

Plate 12.6 Adult typing with child play-typing

young child who would cause no apprehension. A version of this study by Henchy and Glass (1968) confirmed your expectations: expert audiences evince more apprehension.

Yet, of course, children can produce their own impact on performance, via distraction from the activity in hand.

As we shall see in many places in social psychology, the various explanations for the phenomenon of social facilitation and INHIBITION are not so much competing against each other, but should be regarded as partial contributors to an overall explanation. So here we should see that basic arousal processes may predominate in some situations, but a mixture of apprehension and distraction may be a more appropriate explanation in other cases.

INHIBITION

The individual in the social group: beyond conformity pressures

Let us now move to the level of the group: here we can give even stronger instances of individual behaviour being shaped not only by the presence but also the actions of others. Dramatic changes in individual behaviour can be demonstrated, for example, in the classic studies of conformity by Asch, and obedience by Milgram (to be outlined below); but more often, we would stress, social influence is a more subtle process, of individual needs and expectancies being met by the social and information resources offered by the other people in the group, all of them interacting within the norms and role-structures of the group, and each influenced by some level of identification with the group.

Furthermore, we should re-examine these classic studies within the more

481

modern framework, rather than accepting that Asch's and Milgram's subjects (note the word!) were passive acceptors of social pressure.

Subjects in Asch's 'studies of independence and conformity' (1956) came to the lab expecting to take part in studies of perceptual judgement; and found themselves one of eight participants asked to match a standard line to one of three 'stimulus lines' displayed alongside. The task seemed easy, and on the first two trials all subjects were in agreement as they called out their judgements. On the next and subsequent trials something very different occurred. Imagine the position: you are sitting in the last seat, and hear each of the first seven sing out what looks to you to be the wrong answer. The differences were sufficiently clear cut that subjects on their own would not make mistakes; yet here you are faced by a consistent majority . . .

Asch found that on one-third of occasions, faced with this pressure, people complied with the social consensus against their own clear perceptual judgement. None realized that the unanimous majority were in fact carefully programmed confederates of the experimenter. Interviewed afterwards, most subjects talked of their discomfort in the situation, and those who yielded talked about avoiding being 'different', or rationalized the situation by assuming the others had a clearer view, etc.

Note that there was a wide individual variation of interpretation and response:

Plate 12.7
Source: Camera Press.

Plate 12.8 Pop concert: compare plate 12.7
Source: Katz Pictures.

capsule summaries of the Asch studies tend to overstate the 'behavioural conformity' line, as if this is a universal of human behaviour. In practice, situational and cultural factors can change the level of compliance shown: for example, Asch found he could reduce compliance by programming one of the confederates to continue to respond correctly, thus giving social and informational support. Some exact replications of the original study, carried out in more independent minded times and cultures, have found much lower levels of public compliance: for instance, Perrin and Spencer (1981) found British students remaining steadfastly independent. (How do you think your contemporaries today would react?) The historical and cultural settings of our experiments are important – Asch's study was done in the 1950s America of McCarthy, when political correctness was all; Perrin and Spencer took British students at perhaps the height of independent mindedness; while in an almost contemporaneous study, Doms and Avermat (1982) found their Belgian students to be much more like Asch's people. (Perrin and Spencer had indeed found that non-student populations in Britain were still showing some conformity.)

One should also question the very settings within which studies are conducted: the Milgram (1974) demonstration of obedience, again often summarized in textbooks as if it were universal, may instead reflect peoples' view of the subject role in a lab experiment and no more. Imagine yourself recruited as a subject: Yale University has high prestige for its research, and, as an outsider, you are in-

Box 12.2   Should Social Psychology Abandon the Laboratory?

Many of the studies that make up social psychology have been conducted in a laboratory setting, for purposes of standardization, simplification and ease of replication.

Yet even the most confirmed adherent to this 'scientific' procedure must have some sympathy with those critics who have suggested that the average experiment consists of: bringing together groups of strangers into an unfamiliar, rather formal setting, and requiring them to interact on tasks that they suspect have more to them than they have been told. Hardly the neutral situation claimed. Derek Edwards and Jonathon Potter have argued that the published reports of lab studies often fail to address the impact on subjects' responses of relations between subjects and experimenter.

One study in the experimental mould which precisely does address this is Reicher and Levine's work (1994) on 'deindividuation' in the crowd: rather than attempt via interviews in real crowds to capture what Le Bon described as their 'sentiment of invincible power', the researchers sought to create in the lab the conditions wherewith to manipulate its conceptual equivalent: the feeling of deindividuation. Their first study made supporters of the Campaign for Nuclear Disarmament individually identifiable to a powerful out-group; here, they found that people awarded to their own group better rewards than to members of the powerful other group significantly more when they were responding anonymously.

The second experiment constructed a situation where science students had either their 'Scientist' or their general 'Student' identity highlighted; and then were asked to respond anonymously or by name to questionnaires about student life, which they believed would be read by members of staff.

Subjects defined by the 'student' label were more likely to say that they chose psychology for an easy life, and that they might plagiarize essays and fabricate lab data than would 'scientists'. (Remember, they *all* were science students.) And this was true of 'scientists' even when the temptations of anonymous questionnaires were offered. Deindividuation has some effects, but does not necessarily overcome group identity.

Reicher and Levine therefore agree with Edwards and Potter's (1992) reservations about lab experiments in social psychology – up to a point: qualitative studies would capture more of a situation's meaning for the person than quantitative ever can. But this does not mean that experiments should be abandoned: 'Indeed, we would argue that the experiment involves such clear and asymmetrical relations between subjects (the term itself is revealing) and experimenters, it is an excellent domain for the study of power relations' (1992: 161).

As for Le Bon and his notion of the formless, fickle and irrational crowd: by bringing an aspect of the crowd into the lab, we can now see how wrong he was. Crowd behaviour is just as socially meaningful as that shown in small groups: and perhaps it is only in the crowd, where the size of the in-group weakens authority's power to identify people and hold them to account, that people are completely free to give what Reicher and Levine call 'unconstrained expression to their collective understandings of the social world'.

trigued to participate there in an innovative study of the learning process. Given this introduction by an authoritative-seeming and confident young researcher, you are assigned to the 'teacher' role, and your fellow subject (actually, the experimenter's confederate) is sent to an adjacent room in which he has a series of learning tasks to perform, under your supervision.

A plausible story about the value of punishment in the learning process is given to you, before you start into your 'teacher' role: with the experimenter standing by, you are to teach by giving electric shocks for each of the pupil's mistakes, via a remote control to his room. You have been told to increase the voltage each time, moving through mild to moderate, and up the scale to dramatically labelled levels ('450 volts. Danger: Severe Shock'). Of course, you wouldn't obey, as soon as you heard the cries of pain coming from the pupil's room; you would challenge the stony-faced experimenter and leave. If so, as Milgram's headline-grabbing study showed, you would have been an unusually disobedient subject. On average, 62 per cent of his subjects went up to the maximum.

The explanation for his results cannot be that subjects realized that the 'pupil' was really a convincing actor, who never received any shocks: debriefing interviews showed that this was not the case.

Consider all the factors in the experimental situation which support a complying response: the status of the institution, the mystique of 'scientific research', novelty, the authority relations of researcher and subject, etc. Try the thought experiment of systematically removing each of these factors, and see what your predictions would be. (Milgram found that relocating the study to the offices of 'Research Associates' was in itself sufficient to reduce maximum compliance down to 48 per cent: still of course a worryingly high level.)

The institution's prestige may serve to send a message not only of authority, but also of reassurance, a guarantee that all must be well, despite appearances. Here, as elsewhere, people search for meaning and understanding; their unease is assuaged by this implied reassurance. Add a further, disconfirming, factor, and all that doubt comes flooding back: Milgram contrived one version of the study at Yale where two fellow subjects (in fact confederates) refused to participate in the 'teaching'. Compliance plummeted to 10 per cent.

Being in a minority in the group may lead to obedience against one's first inclinations, or outward compliance, to avoid social censure; where the situation is ambiguous or uncertain, it may lead to full conformity. Here not just one's behaviour, but also one's beliefs are changed towards those of the group.

The potential power of the minority

Up to this point, we have been considering majority power. However, the minority may well itself have a disproportionate impact upon the group: before reading on, you might like to consider any cases known to you where this happened, and analyse the reasons why the strength of the majority did not prevail.

Consider, indeed, why majorities are usually assumed likely to prevail: first, you might say 'weight of numbers'. By itself, this is not an explanation: this could either imply social pressure being applied to disagreeing group members to fall into line, or an information exchange process. If a simple social decision-rule were to be to accept the most frequently expressed point of view, then a unanimous majority would always prevail, and minority voices would be lost. However, in addition, the majority's influence may derive from their perceived competence.

A single, wavering minority viewpoint lacks any of these factors. By definition, a minority could not prevail on numbers; therefore its force must stem from the strength of its arguments, its apparent conviction, its coherence and tenacity.

Wishing to examine these suggestions, Moscovici (1985a) devised an experimental setting which took Asch's design and inverted it: Moscovici's groups consisted of a majority of 'real' subjects, seeded with one or more confederates of the experimenter. They were instructed to agree with the majority for the first few trials, and then to start giving alternative responses. Moscovici, like Asch, chose easy PERCEPTUAL DISCRIMINATION TASKS that subjects would have found no problems deciding upon on their own; hence, confirmation of their view by the other group members would have been expected. When one and then a second group member began to disagree, this therefore had to be noticed and reacted to. (Other studies of minorities in real-life groups show how disproportionately many communications are addressed to them by the majority.) Initially the fact of their disagreement draws the attention; then their tenacity leads majority group members to address the nature of their arguments. Where first one and then a second person breaks away from the majority consensus, they are seen as a leader and a follower who has become convinced of his/her views. In a series of experiments, Moscovici, Nemeth and others have varied the behaviour of the minority, in order to ascertain the nature of factors involved (see Nemeth 1996). Consistency of their behaviour leads the majority to perceive them as having a coherent position, as does the leader–follower effect, which offers a public model of a group member (apparently) changing their mind, which others could follow. There may, however be some social embarrassment involved in first opposing a minority and then joining it; this was made clear when the experimenters found a plausible reason for withdrawing the minority from the group: they would be called away to the phone, and the majority then found it easier to examine and perhaps adopt the minority position in their absence. (For the sake of historical accuracy, we should note that Asch himself disliked the conformity bias emphasis that social psychology placed on his experiments: as Moscovici 1996 records, what had interested him was the individual's resisting group pressure, not the individual's acting with the group.)

Most of this initial work was done in the lab, with new and temporary groups working on provided tasks; more recently, the study of social influence processes has moved to studying real-life groups and their workings. Although these are inevitably more complex, having a longer history and a greater sense of member identification with the group, we do not have to abandon the lab findings, but rather we can add new factors specific to each group: the existing role-relationships between group members, the current state of alliances and dependencies between members, individuals' expertise on particular topics, etc. Some 'minority' members of a group might have a pre-existing powerful role within the group, giving them what Hollander (1964) has labelled IDIOSYNCRASY CREDIT. In such a case, are we likely to see outward compliance by group members, followed by a genuine opinion change?

PERCEPTUAL
DISCRIMINATION
TASK

IDIOSYNCRASY
CREDIT

Groups have histories

Why join a group? Why stay? Why leave? What changes and what differentiations occur over time? You must realize that groups, like individuals, have their own histories. Let us review what we know of them.

Joining

Why groups first loosely form – here we are talking of informal groups – is at least in part a function of non-psychological factors, such as geographical, architectural and social factors such as proximity in space, and the opportunities this affords for interaction. In a classic study of student friendships on campus, Newcomb (1961) found that the best predictor of acquaintanceship in the first days of term was where in the student residence people lived: those you see around you in those first, confusing days will provide your first group on campus. The people you happen to sit next to in your first lectures will probably become another early, loose group. (Remember, we are likely to have simultaneous membership of several groups, at every stage of our lives.)

Newcomb, however, was more interested in the longer-term friendships that were to develop; and he had hypothesized that these would form around similarities between individuals. Going back to his students several weeks into term, he found this expectation confirmed: within the small student house he was studying, friendship groups had emerged, predictable in terms of attitude similarities. Many other studies have noted that friends are more similar than the non-friends within the broader population; but Newcomb's design enabled him to answer the question of causality that others had posed: do we seek similarities in others, with whom we then group? Or do other factors, such as proximity or physical attraction, initially bring us together, and we then become more similar in our attitudes and behaviour, as a result of mutual influence? *Post hoc*, it is difficult to tell; but Newcomb cunningly had a before-and-after measure. He knew beforehand which students coming up to college were to be given which rooms in the residence; wrote to each, inviting them to join a study, and including an attitude questionnaire to be returned before they came up to campus. On this basis, he could predict both the initial proximity-influenced acquaintances and the later-emergent similarity-based friendships. So, yes, we do select for similarity of attitudes; we also further converge within these friendships once formed. Yet again in social psychology, we find that both apparently alternative hypotheses can be true. The kind of predictability of human choices, as shown in Newcomb's study, is somewhat awesome and thought-provoking. Several years later, Duck and Spencer (1972) followed the Newcomb design, finding that they could accurately predict, from a prior knowledge of incoming students' 'personal constructs', the groups which would form. (A personal construct is an individual's way of understanding or construing the world.) Kelley (1955; see also chapter 14) had shown how to capture an individual's dimensions for judging the world on these constructs; and Duck and Spencer had shown that similarity on these constructs underlaid the attitude similarities that predicted friend-ships.

Although one might also hypothesize that personality similarity would be a useful further predictor, the evidence of many studies shows otherwise. Indeed, one study by Winch (1967) has shown complementarity of personality was a better predictor of one special type of relationship: successful marriage partner-ships.

Staying and leaving

Joining an informal group can therefore usually offer 'consensual validation' of one's attitudes and world views, and thereby reinforce one's sense of identity. The group is not, however, unchanging, and the reasons for staying in the group may be different from those for initially joining it: one has achieved a role within; dependencies have been set up; personal commitment may have been made to some of the group's objectives; one becomes identified by outsiders with such objectives; as well as one beginning to so identify oneself, etc. Even if the indi-vidual finds himself or herself less than content with the group, they may still remain: either the anticipated social costs of leaving may look too high, or the rewards for entry into alternative groups look too low. In other words, groups may be construed in comparative terms with relation to a known and felt-rel-evant context. Leaving a group or a relationship is likely therefore to involve some cost, all the way from the breaking of some regularities of daily life through to, in some instances, a major re-evaluation of one's identity.

Consider some major life transitions: leaving home to go to college; becoming a parent; retirement from the workplace. Take the social-rewards-and-costs ap-proach to these, and think through what problems of adjustment may occur. What could the individual do in preparation for leaving their groups?

Groups in action

Groups have outcomes, all manner of measurable outcomes.

Formal groups such as work-teams, committees and juries are likely to have agreed targets – for instance, the solution of a particular problem, or the produc-tion of a product, or the adjudication of a case. Our behavioural measures should reflect these tasks of the group. We should also seek to assess the social behav-iour within the group, for this will probably be a strong predictor of the satisfac-tion group members report. What would the *informal* group have as equivalents of the formal group's tasks? It would seem strange to expect them to have tar-gets as obvious, in terms of products or cases. Yet we can see that they are 'work-ing' towards outcomes, for which we could also devise measures: decisions as to which film to go and see tonight, or discussions about the quality of food on campus, will have a mix of task and socializing about them.

Leaders and leadership

What are the characteristics which distinguish leaders from other group members? This apparently reasonable question was one which occupied early social psychology for many years; but which turned out to be the wrong question. The implication underlying it is that there will be an identifiable set of personality traits; yet the aggregate finding of many studies is that such a set does not exist (Stogdill, in 1948, summarized forty years' research which, when added together, came to this conclusion). Leaders, as a whole, are not more extrovert than fellow group members, nor more intelligent, nor more physically striking: these are all reasonable hypotheses, and they are sometimes borne out in particular instances. But each time, as Stogdill's review of the research literature shows, there is a counter-example . . .

You can see why psychology might have been attracted to the idea that there were identifiable traits which distinguished existing leaders from their followers. This would have allowed one to develop predictive tests for use in selection and recruitment of future leaders. (And indeed many recruitment consultants still base much of their procedures on personality testing.) Yet the evidence is clearly against this position: leaders as a whole are not a characteristic type. Nor even if one is trying to predict leadership within one single type of group (military combat group, creative writing circle or whatever) is there any better prediction of success.

The more recent position in psychology is that it is not who leaders are, but how they think, behave and are perceived that distinguishes them. Bales, as early as 1950, had foreseen the need to examine leadership styles: he distinguished between those who were predominantly task orientated, and those who spent more time in social and emotional maintenance of their group.

FIEDLER'S CONTINGENCY THEORY (1981) is still the most widely supported account in this tradition: and it has proved an amazingly simple but reliable predictor of leader effectiveness. (Some other studies of leaders and their groups have, in contrast, occasioned many hours of observations by the researcher, lengthy interviews and detailed recording of a group's activities.) In assessing leadership, Fiedler concentrates on two issues:

FIEDLER'S CONTINGENCY THEORY

Stage 1: How to describe the leader's personal style: The experimenter asks the leader to think about fellow group members, and from them to identify one as their LEAST PREFERRED CO-WORKER (LPC); and then to give a description of them as a person, by checking off a list of pairs of adjectives: 'warm–cold', etc. This LPC scale indicates how far the leader can separate the personal characteristics of his LPC from the work characteristics. Being able to see one's LPC's humanity is a style of thinking that strongly suits some group settings, and the opposite, work-focused style of leadership suits other settings. (This aspect of contingency theory has its parallels with Likert's studies of leader behaviours; and his distinction between employee-centred behaviours and production-centred behaviours: Likert 1967.)

LEAST PREFERRED CO-WORKER

Box 12.3 Where do our Stereotypes of National Characteristics Come From?

We know almost nothing about what gives rise to the content of stereotypes, although a good deal is known about the intergroup and within-person processes which lead to stereotyping.

Hub Linssen and Louk Hagendoorn (1994) decided to investigate, working with 16- to 18-year-olds in seven European Community countries: Belgium, Denmark, England, France, Germany, Italy and the Netherlands.

They designed a questionnaire which asked on a scale of 0 to100 per cent how many representatives of a national group would have a certain characteristic. In all, each person rated each country (including their own) on 22 trait adjectives to describe its people; and went on to ask that each country be scored as a nation state on characteristics such as: 'highly developed culturally', 'capitalistic', 'politically divided', 'directed at equality between men and women'.

Analysis of the perceived national traits as a whole showed that differences between countries could be grouped in terms of four factors:

Dominant (egoistic; proud; assertive; competitive; etc.)
Efficient (scientific; industrious; intelligent; honest; rich)
Empathetic (helpful; sympathetic; friendly)
Emotional (enjoying life; religious)

Using these descriptors, they then looked at the data country by country; and here are their findings:

Efficient		Emotional		Empathetic		Dominant	
G	66	I	75	NL	62	G	66
DK	61	F	65	DK	61	E	61
NL	57	NL	56	I	60	F	61
E	56	B	54	B	60	I	58
B	51	G	52	F	56	NL	55
F	51	DK	51	G	54	DK	52
I	43	E	51	E	52	B	46

Stage 2: How to describe the situation: Fiedler offers an equally simple descriptor of group situations, by asking three questions:

Is the task situation: structured or unstructured?
Is the leader's position: powerful or weak?
Are leader–member relations: bad or good?

By answering each question, one can allocate the group into one of the eight types produced by permuting the answers. Now to bring LPC-measured style together with group type, Fiedler studied many hundreds of different kinds of real-life groups, and comparing, within each type, more with less successful examples, using the groups' individual appropriate criteria for judging that success. (Obviously, criteria for success in leading a sales force would differ from those in leading a research team: or at least, I would hope so.)

The task-oriented style of leader turned out to be more effective where the group was structured and with good leader–member relations, with either a powerful or a weak leader position. Structured situations with poor leader–member relations call for a socially oriented style to make a success of them, again whether or not the leader has a strong personal position. Where the task is unstructured, then the leader's position becomes an important predictor of success along with the other two factors.

Effective leadership, then, depends on (or, as Fiedler would say, is contingent

(where B = Belgium, G = Germany, DK = Denmark, E = England, F = France, NL = Netherlands and I = Italy)

Examine this table: do you see any trends?

Efficiency seems to be a northern European characteristic; emotionalism a southern one. Size of country also looks to be involved: for the countries perceived to be most empathetic and least dominant are on the whole the smaller ones.

When Linssen and Hagendoorn then further analysed the results, they found that, in addition to these purely geographical factors, social factors were also predictive of stereotypes in three of the four traits: efficiency was attributed to nationals of those countries which were seen as economically developed and socially secure; and empathy and lack of dominance were attributed to those whose countries were seen as being low on political power and nationalism. However, the emotionality of inhabitants remains best predicted by the north–south position of each country.

These, as you will realize, are data aggregated over respondents from all seven countries; and, although the results hold very largely true in each, there are intriguing local variations: Belgian and Danish respondents link empathy with lack of militarism, whereas for German respondents empathy and absence of regional antagonism are closely linked.

Geographical features as crude as north–south and size of country clearly are invitations to further investigations. Could climate begin to explain north–south? In colder climes, there are fewer opportunities for the visible demonstration of behaviours which could be described as 'emotional' . . .

upon) style appropriate to the situation; and leadership studies ignore situation at their peril.

Other factors also contribute to the group's success: these include particularized dyadic relations that leaders may establish with some individuals in their group ('vertical dyadic linkage' between them); developing into reciprocity between leader and followers; and altered feelings about the leader's legitimacy and competence. Once safely established in their followers' minds, the leader may tap some shared expectancies about the abilities, behaviour and traits of leaders ('implicit leadership theories').

Thus, curiously, although as we have seen there are in fact no sets of traits which actually differentiate leaders as a group, followers may act as if there were, and attribute leaders' behaviours to these supposed abilities.

Charismatic leadership is extremely uncommon: although the 'great man' accounts of history may tempt us to imagine a mini-Napoleon as the leader of any forcefully led group, the more intriguing reality probably lies in a leader's power arising from the attributions followers make. At one extreme, the regard that followers may develop for their leader can turn into a frightening phenomenon labelled GROUPTHINK (see Janis 1972).

GROUPTHINK

Janis, reading through the memoirs of politicians, was struck by the oft-repeated lapses of judgement to which, with hindsight, they would admit. As individuals, we all make mistakes, but most political decisions are taken in committee, where one person's errors should be recognized and neutralized by the others not making the same error. Political committees are also generally served by advisers, whose role is to give dispassionate and expert advice. That at least is what we fondly believe. How then could the major errors of judgement occur? Janis obtained the records of decision-making which preceded the Bay of Pigs fiasco, the US-led invasion of Cuba in 1961; US inveiglement into the Korean War; and then the Vietnam War; and other, later-regretted decisions. In every case, it became clear to the researcher that the US President and his close group could have been aware of the scale of risks they were running, and yet the available information never seemed to get through. Why? (Lest any modern, non-American reader be tempted to attribute groupthink to one country at one point in time, try seeing if you cannot come up with more recent local equivalents.)

Common to all instances, Janis found the following:

1. excessive optimism arising from a shared illusion of invulnerability
2. rationalizations enabling the group to discount warnings and defend past decisions
3. unquestioned belief in the group's morality, and thus, the ignoring of moral consequences of the group's actions
4. stereotyped views of the opposition and their capabilities
5. direct pressure on any member who might show dissent, by calling on their loyalty
6. self-censorship of any doubts or deviations from apparent group consensus
7. a shared illusion of unanimity, taking others' silence to mean consent

MIND GUARDS

8. emergence of self-appointed MIND GUARDS protecting the group from adverse information.

Cohesive groups, drawing together round a leader, often to tackle a threat, are not confined to politics: instances of groupthink can surely be documented in business and family decision-making. And Janis's suggestions for the prevention of groupthink – including encouraging critical evaluation procedures – would apply in each instance.

Polarization of attitudes and actions

As we have seen in the case of groupthink, decision-making by groups may not be as balanced and rational as perhaps imagined; they can produce some unexpected behaviours from their members. We turn to another instance: the group

POLARIZATION

POLARIZATION of individual attitudes. This is a widely documented phenomenon, in which the effect of group discussion of an issue serves to leave individuals with an expressed view which is slightly more extreme than the one they expressed beforehand.

Would you have predicted this? Many of the social influence processes discussed so far, especially those of majorities, indicate that the best predictor of group outomes is the average of all individual choices. Some management theorists decried the committee as a means of making business decisions, seeing it as inherently conservative, with no member wishing to make suggestions out of line with what they felt would be the acceptable norm. Hence, the world of social psychology was intrigued when came the first systematic studies showing a shift, after group discussion, to greater willingness to take risks.

What was happening? Were the first subject groups atypically keen on risk advocacy? Stoner (1961) had indeed taken young, eager business students as his study population; but subsequent replications of the 'shift to risk' took more diverse populations and found the same results.

Why should we find this occurring? Perhaps, it was argued, the most influential individuals in each group happened to advocate the more risky positions; a reasonable hypothesis, but disconfirmed by closer analysis of the groups' discussions: sometimes leaders were the most risk-advocating ones, but on other occasions it was another member (see Burnstein & Vinokur 1977). The current consensus within social psychology is that persuasive arguments within the group are likely to be part of the explanation for the shift.

The group serves as an information exchange, and thereby a shaper of individual views on issues where there is initial uncertainty; this in a way which is importantly unlike the slavish 'conformity' of early psychology. The group is now seen as enhancing and clarifying the values and beliefs that the individual brings to the group.

Brown (1986) first noted that, on some issues that groups discussed, the shift was regularly towards, not risk, but a conservative position. This shift to conservatism was typically found where the topic involved decisions about marriage, one's family dependants, or issues about their well-being; in contrast, willingness to take greater risk was associated with business decisions, sport, games, etc. What Brown felt was that there is a set of cultural values at work here: it is generally accepted that one should seek others' well-being, and not take actions which might jeopardize it. Equally, there is a widespread feeling that adventurous initiatives should be taken where possible in sport and in business enterprises.

But the problem which often faces the individual is quite what is the appropriate embodiment of these values? How cautious should one be with relation to matters of health and well-being? What is a reasonable level of risk to choose in business or sport?

Coming into a group can therefore give the individual information on what others feel is an appropriate level of caution or of risk to choose. And, to many people's surprise, they find others in the group who more closely embody the cultural norm than they do; and thus are freed to move closer to the preferred pole than they had done previously. Hence we observe a group shifting towards the pole already favoured in their initial individual choices.

Box 12.4 What Marks did You Get for your Lab Report?: A Field Study of Social Comparison

Margaret Foddy and Ian Crundall (1993) have made a virtue out of what is normally considered a disadvantage in using psychology undergraduates as subjects: they studied students' natural tendency for socially comparing themselves by focusing on their interest in how others had done on their lab reports. This task provides a good test of social comparison process, because it is relatively novel to the students (and thus they were motivated to reduce uncertainty); important to them (for these students, labs were worth 25 per cent of their final grade); and conducted in a relatively competitive situation (both with regard to getting onto courses, and into the job market).

How did they conduct the study?

The first-year psychology class recorded details of how they had spontaneously compared themselves with fellow students two weeks before they handed in an assignment, and one week after it had been returned to them. Data was collected on the occasion of three lab reports.

They found that the majority of students did make comparisons with others' performance; that this was particularly prevalent after getting their marked assignments returned to them; and that this became more frequent as term progressed. However, there was a substantial minority (nearly 19 per cent) of students who did not seek to compare themselves at any stage.

For those who did, comparing oneself with others who were similar in ability was the most common pattern; but, people also sought out other students who were better than themselves, particularly after they had received objective feedback on their own reports.

Theories of social comparison have rather simplistically claimed that people will gain the most useful information from others they see as similar to themselves; but you will see that in a case such as this, the reassurance this might provide can be offset by the desire to improve own performance.

Having received back one's marked report, being able to compare one's performance with that of a range of fellow students, including those one knows to be stronger students, enables one to:

interpret the mark one has received
know the range of marks received, and thus infer the task difficulty
place oneself in the ability spectrum of the class
find out how close one is to the best students
and establish what improvement one could make to emulate them.

This study shows that in everyday (student) life, people do make social comparisons, even when objective and expert feedback was provided to them, because this was offering a wide range of extra information, plus reassurance, motivation, tips for the future, etc.

SOCIAL COMPARISON
PROCESSES

For such SOCIAL COMPARISON PROCESSES to produce a shift, three propositions must hold:

1. any given issue evokes in the individuals some cultural value (e.g. for risk, caution, etc.);
2. each individual then adopts a position which they feel is the culturally-desirable one;
3. coming into the group gives each individual information on others' choices, and if this shows them that they were not as risky (cautious, etc.) as they had believed, then this will motivate change toward the culturally valued pole.

In advance of the group, almost everyone thinks their position is like the others, only a little better. Codol (1975) has twenty studies which show this belief to be very widespread: he has found belief in the 'SUPERIOR CONFORMITY OF THE SELF', among children and adults, professionals and blue-collar workers, on a whole range of issues. (You could easily run an informal replication of this with your friends: which person, for example, doesn't believe themselves to have a better-than-average sense of humour?)

Information of others' views without any group discussion is sufficient to bring about the shift, confirming that social comparison underlies the effect. Information plus discussion, however, brings larger shifts, indicating the supplementary role of persuasive arguments in the process. And the more arguments in favour of the pole position are heard, the greater are the chances of a shift. (See the review by Wetherell 1987.)

Attitudes, prejudices, opinions: all have been shown to be susceptible to the social-comparison and persuasive-argument induced shifts we have been discussing. Polarization in groups turns out to be a widespread and important phenomenon: it can occur, for instance, in the deliberations of a jury. Think for a moment about how one might characterize a jury: a group of strangers, making an important novel decision in conditions of uncertainty; here are the prime conditions for shifts. (See for example Myers & Lamm 1976, who ran simulations of jury decisions, actual trials being beyond bounds for the experimental social psychologist.) In contrast, there are situations where a group holds no secrets for its members, and where little or no social influence occurs as a result: Manstead and Semin (1980) found the perfect instance in their observations of medical case conferences where the doctors had been meeting regularly for ages – no changes there.

We have seen here, in the study of groups polarizing individual responses and attitudes, a model for how many group influence processes operate: not so much a matter of majority pressure upon the individual, as a case of the individual having needs (for information, norms of appropriateness, and validation of own ideas and self-concepts) which the other members can fulfil.

We can also draw a broader lesson from these studies: when they first started, social psychology was concerned above all with the exactness and replicability of its studies. As a consequence, most studies were lab-based experiments, using standard, simplified conditions: in this case, shift studies initially used a standard set of 'choice-dilemma' problems, each one consisting of a brief hypothetical situation and a single scale on which to record one's recommendation. Social psychology then seemed to feel that replicability of its experiments was more important than their realism; now the priority has reversed, recognizing that every situation is responded to in subtly different ways, and that the lab is no 'neutral' setting in which to observe universals of human behaviour, but only perhaps a useful first step before testing any generalizations in settings which were 'real' for their participants.

SUPERIOR CONFORMITY OF THE SELF

▧ Society, Groups and Individuals ▧

Awareness of group identity and the origins of conflict

So far, we have been concerned with socially cohesive groups, whose interdependence arises from the satisfaction of individual needs, attainment of goals and mutual attractions. As already suggested, the group may well also give an identity to each individual, and this may have negative as well as positive consequences, as we shall now go on to see.

For it is alarmingly easy to artificially create 'group feelings' which not only lead to positive thoughts about one's own group, but also derogate 'other groups' in contrast with one's own. In examining this, we shall see the origins of prejudices, and of conflicts between groups.

We could then offer a definition of a group as a collection of people who perceive themselves as belonging to the same social category: this is the definition used by Turner and other proponents of the 'social identification model', in contrast to the 'social cohesion models' of groups so far reviewed. In this view, perceived similarity within the group and attraction to in-group members are seen as consequences of this *self-categorization* process, and not the prerequisites of group formation.

Wagner and Ward (1993) have shown that the more a person defines themselves in terms of group-category membership, the more identity with, and liking for, other group members (s)he will show, together with an assumption of similarity of their attitudes and values. What makes one's own group membership more salient, more important to one?

Sometimes, it is precisely an awareness of another, potentially competing, other group that strengthens within-group feelings, heightening our feelings of similarity with 'our own' and accentuating differences with 'the others'. Jost and Banaji (1994) have discussed how the holding of stereotypes about others can offer justification for self, for the group and for the system.

The clearest demonstration of this was given by Muzafer and Carolyn Sherif, in a classic series of natural experiments in summer camps, during which they were able to conjure up a whole miniature society, its strengths and conflicts, and then (being responsible social scientists) set about resolving the conflicts that had been created.

There were in fact a number of years in which the Sherifs carried out these studies (see Sherif & Sherif 1953 for a full résumé), but we will describe them as one experiment.

ROBBERS' CAVE

Going away on summer camp was a normal part of a 12-year-old boy's expectations: and the boys arriving at ROBBERS' CAVE, to participate in the weeks of outdoor activities, found themselves accommodated in the bunk house, getting to know the other boys and the camp's organizers, and settling in for the activities. All as normal, except for the fact that among the organizers were psychologists, there to watch the beginnings of GROUP COHESION. By means of discreet

GROUP COHESION

questions and observations, they recorded the friendships developing, and the group drawing together. In particular, the group was seen to become structured, with some individuals taking the lead and others tending to follow. Camp activities were designed so as to throw the boys back on their own resources, and within days a stable set of roles had developed: one led in organizing the cooking, another in athletics, another gained a reputation as the camp-jester; others were willing followers, and some were usually disruptive.

These leader and follower roles noted by the observers were also recognized by the boys themselves, and the Sherifs saw how the leaders' prowess was exaggerated by the other boys. Similarly, the least-ranking boys' skills (e.g. at basketball) were *under*estimated by the others. Each group developed its own styles, nicknames, legends and ways of keeping order.

The Sherifs concluded that this group identity arose from the pattern of interdependence:

> interdependent activities directed toward goals of high appeal value are a sufficient condition for group formation . . . [and for the] signs of 'we' feeling and pride in joint accomplishments that mark an in-group. (1953: 239)

Note that this is *before* the group became aware that there was in fact another group camping in the vicinity, and before they issued their challenge to compete at sports.

So, if *phase one* of the study was of group formation, then phase two was to examine intergroup feelings and conflict. The Sherifs hypothesized that competition between two groups for outcomes or resources that only one can attain was likely to lead to negative STEREOTYPING of the other group, increased positive feelings about one's own group, and eventually to conflict. How did they engineer this at Robbers' Cave?

STEREOTYPING

The camp observers arranged a series of games tournaments between the groups: baseball, football, tug-of-war, as well as other competitions for prizes. Initial good-humoured rivalry gave way to name-calling; derogation of the other group led into activities to spite the other group.

Systematic errors in estimating own group's and the other group's performances were quickly evident; each group was seen to close ranks and show heightened solidarity with its own:

> After the tournament, the members of each group found the others so distasteful that they expressed strong preferences to have no further contact with them at all. In short, in-group exclusiveness was accompanied by extreme social distance between groups. (1953: 243)

The conclusion drawn from this stage was that sustained conflict over goals that both desired but only one could achieve, is a sufficient condition for the rise of hostile acts, derogatory images of the other group, and what the Sherifs describe as 'the rudiments of prejudice'.

Plate 12.9 Political rally:
civilized intergroup conflict?
Source: Sally and Richard
Greenhill.

Note that none of the usual trappings of society's conflicts (differences in appearance, custom, language, etc.) had been present. Nor had it needed emotionally disturbed individuals to precipitate the prejudices and hostilities. This last point is particularly important, for some theorists on prejudice and intergroup conflict have started with this presumption, and have therefore tackled prejudice as primarily a problem for individual psychology. But, as Brown's (1995) critique shows, this approach underestimates how important is the immediate social situation in the genesis of prejudice (see Further Reading below). Nor does it acknowledge that many intergroup conflicts are years, if not indeed many generations long: and thus they shape the social landscape within which children are socialized.

How can we reduce intergroup conflict?

How could the Sherifs restore harmony in the camp? And what might their efforts say about the possibilities for the reduction of prejudices in society?

The *final phase* of the Robbers' Cave experiment was thus the reduction of conflict. In this, the Sherifs used local versions of strategies which have been advocated on the national scale:

> countering of stereotypes by presenting accurate and favourable information
>   about each group (and thus its humanity);
> appeals to high moral values;

Box 12.5 In a Multi-cultural Society, Who do you Identify With? Or: Why only Some Australians Cringe when their Country is Mentioned

'Apply the cricket test' was the advice of former right-wing British minister, Norman Tebbit. As a test of their identification with Britain, he suggested asking immigrants which team in a Test Match they would cheer for if England was playing their former country at cricket. You may feel that this empirical test of a person's identity could be improved upon (not least to extend enquiries to non-cricket-playing countries!); and a recent Australian test might provide a better basis.

Norman Feather (1994) has developed the Cultural Cringe Scale. He reasons that not all groups exhibit the in-group favouritism that social identity theory predicts, and that some actually derogate their own in favour of others. Such 'cultural cringe' is said to exist when members of a culture devalue their group's products and achievements compared to those of another culture's.

A sample item on the 16-point scale would be: 'It is only when we see top overseas entertainers that we see real talent.'

Some of Feather's Australian respondents showed strong identification with their country by firmly rejecting such statements; others endorsed them. The groups' identifications were further confirmed by their statements about how much they cared about being an Australian: in other words, in-group bias was correlated with national identification.

We can go further: this correlation is stronger for those people whose personal values stressed conformity and security, and who assigned low values to hedonistic values. (Feather had everyone fill in a value survey.)

So it seems as if the collectivists tend to cheer for their own, while individualists are not so vocal!

bringing of rival leaders together in conference; increasing contact between groups.

None of these methods proved effective: as you will realize, information campaigns can be selectively listened to; moral sermons can be ignored in the height of conflict; and leaders have often come to the fore as embodying the own-group pride, and thus they may fall if they suddenly advocate the opposite, and seem too friendly with 'the others'. Indeed, in the camp, increased contacts became the occasion for the renewal of hostilities.

What did prove temporarily effective was the presence of a *common enemy*. How did the Sherifs achieve this? They contrived to invite an outside group to a sports tournament against a joint team from both groups. Hostilities were suspended for the duration, although social distances between the groups scarcely diminished.

As you will realize, even had this remedy been more effective, this would hardly have been a morally acceptable solution, substituting a new enemy for the old. You have probably already anticipated the Sherifs' long-term solution: creating the conditions for interdependence between the groups. Recall that, at the outset, it had been such interdependence between individuals which led to the group forming, because no individual could achieve goals without cooperating. So, similarly, the experimenters contrived a series of situations where the groups' goals could only be achieved by both groups working together. The camp water supply mysteriously broke down, and only a joint effort could mend it; the truck that was to collect their food needed a pull-start from everybody acting together; the film both groups wanted to see, neither could afford to hire

Plate 12.10 Community
action group
Source: Sally and Richard
Greenhill.

without financial contribution from the other. Gradually, working together for these superordinate goals, the separate group identities began to dissolve, and with them, the stereotyped us/them contrasts.

Can we generalize from this study (or rather, series of studies, because the Sherifs repeated the design three times, in different settings and with different populations)? Workshops on human relations in industry, starting with 150 groups run by Blake and Mouton (1962) were the first to show that the Sherif analysis of the origins of conflict was widely applicable, as were their solutions. Superordinate goals – such as the success of the company – may be easier to discern in some situations than others; we may then find that, in order to reduce conflict, governments have to resort to legislation against expressions of prejudice, and to affirmative action, designed to make opportunities in society more equal. In the light of our consideration of the origins of social conflict, how effective would you expect such interventions to be?

The minimal conditions for prejudice

After the Sherifs' suggestion that conflict over scarce resources was the sufficient cause of intergroup hostility, the question then arose: was it the necessary cause? In other words, had social psychology established what were the minimal conditions under which such hostility might arise? (For a general review of this area, see Tajfel 1981.)

A series of studies followed. Rabbie and Horowitz (1969) were convinced that one did not need any major resource issues to start off the stereotyping, and demonstrated this in a simple lab experiment. Subjects were recruited to participate in a study, divided into two groups, told that their payment for attendance would be determined by a coin toss. This duly took place: one group would receive payment, the other none. They were then asked to give their first impressions of the people in the room, those in their own group and those in the other. Uniformly, people gave more favourable accounts of 'fellow members' than of other group members. This, despite the fact that the 'groups' hardly existed, having been created arbitrarily in front of their eyes, and the coin toss that decided the reward was equally random. You might guess that the losers would feel envious of the winners, and therefore disparage the winners; but equally, in fact, the winners disparaged the losers.

This experiment still retains a vestigial resource for which one could see the 'groups' as being in competition. Could one remove even this and still have the beginnings of prejudice?

Tajfel (1974) brought schoolboys into his lab for a day of studies. First off, the experimenter purported to assess their aesthetic preferences: slides of modern art were projected, and each boy wrote down which ones he liked. These sheets were taken away to be scored by the experimenter's assistant, who shortly returned to tell the boys that approximately half of them had preferred paintings by Paul Klee, and the others had preferred those by Wassily Kandinsky. (In fact, no such scoring had taken place, and this was a device to provide an outwardly credible rationale for a division of the group into two on what was in fact a random basis.) The experimenter then suggested that these preferences would give him a way of dividing the boys into two groups for the remainder of the lab session. In fact, the next thing each boy had to do was to suggest how 'real' money should be paid out at the end of the session to two other boys, anonymous save for a Klee or Kandinsky label. Sometimes, the pair was identified as two own-group, sometimes two other-group, and sometimes one from each group. There was a highly consistent tendency to favour own group over other group in a straight comparison, even though, as we have seen, the 'groups' had no basis in reality, and certainly were in no way competitors. Tajfel and Billig (1974) even went so far, in one experiment, as to explicitly assign boys to groups at random; and own-group still was favoured over other. The most striking feature of all was the boys' eagerness to emphasize differences between own and other, even if this meant turning down the possibility of more rewards for both own and other: what Tajfel called 'gratuitous intergroup discrimination'.

So, in seeking the minimal conditions, we may have found quite how basic is a group's capacity to discriminate against another: it occurs

> even when no self interest is served,
> and where there is no explicit competition between groups,

nor any possible history of previous conflict,
let alone a suggestion of disturbed personalities as leaders or followers.

We have therefore to face the fact: inherent in labelling oneself and others in terms of group membership is the likelihood of differential perceptions (often discriminatory perceptions). Categorization works this way: labelling allocates an instance to a category; the category then accentuates differences between adjacent categories (Brown 1995 goes into more detail on the social and cognitive bases of prejudice and conflict than there is room to consider here: see Further Reading below).

However, if each of us has a number of reference groups, which to a greater or lesser extent shape our social identity, and where we have a basic, stable identity given by a long-term social group, then other more obviously temporary subgroupings may not produce the 'us and them' of the Robbers' Cave. Tyerman and Spencer looked for a situation where such a long-term group is occasionally broken down into subgroups for competitive activities; and found it in the annual camp of a homogeneous scout group. In that camp, the scouts were divided into teams for activities and accommodation, and Tyerman and Spencer ran replications of the Sherifs' measures. As the camp progressed, there was keen competition between the subgroups in sports and other activities, but no hostility developed between them. The scout group was superordinate for them, and we can conclude that long-term acquaintanceships can survive temporary segregations (Tyerman & Spencer 1983).

Crowds can be predictable

A small step from the Sherifs' boys' camps to everyday social experiences: downtown shopping, arriving for a football match, attending a big concert. The numbers have increased, but has anything else changed as we move from the behaviour of groups to that of crowds? Or could we use what we have seen so far with the smaller scale to predict the larger?

The first social scientists to theorize about the crowd certainly saw it as a very different sort of animal, with the accent on animal!

Gustave Le Bon (1908) was writing at the end of a century and a half of major social revolutions across Europe, in which crowds on the streets had often been the agents of change, as indeed they have continued to be in countless later examples. Not surprisingly, Le Bon laid stress on the crowd's capacity to alter individual behaviour, and attributed this to 'the crowd soul'. This soul consisted of basic impulses, little influenced by reason, and easily influenced by the suggestions of the leader, who finds it easy to impose his will on the crowd. As a consequence, individuals in a crowd were able to show levels of irrational and primitive behaviour that they would not ordinarily show. ANONYMITY, CONTAGION and SUGGESTIBILITY were the reasons Le Bon offered, and which were uncritically accepted by writers on crowds for many years afterwards, as if these were all

ANONYMITY

CONTAGION

SUGGESTIBILITY

one needed to give as explanations for crowd violence. Even where the crowd has shown negative behaviours, we cannot feel that 'contagion' offers more than a description of the spread of feeling through the crowd: it does not say how or why this should occur. Nor is the 'suggestibility' of the crowd much more than an assertion that individuals are made more open to ideas, as if in an hypnotic trance. 'Anonymity', however, seems worth further investigation.

But there is clearly no inevitability about crowds acting in irrational ways: you will easily be able to think of situations you have been in when the crowd has been peaceable and responsible in its actions, or has been highly emotional but in a positive way. Concerts, religious and political rallies, many sporting events may be examples for you. Is there a way of differentiating between situations where the crowd is unruly and those where it is not? And indeed, when it might seem to the outsider as if there were no rules governing behaviour in crowds, closer investigation can indicate that, for example, the crowd at a football match has its predictabilities, as we shall see below.

Our two foci will therefore be: first, the individual's experience in a crowd – is there a sense of anonymity as Le Bon indicated, and if so does this liberate the individual to act in less social ways? Second, are there predictabilities about crowd behaviour, with perhaps roles and rules ? (For an extended review of this area, see Moscovici 1985a and b.)

Even in the small group, increasing anonymity can subtly change an individual's behaviour: in the kind of decision-making groups we heard about above, the conditions under which people record their decisions – whether they vote on anonymous pieces of paper, or have to declare themselves in front of the group, and have their name identified – may well predict the nature of individual decisions.

One is less socially constrained when in a crowd: you are both less aware of being observed, and also more aware of the fact that those around you do not know you as an individual.

In Le Bon's account, individuals in a crowd lose their own opinions and intellectual faculties, are unable to control their own feelings, and begin to act in surprising ways. Here, Le Bon has in mind the revolutionary crowd, swayed by a demagogue; but most of the time, this is such an exceptional event that to take it as a type example would be misleading, and our range of concern should be of everyday crowds and events.

Le Bon's explanation of unusual and extreme crowd events will be recognizable to you as being related to those theories of social influence and conformity which assume the individual to be pressurized by a majority, rather than those accounts which see the individual as gaining information, meaning and identity from their groups. Groups, in this latter view, help to give the social world a structuring that helps disambiguate it for the individual. Many social situations are unclear; what action is appropriate is thus uncertain, and one seeks clarification. Social psychology found this when seeking to explain why bystanders are often unresponsive (Latané & Darley 1970): it was not so much a question of the bystanders not wanting to become involved, as their not knowing whether the situation was one which needed their involvement. They were surrounded by equally unsure strangers, also doing nothing because they, too, could not read the situation. Thus, each bystander took the others' inaction as signalling a non-event. But when one's uncertainty is resolved the other way – someone shouts 'fire', for example – then established and appropriate ways of responding to that category of situation become available. To continue with the 'fire' example, extensive retrospective studies of many fires in public places, by Canter (1990) and his colleagues, have shown that in the large majority of cases, the ending of uncertainty leads to orderly, rational behaviours, such as warning others, attempting to fight the fire, and evacuation of the building; and that only in a very small minority of cases does panic occur.

> Rather than revealing raw animal instincts, studies of behaviour in fires give strength to the mental nature of our existence as social beings, involved in actions that are structured by perception and thought. (Canter 1990: 3)

So also could we conclude of much other behaviour in crowds: anonymous we may be, but our actions are still determined by our rational understandings. Even in cases where there is, to the outsider, the appearance of disorder, as in, for example, some crowds at football matches, then an explanation is best given in terms of the participants' perceptions of appropriate behaviours, rather than in terms of some untestable 'group mind'. As Harré and colleagues discerned, there are even rules governing 'disorder', (Marsh et al. 1978). They not only were able to observe regular patterns in the actions of their football crowds, on match days; but also, through careful interviewing of key members of the crowd who regularly attended a particular ground, were able to assemble a full account of the subgroups within the crowd, for whom the matches provided the occasion for planned disorder. The picture that emerged was of an organization, with junior and senior roles, acknowledged by all 'members', which were achieved as a result of prowess in action against rival team supporters at earlier matches. Approvals and sanctions were meted out by senior members, and future football fixtures were scanned with anticipation of the nature of the off-pitch skirmishes with rival supporters, each set of opponents carrying a reputation before them. The actions on match days were carefully planned as if a military campaign.

This is not to say that anger and violence do not sometimes spontaneously erupt in crowds – studies such as Reicher's (see Reicher 1987; Emler & Reicher 1995) on the street disturbances in Bristol give examples – but rather that we should not see each occurrence as an example of a mysterious 'group mind' at work: we should examine each case more carefully for indications of how participants understood the developing situation and acted accordingly.

Plate 12.11 Playgroup in action
Source: Collections/Anthea Sieveking

▩ Conclusion ▩

In this chapter, we have been examining social behaviour from the scale of the dyad right through to the crowd, with much attention paid to the small-group level. We have looked at the mechanics of communication, verbal and non-verbal; we examined this at dyadic level, but you will realize its applicability to larger social encounters. We considered how the social group could be seen as defining the individual's world: whether it be via the facilitating (or inhibiting) effect of others' presence; by the perceived pressures to conform to the majority; or through the potential innovations of a minority. We have seen that groups have a history of their own, and that it is possible to examine this via the kind of social setting that has been used to examine the emergence of group identity. Such identity often arises as members of a group compare themselves with another group; and may well lead on to intergroup rivalries and prejudices. We finished the chapter considering whether those looser assemblies we call crowds could be seen as having a predictability to their behaviour: not, as the earliest theorists would have us believe, by resorting to concepts as mysterious as a group mind. Rather, we should look to a looser kind of social organization, and of information flow between individual members of the crowd, to explain crowd behaviour, peaceable and uneventful or more dramatic and volatile.

Let us conclude with some thoughts about themes to which social psychology should in the future pay more attention: gender, class and culture. You may already have thought, as you read through some of the main areas of the subject, that the approach conventionally taken is to look for universals in human social behaviour. Take as our example the treatment above of the phenomenon of social facilitation/inhibition. We examined a range of explanations that have been offered in the literature; but nowhere was there any suggestion that these would only be applicable to certain societies or settings. Psychology as a whole has tended to (conveniently, for it) ignore cultural and historical context: one exception which we met earlier was the query whether conformity pressures experienced in the small group reflect the level of conforming behaviour existing at the time in the wider society. We have also alluded to variations in social behaviour which relate to the immediate local context (you will remember that Milgram found such variations where he studied obedience-affected rate of response), and the chapter on environmental psychology will develop thoughts on how social and physical environments interact as factors influencing behaviour. Chapter 17's consideration of behaviour in the workplace, similarly, emphasizes the local culture of organizations; and socio-cultural context was seen as important in considering the development of social behaviour in chapters 2 and 3. But social psychology has, as yet, really to conceptualize culture in ways which would enable it to do justice to culture's undoubted importance for explanations in the field. Exactly the same point could be made with relation to mainstream social psychology's real neglect of social position ('class') and gender. Other social sciences have so much been focused on these, that one is tempted to believe that experimental social psychology almost chose to differentiate itself by this very act of ignoring culture, gender and class.

CHAPTER SUMMARY

1 The success of social interactions depends in large part on the participants' skilled use of the range of verbal and non-verbal channels of communication to receive and send information.

2 The initial 'work' of an encounter between two or more individuals is to establish a shared definition of their situation; and therein to tacitly negotiate their various roles, rules and expectations. Within this, each individual will attempt to manage their own self-presentation.

3 The verbal channel can offer the most specific and detailed means of transmitting information; and is supported, supplemented and even subverted by the non-verbal channels. These latter can reinforce the points being made verbally; send meta-signals about the encounter which are too sensitive to be verbalized; and on occasions may unintentionally 'leak' our true feelings.

4 Social action in the presence of another person can be either facilitated or inhibited by their mere presence. Which of these effects occurs can depend on the familiarity of the task in hand, and the status and expertise of the person who observes one's action.

5 The individual's experience of the social group may include: social pressures towards public compliance;

a personal desire to conform to socially validated behaviours; and even, in some settings, such an obedience to perceived authority that the individual carries out actions which, uninfluenced, they would not have carried out.

6 However, majorities within a group are not the only source of social influence: the minority may exercise a social and informational influence way beyond its numbers by its consistency and coherence in advocating an alternative point of view.

7 The exercise of leadership may be dependent less upon who the leader is than upon how they think, behave and are perceived by other group members. Effective leadership has been shown to be dependent upon using a style appropriate to the situation: and such style reflects the leader's concept of the group members.

8 Leaders – especially powerful and prominent ones – can contribute to groupthink: a highly close-minded form of group decision-making where any discrepant information and doubt are kept away by 'mind guards'; and where alternative decisions are therefore never properly evaluated, in the mistaken aura of the group's moral rightness and invulnerability.

9 Individuals come to the group not only to affiliate, but also to receive consensual validation for their views. Where the group is able to reinforce a social value they share, then this can lead to a polarization of attitudes consistent with this value.

10 Social identity is given and reinforced by one's own group membership: and this may be further strengthened by favourably contrasting one's own group with others that one perceives to be potential competitors. In this lie the seeds of stereotyping, prejudice and intergroup hostility: these in turn perhaps supported by historical and economic conflicts within society.

11 Empirical studies indicate that stressing the mutual interdependence between groups in society can be a most effective way of reducing such conflicts between groups.

12 None the less, the very act of social categorization may represent the minimal conditions for generating prejudice.

13 The coming together of large numbers of people as a crowd was viewed by early theorists as likely to create conditions for anonymity, suggestibility and contagion. We now view the crowd experience more broadly: it can indeed enhance our emotions, but often in a positive direction; and rather than stressing irrational behaviour in the crowd, the individual in the crowd is best seen as seeking information from the behaviour of others there.

▓ Further Work ▓

1. Why are individuals attracted to particular groups and not others? Does this process reflect individual needs; and how might these mesh with those of other group members?

2. Are we right to accept the popular view of the crowd as primitive, suggestible and potentially dangerous? Or can we offer a more sophisticated view of activities where large numbers of individuals are gathered?

3. This chapter has described the setting up of 'miniature' social situations to study the origins, nature and reduction of prejudice. What other social issues could it apply a similar approach to? Outline a research project on an issue of your choice.

4. Discuss the merits of laboratory-based versus field studies of social behaviour.
5. Do the various channels of communication each have their particular role in maintaining social converse?
6. 'Belonging to a group (of whatever size and distribution) is largely a psychological state which is quite distinct from that of being a unique and separate individual, and it confers social identity, or a shared/collective representation of who one is and how one should behave' (Hogg & Abrams 1988). Has social psychology always fully appreciated this?
7. Using the Box on social comparison ('What marks did you get for your lab report?') as your starting point, design a new study on social information-sharing in another domain of student life.

■ Further Reading ■

Hogg, M. and Vaughan, G. (1995) *Social Psychology: An Introduction*. London: Prentice-Hall/Harvester Wheatsheaf.

> Perhaps more than anywhere else in psychology, European and American traditions of research differ in social psychology: in range of topics, in critical approach and, it has to be said, in breadth of reading. 'European' is here an intellectual/descriptive term, rather than a strictly geographic one – Hogg works in Australia and Vaughan in New Zealand and Singapore.

Hewstone, M., Stroebe, W., Codol, J.-P. and Stephenson, G. (1996; 2nd edn) *Introduction to Social Psychology*. Oxford: Blackwell.

> The European tradition continues.

Brown, R. (1988) *Group Processes*. Oxford: Blackwell.

Brown, R. (1995) *Prejudice*. Oxford: Blackwell.

> Two more detailed, and very thought-provoking, monographs by Rupert Brown.

Argyle, M. (1971; many subsequent edns) *The Psychology of Interpersonal Behaviour*. Harmondsworth: Penguin.

> Argyle is one of the grand old men of British social psychology, and as one who virtually 'invented' non-verbal communication, he is also a great popularizer.

Nemeth, C. (ed.) (1996) Minority influence. *British Journal of Social Psychology*, 35, 1–219 (Special Issue).

> For a vivid insight on 'how psychology is done' look at the opening, very personal, articles by Charlan Nemeth and Serge Moscovici, which preface a volume illustrating a range of research techniques on minorities and their influence. This has been a central topic in social psychology in Europe, but has largely been neglected in the US, as Nemeth, herself an American in the European tradition, points out.

PsyCLE MODULE: NON-VERBAL COMMUNICATION

This module supports the section on 'channels of communication', as it uses video and simple demonstrations to explain the terminology that is introduced and how social psychologists use these features to investigate how we communicate without language.

CHAPTER 13

Environmental Psychology

Christopher Spencer

CHAPTER AGENDA

- Environmental psychology can be defined as: the study of the transactions between individuals and their (socio)physical environments. Note, not just 'the effect the environment has upon behaviour', for as we shall see in this chapter a straightforwardly determinist view is misconceived.

- The first section of the chapter then goes on to introduce the concept of the 'behaviour setting': this integrates the social and physical environments of everyday life in an account which acknowledges that we shape, as well as are shaped by, such settings as our bedrooms, our classrooms, places of worship, sports grounds, etc. (This is what we mean by the word 'transactions' in the definition just given to you.) Before you read on, think of your own day: how many distinct settings have you participated in already today? See whether you were both shaper of and shaped by the settings. What events did you engage in, and how did these relate to your needs?

- Environments can provide for many levels of personal and social need: from shelter and sustenance through social support to the most exhilarating experiences and life-enhancing tranquillity. We shall consider personal space needs in humans, and see whether work on the concept of territory in birds and animals has any relevance for our species.

- When people express needs for privacy, and yet also wish for sociality, how can their spaces provide them with both?

- What happens to well-being when the human density increases? Can we promote a sense of community? Is it possible to 'design out' crime?

- Indeed, does psychology have a key role in promoting well-being by working with architects and other planners to help them identify the needs of building and space-users?

- People are generally not very articulate when asked to envisage their own future needs, nor are planners always successful in communicating the implications of a design plan. We will take the example of schools and places of learning; and then consider how one can plan for special needs, taking the young, the ill, the elderly as our examples. The blind face a special challenge in spatial cognition and way-finding.

- Finally, the chapter considers the personal importance that environments can have for people. Can we predict peoples' aesthetic preferences, and attachments to the places in their lives? All of these issues are on the agenda of environmental psychology.

▓ Environmental Determinism? Assessing the Evidence ▓

Consider your own personal environment and how you might be affected by it: your room and its decor, the building and its setting, the locality in which you live, the weather – an ever-broadening range of potential influences upon your behaviour and well-being. How could studies be devised to assess these effects?

At room level, furnishings and decor could be systematically varied, in an experiment designed to discover their effects upon – what? What outcome variables might one look at? In just such an experiment, Sommer and Olson (1980) took the least attractive classroom on campus, and softened its appearance. Their before and after measures of impact included as variables: observations of student reactions in the room; and instructors' eagerness to book the room for their classes. Student participation in classes showed a clear improvement after the softening occurred. (And in a follow-up study many years later, Wong et al. 1992 found the same soft classroom still outperforming all the other still unmodified classrooms on campus.) Dentists, modifying their surgery, might choose to assess the effect of changes by using physiological measures of patient relaxation during treatment, by their verbal responses, and by numbers of appointments kept. All would be acceptable indicators of change; and you might like to consider whether each would indicate different aspects of patient response.

Moving our investigation up from room to building scale, let us next consider how the environmental psychologist might study differences between two layouts in a student housing block. Keeping room type constant, imagine the rooms either aligned along a through-corridor, or clustered within their own suite. Your own intuition would probably already have presumed that the latter would prove the better, as indeed studies by Baum and Valins (1977) found. But 'better' by what token?

HIGH DENSITY
SETTING

Both are HIGH DENSITY SETTINGS. Yet on every measure, the suite students were better off than those on corridors:

in terms of their perceptions of crowding;
and they were less often in unwanted interactions with others;
and more sociable with those they did want to be with;
and felt themselves to share attitudes with fellow students.

The effects of layout type extended beyond the housing block itself: the corridor students were more likely to be somewhat socially withdrawn elsewhere on campus. Thus, for example, when observed by the experimenters in a waiting room, they tended to sit farther away from and look less at others. The social overload of the corridor seems to lead to a withdrawal strategy, in contrast to the positive social experience of the suites.

Changing scale again, we can ask: does the weather affect our behaviour?

Journalists are often ready to make this attribution for crimes occurring in summer-time, and early criminologists (e.g. Lombroso 1911) logged various kinds of offence against season, temperature and weather. Recently, Ellen Cohn (1993) has investigated an aspect of the question by using as her dependent variables the calls made to the police for assistance in cases of domestic violence and of rape. She found the violence cases to be much more highly related to weather and to time of day than were the reports of rape. Why, you might ask? The latter seem to be more premeditated, in contrast to the more spontaneous nature of domestic violence, which shows this link with unusual heat and with darkness. Cohn suggests a heat/evening drinking linkage as one possible explanation for this pattern: a timely reminder to us that simply finding a correlation between a particular environmental variable and a pattern of behaviour is not an explanation in itself.

For often, as in this last example, the environmental factors do not directly cause or determine a behaviour, but rather make its occurrence more likely, through intermediate factors: here, perhaps increased alcohol intake; in the student housing example of Baum and Valins we cited earlier, frequency of unplanned encounters on the corridors led students to feel lack of control, and lesser identification with fellow students; these in their turn leading to the reduced general well-being on campus as a whole.

Simple ENVIRONMENTAL DETERMINISM seems therefore a much less plausible position than more complex forms of environment–behaviour transactions.

ENVIRONMENTAL DETERMINISM

And what is this as yet undefined 'environment'? Should we just be looking at the physical environment, or rather realize that often the individual is in interaction with a sociophysical environment, experienced as a whole? (Student life situated within a residence; the lecture within a classroom; dental treatment within a surgery.)

Each of these has usefully been described by Barker (1968) as a BEHAVIOUR SETTING: a small-scale social system whose components include people *and* inanimate objects. The classroom as a setting is not only its walls, decor, layout and furnishings, but also those activities and the people engaged in them. The fit between these activities and the physical arrangements is described as behaviour–environment SYNOMORPHY. Does this particular arrangement of seats facilitate the class instructor's style of student-centred learning? Does this waiting-room manage its varied functions without conflict: presenting a public image to potential patients; receiving and logging the incoming patients; holding them until they are called in to see the dentist or medic; providing a work (and social?) base for reception staff; displaying health-campaign literature; etc. As Barker described them, settings are not dependent upon particular persons: the students and staff in the classroom may differ from time to time, but essentially the setting persists.

BEHAVIOUR SETTING

SYNOMORPHY

The first studies to use this ECOLOGICAL APPROACH were conducted way before environmental psychology had emerged as a recognized field: Barker and Wright (1955) were sampling the everyday activities of children in a small American

ECOLOGICAL APPROACH

town, Oskaloosa (and later extending the work to map all activities of the inhabitants, comparing them with those in a similar-sized town, Leyburn, in the Yorkshire Dales). Writing about, for example, one boy's day, they describe a series of behaviour settings that he travels through: starting with the rituals of getting up; breakfasting with family; journey to school; the several settings of the school day; the soda-fountain on the way home; etc. Consider this last as an example: over the day and over the years the setting's personnel may entirely change, yet the same social/commercial interchanges will continue. (Have you ever revisited your old school and witnessed your successors going through all the routines that once were yours?)

Note a second insight from Barker's work: these immediate environments are more important predictors of the individual's behaviour at any point in time than are their personal characteristics. In class, all are engaged in broadly the same, situation-appropriate behaviour as each other; in the soda-fountain, all participate in another and distinct repertoire of behaviours; and so on. Within each setting, of course, behaviour is not so stereotyped that all is identical, with no recognizable individualisms. Personalities exist and persist; but, the claim is, what individuals do is largely determined by the rules and expectations of the settings through which they travel. And this is a view of determinism which still admits much individual action: from the choice of which settings to enter, to the style in which one fulfils a role within that setting. (Reflect on these freedoms and constraints with relation to your own daily life.) Many writers have developed and extended the initial insights of ecological psychology: Walsh et al. (1992) have been able to review several hundred studies of settings as diverse as the workplace, and weddings. And Canter (1984) has offered a conceptual link with social psychology in his account of social behaviour in terms of the roles and rules that are associated with particular situations. The move away from a simple determinism continues: when talking about environment and behaviour, we now tend to stress peoples' understanding of and willingness to observe these situational roles and rules. In other words, these social constructions, associated with places and situations, mediate between environment and behaviour, rather than there being a direct causal link.

▓ Environmental Needs and the Use of Space ▓

Personal space and territory: how does human and animal use of space compare?

Basic to a biologist's description of any animal species would be its needs and use of space: how do its social-spatial living patterns enable it to gain the resources it needs? We would have an account of diet; then the distribution of foodstuffs, and their seasonal variations; the whereabouts and characteristics of predators, etc. From this data, we would be able to understand why some species are solitary, some live in family groups, some in larger societies, some shifting pattern with the seasons. Territories, in the strict sense of the word (as *exclusively occupied and defended areas*), characterize only a minority of species – some songbirds, gibbons, siamang and titi monkeys would be examples. Species living in larger groups would usually have a home range: an area through which they will move, on both daily and seasonal basis, overlapping with other groups. Some species' patterns involve migrations over great distances, others stay within a small area all their lives.

Set against such analyses, modern human needs and thus use of space show considerable contrasts: the important determinants of early hominid life, food gathering and the avoidance of predators, have little direct significance for most of us. 'Territory' could only be used in a metaphorical sense, to indicate some aspects of place attachment and of desires for privacy, which will be discussed later; HOME RANGE might seem better fitted to our species. But the first point that any biologist would note about humans would be the species' sheer diversity of ways of successfully exploiting almost the whole range of Earth's habitats: intelligence, and the cultural transmission of knowledge and techniques, have enabled humans to adapt and shape the environment to a huge range of life patterns. What then defines the spatial needs of a species whose members include crofters and deep-sea fishermen, stockbrokers and monks?

HOME RANGE

Needs for privacy and sociality in balance

Given this diversity of human life patterns, we can still ask whether our species as a whole shares some basic characteristics in the ways it uses space to mediate patterns of social interaction. Is, for example, privacy a basic need? By privacy, I here mean not so much complete social isolation as a 'selective control over access by others to the self or to one's group' (Altman 1975): i.e. management of one's social interactions. (Recall the example above of the corridor students versus the suite-living students.) Note that this conceptualization does not limit privacy to being on one's own, but can often involve the privacy of self and *chosen* others: family, friends, etc.

The empirical evidence is that individuals all recognize the concept of privacy, but express different personal needs for privacy: Marshall (1972), for example, found that those whose childhood denied them much privacy preferred a greater degree of anonymity as adults. Bannerji and Spencer found that men and women students coped with lack of privacy in different ways: assigned to share a study-bedroom with a stranger, males tended to cope by time-sharing, one being out when the other was in; whereas women tended to become a pair, and tolerate each other's presence (Bannerji & Spencer 1986). But do people from different cultures have different average levels of privacy need? Altman had suggested that cultures differ more in ways of achieving it, rather than in their needs. There had been a series of impressionistic articles claiming that some societies – for instance, the Chinese community in Hong Kong – manifestly

Plate 13.1 Driveway of house standing alone: do you dream of isolation?
Source: Roger Scruton.

thrived in dense city conditions; to which came the fierce rebuttal by Loo and Ong (1984), who showed that the desire for privacy was there, but, given the Hong Kong density, individuals had to develop other, non-spatial ways of asserting their control: cut-offs which are recognized and respected by others. For many of us living in less densely populated places, actual withdrawal is a possibility; and in Kaplan's studies (1983) of the values that people place upon the natural environment, she found that many people cited the opportunity for controlled isolation and the rediscovery of self as their main reasons for seeking and valuing the countryside. (People's experience of nature has become a fascinating area of study in itself: see, for example, Kaplan & Kaplan 1989.)

The individual's desired level of privacy will thus vary from time to time: all the way from withdrawal to positive social stimulation. As Altman's diagram indicates, there are several devices which can be employed to achieve the currently-desired level of privacy: these include social, symbolic and physical. Mismatch can still occur between desired and actual: too little privacy may be experienced as crowding (which as we shall see is not synonymous with high

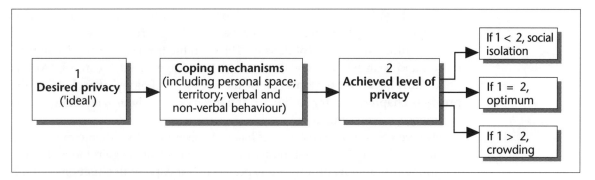

Figure 13.1 Altman's privacy diagram (see Altman 1975)

density); too much privacy can result in feelings of social isolation (we shall later in the chapter look at designing towns so as to bring their inhabitants sociably together, while at the same time affording them the opportunity for withdrawal).

The experience of crowding; and mechanisms for coping

Individuals do not inevitably experience crowding when the social density is high (Stokols 1972). Sometimes, we actively seek a number of people in a small space: parties would be a good example. To get the right atmosphere, most people invite enough guests so that the room is 'full', and further heighten the effect by music and lighting. The same numbers in the same room when one was trying to work would be experienced as oppressive. (Recall Barker's concept of synomorphy, the fit between place and needs.)

What high social density seems to do is to heighten our prevailing feeling: if initially this feeling is positive, as it should be at a party, then the social throng will intensify the feeling. If, however, the feeling is negative, then increased density makes this worse. Freedman, in support of this DENSITY-INTENSITY EFFECT HYPOTHESIS (Freedman 1975), gave four-person groups a task to do. In half the conditions, that task was pleasant, and in half it was unpleasant. Half of the positive groups and half of the negative groups met in a large room, and the others in a small room. Self-report measures bore out the intensification hypothesis: in the smaller room, the pleasant task was seen as more pleasant and the unpleasant task more unpleasant than they were in the larger room. This finding held true for a variety of problem-solving tasks and discussion topics.

DENSITY-INTENSITY EFFECT HYPOTHESIS

What is going on when we are in a high-density situation? Our physiology tends to change: the pulse rate increases, our hands may be slightly more sweaty, and other physical indicators of arousal can be found (Baum & Paulus 1987). If that arousal is also stressful, this could be found from an elevation of cortisol levels in the bloodstream, and the endocrine epinephrine in the urine: studies of people shopping in crowded conditions, and commuting on packed trains have used such measures of stress. However, as Bell has commented (Bell et al. 1990), these stresses can be reduced by increasing the person's feeling of control in the situation: for example, the stress is least upon those commuters who board an empty train at the first station than it is on those joining them at later stations when the train is full, even though they have the longer ride, and experience the same eventual maximums of density. Those on the train early can choose their places, and with whom they sit; those on later have no such control. (At this point, turn back to the discussion of the social psychology of crowds, in the previous chapter, and try to link up the observations there with those on the experience of crowding here.)

Selective control of access to self has thus been one clear theme in environmental psychology's understanding of privacy; control is again the word central to the discussions of how we experience and cope with situations of high density, and whether they are felt to be 'crowded'. Sometimes, it is impossible for the individual to avoid high density which may threaten socially supportive relationships, but (s)he could still retain control via social withdrawal and/or by relying more upon existing social relationships (Evans & Lepore 1992).

■ Designing for People's Needs ■

Environmental psychology had its origins in a practical collaboration between researchers and designers: back in the 1960s, Proshansky and colleagues were asked to evaluate the design of hospital wards and day-rooms, and their effects on patient well-being (see Rivlin 1992). Ever since then, the area has had a commitment to applying its theories, and to developing these theories in 'real-world' field settings. What contributions can psychology make to the designer's need for knowledge of peoples' spatial needs? (Note that here I am using 'designer' as a shorthand to encompass professions such as architect, interior designer, landscape designer, town and regional planner.)

When in the past designers responded to the design brief from a client, they often had little more to go on than their intuitions, plus their informal study of other similar projects. In recent years, there has been an attempt to introduce a more systematic collection of data on user-needs, under the term ENVIRONMENTAL PROGRAMMING (Mazumdar 1992). This can, however, still focus more on groups of users, and what they can be presumed to need as a group, rather than focusing upon actual individual needs.

ENVIRONMENTAL
PROGRAMMING

The temptation is obvious: designers find the rest of us relatively inarticulate when we are asked to specify our spatial needs. We tend to ask for the known environment, with minor modifications; we cannot envisage a range of radical alternatives, or stand back from ourselves to analyse our own needs in abstract.

So the designers have had to develop communication tools to elicit responses from potential users of their designs: these often involve a range of ENVIRONMENTAL SIMULATIONS which are more user-friendly than ground plans. Drawings are easier for the layman to respond to; easier still are three-dimensional models; and the rule seems to be that the closer to reality, the easier: a movie camera within the model gives you movement in the image, almost as good as a movie

ENVIRONMENTAL
SIMULATIONS

trip through a full-scale real setting. Thanks to COMPUTER AIDED DESIGN PROGRAMS (also known as CAD), the designer can work interactively with the user on altering the design on-screen to try out a whole range of alternatives, and then 'walk' round and through the simulated buildings (Marans & Stokols 1993).

COMPUTER AIDED
DESIGN PROGRAMS

There still remains a role for the environmental psychologist, in compiling an aggregate specification based on field research on which of these designs, in reality, work best. What designs of playground are used most: those with standard play equipment or those with features onto which children can impose their own imagination? Which ward designs best balance the well-being of patients with the efficient delivery of nursing care? And, to revert to our familiar example, which student-room layouts produce the most health and happiness in their users?

Whether it is at home, work, or in the city, the promotion of well-being has become the theme of this area of environmental psychology, as a joint enterprise of designer, psychologist and user: 'planning as if people really mattered' in Clare Cooper Marcus's splendidly challenging phrase (Cooper Marcus & Sarkissian 1987). Environmental psychology of course has its conventional science aspects, concerned with the formulation and testing of hypotheses about human–environment interactions; but also is an applied science, with its humane values to the fore. To illustrate how psychologist and designer can work together, we will now consider an example from that very familiar setting, the school.

Designing schools and other places for learning

Social scientists and designers have worked closely together on the planning of schools, so this offers us a good example of what can be achieved, and indeed what a range of factors have to be considered in the design and functioning of any complex setting.

1 Physical features

The physical features of the school premises are determined in part by the design brief: accommodation for what number of pupils, what age range, how many classes, what balance between specialist rooms (e.g. laboratories) and more flexible rooms, what outdoor space needs, etc. Yet for any brief given to the designer, there is a range of possible solutions; and much of the designer's skill comes in balancing competing needs (e.g. ease of circulation with avoidance of noise from human 'traffic') and suggesting compromises. The psychologist's role may then become that of evaluating the impact of such designs and compromises.

Let me give you an example: the architect has suggested that, as a way of utilizing the site most efficiently, some extra classrooms could be squeezed in if they were windowless. What effect might this have upon the pupils and teachers using such rooms? The psychologist could then offer a number of well-

Plate 13.2 A windowless workplace, artificial conditions
Source: Ace Photo Library.

researched studies, and offer a reasoned opinion. Küller and Lindsten (1992), for example, compared 90 primary schoolchildren whose main base was in one of four classrooms:

conventional windows,
top-lit,
windowless with 'warm-white' fluorescent lighting,
and windowless with 'daylight' fluorescent lighting.

The study followed the children for a whole year, and assessed the effects of the different types of lighting on:

stress (as measured by hormones excreted),
classroom performance,
body growth,
and sick leave.

The researchers found that work in windowless classrooms may upset the basic hormonal pattern, which in turn may affect children's ability to concentrate; and over time may affect growth and sickness rates. Artificial light, especially of the more natural spectrum type, may, however, have a part to play in supplementing the short daylight of winter, thus having an impact on the children's

Plate 13.3 Potplant in an office environment: a modest way of softening and personalizing one's workplace
Source: Cefn Newsham.

health. So, although the psychological research favours windowed over windowless, the evidence is not wholly against well-implemented artificial conditions. Other, less extreme variations in school physical features can and have been equally well researched. (Recall the research on 'softening' the classroom by Sommer and colleagues, which we discussed above: how simple physical changes added popularity to the worst-loved classroom.)

2 Building messages for different age groups

The age group of pupils clearly has implications for the basic spatial designs, and for the ergonomics of the classrooms and their fittings; but the design team needs also to consider the 'messages' that the rooms send to the pupils. Warmth, security and enjoyment would be messages the nursery classroom might be designed to send: by careful choice of colours, textures and furnishings. You could also strengthen the messages by using room divisions (perhaps by designing in quiet areas away from the main flow). The ambiance of the nursery would also be influenced by the range of available resources for activities. In contrast, design for teenagers in school would be aimed to send a different range of

Plate 13.4 A nursery
school
Source: Collections/
Anthea Sieveking.

messages about their involvement in the place. (For a review of such considerations, see Gump 1987.)

3 Educational objectives

Educational objectives of the school would be a second level of factors that our school design team would have to consider: what style of teaching and learning characterize the institution – is a discovery approach predominant? Do formal lessons predominate? Will pupils work individually or in groups? Producing a synomorphy between these objectives and the building's form therefore becomes the next aim for the team. Thus, for example, open education would be supported by open-plan architecture; the teacher's objectives of flexibility through multiple, parallel activities. Child-centred, and maybe child-paced work, should be facilitated in the building and fittings, and would need to recognize extra needs for sound-control.

4 The size and organization of the school

The administrative form of the school itself may well be found to be related to pupils' feelings of satisfaction with the school (Gump 1987). Which would you think would be more involving of its pupils: a large or a small school?

Numerous studies show that the smaller school records a higher level of pupil involvement and satisfaction with their school. (The same finding is true of other kinds of organization: small versus big churches, companies, etc: see Wicker 1979.) Why?

Imagine walking into a small school, and reading its notice-board: perhaps sports teams will be posted, there will be a few school clubs announcing meetings, there may be a call to take part in the school play. Compared with the crowded notice-boards of a much larger school, not an enormous amount seems to be going on in the small school.

Yet, *proportionately*, the smaller school may in fact have more activities than the larger one; and, as a result, each individual pupil's chances of participating are greater. Barker and Gump, back in 1964, showed small schools in rural USA might have 35 to 50 pupils, and 60 behaviour settings (these would include these clubs, as well as other, less formal activities, and the formal school activities such as classes); whereas they found that large, urban schools might offer 500 settings for their 2,000 to 2,300 pupils. More settings, but many more pupils competing (or perhaps, not bothering to compete) for involvement in each. Back in those less politically aware days, the researchers described this

Plate 13.5 Quaker meeting: consider how well this space serves the group's purpose
Source: Reproduced with permission of the Library Committee of Religious Society of Friends in Britain.

phenomenon as 'undermanning': nowadays, it has become understaffing.

Evaluation of school designs once they have been built and used (*post-occupancy evaluation*, in the jargon) need also to take into account those aspects of the setting that are purely social and educational: the formal and informal culture of the school and its classes. We have already mentioned the formal educational objectives of the school: we now need to ask how these are instantiated in practice, and how individual teachers and groups of pupils create an ethos in each behaviour setting. For the point is, however well designed is the fit between space and formal objectives, pupil and teacher satisfaction and well-being will ultimately rest on the ethos created: respect between all individuals, enthusiasms, and a lack of disruptions and bullying (see Smith & Sharpe 1994). Other aspects, too, will need consideration: for example, the resources allocated to the school. As Smith and Connolly (1980) found, a scarcity of resources in the nursery class is directly predictive of the level of hostilities!

Planning for special needs, for example those of the young, the ill, the handicapped, and the elderly, could equally well have afforded us our case study of psychologist and designer in collaboration: there is an extensive literature on each (Stokols and Altman, in 1987, edited a handbook of environmental psychology, consisting of nearly 2,000 pages of studies-in-summary!) Instead, we will turn to crime, to give a different kind of collaboration between researcher and designer.

▧ Defensible space: Patterns of Crime in the City and on Campus ▧

DESIGN OUT

Can we 'DESIGN OUT' crime? In practical terms, should this prove to be possible, it would be one of environmental psychology's major social contributions. Equally, this topic poses a major theoretical challenge to the field: 'Environmental Psychology tends to take on the most difficult tasks in the most challenging discipline, and the topic of crime epitomizes this brave or crazed proclivity' (Gifford 1993).

Note: what are *not* being discussed here are the social, political and economic roots of crime itself, but rather whether the incidence and location of crime can be predicted; and whether, from this knowledge, we can make recommendations about redesigning places so they become safer by repulsing crime.

For crime, when you look at the records, is not randomly scattered across time and space, but shows distinct patterns. The crime statistics of my city, for example, show a small but stable peak in 'assaults against the person' at 2.30 in the morning. As a sober citizen, normally safe asleep at that hour, one has to ask why? The answer was very closely tied to place as well as to time: the city's few rowdier nightclubs close at that hour, and all the incidents occur as their unsteadier patrons leave.

Where did burglaries take place? One can ask that question at the level of city district; or at neighbourhood level; or even in greater detail, at the level of the individual house. At each, there is a story to tell, which leads one to treat criminal acts as processes. Much burglary arises from the need to raise money (recent UK statistics indicate that as much as 50 per cent is specifically to pay for drugs): if one then thinks of the burglar's activities as rational, and the gap between home and target as the 'journey to work', then predictions about likely travel distances can be made: and indeed, the city districts in which many burglars live are also the ones with the highest rates of (petty) burglary (Brown & Bentley 1993). Data for such studies comes, I hasten to say, from convicted burglars.

Interviews with such people confirm the pattern which emerges from the statistics about this non-random patterning of crime which is apparent both at the neighbourhood and at the individual-dwelling levels of analysis. From the statistics, for example, one can show that an end-of-terrace house is a more likely target than houses in the middle of the row; and that a whole number of other physical 'descriptors' can be given of places most at risk. For the burglar himself is also judging risks – in his case, of being detected – in selecting his target. Given that each house in a row is likely to contain roughly the same value of stealable goods, his decision which one to enter is mainly based upon his perceived ease of entry without challenge. Surveillance by neighbours is what he least needs, and certain housing layouts maximize and others minimize his perception of being seen. This is an appropriate place to introduce Newman's concept of DEFENSIBLE SPACE.

DEFENSIBLE SPACE

Imagine yourself walking through some housing areas: in one area, each house has its individual fence, a garden overlooked by the windows of the house, and by those of its neighbours. Walking up to a front door here, you would feel that you had entered private space, defended space, and would be quite likely to be observed. Compare the feelings you would have in approaching the front door of a flat in a large apartment block, where no windows look out onto the lobby, and where there are no signs of personalization of the area. Newman in 1972 created quite a stir among psychologists and architects alike when he showed how such physical differences between housing layouts were predictive of crime levels. Using crime-incidence data from the police, he compared patterns of crime on two public housing projects in New York, comparable in their inhabitants, contrasted in their layout. One of these, Brownsville, had the barriers and territorial markers which sent messages about the space being private, or semiprivate and communally shared, and thereby 'defended'. The other, Van Dyke, had impersonal grounds, threatening walkways and entrances, and sent signals about the residents' vulnerability. Newman interviewed residents, visitors and police about both projects:

> All intruders, including police and interviewers, feel more cautious about invading the privacy of residents at Brownsville. By contrast, their attitude toward the invasion of the interior corridors at Van Dyke is callous and indifferent.

Box 13.1 Can We Predict the 'Hot Spots' of Crime and Fear of Crime on Campus?

We know, as social scientists studying the data, that crime is not evenly distributed across our cities; we, in our capacity as ordinary citizens, also have this impression, and are likely to shape our behaviour accordingly. Perceived danger may be at the level of whole city districts: the macro-scale. We are also aware of particular local places where fear of crime is elevated: the micro-scale.

Although one might think of the typical college campus as a relatively safe place, the statistics on crime indicate that there is a rising number of both petty and more serious incidents occuring in many colleges. Students' fear of crime has, as a consequence, risen considerably (see Nasar & Fisher 1993).

Jack Nasar and Bonnie Fisher wanted to look at what campus micro-features were associated in peoples' minds with vulnerability to crime; and they chose to study one campus they describe as having such a climate of fear, Ohio State University. Here, a survey had already reported that crime and violence were students' main concerns.

Their first act was to study the physical layout of the campus, and to identify places where the terrain:

- offered concealment to a potential attacker
- blocked one's prospect and foresight
- blocked one's means of escape.

Each of the sub-areas of campus were rated by a group of 20 observers on each of these aspects (so, for example, a long, narrow and well-vegetated path was rated

as 'low prospect, high concealment, and blocked escape'; another wider pathway was rated as 'high prospect, moderate concealment, and low escape').

Next, in order to study peoples' everyday responses to the campus, Nasar and Fisher used several kinds of measures: open-ended questions to students; rating scales; and observations of pedestrian behaviour. Over 250 students answered questionnaires about the campus as they saw it (with no explicit mention of crime or fear, so as not to bias responses). After completing this, people were then asked to rate key areas of the campus for perceived safety. Finally, trained observers watched ongoing pedestrian traffic throughout the campus over a two-month period, covering both daytime and evening hours.

They found that people did indeed report being afraid of certain areas of campus; that these areas were the ones predicted by the study of the physical layout of the campus; and that the reported fears were mirrored by the actual observed behaviours. After dark, the pattern of behaviours was especially 'safe': pedestrians avoided the areas which had low prospect, high concealment and blocked escape. Walking in a group may also be a response to fear, and there was a greater tendency towards this in the evenings past the feared places.

Discovering hot spots of fear of crime has implications for the surveillance of existing campuses (patrols, cameras, etc.), as well as perhaps prompting some physical modifications to reduce fear-inducing features. Where a new campus is being designed, studies like this one could help design out crime.

The two projects had very similar populations, by whichever social indicator you choose; yet in the study period, there were 92 robberies in Van Dyke, compared with 24 in Brownsville; and there was twice as much 'malicious mischief' in the former as the latter.

Subsequent research on crime and the environment has, not surprisingly, shown that Newman's pioneering study oversimplified the patterns to be found (Brantingham & Brantingham 1993); yet, as the more detailed studies show, there are many design recommendations to be made. 'Designing out crime' is much more than just fitting better security hardware; and is indeed closely related to which design factors can promote a sense of community, belonging and well-being among residents.

▨ Individual Perception and Understanding of the Environment ▨

In this section, we shall see why environments are more than a collection of objects: basically, the perceiver is surrounded by what is being perceived. Environmental perception and cognition demands separate treatment (above and beyond chapter 6, here, on perception) in that it differs from object perception in its complexity, its multisensory nature, and its intimate connection with the activities of the individual: whether as learner about or user of the environment, the individual is within the observed in a way not parallelled in object perception.

ENVIRONMENTAL COGNITION is, by definition, concerned with real-world perception, at molar (i.e. comprehensive) rather than molecular level. Environments are continuous, hugely complex, and potentially rich with meaning. Characteristic of many individual transactions with them is that of purposiveness: individuals in using space are seeking resources, association, privacy; they are travelling or searching to fulfil some goal or plan. Such purposeful encounters probably characterized the individual's very first, learning-phase, transactions with particular environments; and thereby they serve to organize the complexity of environments into coherent, knowable wholes. Common language and environmental psychology both describe these as 'places'; and one of the distinctive enterprises of environmental cognition research has been to describe what distinguishes places from 'PLACELESSNESS' (Relph 1976). In addition to the coherence of the physical elements of place, researchers soon realized that the defining characteristics also included socially acknowledged place rules and expectations (similar to the 'scripts' which enable individuals to recognize and react appropriately to social situations). 'Places' also have an aesthetic dimension to them, as will be discussed in the concluding section of this chapter: in other words, they are non-random assemblages of socially significant physical elements, which evoke affective responses in the traveller.

Knowledge of space – the spatial layout of resources, refuges, kin, dangers, predators – must rank as one of the most basic universal aspects of cognition. The *range* over which the organism is knowledgeable will reflect the species' activity patterns – from a few centimetres of rockpool for some molluscs to the pole-to-pole migratory journeys of some terns and shearwaters.

Accurate travel from point to point demands a knowledge of orientation – the 'vector direction' – and the distance to travel. Animal behaviour studies have identified the range of information sources that are variously in use to plot such routes: these range from the social to the celestial – from, for example, the waggle-dance of bees returning to the hive, which communicates the direction from there back to a food source; through to the use of star patterns and the earth's magnetic field by some birds in night migration.

Gibson (1979), in his accounts of the senses as perceptual systems, has empha-

ENVIRONMENTAL COGNITION

PLACELESSNESS

AFFORDANCES

sized the importance of taking an information-processing approach to environments. In his account, places are perceived in terms of their AFFORDANCES: the kinds of activities that a place permits or encourages. Perception of environmental features is thus seen in functional terms; similarly, storage, access and use are guided by functional properties. Gibson's account has been perhaps better received by environmental psychologists than by mainstream perceptual psychology; and has helped to shape accounts of the child's development of environmental competencies. It also converges with Barker's 'ecological psychology' account of how children come to realize the social potential of places, which are there usefully described as 'behaviour settings' – a concept which, as we have already seen, integrates the social with the physical.

Environmental cognition research shares with much of contemporary cognitive psychology an increasing concern for the development of knowledge structures; it too has offered computer models of such structures, and their use in navigation through space, as will be discussed below. It is clear that the amount of central processing capacity available at any one moment is limited; that spatial navigation can claim a considerable portion of this, and thus that any further complex task imposed upon the traveller is likely to compete for this cognitive resource.

We have now seen the role of environmental cognition in promoting the biological survival of the organism, and in aiding its *cognitive efficiency* in using the environment. Its final, most sophisticated role is in developing and maintaining personal and social well-being through identification with and ATTACHMENT TO PLACES. Here, the empirically minded psychologist may feel ill at ease, dealing with concepts which are altogether less easy to define and to measure.

ATTACHMENT TO PLACES

However, there exists an extensive literature about the 'sense of place': the awareness that some locations have a coherence and identity that allows individuals themselves to identify with these places; to gain pleasure, security, self-understanding from them; and to place considerable importance upon such places in their memories, their self-descriptions and their decisions. The 'sense of place' literature – in geography, and in planning – points up a need for psychology to examine more closely the higher importance of places for people.

Within psychology, there is a well-developed understanding of the nature of attachment – yet in nearly all of it the attachment is to people. There is only a small literature on displacement: on the nature of homesickness (think of, say, children sent away to boarding school); on the deleterious effects of separations when a child is hospitalized; and on the psychological functioning of those who are away from familiar places, whether through enforced exile, or travelling as students to a foreign country. (Even the new interest environmental psychology has shown in periods of short voluntary exile – such as tourism – the possibility of some negative effects amid all the positive effects such travel is usually assumed to bring. For a review of the developing literature on people's attachment to places, see Altman and Low 1992.)

Similarly, practically all of psychology's literature on the development and

Box 13.2 The Essential Qualities of a Home

'A home is more than a house': can we give credence to this old slogan? Would people agree on those features which lead them to become attached to a residence?

Jerry Tognoli in a 1987 review found many theorists had written about the home, but that there was a dearth of empirical evidence to support their conclusions. He offered a plausible list of concepts to investigate:

Centrality: the home is the individual's primary 'territory'
Continuity: stability and continuance of occupation
Privacy: control over access to self
Self-expression and personal identity: home as a vehicle for expressing one's individuality, and 'being oneself'
Social relationships: not only family but also social network
Warmth: an atmosphere of friendliness and support for self
Physical environment: the setting for all the above

Sandy Smith decided to test the importance of these themes in people's perception of their houses/homes; and interviewed two groups of fellow Queenslanders.

The first group recorded the range of everyday activities they and their partner engaged in around the home: what, when and where. This gave Smith the repertoire of commonplace activity patterns (25 main activities, all of which you would recognize in your own life: tidying up the house; speaking on the phone, etc.).

These then were written out on cards, to become the prompts for discussions with a second sample drawn from the same community. But, rather than having an open-ended discussion, the logic of 'repertory grids' (more often used in personality research) was used to elicit people's 'constructs' about the home. Repertory grids, originally used in the field of personality, enable the researcher to elicit a person's own important dimen-

sions of judgements ('personal constructs') by asking the person to compare and contrast people (or here, places) which have particular significance for them.

The concept of a construct, as an idea which enables one to differentiate between stimuli, was explained: and they were then asked to sort the activity cards into two packs to illustrate such a constuct ('personal control' might be one such; 'social interaction' another one; and so forth).

Statistical analysis of the pooled results of these sortings into piles showed that there was wide agreement among the whole sample that the activities had meaning and importance in one of four clear clusters:

Recreation (e.g. reading; speaking on the phone)
Social Interaction (e.g. caring for children; having a meal with one's partner)
Personal (e.g. spending time with pets; personal hygiene)
Housework (e.g. tidying; preparing food)

Males and females were equal in valuing activities in terms of their affordance of social interactions; but, for women, the dimension of personal control within the home was more salient than for the men. Men with children at home were closer to the women's pattern of construal than were men with no children at home.

But the main finding of the study was that there was a high degree of consensus between men and women in their understanding of situations around the home (as shown by the way they structured them in their responses). And in further interviews with his householders on what they thought to be the essential qualities of their home, Smith was able to confirm that they saw these to be: the qualities of continuity, privacy, self-expression, social relationships, and warmth, as well as aspects of the physical features of the dwelling. (For background, see Smith 1994a, 1994b.)

sustenance of self-identity and well-being tends to describe this solely in terms of the individual's social environment, without considering the possibility that identification with places may interact with those processes. Does self-identity shaped by the earliest memories of place, through to an account of those places where one feels 'most at home', 'most oneself', seem implausible to psychology? Such an account is certainly not far-fetched for the autobiographer, for the

Plate 13.6 Exterior of a village school. Consider how often school crops up in autobiographical accounts as a significant shaper of self-identity
Source: Roger Scruton.

AESTHETICS OF
PLACE

historian, for the political scientist. Think how often such writers attribute significance to earliest experiences of place.

Nor is such discourse unfamiliar to those design professions whose very aim and claim is to be able to 'create places': interior designers, architects, city planners. In such disciplines, there is perhaps a greater belief in an environmental determinism of behaviour, and of feelings and well-being, than is common within psychology.

There is, however, some clear empirical evidence within both environmental psychology and planning that the AESTHETICS OF PLACE can be directly linked to personal well-being in studies of satisfaction with housing: the outward image of a housing project ranks high on the list of factors predictive of satisfaction and well-being in many studies. Similarly, the appearance of particular behavioural settings has been shown to affect behaviour within them: we have already seen, for example, Sommer's classic experiment in 'softening' a university classroom by changing its decor, which led to the least popular and effective room on campus becoming the best used. There is clearly an important and diverse future research agenda here for environmental psychology.

This section of the chapter has argued for the study of the cognition of the environment above and beyond the main psychology of cognitive processes, on the grounds that: environmental cognition has an immediate biological survival value; that the properties of the 'object' of the cognition are so mucg2more complex than in usual object perception; and that environmental cognition leads one to discussion of the sense of place, of self-identity, and of individual well-being.

Hence, any simple definition of environmental cognition which does not admit to all three of these levels will be incomplete.

In order to understand a skill, it is often instructive to study its development. Much of environmental psychology's cognition research has been concerned with the two kinds of development: ONTOGENESIS – the development from infancy of cognitive skills for environmental understanding; and MICROGENESIS – the development of knowledge about the novel area, using these skills.

ONTOGENESIS

MICROGENESIS

▦ The Ontogeny of Environmental Cognition ▦

The child develops skills for gaining, referencing and using environmental information

In this section we will examine Piaget's account of cognitive development as applied to this area; indicate how environmental psychology has extended this account; and show how, with increasing experience, the child can begin to 'parse the grammar' of the environment. Much of the process is visually led: hence, the blind child has to use alternative sources to construct images of the environment. The section ends considering how the process continues through the lifespan, with differentiating environmental cognitions reflecting the individual's activities and interests.

The Piagetian perspective

The account given by Piaget of the child's developing concepts of space is based closely on his general stage theory of cognitive development: see, for context, chapter 2. The child moves from a SPATIAL GEOMETRY constructed on *topological* principles, through a *projective phase* to one derived from *Euclidean* principles. Piaget is particularly concerned with small-scale space, but extends some of his discussion to the geographical scale.

SPATIAL GEOMETRY

Proximity, separation, order, openness and closure are the basic topological principles, which the child by the age of two is beginning to apply. Perspectives, and in particular the realization of how objects interrelate in space independent of the child's own position, is slowly developed alongside topology: such projective principles may be discerned at the age of three, but, according to the Piagetian view, it takes another eight or nine years for their full development. The ability to apply metrics to space – the basis of Euclidean principles – may emerge at age 4, and continue developing into adolescence. The child will become better able to estimate distances and bearings, and to operate with proportional reductions in scale.

The environmental psychologists Hart (1979) and Moore (1986) have extended this approach to the child's understanding of large-scale places. During the sensorimotor stage, the child is capable only of EGOCENTRIC ORIENTATIONS: the environment is understood only as it relates to self. During the preoperational stage, the child begins to use a FIXED SYSTEM OF REFERENCE: known locations – home, friends' houses, shops, school – provide the bases for this system.

By the end of Piaget's concrete operations stage, children will begin developing a COORDINATED REFERENCE SYSTEM, with abstract geometric patterns and, arguably, which will be referenced against the cardinal directions: i.e. north–south.

Since Piaget's pioneering studies, much more systematic evidence has been collected; and contemporary environmental psychology characteristically goes beyond the Piagetian account. It lays more emphasis upon experience, background, values and interests as differentiating children's learning about the broad environment: here, as elsewhere, it has adopted the transactional perspective discussed at the opening of the chapter. (See, for example, Blades & Spencer 1995.)

▓ Expanding Frames of Reference; and Individual Differences ▓

As the infant and child grows older, there is an expanding range of geographical experience. Is there a corresponding developmental sequence?

Does the child first achieve an integrated image of body layout (with much effort expended in body-part coordination), then extend this frame of reference outward to the immediate world (with the focus now being on the location of objects); and thence outward from this, as the child explores ever more widely, to consider the spatial interrelationships between places? (These have been labelled the EGOCENTRIC, ALLOCENTRIC and GEOCENTRIC FRAMES OF REFERENCE.)

Pick and Lockman (1981) have shown that the individual does not have to achieve complete mastery of the first frame of reference before working on to the next. Nor does the individual necessarily dispense with earlier frames: the individual can call upon a multiplicity of reference systems. Some life tasks call forth an egocentric frame, others an allocentric, still others a geocentric; and many tasks implicate several frames of reference. (Pick's definition for a FRAME is 'a locus or set of loci with respect to which spatial position is defined'.)

The case for a relationship between adequacy of BODY-IMAGE (the first such frame) and success in other, broader, spatial skills is not supported by empirical evidence (Spencer et al. 1989). There is, however, evidence for a general age-related trend from egocentric-responding to allocentric-responding on spatial tasks; although when this shift occurs, it varies dramatically both with task type, and with the availability and salience of environmental cues. And, note, 'egocentricity' is not here being used in the strict Piagetian sense, but simply to indicate the literal self-centredness of the frame.

EGOCENTRIC ORIENTATIONS

FIXED SYSTEM OF REFERENCE

COORDINATED REFERENCE SYSTEM

FRAMES OF REFERENCE: EDOCENTRIC, ALLOCENTRIC AND GEOCENTRIC

FRAME

BODY-IMAGE

So far, we have discussed the development of spatial competence as if all individuals had equal abilities; but as anecdotes will have often suggested to you, there may be strong differences between people in spatial performance. What is the evidence?

Many studies have been done, and they indicate that indeed there is evidence that there are stable individual differences in performance on spatial tasks. Similarly, sex differences have been widely reported in measured spatial abilities:

1. There is evidence that sex differences in *spatial perception* as measured by, for example, the water-level test, exist by age 8 and persist across the life-span.
2. There is also a small effect for *mental rotation* – as measured by the rotating figure test.
3. But the task of *spatial visualization* has been found to be equally difficult for most males and females: tasks to test this usually consist of complex, multistep manipulations of spatially presented information.

▓ Developing an 'Environmental Grammar' ▓

Not only does the child develop their cognitive skills for processing and retrieving spatial information, but they also, as a result of their transactions with a variety of environments, develop a set of expectancies about the layout and components of typical behaviour settings. Just as ecological psychology has demonstrated that individuals learn and apply generalizable scripts about the behavioural roles and rules of behaviour settings, so too does the individual come to learn an ENVIRONMENTAL GRAMMAR of spatial expectancies.

ENVIRONMENTAL
GRAMMAR

We can usefully illustrate this with relation to the ever-broadening range of settings the child will encounter: *rooms* are likely to have standard components (e.g. furniture, doors, windows); *houses* are likely to have a specified subset of designated-use rooms; *neighbourhoods* will usually contain a range of domestic, public and commercial buildings; and *cities* can usually be expected to have differentiated regions. Learning an environmental grammar, at any of these scales, consists of developing the appropriate expectancies and, hence, the corresponding search strategies.

Note how far the actual *rules and contents* of such grammars will be very largely determined by local cultural patterns. (For example, David Canter has written about the striking differences between Japanese and European houses: not just in terms of their appearance, but also in terms of which activities normally are performed where: Canter 1977.)

The individual's ability to parse the environmental grammar of a place again represents not just their 'developmental stage' but, most importantly, their personal range of transactions with similar types of setting: Roger Hart (1979) found that he could best predict children's knowledge of their New England town by reference to their free-ranging activities in it, rather than their chronological age or stage.

▨ Using Alternative Sources of Input: The Task of the Blind Child ▨

Not until one examines the blind child's ways of coming to know the physical environment does the centrality of vision to the sighted child's spatial understanding become fully apparent. For the latter, the visual overview – whether of room or region – serves to articulate the elements of experience into a spatial whole. For the blind child, nothing can be so directly realized, all has to be constructed, either through one's individual, sequential experiences, or through such spatial aids as maps and models.

And, as a consequence, the unaided and untutored blind child tends to be less mobile than the sighted, fearing collision with obstacles, and becoming disorientated or lost. Hence, in this area, environmental cognition research has one of its practical applications, in developing and evaluating the mobility education of the blind.

One of the basic (but until recently untested) assumptions of mobility education has been that the body-image provides the base-line frame of reference for cognizing space beyond the body: and hence much practical work has tended to be done with young blind children to develop this image. However, as already noted, the recent empirical evidence does not support this assumption. It would seem more profitable to work directly with the blind child's strategies for exploring and knowing about immediate and then more distant space.

INTEGRATED INTERNAL REPRESENTATION

Direct experience is important for building up an INTEGRATED INTERNAL REPRESENTATION of an area: indeed, the single most important predictor of a blind child's spatial ability (holding level of visual handicap constant) is the amount of lifetime freedom to explore space the child has been allowed. Over-protective parents, who limit this experience, may inadvertently produce children who arrive at school age with self-protective, non-exploratory styles.

Whereas 'mobility training' used to concentrate upon route and landmark learning, to equip the individual for the most likely routes through their area, modern mobility education attempts to build up exploratory skills and to encourage the child to integrate geographical information into a coordinated spatial whole. The use of 'tactile maps' not only imparts specific knowledge about an area, but also develops this spatial thinking, which frees the blind child from over-dependence on taught routes. And a range of audio tactile graphics processors, that the child can interact with, interrogate and input own discoveries into, are likely to become more widely available as technology becomes more affordable.

Box 13.3 Can Visually Impaired People Use Tactile Maps to Navigate?

If you are a sighted individual, your vision gives you more than awareness of all the objects present in the world around you: it also gives you an immediate frame of reference which places all of these in relation to each other, as well as to your current position in space. Imagine yourself walking into a strange room, and, after a few seconds there is a power cut, and you are completely unable to see. You might not have had time to notice all objects in the room, but you would have established sufficient of an idea of layout that you could navigate through it. Although you might be clumsy, and bump into things (you had not gained precise locational information) you would know what the approximate dimensions and layout of the room were.

Maps have a similar property to that snapshot view of space: they not only indicate the presence of features, but they give one the spatial frame for locating them, and thus for informing navigation through the area.

Could maps, created specially for the blind by replacing visual symbols with tactile ones, offer the blind a means of gaining overview of a space that they would otherwise have to construct by journeying back and forth through the space? Tactile maps have been used for many years, but Simon Ungar and colleagues (1994) wished to evaluate how well they provided a frame of reference for navigation.

As in many experiments in psychology, they cut the problem down to basics: the map in this case was simple, and the space it represented was a large room containing six unique objects as places within it: large boxes, each containing a unique toy.

Participants in the study were 15 congenitally blind children and 23 children who had some residual vision; there were two age groups, aged 5–7 and 8–12 years;

and they were introduced to two layouts of the toys, either by direct locomotor experience or with a tactile map.

In the first layout, children were initially led by the experimenter from the centre of the layout to each of the toys in random order. The children were then asked to make direction estimates from this centre point to each of the landmarks using a specially constructed pointer. Next, the children were given a tactile map of the same layout and allowed to explore it until they claimed to be familiar with it. After this, they were again asked to make direction estimates.

A week later, the procedure was repeated for a second, different layout, but this time the children were given a map first, and that was followed by locomotor exploration.

When they were introduced to a novel layout by direct experience, the totally blind children, as expected, performed very poorly relative to the residual vision group. (Even having just a small amount of vision helps one learn something of the world's stucture.) However, the accuracy of their direction estimates improved dramatically when they were shown a tactile map of the same environment. Their performance was about the same when they had the tactile map of the second layout, and this remained the same after locomotor experience was added. In contrast, having a map led the residual vision group to perform more poorly than they had with direct locomotor experience: for them, it was an unnecessary extra source of information to be attended to.

So, Ungar and company conclude, it is clear that tactile maps are demonstrably able to do for the totally blind child what direct experience is doing for the sighted, including even those with reduced vision.

Later Life-span Developments in Environmental Cognition

Development continues through the life-span, even if the most dramatic changes occur during childhood. We should thus conclude this section with a brief review of such life-span developments in environmental cognition.

During adolescence and early adulthood, the range of an individual's

Plate 13.7
Orienteering
Source: Collections/
Anthea Sieveking.

activities increases considerably; and with it increase not only the range of environmental knowledge but also the subtlety of understanding of environmental grammars. *Diversity* of knowledge between individuals also increases, as a function of activity patterns, salience and, in some cases, some formal environmental awareness training.

Thus, for example, architects, planners, pilots, and orienteers have all been populations whose spatial and environmental awareness has been studied and compared with untrained control groups. Training in many of these cases offers the individual a novel and extended vocabulary for environmental descriptions – such as architectural styles, and land features useful for navigation. But more than that, such specialist training in matters spatial heightens the individual's ability to learn, and operate efficiently in, new places.

And in general the activity patterns of the individual, as they change through the life-span, predict the nature of selective inclusion into our environmental images of the city, region or world. Clearly, not all 'environmental facts' are sought or retained in this schema; and the pattern of search and retention serves the individual's salient activities. The same city district, as known to the young adolescent, the lover, the businessman, the retired oldster, will be remembered (and reported back to the experimenter) in importantly different ways.

Particular research attention has been paid to the environmental needs – and hence patterns of cognition – of two of these: the adolescents and the old. Both groups are heavily dependent upon what the neighbourhood affords them; both are likely to discover, at least in Western cities, that environments appear to be designed by and for the mobile adult of middle years, and that as a result, their needs are not fully satisfied.

▒ The Microgenesis of Environmental Cognition ▒

The spatially skilled adult develops knowledge of a new geographical area

The previous section described the development from infancy of the basic skills to process environmental information; but so far we have not fully described what it is that develops, or how the information is stored. Is this spatial information stored spatially: a map in the head? In this section we address this issue, while considering how the skills are used to learn about a newly encountered area.

During the 1940s, many rats ran many mazes in the interests of science; and occasionally they escaped the confines of the maze and were able to run in a direct line to the end point of the maze. Tolman, noticing this, suggested that, rather than learning a rigid series of left and right turns, the rats were in fact aggregating all of this information about turns, angles and distances into a *cognitive map*, which enabled them to realize the relative positions of places (Tolman 1948).

This metaphor of a map has become so persuasive that it threatens to convince us that *all* spatial information is STORED ANALOGICALLY: an internal spatial representation. Yet there is clear evidence that spatial information can also be STORED AND RETRIEVED PROPOSITIONALLY – in other words, almost as a string of instructions for movement along a route. One can visualize a route; equally, one can access a sequence of information about it.

ANALOGICAL STORING

PROPOSITIONAL STORAGE AND RETRIEVAL

After Tolman, the city planner Kevin Lynch (1960) was next to shape our thinking on the nature of the 'cognitive map'. In his empirical investigations of the images travellers developed of the city of Boston, he identified the key elements of the image as people drew it for him as sketch-maps: routes, NODES (places where routes intersect) and landmarks; with at a larger scale, city regions and PHASE CHANGES (boundaries where, for example, land gives way to water).

NODES

PHASE CHANGES

Because routes and landmarks are clearly basic elements in both the ontogenic and the microgenic accounts, the literature has often tacitly assumed that microgenesis recapitulates ontogenesis: that what we are doing, as adults, meeting a new place, is going through all the stages that the child went through when learning how to learn about places. Perhaps the predominant reason for this has been the influence of Siegal and White's (1975) theory.

They have argued that children first learn as landmarks those places which are of particular interest to them. Once these are established, information about MINIMAPS local routes can be fitted to them, forming MINIMAPS. These may be locally accurate and usable; yet children will not initially realize how their several separate minimaps could interrelate. Only later in the developmental sequence can children integrate these minimaps into an overall representation of the environment.

Many published studies support the Siegal and White sequence for both ontogeny and microgeny: adults learning new areas do seem to re-enact the child's developing sequence. First, a few landmarks in the new city, then local routes linked to them; and finally, an assembly of these into an overall structuring. (Often, it must be said, using a map to aid this integration process.)

A note of caution, however, should be entered here: many of these studies use 'indirect' methods of testing people's knowledge of the environment – for instance, drawing sketch-maps or giving distance estimations – and these methods may not fully reflect such place knowledge. Studies have been conducted in which environmental cognition is tested more directly (e.g. by asking a young child or a newcomer to re-walk a complex route that they had just encountered). Such studies suggest that much more information can be recalled and acted upon than would be represented in a sketch-map.

Route learning, in other words, may not be the later, constructed process of the Siegal and White account: much important learning is taking place on the first encounter; and indeed being able to accurately and swiftly retrace a once-travelled route may have high survival value!

How the researcher collects data on environmental cognition is so crucial that the next section of the chapter will look at measurement techniques and their implications.

▧ Measurement Techniques: How to Represent the Cognitive Representations of Environment ▧

Any investigation of the cognitive world of an animal or of a very young child necessarily has to rely heavily on behavioural data – either in natural or experimental situations. We might, for example, be researching whether cetaceans use magnetic fields to navigate. Data on whale-strandings and their association with measured geometric anomalies may provide an answer. Or the issue might be: does the pre-verbal child use an egocentric or an allocentric coding of places and events? One would probably devise an experimental setting to test the question.

When working with older children and with adults, however, most researchers have preferred to use methods in which the person represents to the researcher their representation of the environment: methods used include sketch-mapping, model building, and making distance and bearing estimations. Such productive methods clearly impose demands upon the person's general representational capacities: their level of 'graphicacy' (cf. 'literacy'), for example – their general capacity to draw anything. Young children's spatial knowledge so clearly outstrips their graphic skills that the point is obvious; but it is one which is often forgotten when the investigator asks apparently competent adults to sketch their 'knowledge'. A thin or inaccurate map may mislead. Second, each method of representation (sketch-map, verbal description or whatever) can be shown to elicit from store a subtly different subset of the information the person holds: some elements are clearly to the fore when the demand is for a 'map'; others, when one asks for a 'route description' as a means of elicitation.

Other experimenters have attempted to construct the implicit 'cognitive map' from apparently more objective questions on – for example – distance estimates. These methods have their advantages – but also begin to reveal the non-transitivity of such estimates. (One famous, early finding of environmental psychology was that the distance estimates for the same route between town centre and suburb was estimated differently according to direction of travel.) Multi-dimensional scaling is conventionally used to integrate such estimate data.

Some experimenters have been bold enough to leave the laboratory and investigate environmental cognition in action: for example, having people navigate through an area while tape-recording as full a 'verbal protocol' as they could. Such methods elicit exciting data, but often involve as much a voyage of discovery for the navigator as for the investigator, bringing to the surface decisions that the individual had not previously been aware of. Measurement, in other words, may alter the process being measured.

▦ Research Techniques to Capture Individual Strategies ▦

Intensive work with individuals in the 'real world' can eventually build into a detailed model of environmental knowledge. Golledge and colleagues (1985, 1993), for example, have studied one individual's route learning over a period of a week; and have combined many of the above methods of investigation to produce such a cognitive model, which they have then been able to computer-simulate using artificial intelligence techniques. (Much of the work on human environmental cognition and navigation has strong implications for those in the Artificial Intelligence community concerned with, for example, robot guidance systems.)

Other studies have observed individual styles in the application of environmental cognition: Ottosson (1987) has, for example, spent much time running

Plate 13.8 Shopper
formulating a plan of
action
Source: Roger Scruton.

behind orienteers, making detailed commentaries about their behaviour, to discover their personal strategies for planning travel. Passini (1984) has studied shoppers' strategies in planning travel through a shopping precinct; and Gärling has assessed the evidence for their approximating to a 'least distance minimizing heuristic', to which we shall return below.

Most of the naturalistic, long-term studies of people's spatial behaviour have been done with children and adolescents: Torrell and Beil (1985) asked 6- and 10-year-old children to keep detailed diaries of their outdoor activities; Moore (1986) had 9- to 12-year-olds take him on a lengthy field-trip round their neighbourhoods, and, from extensive interviews, has elicited the private worlds of these children. And, as we have already seen, Hart (1979) lived among the children of a New England town as would an anthropologist, vividly documenting the way the cognized world expands with the roles and freedoms allowed to children as they grow older.

What are the Implications of Environmental Cognition?

The prediction of action and of aesthetic responses

Throughout the earlier discussions, environmental cognition has been presented as intimately connected with action. In this section we now will consider its role as the basis of spatial decision-making (i.e. overall strategy choices and the level of broad implementation); and also of movement through space and spatial updating (the level of detailed implementation of journey plans). The final section of the chapter will examine the link between our environmental cognition and our aesthetic responses to places, from the large scale – the cognitive image of places (e.g. holiday destinations, shopping areas) as determinants of travel and relocation decisions; through middle scale – the appearance and layout of towns (their 'legibility'); to the small scale: the dimensions of aesthetic judgement of buildings or rooms.

Environmental cognition as the basis for spatial decision-making

Knowledge of the environment influences both our evaluations of and actions within it; such knowledge uptake is itself selectively filtered by the individual's goals and personal plans; and the extent to which a place satisfies these goals and plans affects the individual's evaluation of places.

Plate 13.9 Village: pleasing aesthetics
Source: Roger Scruton.

Traditionally, cognitive psychology and behavioural/economic geography have concentrated specifically upon the relationship between cognition and action, leaving out any account of aesthetics. Individuals are seen as making decisions about how to choose and act in the world: actions are taken after the individual perceives and forms preferences for different possible action alternatives, following specifiable decision rules, and observing constraining factors.

The kind of cognitive factors involved include previous experience, perceptual abilities, hierarchical goals and the decision rules mentioned above. As Gärling and Evans (1991) have indicated in their review, the formation of plans and their influence on actions in the environment has become a topic of increasing interest within cognitive psychology. A typical research issue is the influence of individual goals upon travel plans and decisions: spatial problem solving in a world constrained by time pressures, geographic layout, available transport and so on.

Gärling and colleagues, for example, have asked whether a shopper's travel plans through town could be described by a heuristic for achieving the least possible total distance between all the shops to be visited. Their findings are instructive: under a laboratory simulation, where the spatial relationships between targets are clearly visible (e.g. on a town plan), people do choose paths and sequences which approximate this most efficient heuristic. However, in the equivalent task, travelling in the real world, they found that real shoppers are much more prone to take less efficient routes, partly as a result of distractions and partly, one can hypothesize, because the real world is less easy to conceptualize in plan-relationships between target places.

Hence, a coldly 'rational' decision rule is unlikely to give a full prediction of much human spatial behaviour: actions are based on more than just a clear geographical 'cognitive map', with a mathematical decision rule for travel plans. We know that any account, to be adequate, must include some reference to preferences and motivations.

And even such a motivational analysis may overstate the purposive, rational character of many of the journeys we make: in many cases, we start out with only a very general overall plan, and our particular actions are guided by events and places encountered en route. We can analyse even a relatively simple way-finding task to show that it is composed of many sub-processes In an extensive study of way-finding, Passini (1984) recorded travellers' descriptions of their routes and actions as they walked through urban shopping malls. Some subjects recorded more than 100 discrete route decisions in completing a task taking 20 minutes.

And analysis of such protocols indicates how responsive rather than thought through and pre-planned is such a decision process. Most people have often only global initial plans, with a few general decisions and a number of specifics at the outset. Particular problems are then tackled as they emerge: Passini observes that generally a new detailed plan is formulated only after the previous

Plate 13.10 A child in a shopping mall, practising spatial protocols
Source: Sally and Richard Greenhill.

plan has been executed. The execution of travel plans is controlled by matching and feedback: matching relates the expected place image to the perceived place. Where there is a match, feedback sets the action part of the decision in motion; where there is a mismatch, it leads to further problem solving.

Environmental psychology and Artificial Intelligence have both a keen interest in the maintenance of orientation during travel: the tasks include place recognition, keeping track of one's location when moving about, and anticipating features of the environment. Successful travel may appear to be an automatic process, but can be shown to involve a continuous and complex updating process.

▨ Environmental Cognition and Aesthetics ▨

Cognitive maps, as described above, were first conceived by Tolman as the internal representation of space and its routes, junctions, distances, angles. The apparently similar term 'mental maps' was used by the geographers Gould and White (1986) to indicate an altogether less factual representation of space: they were concerned to account for the preferences, prejudices and images of places that lead individuals to make spatial choices. Thus, for example, some places within one's country are widely agreed to be attractive holiday destinations; others would be seen by most people as being less attractive. Such consensual views can be aggregated and drawn over a cartographic map outline as contours of preference, as an outward graphic representation of these inward

Box 13.4 The First Recorded Environmental Psychology Experiment? The King of Kerman Commands an Investigation

Although people must have discussed the transactions between environment and behaviour from time immemorial, certainly one of the first systematic experiments on the subject is recorded in the travels of Marco Polo, some seven hundred years ago.

Marco Polo had been making his way east from Venice, bound for Cathay, and was travelling through the kingdoms of what we now know as Iran or Persia. He recounts the experiment thus.

In the kingdom of Kerman, the people are known for being peace-loving, slow to anger, good to each other, and altogether most pro-social. The king, noting this, asked his court philosophers why this might be, given that the peoples of all the neighbouring kingdoms of Persia had the opposite reputation: they were always arguing among themselves, and violent even to the

point of murder.

The king's wise men offered the opinion that the answer lay in the soil.

Intrigued still further, and being a good empiricist well before his time, the king set up this experiment.

He sent for soil to the unruly kingdoms of Persia (and in particular to the the most notorious of them all, Isfahan); and there returned to Kerman seven laden ships.

The king ordered that this soil should be spread out on the floors of particular rooms, and be then covered up by carpets. A banquet was then held in these rooms, and as soon as they had eaten, the guests started to argue and fight with one another.

Seeing this, the king agreed: the answer truly lay in the soil.

preferences. Similar 'mental maps' were also constructed to demonstrate consensus about willingness to relocate when seeking employment.

These were early, relatively crude exercises; yet they none the less serve to reinforce the point that environmental cognitions and actions are closely linked to preferences. Later work on the images of distant places has shown how initial preferences can act as a selective filter in the seeking and processing of new information about these places: in this, environmental psychology links up with the psychology of prejudice and stereotyping of peoples (see chapter 12).

We can move from this broadest geographical scale to research at the middle scale – the preferences people express for aspects of man-made environment and natural landscapes.

Lynch (1960), in discussing the image we develop of the city, introduced the concept of the LEGIBILITY OF PLACES. Interestingly for the present discussion, the concept as he uses it links ease of understanding the physical layout with aesthetic response.

LEGIBILITY OF PLACES

A legible city (or district) would be one which is relatively easy to comprehend and to remember – with implications for distinctiveness and discriminibility. Areas lacking in clear landmarks, nodes, districts, etc., would rate as low in legibility. And, interestingly, it is these poorly structured areas which are also rated as less aesthetically appealing, a finding which has led many researchers after Lynch to examine in more detail the relationship between particular physical features (and their interrelationship) and peoples' aesthetic response to them.

But, you might reasonably ask, can aesthetics be looked at scientifically? In fact, EXPERIMENTAL AESTHETICS has cropped up at several stages in the history of general cognitive psychology. Within the specifically environmental domain,

EXPERIMENTAL AESTHETICS

Plate 13.11 High Mass at a Roman Catholic Cathedral: compare this behaviour setting with the Quaker meeting in plate 13.5
Source: Andes Press Agency/Carlos Reyes Manzo.

recent work has been particularly promising, and has introduced some romance back into psychology: where else in psychology would one find empirical work on what predicts people's feelings of mystery (to take a concept researched by Kaplan)?

Nasar, in identifying the evaluative image of the city as a whole, distinguishes between: identity; location; and what he calls LIKEABILITY – the qualities accounting for preferences. His empirical work shows that likeability has two broad dimensions: AFFECT and IMAGEABILITY.

Peoples' affect for environments (Nasar works principally with American cityscapes, it should be noted) are predicted by: the naturalness of the place; its upkeep; openness; order; and historical significance. Imageability relates to distinctiveness of form; visibility; and patterns of use – which in turn relate to a place's symbolic significance.

And at the scale of an individual building or room, there has again been much recent research linking form to aesthetic response. Despite perhaps the lay-presumption that tastes may differ widely, in practice there tends to be a high public agreement on choices between places: i.e. one can indeed see an emergent consensus on aesthetics. (Group differences, cultural differences, and 'expert–group' differences of course can overlay this observation.)

LIKEABILITY

AFFECT

IMAGEABILITY

Such emergent consensus has encouraged work on the predictors of preference at this level. Visual arousal and complexity are among the factors implicated (along with Kaplan's mystery!), there being an empirically determinable optimal level of complexity for a particular building type.

Aesthetic responses might perhaps be thought of as a superficial by-product of environmental cognition. But Nasar argues that cognition and aesthetics are both crucial to the public experience of urban areas:

- aesthetics is a major dimension of environmental perception;
- pleasure and beauty rate as the central dimensions of environmental assessments; and, most importantly,
- aesthetic factors have consistently been found to be closely associated with judgements of community satisfaction.

Yet, says Nasar, planners and urban decision-makers gloss over aesthetics as subjective and unquantifiable: it is neither. (And, most worryingly, such design professionals have consistently been found to differ from the general public's consensus in appraisals of the built environment.)

There is, in addition to all of the above research on the man-made environment, an equivalent empirical literature developing on what factors predict the aesthetic response to the natural environment (e.g. Kaplan & Kaplan 1989). In both areas, environmental psychology has contributed to this by moving discussion on from the speculative level of early aesthetics research to the well-supported principles of current theories of environmental aesthetics.

CHAPTER SUMMARY

1   How far is our behaviour shaped or even determined by aspects of the physical environment? If environment was initially ignored within psychology, we should now be aware of the opposite danger, of exaggerating its importance: instead, the transactions between people and their places are the focus of this field.

2   Such transactions can be studied empirically, at all scales, from the room to the region and its weather.

3   Ecological psychology gave the lead to an integrated view of places and behaviour therein with its concept of a behaviour setting, a small-scale social system comprising both the physical place, and people's expectations of behaviour there.

4   Personal control over space is clearly an important factor in well-being, whether at the micro-level, of the personal space around the body; the more macro-level controlled access to the self which may be achieved via having places which are private to oneself and chosen others; and most macro, feelings about places within one's 'home range'.

5   We must distinguish between density and crowding: it is useful to see density as the objective measure of people to space; and crowding as the

subjective response that there are too many people within a space, compared with one's desired level for that place and activity.

6   Environmental psychology originated with a practical collaboration between researchers and designers; and has retained its commitment to practical applications of its research to architecture and design, in, for instance, researching and communicating user needs, via techniques such as the simulation of to-be-built places.

7   As an example of theory and practice working together, the chapter considers the designing and use of the school: their physical design (e.g. windows and well-being); their symbolic meanings (the 'building messages'); the fit with the school's educational objectives; and implications of the size of the institution for pupils' feelings of involvement.

8   The location of crime is not random: environmental psychology, by studying its patterns, can test hypotheses about the criminal act as a located process – why what happens where. Does this give us the opportunity to 'design out' crime? A useful concept is that of defensible space, a concept where the perceived ownership of space, (lack of) surveillance of potential intruders, and risk of detection meet.

9   People's understanding of the environment includes, but goes beyond, the cognitive map of particular places: it also includes an experience-derived 'environmental grammar' and an aesthetic response to spaces and places. Such aesthetic responses may well influence choices and behaviour, as well as the person's well-being.

10 We can study environmental cognition both microgenetically and ontogenetically: the child's developing skills in integrating spatial knowledge; and the way in which the newcomer assembles spatial knowledge of a place. We now know far more of the child's developing place-skills than was given in the account given by Piaget.

11 How dependent upon vision the processes of environmental cognition are is illustrated by considering the tasks of the blind child; and the chapter shows how far the provision of space-summarizing devices such as the tactile map can substitute for the visual overview.

12 What is the nature of the cognitive store for environmental knowledge? There is evidence that it is both analogical (map-like) and propositional (like a set of route instructions).

13 And how can we find methods of investigating this cognitive store which do not, in themselves, impose impossible additional tasks as the person attempts to publicly represent this knowledge as they draw, model or describe it for the investigator?

▓ Further Work ▓

1. Why is knowing where you are so important?
2. Can we design places?
3. Has psychology underestimated the environmental skills of the young child?
4. How does the child's increasing mobility affect their environmental cognition?
5. Can we predict people's aesthetic responses to a place? And do they matter?
6. Conduct a thought experiment to redesign an area of college which you feel does not support people's needs. How would you assess these needs? Communicate them to a designer? And assess the success of the changes?

7. Compare what information is included when you (a) ask for a sketch-map to show you your route; (b) ask for verbal instructions to the same place.
8. Is a cognitive map like a 'real' map?
9. Describe some of the behaviour settings you frequent; and examine the transactions between place, roles and rules in shaping your actions there.
10. How would Baum and Valins, and Oscar Newman, assess your current accomodation?
11. How do the concepts of privacy, crowding, control and defensible space interrelate?
12. Study your own acquisition of spatial knowledge as you learn a new area of town: you could keep a diary of the first few days; draw sketch-maps each night; and afterwards compare your records with those on a local map.

▧ Further Reading ▧

Bonnes, M. and Secchiaroli, G. (1995) *Environmental Psychology: A Psycho-social Introduction*. London: Sage.

> If you would like to read further on the intellectual origins and current issues of environmental psychology, this is an authoratative (but by no means easy) source book.

Matthews, M. H. (1992) *Making Sense of Place*. Hemel Hempstead: Harvester Wheatsheaf.

> A very approachable text, which lays most stress on the child's understandings and use of the world around.

Spencer, C. P. (ed.) (1995) *The Child's Environment*. London: Academic Press.

> Spencer covers the same aspect in a book of readings.

McAndrew, F. (1992) *Environmental Psychology*. Pacific Grove, Calif.: Brooks/Cole.

Veitch, R. and Arkkelin, D. (1995) *Environmental Psychology: An Interdisciplinary Perspective*. Englewood Cliffs, NJ: Prentice-Hall.

> These two are typical of the American texts in this field, which stress the person–environment transaction with less emphasis on its cognitive aspects.

Stokols, D. and Altman, I. (eds) (1987) *The Handbook of Environmental Psychology*. New York: John Wiley.

> From its relatively recent origins, environmental psychology has grown rapidly: witness the existence in the subject's second decade of the *Handbook*. You should note that the *Handbook* is a huge reference work, and not a conventional text, but even so it has many detailed yet accessible chapters on environmental psychology applied to, for example, schools, the crowd, transportation, etc.

PART 6
The Individual

CHAPTER 14

Personality – The Individual and Society

Christopher Spencer

CHAPTER AGENDA

- We first ask why there seem to be so many theories of personality, and find many users of such theorizing.

- The review of theories starts with those that the layman probably most associates with the term 'psychology' – the dynamic theories of Freud; and we assess their current standing within psychology.

- Seeking the dimensions on which personality can be measured has been a major enterprise of personality psychology, but even here, we find important differences between theorists such as Eysenck and Cattell.

- Has resolution come, in the shape of the 'big five' dimensions? Although different theorists' terminology may differ, there is now evidence that personality can be measured on five broad dimensions.

- A challenge to all these approaches to personality comes from those who can present evidence on the power of situations to shape an individual's behaviour. Modern theories have now come to see an interaction between stable aspects of personality, and what the situation affords the individual.

- All of this is personality studied from 'outside' the person; but how do people experience themselves? The chapter concludes by reviewing the work of three writers, Carl Rogers, George Kelly and Abraham Maslow, who have asked this question, and whose different answers may help humanize and broaden the 'scientific' approach to personality represented earlier in the chapter.

▓ Introduction ▓

Psychologists have studied personality for at least one hundred years; philosophers have pondered and analysed it for perhaps two and a half thousand years; and human beings have probably been involved observers and theorists about personality since there have been human beings. It is thus clearly important to us, whether as laypeople or professionals: yet, because the research goes on, it might seem as if this area has yet to achieve any firm conclusions. This chapter brings you a progress report, whose conclusion, I hope you will agree, is that there are many definite and worthwhile statements we, as psychologists, can contribute to the debate.

You will see why, initially, there were so many theories of personality within psychology – indeed so many kinds of theory: there are several different groups of psychologist needing personality psychologies to fit their requirements – social, developmental, clinical, educational, industrial, organizational psychologists all wanted to be able to talk of individual differences in their own ways.

We will then visit a number of these approaches and characterize them for you: those which have sought personality types for clinical psychology; traits or dimensions of personality for the predictions of social psychology; continuities for developmental and life-span psychology; and situational dependencies for social and environmental psychologies. As we consider specific major theories, you will become aware of some of the classic debates in this field: should we see personalities as unique wholes or as variations on universal themes and dimensions? Do we remain pretty much the same personalities from childhood on? Or are there aspects of life stages which come to dominate individual differences? Are we consistent in our core behaviours and beliefs regardless of where we are or with whom, or do social and physical situations override and obscure any longer-term stabilities?

What, in other words, is the evidence for stability across the life-span? Across situations? And, if we do find strong evidence of variability across time and place, does this do damage to popular (and some scientific) concepts of personality? Should we seek altogether more sophisticated conceptualizations of personality; or rather, would the solution be to improve our measuring techniques? (When we tell you that two, conceptually quite similar theorists can claim that you need either two/three or sixteen dimensions to measure personality, you may well feel some need for resolution – and, we are happy to say, a widespread agreement on this is breaking out: it looks as if we can agree on five major dimensions.) Of this, and more, later.

There are some other, related issues which we will consider: for instance, can we use personality tests (or indeed interviews, or any other such procedures) to select people for jobs with any reliability, if people's behaviour turns out to be as variable as some theorists suggest? Should we, rather, see the main contribution of personality psychology as getting people to understand each other, and themselves, rather than as working towards a scientist's precise prediction of behaviour?

The first justification for a psychology of personality is that there already is an intuitive lay-version of it which we all employ, and which we as psychologists could and perhaps should develop and refine.

Is every person a personality theorist? There does seem to be an apparent human need to see stability and predictability in others' behaviours, which is in line with the need to cognize the rest of the (non-human) world as possessing continuing and therefore predictable characteristics. This helps us as actors to anticipate social behaviour, and search our repertoire for appropriate responses.

ATTRIBUTION
THEORY

We would also seem to have the need to explain those behaviours by attributing them to some core characteristics of the individual person. ATTRIBUTION THEORY, as we saw in chapter 11, shows that, especially when accounting for others' behaviour, we are more likely to explain it with reference to their characteristics than to any situation they might be in. (In contrast, where we are trying to explain our own behaviours, especially where these are less than perfect, situational explanations are to the fore!)

Personality also is a concept useful to us in our everyday communications. Witness the huge number of entries in the dictionary for aspects and types of personality: Cattell, following Allport, claimed to have found 18,000 such words in the *Webster* dictionary! These words have arisen from the vast interest and

Plate 14.1 Filling out a questionnaire: one way to profile personality
Source: Roger Scruton.

need we have to classify stable and continuing aspects of other human beings. Most introductory chapters on language make much of the calculation that the Inuit have dozens of words for snow, or that Arabic has quite a few for camels and/or sand, as indicating the great salience each has for that culture. Your personality chapter has offered you this statistic of quite a different order, and leaves you to draw your own conclusions.

Before turning to the systematic and professional theorizing of personality, we must warn you that we are not quite done with everyday theorizing about it. Later in the chapter, when talking about methods used in measurement of personality, we will note that many of these involve lay-people either assessing themselves (e.g. via questionnaires) or assessing each other (e.g. via rating scales); and that, furthermore, these methods often come up with greater consistencies than an objective observer has noted. Could you anticipate why this might be?

▓ Why Are There So Many Theories of Personality? ▓

After a century or so of research, you might expect there to have emerged a consensual view of personality – how it emerges, whether biology and life experiences have equal part in its origins, how stable it remains through life and across situations, how much of behaviour it can explain, how it relates to the individual's self-concepts, personal constructs and attitudes, how we might best offer a structured description of personality, etc.

Yet if you were to search out one of those hefty texts entitled 'Theories of Personality', your first impression might be somewhat disheartening: chapter after chapter of apparently dissimilar theories, usually each using a distinct and often obscure descriptive vocabulary. How can this be? Can they all be wrong, save one of them? And which one?

Think back to the varied reasons why psychologists might want to study personality.

Some of the earliest theorists were involved with treating patients on an individual basis, over many sessions, in a quasi-medical mode, laying emphases upon the organic (and at that time largely inaccessible) origins of the individual's condition. Other clinicians, coming from a humanistic and whole-person approach, were equally inclined to theorize about the person holistically, but with more of a forward perspective. Yet others, equally concerned with patients, were employed within a medical setting to conduct the preliminary assessment of whole batches of patients and to assign them to diagnostic categories: this classificatory approach might then shade into the more scientific consideration of personality.

The interest in individual differences that the 'scientist-psychologist' might have would often be less person-centred, more focused on a comparative analysis of many humans' behaviour than would be that of the clinic-based

Plate 14.2 Boys playing around tree
Source: Collections/Anthea Sieveking.

MULTI-TRAIT
PERSONALITY
INVENTORY

psychologist. Imagine that you were investigating, for example, drivers' behaviour on motorways; and one focus of your study was to be individual differences in reactions to police warning signs. You would have no need (or time!) to investigate individual personalities in any great depth, especially if your study was to include several hundred drivers as its sample. A quick-to-administer test would be your operational requirement: but a test of what? You might here want a quick overall summary of individuality, offered in a test format which would enable you to compare across the whole sample, and indeed other researchers' samples. Here, a MULTI-TRAIT PERSONALITY INVENTORY would seem appropriate. You might, in contrast, be concerned to study individual differences with respect to one particular trait: for example, your research might be into children's need to achieve as a predictor of how they responded to a competitive classroom situation. Here, focus upon this single trait would be appropriate.

Yet other groups of psychologists would be using personality to predict individuals' future performance in, for example, work settings. In format, their personality-measurement tools may look very similar to the questionnaires used by the scientist-psychologists; but their underlying rationale may differ somewhat: for their aim is to select the best candidates for employment in a particular post. Similar uses of tests to predict might take place in education; in career guidance; in the prison service; and so forth.

Rather than attempting a survey of the dauntingly large number of separate theories of personality that have been devised, this chapter will illustrate some of the main issues, by concentrating upon:

- Freudian theory as an example of a dynamic approach to the origins of personality;
- Trait theories as a way of classifying individuals with relation to each other;
- Mischel's demonstration that we need to consider the situational determinants of behaviour;
- A range of person-centred and/or 'phenomenological' theories, which highlight the person's own self-understanding.

▨ Dynamic Theories of Personality: More to Behaviour than We are Aware Of? ▨

The model of humans as fully rational and aware beings is challenged by a number of observations. For instance, we may meet individuals who show persistent and apparently inexplicable irrational behaviours: an obsession with washing and rewashing their hands in the Lady Macbeth manner. Phobias about creatures or places which hold no apparent real dangers. Feelings of worthlessness despite evidence to the contrary from friends. And, in the arena of more everyday experiences, are we convinced that we are aware of the motivations of all our behaviours? Or may we 'forget' those things which we would rather not do?

Freud suggested that we reverse the assumption of rationality: he suggested that, in reality, most of our motivations are unavailable to us, or at least we are unaware of them.

The most dramatic and immediate demonstration of this is given by hypnosis. Suggestions given by the hypnotist are responded to by the person once released from the trance; yet if we question them on why they are acting in this way, they can give us a perfectly coherent account in terms of their own motivations, even though we will have witnessed the 'real' external cause.

Freud, who was originally trained in medicine, came across instances of obsessional behaviours and other inexplicable behaviours – such as a child's irrational fear of horses – for which current conventional medical explanations seemed unconvincing. He was also impressed by a colleague's use of hypnosis in treatment. In these two factors lay the seeds of his own approach to personality.

But how to get back to things beyond consciousness? Freud distinguished between the preconscious and the unconscious. Freud argued that we should first note the significance of dreams: during dreams, things which we do not acknowledge when we are awake can come closer to awareness, albeit in altered and often symbolic form. Freud analysed his own dreams as a means of developing a symbol system to interpret elements of the dream. He then applied this

Plate 14.3 On the
analytical couch
Source: Collections/Anthea
Sieveking.

system to the dreams that he had his patients recount to him. This they did
repeatedly over a long series of appointments, both to bring out the consistent
themes and, dynamically, to produce in the patient a greater awareness and
acknowledgement of what thoughts lay beyond consciousness.

FREE ASSOCIATIONS

A second access route used by Freud was the technique of FREE ASSOCIATIONS.
He argued that, if one were at one's most relaxed in dream-sleep, then a similar
relaxed state could be induced by the combination of a reclining posture (hence
the famed couch), an encouraging and permissive analyst, and instructions to
move freely from thought to thought.

PSYCHOPATHOLOGY

Everyday life, and what Freud called its PSYCHOPATHOLOGY, was a third rich
source of insights: the verbal slips made in conversation were not mere accidents, but were significant, and their analysis would often reveal an underlying
motivation.

From many encounters with patients, and the use of these three techniques
for building up a case, Freud found it useful to conceive of a tripartite architect-

ID

ure of the personality: the ID, the EGO and the SUPER-EGO.

The *id* is present at birth, and is entirely unconscious. It includes all what

EGO

Freud considered to be 'basic instincts': 'sexual' (pleasure, self-preservation);
and destructive-aggressive.

SUPER-EGO

The *ego*: at 6 to 8 months of age, the ego develops out of the id as a result of
early life experiences; the ego spans conscious, preconscious and unconscious;
is logical, self-preserving and reality-testing; and is the locus of the emotions.

The *super-ego*: at about 3 to 5 years, the super-ego emerges out of the ego; it is seen as the seat of the conscience, and develops from internalizing the standards of behaviour expected by one's parents.

The British therapist Don Bannister once mischievously but memorably likened this three-part conceptualization of personality to 'Dialogues between a maiden aunt and a sex-crazed monkey who are locked in mortal combat, the affair being refereed by a rather nervous bank clerk' (Bannister 1966).

Testing Freud's theories

Evidence in favour of Freud's approach to personality comes from the internal consistencies in the individual cases of his patients. Indeed, one of the great legacies of the method lies in these case studies; yet curiously, few of them were prepared for publication: Freud only published case studies in order to illustrate and develop theoretical points.

Yet even here the Freudian method is open to challenge. Consistency in patients' accounts can be suggested by the analyst: and indeed shaping of the recurrent dreams can be detected in the accounts. It has been said, only partly in jest, that Freud's patients quickly learned to dream in Freudian symbols, Adler's patients in Adlerian, and so on (Freud was the first of many practitioners and theorists following a broadly analytic, dynamic approach to psychology, each one of whom offered their own variations on the broad dynamic theme).

Freud and the psychoanalytic tradition have been important to psychology in emphasizing that much of personality and motivation operates beyond the level of consciousness and rationality. One can accept this proposition without then subscribing to Freud's particular personality model of id, ego and super-ego, or to his account of the psychosexual stages (oral, anal, genital, etc.; which we shall not elaborate here) through which it was said to evolve in childhood. These stages were hypothesized on the basis of Freud's interpretation of adult analyses, and were never checked against either biographical details of the specific person's childhood; or, perhaps more significantly, compared with any empirical investigations of childhood in general. Set against the subsequent ninety years' research work of developmental psychology, the proposed 'stages' of childhood in the Freudian account look now to be an historical curiosity to most empirically based developmental psychologists. (Recall how little of a dynamic account of childhood was given in chapter 2.)

Consider this: proving causality within Freudian accounts of personality via the case studies must always be difficult – they are after all retrospective and, in at least one case, actually second-hand. Adults reconstructed for the analyst what they had been like in early childhood; or, in the case of Little Hans, described to the analyst what someone else's experiences had been – not the best data source! A predictive, 'longitudinal' (i.e. taking place throughout the subjects' lives) design would have been preferable, but its practical difficulties are obvious: imagine applying for research monies to study the same large cohort of people in sufficiently intimate detail from birth until at least well into their middle age.

Box 14.1   Can We Measure Personality in Monkeys?

Anyone who has kept a pet will be happy to give you a description of its endearing character; but could we move from the anecdotal to the scientific, and offer a way of reliably measuring it?

For those personality theorists who see personality descriptions as arising from consistencies in observed behaviour, this question should pose a welcome challenge to demonstrate their technique in action.

Eysenck once accepted this challenge, and joined forces with the primatologists Chamove and Harlow, who had large captive colonies of macaques. Eysenck's technique when working with humans was to use self-report questionnaires, and imply behaviour from the responses. With the monkeys, self-report is a less useful technique (at least until we can recruit more monkeys as psychologists), and the analysis is based directly on observed behaviour.

But which behaviours to sample?

The authors selected ten: examples of which are social exploration; social play; non-social play; social cling; hostile contact – behaviours which observers can rate with high reliability.

Each individual was observed in free activity in their home group on 30 occasions for 60 minutes; and data were also collected from one-on-one encounters with a playful infant and with a docile adult.

Analysis of the records over all these sessions showed a striking result: three clear factors emerged, with very little intercorrelation:

> level of hostility
> level of fear
> level of sociability/affection

To quote the authors, 'These patterns of behaviour are not dissimilar to those which gave rise to the three major factors in research on human personality: neuroticism–stability; extraversion–introversion, and psychoticism.'

Marked individual differences exist between monkeys in their social behaviour, differences which are sufficiently stable to be evident in a study such as this one, and thus be regarded as aspects of 'personality'.

(Some have tried to subject limited aspects of Freudian theory to such tests, with a measure of success: the data by no means support Freud.)

More problematic still is the status of Freudian theories as theories of science at all. Are the propositions stated in ways which would enable one not only to test them, but to falsify them? (This is the standard way that philosophers of science say is the basic test.) Here, we could spend much time in interesting debate between those who argue that Freud framed his theories with so many 'get-out' clauses (such as mechanisms of denial, repression, reactance) that testing becomes meaningless; and those who argue that they could be reformulated so as to subject them to rigorous test.

'Instinct'

Freud's attempts to use the concept of instinct to explain human behaviours again makes his writings seem creatures of a former age. Other writers at the beginning of the twentieth century were 'discovering' many more, and indeed even more elaborate, 'instincts'. Take for instance McDougall, writing in 1908, who discerned that social behaviour was shaped by eleven such 'instincts', which ranged from the Instincts of Flight, Pugnacity and Curiosity to those of Self-abasement, Self-assertion and Acquisition. The circularity of such 'explanations' had yet to strike home. Consider: the existence of an 'acquisitive instinct' is attested to by people's collecting and hoarding behaviours; yet one then explains these behaviours in terms of the instinct.

Freud himself doubted the usefulness of his postulated instincts towards the end of his career: 'Thanatos', the famous self-destructive force, drops from his scheme of things. Later members of the analytic family of theorists, too, have varied in their reliance on 'instinct' as a concept. We would need a huge chapter to do justice to the variety of insights, theories and terminologies offered.

Dimensions of personality: how to compare people for scientific purposes while still respecting their individuality

'We are all different: let us celebrate our individuality', is a humane sentiment that I hope all psychologists share in their personal capacity, including clinical and phenomenological psychologists.

But for some purposes, we may wish to compare individuals – say, in their susceptibilities to stress, or in their likelihood to participate in an election, or their characteristic level of generosity, or their commitment to healthy eating . . .

And, in order to compare, one has to discover or invent criteria by which individuals can be described as similar or different: dimensions of variation.

Consider: we do it all the time in our everyday descriptions of people:

She's about three feet tall, with light brown hair and blue-grey eyes.

This physical description of an individual uses three dimensions upon which all emphasis could be placed: height, hair colour and shade of eyes.

Could we do the same for personality descriptions? In doing so, we would be looking for universally applicable dimensions of personality. As with the physical descriptors, each person would have their position on a dimension (as with height, you may be six feet tall: Toulouse-Lautrec was 4 feet 11 inches). Your individuality would thus be summed up by your position on this dimension and – how many others? The number of dimensions need not be huge, given all possible permutations, to capture a wide range of individualities. And, as we shall see, some have claimed we can capture much that is important with a mere two or three dimensions.

Who, typically, might be most likely to be measuring individuality via dimensions of personality? Many areas of psychology – experimental, social, organizational, developmental, health – might well wish to use such an approach: this would give them standardized tools with which to measure individual differences. Consider: you are conducting a health education campaign, and, in evaluating its success, find one group of people most resistant to the message. Among other factors (for instance, their past experience of such campaigns) you might wish to see whether such resistance was related to stable individual differences – aspects of personality.

Box 14.2   Perceived Material Wealth and First Impressions

How far are our impressions of a stranger's likely personality affected by particular aspects of their appearance? Helga Dittmar (1992) has illustrated that our impressions can be shaped by the apparent wealth of the individual.

She devised a set of four brief videotapes: a young male actor seen coming back to a relatively affluent home setting; and the same actor returning to a poorer home setting; and a young female actress in the same two settings. Groups of adolescents saw one out of these four videos, and were asked to describe the stranger they had seen depicted. The adolescents themselves were drawn from either a wealthy or working-class background.

The wealthy person (male or female) was seen as more intelligent, successful and educated; and as being more in control of their life and environment than was the less affluent person. In contrast this poorer person emerged as warmer, friendlier and more self-expressive. (Which would you prefer to be?) The female video character was seen as less autonomous and self-reliant when poor than wealthy; whereas the opposite was true for the male character.

These impressions were common across all the adolescent viewers, regardless of which home background they declared to be most like their own: in other words, similarity between self and perceived person had little or no effect on the inferences one made from these first impressions.

This is perhaps against what the social-psychological theory social identification theory (Tajfel 1984) might have predicted; but in line with a dominant representations approach, which stresses a consensual view of social phenomena such as wealth and identity.

Some ideas about social phenomena are shared between members of particular groups within society; and lead individuals to perceive reality within the context of this shared belief system (see Moscovici 1988, who was developing Gergen's 1985 social constructionist perspective).

Other ideas, such as notions about wealth and material possessions, are, as we have seen in this study, still more widely shared, and become society's dominant representation. Dittmar's findings are in line with many earlier studies of how Western children are socialized into a view which endorses the legitimacy of wealth differentials, seeing them as the outcome of individual merit. This they do, regardless of where in society their families are placed. Furnham and Lewis (1986) have summarized person perception research which favours the affluent over the poor: attributional studies indicating that the wealthy are seen as intelligent, responsible, hard working and attractive; while the poor are described as lazy, unmotivated, and lacking in proper money management skills. (Sounds like the stuff of political speeches, does it not?)

If one takes just three dimensions, with all their possible permutations, one has a large number of possible positions, and this approach has attracted psychology for much of this century. During the 1930s , Sheldon proposed that personality and physique were related and that each could be described using a three-dimensional scheme, each dimension having seven possible positions. Thus using his notation, a person could range from a 7-1-1 (maximum on first dimension, minimizing on the other two) to a 1-7-1 or a 1-1-7. Most individuals would be less extreme, scoring, for example, a 4-3-5 as medium on each dimension.

We give you this as an early instance of dimensionalizing individuality. Sheldon's particular dimensions do not have any current acceptability within psychology: subsequent research has shown his investigative methods to be faulty. He claimed to have found evidence for a high correlation between his three personality dimensions and 'three dimensions of physique':

mesomorphy
endomorphy
ectomorphy

which, being translated, mean roughly muscularity, fatness and wiriness. The trouble was that those who were assessing the individual's personality knew what the person's physique was, knew Sheldon's hypothesis and could hardly then fail to be influenced by this in their ratings of personality. During the 1930s, there was little awareness that psychology needed to make its measurements blind to the hypotheses of the study.

An apparently even simpler, but this time scientifically based, two-dimensional solution was proposed in the 1940s by Eysenck, who has subsequently discerned the need to add a third dimension.

Eysenck was working as a psychologist alongside psychiatrists for whom he made the preliminary assessments of patients. Psychiatric diagnoses could, Eysenck believed, be cross-checked with behavioural data about the patients, and so he set about seeing empirically how many dimensions it would take to sum up the variations in this behaviour.

By the statistical technique of factor analysis, which rotates the data to find the dimensions which best fit the data, Eysenck initially proposed that two, orthogonal (i.e. at right-angles and therefore independent) dimensions were adequate to account for a large percentage of the variability. (Rotating data is not easy to explain, but a working definition would be this: where the data consist of a large matrix – where every variable is related to every other variable – then there is more than one way of 'inspecting' these relationships: statistically, one can alter the search questions asked.) He labelled these 'EXTROVERSION–INTROVERSION' and 'NEUROTICISM–NORMALITY', borrowing the terms from earlier psychologists. But note that while the dynamic psychologist Jung had thought of extroverts and introverts as separate personality types, here Eysenck proposed them as end points of a continuum, upon which we can all be placed.

'EXTROVERSION–INTROVERSION'

'NEUROTICISM–NORMALITY'

As you can imagine, few psychologists have the time or opportunity to collect behavioural data on the people they are studying, and would prefer to have a standard measuring instrument which is quicker and more portable. Eysenck thus moved to construct questionnaire scales to capture the dimensions. So was launched the EPI (the EYSENCK PERSONALITY INVENTORY), and several years later its modification, the EPQ (Q for Questionnaire). This latter scale incorporated a third dimension, 'PSYCHOTICISM', whose presence extensive empirical work had shown to be necessary to account for more of the variance in the data.

EYSENCK PERSONALITY INVENTORY

'PSYCHOTICISM'

There has been a huge amount of use made of this way of conceptualizing and then measuring personality. In a robust defence of the approach against his critics (whose points we shall come to shortly), Eysenck can present a many and varied listing of behaviours he has found to be related to scores on the introversion–extroversion dimension: sensory threshold; pain threshold; time estimation; sensory deprivation; perceptual defence; vigilance; reminiscence;

sleep–wakefulness patterns; rest pauses in tapping; speech patterns; conditioning; expressive behaviour, etc., etc. You will see that this list ranges from very specific motor patterns up to more major descriptors of individuality. But the correlations do not stop here: from the social, health and developmental literatures, Eysenck draws similarly long lists of correlates between one or more of his dimensions and behaviours as varied as: the reasons for smoking; people's voting patterns; and their religious observances.

How many dimensions?

Not all within this camp of personality theorists would accept that we can reduce all data down to as few as three dimensions. Raymond Cattell (1965), for instance, has advocated sixteen. He started from an ingeniously different perspective, from the wisdom of the ages as collected together in a dictionary. As already mentioned, there are tens of thousands of personality descriptors in the English language; Cattell then identified a further eleven terms stemming from psychology research which seemed to have no everyday language equivalent; and then set about reducing this aggregate list to manageable proportions .

Factor analyses of this subset led to a 16-factor solution, and Cattell then set out to capture these by means of a now widely used scale, the 16-PF, which like Eysenck's has been used as a predictor of a wide range of behaviours.

But why the discrepancy? Sixteen as against three?

The answer is not very interesting, except for enthusiasts; and relates to the statistical strategy you use to rotate your data, and what you choose to use as cut-off points in the analysis.

Many other theorists have offered their methodological variations on this theme, to the point that, had you been reading in this field some years back, we suspect that you would have been justifiably irritated, and would have asked why they could not have attempted to work towards some unification. You will therefore be pleased to hear that there is now emerging a consensus that five dimensions are about the appropriate number to capture human richness without resorting to minutiae. When the various theories are laid side by side, under the banner headline of these, THE BIG FIVE, you realize that often what was separating them were differences in nomenclature, rather than anything more fundamental.

THE BIG FIVE

Hope is thus in sight, and, with the coming of new, integrative Big Five questionnaires, you would expect research on personality traits and their relationship to behaviour to surge ahead. But there is a much more fundamental attack underway on the assumptions underlying the personality theories we have seen so far. Whether they be dynamic typologies, or dimensionalizing trait theories, they would seem to make the central assumption that personality is a relatively stable, broad characteristic of the individual.

Yet the empirical evidence would seem to suggest that an individual's behaviour is variable from situation to situation. To quote from the most vigorous critic, Mischel (1973):

Box 14.3   Anticipating, Experiencing and Remembering Becoming a Mother

One of the major life events must be becoming a mother; and Jonathan Smith's (1990) longitudinal study of this process therefore has intrinsic interest: few psychologists have given us as clear a picture of the mixture of hopes and fears, cultural myths, socially given information and personal beliefs that characterize pregnancy, birth and motherhood.

The study also enables us in this chapter to see how stability and change can both be found in a person's life as they anticipate, undergo and look back upon an important life event. The way Smith collected his data enables us to see how these anticipations, experiences and memories may significantly mismatch, without the person being fully aware of the fact.

'Clare' was 29 years old; and was visited by the researcher on four occasions, at three, six and nine months pregnant, and five months after the birth of 'Rebecca'.

On each occasion, Clare expressed her feelings via a standard Repertory Grid, with elements provided by the researcher, and constructs which she generated. After Clare had completed the fourth, post-birth grid, she then completed two further grids: for how she thought she had responded at three months and at nine months pregnant. After Jonathan Smith had analysed the grids, he brought them back to Clare for her interpretation.

During pregnancy, there were dramatic changes in self-rating for control of responsibility, as the foetus grows and as one prepares to go into medical care for the birth. After the birth, Clare reports a feeling of constant responsibility; and needing to be, and actually being, more decisive.

During her pregnancy, Clare's constructs became more tightly clustered, focusing in on how much people are 'together', resilient, and decisive; this clustering only slightly loosens at the time of the post-birth grid. And, when asked to think back to how she had been at three months, she finds this difficult to recapture: 'I cannot imagine what my life was like before Rebecca. . . . I can't make that leap back, she's so inextricably entwined.'

Overall, pregnancy was the time when a more coherent and determined self-concept developed for Clare; closer relations with her partner; and an initial coming together and then slight distancing from her mother.

Using the grid enabled the researcher to chart changes and continuities in the self, and when looking retrospectively, to demonstrate that the 'self is a selective personal historian'.

Table 14.1 The Big Five dimensions: the coming together of theorists. E = Eysenck 1970; C = Cattell 1957; B = Buss 1985; F = Fiske 1949; D = Digman 1990. Note in Digman 1990 there are listed altogether 14 separate recent dimensional theories, all of which more or less fit the big five paradigm. A few of them (such as Buss & Plomin) have one empty cell. Only Eysenck attempts a three-dimensional solution.

Theorist	1	2	3	4	5
E	extroversion	— psychoticism —		neuroticism	* * * * *
C	exavia	cortertia	super-ego strength	anxiety	intelligence
B	activity	sociability	impulsivity	emotionality	* * * * * *
F	social adaptability	conformity	will to achieve	emotional control	inquiring intellect
D	extroversion	friendly compliance	will to achieve	neuroticism	intellect

There is impressive evidence that on virtually all of our dispositional measures of personality, substantial changes occur in the characteristics of the individual over time, and even more dramatically, across seemingly similar settings cross-sectionally.

In order to give any meaning to the concept of personality, would we not need such consistencies, both across the life-span, and also across situations?

The situational challenge to the trait approach to personality; and the interactionalist resolution to the problem

Mischel's critique, in summary, is this: only 5 to 10 per cent of the variance of actual observed behaviour is related to individual differences in personality traits, and therefore the emphasis on a trait-based approach to understanding behaviour is misplaced.

For some fifty or sixty years, Mischel argues, psychology's fundamental assumptions have remained unaltered: that

- Personality comprises broad underlying dispositions which
- pervasively influence the individual's behaviour across many situations
- and lead to consistencies in their behaviour.

Yet Mischel argues: look at the empirical evidence: it does not support these assumptions. (See, for example, Mischel 1994, in Further Reading below.)

Trait theorists seem to assume that traits apply universally, across situations; environmental psychologists lay their emphasis on the situation as the main determinant of behaviour. (Neither, in practice, is as 'uni-deterministic', as one-track, as we are making them sound.)

What resolution can we reach? Is there a mid-point, where we can study behaviour as a product of traits expressed in interaction with situations? This section will ask what evidence we can draw upon, and then offer an INTERACTIONALIST resolution which has recently gained much favour.

INTERACTIONALIST
RESOLUTION

What is the evidence for consistencies across situations?

There are many studies which show that even those traits we might expect to be 'core', such as high/low dependency, may vary according to the social situation. Let us take dependency as a thought experiment: consider yourself when back at home with your family; as you were at school; as you are now, perhaps at college; as you are with your partner or close friend. Does your dependency level remain the same? Now, let us continue the thought experiment: hold the people constant and now vary the situation. Consider yourself and your partner/friend when you are: dealing with financial matters; choosing decorations for your flat; planning a holiday trip; entertaining guests . . .

Plate 14.4 'Reflection': note the metaphor
Source: Collections/Anthea Sieveking.

Realize that the variability you will have noticed is not random; it is simply that its complexity has not been fully recognized or documented. Persons acting in situations are not infinitely varied, but follow a finite number of personal 'scripts'. And were we to examine your particular scripts (with-partner, entertaining, decorating, holidaying, etc.), we would begin to observe stable patterns of behaviour within types of situations which have similar psychological meaning for you and your partner. There is much variability, but it is rule-following.

But surely, you will say, we do see a great stability in personality, both within ourselves and in those we know well?

Exactly: it is our nature as everyday perceivers to see stability of characteristics; but is it really there when as psychologists we come to measure it?

Consider the three categories of data conventionally used in personality assessment:

Q-DATA: self-ratings (e.g. questionnaires)
R-DATA: others' ratings of a target individual (e.g. a teacher's rating of a pupil)
T-DATA: objective tests of behaviour

Q-DATA
R-DATA
T-DATA

Box 14.4   Offender Profiling: Personality Assessment of a Person you have yet to Meet

Psychologists have been able to offer assistance to the police in the field of crime detection via a technique that has come to be called 'offender profiling' (see, for example, Canter & Larkin 1993). The logic of this should intrigue you: for it almost reverses the usual way personality testing normally proceeds. Normally, the psychologist is face to face with someone to whom he can apply some kind of test, and from that perhaps attempts to deduce likely future behaviour. The forensic psychologist is instead faced with an account of past behaviours from the crime record (a series of similar attacks, say), and the challenge is to conjure up a profile of the person likely to have committed them.

Consider the situation: you do not necessarily know that all the crime incidents are connected (unless it is a rare case where perhaps one has DNA matched samples from each), but are linking the incidents because of proximity in time and space, and by *modus operandi*. Canter, for example, was faced with the record of a series of attacks on women that happened over a period of months in adjacent settlements that were all served by the same commuter railway. Details of how the attacks had been carried out were sufficiently similar to suggest the same perpetrator had been involved; and so the investigative team decided to build up a profile of the likely attacker.

Who would be in a position to travel the route? Who would have the familiarity with the hidden places where the attacks took place? So far, the investigation is using the usual police methods of narrowing down the field – down to about the last ten thousand!

Witness statements, traces at the scenes and other evidence would next come into play, to try to build up a picture of offender appearance, style, and perhaps motivations. All partial data sources that the conventional personality theorist would despair of: yet they are the only data available.

Forensic psychologists have indeed successes to claim from their painstaking analyses. The process is far from the instant inspiration of the television portrayal: 'The man we are looking for is a bank clerk aged 34 with a passion for leeks.'

Can psychology then build up general theories from such specific cases? David Canter and Paul Larkin were able to aggregate the records on 45 convicted rapists, who, between them, had been responsible for 251 offences in the London area. This data enabled the researchers to pose and to answer the question: do serial offenders tend to commute away from their home base to offend (the Commuter Model); or rather, did they tend to live within the circle of their activities (the Marauder Model). Results from their study indicate that 87 per cent of the sample were 'marauders' in their home area, and that 'commuting' was atypical.

From this (essentially) geography of crime analysis, Canter and Larkin then extend their hypothesis to include more detailed psychological factors: the potential offender's assessment of local and more distant areas as likely places to find victims, avoid risk of detection, etc. Over the 'career' of a serial offender, the observable patterns of offending seem to change in the geographical record: local attacks characterizing one phase, wider-ranging activity other phases.

You might now consider what interviews with convicted offenders would add to the study. How would their accounts test or elaborate theories of offending? And how might this developing area of theory, linking personality, and environmental psychology, feed back into the prevention and detection of crime?

The evidence tends to show large and enduring correlations of personality and behaviour across situations where the researcher has used either Q- or R-data, i.e. when people rate themselves or rate others using broad trait terms.

Yet when 'ongoing behaviour in specific situations is sampled objectively by different objective measures' (in other words, when we are using T-data), the correlations tend to be much smaller.

Let us consider some examples of each type of data.

LONGITUDINAL STUDIES   Q- and R-data were the bases of Block's much-cited LONGITUDINAL STUDIES (for example, 1971), often cited in textbooks because they apparently show how consistent are the manifestations of personality even in those years of change that stretch from early adolescence through into adulthood. Block asked teachers and friends to rate students they knew well, first when the students were at junior high school level, then again at senior high, and finally as young adults. Each rating was on a series of character traits, and we can take the findings on ratings of impulsiveness as representative of the whole. Block found a correlation of 0.57 between the rating of individual boys' impulsiveness at junior high and at senior; with a 0.59 correlation between senior high and young-adult ratings on this trait. (A correlation of 0.57 would indicate a very high degree of stability of ratings, over time.)

This sounds impressively high: amid all life's changes, people were still rated as consistently as this over something like a ten-year period. (And you might like to note that they were also similarly consistent over this period when rating themselves for impulsiveness.)

But are these ratings really to be regarded as summaries of the individual's actual behaviour over this period? Or does the R-data technique measure enduring reputations? Reputations, stereotypes, images: all of these are remarkably resistant to change, even in the face of contrary evidence. Elsewhere in this book, you have seen how unreliable eyewitness testimony can be, and how subject it can be to EFFORT AFTER MEANING. If this is true of witnesses describing one recent specific event, how much more true is it likely to be where one is asked to describe a person, to rate the generality of an individual's behaviour over time?

EFFORT AFTER MEANING

Traits, in the eye of the beholder, can be seen as *our* explanations for behaviour, rather than *the* explanations: which is to say that we summarize our expectations

Plate 14.5 Boy playing with a car
Source: Collections/Anthea Sieveking.

by using a trait label ('John is a confident person'), but to then explain his confidence by resort to this trait of 'confidence' is to be circular (traits as summaries rather than causes). But are we even overstating their value as worthwhile summaries?

Mischel challenged the assumptions of such personality theorists by getting back to the data itself. Quite how consistent are behaviours over even quite a short period? Take what would seem quite a central trait, moral behaviour. Most people would probably agree with you if you said that children could reliably be ranked from the most amoral through to the most consistently morally pure!

Yet if you were to set up a series of practical tests (T-data) of how a set of children would respond in a series of moral choice situations, you would find that this rank ordering was not consistent across situations Early this century, Hartshorne and May (1928) worked with thousands of children in many situations: around the home, at parties and in athletic competitions. In each situation the experimenters contrived to offer the children chances to mis-

Plate 14.6 Child with plate of marshmallows
Source: Roger Scruton.

behave, by lying or cheating or stealing. Prior to these field tests of moral behaviour each child had filled in a number of self-report questionnaires about their moral thinking, and this Q-data showed considerable internal consistency. But out in the field, children showed much less consistency: one child might be sternly moral at home, but willing to cheat at one particular sports meeting. Another might be dishonest at class, but fair in sports and Sunday School. This, Hartshorne and May suggested, was not evidence that human beings were 'capricious' in their behaviours, but that the consistencies that were there, were more subtle and situation-related than trait theorists realized.

How does one conceptualize the situation?

Mischel's own work (1983) on children's moral behaviour and their self-control has, more recently, shown it is the individual's conceptualization of the situation which is central. Sit one child down in front of a packet of tempting sweets, tell him/her to wait, and then leave them alone: temptation at some point is likely to prevail.

But now transform the situation, cognitively, by getting the child to imagine that, for example, the marshmallows are fluffy white clouds, and the child now has a device for delaying.

Mischel's results show that it is what is in children's heads, and not what is actually in front of them, that determines their ability to delay a reward. And in life, instead of an experimenter's instructions transforming the situation, it is more often the person's own thoughts which produce the transforms. Now perhaps you can see why the prediction of behaviour with even a 'full' knowledge of personality and situation will always be a subtle art.

Replacing single-act with multiple-act criteria

Nowadays, many psychologists would respond to all these challenges to traditional ideas of personality by using a MULTIPLE-ACT CRITERION – a pooled combination of many behaviours deemed to be related to a particular trait or characteristic; and by using many observers. Compare this with a SINGLE-ACT TECHNIQUE, where we use a single behaviour to be measured as if actions here will generalize to all similar situations. By aggregating one's data, and measuring the person's behaviour across many behavioural acts, one gains a more reliable measuring tool.

MULTIPLE-ACT CRITERION

SINGLE–ACT TECHNIQUE

So where do we stand? We are not denying that techniques like multiple-act do not reveal broadly described stable differences between individuals. Nor yet are we seeing all behaviours within any one situation as being uniform: there will be variations within the general script for the situation.

Person-in-situation

Sophisticated trait research is now taking situations seriously into account, and indeed much work is now done under the interactionalist banner: behaviour being seen as a result of person-in-situation.

How then to characterize situations? You may wish to refer back to the environmental psychology chapter for a consideration of this, reminding yourself that there we saw situations as sociophysical. Here, in the chapter on personality, our goal must be to characterize types of situation as they interact with differences in individual personality.

One way of assessing types of situation – see Bem and Funder (1978) – starts precisely with the interaction, by characterizing situations by the personality types who function most effectively in them. Another approach has been to attempt situation-measuring scales, such as ERI: the Environmental Response Inventory; and its equivalent for children, CERI.

So far, there has not been enough of the (potentially time-consuming) direct study of persons-in-situations. One promising line has, again, come from Mischel and colleagues. With Shoda (Mischel & Shoda 1995), he has mounted a series of studies of children's camps. In these, they had observers rate *interpersonal situations* – such as being praised or blamed by adults, being teased by other children on the camp. Then they separately rated child reactions to these situations (were they accepting or rejecting of blame?; etc.). As you can imagine, over the summer of the camps, there were many occasions on which each child found her/himself in each of the situations listed; and on each occasion, the observers noted and classified the child's reaction. The research question is then formulated thus:

> What is the probability that a particular social situation was followed by a particular response in each child?

IF–THEN PROFILE

The data from these observations is then plotted in what Mischel calls an IF–THEN PROFILE for each child on each type of behaviour.

The analysis of this data showed convincing stable individual differences.

THE COGNITIVE-SOCIAL APPROACH TO PERSONALITY

Plotting these conditionals, the if … then's, of behaviour is located within what has come to be called THE COGNITIVE-SOCIAL APPROACH TO PERSONALITY, in which personality studies have joined the cognitive revolution of the rest of psychology. We are thus emphasizing the individual's expectations and hypotheses about the social world. Stimuli are not just stimuli; they can be cognitively transformed, just as you will remember that the children's marshmallows became clouds, and were thus less immediately tempting.

How is a situation encoded or understood by the individual?

Take a personal thought experiment: compare your first day in college with the college you know now. Essentially the same physical environment, yet your early bewilderment has (I am sure) been entirely replaced by an appreciation of the behaviour settings that college affords; and of one's roles within the college; as well as the expected values, attitudes and behaviours that exist among one's social groups, etc. Your encoding of the situation when you first arrived at college probably drew upon similar situations you had earlier known; but was in no way as sharp or well attuned to the local nuances of meaning as it has become since.

In addition to local strategies, individuals also bring to a situation their own relatively stable explanatory strategies: see the discussion of attributional styles in chapter 11. These will shape the expectancies of what is likely to happen in a particular situation, and how far they may be able to influence it: optimism/pessimism; potency; perceived competence; etc. If the modern cognitive-social approach stresses individuals' subjective value systems, self-regulatory systems and perceived self-competencies, then there are precursors of this emphasis within Kelly's attribution theory, and Rotter's EXPECTANCY–VALUE APPROACH, as well as a close parallel in Ajzen's work in the field of attitudes, where the 'theory of planned behaviour' has shown that the individual's beliefs about their past competence can predict how their attitudes translate into their future behaviour. (See the chapter 11 for background on all these concepts.)

EXPECTANCY–VALUE APPROACH

The view of the person in modern personality studies

The view of the person that you will have noticed emerging as we have moved through a review modern personality studies is of an active individual, who is construing and then processing social information; who is responsive to the nuances of social situations, and who adjusts their self-presentation to match. We are witnessing the coming together of two erstwhile separate fields of psychology: personality psychology and social psychology (see Krahé 1992 for an extended discussion). Both fields have realized that their main constructs are just that: attitude, personality, traits, social influence, etc. are constructs which enable us, both as social scientists and in our everyday lives, to make sense and order out of a complex diversity of events. You will also realize that the study of situations within environmental psychology (see chapter 13) has a major contribution to make here.

As we have been considering personality in this chapter, you will have been reminded of discussion in earlier chapters of such constructs as: self-identity; self-esteem; self-control; self-focus. Individuals differ in the extent to which they are self-aware: Duval (e.g., Duval et al. 1992) has suggested that the highly self-aware person tends to be more likely to impose personal standards on themselves than the less self-aware; and as a result, tends to be more honest, helpful and harder working. Topics such as aggression and altruism now demand an integrated social/personality approach to conceptualize them, and this may well also demand an awareness of how the adult person has developed from childhood experiences, and in a cultural context. To take an example, Gilligan (1982) has argued that men and women may achieve and define their identities in importantly different ways:

Box 14.5   How Men and Women View Aggression

There is a growing body of evidence that, in Western societies at least, men tend to hold an instrumental social-representational view of aggression, which sees it as a functional act which allows one person to impose control over another; while women view it in *expressive* terms, as breakdown of self-control over anger.

If this is so, how can we account for the difference?

Do the differences arise from basic personality differences between the genders, or from social role (for example, the occupational roles)?

Anne Campbell and Steven Muncer (1994) designed a study to examine the relative contribution of these personality and role factors. Their subjects were drawn from the armed forces and from the nursing profession. These were asked to complete the Personal Attributes Questionnaire, and a psychometric measure of their view of aggression as expressive or instrumental.

Previous literature (e.g. Gilligan 1982) had suggested a basis for the expressive/instrumental difference in female/male traits:

Men have been characterized by: self-assertion; independence; competitiveness; and ability to stand up under pressure.

Women by being more interpersonally orientated; devoting self to others; kind; understanding of others.

Alice Eagly (1987) has, however, in her social role theory, argued that occupational roles typically occupied by men incorporate and legitimate elements of aggressiveness, whereas typically female occupations emphasize a caregiving, non-aggressive role.

So you will realize the logic behind Campbell and Muncer's study design: measure the personality and beliefs of both males and females in typically male and female occupations. They used the masculinity (M) and femininity (F) scales from the Personal Attributes Questionnaire as measures of 'gendered personality' and their own Expagg scale, on which subjects had to select one of two responses for each item, expressive or instrumental aspects of aggression.

They found that occupational role was the strongest predictor of scores on the way people represented aggression on the Expagg. Thus, independent of their sex, men and women in the military thought of aggression one way, and those in nursing the other.

However, remember that only small percentages in the military are female, and in nursing, male. What might this suggest? Perhaps selective entry into the occupations by those already closer to that occupation's norms?

And note that Campbell and Muncer found that the men in the army showed a particularly instrumental view of aggression, well ahead of the army's women, with all of the nurses way behind. What does this suggest? Males and females in the army are both in a profession which legitimizes aggression, but may have different opportunities to realize this. They may also differ in the amount of power they can exercise within their job.

men define and value themselves mostly in terms of achievements and autonomy; women . . . through close relationships with people.

Gilligan suggests that from childhood, male and female experiences differ significantly: male and female children are systematically treated in different ways, and as a result their expectancies of social interaction styles diverge. In Gilligan's phrase, they develop different voices.

So – psychology should see both persons and situations as being important in the explanation of behaviours; and should reject as unhelpful those questions which seek to separate or oppose them: for people and situations interact.

On some occasions it will be found that situations predominate in our explanations, while on others, individual variation will predominate; but in the

Plate 14.7 Ranks of students in a lecture theatre
Source: Ace Photo Library.

majority, an interactive account should be sought. As we saw in the 'Environmental Psychology' chapter, some behaviours are better explained in terms of the situation. Here, the scripts, the shared expectations, the common construal of roles, etc. are all better predictors of behaviour than would be anything based on personality variables. Think back to our example of lecture-room behaviour.

At the other extreme, where situations are very unstructured, we may attempt an explanation based on the individual's characteristics alone. But consider even your most apparently unstructured time, away from college's formal settings, just 'being with friends'. Even here, careful analysis would surely uncover some sets of shared expectations, behaviours, and so forth.

For situations differ in the prescriptiveness of behaviours, and hence in the variety of behaviours an observer would see. Now, individuals as part of their social and cultural learning, both during childhood and afterwards, learn the range of expected and appropriate behaviours; and can, if skilfully questioned, indicate what this social knowledge consists of. As Garfinkel (1967) once suggested, one of the quickest and most dramatic ways of eliciting these expectations of role-appropriate behaviours is to start acting in ways appropriate for a completely different situation: going home after term, and acting out the role of a paying lodger in your own family home. What reactions would you get?

But how do people experience themselves?

Phenomenology and the personal approach to personality

Common to many of the approaches reviewed thus far in the chapter is an external view of the person, rather than an emphasis on how individuals themselves see their individuality. This is clearly true of those approaches which rely upon behavioural observation as data source. But consider how it is also true of those approaches whose database at first looks more subjective: ratings by others; ratings of self; self-generated accounts of dreams and childhood; etc. The data themselves may be more or less freely generated by the individual (or by their acquaintances), but the interpretation, classification and analyses of these data use external, prior-established standard criteria, rather than ones which grow out of the data. Often, standardization is the aim, so that people's scores can be compared; and, as we have seen, such an aim characterizes much scientific, explanatory research.

However, not all those working in the field of personality have such aims: for a variety of reasons they instead wish to understand the person's own world-view in their own words. How to do this, without imposing a standardized data-collection vehicle, or shaping up the person's account to fit the researcher's schema, and then interpreting individuality into a standard set of categories?

As chapter 11 has shown, in recent years, social psychology has witnessed an enormous growth in research interest in the self and self-systems. Some personality theorists were there first, and you are coming to psychology at the time when these two fields are about to achieve exciting synthesis.

How can we explore subjective experiences? How can we make statements about an individual's self-systems without, as researchers, losing this individuality?

Within personality psychology, there exists a group of writers who as phenomenological theorists take as their main focus the individual's expression of their own world-view. You will notice as we review a small selection of this important but diverse field that what they have in common is:

1. a rejection of the determinism that characterizes many other personality theories (e.g. early trauma in dynamic theories; biological underpinning of traits for Eysenck; etc.), and hence their accounts of human motivations;
2. an alternative view of the person, as an active, interpreting experiencer of the world;
3. an emphasis on the individual's current world: their current circumstances, relationships and roles. (Contrast this with the emphasis that dynamic theorists, for instance, place on the past events of life.)

An historical account of this field would have to acknowledge the early thinking of existential philosophers and essayists; and also the advocacy of major founding figures of psychology: William James, C. G. Jung, G. H. Mead, and Kurt Lewin.

We will here consider the influential work of the somewhat more recent writers: Carl Rogers, George Kelly and Abraham Maslow. Their mid-twentieth-century work has inspired contemporary approaches to social understanding, as well as to therapy and family relations; and has given rise to an altogether more positive and optimistic view of possibilities for the person.

Carl Rogers: celebrating and actualizing individuality

Why should the individual's unique way of viewing the world matter to the psychologist? To the novelist; to the person him/herself and to their friends, yes – but why to the psychologist?

Rogers says because this unique view of the world helps to explain behaviour: how you interpret the world explains how you will respond to it. What the person's 'internal frames of reference' are determines the person's actions: and therefore the psychologist has a clear interest.

Rogers talks of the person as striving to fulfil, of ACTUALIZING THE SELF. Whereas other psychologists tend to explain behaviour by a series of separately described motivations, Rogers sees a wholeness:

ACTUALIZING THE SELF

> The organism has one basic tendency and striving – to actualize, maintain and enhance the experiencing organism.

Until these last few words, about the 'experiencing organism', one could almost have been hearing any *biologist's* description of a species: 'the barnacle, by all its behaviours, is designed to . . . ' But the essential difference is that such a species operates and adapts to the world in a uniform way: whatever its subjective experiences are, they do not seem to lead to any great varieties of outcome. In contrast, humans manifestly react in many different ways to the 'same' situations because, for them, they are not the same.

Does the barnacle start from a perception of itself as strong or weak? Valued by others, or worthless? Competent or naive in the ways of the world? As Rogers shows, human self-images are key filters in behaviour.

Rogers makes the point that, for some individuals, this image of the self is in harmony with the organism; for other individuals these two systems can be in opposition. When they are in opposition, the individual may seek to maintain the self-concept against the reality which the organism is facing. An important part of this reality is the regard with which others hold us.

From his extensive clinical experience, Rogers confirmed that there is a universal need to receive positive regard from important others. But how do these others give us this regard? On some occasions, we receive positive regard for the positively evaluated actions we have performed: a lecturer praises our coursework, for example. Here, the acceptance is conditional. Or we may receive regard unconditionally: we are positively regarded just for who we are.

Where there is a lack of harmony between self and organism, this may reach a

CLIENT-CENTRED
THERAPY point where a therapeutic intervention is called for. In CLIENT-CENTRED THERAPY (also known as person-centred or Rogerian therapy), we see the above theories of personal needs being brought into action. Thus, the therapist:

- views the client as intrinsically good, and thus capable of self-development;
- offers a sense of unconditional acceptance and regard for the client;
- establishes an accepting, unconditional relationship.

The client:

- as a result, becomes less afraid to face and accept their own feelings and experiences, which may have been denied or distorted to protect the self-concept;
- and, we hope, experiences personal growth and self-actualization.

Rogers, whether as theorist or therapist, stresses the 'reality and significance of human choice' as much as any other writer – and considerably more than most do!

George Kelly: eliciting personal constructions of the world

As we have seen earlier, psychologists often approach personality study with a system of categories which they have derived from theory, or from earlier data (or from both). These they impose via questionnaires, interview schedules, tests or whatever. Now, their 'subjects' manifestly can and do fill these in, respond, etc., to the satisfaction of the psychologist; who goes away from the encounter, feeling that this measurement has captured the essence of the person.

But this is to ignore the diversity of ways that people could have told the psychologist about themselves, and their friends, and their world-view. Contrast the (apparent) certainty of the pencil tick as a response on a closed-ended questionnaire with the range of responses that the same person would give during an open-ended and unstructured discussion on the same topics as had been in the questionnaire. Try it with some of your friends: you will never be able to think quite the same about simple questionnaires again.

Apply this approach to studying personality via people's world-views. Instead of arriving with a closed-ended set of categories, why not ask each individual for their own dimensions or categories?

For, as George Kelly argued, the psychologist in explaining behaviour is in effect only doing at a professional level what all of us in our own lives have been doing all the time: explaining our own and others' behaviour. This could well be seen as a central life skill, not just the satisfying of curiosity. We can anticipate and respond appropriately, and so influence, cajole, appease, etc. No one of these could work, nor would social life be possible, if we did not operate a detailed 'theory of mind'.

But – and here is Kelly's distinct contribution – each of these 'people-as-scientists' is operating by their own set of analytic rules. How does the individual construe, or understand, the world and all the social events therein? What are their personal dimensions for understanding other people? And how could we as scientists ourselves study these personal constructs without then crushing this individuality in our data-gathering?

The answer from Kelly is: let us find a way of eliciting these constructs while they are talking about familiar persons in their life: we would offer no leading suggestions. The method Kelly adopted was this. Ask the person to nominate a number of people who are significant to them: one can suggest a number of likely role-titles – a parent; a teacher; a close friend; etc.; plus the self.

Then ask the person to say in what ways these people are similar to each other, and how they differ. This is done by working successively through the list, picking persons A, B and C, and asking how two of them resemble each other and differ from the third.

'A and C are always cheerful, and B tends to be depressed.'

Next, repeat the process for persons B, C and D:

'Well, B and C are selfless whereas D is a go-getter.'

And so on, through all possible triplets, generating these bipolar constructs (Cheerful–Depressed; Selfless–Go-getter; etc.). After all combinations have been completed, you will have facilitated the person in generating a whole list of their own dimensions for talking about people (and themselves). But it is likely that in this list you would find some constructs repeated, or at least some apparent synonyms. The question then becomes: does the individual use all of these dimensions to judge the world, or are some of them effectively the same? To answer this, ask the person to take each construct, and to apply them successively to each person on the grid. When they have worked right through, saying how much each construct describes each person, you will then have the data to ascertain whether some of the dimensions are being used as effective synonyms. Finally, from a comparison of these patterns on the grid (for example, by computer program such as the purpose-designed and charmingly named INGRID), you can discover the factor structure of the person's constructs.

Bonarius (1965) and other researchers quickly followed up Kelly's initial insights, and gave them a firmer empirical foundation. Their research has shown there to be a considerable consistency over time in a person's construct system; and Kelly was indeed justified in seeing this novel way into a person's world-view as a contribution to the PHENOMENOLOGY of personality. Starting from a person-centred method of eliciting the data, we, as scientists, now can finish up with a measurable, repeatable data set which we can then

PHENOMENOLOGY

Plate 14.8 Role play
Source: Collections/Sandra
Lousada.

analyse for complexity, structure, similarity to structure of others, change over time, etc.

But, you may ask, are these constructs true of the target persons? This, emphasizes Kelly, is not the point: instead, we should see them as being the dimensions the person finds convenient for their purposes.

REPERTORY GRID

And this would also be the approach of the therapist using a Kellyian REPERTORY GRID; first use the grid method to elicit the constructs and then use interviews to elaborate these constructs. If this reveals concerns, obsessions and ill-fitting constructs, then these can be explored with the person. Psychotherapy, if needed, would then provide a setting in which the person can elaborate their constructs, test them through for their implications, and set about modifying them. Kelly himself found that role-play was a useful technique with clients: people developed an understanding of other, key people's subjective worlds, by role-playing them and then asking questions. How does your partner see the world? How do they see you?

And Kelly's own philosophy enables him to predict change: if people are indeed able to construe themselves and others in alternative ways, then change is possible. (Similarly, one can show that, in the realm of people's political constructs, people with elaborated and self-aware systems are much more able to contemplate such divergent acts as voting tactically than are those people who view the political world as simply dimensioned.)

Abraham Maslow: getting one's needs in order

Rogers, Kelly and other phenomenologists stress the potentials of people: towards fulfilment, self-as-experienced, individuality of world-view, openness, awareness. Sometimes their approaches have been criticized for being a celebration of self, rather than a systematic use of data about the self (and self-systems) to offer explanations of behaviour. For a discussion of this, see chapter 11.

One figure who overlaps both the celebratory and the scientific approaches to the self as personality is Abraham Maslow. The language that Maslow uses is similar to that of others whom I have called celebratory writers: he talks of 'being in touch'; of the possibility of 'total fulfilment'; and of 'actualizing the potential self'.

His contribution to the science of personality is to bring an order to what may seem a complex and competing set of needs that the individual experiences. These needs, Maslow indicates, can be logically arranged into a hierarchy, from the most basic to the highest, most abstract (and most distinctly human).

And the existence of this hierarchy can be empirically demonstrated, in that the basic needs:

> physiological needs
> the need for safety and security

are initially most powerful in shaping behaviour; and only when these are at least partly satisfied does the striving move up the hierarchy to:

> love and belongingness
> self-esteem
> self-actualization.

Social membership, which we can see as being included in 'belongingness', is the means of moving upwards towards self-esteem – for instance, social acknowledgement may lead to the recognition by the self of own social competencies; and it is through this recognition that the final stage – actualization – can occur, as one realizes one's achievements. These may be creative, social, sporting, spiritual; with sometimes, as Maslow notes, an identifiable ecstatic experience, a 'non-striving state of perfection', which has been labelled the peak experience.

Who is truly self-actualized and fully functioning? Maslow found it useful in his thinking and writing to identify exemplars in both public life – Beethoven, Einstein, Lincoln – and from among those he personally knew and admired.

This leads one to ask whether one could specify a common set of attributes characterizing such truly actualized people. From Maslow's suggestions, we can offer the following list:

1. They are accurate in their perceptions of reality.
2. They accept the world, other people and themselves.
3. They have a broad perspective, which they bring to problems outside themselves.
4. While they are spontaneous and natural, they also require privacy.
5. They are little dependent upon popularity, and their satisfactions are predominantly internal.
6. Their responses to the natural and social worlds have a continuing freshness, with, at times, a feeling of at oneness with nature which approaches the mystical.
7. They may have a similar sense of identification with humanity as a whole.
8. They are respectful of others and lack prejudice.
9. Their ethical principles run deep.
10. Their creativity comes from their freshness of approach; and from their relative detachment from their surrounding culture.

Self-actualization is, when you survey these characteristics, what many of the world's philosophies and religions are indicating we should be striving for as mature human beings: both a detachment from the immediate rewards of the world, and yet an identification with humankind and with the world as a whole. You will also recognize, at the level of personal functioning, that Maslow's description of the self-actualizer picks up many other writers' prescriptions for mental health: from self-acceptance and tolerance of others to a lack of worry over minor details, and a personal commitment to issues of major importance.

DEFICIENCY MOTIVES

GROWTH MOTIVES

Maslow's approach to motivation has been to distinguish between the DEFICIENCY MOTIVES, those which reduce the needs lower in the hierarchy (reducing one's hunger and thirst, obtaining security), and the GROWTH MOTIVES, which move one up to the higher parts of the hierarchy. His approach has been enthusiastically received and developed by some organizational psychologists (see chapter 17), given that work is seen as one of the most important means of self-fulfilment.

Plate 14.9 Boy playing with cars
Source: Collections/Anthea Sieveking.

The impact of the phenomenologists upon wider psychology

At the outset, when asking why there were so many strands to the psychology of personality, we stressed that the answer lay, at least in part, in the uses that each theorist intended for their theory: were they scientists, with a focus on predicting and explaining, or therapists, with client change in mind? Which tradition did they come from: positivist, existentialist, eclectic? Were they working with or on their people/subjects? (The very terminology they choose is significant.)

Phenomenological approaches to personality, you will not be surprised to learn, have had the least impact upon quantitative, lab-based experimental studies; a greater impact on social psychology, where for example, self-research has benefited from its insights; and an even greater impact on some areas of clinical psychology, counselling, and community psychology where humanistic therapies at both individual and group level have taken their place in the range of widely used techniques. (Evaluation of their efficacy in comparison to other approaches will be considered in chapter 16; suffice it to say here that, amidst the testimony of enthusiastic advocates of what sounds like the most positively patient-centred therapies, there is some evidence of negative outcomes in some situations.)

▨ The Future of Personality: Learning from the Mistakes of the Past ▨

David Magnusson, one of the contemporary visionaries of the field, has reminded us of both its achievements and its problems (e.g. Magnusson & Törestad 1992). Whereas other fields of psychology – for instance, cognition or neuropsychology – tend to concentrate on a single aspect of the individual, the special contribution of personality psychology is to develop theories of the whole person. As we have seen, personality psychology is now realizing its common cause with social and environmental psychologies (see Walsh et al. 1992). We can hope for still further integration of its way of approaching humans as whole people to infuse other areas of psychology in the future.

CHAPTER SUMMARY

1   The field of personality contains an almost bewildering variety of approaches, from the biological to the phenomenological; and within each, a range of theories. This variety reflects both the intellectual origins of each theory, and its potential field of application, whether clinical, scientific, etc.

2   As an exemplar of the clinic-based approaches, the chapter first examines the assumptions underlying Freud's psychoanalytic theory: including the hidden nature of many of our motivations. From this, it follows that ingenious and indirect methods of exploration of the personal dynamics must be used: these for Freud would include the analysis of dreams, and of everyday slips in speech, and the insights from free association techniques. The scientific status of such data is then discussed.

3   As an example of a more scientific range of approaches, trait theories are next considered: these rate personality characteristics on a range of dimensions, with data usually derived from either self-ratings, or ratings of the person by others; and much less often derive from the direct observation of behaviour.

4   But how many dimensions? Although there has

been considerable disagreement between theorists, arising mainly from procedural and statistical differences, there is now an emergent consensus that five dimensions can capture most of the variance.

5   Much of the foregoing is predicated on the stability of the personality, both across time and across situations. Now, whereas there can be impressive stability in self-ratings and the ratings of others of a person across time, there will also be considerable variations in the observed behaviour of the same person at the same point in time as they move between situations, each situation having its own set of expected behaviours that most participants will adopt.

6   Rather than relying on a single behavioural act as the criterion for assessing personality, we can sum across many acts deemed to be indicative of a particular trait, and make use of many observers.

7   Person-in-situation, rather than either personality- or situation-determined accounts of behaviour would now seem to have their advantages for both the clinical and the scientific interests in personality. This view will emphasize the active, situation-construing individual, and is now coming to characterize current social psychology.

8   How people experience themselves – the focus of phenomenological psychology – then becomes highly relevant to the future progress of personality psychology, having previously been confined to one therapeutic tradition.

9   Rejecting a deterministic and past-oriented view of personality, theorists such as Rogers, Kelly and Maslow emphasize the individual's understanding of their current and future worlds; their acceptance by their fellow human beings; and the level of fulfilment of their perceived needs.

10 Implications for personal change, reconstrual of the world, and realization of one's own potential flow from such an approach.

Further Work

1. Should we see personalities as unique wholes or as variations on universal themes and dimensions?

2. Do we remain pretty much the same personalities from childhood on? Or are there aspects of life stages which come to outweigh individual differences? OR: Are we consistent in our core behaviours and beliefs regardless of where we are or with whom, or do social and physical situations override and obscure any longer-term stabilities?

3. If psychological research finds strong evidence of variability in an individual's behaviour across time and place, does this do damage to popular (and some scientific) concepts of personality?

4. Discuss the potential advantages of studying personality longitudinally. What problems – practical, ethical and theoretical – might be encountered?

5. Has psychology lost powerful potential insights into the motivation of the individual since the majority of personality theorists turned away from Freud?

6. 'In the psychodynamic approach, the motive is the chief unit, unconscious conflicts are the processes of greatest interest, and the clinical judge is the favoured instrument' (Mischel 1994; see Further Reading below). Contrast this with the phenomenological approach, where the person's view, and not the hypotheses of the psychologist, is predominant.

7. If you were seeking personal understanding, would you seek out a different tradition of psychology than when you sought a scientific account of behaviour?

▨ Further Reading ▨

Ewen, R. B. (1993) *An Introduction to the Theories of Personality*. Hillsdale, NJ: Erlbaum.

> At general textbook level, we have clearly not the space to even list the full range of theories that have been proposed, let alone elaborate on them. Ewen provides a much fuller (and perhaps less opinionated) view.

Mischel, W. (1994) *Introduction to Personality*. New York: Holt, Rinehart and Winston.

> As this chapter has indicated, one of the most innovative thinkers in the recent history of personality has been Walter Mischel. Despite having a strong position of his own, he has none the less produced a most balanced and lucid textbook.

Barnes, P. (ed.) (1995) *Personal, Social and Emotional Development in Children*. Oxford: Blackwell.

> This book will really help you to link this chapter's treatment of theories of personality with the book's developmental opening chapters.

CHAPTER 15

Intelligence

Mark Blades

CHAPTER AGENDA

- This chapter explores some of the issues related to the concept of intelligence and intelligence testing. The focus will be on the way that the term 'intelligence' has been described and defined by different researchers. This approach is taken because the history of research into intelligence has been dominated by the way that different researchers have defined the concept.

Issues running through the history of intelligence research will be discussed. These include the following:

- How should intelligence be measured? Does a researcher's definition of intelligence influence the way he or she designs a test of intelligence?

- Is intelligence a single factor in each individual which can be measured? Or is 'intelligence' just a convenient label for all the different and varying abilities that an individual might possess?

- Have traditional definitions of intelligence been too narrow? Or should 'intelligence' also take into account a person's social skills, musical talent, and sporting prowess?

- Is a person's intelligence inherited? Or is it the result of their environment and education?

▨ Defining Intelligence ▨

'Intelligence' is not an easy concept to define. You may want to pause for a moment and think of a half-dozen different definitions of the word intelligence, or alternatively think about a few activities which could be described as 'intelligent' behaviours. When people are asked to do this, most people produce one or, at the most, two definitions of the word. Despite the fact that everybody uses the word 'intelligence', most people find it not only surprising to be asked to define it, but also very difficult to do so.

It is also notable that the types of definitions which are given by different people vary quite a lot. This is what Sternberg et al. (1981) found when they gave people a blank piece of paper and asked them to list the kind of behaviours which characterized 'intelligence', 'academic intelligence', 'everyday intelligence' and 'unintelligence' – they collected 250 different types of behaviour under those headings. The behaviours most frequently listed as intelligent included items such as 'reasons logically and well'; 'reads widely'; 'keeps an open mind', and 'reads with high comprehension'. The behaviours which were most often given

LAY-PEOPLE'S CATEGORIZATION OF AN IDEALLY INTELLIGENT PERSON	EXPERT'S CATEGORIZATION OF AN IDEALLY INTELLIGENT PERSON
Practical problem solving	**Verbal intelligence**
reasons logically and well	displays a good vocabulary
identifies connections among ideas	reads with high comprehension
sees all aspects of a problem	displays curiosity
keeps an open mind	is intellectually curious
responds thoughtfully to others' ideas	sees all aspects of a problem
sizes up situations well	learns rapidly
gets to the heart of problems	appreciates knowledge for its own sake
interprets information accurately	is verbally fluent
makes good decisions	listens to all sides of an argument
goes to original sources for information	displays alertness
poses problems in an optimal way	thinks deeply
is a good source of ideas	shows creativity
perceives implied assumptions	converses easily on variety of subjects
listens to all sides of an argument	reads widely
identifies connections between ideas	likes to read
	identifies connections between ideas
Verbal ability	
speaks clearly and articulately	**Problem-solving ability**
is verbally fluent	applies knowledge to problem at hand
knowledgeable about a particular field	makes good decisions
studies hard	poses problems in optimal way
reads with high comprehension	displays common sense
reads widely	displays objectivity
deals effectively with people	solves problems well
writes without difficulty	plans ahead
sets aside time for reading	has good intuitions
displays a good vocabulary	gets to the heart of problems
accepts social norms	appreciates truth
tries new things	considers the end result of actions
	approaches problems thoughtfully
Social competence	
accepts others for what they are	**Practical intelligence**
admits mistakes	sizes up situations well
displays interest in the world at large	determines how to achieve goals
on time for appointments	displays awareness of immediate world
has social conscience	displays interest in world at large
thinks before speaking and doing	
displays curiosity	
does not make snap judgements	
makes fair judgements	
assesses well the problem at hand	
sensitive to others' needs and desires	
frank and honest with self and others	
interested in immediate environment	

Figure 15.1 Examples of the behaviours given by lay-people and experts when describing an 'ideally intelligent person'.
Sternberg et al., 'People's conception of intelligence' in *Journal of Personality and Social Psychology*, 1 (Copyright © 1981 American Psychological Association. Reprinted with permission).

as typical of unintelligent behaviour were items like 'does not display curiosity', or 'does not tolerate diversity of views'.

In a second survey, Sternberg et al. (1981) asked 'lay-people' (i.e. people from a variety of backgrounds, but specifically not university students or researchers) to choose which of the 250 behaviours were characteristic of an 'ideally intelligent person', and found that the behaviours which were selected could be grouped into three main categories: practical problem-solving ability; verbal ability; and social competence. The typical behaviours which were included within those three categories are shown in figure 15.1. Sternberg et al. also asked 'experts' (who were all working in universities and carrying out research into intelligence) to use the list of 250 behaviours to describe an ideally intelligent person. The experts categorized such a person in a slightly different way from the lay-persons; their responses could be categorized under the headings of verbal intelligence, problem-solving ability and practical intelligence.

Despite the different groupings of behaviours there was an overall similarity in the categorization by both lay-people and experts – problem solving was seen as an important factor in relation to all aspects of intelligence and practical abilities were also seen as important. However, Sternberg et al. pointed out that there was a difference in emphasis in lay-people's and experts' views of intelligence – some behaviours received more emphasis from the lay-people (for instance, 'acting politely', 'displaying patience', 'expressing emotions appropriate to the situation') and these can be described as interpersonal abilities – they are ones which reflect social competence. In contrast the experts put more emphasis on behaviours such as 'showing flexibility in thought and action', displaying curiosity and reasoning logically – all of which may be called intrapersonal abilities – they are ones which reflect a person's own competence and motivation. What is most striking about the differences between experts and lay-people is the emphasis of the former on social intelligence – this is not an aspect of intelligence which is directly assessed by traditional tests of intelligence; nor is it one which has been included in the definitions of intelligence put forward by the most influential researchers into intelligence (see Box 15.1).

Sternberg's analysis of different descriptions of intelligence is important because it shows just how many different behaviours can be considered as reflections of intelligence. This is not to say that there will, or should, ever be a single and agreed definition of the term. It is likely that intelligence is a word or concept which will always be used in different ways by different people. However, its variety of meanings is one of the main problems in discussing intelligence, and most of the rest of this chapter will be concerned with the ways that researchers have tried to clarify the nature of intelligence.

One other point should be made here. Both the descriptions collected by Sternberg, and the formal definitions of intelligence put forward by researchers, have been collected from Europe and North America. 'Intelligence' may be described with different emphases in different cultures. Wober (1974) examined the concept of intelligence in Uganda and found that it was seen less as an internal

Box 15.1   Some Researchers' Descriptions of Intelligence

Galton: intelligence is a natural ability which qualifies a man to perform acts which lead to reputation and climb the path that leads to eminence.

Binet: intelligence is a faculty which includes good sense, practical sense, initiative and the ability to adapt to circumstances; it is the ability to judge well, understand well, and to reason well.

Thurstone: intelligence is the capacity to inhibit instinctive judgements and instead, to consider different responses, and to learn from experience.

Wechsler: intelligence is the global capacity of the individual to act purposefully, to think rationally, and to deal effectively with the environment.

Gardner: intelligence is the ability to solve problems or to fashion products which are valued in one or more cultural settings.

Sternberg: intelligent behaviour is shaping one's environment; dealing effectively with novel tasks; and employing appropriate meta-components, performance components, and knowledge-acquisition components.

The above descriptions simply summarize the formal definitions of intelligence put forward by some of the researchers who are discussed in this chapter. Even though most of the descriptions of intelligence can be categorized under a few headings (for example, descriptions which emphasize cognitive abilities, and ones which stress learning and adaptation) the variety of descriptions indicates the lack of any single agreed definition of intelligence.

aspect of a person, and more as a public and external characteristic. According to Wober (1974: 267), intelligence was 'a public spirited orientation of the mind', with connotations which include the idea of shared knowledge and wisdom applied for the benefit of the community. In another survey, Serpell (1977) asked adults in Zambia to explain why they thought specific children were intelligent – the adults not only referred to the children's mental abilities by describing them as clever and wise, but also said that intelligent children were ones who listened to what they were told, could be trusted to carry out what they had been asked to do, and had respect for their elders. Other studies have also found that many cultures place emphasis on trustworthiness and social responsibility (e.g. Super 1983, in Kenya), and this emphasis contrasts with European and American definitions of intelligence which focus primarily on an individual's cognitive abilities rather than a person's behaviour in a social context.

■ The Psychometric Approach to Intelligence ■

PSYCHOMETRIC

The term PSYCHOMETRIC can be translated as 'mental measurement' and covers all those aspects of intelligence research which are concerned with the design and the use of intelligence tests, and related research (such as that into the nature of intelligence) which has been based on the results of intelligence tests.

Intelligence testing focuses on the assessment of individual differences, and was first stimulated by early researchers' interests in discovering ways to quantify differences in peoples' ability (e.g. Galton 1869), but the main reason for the continuing importance of intelligence testing is the practical one of selection.

Effective intelligence tests were first designed to measure individual differences in educational achievement (Binet & Simon 1905); then they were extensively used during the First World War as a way of assessing recruits for appropriate roles in the army; and since then intelligence tests have become endemic. Very few people will get through life without taking one or more intelligence tests, because testing is seen as a convenient (and quick) way to select people for educational courses; for jobs and careers; and, in most European countries, for national service. In other words, the influence of intelligence testing cannot be underestimated (see Gregory 1992).

The psychometric approach also includes the research into the nature of intelligence which is concerned with how different abilities may relate to each other and to intelligence overall. The debate here (at the risk of simplification) is between those researchers who have considered intelligence to be a single general attribute which influences everything which a person does (e.g. Spearman 1927) and those who have argued that rather than a general intelligence, people possess distinct abilities (e.g. Thurstone 1931).

History of intelligence testing

Galton, in England, was the first to attempt the measurement of intelligence. In fact Galton tried to measure a whole range of qualities from female beauty to the boringness of lectures, but he is best known for introducing the idea that intelligence was something that could be quantified. Galton's tests were very much influenced by his own concept of intelligence – he thought of intelligence as an underlying trait which would be manifested in many different aspects of a person's performance. Given this belief, Galton designed a large number of different tests in the expectation that some or many of them could be used to reflect intelligence. The tests included both physical measures such as the capacity of the lungs and the strength of hand squeeze; and behavioural measures such as reaction time (for instance, the speed with which a person responds to a sound). Over a period of several years in the 1880s Galton tested many thousands of people at his 'laboratory' which was set up at London exhibitions and museums (quite often charging people for the pleasure of being tested – one of Galton's innovations which later psychologists have failed to exploit). Galton wanted to identify those tests which best correlated with social status and 'reputation', but was unable to find any relationship between a person's test performance and their social rank.

Despite Galton's failure to find a test which could be used to measure intelligence, other researchers pursued the same aim. James McKeen Cattell (1890) in the United States also designed a series of tests to measure sensory, motor and perceptual processes – for example, he measured how quickly a person's hand could move through a distance of half a metre; the length of time it took to name ten colours; speed of reacting to a sound stimulus; and how well a person could judge a time span of ten seconds. Even more so than Galton, Cattell believed

1. Follows a moving object with the eyes
2. Grasps a small object that is touched
3. Grasps a small object that is seen
4. Recognizes the difference between a square of chocolate and a square of wood
5. Finds and eats a square of chocolate wrapped in paper
6. Executes simple commands and imitates simple gestures
7. Points to familiar objects (e.g. 'show me the cup')
8. Points to objects represented in pictures (e.g. 'put your finger on the window')
9. Names objects in pictures
10. Compares two lines of markedly unequal length
11. Repeats three spoken digits
12. Compares two weights
13. Shows susceptibility to suggestion
14. Defines common words by function
15. Repeats a sentence of fifteen words
16. Tells how two common objects are different (e.g. paper and cardboard)
17. Names from memory as many as possible of 13 objects displayed on a board
18. Reproduces from memory two designs shown for ten seconds
19. Repeats a series of more than three digits
20. Tells how two common objects are alike (e.g. butterfly and flea)
21. Compares two lines of slightly unequal length
22. Compares five blocks to put them in order of weight
23. Indicates which of the previous five weights the examiner has removed
24. Produces rhymes for given words
25. Word completion test
26. Puts three nouns in a sentence (e.g. Paris, river, fortune)
27. Given set of 25 comprehension questions
28. Reverses the hands of a clock
29. After paper folding and cutting, draws the form of the resulting holes
30. Distinguishes abstract words (e.g. boredom and weariness)

Figure 15.2 Items used in the 1905 Binet–Simon scale. Gregory, *Psychological Testing: History, Principles and Applications.* Copyright © 1992 by Allyn & Bacon. Reprinted/ adapted by permission.

that mental energy and bodily energy were inseparable and that measures of physiological performance were appropriate ways to test intelligence. However, when Wissler (1901) used Cattell's measures to test 300 American college students, he found that there was almost no relationship between the students' test performance and their success in college. Wissler's failure to find a relationship led to a decline in the use of sensory, perceptual, and reaction-time tests (though this might have been a premature dismissal of these tests, because more recent researchers have argued that there is a relationship between such measures and intelligence – see below). At the time the rejection of such measures left the way open for the development of other tests of intelligence in the early 1900s.

The introduction of compulsory education in France at the turn of the century resulted in many more children attending school, many of whom performed poorly. The French government realized the need to identify which children required special education, and in response to this need Binet and Simon (1905) designed the first INTELLIGENCE SCALE. Their intelligence scale was designed in a very practical way: they collected already-existing tests of memory, comprehension, vocabulary and reasoning, and invented new ones as appropriate. Then they spent a long time in schools using the tests with pupils with a range of ability to find out which tests distinguished between younger and older children and between good and poor learners. In other words, their selection of test items was based on choosing those items which generated good performance from children rated as bright by their teachers, and poor performance from children who were considered less able by their teachers.

Having identified the most effective tests Binet and Simon listed them in order of difficulty (see figure 15.2). The 30 tests were administered in the order of the list until a child was unable to complete any more of the tests, and the child's performance could be compared to the expected performance of other children of the same age. The use of a single test provided a common measure of performance; it could be administered by a teacher; it was brief; and most important of all, it was successful in distinguishing between children – children who did well on the test were likely to be successful at school, and those who did poorly were likely to be in need of special education. Perhaps it was not surprising that THE BINET–SIMON TEST predicted children's school performance, as each item on the test had been selected precisely because it did differentiate between children of different abilities. In other words, Binet–Simon's test was an excellent predictor of scholastic performance, and served the purpose for which it was designed.

However, as Richardson (1991) has pointed out, knowing that children who do well in school do well in a test like the Binet–Simon test (which is made up mainly of school-based items) does not in itself say anything independently about intelligence; or, put another way – good performance on the Binet–Simon test does not explain *why* a child has a good performance. There may well be the temptation to say that a child has good test performance because he or she has high intelligence, but here, the justification for claiming that the child has high intelligence is based on her good performance on the test. In other words, such reasoning may sometimes be no more than a circular argument – a person does well on a test because they are intelligent; they are intelligent because they do well on a test.

The Binet–Simon test went through a number of revisions: the number of items was increased; it was extended to include adults; and in 1911 it was divided into age levels and every age level had five items in it. It then became possible to discuss performance in terms of specific age levels. If a child completed the items at (for example) the 8-year-old age level (but not the items at the 9-year-old level) she could be said to have a mental level of eight years. This example indicates why intelligence tests are often called scales – a child's intelligence is measured in terms of how many items (or how far 'along' the scale of questions) she answered correctly. What was originally known as 'mental level' quickly became known as MENTAL AGE (MA), and to compare a child's mental age with her actual,

INTELLIGENCE
QUOTIENT

STANFORD–BINET
TEST

LEARNING
DIFFICULTIES

WECHSLER ADULT
INTELLIGENCE
SCALE

chronological, age (CA), a ratio can be calculated by dividing MA by CA and multiplying by 100 to give an INTELLIGENCE QUOTIENT (IQ). For example, a child who achieved the items for a 8-year-old, but had an actual age of 10 years would have an IQ of 80. Given the formula for IQ calculation, an age-appropriate IQ is always 100.

The Binet–Simon scales were revised by other researchers and also translated into other languages. The most extensive revision was by Terman at Stanford University in the United States, and this revision became known as the STANFORD–BINET TEST. The Stanford-Binet was an important IQ test for several reasons: it provided a scale of ninety items which could be used to test all people from individuals with LEARNING DIFFICULTIES to 'superior' adults; there were precise instructions about how to use the test so that it could always be administered in the same way; and examples of acceptable and unacceptable answers to test items were given in a manual so that scoring could be carried out with precision. For a long time the Stanford–Binet test was the predominant test of intelligence, and as such it was the test against which most other tests were measured.

However, the original Stanford–Binet was limited in several ways because, for example, it emphasized verbal ability, and a person's performance was expressed as a single (IQ) score. To overcome such limitations Wechsler designed a further intelligence test specifically for adults which was first published in 1939. A distinctive feature of the Wechsler test was the inclusion of different sub-tests. Half the sub-tests make up a verbal scale and the other half contribute to a performance scale; both scales can be scored separately to give a verbal or a performance IQ as well as an overall measure of IQ based on a person's score for the whole test. Examples similar to the ones used in the WECHSLER ADULT INTELLIGENCE SCALE (WAIS) are shown in figure 15.3. Unlike the Stanford–Binet intelligence scale, a person who takes the Wechsler test attempts all the items, and this has the advantage that it allows a 'profile' of a person's ability to be constructed – performance on the different tests can highlight a person's strengths and weaknesses. Since the invention of the original Wechsler scale for adults there are now versions for children and for pre-school children.

For both the Wechsler tests and the more recent versions of the Stanford–Binet scales IQ is no longer calculated by a formula. Instead, after a mathematical transformation, a person's score is compared to the distribution of all IQ scores. The mean score of this distribution is, arbitrarily, set at 100 with a standard deviation set at 15. (If the standard deviation is set at 15 it means that approximately two-thirds of all IQ scores fall between a score of 85 and a score of 115.) In other words, average IQ score is taken as 100 and there is a symmetrical distribution around this average score. By comparing an individual's transformed score with this distribution, his or her IQ can be calculated.

The Stanford–Binet and Wechsler intelligence tests are the most frequently used intelligence tests, though there are now many more tests available. In Britain the British Ability Scales (BAS) for children and young people were specifically designed to measure up to six different cognitive processes: speed of

---

Verbal Scale

Information: this subtest examines general knowledge. The examiner asks a number of questions, of increasing difficulty, like:

How many days are there in a week?
Who wrote *Pride and Prejudice*?
What is the large bone in the thigh called?
How far is it from London to Moscow?

Digit Span: the examiner reads a list of numbers and asks the person being tested to say them from memory. The examiner begins with a short list and on each trial increases the length of the list up to eight items, e.g. 4 – 9 – 6 – 1 – 8 – 3 – 2 – 7. The person is asked to repeat these in the same order, and also, on other trials, repeat similar lists in reverse order.

Vocabulary: a person is asked to define words. The list is of increasing difficulty (e.g. house, income, articulated, onomatopoeia).

Arithmetic: the examiner says a mathematical problem which has to be answered without the use of paper or pencil. For example:

If a suit was originally priced at £150 and the seller increases the price by 10 per cent, how much does the suit cost now?
If it takes eight women six days to finish a job, how long would it take twelve women to finish the same job?

Comprehension: these are items which need to be explained (i.e. understanding them does not depend just on factual knowledge). Items might be:

Why do people use umbrellas?
If you are driving a car why should you obey the speed limit?
What does the saying 'Give her an inch and she'll take a mile' mean?

Similarities: the person being tested is asked to explain why two things are alike. For example, 'Why are shoes and sandals alike?' Of course, there may be several ways in which the two items are alike (both words begin and end with an 's'), but a correct answer for this example would include a reference to the category to which both items belong (i.e. footwear).

Picture completion: a person is shown several pictures of objects and asked to say what is missing; for example, simple items might be a picture of a chair with a leg missing, or an airplane with a wing missing. The items become progressively more difficult.

Picture arrangement: the examiner spreads out up to five pictures on the table and asks the person being tested to re-arrange the pictures so that they tell a story. There are no words in the pictures and therefore the relationship between different pictures has to be worked out visually. A set of pictures might include, a child playing with a doll, a child with a wrapped box, an adult putting a bow on a wrapped box, the child putting her hands in the opened box, the adult giving the box to the child.

Block design: in this test a person is given nine cubes, and a specific pattern. The sides of each cube are painted red or white, or half red and half white. The cubes have to be placed together so that the upper faces of the cubes display the given pattern.

Object assembly: a person is given the pieces of a jigsaw and has to make the appropriate object. For example, there might be five pieces, which when put together show the outline of a dog.

Digit symbol: a person is given a set of symbols associated with the numbers 1 to 9. Below this key there is an extensive set of randomly ordered numbers above blank boxes. The appropriate symbols have to be filled in below the numbers. This test is measured by how many symbols a person fills in correctly in 90 seconds.

1	2	3	4	5	6	7	8	9
L	O	コ	∨	△	II	↑	✗	⊥

2	6	9	5	4	1	6	7	2	5	3	8

Figure 15.3 Examples of items which are similar to the ones used in the Wechsler Adult Intelligence Scale (WAIS)

Box 15.2   Reliability and Validity

To be useful and effective intelligence tests must fulfil certain criteria.

Reliability

Tests must be reliable – this means that when the same group of people take the same test on two different occasions there should be a high *correlation* between the group's scores the first time they take the test and the second time they take the test. In practice there is a difficulty in giving the same test twice, because the second time people will have the benefit of having seen the test before and may recall the answers. This problem can be avoided when there are two different but equivalent version of the same test – one version can be given on the first occasion and the other version can be given on the second occasion. For most established intelligence tests the correlation between test group's scores on the first and second administration is usually very high, and therefore such tests have an acceptable level of reliability.

Validity

There are several types of validity which have to be considered in relation to intelligence tests. Unfortunately, the same types of validity are sometimes given different names, and different degrees of emphasis, but the important point is that acceptable tests should fulfil all aspects of validity.

External or empirical validity refers to two related aspects of validity – concurrent validity and predictive validity. Both types of validity involve the comparison of a test with other measures which are assumed to be testing the same abilities. If the other measures relate to a person's contemporary performance the comparison is an examination of concurrent validity; if the other measures are ones which refer to a person's performance in the future the comparison is one of predictive validity.

Concurrent validity usually involves correlating one intelligence test with another, established, intelligence test (and usually the Stanford–Binet and the Wechsler scales are taken as the standard against which new tests are validated). Of course, this only means that a validated intelligence test is one which produces the same results as another, earlier, intelligence test and it requires the assumption that the earlier intelligence test itself has concurrent validity. As Richardson (1991) has described, this assumption may be weak; for example, each revision of the Stanford–Binet has been justified on the grounds that the revision measures the same thing as the previous revision – all the way back to the original Binet test! Therefore, in a sense, the concurrent validity of many new tests is assessed by a rather indirect comparison with Binet's original work.

An alternative way to assess concurrent validity is to take other measures of current performance – for example, children's current performance in school can be used to validate a test by examining whether their school performance correlates with their performance on the intelligence test. This procedure makes the assumption that children's school performance is itself a valid measure of intelligence, but of course, school performance depends on many factors which may or may not be related to intelligence (motivation, home background, health, quality of teaching, and so on).

information processing; reasoning; *spatial imagery*; *perceptual matching*; short-term memory; and verbal comprehension. These aspects of intelligence are assessed by a large number of different sub-scales. Unlike other commonly used IQ tests the BAS permits the construction of a very detailed profile of performance and the detection of unusually good or poor performance on individual sub-tests. Such tests are particularly useful for diagnosing specific learning difficulties or relative changes between different abilities over a period of time.

The tests described above are administered individually; other tests have been designed so that they can also be administered to groups of people (an advantage when large numbers of people need to be tested rapidly). One of the better-

Predictive validity means that a test should be a predictor of future related performance; for example, a child's score in an intelligence test should predict later school performance, and there is no doubt that tests such as the Stanford–Binet do predict later academic success and clearly have predictive validity when compared with school performance. Though it should be noted that the very relationship between standard intelligence tests and academic achievement has prompted some authors to argue that such intelligence tests are better thought of as tests of educational ability rather than as tests of intelligence (Richardson 1991).

Content validity or *face validity* refers to the appropriateness of a test. For example, if a test designed to examine an aircraft pilot's navigational skills only measured her vocabulary and memory span, it might not be thought very appropriate. Most people would probably agree that a test of navigational skill should at least include items related to map reading, spatial abilities, and geographical knowledge. Content validity is rather obvious when the test is easily defined (like navigational ability), but as emphasized throughout this chapter, there is no commonly agreed definition of intelligence, and therefore 'content validity' in the case of intelligence tests is more difficult to assess. It may often only mean that the designer of the test believed that the items included in the test were appropriate measures of intelligence. Even the latter may not always be the case – for example, Binet was concerned with designing a test which identified children with *learning difficulties* and chose test items which were effective in distinguishing between children; in other words, the items were selected empirically, rather than because of any particular beliefs Binet had about the nature of intelligence. This point overlaps with the issue of construct validity.

Construct validity refers to psychological 'constructs' or concepts which depend on theoretical assumptions. In contrast to some specific physical or cognitive abilities (e.g. strength of hand grip or memory span) which are comparatively well defined and testable, some psychological concepts such as 'intelligence', 'depression', 'leadership' are theoretical constructs – they cannot be identified directly but only indirectly. A person's intelligence cannot be tested directly – it can be inferred only from her behaviour (e.g. solving a problem successfully), but intelligence is more than just the behaviour on a single task because intelligence implies a construct which is a broad influence over a number of tasks. In other words, to identify and measure a person's intelligence involves making inferences from a range of tasks and behaviour. Construct validity is the process of ensuring that these inferences are the appropriate ones to make. Herein lies a difficulty, because the appropriateness of any inference will depend on a researchers' theoretical view of intelligence. For example, if one researcher theorized that intelligence influences performance on every task, she would be entitled to argue that inferences drawn from mental arithmetic, vocabulary tests, crossword-puzzle solving, snooker playing and ballet dancing were all appropriate indicators of intelligence. A second researcher might have a different theory of intelligence – she might accept that mental arithmetic reflected intelligence, but feel that it would be inappropriate to draw inferences about people's intelligence from their crossword-puzzle solving ability.

known group tests is the Progressive Matrices test designed by Raven in Britain in the 1930s – this test also has the benefit of requiring a minimum of verbal instructions and can therefore be used with people with language difficulties. People are presented with eight items in a matrix; the ninth item is missing and the person has to select (from a given choice) which item best completes the matrix (see figure 15.4).

There are now a number of different intelligence scales, as well as numerous tests of specific abilities (for a summary of tests see Aiken 1991; Gregory 1992). Irrespective of the type of test, every test must fulfil the criteria of reliability and validity, and these criteria are described in Box 15.2.

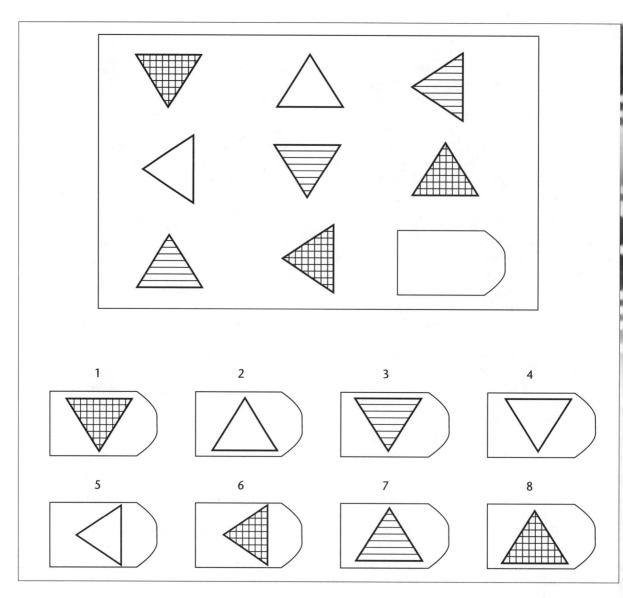

Figure 15.4 An example which is similar to the items in Raven's progressive matrices. One of the eight choices is selected to complete the pattern

The nature of intelligence

Galton was the first to suggest that intelligence was a global ability which influenced a person's performance on a range of tasks; but it was only much latter that Spearman (1904) used statistical techniques to investigate the relationship between scores on different measures of intelligence. In his early research, in Britain, Spearman noticed correlations between children's performance over a range of different measures – for example, children who performed best in school examinations (e.g. maths and English) also tended to do best on sensory tests (e.g. pitch discrimination) and also tended to be given better ratings by teachers for other subjects (e.g. musical ability). Spearman argued if performance on one test showed a high correlation with performance on another test it was likely that the same factor was influencing performance of both tests.

Spearman (1927) used a mathematical technique called FACTOR ANALYSIS as a way to identify the underlying factors which could account for the correlations between different tests. If the same group of people take a large number of tests it is possible to calculate the correlation between all the scores for each pair of tests. The calculated correlations (the *correlation coefficients*) give an indication of the similarity for each pair of tests (where a high, positive, correlation indicates that the group of people performed similarly on both tests of the pair). Table 15.1 shows an (invented) table of all the correlations between several pairs of hypothetical tests. Such a table can be 'reduced' by factor analysis to a smaller set of values which summarize the intercorrelations between all the tests – the actual set of values will indicate the minimum number of factors which can be used to describe the data. Spearman demonstrated that, for his data, all the correlations could be accounted for by just two factors. One was a factor that applied to all tests that he called '*g*' (which is usually referred to as GENERAL INTELLIGENCE); the other was a factor specific to each test (called '*s*'). It was Spearman's belief that when two people performed differently on the same test it was because they had different levels of *g*. Using a rather mechanical analogy Spearman referred to the set of mental processes required for a particular task as an 'engine' and the effectiveness of this engine would depend on the 'energy' (or *g*) which could be supplied to it – people with more *g* would perform a task better. Spearman's view of intelligence is usually called a 'two-factor' theory, or alternatively a 'monarchic' theory because it emphasized the all-pervasive influence of a single *g* factor.

Spearman was criticized for ignoring 'group factors'. Group factors arise when some tests correlate well with each other, but not with other tests. For example, in the hypothetical example given in table 15.1, the group of spelling, reading and vocabulary tests all correlate highly with each other; and similarly, the group of drawing, jigsaw and maze tests all correlate highly with each other; but there

FACTOR ANALYSIS

GENERAL
INTELLIGENCE

Table 15.1 Correlation coefficients between performance on six hypothetical tests (invented data). The higher the coefficient the more similar the performance on two tests. The table shows that correlations between tests may vary – in this fictitious example, vocabulary scores have a higher correlation with reading scores than they do with scores on a test of making jigsaws.

	spelling	vocabulary	reading	mazes	jigsaws
vocabulary	0.75				
reading	0.75	0.60			
mazes	0.41	0.50	0.59		
jigsaws	0.45	0.43	0.49	0.79	
drawing	0.52	0.47	0.55	0.68	0.73

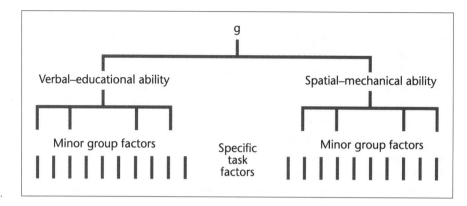

Figure 15.5 A diagrammatic
description of Vernon's
hierarchical model of
intelligence.
Vernon, *The Structure of Human
Abilities* (Methuen, London, 1950).

is only low correlation between tests in the two different groups. To take both general and group factors into account, Vernon (1950) in Britain proposed a model of intelligence called a 'hierarchical model'. In his model general intelligence is a factor permeating performance on all tests, but there are also two major group factors (labelled verbal–educational ability and spatial–mechanical ability) which influence distinct groups of tests, and in addition there are minor group factors and specific factors. Vernon's model is best described diagrammatically in figure 15.5.

British researchers such as Galton, Spearman and Vernon all held the view that intelligence involved an important general factor. In contrast, many American psychologists developed theories of intelligence which emphasized the independence of different factors. For example, Thurstone (1931) used factor analysis to identify seven separate factors in the performance of intelligence tests. He called these 'primary mental abilities', and named them as follows (with examples of tests which reflect each factor):

1. verbal meaning (e.g. vocabulary and comprehension tests)
2. word fluency (e.g. speed of naming words from a specific category, such as all the animal names beginning with a B)
3. numerical reasoning (e.g. speed and accuracy at mental arithmetic)
4. spatial (e.g. imagining what a three-dimensional object looks like after it has been rotated)
5. perceptual speed (e.g. quickly checking lists for specific items or errors)
6. memory (e.g. recalling a list of words)
7. inductive reasoning (e.g. solving number completion tests)

GROUP FACTOR
THEORY

Thurstone's approach is usually called a GROUP FACTOR THEORY, or sometimes an 'oligarchic' theory, because he originally claimed that the seven factors were independent of each other.

Although factor analysis is an effective way to identify the different aspects of intelligence, the technique has limitations, because the solutions obtained through factor analysis will depend on the number of ability tests which are used, the type of tests, and the type of people who are given the tests. The solution will be influenced by the researcher's choice of factor analytic technique – the same data can be analysed in different ways to obtain different solutions. None the less, there has been sufficient research to demonstrate that intelligence can be discussed in terms of different factors and that hierarchical models of intelligence with a single factor for general intelligence at the top of the hierarchy are more appropriate than other models which do not include a general factor (Gustafson 1984). However, it should be remembered that any model of the relationships between test scores may indicate no more than patterns of performance on those tests, and such a model cannot say anything about the nature of the cognitive structure underlying intelligence (Gould 1981).

The debate about the structure of intelligence and the importance of different factors is not simply an academic debate about the validity of various mathematical techniques, because the way that people think about intelligence has important practical and social consequences. The belief in a general factor of intelligence which underlies all performance implies that intelligence can be tested using a small number of 'paper and pencil' tests because such tests will reflect intelligences as well as any other tests. It was this type of reasoning that led to the British '11-plus' examination which, in the past, was used to segregate 11-year-olds and determine what type of secondary school they would attend.

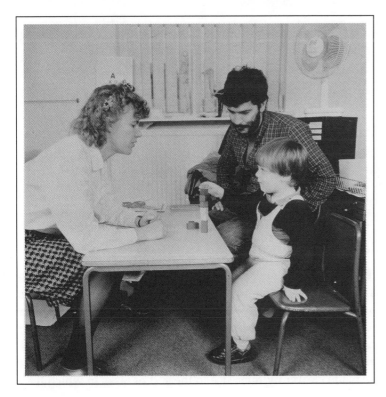

Plate 15.1 A young boy undertakes an intelligence test
Source: Science Photo Library/St Bartholomew's Hospital.

Box 15.3 People with Exceptional Abilities

Plate 15.2 Drawing of the Kremlin Palace by Stephen Wiltshire, 1991. Wiltshire is a young person with autism who has a remarkable (and untrained) talent for drawing.

There are some people who have a generally low level of intelligence who are capable of outstanding performance in one, or very rarely, more than one area of intellectual ability. Such people have been referred to as *idiots savants* ('wise fools') or less pejoratively as *savants*, and

their performance can be illustrated by a few examples:

Calendar calculating. Howe and Smith (1988) reported the case of 'Dave', a boy age 14 years who had a very low IQ (about 50); the reading age of a 6-year-old, and very few social skills. None the less, when he

Fluid and crystallized intelligence

Cattell (1940) and Horn and Cattell (1966) also used factor analysis and identified, not one, but several general factors which influenced performance across many tasks. Cattell called the two most important general factors 'fluid' and 'crystallized' intelligence. FLUID INTELLIGENCE refers to a person's capacity to solve new problems and to learn; and CRYSTALLIZED INTELLIGENCE refers to performance on well-learned and familiar tasks. The distinction between these two types of intelligence can be made clearer by reference to the sort of tasks in which they

FLUID INTELLIGENCE

CRYSTALLIZED
INTELLIGENCE

was asked a question like 'on what day of the week is the 1st of July 1940', he could work out the correct day of the week within 10 seconds. Dave could also work out the correct responses to questions which required several answers, such as 'in what years does the 9th of October fall on a Wednesday?' For a discussion of the ways that calendar calculators might perform such tasks, see Howe (1991).

Other calculating skills. Sacks (1985) observed the abilities of Charles and George, adult identical twins who lived together in a residential home. Sacks noticed that the twins spent their time taking it in turns to say different six-digit numbers to each other, and he realized that they were 'swapping' prime numbers. In some way they were able to examine numbers and identify which ones were primes. When Sacks took part in this activity (he looked up the prime numbers in a book!) by saying additional prime numbers to the twins he found that with the added stimulus of being presented with 'new' primes the twins progressed to identifying twenty-figure prime numbers.

Musical skills. The case of Leonard, a 40-year-old with the mental age of a 10-year-old, is summarized by Howe (1991). Leonard had major problems with everyday tasks – for example, when getting dressed he put on the first item of clothing which came to hand. In contrast to such failures he was able to memorize several pages of writing after a single reading; he was also an expert on music, having an encyclopaedic knowledge of musicians and composers. He could play music from sight and played the piano so well that he acted as a pianist during the rehearsals of professional orchestras.

Drawing skills. Several savants have demonstrated exceptional drawing skill. The teenager Stephen Wilt-shire is autistic, but can produce remarkable artistic views of buildings and architecture which he draws rapidly and without preparation. Whether he is directly looking at a building or just drawing from memory, he can reproduce architectural scenes very accurately.

Although several individuals with exceptional abilities have been observed and studied extensively, as yet very little is known about why or how savants develop the often outstanding specialized skills which are so unusual. One commonly noted aspect of savants is their often obsessive involvement in a single activity, and there is no doubt that most have extensive practice of calendar calculating, piano-playing or whatever other skill they have developed. But apart from such generalizations, it is difficult to say much at all about the phenomenon of savants. Their existence is a problem for any theory of intelligence. Some theories of intelligence (e.g. Gardner's 1983 theory of multiple intelligences) which emphasize separate abilities can incorporate the existence of savants without difficulty – the argument can be made that anyone may be good at one activity and poor at another, and therefore savants are only an extreme example of such differences. In contrast, it is more difficult for theories which emphasize g (a *general intelligence* which pervades all performance) to explain the presence of savants. Savants, by definition, always have very low g and yet with such low general intelligence they can still achieve specific feats of memory, music, art, or calculating well beyond the level of most people. Some recent researchers have tried to explain the latter 'contradiction' (see e.g. Anderson 1992), but other researchers who have put forward general theories of intelligence that have ignored the existence of savants (e.g. Sternberg 1985).

occur. A vocabulary test depends on well-learned knowledge about the meaning of words, and this knowledge is part of crystallized intelligence. Similarly, a test of social ability would tap into crystallized intelligence because social skills and knowledge are typically well learned and practised. In contrast solving a new problem such as finding the next number in a series (4, 9, 15, 22, 30, . . .) requires flexibility, and an original response and is therefore dependent on fluid intelligence. Similarly, performance on tests like Raven's matrices requires new reasoning and is also a test of fluid intelligence.

Crystallized and fluid intelligence are not entirely distinct. Any task (e.g. learning the meaning of a word or developing a specific social skill) originally depended on fluid intelligence before it became a habitual part of a person's knowledge (and thus part of her crystallized intelligence), and many tasks involve both types of intelligence. For example, in solving a mental arithmetic problem $[(2 \times 2) + (2 \times 2)] \times (3 + 3)$ the symbols and some elements of the calculation (e.g. the sum of $2 + 2$) will be well known (crystallized intelligence) but the efficiency with which the problem is solved will also depend on appropriate abstract reasoning (fluid intelligence). The relative importance of the two types of intelligence varies with age – fluid intelligence declines with age, as older people lose some of the ability and flexibility to deal with new problems and situations. In contrast, crystallized intelligence, which is the sum of everything which a person has learned, is likely to go on increasing, and to some extent compensate for any decline in fluid intelligence.

Multiple intelligences

Gardner (1983) proposed a theory of multiple intelligences, and by this he meant that there may be several different 'intelligences'. Because Gardner argued for several distinct types of intelligence his theory can be seen in the tradition of Thurstone (who suggested that people have separate abilities), but whereas Thurstone derived his theory from factor analysis, Gardner argued the case for separate intelligences on the basis of several criteria. He suggested that an intelligence can be identified in the following way:

Brain damage: if a specific skill can be lost while other skills remain intact, it implies that the lost skill is to some extent independent of other skills.

People with exceptional abilities: some individuals may have a generally low level of intelligence, but have one exceptional talent (see Box 15. 3) which suggests that a particular intelligence can function separately from other abilities.

Developmental history: Gardner argued that an intelligence which is independent will have a distinct sequence of development in an individual.

Evolutionary history: if compared to other intelligences an intelligence also has a distinctive evolution this is further evidence for it being independent of other intelligences.

Core operations: this refers to the idea that a separate intelligence is likely to be dependent on a particular set of cognitive processes.

Experimental evidence: independence of intelligences can be shown in at least two ways – first, if there is evidence from factor analysis that a performance on a task which requires a particular independence is uncorrelated with performance on other tasks which require other intelligences. Second, in experiments when people are asked to perform two different tasks at the same time there will be pairs of tasks which are comparatively easy to per-

Plate 15.3 Training in ballet
technique often begins at a
very young age
Source: Ace Photo Library.

form simultaneously (with the implication that the two tasks rely on different intelligences) and there will be some pairs of tasks which are difficult to perform at the same time (implying that they both require the same intelligence).

Symbol system: a particular intelligence may have its own symbol system (e.g. words, pictures, numbers).

On the basis of the above criteria Gardner (1983) described six distinct intelligences: logical-mathematical intelligence, spatial intelligence, linguistic (i.e. verbal) intelligence, musical, personal, and bodily-kinesthetic intelligence. The first three of these are typical of many classifications and are abilities which are examined in many standard intelligence tests. The other three are less frequently included under the heading of intelligence, but Gardner argues that they do fulfil most of his criteria. For example, with reference to musical intelligence, there are some brain-damaged individuals who retain unimpaired musical ability; some people with generally low intelligence do have outstanding musical skills (Box 15.3); musical ability may involve distinctive 'core operations' such as recognizing pitch, rhythm and timbre; and music is supported by a distinctive system of musical notation.

Personal intelligence includes both an understanding of one's own and others' emotions and behaviour; and bodily-kinesthetic intelligence refers to the abilities that might be used by people who are skilled in movement (e.g. dancers and athletes) or in handling intricate objects (e.g. watchmaking).

Gardner's (1983) theory of multiple intelligences is unusual because it extends the concept of intelligence to areas such as personal, musical and bodily skills, and these have largely been ignored in conventional intelligence assessment. Therefore Gardner's approach is important for extending the concept of intelligence, and putting emphasis on aspects of behaviour (such as personal and social abilities) which are often cited in lay-people's views of intelligence (see above).

The existence of many individuals with average intelligence who have one exceptional ability or skill is often cited as evidence for Gardner's theory of separate intelligences. The most dramatic examples of people with an exceptional ability are 'savants' (Box 15.3), individuals with a level of intelligence well below average but who have a single outstanding skill. The existence of such individuals is strong evidence in favour of abilities being independent. Indeed, it is not easy to explain how a person with a very low level of intelligence can achieve feats of memory, of music, or of art, which far surpass what most people can achieve, and therefore it is tempting to conclude that certain abilities are indeed independent and that they can exist separately from other abilities.

However, Gardner's approach has been criticized because some of his criteria are vague and speculative (for example, little can be known for certain about the history and evolution of any ability), and a major problem is that his theory is in direct contrast to the research based on factor analysis. Most recent researchers using factor analysis have concluded that there is a general factor in intelligence, and this runs counter to Gardner's emphasis on the independence of different intelligences.

In summary, there is evidence that abilities can be separate and independent (as in the cases of savants), but there is also evidence that underlying different abilities there may be a common general factor (from the factor-analytic research). The debate between those who have believed in separate abilities (e.g. Thurstone, Gardner) and those who have emphasized intelligence as a unitary factor (e.g. Spearman, Vernon) has had a long run in the history of intelligence research. It is unlikely to be resolved by pointing to selective aspects of the evidence; what is needed is a theory which can satisfactorily explain both the apparent general nature of intelligence and the fact that some individuals have unique abilities.

The Information-processing Approach to Intelligence

The psychometric approach to the study of intelligence is essentially a descriptive approach. Scores on IQ tests can describe the differences between individuals, and factor analysis can be used to describe the relationship between tests of different abilities. But the psychometric approach can contribute little of explanatory value – knowing that one person is better than another on the Stanford–Binet intelligence scale says little about the reasons for that difference. Researchers trying to find the reasons for differences in intelligence have adopted the information-processing approach. The aim of this approach is to relate intelligence to aspects of cognition, such as the speed that people process information or the strategies they use in reasoning tasks.

Speed of information processing

Any task requires processing information, and several researchers have considered the relationship between the speed that people process information and their level of intelligence. In particular researchers have concentrated on measuring basic information-processing skills to find out if individual differences in basic processing are related to individual differences in intelligence.

Hunt (e.g. 1978) carried out a number of experiments in which he typically included two groups of participants: one group had high verbal intelligence scores (as measured by standard tests) and the second group had low verbal intelligence scores. Both groups were given a task which involved processing information, and the speed they performed the task was measured. For example, Hunt et al. (1973) showed participants, on a screen, pairs of letters like AA, Aa, or Ab. In a 'name match' condition participants were asked to respond 'yes' if the letters were the same (e.g. Aa, AA, Bb), but in a 'physical match' condition they only responded 'yes' if the two letters were exactly the same (e.g. AA or bb). A physical match can be made more rapidly than a name match because a physical match can be made quickly on the basis of what the letters look like, but a name match requires searching memory for the names of the letters before responding. Hunt et al. (1973) found that it took participants with high verbal intelligence scores 33 milliseconds longer to make a name match than a physical match, and this reflected how long it took them to search their memory for the names of the letters. In contrast the participants with low verbal scores took 86 milliseconds longer – in other words, they were much slower at searching memory.

This approach to the study of intelligent performance is often known as the 'cognitive correlates' approach, because Hunt's research demonstrated that there was a correlation between basic cognitive processes (in the example above, the speed at which people could search memory) and intelligence scores (on a test of verbal intelligence). He suggested that better verbal ability might depend on having faster access to letter names in memory. However, as Hunt (1980) himself pointed out, the correlations between verbal intelligence and processing speed in the cognitive tasks he used are often quite low, and therefore individual differences in processing speed are unlikely to account for many of the individual differences in intelligence.

Hunt chose 'simple' tasks, in the expectation that performance differences on such tasks would be the consequence of differences in low-level processes like processing speed. However, performance on even apparently simple tasks may often involve the higher-level judgements. For example, in most tasks which require participants to make rapid responses, participants are typically given instructions to go as fast as possible, but to make as few errors as possible. Such instructions mean that participants have to make decisions about how to approach the task to achieve a good performance (e.g., go fast and tolerate some errors; or less fast to avoid all errors). Decisions like these involve strategic judgements – it may be the case that more intelligent participants are better at the task because they are better at identifying an optimal strategy. The point here is that if different people attempt the same task using different strategies, measuring how long they take to perform the task will not necessarily be a pure measure of their processing speed; rather the measure will reflect a mixture of different processes. If a task involves both basic processes and strategies it is impossible to know whether more intelligent people perform the task faster because they have better speed of information processing, or because they have better strategies (or both).

To find 'purer' measures of information processing other researchers have adopted tasks which do not involve response speed. For example, in 'inspection time' tests a person is shown a simple stimulus which includes a short and a long vertical line. The stimulus is presented on a computer screen and the participant is asked to respond by indicating whether the longer line is on the right or the left. The stimulus is presented for different lengths of time (from a few milliseconds to half a second) – and a participant responds *after* the stimulus has been displayed, so there is no requirement to respond quickly. For long presentations the task is straightforward, and at very short presentations a person is reduced to guessing the correct answer. A person's 'inspection time' is the shortest stimulus presentation time which a person can respond to without making errors. Different people have different inspection times, and several studies have found that there is a negative correlation between individuals' inspection times and their intelligence scores (Nettelbeck 1987). It is negative because people with higher intelligence scores have lower inspection time. This implies that people with higher intelligence are also better in a task which is assumed to reflect basic processing of information.

The inspection-time task is not open to quite the same criticisms as Hunt's cognitive tasks, because there is less opportunity for higher-level strategies to be involved in the inspection-time task. Participants in the latter task are not asked to respond quickly; all they have to do is report which line of the stimulus is longer. None the less, some researchers have argued that inspection-time tasks do involve higher-level processes and that they are not entirely pure measures of basic processing (for a discussion, see Anderson 1992).

There are now a number of studies, using various tasks, which have shown a correlation between intelligence and the speed of low-level cognitive processes, and some researchers have argued that this correlation implies that a person's intelligence is influenced by the efficiency of his or her 'basic processing mechanism' (Anderson 1992). However, other researchers have disputed such an interpretation – for example, Howe (1988) pointed out that such a correlation could be the result of factors other than a direct relationship between intelligence and processing speed. He argued that there are underlying performance factors, common to both intelligence tests and processing tasks, which account for the correlation between them (e.g. factors such as attentiveness, motivation and confidence).

The interpretation of measures such as inspection time has generated much debate (for a summary of this debate see Howe 1990 and Nettelbeck 1990). Even if there is a relationship between low-level information processing and intelligence, it is unlikely that processing speed has more than a small influen on a person's intellectual performance (see Kline 1991), and therefore some researchers have argued that understanding intelligent behaviour can better be achieved by focusing on higher-level cognitive processes. The latter approach is exemplified by Sternberg's (1985) 'componential' analysis of tasks which require complex reasoning.

Componential analysis of information processing

Sternberg (1985) has stressed the importance of examining the way that people carry out the type of tasks and problems which are typically included in tests of intelligence. He argued that problem-solving tasks can be analysed in terms of the information processes or 'components' which are required to complete the task.

Sternberg has been particularly interested in the processes or components which are required in tasks of ANALOGICAL REASONING. In an analogical problem a person might be asked to complete a task like the following: Bird is to air as fish is to (a) land (b) water, where the person has to select the most appropriate response from the alternatives which are provided. An example of a picture analogy used by Sternberg and Rifkin (1979) is given in figure 15.6.

Sternberg and Rifkin suggested that such tasks required the following component processes:

ANALOGICAL
REASONING

Encoding: refers to the initial processing of all the information which is presented in the task; for example in figure 15.6, a person might consider all aspects of the five figures (type of hat, type of footwear, pattern on clothing, object being carried, and so on).

Figure 15.6 A picture analogy. One of the figures (1 or 2) from the right must be selected so that the relationship between that figure and figure C is the same as the relationship between figures A and B.
Stern & Rifkin, 'The development of analogical reasoning processor' in *Journal of Experimental Child Psychology*, 27 (Academic Press, 1979).

Inference: means working out the changes be needed to make A into B (i.e. changing A's hat to match B's hat).

Mapping: refers to the relationship between figures A and C (noting that they have the same hat, but all other features are different).

Application: means applying the changes worked out by the inference component to C (i.e. changing C's hat) to produce an 'ideal' answer for the analogy. The ideal answer can then be compared to the given alternatives and figure D1 selected.

Justification: if the given alternatives do not include one that matches the ideal answer exactly, it is necessary to choose the alternative which is closest to the ideal answer and justify this choice.

Respond: simply means giving the selected answer.

The above analysis describes only one possible way to solve an analogical problem of the form A is to B as C is to D. Some of the components may not be necessary for all analogical tasks – for instance, for the picture analogy task in figure 15.6 there is no need for the justification component (because the 'ideal' answer is one of the alternatives) and there may be no need for the mapping component (because this analogy can be solved without the mapping component).

Reducing performance on a task to a number of components is important because the way that different people solve analogies can be compared in terms of the components they use, and how they use those components. For example, people with higher intelligence tend to spend longer in the encoding stage of a problem. This finding goes beyond descriptive conclusions like 'people who are more intelligent are better at solving analogies', because knowing that more intelligent people spend more time encoding a problem begins to explain why there might be differences in performance between people with high and low intelligence. Therefore, Sternberg's componential approach offers an insight into the relationship between complex cognitive process and intelligence.

Sternberg (1985) called processes like the ones described above, which are used in a particular task, 'performance components'. Such components have to be selected and ordered in an effective way if they are to be made appropriate for a task, and therefore Sternberg suggested that there was another group of processes called 'metacomponents'. The latter are the high-level strategies which are necessary to decide what type of problem has to be solved, and which performance components are needed to achieve a solution to the problem.

In addition, Sternberg (1985) also defined 'knowledge-acquisition' components, which include the processes which are needed during the course of learning new information. Under the latter heading Sternberg described the following components:

Selective encoding components – which include the processes required to sift relevant information from irrelevant information when solving a problem. Sternberg has illustrated the type of problem which requires selective encoding with the following example:

> If you have black socks and brown socks in a drawer, mixed in the ratio of 4 to 5, how many socks will you have to take out to make sure of having a pair of socks of the same colour?

In this problem the information about the ratio can be ignored because it is irrelevant.

Selective combination components – which means putting new information together in a coherent whole. Sternberg's example of a problem which emphasizes both selective encoding and selective combination is:

> Water lilies double in area every 24 hours. At the beginning of the summer there is one water lily on the lake. It takes 60 days for the lake to become covered with water lilies. On what day is the lake half covered?

Selective comparison components – which means linking new information to information which is already known.

Sternberg has pointed out that knowledge-acquisition components are important, and has argued that people who are better at solving problems (like the examples given above) which require knowledge-acquisition components also perform better on standard intelligence tests.

Sternberg's componential approach is an attempt to analyse the most important processes which underlie performance on the type of problem-solving tasks which have typically been seen as tests of intelligence. Although Sternberg's approach has generated several insights into the way that people perform different tasks, his componential analysis has been criticized. There is a difficulty in selecting the level of analysis – for example, the performance components which Sternberg described are not single, identifiable processes, but summarize many different cognitive processes, and there could be a number of further levels of analysis dividing each component into subcomponents, and so on. Sternberg does not always justify why his level of analysis is the most appropriate one.

Some researchers have been particularly critical of Sternberg's approach – for example, Kline (1991) has pointed out that analogical problems inevitably require 'inferences' and 'applications' (if they did not they would not be analogical problems); and similarly, all problem-solving tasks require a 'response'. Kline's argument is that, for the most part, Sternberg has only described what is necessary to solve a problem (which is inherent in the type of problem); he has not explained how people solve the problem. In other words, the main criticism of Sternberg's componential approach is that his analysis *describes* the information processing which is required to complete tasks (like analogies) which involve intelligence. The fact that people succeed on such tasks means that they must have employed 'encoding' and 'inference', but simply labelling these aspects of the task does nothing to explain the psychological processes which people use in intelligence tasks.

Sternberg's triarchic theory of intelligence

Sternberg's componential approach is part of a larger theory of intelligence which he put forward as the 'triarchic theory of intelligence' – it is called triarchic because it includes three sub-theories; these are shown diagrammatically in figure 15.7. One is the 'componential sub-theory' which considers the cognitive processes (i.e. metacomponents, performance components and knowledge-acquisition components) involved in intellectual tasks; this sub-theory was described in the previous section.

A second sub-theory is the 'experiential sub-theory'. Sternberg (1985) pointed out that most of the tasks used in intelligence tests include both familiar and unfamiliar aspects – for example, most adults will be familiar with the form of analogies even if the particular analogy which they are asked to complete is new to them. Sternberg argued that such tasks inevitably confuse intelligence with

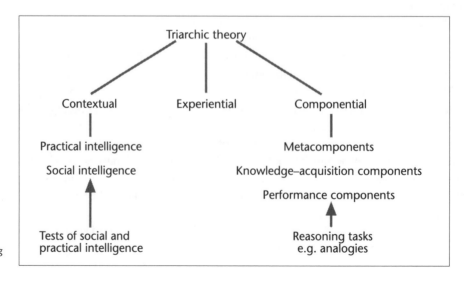

Figure 15.7 A simplified diagram of Sternberg's triarchic theory of intelligence to show relationships between the sub-theories
Source: adapted from Sternberg 1985.

Box 15.4 Tests of Practical and Social Intelligence

In contrast to standard *intelligence scales* (like the WAIS), which measure intelligence with tasks of problem solving and general knowledge, a few tests have been designed to measure people's practical and social skills. It is not easy to design such tests because practical and social abilities are typically ones which are expressed in real-life situations rather than in the context of a formal test. None the less, there are now a few tests which can give an insight into people's ability to cope with different social and practical situations.

Tests of Practical Intelligence

ETS Basic Skills Test – ETS stands for the Educational Testing Service (in the USA). The Basic Skills Test includes items which test the ability to read street maps; understand transport timetables; comprehend written text, technical instructions, advertisements and bottle labels; and fill out typical forms.

In-basket test – designed by Fredericksen (1962). For this test a person is, literally, given a basketful of telephone messages, letters, memoranda and documents which simulate the items which might accumulate on the desk of a business manager. The person has to decide how to deal with all the items. Her performance is scored for both the appropriateness of the action chosen in response to individual items, and also for the effectiveness of her overall approach (e.g. planning in what order to deal with the items, or setting deadlines for completing the task).

Tests of Social Intelligence

Profile of non-verbal sensitivity – designed by Rosenthal et al. (1979), this test consists of examples of one woman's non-verbal communication presented on videotape. For example, a person might be shown a two-second extract (without sound) showing just the face of the woman as she acts out an emotional scene. After this brief viewing the person has to select one of two given interpretations: (i) the woman was expressing jealous anger, or (ii) the woman was nagging a child. Performance on this test measures how well a person can use non-verbal information to interpret another person's emotions; the ability to do this successfully is one aspect of social intelligence.

Sternberg's test of social intelligence – described in Sternberg (1985). This test includes a number of black-and-white photographs each showing two people. One set of photographs shows a man and a woman standing together; some of these are photographs of genuine couples, and some are photographs of two strangers who have been asked to stand together posing as a real couple. The photographs are shown to people who have to say which photographs portray real couples and which show the 'fake' couples. The other set of photographs show two individuals, one of whom is (genuinely) the supervisor of the other. People are shown the photographs and asked to say which of the two individuals is the supervisor. Success on this task is related to how well people interpret the non-verbal information in the photographs (e.g., for the couples: how far apart they are standing; how relaxed they appear; and the similarity of their appearance). Such interpretations are an important part of social intelligence.

experience, and so he suggested that the most appropriate way to assess intelligence was with novel tasks or with highly practised tasks. The way that people perform novel tasks is more likely to reflect intelligence because people will not be able to draw on past experience. Novel tests include problems which require insight rather than previous knowledge (for example, the water-lily problem described above).

In the case of highly practised tasks performance will become automatic. For example, for most experienced motorists, driving a car will be automatic, and this leaves cognitive resources available for other tasks (such as taking part in a

Box 15.5 The Genetic–Environment Issue

The focus of this chapter is on concepts and theories of intelligence, but a reference should also be made to the genetic–environment debate about intelligence. Some researchers (e.g. Eysenck) have argued that the genetic basis is the most important influence on a person's intelligence, while others have argued that intelligence is mainly determined by the environment (e.g. Kamin) – for a summary of this debate see Eysenck and Kamin (1981). Such strongly held positions are only possible by selective use of the available evidence. Scarr and Carter-Saltzman (1982) have reviewed much of the research into the influence of inherited and environmental factors on intelligence, and it is clear that both factors have a role in the development of intelligence.

It is difficult to distinguish genetic and environmental factors – if a child's intelligence is similar to her parent's intelligence, the similarity may be the result of the child and parents sharing common genes, or it may be because the child and parents share the same environment. Therefore, researchers have had to devise studies in which genetic and environmental factors can be distinguished:

Twin studies – Monozygotic (MZ) twins are twins formed from a single fertilized egg which splits and develops into two identical twins who each have exactly the same genes. Most twins will, of course, be brought up together, but there are a few cases where such twins have been separated and brought up in different families. Each pair of MZ twins who have been reared together share the *same genes* and the *same environment*, but each pair of MZ twins who have been reared apart share the *same genes* but have *different environments*. Dizygotic (DZ) twins develop from two different eggs. They share some genes in common, but they have no

more genes in common than any other pair of siblings. Therefore, a pair of DZ twins who are brought up together have *different genes* but share the *same environment*.

MZ twins reared together have very similar scores on intelligence tests (i.e., if one twin of a pair has a high score it is likely that her twin will also have a high score; if one twin of a pair has an average score it is likely that her twin will have an average score). By considering a number of MZ twins reared together, the similarity of their scores can be expressed by a correlation coefficient – the higher this figure (up to a maximum of 1.00) the more closely related are the scores. The correlation for pairs of MZ twins reared together is high (about 0.85). The correlation for pairs of MZ twins reared apart is also high (about 0.76). The correlation for pairs of DZ twins reared together it is about 0.60.

If there is a genetic component in intelligence, people with the identical genes should have more similar intelligence scores than people who do not have identical genes. This is demonstrated by comparing the MZ twins reared apart and the DZ twins reared together. Even though the latter have the benefit of a common environment, the correlation of their intelligence scores is much lower than the correlation for the MZ twins brought up in different environments. In other words, there is a genetic component in intelligence.

If there is an environmental component in intelligence, people with the same genes who share the same environment should have more similar intelligence scores than people with the same genes who do not share the same environment. This is demonstrated by comparing MZ twins reared together and MZ twins reared apart, because the correlation for the former is higher. In other

---

complex conversation at the same time as driving). Sternberg suggested that how well and how extensively a person can make aspects of performance automatic will depend on the intelligence of that person. In other words, a more intelligent person will be able to achieve a greater degree of automaticity on a task, and as tasks become more automatic, cognitive resources are freed for yet further tasks.

Sternberg's third sub-theory is called the 'contextual sub-theory', which refers to the way that people interact with their environment (where environment includes every aspect of a person's life – their culture, family, career, and so on).

words, the environment also has an influence on intelligence.

Adoption studies – Adoption studies focus on children who have been separated from their natural mother at birth. The intelligence scores of such children can be compared to the scores of their natural mothers and the scores of the mother who adopted them. Children's intelligence scores tend to be more similar to their natural mothers' scores than to their adoptive mothers' scores. In other words, even though adopted children have shared the same environment as their adoptive mother, their intelligence is more closely correlated with their natural mothers (with whom they have never had any contact). This finding indicates a genetic component in intelligence.

Adoption studies have also demonstrated the relevance of the environment. For example, Schiff et al. (1978) investigated children from working-class families in France who had been adopted by upper-middle-class families. In each case the children who were adopted had siblings who remained in the working-class environment. Schiff et al. found that the average IQ of the adopted children was 111, but the average IQ of their siblings was 95. This finding implies that the better environment of the middle-class homes contributed to the better intelligence scores of the adopted children.

Although the results described above are typical of many studies, it should be noted that both twin studies and adoption studies have frequently been criticized – for a discussion of the problems associated with the methodology and interpretation of these studies see Scarr and Carter-Saltzman (1982).

One final point should be emphasized. Intelligence, at least as it is typically measured in terms of IQ based on standard tests, is not necessarily a fixed and unalterable value for each person. From studies like Schiff et al. (1978) it can be inferred that children benefited from being placed in better environments. More specific evidence for the advantage of an improved environment was found by Kirk (1958), who compared two groups of young 'retarded' children from different institutions. One group attended a pre-school in the community, but the second group received no pre-school education. During the period of the study the first group showed a gain in IQ of 12 points; the second group had a decline of 6 points. For a discussion of how environmental and educational factors can contribute to an increase in IQ scores see Ceci (1990).

A dramatic of example of environmental effects on IQ is the case of the twins described by Koluchova (1972). The monozygotic twins were born in Czechoslovakia in 1960 and from the age of 18 months were kept together in a bare, unheated room; they had minimal contact with anyone else; and they were frequently beaten. When they were discovered, at the age of 7 years, they were unable to walk, had very little language, and an estimated IQ of only 40. The twins were placed in a special school and then in a supportive foster home. They rapidly improved, so that by the age of 8 years both twins had IQs of about 70; by 14 years both had achieved an IQ of about 90; and at 20 years they were described, by Koluchova, as above average intelligence (i.e. as having IQs over 100). Clearly the twins' experience of a beneficial environment after the age of 7 years was able to compensate for their previous severe deprivation. For a detailed review of the studies relating to deprived children see Skuse (1984).

He suggested that people can interact with the environment in three principal ways: they can either *adapt* themselves to the environment; or they can try to *shape* their environment to match what they want; but if both of these prove impossible they can *select* an alternative environment. Sternberg emphasized that a description of intelligence has to make reference to the way that people behave in their environment; in other words, one aspect of intelligence is how effectively people operate within, or change, the contexts in which they live.

Sternberg's experiential and contextual sub-theories raise many important issues about the nature of intelligence, and in pointing out these issues, Sternberg has shown how difficult it is not only to pin down the concept of intelligence, but also to measure intelligence. For example, the contextual sub-theory emphasizes that one aspect of intelligence is successful adaptation to the environment. Many researchers and lay-people would agree that successful adaptation is indicative of intelligence (see figure 15.1 and Box 15.1), but this is not something which can be measured by a standard test of intelligence. In fact, it may not be possible to measure such general notions as 'adaptation' in any meaningful way. None the less, there may be specific aspects of contextual intelligence which it is possible to test – these aspects involve a person's ability to deal with practical problems or to interpret social situations, and examples of some of the tests which have been used to measure social and practical intelligence are given in Box 15.4.

Although Sternberg's (1985) triarchic theory is the most ambitious attempt to bring together the many different aspects of intelligence in a single theory, it is not clear how the three sub-theories are integrated, and this very much weakens the attempt to produce an overall theory of intelligence. What the triarchic theory has demonstrated is the difficulty of describing any individual as intelligent or unintelligent. A person may be excellent at dealing with novel problems which require insight; poor at solving analogies; have an average score on a test of social abilities; have an unsuccessful marriage, a very successful career, and so on. According to Sternberg all these aspects of a person's life and performance are related to intelligence, and therefore it is impossible to summarize any one individual, who has a range of different successes, along a single (traditional) scale of intelligence. Making comparisons between people is also difficult, because two people may have very different patterns of abilities. Sternberg (1985) himself came to this conclusion, though at the same time he salvages a role for testing by saying that there may often be practical reasons for distinguishing between people (for instance, when selecting candidates for a job).

▓ Summary and Conclusions ▓

This chapter has focused on the different definitions of intelligence which have been discussed by researchers for more than a century. These definitions range from the cognitive ones which have stressed that intelligence is related to the efficiency of basic mental processes (especially the speed of such processes), to the very general definitions which consider intelligence in the widest possible context as a person's successful adaption and control of his or her environment. The different definitions of intelligence are not necessarily mutually exclusive – for instance, there would be nothing wrong with suggesting that people who have better cognitive processes will be able to think and reason better, and therefore they will be more likely to make a success of adapting to their environment.

One of the debates which runs through the history of intelligence is the debate between those who believe that intelligence is an underlying, all-pervasive quality

which will be reflected in any task (in other words, a person who is good at one task will also be good at another, because she has good general intelligence), and those who believe that different abilities are largely independent (someone can be an excellent linguist, but awful at mathematics). There is evidence to fuel both sides of the debate about 'general intelligence' and 'separate abilities': the former position can be argued from the factor-analytic research which has demonstrated a general factor in performance; and the latter position is supported by the existence of savants. The debate will only be resolved by a theory of intelligence which accounts for all the diverse evidence, but despite recent attempts to do this (such as Anderson 1992) there is no theory which satisfactorily incorporates all the different views of intelligence.

Plate 15.4 Chinese musician: some researchers, like Gardner, consider musical ability as a distinct intelligence
Source: Andes Press Agency/ Carlos Reyes-Manzo.

In more recent discussions of intelligence (Gardner 1983; Sternberg 1985) there has been an increased emphasis on aspects of intelligence which are not measured in conventional intelligence scales. For example, Gardner included social, physical and musical skills as examples of intelligent performance, and Sternberg's contextual sub-theory refers to practical and social intelligence. The inclusion of a wider range of behaviours under the heading of intelligence has been influenced by a recognition that the traditional definitions of intelligence have concentrated on skills (such as academic abilities) and excluded performance in the real world, but it is the latter which is given the greatest prominence when ordinary people label someone as intelligent. On the one hand, the recognition that social, practical and adaptive skills are appropriate aspects of intelligence, may be seen as a positive step in providing a richer and more intuitively satisfying description of intelligence which reflects the way that the term is used in everyday language. On the other hand, the more the concept of intelligence is extended to include an ever greater number of skills and behaviours, the more difficult it becomes to provide a measure of a person's intelligence, or to make valid comparisons between the intelligence of different people. This may or may not be a good thing. In areas of psychology which have traditionally involved extensive intelligence testing there are some psychologists who consider that conventional tests (such as the WAIS) are based on too narrow a concept of intelligence and are therefore too limited to measure intelligence – those psychologists may dislike the idea of using conventional tests at all.

Other psychologists may view conventional testing as a quick and practical way to find out if a person has specific difficulties which can then be investigated in more depth. For example, a profile based on the different sub-tests of the WAIS might show that a person with average or better than average intelligence overall performs well on several sub-tests, but has particular difficulties on other sub-tests which reflect working memory performance and speed of processing – such a profile might be indicative of dyslexia. If a psychologist finds such a profile then she could go on to carry out further investigations to reveal the extent of the person's dyslexia. Yet other psychologists consider that intelligence and ability testing is important and necessary, and they would have no hesitation in making judgements about people directly from the results of conventional tests.

It is unlikely that people will omit the word 'intelligence' from their conversations, just as it is unlikely that society will abandon the intelligence tests which are now ubiquitous. If people and psychologists are to continue to use 'intelligence' as a concept with meaning, it is important to clarify that meaning as precisely as possible. However, even after more than a century of research the notion of intelligence remains, as Richardson (1991: 1) says, 'a flexible concept with many meanings . . . it is one of the most elusive and slippery of ideas'.

CHAPTER SUMMARY

1 The word and concept 'intelligence' is difficult to define – it may be used in different ways by different people. The lack of an agreed definition makes if difficult to investigate intelligence or compare theories of intelligence which are based on different concepts of intelligence.

2 There is a long tradition of research into intelligence. Galton was one of the first to attempt to design a measure of intelligence. The early tests included a variety of physical and cognitive measures and were not always successful at predicting a person's later performance.

3 Binet designed the first effective intelligence test – to identify children who had learning difficulties in school. A large number of later intelligence tests have been based, directly or indirectly, on Binet's original intelligence scale. The measurement of intelligence is referred to as the 'psychometric approach'.

4 Another approach to intelligence research has been taken by researchers such as Spearman and Vernon. They investigated the relationship between different abilities using a mathematical technique called factor analysis. Some researchers came to the conclusion that there was a single, important, underlying factor (usually labelled 'g') that affected an individual's performance across all tasks – if someone performed well on one task they were likely to perform well on another task as well.

5 Other researchers (such as Thurstone) placed more emphasis on separate factors which were thought to be largely independent of each other. Gardner argued that rather than a general intelligence, there are several distinct 'intelligences', and an individual may perform well on one, or more, of these but not necessarily on all.

6 Savants are people with generally very low intelligence who do have a remarkable ability to excel in one ability (music, drawing, memory). Such cases support the idea that abilities can be independent of one another.

7 Researchers who have adopted an information-processing approach to intelligence concentrate on the cognitive processes which may contribute to intelligent performance. Some researchers (e.g. Hunt) have emphasized the relationship between individuals' speed of information processing and their scores on intelligence tests.

8 Other researchers in the same tradition have considered wider aspects of intelligence. Sternberg has not only considered the cognitive processes involved in solving tasks (such as analogies) which are a common part of intelligence tests, but has also stressed the need to take into account other aspects of intelligence (such as practical and social skills). He put forward the 'triarchic theory of intelligence' to integrate these different aspects of intelligent behaviour.

9 All tests of intelligence should be reliable (produce a similar result each time they are used with the same person) and valid (be testing what they are meant to be measuring).

10 There is evidence that intelligence is inherited. There is also evidence that people's intelligence scores are influenced by environmental factors. In other words, both genetic and environmental factors contribute to an individual's intelligence score. These factors are inseparable in practice. Intelligence is not necessarily 'fixed' for any one person, because education and positive environmental experiences can result in an increase in that person's intelligence score.

■ Further Work ■

1. Collect as many definitions of intelligence as possible from journals, textbooks or dictionaries; or better still, carry out surveys directly with people by asking them how they define intelligence. Try to categorize all the definitions collected and discuss which ones could be tested to measure a person's intelligence.
2. Consider the differences between intelligence tests and school or college examinations. Do the latter measure intelligence?
3. What implications do recent theories of intelligence have for the design of intelligence tests?
4. The term 'intelligence' is sometimes used as if it describes a single underlying ability, and sometimes used as if it refers to groups of separate abilities. Why?

■ Further Reading ■

Richardson, K. (1991) *Understanding Intelligence*. Milton Keynes: Open University Press.

> This book discusses, in a critical way, the issues and debates which have surrounded the concept of intelligence.

Gregory, R. J. (1992) *Psychological Testing: History, Principles and Applications*. Boston: Allyn and Bacon.

> An excellent compendium of all intelligence tests (and other psychological tests). Despite the technical nature of many tests, Gregory describes them clearly and discusses the merits, or otherwise, of each test.

Gould, S. J. (1981) *The Mismeasure of Man*. Harmondsworth: Penguin.

> Gould discusses the history of intelligence measures and intelligence testing. He takes a critical approach which highlights many of the underlying motives, often very dubious, which have influenced the use of intelligence tests. Always very readable, this book is not only about measuring intelligence, it is also about the practice, honest or otherwise, of researchers who have used results from intelligence tests to further their own political beliefs.

PART 7

Applied Psychology

CHAPTER 16

Clinical and Health Psychology

Graham Turpin and Pauline Slade

▓ Introduction ▓

If you were to ask a lay-person what a psychologist did or why someone might study psychology, the usual answer concerns how psychology provides a better understanding of human behaviour. It is people oriented and focused on how individuals experience and function in the social world around them. Lay-accounts of psychology also tend to associate the therapeutic role of psychologists with the experience and treatment of mental illness. Indeed this frequently gives rise to the public's confusion surrounding the terms 'psychologist', 'psychiatrist' and 'psychoanalyst'. Accordingly, many people motivated to study psychology do not wish only to gain insight into human behaviour, experiences and feelings, but also to use this knowledge in order to resolve perhaps their own or other peoples' psychological problems.

This desire to apply psychology to human problems is a powerful motivating force, and also accounts for why applied and professional psychologists have an ever-growing influential position within public services responsible for providing education, childcare, health and social care. Young parents studying psychology for the first time will find it irresistible not to apply their newly acquired knowledge to their child's development and progress. Similarly, psychology students will be tempted to validate different psychological approaches in terms of how useful they are in understanding their own individual personal problems and dilemmas, and those of their friends and acquaintances. However, we need to be cautious, since as we will learn later in this chapter, gaining an understanding of human problems and disabilities is often complex, and the application of psychological treatment is a highly skilled and responsible professional activity.

The area of psychology, therefore, where the lay-person has traditionally recognized its greatest potential impact is in understanding mental health and mental illness. Indeed, the most popular psychology classes tend to be those on 'psychological disorder', 'abnormal psychology' or PSYCHOPATHOLOGY, and many psychology graduates seek further training as clinical psychologists. This popularity reflects the traditional application of clinical psychology to explain and treat mental-health problems such as anxiety, depression, psychosis, eating disorders, etc. However, there has been a recent development which has had a major impact on the application of psychology to healthcare. Within the past thirty years, psychological research and theories have been applied not only to 'mental' health problems but also to 'physical' health problems. Today, there is widespread recognition of the influential role of psychological and behavioural factors in the expression, maintenance and treatment of many physical illnesses (heart disease, diabetes, renal failure, pain, etc.). Consequently, clinical psychologists have extended the range of clinical problems and client groups with whom they work, and have moved from psychiatric hospitals or mental-health clinics, out into primary-care and general hospital settings. New terms for this psychological discipline have also evolved, including PSYCHOSOMATICS, 'behavioural medicine', 'medical psychology' and 'health psychology'. We shall use the latter term here.

Within the profession of applied psychology, a controversial debate is being held regarding the boundaries between clinical and health psychology. Proponents of health psychology argue for a separate discipline, with distinct boundaries between clinical and health psychology with respect to theory and research, the nature of health problems, methods of treatment, and professional organization and training. An emphasis is also placed on non-individual forms of intervention, such as health education and health promotion. The opposite view considers health psychology to be an extension of clinical psychology, focusing specifically on people with physical health problems and their associated psychological needs.

The latter approach described above will be adopted within this chapter. Rather than trying to identify the differences between clinical and health psychology, or mental and physical illnesses, we wish to stress the commonality of psychological approaches to mental and physical health. Indeed, we would argue that health and well-being should not be arbitrarily separated into 'mental' and 'physi-

PSYCHOPATHOLOGY

PSYCHOSOMATICS

cal'. An approach that emphasizes psychological, social and biological factors will be necessary for the understanding of all health problems. Our belief is that it is essential to consider all three factors when seeking to account for experiences of health and illness.

The aims of this chapter, therefore, are to survey psychological theories and perspectives on both physical and mental health. Where possible we will seek to address both aspects of health and illness, although it may be that some theories or models have been developed specifically with either mental or physical health problems particularly in mind. Our approach will be essentially integrative, and we hope to illustrate each approach where possible with examples of both physical and mental-health problems. Case studies will be included to illustrate particular clinical problems and to provide examples of various psychological therapies and interventions. Finally, we will briefly describe the professional roles and activities of both clinical and health psychologists as they currently exist within the UK.

▦ Concepts of Health and Illness ▦

When someone feels ill there is often clear evidence of infection, indications of physiological changes or some pathological process. However, the term 'illness' in reality requires a much broader conceptualization. When someone is 'ill' does this inevitably imply that there is evidence of physical damage or an ongoing damaging physiological process, or just that an individual is experiencing symptoms which are generally viewed as unpleasant? Indeed, is it necessary for an individual her/himself to view these symptoms as undesirable or be aware of any problem? Consider the circumstances in which an individual who feels well, attends for a routine health check for employment purposes, and raised blood pressure is detected. Can this person now be considered as being 'ill' in some way? In this chain of events the individual has not been aware of any unpleasant symptoms and yet there are indications of an ongoing pathological process. In other circumstances lack of awareness or insight may itself be a recognized feature of some mental conditions. For example, in paranoia involving delusions of persecution, one characteristic is that individuals may lack understanding that their interpretation of the world is in any way unusual. In such circumstances the individual is often brought to the attention of healthcare services, not through their own volition but because of the impact of their behaviour on others or through others' concerns. There are certainly instances in which 'illness' may occur without the individual's personal awareness of symptoms.

If personal awareness is not a requirement for illness, then is it necessary for there to be evidence of physical abnormality or a damaging physiological process? There are many occasions when individuals experience symptoms but doctors are unable to find any evidence of physiological or physical abnormality. For example, many women experience abdominal pain for which after numer-

Plate 16.1 A child regards
her mirror image: what
am I?
Source: Collections/Sandra
Lousada.

ous investigations gynaecologists can find no physical explanation. Clearly, in
such circumstances the distress is real, but would the person be considered as
ill? The woman herself is certainly likely to take this point of view, and yet her
difficulties may be viewed as insignificant by doctors because they are unsub-
stantiated by medical evidence.

The concepts of the sick role and abnormal illness behaviour are also of value
in understanding the meaning of the term illness. Parsons (1951) suggests that
the experience of illness leads to certain benefits but also involves certain responsibilities. Whilst an individual is 'ill' they are at liberty to relinquish many
of their social and occupational roles. This entitles an individual to rest in bed, to
avoid many routine duties and receive help from others. However, the 'ill' individual is expected 'not to want to be ill' and to take reasonable steps to become
well again; hence to seek and cooperate with appropriate medical help. In some
circumstances important social factors may maintain an 'illness'. For example, if
a previously non-attentive partner becomes highly solicitous because of the ill-

ness then the advantages of recovery may be outweighed by the disadvantages. In some such cases the behaviours associated with the illness, staying in bed, avoiding activities, etc., may be maintained when physiological indicators suggest that recovery should be in progress. In such circumstances the person may be considered by others as experiencing 'abnormal illness behaviour'.

In understanding the concept of illness the role of cultural values is also worthy of attention. After the birth of a child in Western societies women are expected to return to so-called normal activity and resume responsibilities in their lives after a matter of hours, or at most several days. Consider the example of a woman who has remained in bed, requiring all her needs to be provided for by others, for the duration of a month after giving birth to her child. Other than feeding the child, she has relinquished all other responsibilities. Could this woman be considered as ill? It is most likely that concerns about her health would be voiced and medical opinions sought. However, in some other societies it is expected that for the month after childbirth the new mother should be cared for in this way, and the behaviour outlined would be considered as unremarkable and indeed the norm. In our own society in the recent past, two weeks of hospital bed-rest was the typical care provided after giving birth. These examples illustrate the need to distinguish between disease, illness and sick role. Illness, it should be stressed, requires a much broader conceptualization, and although it is usually associated with medical evidence of abnormality, it also incorporates aspects of the individuals' wider functioning, self-perceptions and behaviours, and requires consideration of social context and societal norms.

Definitions of physical and psychological well-being

When we say a person is 'healthy' what is the meaning of this term? Can the experience of health be equated with the absence of 'illness' or merely indicate that the person shows no evidence of disease? If an individual is free from the experience of unpleasant symptoms, shows no evidence of physiological abnormality and does not report experiences or exhibit behaviours considered beyond the realm of 'normality', are they 'healthy'? Surely the concept of health must involve more than the absence of illness. Attempts have been made to define this concept in terms of ability to fulfil family and occupational roles, being integrated into a social network, and experiencing positive thoughts and emotions. Such ideas view health as incorporating aspects of behaviour, thoughts and feelings in addition to judgements about physical status. However, it must be noted that such ideas themselves involve value judgements about the desirability of maintenance of various roles and social relationships, all of which may differ between cultures. If health and illness are considered as incorporating biological, behavioural, cognitive, emotional and social functioning, and as representing the two poles of a continuum, then the majority of individuals are likely to be represented in the middle area. One implication is that the exceptionally healthy individual may be as, or even more, uncommon, than the very ill individual, and as such could be considered as abnormal. At this point it is important to consider what we mean by normality and abnormality.

Problems of defining normality and abnormality

As we have discussed above, exceptional health and longevity may be as rare as chronic physical illness. However, neither longevity nor physical illness are considered particularly 'abnormal' by society; they are a natural consequence of the human condition. In contrast, mental illness is often viewed differently, resulting frequently in people with a mental-health problem being stigmatized, considered abnormal and labelled with derogatory terms such as 'mad', 'bizarre', 'idiot', 'insane', 'psycho'. This section will address questions of abnormality.

It has traditionally been assumed that people suffering from a mental or sometimes physical illness, are in some sense 'abnormal' or are experiencing some 'abnormal' psychological state or level of functioning. In contrast, 'normal' people are said to be 'healthy' or, at the very least, not displaying signs of

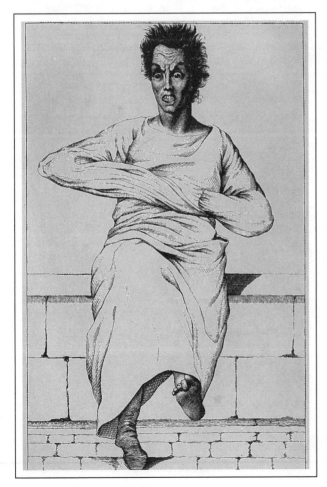

Plate 16.2 'The Lunatic'
Source: Mary Evans Picture Library.

Box 16.1 Identifying Normality and Abnormality

Recognizing abnormal behaviour is essentially a subjective judgement that each of us makes. It is influenced by many implicit values and factors. The exercise below is to help you appraise how you and your friends recognize and identify 'abnormality' in others. Please read the short vignettes below, which describe different individuals.

1. Mr Smith has always lived alone in an isolated cottage. He has six dogs which he looks after. He never goes out of the cottage unless absolutely necessary, and has no friends or visitors.

2. Mr Jones is intensely afraid of heights. He has left a job because his office was on the fifth floor, and refuses to visit his daughter who lives in Austria because of the mountains.

3. Mrs Jarvis, who was born in Jamaica, is a follower of the Pentecostal Church and believes that on occasions she is possessed by Spirits which make her 'speak in tongues'.

4. Mrs Smith was arrested for shop-lifting two weeks ago. She blamed the tablets (valium) that she has been taking for the last five years but had recently discontinued.

Now rate them on the two scales below as to whether the person has psychiatric/psychological disorder and also whether in your opinion they should seek treatment. Having rated each case vignette, compare your ratings with your friends and discuss any agreements or disagreements in your judgements.

	The person suffers from a psychiatric/psychological disorder				
	Strongly agree 1	Moderately agree 2	Do not know 3	Moderately disagree 4	Strongly disagree 5
1	1	2	3	4	5
2	1	2	3	4	5
3	1	2	3	4	5
4	1	2	3	4	5
5	1	2	3	4	5
6	1	2	3	4	5
7	1	2	3	4	5
8	1	2	3	4	5
9	1	2	3	4	5
10	1	2	3	4	5
11	1	2	3	4	5
12	1	2	3	4	5

5. Mr White is a successful executive who has just been told by his GP that he has high blood pressure.
6. Bob is a street musician who recently dropped out of art school. He likes to 'perform' using a variety of vegetables and dead fish!
7. Mrs White is a housewife who spends nearly every day at home keeping the house 'spick and span'. Her husband returned early from night work last week and found her dusting at 2 a.m.
8. Jane is 22 years old and a dancer. Although she weighs only 6 stone she is continually dieting.
9. Bob is a loner who keeps to himself because he believes that the social-security snoopers are out to kill him. Although unemployed he refuses to seek any welfare benefits.
10. Sue is a 6-year-old girl who is extremely shy and seldom speaks. She becomes very upset if her parents alter her playroom furniture.
11. Joe is 9 years old and wets the bed five times a week. His parents' marriage broke up when he was 5 years old.
12. Mrs Black is married with two daughters. Last week she confided to her best friend that she had never experienced an orgasm.

The person needs treatement for his/her problems				
Strongly agree 1	Moderately agree 2	Do not know 3	Moderately disagree 4	Strongly disagree 5
1	2	3	4	5
1	2	3	4	5
1	2	3	4	5
1	2	3	4	5
1	2	3	4	5
1	2	3	4	5
1	2	3	4	5
1	2	3	4	5
1	2	3	4	5
1	2	3	4	5
1	2	3	4	5
1	2	3	4	5

abnormality. This distinction between 'normal' and 'abnormal' has been a question which has vexed psychologists for many years. Clearly, there are many experiences, such as anxiety, sadness, malnutrition, which are common human experiences and represent the 'norm' for many individuals, cultures or societies. However, society also attributes some value judgements concerning these human conditions and distinguishes between acceptable limits of normality and unacceptable limits of abnormality.

In order to resolve such inconsistencies, attempts have been made to identify particular dimensions or definitions of 'normality' and 'abnormality'. Unfortunately, all such attempts have failed, and it would be wrong to presume that any simple dimension would be adequate to define abnormality. Many separate judgements are made on a range of dimensions and values as to what constitute normality or abnormality, and accordingly resultant norms or socials rules will vary across cultures and subcultures. Indeed, different individuals will make quite differing judgements of abnormality and as to whether an individual is suffering from some form of mental or physical illness. Box 16.1 provides an exercise for you to explore your own implicit definitions of normality and whether you believe an individual might seek treatment for a mental-health problem. If you compare your responses with those of friends or fellow students who have completed the same ratings, you will understand that people differ considerably in how they judge normality and abnormality.

Nevertheless, it is useful to consider whether a particular feeling, experience or behaviour might be thought to be intrinsically abnormal and require some form of psychological treatment or amelioration. For clinicians this is a real dilemma since many clients consult therapists with day-to-day problems and troubles which perhaps ought not to be labelled as clinically abnormal and, therefore, require some specialized therapy or treatment. For example, George Brown (cf. Brown & Harris 1989) has shown many times that women with young children, living in inner-city areas, from working-class backgrounds, and without the support of a close confidant are at risk of becoming depressed. Should we label this depression 'abnormal' and treat it with antidepressant medication, or see it as a 'normal' response to an adverse set of life circumstances? Since not all women under these circumstances become depressed, some therapists would consider that the depression is an abnormal response and that treatment is appropriate. In contrast, others would see depression as a 'normal' response but argue that such women need to be enabled to overcome the adversity within their lives, and hence defeat their depression by a process of personal development and growth. The latter, it is argued, is more likely to come about through cultural and political changes than necessarily through individual psychotherapy.

Approaches to abnormality

What factors should psychologists consider, therefore, in order to make these judgements? Several different dimensions have been traditionally identified

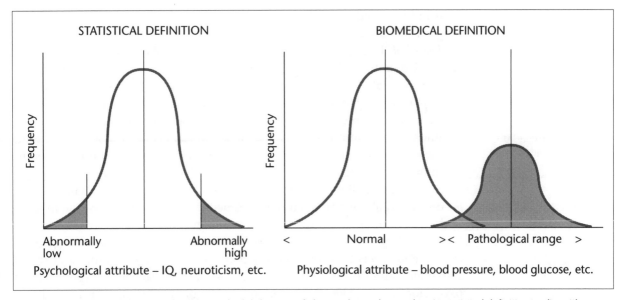

Figure 16.1 Comparison of statistical and biomedical definitions of abnormality and normality. (A statistical definition implies either abnormally high or low values of a psychological variable which is normally distributed. A biomedical definition of abnormality implies a separate pathological distribution outside of the normal range. A hypothetical disease process is said to be responsible for the shift from normal to abnormal functioning.)

which inform how judgements of abnormality are made. These include:

Statistical. Psychologists in particular have sought to identify abnormality by measurement. With reference to a normal distribution, abnormality may be defined as being attributes with infrequent values. This is illustrated in figure 16.1. Examples of such an approach have included Eysenck's personality theory, and also the classification of intellectual ability and disability. Eysenck (1967) has sought to explain common forms of personality as measured by NEUROTICISM, INTROVERSION and PSYCHOTICISM. This implies that mental illness is a question of degree and represents on a continuum a quantitative and not a qualitative difference from 'normal' functioning. Critiques of this approach, however, dispute that 'abnormal' behaviour is on a continuum with 'normal' behaviour.

Another example concerns intellectual functioning and refers to a discontinued practice of classifying individuals as mentally subnormal or severely subnormal on the basis of their IQ score. Although such distinctions are based on the distribution of IQ scores, certain value judgements have been implicitly made. For example, a person with a severe intellectual disability has an IQ score of the same order of statistical rarity as a genius, but at the opposite end of the dimension. Although in statistical terms their 'abnormalities' are equivalent, high IQs are more respected than low IQs.

Although the above examples relate to psychological constructs, statistical definitions of abnormal functioning are also relevant to physical illnesses. Most physical conditions are characterized by doctors with respect to normal measures of functioning. Hence, hypertension (raised blood pressure) or hyperthy-

NEUROTICISM

EXTROVERSION–
INTROVERSION

PSYCOTICISM

roidism (increased thyroid activity) are defined as deviations outside a normal range of functioning.

Biomedical. This approach, in direct contrast to the above statistical approach, emphasizes both qualitative and quantitative differences. Hence, as already described, a deviation in normality may be indicated either by the presence of some self-reported symptom or some abnormal measurement or sign. However, it is assumed that the mere description of an extreme value or function is itself an insufficient definition of abnormality. The BIOMEDICAL APPROACH assumes that some qualitatively different pathological process is underlying the expression of the symptom or deviation of a diagnostic sign (see figure 16.1). Hence, in the previous example an individual with elevated blood pressure or thyroid functioning is considered abnormal when it is assumed that the elevation is due to some underlying pathological process (such as kidney failure or thyroid tumour), and is not an extreme physiological response to some environmental challenge. Similarly, an adolescent with a very low body weight might be either a victim of starvation, suffering from a physical illness such as cancer, or experiencing a psychological disorder such as anorexia. The biomedical approach would assume that, in the latter condition, some underlying pathological physiological process might explain the antipathy towards normal body weight.

Although the biomedical approach provides sufficient explanations for many physical conditions, it is not without its critiques. In particular, it is argued that many psychological disorders may not have an identifiable and specific physiological or organic cause. Instead, such disorders are described by psychiatrists as functional or psychologically caused. Even where a pathogen may be identified (as in many physical illnesses), psychological factors may well moderate how well an individual functions and their level of physical and psychological well-being. Hence, many health problems have multiple determinants and not a single pathological cause. Finally, note that many socially derived patterns of deviant or illegal behaviour have been controversially (and inappropriately) labelled in the past as exclusively biologically determined and pathological – for example, delinquency, homosexuality, single-parenthood, moral deficiency, and so on.

Cultural. Many forms of 'abnormality' are culturally defined, particularly with regard to the value judgements associated with particular norms, and the societal response to such norms. Some sociologists and psychiatrists have argued that much mental illness is not actually an illness but social deviancy (see Bootzin & Acocella 1988). Social deviancy is behaviour that violates social norms and elicits strong disapproval or stigmas. A person who, according to Scheff, is labelled as 'mentally ill' will display what are considered as 'strange, bizarre and frightening' behaviours which break fundamental norms of social behaviour; this in Scheff's terms constitutes 'residual deviance'. The social context is particularly important in determining such deviancy. Sunbathing naked on a nudist beach in Brighton may be culturally acceptable, but would be deviant if such behaviour occurred in the main square of your home town.

BIOMEDICAL
APPROACH

The importance of cultural factors is often undervalued, although they may play an important role in explaining many social inequalities in health and illness. The incidence of both physical and mental illness varies widely across gender, social class and cultures, and as a result of cross-cultural translocation, unemployment, etc. Moreover, an understanding of social influences also helps to understand society's responses to illness. Different moral (e.g. in the cases of homosexuality and gender identity) and legal (e.g. in the case of definitions of insanity) judgements are made concerning people with mental-health problems. In addition, society has adapted many different postures towards illness and disability, including custodial, moral, medical and equal-rights approaches. Positive social attitudes towards illness, disability and handicap need to be engendered and people given the opportunity to exercise their basic human rights and civil liberties.

Idiographic. Perhaps the approach which is most pragmatic and approximates to the clinician's individual judgement is the idiographic approach. Essentially, a psychological disorder is termed such if it causes the individual undue distress, discomfort, life dissatisfaction, or causes dysfunction either socially or occupationally. For example, most people would experience some anxiety at the prospect of delivering a short speech to an audience of close friends or acquaintances. Clinically, this might be judged as abnormal if the individual's level of anxiety was excessively distressing (highly anxious and physiologically aroused), if it brought about discomfort (tense and trembling), life dissatisfaction (feeling inadequate and a failure) or caused dysfunction (unable to perform at an appropriate level). The four 'Ds' can be a useful rubric by which to weigh up the clinical severity of a problem. Other factors which contribute to idiographic description of abnormality have been defined by Rosenhan and Seligman (1995). These are suffering, maladaptiveness, irrationality and incomprehensibility (i.e. bizarreness), vividness and unconventionality (i.e. eccentricity), observer discomfort (i.e. distress of others and onlookers) and violation of moral and ideal standards (i.e. outrage).

Disability and handicap

We have tried to distinguish between health and illness, and normality and abnormality. However, we wish to stress that such distinctions are more difficult to make than they would first superficially appear. Society also uses other terms such as 'disability' and 'handicap' to describe a variety of so-called physical and mental conditions. Unfortunately, each new term brings with it different values and interpretations. People who have been born with innate brain disorders, and hence have only limited cognitive functions and abilities, have been labelled using numerous derogatory and devaluing terms such as idiot, moron, imbecile, feeble-minded, mentally deficient, subnormal or handicapped, learning disabled, challenging behaviours, etc. These terms reflect different models and approaches to the disabled in our society. Their tendency to alienate and stig-

Plate 16.3 An impoverished environment
Source: Andes Press Agency/ Carlos Reyes-Manzo.

matize the individual reflects the real sense of apprehension and suspicion with which the lay-people often view individuals who act and behave differently to themselves.

Recently, there has been an attempt to use terms such as disability and handicap in a more constructive fashion. The World Health Organization has suggested the following usage for the terms deficit, disability and handicap. The term 'deficit' is used to describe a fundamental and intrinsic dysfunction within the individual which will have some physiological or psychological basis. For example, a deficit might be a memory loss, or an inability to finely control physical actions. These deficits can then give rise to a variety of behavioural and social difficulties which will be recognized as a disability by the individual and those around him or her. However, it would be wrong to merely equate any disability to intrinsic deficits caused by physical or mental illness. Illness usually has associated social consequences, such as difficulty maintaining or gaining employment, poor living standards, poor quality of life, housing and accommodation problems, and so forth. These economic and social consequences, together with society's negative values and social stigma, can be seen as an associated set of handicaps that accompany disability. Such disadvantages, however, do not arise directly from the deficit or illness, but are extrinsic to the individual and are socially caused.

▦ Models and Explanations of Health and Illness ▦

In the previous section, we attempted to distinguish between health and illness, normality and abnormality, and dysfunction and disability. Implicit in many of these accounts are particular theoretical approaches that have been applied to mental and physical health. The purpose of this section is to review these different theoretical models. The first half will focus on models which have traditionally been applied to mental-health problems, whereas the second half will address more general theories relating to health and illness. Some models (for instance, the PSYCHODYNAMIC and BIOPSYCHOSOCIAL) have been applied to both physical and mental-health problems. The interested reader who wishes to read further about these models should consult the many introductory textbooks on abnormal psychology (see Further Reading below).

PSYCHODYNAMIC MODEL

BIOPSYCHOSOCIAL MODEL

Overview of major models used to understand mental health and illness

Before we examine each approach in turn, we need to be clear about what aspects of mental ill-health they are exactly seeking to account for. We will assume, therefore, that it is sensible to consider certain psychological or physical disorders which can be identified as a particular profile of symptoms (i.e. a syndrome). A series of questions can be posed, therefore, about how certain individuals have come to display a particular syndrome or disorder. First, there is the epidemiological question which seeks to explain the differences between certain individuals in a population who will display a specific disorder and those who will not exhibit such symptoms in their lifetimes. (EPIDEMIOLOGY is the study of how diseases spread.) Risk or VULNERABILITY factors associated with the individual expression of the disorder will be identified. Secondly, there is the question of timing. Assuming a group of individuals have identical risks for a disorder, why does one individual suddenly exhibit symptoms and another remain symptom-free? Essentially, this question implies that the pattern of severity of most disorders is episodic in nature and fluctuates over time. Hence, to answer it we need to identify the factors that have triggered or precipitated a particular episode. Thirdly, there is the fundamental question regarding the causal mechanism underlying the expression of the disorder. Sometimes such accounts address the syndrome collectively (for instance, a cause for schizophrenia is thought to be an overactive neurotransmitter system called dopamine) or might refer to individual symptoms or phenomena (psychological models of hallucinations, DELUSIONS, etc.). Finally, there may also be a series of models which account for why certain treatments are effective or not. Usually, the theories which are directed at treatments overlap with those that account for causal mechanisms, but this may not always be the case.

EPIDEMIOLOGY

VULNERABILITY FACTOR

DELUSIONS

It is important, therefore, when reading about theories of both mental or physical illness that you are able to discern what exactly the theory or model is seeking to explain. Is it an epidemiological account, causal model, description of the factors maintaining the disorder, or an explanation of treatment?

Biomedical models

These models are based on the assumption that the transition from health to illness is caused by the presence of a pathogen which disrupts the physiological functioning of the individual and gives rise to the expression of a particular disease or illness. The disease is identified specifically by the nature of the pathogen or pathological mechanism. Pathogens may arise due to chromosomal abnormalities, biochemical dysfunction, immunological dysfunction, infectious agents (viruses or bacteria), ingestion of chemical substances (poisons or substance abuse), or trauma (head injury, psychological stress). The illness or disease expresses itself as a set of symptoms experienced by the patient and observed by the physician. It can also be identified by objective tests of physiological signs of dysfunction. Together these lead to a diagnosis which identifies the likely cause of the pathological mechanism. Finally, treatment is conceptualized as an intervention which corrects the underlying dysfunction (a cure) or controls and suppresses the symptoms associated with it.

Biomedical theories provide the bedrock of physical medicine and account for many of the objective features of specific physical illnesses. However, solely biomedical explanations are unable to account for psychological factors associated with increased risk for a specific illness. Similarly, they are unable to account totally for how individuals cope with or adapt to their illness or disability, and hence for their overall response to treatment and clinical outcome. Accordingly, even within physical medicine, there are those who propose more holistic approaches based on a synthesis of biomedical and psychosocial models (discussed below).

Justification of a strong biomedical model of mental-health problems is a controversial subject. On the one hand there is irrefutable evidence that some forms of mental-health problems or disability are associated with chromosomal abnormalities (e.g. Down's syndrome; Huntington's chorea – an inherited neurological disease) or brain damage (e.g. Korsakoff's psychosis – an acquired organic dementia arising from alcohol abuse). In addition, advances in neuroscience such as genetic markers, brain imaging and so forth, hold great promise for biobehavioural accounts of mental-health problems. On the other hand, for many forms of mental-health problem, there is little direct evidence for a biological pathogen or few objective signs from which to diagnose it. Moreover, biological treatments for many mental-health problems are at their best insufficient and in some cases may even lead to further symptoms or disabling side-effects. (See chapter 5 for further discussion of biological treatments for mental illness.) It is also even more likely that, as in the case of so-called physical illnesses, mental illnesses will be multidetermined by a combination of biological, psychological and social factors (see later accounts of biopsychosocial models).

Intrapsychic models

Intrapsychic models include various psychodynamic accounts of personality development. They are similar to all deterministic accounts, such as the medical model, in that they seek a set of identifiable causes. However, they assert that abnormal behaviour and emotional distress arise from an underlying pathological psychological process. These processes arise due to abnormal personality development and result from the dynamic interplay between various drives and instincts. Abnormal behaviour, therefore, is not learned *per se* but is a product of abnormal personality. Psychodynamically based accounts of certain so-called psychosomatic illnesses (e.g., asthma, headache, ulcers) have also been said to arise from personality dysfunction. Treatment is concerned with redirecting personality development.

The foundations upon which many intrapsychic models are based are the psychodynamic theories of Sigmund Freud. According to Freud (see chapter 14) personality and behaviour are the products of various dynamic energy systems based around primal instincts or drives (e.g. sexual or libidinal impulses). If these drives are blocked, this results in unconscious conflicts, giving rise to DE-FENCE MECHANISMS which manifest themselves as predictable patterns of dysfunctional behaviour. These conflicts are accompanied by anxiety and result from interactions between the different personality structures named: the id, ego and super-ego. The id is concerned with gratification of basic biological instincts and the pleasure principle; the ego is manifested as consciousness and the reality principle; and the super-ego constitutes moral conscience and idealistic striving. The development of an individual's personality structure arises as a result of a maturational process from birth into adulthood, whereby the individual passes through a series of psychosexual stages. Conflicts that arise and are defended against at particular stages are said to result in specific personality types such as anal-obsessive personality (which is characterized by excessive attention to detail, and related to the anal stage of psychosexual development when the infant is said to become preoccupied with toiletting and retention of faeces). Examples of defence mechanisms include: repression, whereby unwanted thoughts or prohibited desires are forced out of consciousness; projection, whereby individuals attribute their own thoughts and feelings to others; displacement, when feelings are redirected to a less threatening target or individual; identification, whereby individuals internalize the thoughts and values of others; and sublimation, when undesirable goals are replaced by more socially desirable aims. Each of these defence mechanisms may be associated with particular neurotic disorders or psychosomatic personalities.

Psychodynamic theory and psychoanalytic treatments have always been subjects for debate. Traditionally, psychoanalysis has been criticized for being unscientific because many of its constructs are not easy to theorize, or objectively measure or quantify in some way, and the ideas are very difficult to test experimentally. Nevertheless, several hypothetical psychodynamic concepts surrounding unconscious processes have recently been studied experimentally with some

DEFENCE
MECHANISMS

Plate 16.4 Potty training
Source: Stephen Lovell-Davis.

success, using paradigms from cognitive psychology. Another major area of debate concerns Freud's reliance on reports of sexual abuse from his female patients, and his later interpretation of these reports with respect to psychosexual fantasies. This raises a fundamental question regarding the validity of the case material from which Freud generalized his psychodynamic theories: many recent theorists assume that abuse had in fact taken place and had not been the subject of fantasy. Finally, psychoanalytic psychotherapy has also been questioned by some both in terms of its effectiveness and the overriding influence that therapy has on individuals' lives (e.g. Masson 1992), particularly as a result of private practice within the US.

Humanistic approaches
A series of different approaches, particularly to therapy, have become known as 'humanistic' (see chapter 14). Essentially they are oriented towards self-awareness, personal development and growth rather than deterministic accounts

of psychopathology. A typical example of a humanistic model is Maslow's 1954 hierarchy of needs. He described a hierarchical structure of human needs which included physical need, safety, belonging and affection, self-esteem and (the most superior need) self-actualization. This latter term describes essential human and creative activities and desires. Similar ideas have been developed by Rogers (1960) in relation to 'client-centred therapy'. Here the therapist provides the client with unconditional positive regard and acts as a listener to the client's concerns and anxieties; any comment expressed by the therapist is delivered in a non-judgemental and non-interpretive fashion.

Other humanistic models and theories include Kelly's self-theory and various different encounter-group therapy approaches. Indeed, together with psychodynamic theories, many of those approaches have merged to evolve new forms of therapy, such as family therapy or systemic therapy, which seek to account for interactions between family members.

Learning and situational perspectives

Many different theories from experimental psychology have been applied as explanations of abnormal psychology. The most influential of these approaches have relied on various applications of learning theory (see chapter 8). Essentially, all abnormal behaviour is viewed as learned. For example, a phobia such as a fear of a snake or spider will have been acquired via a process of classical conditioning. Moreover, the characteristic avoidance of snakes or spiders will be further reinforced and learned, since it leads to a reduction in anxiety. Other learning processes, such as observational learning, may also lead to the acquisition of maladaptive behaviours. Treatments based on the principles of learning theory have been developed and are collectively known as behaviour therapy or modification. These approaches have been used to help disabled people learn new or more adaptive behaviours, or to eliminate maladaptive responses such as phobias, panic attacks, etc. Specific therapeutic techniques include systematic desensitization, '*in vivo* exposure', 'flooding', response prevention, and a range of self-management and self-control strategies. Most of these therapeutic techniques involve the exposure of the client to their fear either in imagination (systematic desensitization) or directly (*in vivo* exposure and flooding), or are aimed at either increasing the person's ability to cope with fear or inhibiting their fear or avoidance behaviour (response prevention).

Solely behavioural approaches, which have been termed 'radical behaviourism', have been criticized due to their narrow approach. In particular, the failure to deal directly with patients' thoughts or cognitions was considered a weakness. For example, many disorders are characterized by major disruptions of thought processes (for example, schizophrenia). However, a radical behavioural approach fails to account for the full-range schizophrenic experience (i.e. delusions, hallucinations, thought disorder), since these processes are not directly observable.

Plate 16.5 'Fear'
Source: Collections/Anthea
Sieveking.

Cognitive and attributional models

As a consequence of the limitations of radical behaviourism, more flexible theo-ries were applied from mainstream psychology. These tended to emphasize the importance of not just learning, but also attentional and ATTRIBUTIONAL PROCESSES – how individuals assign causal meaning to events (see chapters 7 and 11). At the same time, therapists such as Beck and Ellis were attempting to account for disorders such as depression in terms of dysfunctional thinking. Beck suggested that depression might be due to a cognitive distortion whereby a depressed in-dividual has a negative view of themselves, the world and the future. These negative feelings are maintained by the presence of automatic negative thoughts, arising from a negative schemata. These important ideas gave rise to an influen-tial therapeutic approach known as cognitive behaviour therapy, or just cogni-tive therapy. Moreover, Beck's propositions relating psychological dysfunction to abnormal thinking also prompted a major expansion in experimental and cognitive research directed specifically at mental-health problems. For example,

ATTRIBUTIONAL
PROCESSES

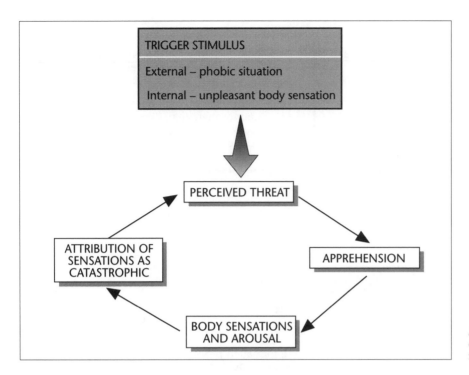

Figure 16.2 A cognitive model of panic attacks
Source: Clark 1986.

the experience of depression has been associated with negative attributions and biased memory processes. Similarly, anxiety disorders such as panic attacks have been accounted for by Clark (1986) as arising from cognitive misinterpretation and 'catastrophization' of physiological events (these are psychological terms for when we misread a situation entirely and interpret it as dangerous or threatening; see figure 16.2). Experimental evidence to support the idea that anxious people experience a bias towards threatening material (e.g. cancer or sickness-related wards) has been demonstrated in studies of attention and implicit memory within these subjects. Finally, attributional models have also been applied to more serious mental-health problems such as paranoid psychoses and schizophrenia. For example, Bentall (1990) has shown that paranoid patients differ from normal and depressive patients in relation to their attributional style. Similarly, deluded patients also show errors of judgement and attributional analysis.

The cognitive paradigm, therefore, represents a major contribution to understanding mental-health problems and has originated from both cognitive psychology and psychotherapy.

Integration

It would be unsurprising if a novice reader were confused at this point in the chapter. A great diversity of models has been presented, each deriving from separate philosophical, psychological or therapeutic influences and backgrounds. How can these models be judged and evaluated? Some criteria might include:

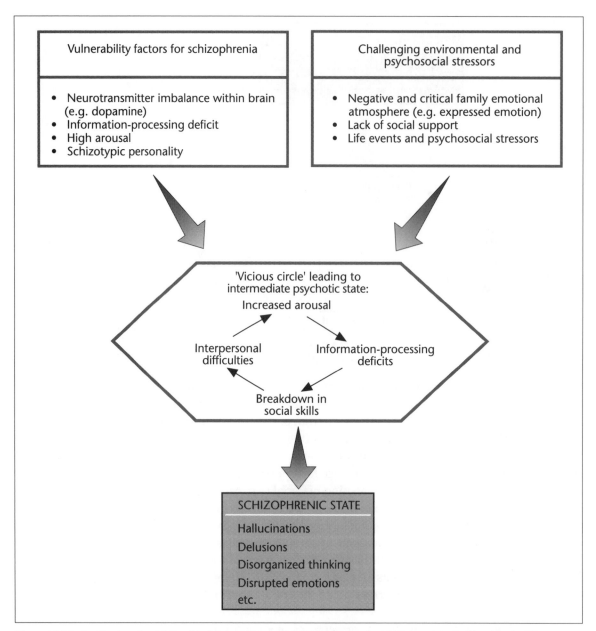

Figure 16.3 A simplified version of Neuchterlein and Dawson's (1984) 'stress-vulnerability' model of schizophrenia. (The model emphasizes the interaction between psychobiological vulnerability factors with psychosocial and environmental stressors which trigger individual episodes of schizophrenia.)

whether a theory or model lends itself to scientific proof; whether experimental evidence exists to uphold its major assertions; how clinically effective the therapeutic approaches derived from the theory or model have actually been; how clients or therapists view the utility or face value of a theory or explanation. One of the satisfying challenges of studying 'psychopathology' is the opportunity to personally evaluate and validate different models and explanations.

With so many different models, should we espouse only one, set one against another in competition, or try to be integrative? Therapists frequently adopt several models and use them differentially, depending upon the nature of the individual and their problem. Similarly, theoretical explanations of illness phenomena are becoming equally eclectic and may involve many multiply-determined models.

A recent example of a type of model which spans several different levels of explanation is the biopsychosocial model. These models have been advocated with respect to both mental-health (schizophrenia and depression) and physical health (diabetes and cardiovascular disease) problems. In relation to schizophrenia, Neuchterlein and Dawson (1984) suggest a biopsychosocial model which they believe provides an explanatory framework for vulnerability in schizophrenia, which is one of the most common and severe forms of mental illness which involves disruption of cognition (thought disorder and delusions), perception (hallucinations), affect (misinterpretation of emotions) and behaviour (lack of motivation and drive).

Essentially, they have tried to link several distinct factors (genetic, biochemical, environmental, social, familial, cognitive) which have been implicated in a person having a greater risk or vulnerability for a schizophrenic breakdown. A simplified version of this model is drawn in figure 16.3. An advantage of such an integrated model is that it suggests complementary ways in which different approaches (cognitive therapy, family therapy, medication, psychosocial, rehabilitation) might be targeted together at alleviating problems and symptoms associated with schizophrenia.

How may psychological factors influence both physical and mental health?

The previous sections have identified a series of different ways of using psychological ideas to understand health problems. However these conceptualisations have primarily been derived from work with individuals with mental-health problems. Aspects of the same models can be applied and extended to aid our understanding of physical health issues and the very major role that psychological factors play in this area. While it is immediately apparent that psychological factors are of importance in mental health and illness, their role and relevance in physical health is less widely recognized. At this point it is important to remember that the concepts of health and illness, as already discussed, incorporated both physical and psychological aspects. We will attempt to demonstrate the importance of psychological influences by describing a series of case vignettes. It will become apparent that even where conditions or experiences may be considered as primarily physical, their onset and course may have involved the operation of psychological factors, and indeed the experience of the condition may have led to psychological consequences.

What evidence is available to support the assertion that our health, in particular our physical health, is influenced in any way by psychological factors? Over the last few hundred years the major developments in knowledge about the workings of our bodies have focused on biological information such as understanding the circulation of the blood, the internal structure of the cell and the role of infectious agents in illness. Until the latter part of this century the primary conceptualization was that illness occurred as the result of physiological malfunction. This can be seen as akin to the biomedical model described in the previous section. However, the inadequacies of this model are becoming more clearly apparent. Consider the case of Mr A:

> Mr A aged 66 was hospitalized for a chest infection and died shortly afterwards. He lived alone, had been eating poorly and had recently lost a lot of weight. It transpired that 4 months ago his wife, whom he had been married to for 40 years, had died suddenly of a heart attack. Since then Mr A had been out very little and had been very preoccupied with his wife's death.

The biomedical model would explain Mr A's death in terms of the fact that he had been exposed to an infectious agent. However it would certainly be correct to consider that he had recently experienced a very important negative event in his life – the death of his wife. Is this likely to be related in any way to his experience of infection? Studies have shown that during the year following the death of a partner the survivor is more likely to suffer, be hospitalized for or die from an infectious illness than individuals who have not experienced such an event. Why might this be the case? One possible explanation lies in the fact that defences to infection are mediated by what is called the immune system, a system which recognizes and renders foreign bodies harmless. Is it possible that the experience of a strongly negative event may adversely affect its functioning? Although the lay idea that someone may die from a broken heart is not itself correct, it does seem that the bereaved partner may have an increased risk of illness and indeed death. We need to look at how these events may influence emotions, and for possible pathways of effect we must turn to models of stress.

Models of stress

The concept of physiological stress was first coined by Cannon in the 1920s. He suggested that when threatened, animals reacted with a 'fight or flight' response. Selye went on to develop a theory of stress. He coined the terms 'stressor' to describe the physical stimulus, and 'stress response' to describe the organism's physiological response. He suggested that, whatever the stressor, the body responded in a predictable way which could be divided into three specific phases. He used the phrase 'general adaptation syndrome' to describe the associated physical changes. In phase 1 the individual shows an initial arousal response to the stressor, which involves increases in breathing, heart rate and sweating, and can be considered as activation of the sympathetic nervous system. The following phase is the phase of resistance, which involves the individual being in a highly aroused state over a longer period of time, with concomitant hormonal changes. Thirdly and finally the phase of exhaustion may be reached. Selye (e.g. 1976) suggested that this occurs when efforts to terminate the stressor have failed, and that diseases of adaptation may occur as a result of prolonged exposure to high levels of hormones and other changes in the phase of resistance. Such conditions might include cardiovascular disease as a result of prolonged high blood pressure, stomach ulcers from prolonged exposure to gastric acids, and cancers in response to changes in the effectiveness of the body's natural defence system.

Selye's original model does not focus at all upon perceptions of the stressor but just documents physiological responses to forms of physical assault on the body. Thus it would be presumed that consciousness was not a necessary prerequisite for the physiological arousal to occur. Work by Mason in the 1970s (e.g. 1975) questioned this assumption and indicated that perception was important; and so psychological factors were drawn into the stress equation. Further developments took place in the 1980s, when Lazarus and Folkman proposed their model of psychological stress based upon two appraisal processes. Cox (1988) provides a useful summary of models. First, it was suggested that an individual appraises the threat inherent in a situation (PRIMARY APPRAISAL), and that the person then appraises their ability to cope with that threat (SECONDARY APPRAISAL). Where the former exceeds the latter, the individual is presumed to experience feelings of stress, and presumably stress responses. Just as the role of psychological factors in the experience of stress responses has been clarified, it is also clear that different emotional responses may lead to different physiological concomitants.

PRIMARY APPRAISAL

SECONDARY APPRAISAL

In attempting to understand how psychology may exert an impact on health and illness it helps to see that, for example, an event perceived as stressful leads to long-term increases in arousal, and ultimately to physical harm through a prolonged stress response. Prolonged raised blood pressure might be a contributory cause in coronary heart disease. Had Mr A also experienced a heart attack then a prolonged stress response might have explained his sudden death, and indeed his susceptibility to infection could be explained in this way.

There are other explanations also incorporating psychological factors. Another pathway might be mediated through emotional responses to stressful events. There is evidence to suggest that when individuals suffer symptoms of depression, feeling miserable and hopeless, with crying spells, lack of interest in activities, poor sleep and appetite, etc., that not only is their mood depressed but their IMMUNOLOGICAL FUNCTIONING may also be less effective. Looking back to the case of Mr A, the death of his wife had clearly led him to experience low moods which may have increased his vulnerability to infection and illness.

IMMUNOLOGICAL FUNCTIONING

It is of interest to consider whether the ideas of Lazarus and Folkman relate to the models developed to account for distress (see previous section). There are similarities with what have become known as the cognitive models of depression and anxiety already described. Essentially the cognitive model considers that events themselves do not cause depressive or anxiety symptoms, but that the way an individual perceives or attributes the event is the important factor. Consider the following:

Ms P and Ms A share a house. One night Ms P is at home alone when she hears a rattling sound downstairs. Her immediate thought is that a burglar has got into her home and she feels very anxious and fearful. Another night Ms A is at home alone and hears the same sound, she thinks to herself that it is the wind rattling the window and consequently feels irritated at the disturbance to her sleep.

In both of these situations the event is identical, but the different constructions placed upon the event lead to different degrees of anticipated threat and different emotional responses. Ms P has developed a pattern in her thinking which leads her to interpret numerous day-to-day situations as highly threatening, and consequently she suffers frequently with unpleasant symptoms of anxiety. Her appraisal of threat within the events she experiences plays a major role in creating her symptoms. Similarly, according to Lazarus and Folkman, appraisal of threat is important in the experience of stress and physiological responses which may impact negatively upon physical health. In some cases, patterns in cognitive appraisal may lead primarily to the experience of physical symptoms, but in other cases emotional symptoms may mediate between events, physiological responses and physical illness.

There is certainly evidence to suggest that the same event can trigger different responses in different individuals, or indeed the same individuals at different times. For example, Brown and Harris (1989) found that 80 per cent of women who began to experience significant depressive feelings had recently experienced a major unpleasant event such as a serious illness, death of a loved one, or redundancy. In their subsequent work it was recognized that such events often involved some sort of loss experience, whether it be the loss of a relationship through death or marital breakdown, the loss of a job, or even the loss of a cherished ideal such as pursuing a particular career or being able to start a family. However, while in almost all those with the onset of depressive symptoms one could identify a preceding negative event, only 20 per cent of those experiencing such events subsequently experienced depressive symptoms. Why should this be the case? The cognitive theory would suggest that people may appraise events differently. Why does this individual variability exist?

It appears that the concept of vulnerability may be helpful in this context. Are there certain aspects of an individual that may lead them to respond more negatively to an unpleasant event? If this is the case, can these aspects be related to events individuals have experienced, their GENETIC PREDISPOSITION, or features of their current environment? As we have already discussed, Brown and Harris certainly identified several factors which if present increased the probability of an individual becoming depressed in the aftermath of a negative life event. These factors were the loss or separation from mother before the age of 11 years, having three children under the age of 5 years, the absence of a confidant, and not being in paid employment. How might these factors derive their influence? The

GENETIC
PREDISPOSITION

Plate 16.6 Social support
Source: Sally and Richard Greenhill.

early experience of separation from mother may lead to the presence of a cognitive schema relating to loss which is easily reactivated in the presence of an event with similar features – i.e. the individual is cognitively sensitized. The other features may relate to aspects of the current environment, degree of demand upon the individual (number of children) and their resources to cope with demand. The absence of a confidant can be seen in this context as limiting COPING resources. This work stimulated the development of interest in the concept of SOCIAL SUPPORT, and its relationship to responses to stressful situations. While not being in employment might be construed as low demand, it can also be considered as restricting access to social contacts and therefore potential support, as well as being associated with greater financial hardship.

The example of bereavement also provides an important illustration with regard to social support. Thinking back to the case of Mr A, not only must he experience the unpleasant feelings associated with any major loss, but he has also probably lost the person who may generally have helped him to cope with difficulties. Had the person who had died been a relative or even close friend, it is highly likely that Mr A and his wife would have discussed this event. Through sharing the experience of loss, they would to some extent have provided social support for one another.

COPING RESOURCES

SOCIAL SUPPORT

Social support

Social support is a broad concept with varied definitions. It often refers to the feeling that one is valued by others or that one has someone to confide in. It may also encompass having access to practical help and information from others. As already noted, Brown and Harris suggested that the lack of a confidant was a predictor for depressive symptoms after an adverse event. There is certainly evidence to suggest that lack of social support (although variously defined) is associated with more adverse health outcomes. How may this effect be mediated? We need to consider what happens when we talk over our problems with an individual who has genuine concern for us. There are a variety of potential mechanisms.

Simply the fact that another person is prepared to spend their time and show their concern for our plight may help us to feel better about ourselves as individuals. It emphasizes that there are people close by who believe us to be important to them. The experience of support may therefore enhance damaged self-esteem. The process of talking about the difficulties may help us to feel more relaxed. This is recognized in lay-terms as the value of 'getting things off one's chest'. In addition, having to explain the problem to another often helps a person to improve their own understanding of the situation and therefore to generate solutions. Another person may offer their own different perspective both on the situation and potential solutions; they may also offer practical help. Thinking back to our examples, the impact of Mr A's bereavement is probably intensified because it has involved the loss of the individual in his life who has typically provided him with the most help in coping with his difficulties both in terms of emotional support and with respect to practical help in his daily living. Following her death in all probability he was required to take on roles and responsibilities previously carried out by his wife. Social support therefore implies availability of assistance in a range of different guises. The case of Ms C is also of interest in this context:

Ms C is a secretary for a small firm which first started two years ago. She has always worked conscientiously but has found it increasingly difficult to complete the work expected of her as the turnover of the firm has increased. One day the owner tells her that they have just lost a very lucrative contract as a result of the fact that their tender did not reach the required place in time, and that this is her fault, as it should have been dispatched by an earlier post. Ms C goes home feeling upset and guilty about this. She lives alone, has recently broken up with her boyfriend and has no family or friends close by. She finds that she can't get this incident out of her mind and continues to feel distressed. Unexpectedly her sister calls. She can tell that Ms C is not her usual self and asks her what is the matter. Ms C talks over her distressing experience in detail with her sister. After the conversation Ms C realizes she feels much more relaxed and less upset. She can face going back into work tomorrow. What has happened?

Ms C's sister helped her to put the problem into perspective: her job is only one part of her life. She also helped her to realize that the demands upon her time had been highly inappropriate for many months, and suggested how she could deal with the problem of work overload by discussing it with her boss and suggesting various ways of rationalizing demand and improving efficiency through access to additional equipment. In this case the social support provided had facilitated a simple cognitive restructuring that is a different way of thinking about the situation, and a change in her view of the significance of this event in her life as a whole. It also gave an opportunity to ventilate feelings, develop a better understanding of the issues and her own role in these, together with a sense of shared experience and suggestions for taking practical steps to resolve the problem. It is little wonder that access to social support is now considered an important factor in preventing illness responses and promoting well-being.

It seems that the availability of social support may influence coping, and this concept needs to be explored further. What do we mean by coping and how might it affect health and illness?

Coping

When we talk about coping we mean the efforts people make to deal with unpleasant experiences. These may take many different forms, varying from trying to find out more about a problem, taking active steps towards resolution, saying to oneself that it isn't important (and thereby downgrading the importance of the issue), pretending the problem doesn't exist, drinking more alcohol, exercising. All these responses, and there are many more which could be considered, are attempts at coping. Lazarus has introduced the idea of dividing coping attempts into two groups based upon their function: 'problem focused' and 'emotion focused' coping. The former would include attempts to resolve the problem itself, and the latter, to deal with the emotional consequences. For example, in the case of Ms P, deciding to seek help from a therapist and trying to identify and alter her problematic thoughts could be considered as problem-focused coping, whereas drinking alcohol to blank out the feelings of anxiety could be considered as emotion focused. Similarly, Ms C has used discussion with her sister as an emotion-focused coping strategy to deal with her feelings, and this has enabled her to think about using a problem-focused strategy, talking with her boss about his expectations of her. In some situations where, for example, it is difficult to change the situation, emotion-focused coping may be particularly desirable; and in others, where resolution of the problem is possible, then problem-focused coping may be more helpful. However, it seems that some emotion-focused strategies such as wishful thinking may be particularly unhelpful. In other cases failure to use problem-focused strategies may mean that a problem which is resolvable remains, and the individual continues to experience its negative consequences as a result of their own passivity. There is evidence to suggest that in many situations an active problem-focused approach is beneficial to health.

The parallel concept of 'perceived control' is important. Where individuals feel that they can influence important aspects of their current circumstances they are, in general, less likely to experience emotional distress. In addition, in terms of physical health, there is evidence that people in occupations with low control but with high demands being made upon them, such as air-traffic controllers, suffer from high rates of physical illness. How we attempt to cope and the control we feel we can exert over aspects of our lives seem to have important implications for physical health. Again there are parallels from within theories developed to explain mental-health problems. One of the main theories developed to explain the experience of depression is 'LEARNED HELPLESSNESS' (Seligman 1975), which derived from experiments in which animals were subjected to inescapable aversive stimulation. As a consequence some animals became very passive in their responding, failing to escape when this became possible. Analogies were drawn with the apathy often associated with the lowered mood considered a feature of depression. This learning theory of depression has since been extended to incorporate feelings of hopelessness about the future, with their implications about lack of control. Again it can be seen that coping strategies and perceptions of control relate to physical and psychological conditions.

LEARNED HELPLESSNESS

The biological characteristics of the individual

In addition to considering the experience of life events and coping responses together with factors such as the availability of support, it is also important to consider the biological constitution of an individual.

Each individual carries genetic information which may influence their propensity to certain disease processes or psychological conditions. For example, comparisons of male students with and without a family history of high blood pressure have indicated no differences in their blood pressure under resting conditions, but under task stress those with a family history showed greater elevations, demonstrating their biological propensity to such reactions. Repeated elevations may increase the probability of the development of heart disease.

Enduring psychological characteristics of the individual

Other features which may be important are the enduring psychological aspects of individuals' approach to life and themselves. One feature recently proposed is 'dispositional optimism' (Scheier & Carver 1992) – the tendency to believe that one will generally experience good rather than bad outcomes in life. This can be considered as a generalized expectancy which is conceptualized as stable over time and situation. Scheier and Carver suggest that individuals high on this dimension may show better adaptation in terms of lower levels of depressive symptoms and higher levels of happiness at times of difficulty. For example, when the subjective reactions of a group of men having coronary artery bypass surgery were investigated, optimists reported lower levels of hostility and depression than pessimists before the surgical procedure. In the week following the operation optimists reported greater relief and happiness, and at six months they reported a much more favourable quality of life. Such reports were independent of medical factors such as the original seriousness of the disease or the extent of surgery.

How might the optimism create its impact? One suggestion is that optimists may approach problems differently. This relates to the previous discussion of coping strategies. Another suggestion is that optimists tend to use coping strategies which focus upon influencing the problem rather than just dealing with its emotional effects – a bias to problem-focused rather than emotion-focused coping strategies. For example, a person who felt overloaded at work might talk to their superior about ways of adjusting workload, rather than just trying to relax or drink more alcohol as ways of dealing with the unpleasant feelings created. There are also suggestions that optimists accept the reality of adverse events rather than denying their existence, but also attempt to make the best of the situation by construing it in a positive way and learning from the experience. Therefore it may be that optimists tend to cope with difficult situations in rather different ways from pessimists.

Other psychological concepts which focus upon individual variations in how people view difficult situations are 'hardiness' (Kolbasa et al. 1982) and 'sense of coherence' (Antonovsky 1988). These may relate to positive health outcomes via some sort of emotional resilience. The former suggests that individuals who view change as challenge rather than threat, who commit themselves fully in their activities, and who exert control over situations may fare better in emotional terms than 'less hardy' individuals. Similarly, the sense of coherence hypothesis proposes that people who are able to make sense of their worlds, experience them as a predictable, and who have a sense of purpose in their lives, may also fare better than their counterparts with lower ratings on these dimensions.

In summary, there are substantive variations in how individuals view their worlds and respond to equivalent events. These differences may influence both their psychological and physical health. The origin of these differences is unclear and complex, and indeed may be attributable to constitutional propensities and shaping life experiences. It is important to note, however, that there is evidence from psychological therapies (particularly cognitive therapy) that people can modify their appraisal patterns and the way they respond to stressful events.

Aspects of unpleasant events

Considerable time and attention has been devoted to factors which may influence a response to a stressful event. These factors include biological, psychological, social and cultural factors. It is also necessary to consider the nature of the event itself, since this may influence access to social support. If the event involves the death or serious illness of a major source of support such as a partner

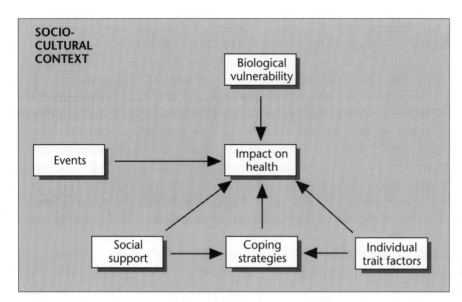

Figure 16.4 A biopsychosocial model of the influence of events on health

this may have a direct detrimental effect. If an event is a catastrophe affecting large numbers, then the shared grief of relatives may provide some access to support. The cultural context is also important. For example, miscarriage is often a hidden event in our society, occurring before knowledge of a pregnancy is widely shared and without associated ritual. It has been suggested that the lack of public acknowledgement may contribute to difficulties in coming to terms with the experience.

Events may be single, acute experiences with or without clear long-term consequences. Alternatively individuals may be subject to chronic low-level stressors, a single incidence of which may be unimportant, such as in the case of noise nuisance from neighbours or financial hardship. Events may not involve a tangible loss but a loss of potential, such as in the case of infertility. Thus events may vary in initial severity, time course and social context; and these dimensions may all influence implications and consequences.

In summary, one important mechanism through which psychological factors may influence both physical and emotional health is through responses to unpleasant events, whether these are major traumatic events or long-term low-level difficulties. In understanding the impact it is necessary to take into account the biological vulnerabilities of the individual, enduring aspects of their personality, their patterns of appraisal, coping strategies, and access to and use of social support. The influence of the cultural context in affecting patterns of responding also requires acknowledgement. It is clear that a biopsychosocial model is required to understand the development of illness and facilitation of health.

▨ Beliefs about Illness and Stressful Events ▨

Up to this point we have considered how psychological factors may play a role in causing physical symptoms primarily as a result of stress responses, but there are also other pathways of impact. In a study of people in the community Pennebaker reported that on average a person routinely experiences several minor symptoms per week. The frequent experience of a number of minor symptoms can be considered as normal. How an individual responds to their symptoms may have important implications for their health. Indeed, in some circumstances the action taken or not taken may literally mean the difference between life and death. A substantial proportion of individuals experiencing a first heart attack will die as a consequence. One of the major determining factors of outcome appears to be whether a person is given medical attention at an early stage. How an individual responds to the experience of symptoms is influenced not just by their severity but by individual patterns of thinking about symptoms, willingness to communicate pain to others, and availability of others around them. The problem is in determining when pain is related to a heart attack and when similar symptoms are caused by minor conditions such as a strain, indigestion or heartburn. Therefore the beliefs of the sufferer and those around them may be crucial.

Consider the two extreme cases of Mr B and Mr H:

Mr B was a man who never complained. He was brought up in a household where it was considered a weakness to be ill. He had almost never taken time off from work, and refused to see doctors. When he experienced chest pains he put it down to 'a bit of indigestion' and, not wanting to make a fuss, went to sit on his own in his lounge. He did not mention how he felt to his wife, who later found him doubled up with pain and called an ambulance.

In contrast, Mr H had always worried about his health. He had been very sickly as a child and his parents had always paid his health considerable attention. As a child he was kept at home for the slightest ailment. His mother would be particularly attentive at those times. As an adult he had always worried about his health, and when he experienced chest pains feared the worst and called his doctor immediately.

Clearly Mr B and Mr H, as a result of psychological factors, responded very differently to their experience of symptoms. Understanding the determinants of health behaviours is important. Although this encompasses how we respond to the experience of symptoms in terms of when we contact a doctor and whether we comply with treatment suggested or prescribed, it is actually a much broader question than it may at first appear. Health-related behaviours may include those engaged in to promote well-being (for example, exercising), together with the avoidance of harmful behaviours such as smoking. In addition, we need to consider the extent to which individuals engage in behaviours, such as attending for screening for cervical or breast cancer, which will alert to early signs of illness. Finally, in cases of chronic illness, behavioural responses to that condition may be crucial in minimizing progression and the onset of additional symptoms. For example, in diabetes, if individuals comply with a regime of diet and monitoring which maintains their blood sugar within specified limits and avoids the extremes of hyper- and hypoglycaemia (high and low blood sugar), then the frequency of other complications arising as result of the condition can be minimized. However, psychological factors exert a powerful impact on these behavioural responses and therefore physical health.

Understanding factors influencing health-related behaviours

Initially it was considered that providing information was the key to behaviour change. The premise was that if people knew they were at risk then surely they would do something to ameliorate the situation. This was the assumption behind a recent initiative of the Department of Health in Britain to promote annual health checks at health centres. Whilst this has been done and considerable proportions of the population have received information about their risk behaviours, the information has failed to trigger significant changes in behaviours. The whole initiative must be considered a costly failure. Why did it fail? Perhaps because it is clear from the psychological literature that being presented with the information that one is at risk has little impact on actual behaviour in a whole range of conditions. Although it is clear that information and knowledge in themselves are insufficient conditions for behaviour change, it is less easy to provide a full understanding of the factors which are influential. Indeed, this is perhaps one of the greatest challenges for psychology of the next decade. It is important to state that the current models available are relatively poor predictors of actual behaviour and without doubt will be subject to considerable modification. However, they are worthy of outline at this stage.

The 'health belief model' initially suggested that an individual's beliefs about the seriousness of, and their vulnerability to, a particular condition, together with the cost/benefit analysis of executing the behaviour in question (such as attending for treatment or screening), predicted whether the behaviour would be executed. Modifications incorporated to enhance the model's predictive power have included the effects of prompts to action by others, together with the notion of 'self-efficacy' (Bandura 1977), which is the belief that one is able to carry out the behaviour. Other models (Ajzen & Madden 1986) have included behavioural intention (the specified intention of a person to carry out a behaviour), and adherence to cultural norms which determine whether the behaviour is considered desirable for the particular group in society with which the individual personally identifies. (See chapter 11 for a more detailed consideration.) Recent contributions to this literature have suggested that whether an individual develops an 'implementation intention' (that is, some plan concerning where and when he or she may actually carry out the behaviour) is important in determining the probability of its execution. Understanding health- and illness-related behaviours is a complex area. It is clear that a variety of psychological factors are important, but their relative weightings, their interrelationships and their specificity or generalizability across conditions and individuals remain to be resolved.

In summary, psychological factors are important in influencing aspects of physical health and illness through a variety of pathways:

1. Unpleasant events may lead to stress responses and physical illness may develop as a result of consequent changes in physiological functioning.
2. Conditions may also be mediated by appraisal factors, psychological distress and the physiological concomitants of lowered mood.
3. Psychological responses to the experience of symptoms may influence subsequent health.
4. Specific behaviours (e.g. smoking, drinking, exercise or uptake of screening) may either reduce or increase the probability of certain conditions.

We have established the importance of psychological factors in both emotional and physical conditions, but haven't yet considered the work of clinical and health psychologists. The aim of the next section is to provide an overview of the principles involved in psychological approaches to intervention and to illustrate these with some case examples. There is no attempt to cover the range of different client groups and settings which may be involved.

▥ Psychological Approaches to Intervention ▥

It is important to understand some of the important general principles governing psychologists' work with individuals. Then we shall consider some sample cases.

The 'biomedical model' assumes that illness is due to some disruption of normal physiological functioning leading to the expression of symptoms. If the physiological abnormality can be remedied then the person will become well again. The patient consults an expert who, through their skills in identification of the problem and their knowledge of the range of medical treatments, is able to restore the person to health. Within this relationship the doctor is the expert and the patient the passive recipient.

In contrast (we hope this is clear from earlier sections of the chapter), psychologists are likely to adopt a biopsychosocial approach to understanding a person's health problems. This has implications for the process of intervention. First, a psychologist will attempt to work collaboratively and create an understanding that change develops from the individual themselves. While a psychologist can assist in this process, the ultimate responsibility for change rests with the patient. It is acknowledged that patients have their own theories and assumptions about the nature of their problems which they bring to the therapeutic situation. The initial tasks for the therapist are to develop a trusting relationship, an understanding of the nature of the patient's problems, and a shared conceptualization of the factors that have contributed to the causation and maintenance of the person's current difficulties. From these understandings the therapist will negotiate and agree with the patient ways of working to ameliorate distressing symptoms. It can be seen that, throughout, the emphasis is upon understanding the person's own perspectives, working to develop new shared understandings and a collaborative relationship. Change achieved through psychological methods requires that the patient should be an active participant rather than a passive recipient of care.

Individual psychological therapy

Another feature of psychological work is that it typically involves four processes: *assessment, formulation, intervention* and *evaluation*. During the phase of assessment, the nature and extent in terms of frequency and severity of the individual's problems are identified together with the development of an understanding of origins and maintenance of the problems. This requires gathering information from the person themselves, and perhaps the use of psychological tests and information, collected from diary records, about the frequency, intensity and triggering factors relating to the identified problems. On the basis of the assessment, filtered through the psychologist's understanding of various psychological theories and models, a formulation will be made by the therapist. The formulation is essentially a hypothesis as to the causes of the presenting problem, and is based within a psychological theory or approach. The understanding developed within the formulation should have clear implications for the intervention strategies which will form the basis of the next phase. Throughout this process, or at certain points within it, the impact of the intervention should

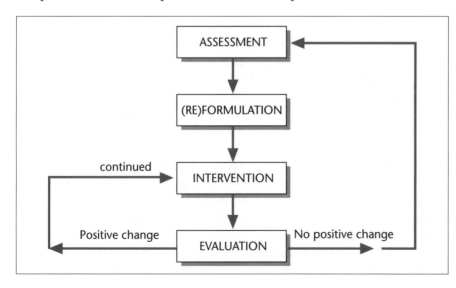

Figure 16.5 Four processes in clinical work

be evaluated in comparison to pre-intervention frequency levels so that the validity of the initial understanding can be reconsidered and intervention revised as necessary.

The following examples illustrate clinical casework, and the four processes, in two patients presenting with mental and physical health problems respectively.

Ms C, as already noted, had developed symptoms of anxiety. She often felt panicky. At these times she noticed her heart racing, her palms became sweaty and she felt dizzy. Her symptoms had begun approximately 18 months earlier, shortly after the death of her mother from a heart attack. When her symptoms worsened 6 months previously she was referred to a psychologist by her family doctor. In the assessment phase it was clear that she was experiencing two to three episodes of panic per day, and these tended to be between 2 and 10 minutes. She completed daily diaries for two weeks to try to identify the triggers for the episodes. It became clear that they occurred generally in an evening when she was alone. Exploration of her thought patterns in these episodes indicated that when she noted her heart racing she would become frightened. Her attention would focus on her pounding heart and she would think to herself: 'I'm going to die. This is how it started with my mother. I'm all alone, there's no one to help me. What shall I do?' On other occasions she would just start to think about being alone and begin to feel shaky and dizzy. The psychologist worked with her using a cognitive approach to identify these patterns. She was able to learn to monitor her thinking and to 'short-circuit' the sequence of negative, anxiety-producing thoughts. Through relabelling the symptoms she was experiencing as due to anxiety rather than indicative of impending death, she was able to remain more calm. In addition she was able to effectively challenge the notion that 'she could not cope on her own' and replace this thought with a more positive coping statement that decreased rather than elevated her anxiety. After five weekly sessions her panic attacks were occurring only about twice per week and were causing minimal distress.

The second case is that of Mr B, who had experienced chest pains. He in fact had experienced a heart attack but fortunately survived. As part of his reintegration into a more normal life he took part in a rehabilitation programme. This involved input from a variety of professionals including physiotherapists and dieticians. However, he was unable to change the behaviour which increased the risk of a second attack, and was referred to a psychologist. Psychological assessment indicated that Mr B was experiencing depressive symptoms: his mood was often low, he could not get off to sleep and he felt that he could no longer do anything that he had done previously. He thought his life was not worth living and his future was bleak. His perceptions of his world led him to feel that there was no point in changing his behaviour with respect to diet and exercise. He had stopped virtually all his previous activities and shut himself off from friends. His wife was very sympathetic and spent a lot of time trying to console him, but this only seemed to make matters worse. The clinical psychologist worked with Mr B to identify these issues. Mr B was encouraged to test his assumption that he could no longer engage in valued activities. Using a behavioural framework, a programme of graded activities was drawn up and agreed. These were to be prompted by his wife, and completion of the small steps to be given particular attention and praise from her. She, with his knowledge and consent, agreed to attempt to ignore his inactivity and no longer provide a sympathetic response. Effectively his wife was providing positive reinforcement for activities; it was also hypothesized that the experiences themselves would be slightly pleasant and therefore rewarding. At the same time she was no longer providing attention for his expressions of distress and his inability to become involved in anything, in the hope that these behaviours would reduce in frequency through the process of 'extinction' (the mechanism through which behaviour which is no longer reinforced reduces in frequency). Through this method he was able to build up more of his previous activities. All this was monitored and reported back to the psychologist on a weekly basis, with accumulated daily charts. Over a six-week period there was a marked increase in pleasant activities and a concomitant reduction in depressive symptoms. He began to take a more optimistic view of his future and was ready to consider longer-term changes in life-style to facilitate health.

Working indirectly through others

While much psychological work is carried out directly with the individuals concerned, there are many occasions when psychologists work primarily with people other than the person exhibiting the problems. They may work with carers, staff or parents. Being prepared to work indirectly on an individual's problems, in association with carers or relatives, distinguishes a clinical psychologist's approach from that of many other kinds of therapy. Indirect work may involve giving specific advice, facilitating group or family therapies, training staff in the acquisition of particular psychological skills, and so forth.

Working at an organizational level

Psychologists may also be asked to consider a process of care from an organizational perspective. For example, women experiencing miscarriages are cared for within gynaecological services. It is recognized that the loss of a baby, even very early in pregnancy, can be an unpleasant and traumatic event for many individuals. A service may be interested in how they can manage their provision of care in order to facilitate the best possible psychological adjustment. A clinical psychologist may interview women about their experiences of care and carry out some observational work of care processes. They may interview the staff providing care about how they handle sensitive situations and analyse their perceptions of the difficulties they face. Psychology provides a theoretical framework for understanding how individuals adapt and cope with unpleasant events. There is also a wide psychological literature focusing upon the concepts of satis-

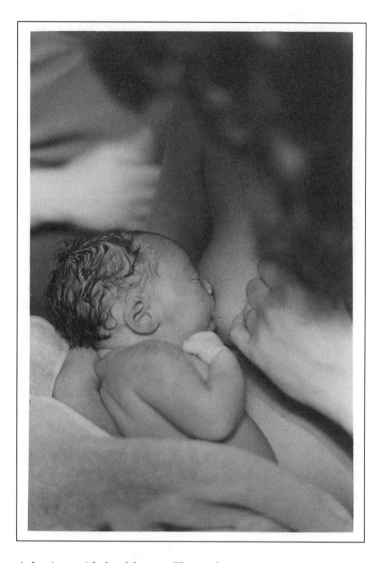

Plate 16.8 Baby at breast
Source: Sally and Richard Greenhill.

faction and dissatisfaction with healthcare. Through integrating information gained from the specific service and relating provision to the psychological principles derived from the literature, it is possible to draw up recommendations to improve care provision. Such issues may involve providing training to help staff understand the normal range of responses to stressful events, or facilitating the development of basic skills involved in relating effectively with people who are distressed. Through this type of work clinical psychologists may influence the provision of care throughout a service.

Clinical psychologists work in a variety of ways. Although therapy is often carried out on a one-to-one basis with individuals, psychologists also work through others and work to change the provision of care for many through organizational initiatives.

Clinical and Health Psychology as Professions

Clinical psychology in the UK has only relatively recently developed as a profession. Moreover, the structure of the profession has been very dependent upon the development of the National Health Service. Unlike other countries where healthcare has been based on private insurance schemes, the UK has benefited from a service free at the point of access. Psychologists have largely been employed within the NHS, and few clinical psychologists have established private practices. However, with the recent changes to healthcare in the UK, private practice may become more prevalent with clinical psychologists.

The first clinical psychologists were employed within the NHS as graduate psychologists in 1948. Since that time there has been a steady increase in the numbers employed: around 200 in 1962, 585 in 1973, 1,000 in 1982 and around 3,000 in 1994. To be employed as a clinical psychologist in the NHS you have to have successfully completed a recognized three-year course of postgraduate training. Currently there are around 24 courses in the UK, training annually about 200 trainees. Competition for places is high, with around 1,400 applicants for these places. Most clinical psychologists on qualification become Chartered Psychologists of the British Psychological Society.

Once qualified, clinical psychologists work in a range of settings and services, such as adult mental health, child care, care of older adults, and in the field of learning disabilities. Some clinical psychologists are employed within Social Services as opposed to the NHS and provide specific inputs typically to residential services for children or disabled people. The demand for clinical psychologists is ever-increasing and reflects the wide-ranging contribution that psychology has to offer services.

Recently other applied psychologists from backgrounds in health, social and forensic psychology have become increasingly employed with human service organizations to offer psychological advice on the delivery and evaluation of such services. As we discussed in the introduction to this chapter, this has led to the establishment of other applied psychology professions (such as health psychology). Currently, these new professional groups are only just becoming established in their own right. For example, many health psychology practitioners would originally have trained and practised as clinical psychologists. New schemes of training are being developed and the boundaries between different professional roles are being clarified. However, just as we have stressed that the Cartesian divide between mind and body or physical and mental health is no longer a useful distinction, many applied psychologists within health settings are also sceptical of proposed professional distinctions to separate health and clinical psychologists.

CHAPTER SUMMARY

1 Psychologists for many years have sought to understand mental illness. Increasingly the role of psychological factors in physical health and illness is now being explored. We have stressed the commonality of psychological approaches to both mental and physical functioning.

2 The concept of illness is much broader than disease. While it is often associated with medical evidence of abnormality, it incorporates aspects of the individual's wider functioning, including self-perceptions and behaviours, and requires consideration of social context and societal norms.

3 Treatment or therapy may often be deemed appropriate when some aspect of functioning is considered to be outside of the 'normal range'. However, deciding what is 'normal' is complex and a number of different approaches can be adopted.

4 Ways of understanding mental and physical illness extend from the biomedical model (emphasizing physiological disruption of the system as causative), to psychodynamic ideas (emphasizing the importance of primal instincts and drives), to learning perspectives and those putting the onus on thought and attentional processes. Aspects of these theoretical perspectives can be integrated into a biopsychosocial model of mental and physical health and illness.

5 Reactions to situations which are appraised as stressful involve the activation of the sympathetic nervous system. Stressful experiences may be related to increased arousal, which may in turn lead to adverse health consequences.

6 The availability of social support and use of certain coping strategies may be important in weathering stressful situations. Biological vulnerability and personality variables may also exert influences on health status.

7 People's behaviours are important factors in their health. There are individual differences in how people respond to the experience of symptoms, for example at which point they seek help. In addition people vary in whether they engage in behaviours which are risky (smoking, use of alcohol, unprotected sex) or are protective of their health (exercise). Psychologists have attempted to develop models to predict such behavioural patterns.

8 Clinical psychologists may work with individuals to reduce their psychological distress directly, but may also seek to work with staff or other family members to affect the well-being of an individual through influencing their care and environment. In addition they may seek to influence the process of psychological care more generally within a unit or hospital, through the development of care protocols or provision of staff training in psychological issues.

▓ Further Work ▓

1. How would you distinguish between a person who described herself as (i) well and healthy, (ii) ill and (iii) disabled? Discuss in relation to both physical and mental-health problems.

2. Discuss the different approaches that have been adopted in an attempt to distinguish between abnormality and normality with respect to mental and physical health.

3. Compare and contrast two different models of psychopathology. Identify the strengths and weaknesses of each approach.
4. Critically evaluate the claim that stress is a major cause of both physical and mental illness.
5. Identify five psychological factors which might help determine how successfully an individual recovers from a serious physical illness. How may each of these factors exert their influence?
6. Describe the ways that a psychologist might contribute to the healthcare of a person experiencing either a physical or mental illness.
7. Consider how psychological factors may be useful in promoting and maintaining good health.

▓ Further Reading ▓

Pitts, M. (1991) An introduction to health psychology. In M. Pitts and K. Phillips (eds), *The Psychology of Health*. London: Routledge, 1–14.

> A simple introduction to the area of psychological factors in physical health.

Evans, P. (1991) Stress and coping. In *The Psychology of Health*, pp. 30–45.

> This covers ideas about stress and coping very well.

Cohen, S. and Herbert, T. B. (1996) Health psychology: Psychological factors and physical disease from the perspective of human psychoneuroimmunology. *Annual Review in Psychology*, 47, 113–42.

> A more difficult read, but a critical consideration of the role of psychological factors in physical illness and the potential role of immunological factors.

Neale, J., Davison, M. and Haagan, D. A. F. (1996) *Exploring Abnormal Psychology*. London: John Wiley and Sons.

> An abridged version of Dawson & Neale, a classic textbook within abnormal psychology.

Lemma, A. (1996). *Introduction to Psychopathology*. London: Sage Publications.

> An introductory reader.

CHAPTER 17

Psychology in the Workplace

Nik Chmiel

CHAPTER AGENDA

- This chapter seeks to provide a concise introduction to the field of occupational psychology. It is not an exhaustive review but sets out the main areas connected to psychology in the workplace.

- The context within which occupational psychology is investigated is raised. The needs of the workplace and the person giving permission for research access are important influences on the topics studied. Knowledge about psychology at work is gained through experiments, correlational studies and case studies.

- The chapter is divided into three main sections: People at Work; Human Factors and the Work Environment; and Organizations. The section order reflects work psychology from the perspective of the person at work, the work environment of the person, and the organization of groups of people at work.

- The People at Work section describes main areas

of work psychology often subsumed under Personnel. Thus the section covers job analysis, personnel selection, training, performance appraisal, motivation, job satisfaction and job stress.

- The Human Factors and the Work Environment section describes some of the areas dealt with by psychologists strongly interested in performance at work. The section considers, in particular, mental performance as a function of aspects of the work environment such as noise and heat; and the issues involved in accidents and errors at work. A key theme in human factors is the relationship between the demands placed on a person by the tasks they do, and the mental capacity they have to perform those tasks.

- The section on Organizations describes issues to do with how companies structure themselves, and how they develop. A key theme is that organizations are not unchanging, but can adapt to meet changing market circumstances.

Introduction

The psychology of work is concerned with the feelings, attitudes, behaviour and performance of those at work. It is also preoccupied with those factors of jobs, work environment, organizational structure and management which influence workers' attitudes and behaviour.

Box 17.1   Workplaces and Research

Work organizations have purposes different to those of psychologists, although their interests may overlap. Work organizations exist to fulfil their own aims and objectives. In the manufacturing-industry sector these objectives could include the production of a quality product at minimum cost. In the public sector the aim could be the provision of a diversity of services within existing resources. Organizations are usually under pressure, commercial and/or political, to achieve their aims. Psychologists, on the other hand, are trying to understand people at work, and base advice on this understanding. However, psychologists research, and advise, dynamic, changing organizations subject to the pressures just outlined. It is, therefore, difficult for psychologists not to be influenced by the pressures organizations are under. Such influence can, and often does, determine the kinds of research psychologists do, and the sort of advice it is possible to give.

The person(s) giving permission to do research in the workplace are often at managerial level within the work organization. The issues management may be concerned about could differ markedly from the concerns on the 'shop-floor' or elsewhere in the organizational hierarchy. An example of the foregoing is that often it is the management who want to know the best way to select a person for a particular job, or who want to know the best way of organizing work teams in order to get maximum work efficiency. Stress at work, or job dissatisfaction, may only be important in so far as they stop workers carrying out their jobs efficiently, rather than as ends in themselves. Performance at work is a very prominent theme in work psychology.

In Britain this area of study is covered by OCCUPATIONAL PSYCHOLOGY. In Europe it is called 'work psychology' or 'work and organizational psychology', and in America it is called 'industrial and organizational psychology'.

OCCUPATIONAL PSYCHOLOGY

▨ Contexts ▨

Socio-political context

One point that needs to be made explicit from the start is that occupational psychology is an applied discipline. Thus the issues which commonly arise are connected with how and why workers behave as they do. Companies, on the whole, want to know the answers to these questions in order to improve productivity, although they may have an interest in how satisfied their employees are. Academics, while possibly being concerned with productivity, are concerned to understand the fundamental aspects of human nature at work. Consultants are asked to give advice to companies and industry, usually on a case by case basis.

The relationship between academics, consultants, and work organizations influences the type of questions, and thus the type of research that is done. Psychologists with an interest in work-related issues can adopt different roles in relation to the organizations and work culture they study. A broad division is whether the psychologist works within, and is employed by, the organization, or whether he or she is an outsider. The psychologist could be motivated by an academic concern with theory, or by a desire to give consultancy on best practice. In most situations, though, the ability to do research or provide consultancy is heavily dependent on the cooperation of work organizations.

The kinds of psychological topics researched in the workplace are influenced to some degree by at least two large concerns: the needs of the workplace; and the person(s) giving permission for research access to the workplace. See Box 17.1.

Early studies

Three studies serve to illustrate the way that workplace behaviour, and hence occupational psychology, has been formed in the twentieth century. The first concerns the philosophy of 'scientific management' espoused by Frederick W. Taylor, an industrial engineer at the Midvale Steel Company, USA, at the beginning of the century. His views were founded on the premise that people are motivated primarily by economic factors, and hence hard work should be linked to pay. He argued that work should be standardized on the most efficient way of doing it, and 'time and motion' studies of metal cutting were carried out to establish this. Thereafter workers were paid on a piecework basis. In other words, so much pay for so much work.

The second study was done at the Hawthorne plant of the Western Electrical Company in the USA from about 1924 to 1932. The researchers demonstrated that social relations at work, and not just economic self-interest, were important for productivity. In one set of observations a small number of women workers were transferred from their usual work area to a separate test area. There the workers experienced a series of controlled changes to their conditions of work, such as hours of work, rest pauses and provision of refreshments. During the changes the observer maintained a friendly manner, consulting with the workers, listening to their complaints and keeping them informed of the experiment. Following all but one of the changes there was a continuous increase in production. The researchers formed the conclusion that the interest shown in the workers, and the additional attention given to them, was the principal reason for the higher productivity (since called the Hawthorne effect). Another set of observations involved a group of men. It was noted that the men developed their own informal pattern of social relations and 'norms' for working behaviour. Despite a financial incentive scheme which offered more money for more productivity, the group chose a level of output well below what they were capable of producing.

The third influential study took place in textile mills belonging to the Ahmedabad Manufacturing and Calico Printing Company in India. In 1952 automatic looms were introduced into the factory in the belief that automation would increase productivity. However, the result was lower productivity and a higher percentage of damaged goods. The technology had been introduced while retaining the old organizational management structure based on scientific management. When workers were asked to suggest changes to the way their work was organized, the result was the setting up of autonomous work groups, multi-tasking by individuals, and a flattened management hierarchy.

These three studies demonstrate that the early agenda of occupational psychology concerned individual motivation at work, the workplace as a social environment, and the influence of the way work roles are organized in conjunction with technological developments. These concerns are still part of the concerns

Plate 17.1 Interviewing
Source: Tony Stone/Bruce
Ayres.

of occupational psychologists today. In addition to the above studies other areas of concern in the first half of the twentieth century were army recruitment, which was a personnel selection issue, and fatigue at work, which related to workload, and the limitations in workers' capabilities.

However, the psychology of work has expanded dramatically in the time since the Second World War, and is now an important part of professional psychology. There is an increasing recognition of the usefulness that contemporary occupational psychology can provide in the understanding of work activity.

Although much of the work of occupational psychologists is practical in nature, the strength of their advice is based on knowledge acquired systematically, through scientific means where possible. Thus research into behaviour at work plays an extremely important part in informing professional practice, as well as in developing more fundamental theories into the psychology of people at work, and how this is influenced by the context of work organizations.

Research in occupational psychology

There are two traditional types of ways to gather knowledge about work: the experiment, and the correlational study. Recently other ways, such as case studies, have also become more accepted (see Robson 1993, below in Further Reading, for a detailed discussion). Within these three main approaches a variety of information-gathering techniques and analyses can be deployed, ranging from interviews and questionnaires on the one hand, to behavioural observation on the other. Some techniques fit better within some approaches than others, though.

Box 17.2 Occupational Psychology in Britain

Since 1971 the British Psychological Society has had a division of occupational psychology which has three main aims. These are: to develop the practice of occupational psychology; to promote high standards of professional competence and behaviour among occupational psychologists; to increase public awareness of occupational psychology for the advantage of individuals and organizations. The division oversees professional development and sets the standards for becoming a Chartered Occupational Psychologist. Chartered Occupational Psychologists are concerned with the performance of people at work and in training, with developing an understanding of how organizations function and how individuals and groups behave at work. Their aim is to increase effectiveness, efficiency and satisfaction at work.

The main areas in which occupational psychologists have skills are: personnel selection and assessment; identification of training needs; organizational change and development; interviewing techniques; performance appraisal systems; vocational guidance and counselling; job and task design; group and intergroup process and skills; design of and adaptation to new technology; career and management development; industrial relations; ergonomics and equipment design; attitude and opinion surveys; occupational safety; design and evaluation training; equal employment opportunity; and stress management.

Clearly not all these skills could or should be acquired by one person, but the division of occupational psychology delineates eight main knowledge areas for occupational psychology which members of the division should demonstrate knowledge in. These are: human–machine interaction; design of environments and work, health and safety; personnel selection and assessment, including test and exercise design; performance appraisal and career development; counselling and personal development; training (identification of needs, training design, and evaluation); employee relations and motivation; organizational development. Applicants for membership of the division then need to demonstrate they have practical/application skills in at least five of the eight areas. Following this, applicants will then need to show their competence to practice independently and unsupervised in working with the public. They will generally have in-depth experience of at least one of the four main practice areas of occupational psychology, which are: work and the work environment (including health and safety); the individual (including assessment, selection, guidance and counselling); organizational development and change; and training.

Thus the case study approach often goes with interviews, whereas there are difficulties in using interview data in an experimental analysis.

Experiments, whether in the laboratory or the field, allow inferences to be made about causality between the variables studied, whereas correlational studies only observe whether factors change alongside others, but causality cannot be inferred. Case studies provide a very rich picture of a particular work setting, but the picture may not generalize to other settings. Occupational psychologists are often limited to observing natural variation and change within organizations and work settings, and hence experimentation is difficult. Many studies tend to be correlational in nature. However, despite the constraints of the work environment some field experimentation is possible and fruitful.

Field experimentation has the same procedure as laboratory-based methods, and tries to follow them as closely as possible. Thus the experiment involves forming a hypothesis, selecting experimental and control groups, introducing an experimental manipulation, measuring the change and making inferences as to causality. However, it may not always be possible to achieve the ideal experimental constraints in the field. Thus control and experimental groups may not

Plate 17.2 Training session
Source: J. Allan Cash.

be randomly determined, and other factors may alter along with the experimental manipulation. There are techniques, such as analysis of covariation, which can aid interpretation.

The advantage of the field experiment over a laboratory-based one is that the real-life conditions of the work setting can be preserved, in contrast to the artificial environment of the laboratory. For some investigations this is crucial, for others it is not, and the laboratory is the best place to produce the knowledge required. In addition to deliberately changing workplace factors to investigate their effect, experimenters can take advantage of naturally occurring change, especially when there is no control over the workplace, or it is undesirable. Here quasi-experimental methods are used to set up comparison groups, measure them before any change, measure them after the natural change, and analyse the results and draw causal inferences as appropriate. Often other factors also change in addition to the factor(s) of interest, and the effects of these need to be taken into account.

The experimental approach has the advantage of allowing causal inferences between variables to be drawn. However, it is often the case that such experimentation is difficult to achieve in the field, and the artificial environment of the laboratory is an impediment to finding satisfactory connections between work-related variables. Under these circumstances the correlational study comes into its own.

Plate 17.3 Automated assembly, workers on a truck factory production line
Source: Ace Photo Library/ Benelux Press.

Correlational studies concentrate on examining what factors change together, without making any inferences as to the causal nature of the relationships. Thus manipulation and control of variables are not as important, and natural variation in the workplace is central. What matters is the degree of relationship (the correlation) between factors, and its direction; that is, whether both factors increase together (a positive correlation) or whether one factor decreases as the other increases (a negative correlation). A fictitious example would be whether people who work longer hours feel less alert, but more satisfied with their work. In this case the length of the working day would correlate negatively with alertness (as the length increases, alertness decreases) but positively with satisfaction (as length increases satisfaction also increases).

Finally, case studies look at individuals or small groups of people at work. Focusing on a small number of people, or a small company, provides an opportunity to look at the group in depth, and over a period of time. Case studies are most useful in an exploratory context. The case study provides for studying a situation in depth, and from a variety of angles, through interviews, observations, and the analysis of documentation. However, a case study doesn't allow statistical generalization.

The usefulness of any of these approaches to understanding psychology at work can be greatly enhanced if the results from one work situation can be generalized to others. In order to generalize successfully certain conditions need to be met. The key factor is representativeness. First, if a particular finding is to generalize beyond the people involved in a study, the people studied must be representative of the larger population to which generalizations are to be made. Second, the context of a study should not constrain generalizability by findings being specific to it, or to the people studied. A fictitious example of a non-generalizable context might be work groups studied on the shop floor. A study of such groups could suggest that certain personality aspects are important to successful team-working. However, a group of office managers might work well together, but exhibit completely different personality profiles. Successful team-working attributes do not generalize across work groups in this hypothetical example.

People at Work

The starting point for considering the individual person at work is to assess the kind of job they do, the abilities and personality they need to do it, and their willingness to perform in the job. These issues are considered by work psychologists under the headings of job analysis, personnel selection and motivation, respectively. These topics are often thought of as central to the endeavours of occupational psychologists.

Job analysis

Job analysis is a logical companion to scientific management. In order to determine what can be done, and how efficiently, it is necessary to analyse the components of a job. With the decline of scientific management, the interest in job analysis also declined, being used largely to set wage levels. However, there has been increased interest since the 1970s because of the need to try and compare different types of job in order to evaluate their comparative worth. This relates to equal pay for people who do different jobs, but who carry out work that draws on similar knowledge or level of responsibility. Another reason for an interest in job analysis is that analysing the requirements for a job means that the abilities needed to do the job can be determined, and then used in picking a suitable person for the job. Using job analysis can help in setting salary levels, and in highlighting any unfair discrimination in selection, for example, in the standards being set for recruiting, and in the procedures being used to make selection decisions. However, understanding what a job consists of forms a central plank to many other activities. It can be the basis for making decisions about job descriptions, critical job needs, the pay level relative to other jobs, the staffing levels needed, the training required, the performance to be expected from job-holders, and the consequent assessments for promotion or continued employment.

Job analysis itself is concerned primarily in identifying those responsibilities and tasks that constitute a job. In order to do this information about the jobs has to be gathered and analysed. Several methods have been proposed, but not all of them will be described for space reasons. The ones that will be outlined here are chosen to give a broad view of the kinds of approach that can be taken to job analysis.

Functional job analysis

Functional job analysis attempts to identify job tasks, set performance standards, and delineate the training needs of workers. It relies on trained persons to use interviews with workers, training and other materials, and observation to analyse jobs using five components. These are: first, purposes, goals and objectives; second, specific tasks; third, abilities required; fourth, performance standards; and fifth, training needs. The abilities needed are related to data handling, communication, machines, language, mathematics, reasoning, and autonomy in the job.

A related system is the Position Analysis Questionnaire (McCormick et al. 1972), which analysts use to classify jobs according to six dimensions. These are: information input; mental processes; work output; interpersonal activities; work situation; and miscellaneous. Rating scales are used which look at the extent, importance, time, applicability, and so on, of the dimensions to jobs. The PAQ attempts to provide a method of analysing any job. Job analysts use the PAQ as the basis for structured interviews of workers and supervisors. From these interviews a job element profile is identified, and this can be used to draw up a job description and compare different jobs. Thereafter a profile of the attributes needed to perform the elements can be produced. The attributes consist of the aptitudes, interests and temperament required for the job, and can be used to detail a person specification for the job. The attribute profile allows recommendations for the types of psychological tests which will assess the attributes in a person, and aid the selection of the right person for the job.

Critical incidents technique

This method is based on asking workers for examples of on-the-job behaviours or critical incidents which were either extremely effective or ineffective in realizing the objectives of the job. Once collected, incidents are grouped by raters into job functions incorporating particular job responsibilities. The 'job elements approach' is similar but tries to identify job elements such as skills, knowledge, abilities, willingness, interest and personal qualities necessary to do a specific job. Other approaches to job analysis have focused on the physical and human abilities needed to do a job.

Whatever the centre of interest, however, job analyses encounter several problems. First, jobs are often changing, and this is particularly so with the introduction of computerized technology, the trend towards team-based working, and the associated drive towards more flexible jobs. Thus a job analysis may be out of date before it can be used effectively. Second, the analysis is only as good as the sources of information on which it is based, and often this boils down to subjective opinion. Third, like any measure, a job analysis should be examined for *reliability* and *validity*. This is rarely done, and would be very time-consuming to do, as well as costing a lot of money. Despite these problems there are benefits to be had through analysing jobs. Job evaluation is a method by which jobs are ranked with respect to their value to an organization, and this value is often reflected in the salary paid for doing that job. The salary can also be set according to market rates based on economic factors, of course. If the salary is influenced by what the job contains, however, then a job analysis can identify the skills and responsibilities which should be rewarded by pay.

Personnel selection

The most obvious requirement for a company or organization is to find the right people to do the jobs needed to achieve the company goals. Picking bad employees also costs a great deal in wasted time spent on recruiting, training, supervising and sacking that person. Recruiting good employees is essential to success, and so effective selection methods are crucial to this process. The essence of selection is to choose somebody who can confidently be predicted to be able to do the job well, and to get on with others in the organization. It is not always possible, however, to realize these joint objectives using one selection method. Research supports the idea that selection tests are useful predictors of job performance, but traditional interviews are poor substitutes. None the less many employers prefer interviews, presumably because of the opportunity to assess whether the interviewee will 'fit in'.

Interviews
The problems with the job interview as a selection technique are very well documented (see, for example, Anderson & Shackleton 1993, or Cook 1993, both in Further Reading below). In general, earlier analyses of research on interviews concluded that they were not a valid or reliable way of identifying good candidates. Interviewers tend to concentrate on negative rather than positive material, training is of limited use in improving interviewer performance, interviewers' impressions may depend more on non-verbal information than what the candidate is saying. Valid and reliable PSYCHOMETRIC TESTS, for example pencil and paper tests of specific abilities such as reasoning, outperform interviewers in selecting good candidates. For a test to be valid it must measure what it claims to measure, and for it to be reliable the test must measure performance in the same way each time it is used.

PSYCHOMETRIC TEST

Interviews can be done in ways different to the traditional wide-ranging discussion of an applicant's background and interests. Panel interviews improve matters (Landy 1976), for example. Structuring the interview so that every candidate is asked the same questions improves reliability. In this type of interview questions and topics outside the structure are not allowed. This does restrict the ability of the interviewer to follow up on interesting areas which arise during the course of the interview. A way round this is to use a semistructured interview, where each candidate is asked about the same broad areas, but supplementary questions can be used to pursue other points as they arise. Both these structuring techniques improve the reliability of the interview (Schmitt 1976).

More recent views of the interview process (Anderson & Shackleton 1993) propose that, if appropriate precautions are taken, the interview can hold its own as a selection technique. In particular, if an interview is structured, and based on a detailed job analysis, then reliability and validity are improved. Anderson & Shackleton also point out that the interview is appropriate for assessing job-relevant social skills.

Another source of information supplied by the candidate is the *curriculum vitae* (cv). In essence the cv is a record of past experience and achievement, and as such could be a rich source of factual information relevant to the job. However, there is usually no external check on the accuracy of the information on a cv, and it is clearly in a candidate's interest to present themselves in the best possible light. In this context references are also often required, but again are problematic with regard to interpretation. At the very least a selector will need to know for how long, and in what capacity, the referee has known the candidate, and what kind of work was undertaken.

Employment testing

The essence of employment testing is to administer a test, or a series of tests, the results of which predict success in the job. Since there are literally hundreds of jobs then, as you would expect, there are a considerable number of tests. These can be grouped under several headings: ability tests, personality measures and job sampling.

Ability tests

There are two main sub-headings related to ability: mental and physical. Mental ability covers a wide range of tests from those connected to intelligence, through deductive reasoning to spatial and mechanical ability. Deductive reasoning tests examine the person's facility with logic inferences, whereas a test of mechanical ability would examine how the relationship between parts of mechanical objects was understood. Physical ability tests measure things like strength, stamina, reaction speed and so on. Tests of ability have been shown to predict performance very well, and so are well validated as a selection tool (Cook 1993).

Personality measures

You may wonder why personality is considered in selection tests when performance can be assessed through the use of ability tests. Clearly personal qualities are important in a variety of jobs, and personality measures are used to identify characteristics that are associated with successful performance, and to screen out people who are clearly unsuited to the job. However, the area of personality testing is subject to some controversy, and it remains to be seen whether personality tests achieve the degree of validity and reliability of ability tests in the job selection context.

Plate 17.4 Factory workers in a car plant, assembling panels on a conveyor belt
Source: Ace Photo Library/Latin Stock.

Job sampling

A job sample is a piece of work provided by the applicant which is considered pertinent to the job being applied for. Examples would be a photographer's portfolio, letters produced by a secretary, and so on. Work already done is used to make judgements about future performance and training needs. A related idea is the work-sample test, where applicants are observed carrying out a piece of work related to the job. For example, Campion (1972) devised work-sample tests for maintenance mechanics, comprising four tasks: installing pulleys and belts; taking apart and repairing a gear box; fitting a motor; and preparing a sprocket to fit a shaft.

Work-sample testing obviously can only work if a person already has the skills necessary to carry the test out. Trainability tests are a form of work-sample test which examines how effectively a job applicant can learn a new skill. The instructor gives standardized instructions and a demonstration, and then uses a checklist to rate how well the trainee does.

Although work-sample and trainability tests have been shown to be popular with applicants, some analysts have pointed out difficulties with them. Robertson & Downs (1989) reviewed several trainability studies and found the tests predicted training success better than job performance. Barrett (1992) suggested that work-sample tests are uninformative, because they test too many job components at the same time, and they are unlikely to be valid over time because of changes to parts of the job over time. For example, a motor mechanic work sample might test knowledge of carburettors, skill with small tools, and reasoning ability. The work sample doesn't separate these. If car engines change, for

Plate 17.5 Operators at a computer control panel
Source: Ace Photo Library/Gabe Palmer.

instance with the introduction of fuel injection, then the test loses validity.

An assessment centre is where candidates for management posts are observed in management games, group discussions and other exercises designed to produce the kind of behaviours expected of managers. Thus the approach is aimed at observing samples (or a profile) of behaviours related to managing. However, these behaviours are produced during the candidates' time at the assessment centre, and so are not a past record of job-related achievement. Whichever approach is taken to job samples there is a need for criteria to be established relating to the performance and its interpretation.

Training

It would be rare indeed if new, and established, employees did not have to learn some new skill related to the job they do. The means whereby this is achieved is usually called training, especially if the learning programme is formally instituted by the employing organization. Training at work can usually be divided into two types: on-the-job; and classroom based. On-the-job training can take the form of apprenticeship schemes on the one hand, and informal tuition from an experienced colleague on the other. Classroom-based instruction involves much less showing the trainee how to perform a particular skill in contrast to explaining why things work, and giving instruction in how things ought to be done.

Traditionally training is constituted by a trainer providing some formal knowledge to the trainee, whether when doing the job or in the classroom, which is then developed into a skill through practice. However, this perspective is being increasingly challenged by arguments that competitive edge and new technology are also served by the use of knowledge which may not be 'teachable' by formal, instruction-based methods because the knowledge is connected with how to do tasks and cannot be readily articulated and communicated. Such knowledge has been called 'implicit' knowledge (Chmiel & Wall 1994).

The type of training done has, and still is, undergoing considerable change with the advent of new technology on the shop floor. Traditional manual skills like lathe work, cutting and drilling operations and the like, are being replaced by computer-controlled machinery, which requires a different set of skills to operate. These skills are much more mental in nature than hitherto, and are likely to require updating throughout a working lifetime.

Training needs

Prior to successful training programmes lies an analysis of the needs the programme is designed to meet. If training needs are not identified beforehand, it is impossible to evaluate the value of training later. Training needs can, and perhaps should, incorporate different levels in an organization. Three main levels are organization, task and person. Organizational analysis concerns issues such as the parts of the organization that need training, in light of the short- and long-term goals of the organization, the cost-effectiveness of the training, and the commitment to training by employees. The task level concerns the knowledge, skills and abilities needed by employees to perform specific jobs. The requirements for a specific job can be derived from a job description generated through a job analysis. The person level is concerned with individual employees and their capabilities. The latter can be determined from performance appraisal systems, recruitment tests for new workers, and from workers' self-assessment of their own training needs. Individual training provides the opportunity for individual development at work.

Training programmes

The ways training programmes are organized and run are often the product of experience as to what works, rather than being based on strong scientific learning principles. There is therefore a gap between theory and practice which hopefully will narrow in the future. The training process has several parts: identification of training needs and objectives; development of training materials; implementation and evaluation of the training programme. Certain practical constraints can guide this process. Training needs can be set in relation to organizational goals and current effectiveness, a task analysis focused on what the trainee needs to learn, and the background and abilities of the trainees themselves. Training objectives should be measurable rather than vague aspirations. Specific goals will help job performance and learning (Latham et al. 1982). The general aim of many training programmes is to facilitate an employee's learning, retention and transfer of job-related skills.

Although training at work often is guided by experience on the part of train-

Plate 17.6 Heavy
manufacturing
industry
Source: J. Allan Cash.

ers, there are several theories of learning based in psychology which can provide some assistance. These theories could be considered as falling into two main
categories: behavioural and cognitive.

Behavioural theories

Behavioural theories are based on studies of conditioning in animals, and they
encompass classical (Pavlov), operant (Skinner), and social-learning theory
(Bandura 1977). In essence the ideas contained in these theories are that reflex
behaviour can be conditioned to different types of stimuli, that behaviours are
learned and maintained by being rewarded, and that behaviours can be learned
by observing and imitating another person's actions. Thus training programmes

could make use of paired associations, rewards and punishments, and role modelling and videotapes.

Plate 17.7 Sellafield nuclear power station, UK
Source: Barry Lewis/Network.

Cognitive theories

Cognitive theories are based on the study of skill acquisition in people, and concentrate on the knowledge and abilities gained through the learning experience. The way knowledge is acquired and whether it is transferable forms the focus of a consideration of whether knowledge is declarative or procedural, implicit or explicit, automatic or requires conscious effort to implement (see Stammers 1996 for further discussion). Thus training programmes could consider whether a trainee is an expert or novice, how they organize their knowledge, whether they are able to articulate their knowledge, and hence transfer it across different job contexts, and whether employees have the understanding necessary to handle the complexity of modern, technologically based jobs.

Training evaluation

There is a common perception among writers on training that not much evaluation of training is done, and when it is done evaluation is frequently rudimentary, often merely gaining the reactions of trainees (Patrick 1992; see Further Reading below). This is surprising given that training costs money and involves time away from the job.

Evaluation of training depends on a clear understanding of why the training was done, what goals it met, individual and organizational, how its effectiveness was measured, what resources were allocated, and what was expected of the training programme. In short, training needs should have been identified against which the effects of training can be compared.

There is a variety of frameworks within which training effects can be evaluated (see Patrick 1992 for an extended discussion). Important are the criteria needed to assess training effects. The main measures include: those based on trainee impressions including their enjoyment of the training, and its perceived value; those concerned with how much has been learned through training, often measured through tests of some kind; those which concentrate on the new skills demonstrated on the job, that is, the transfer of training to the job; and those which centre on organizational objectives such as increased production, or production quality.

Performance appraisal

Performance appraisal is concerned with the criteria, and methods for deriving them, relating to effective job performance, and with the fair means by which individuals can be evaluated against appraisal criteria or standards. Appraisal schemes can be used to decide promotions, salary levels, training needs; set job goals; and validate employee selection procedures. In addition, appraisal schemes can be devised to help employees identify the skills needed to perform current and potential jobs, and thereby form the basis for individual development at work.

Appraisal depends on the establishment of adequate measures of job performance on which judgements about effectiveness can be made. Criteria could include behaviours like 'is always on time', personality traits like 'ambitious', or outputs like 'sales volume'. Once criteria are settled upon, the scale of what is acceptable and unacceptable performance also needs to be defined. For example, how many sales constitute average, good, or excellent job performance, and what is the minimum level necessary to be acceptable? Clearly job appraisal criteria depend in part on adequate job analysis. The criteria should be relevant to the job at hand, and ideally other factors should not affect performance judgements. For example, 'dress and appearance' could be considered central to the job of a receptionist, but not a garage mechanic. Equally, all relevant criteria for job success should be considered for inclusion in the appraisal scheme if possible. If relevant factors are omitted then the criteria are said to be deficient. This can be serious for organizations because it is easy for perceptions about the fairness of the appraisal system to be influenced by a mismatch between appraisal criteria and job-relevant performance factors. Other structural factors affecting fairness are equality of opportunity to perform, and whether individual performance is influenced by co-workers.

Errors in appraisal can also be due to biases on the part of the appraiser, even if these are subconscious. Appraisals based on subjective assessments, for example, ratings of personality, rather than on performance outcomes, can be subject to several sources of bias. Typical are the 'halo effect', one-sided ratings, 'central tendency', similarity to the rater, and conflating dimensions. The halo effect is where the appraiser identifies a positive or negative aspect of an employee, and bases his or her ratings on just that one aspect. One-sided ratings are where an appraiser may be unduly lenient or severe on all dimensions, for reasons not to do with performance. Central tendency is another form of one-sidedness, but in this case ratings are all average. Appraisers can also base their ratings on whether the employee is like, or similar, to them; and, finally, conflating occurs if particular dimensions are wrongly linked, like absenteeism and lateness.

More pervasive aspects of bias can depend on characteristics of both appraisers and those being appraised. For example, older employees may be judged to be less effective than younger ones (Waldman & Avolio 1986). Experienced raters have been found to be better at rating, as have employees who are high performers (Landy & Farr 1980). A way to moderate biases is to use more than one appraiser, but in practice this can prove difficult.

Appraisal methods

Appraisal methods are ways of judging an employee's performance. Common approaches include ranking workers relative to each other, usually along one dimension. Ranking methods are easy to use, but they have a number of problems. Chief among them is that a ranking gives no idea of the level of performance achieved. For example, the top worker may make 200 washers an hour, the next highest 100, the third 98 and so on. Second, ranks do not indicate whether the performance achieved is effective because they do not relate to any performance criteria. A third problem is that the procedure becomes cumbersome with large numbers of workers. Checklists address some of these problems by providing a list of traits or behaviours that the appraiser can check as relevant to performance. However, simple checklists are all-or-none; for example, 'punctuality' is either ticked or not. Another disadvantage is that the checklist doesn't distinguish between different job behaviours. They are all treated as of equal importance. This can be overcome by using weighted checklists. So 'punctuality' might get 20 points, and 'production rate' might get 100 points. This has the further benefit of making the appraiser and worker aware of the relative importance of the various facets of the job.

Rating scales involve the appraiser assessing performance scales that, for example, can range from 'all of the time' to 'never'. Thus some of the disadvantages of simple checklists can be avoided. Scales can be linked to behavioural descriptions at different levels. For example, using 'mixed standard rating scales' (Blanz & Ghiselli 1972), critical incidents of good, average, and poor performance are put into statements on the appraisal form and raters indicate whether the worker exceeds, equals or falls below the standard.

A different way of appraising is to use 'Management by Objectives' (MBO)

(Drucker 1954). Performance outcomes or objectives and the dates they are to be achieved are set. Action plans by which the objectives will be realized can also be outlined. In principle MBO can be imposed on employees, or objectives and plans can be arrived at in discussion and negotiation with employees. Some research suggests that MBO is better suited to participative management styles (McConkey 1983). The advantage of this method of appraisal is that managers and employees know what is expected of them. A disadvantage is that outcomes may not be wholly under the control of the employee. See Box 17.3.

Motivation, job satisfaction and job stress

The effects of work rewards and demands have a central place in occupational psychology. The topics that relate most directly to these are how motivated, how satisfied, and how stressed workers feel in response, and what effects these states have on performance.

Motivation

Motivation can be defined as a force which: causes people to act; that directs behaviour to the attainment of specific goals; and that sustains the effort required in reaching those goals (Steers & Porter 1983). The views of Taylor (which were discussed in the historical section at the opening of the chapter) held that workers were motivated by material gain and money. Since that time theorists have suggested that individual needs are important, or that the costs and benefits of work are judged in a rational way, or that a wide conception of rewards is critical.

Maslow's need hierarchy

One of the most well known need theories is that of Maslow (1965, 1970). In essence the theory states that motivation is the product of realizing needs which could be ordered into five categories. These were: physiological needs like food, water, sleep and sex; safety needs like the need for shelter and physical well-being; social needs like the need to be accepted by others, love, affection, and friendship; esteem needs like the need to be recognized for achievements, to be admired and respected; self-actualization needs like the need to attain a sense of fulfilment. Maslow suggested the lower-order needs had to be met before a person could move to the higher-order needs. As needs are met they no longer act as a motivator and the dominant motivator is to be found at the next level. In the world of work a salary meets survival and safety needs, and social interaction with fellow workers satisfies some social needs. Making a success at work can meet esteem and self-actualization needs. The effect of Maslow's need hierarchy has been to delineate potential needs beyond basic ones, and thus focus consideration on non-monetary incentives to motivate workers.

McClelland's 'need for achievement' theory

Maslow's hierarchy of needs was not developed specifically for the work context. McClelland (1961, 1975) on the other hand proposed three needs central to work motivation which are encompassed by his Achievement Motivation Theory. The three needs are: need for achievement, for example, to get the job done and succeed; need for power, for example, to control others and have influence; and the need for affiliation, for example, to be liked and accepted by work colleagues. Workers are supposed to have a mixture of these needs, which may vary from person to person. However, one or more may be dominant. To assess a person's motivational needs McClelland used a version of the 'thematic apperception test' (TAT). This test involves studying ambiguous pictures for a short time and then writing the story it suggests. The stories are then scored in a standard way to obtain a motivational profile of the person. Like any projective procedure the TAT is open to criticism concerning how it is scored, because different scorers can interpret the stories differently. Research into worker motivation suggests that those with a high need for achievement do attain personal success in their jobs, provided the type of work they do promotes personal achievement. An example would be where there is a direct relation between individual effort and job outcomes like salespeople working on commission. The theory has led to programmes to improve worker motivation in the workplace by matching profiles with jobs to allow individuals to realize their dominant needs (McClelland 1980).

In contrast to need theories which focus on the individual, other motivational theories concentrate on the nature and structure of jobs as instrumental in motivating workers. Foremost among these are Herzberg's two-factor theory, and the job characteristics model.

Herzberg's two-factor theory

The two-factor theory developed by Herzberg (1966) was concerned with the factors which affected job satisfaction, rather than motivation directly. The theory asserted that job satisfaction was the result of the presence of certain job aspects. These were responsibility, achievement, recognition, job content, advancement and personal growth. These aspects he called 'motivators'. In contrast, aspects whose absence resulted in job dissatisfaction were called 'hygienes', and were company policy and administration, supervision, interpersonal relations, working conditions, and salary. The theory emerged from the analysis of the survey responses of white-collar, professional workers. Motivators relate to job content, and hygiene factors relate to job context. Subsequent research has not replicated the presence of two distinct factors (Schneider & Locke 1971), and others have suggested the theory applies more to white-collar workers than other groups.

Herzberg's theory helped to introduce strategies of 'job enrichment' designed to increase worker motivation. These programmes involved redesigning jobs to give more responsibility in planning, execution and evaluating to workers. Job enrichment programmes have been implemented in a number of European and American companies, but their success has been difficult to determine due to methodological problems. Typically, large numbers of jobs are altered at the same time in any one situation, making rigorous comparisons impossible (Miner 1983).

Job characteristics model

The job characteristics model (JCM) proposed by Hackman and Oldham (1976) suggests that worker motivation is affected by whether workers perceive their jobs as meaningful, and whether they have a sense of responsibility in the job and some knowledge of the results of their work. These perceptions are the result of five core job characteristics which are:

1. Skill variety: the extent to which a job demands a diversity of skills and abilities, and hence is perceived as meaningful.
2. Task identity: whether a job is seen as a coherent whole with an identifiable outcome which the worker can relate to his or her work effort.
3. Task significance: the degree to which the job impacts others in the company or its customers.
4. Autonomy: the amount of latitude the worker has to carry out the job.

5. Feedback: whether the job allows the worker to get direct information on performance effectiveness.

The theory asserts that skill variety, task identity and task significance affect the perception of job meaningfulness, autonomy affects the perception of responsibility associated with the job, and feedback affects the experience of work outcomes. Motivation depends on the three perceptions. However, the latter can be moderated by other variables such as 'GROWTH NEED STRENGTH'. Those low in growth need will not be motivated by increases in the five job characteristics, whereas those high in growth need will benefit. Research has tended to support the job characteristics view of worker motivation (Fried & Ferris 1987).

GROWTH NEED
STRENGTH

Equity theory of motivation

In contrast to need theories, several alternative accounts stress the rational, logical element in workers. The equity theory of motivation is one of the latter. In essence the theory suggests workers conduct a cost–benefit analysis of their job (Adams 1965). If the analysis results in the worker perceiving that he or she is being treated fairly, then motivation will be maintained. The cost–benefit analysis is calculated on 'inputs' like worker experience, education, and qualifications; 'outcomes' like pay, perks, recognition, and challenging work; and 'comparison to others', like co-workers, similar jobs, or other work experience. Demotivation is one of the results of 'underpayment inequity' where workers perceive they receive fewer outcomes relative to inputs. Interestingly, the theory suggests that workers can take several actions in the 'underpayment' context. One that follows demotivation is reducing the amount of input to the job, another is to try to increase outcomes, a third is to change who the comparison is made to, and the fourth is quitting the job. Where outcomes are perceived to exceed inputs in comparison with others, an 'overpayment inequity' is created. The possibilities here are to decrease outcomes, increase inputs, change the comparison group or job, or distort the situation by, for example, imagining that your work is of higher quality than your peers. Research has shown that equity theory has potential as an explanation of worker motivation, and that individuals differ in their sensitivity to inequities. For example, giving workers a higher-status job title can lead to increased inputs without any increase in pay (Greenberg & Ornstein 1983).

Expectancy or VIE theory

VIE stands for valence, instrumentality and expectancy, and is associated with Vroom (1964). The theory is concerned with the rational costs and benefits workers associate with their jobs. Benefits include things like recognition and job satisfaction, and costs encompass reprimands and sackings. Motivation is the result of a combination of valence, which is the desirability of an outcome to the worker, instrumentality, which is the perceived likelihood of an outcome given a particular work behaviour, and expectancy, which is perceived connection between the worker's effort and performance.

It is clear that many of the theories of motivation outlined above include similar ideas about what are important motivators at work. Rewards, recognition and responsibility appear constant components in the theories discussed. Where need theories differ from rational theories is in how the components have their influence on workers. In the former needs must be satisfied, in the latter a rational weighing of pros and cons must be perceived as positive.

Job satisfaction

Work is a large part of life for those in employment. An important part of work, therefore, is the enjoyment to be gained from it, and the consequences of such satisfaction for job performance as well as feeling of well-being. Job satisfaction can be viewed as an all-embracing attitude or feeling, that is, a worker can be questioned about their overall approach to their job; or it can be seen as the amalgamation of many different attitudes to specific parts of a job, such as the type of work, working conditions, workmates, company policy and promotion opportunities.

The perspective from the employer's standpoint is focused on productivity, quality of work, absenteeism and staff turnover. All these have a direct bearing on the profitability of the company. The workers' point of view, on the other hand, is almost certainly going to emphasize job satisfaction. One interesting question is whether the latter has any influence on productivity, quality and so on. Reports which have looked at a meta-analysis of many studies of the relationship of job satisfaction to job performance have shown that at best the relationship is a weak one (Iaffaldano & Muchinsky 1985; Petty et al. 1984).

The relationship of job satisfaction to other aspects of work behaviour can be stronger. Muchinsky and Tuttle (1979) found a negative correlation with staff turnover, and Clegg (1983) observed increases in tardiness and absenteeism were accompanied by increases in job dissatisfaction. The factors just mentioned are expensive for organizations. Turnover means that further recruitment and training needs to be done, and lateness and absenteeism means lost production. Organizations have tried to increase employee satisfaction, therefore, through a variety of ways. Job enrichment, based on the job characteristics model of Hackman and Oldham (1976), gives workers extra responsibility. Job enlargement gives workers additional tasks to do. Other ways relate to the salary structure and profit-sharing for employees. The general idea of these schemes is to involve the worker more closely with the organization, and satisfy their job-related needs. They are close cousins of motivational schemes at work.

Individual development

Individual development is about how the person him/herself develops at work. Is the worker motivated at work? Is good work recognized, and hence rewarded, and is the worker encouraged to go further? Does the worker volunteer for training? Is the worker satisfied by his or her job and hence keen to develop into it? Performance appraisal, training, motivation and job satisfaction all clearly relate to individual development by the worker.

Organizations, too, can take an interest in individual development, both because of an interest in employee well-being and quality work, and in order to develop employees so they can take up jobs further up the company. In short, it can be in an organization's interest to promote career development programmes for their employees.

Gutteridge (1986) reports on the goals of the career development system at Disneyland in California, USA. The goals were: to develop a pool of human resources to staff future expansion, and employee turnover; to increase the match between employee's career interests and Disneyland's employment needs and job availability; to assist individuals in their preparation for promotion; and to help individuals raise their awareness of their own abilities and shortcomings.

Work-related stress

Work pressures, deadlines, overwork, difficult colleagues or impossible job demands can all affect how a worker feels about his or her job. The feeling of being under strain is a negative consequence, whereas the feeling of being challenged and meeting those challenges is positive. Thus the impact of work-related stressors and a person's reaction to them is moderated by how they are perceived. Another way of viewing stress is as a physiological reaction to environmental stressors. Selye (1976; first published 1936) identified a common 'fight or flight' nervous system response to a variety of physical stressors. The response included increased heart and respiratory rate, and sweating.

Weiman (1977) studied over 1,500 managers and found that having too much or too little to do, having unclear or inflexible job demands, having too much or no role conflict and having no or a very high level of responsibility led to the incidence of hypertension and heart disease amongst other health-related outcomes. Karasek (1979) has argued that jobs with high demands, but where there is low control or decision latitude over when and how those demands are met, lead to job strain.

Individuals can differ in their response to stressors. Type A personalities (Friedman & Rosenman 1974) are characterized as hard-driving, have a chronic sense of time urgency, and are impatient with obstacles in their way. Type B personalities, on the other hand, are viewed as relaxed, satisfied, and unhurried. Research shows that type A people are at greater risk for heart attacks and strokes.

There is a widespread belief that many physical illnesses are stress-related, including ulcers, heart disease, migraines and hypertension (Beehr & Bhagat 1985). Recent research has implicated stress in effects on the immune system (Dienstbier 1989).

At work these health outcomes affect absenteeism and turnover, and stress can also affect performance and accidents through effects on depression, anxiety and chronic fatigue amongst other things. At the extreme, workers can experience 'burnout', a process whereby increased work demands lead to emotional exhaustion, followed by an insensitive attitude to others at work, and finally leading to feelings of low self-achievement, frustration, and helplessness (Jackson et al. 1986). Burnout is characterized by becoming less committed, withdrawing from the job, and can lead to increased tardiness and absenteeism. It has been found to be more prevalent in occupations which involve helping others, for example, nurses, teachers, social workers and the police (Cherniss 1980).

There has been a variety of suggestions and plans for coping with work-related stress and its effect. At the individual level, coping strategies targeted at stress outcomes range from exercise and diet to relaxation programmes. Work-related strategies targeted at the source of stress include time-management techniques and job rotation. At the organizational level some companies have introduced stress management courses for their employees. Matteson and Ivancevich (1987) propose that effective stress management programmes should impart knowledge, skills and attitudes that are useful in coping with stressors. An alternative or complementary perspective is to alter the jobs that employees do, or change the organizational structure so that employees have adequate training, have a sense of control over their work, are not subject to punitive management, do not work in unnecessarily dangerous conditions, and are facilitated in communicating effectively with others in the organization. In the USA, a 'quality of work life' movement incorporating these percepts was begun in the seventies, and early studies suggested that there were increases in productivity and quality as a result (Herrick & Maccoby 1975).

▒ Human Factors and the Work Environment ▒

The 'Human factors' perspective is mainly concerned with the design of machines, work systems and places to suit human capabilities. The advent of computer-controlled machinery in manufacturing, utilities and even office environments has meant that human factors have become a very much more important part of occupational psychology. In certain industries like aviation and nuclear power, where complex machinery is in operation, and the cost of a mistake is very high, the design of machines is given very careful consideration. Several of the major incidents that could have had potentially catastrophic consequences for the world, like Three Mile Island (TMI) in the USA, and Chernobyl in the USSR, have been, at least in part, attributed to human error when operating complex systems. A main interest, therefore, is in the reasons humans make mistakes with these systems. See Box 17.4.

Traditionally, human factors and ergonomics have concerned themselves with the physical working environment and how people behave as components of the human–machine system. They have been concerned with the design of seating, knobs and dials, lighting, heat and noise effects on performance, to name a few. Interest in human factors has remained high with the advent of computerization in the workplace, because more and more people are required to operate sophisticated systems through computer control or support. The field, along

Box 17.4   Three Mile Island

At Three Mile Island the flow of water to the nuclear reactor's secondary heat removal system was interrupted. This caused alarm lights to flash, and an auditory alarm to sound in the control room. The time was 4.00 a.m. For the following two hours or so the control room operators tried to get to grips with the cause of the alarm. As a consequence of the incident there was a serious risk of a 'meltdown', or that hazardous radiation could escape from the plant. Neither of these things happened, but the incident cost millions of pounds, and the US halted all further building of nuclear power plants. Accident investigators observed that the control panel presented operators with too much complex data, 1,600 displays and gauges had to be scanned when the alarm sounded to try to establish the source of the problem. At the time there were already 200 flashing displays and gauges, making the diagnosis of the fault difficult. In addition the control panel did not contain certain critical information, especially the fact that an automatically controlled valve had not closed, allowing coolant to escape and uncover the reactor core. This could have been discovered by looking at a drain tank water level indicator, but this was positioned behind the main controls. A further problem was that backup valves which, if open, could have allowed water into the secondary heat removal system, were closed. They should have been open, but the fact they were closed was not recognized by the operators because maintenance tags on the control panel partially obscured the lights indicating their status. In addition the diagnostic system designed to keep operators informed about the plant used a computer printer. During the incident messages were being transmitted to the printer at around 10 to 15 per second, overloading it. Information was thus not available until later, and just over an hour into the incident the printer jammed, and some data was lost for good. The report of the analysis of the causes of the incident attributed a number of errors to the operators, but highlighted inadequate control room design, procedures and training rather than inadequacies on the part of operators.

with cognitive ergonomics, has become much more concerned with people as a cognitive part of the system, that is, with how people process information from, think about, control and react to the systems they are engaged with. A consequence is that system designers have the opportunity to consider the relative strengths and weaknesses of humans and machines, and what functions should be performed by each. Machine operators, for example, are adaptable, can handle unexpected events, can think, can learn from mistakes, can get tired and stressed, and react differently in hot or noisy conditions. Machines, on the other hand, do not get tired, can handle routine and automated functions easily, and are less affected by variations in temperature and noise.

Human factors research has thrown up some general principles concerning displays, controls and the working environment. These are far too extensive to detail here, but a summary of some recommendations will convey the type of outcomes traditionally dealt with. The most common displays used to transmit information are visual and auditory, although smell is also used, for example, in natural gas, to warn of a leak. Visual displays are good for conveying complex information, and can carry several messages at once. Auditory displays often serve an alarm function, and are good for urgent messages. Controls (for example, switches, knobs, buttons, levers, etc.) should be compatible with the operator's physical dimensions, should mirror the machine actions they produce, should be clearly marked, adequately spaced and arranged to avoid unintentional use, should be easily discriminable from one another, and standardized if possible. Workspaces should be designed with performance efficiency, operator comfort, safety, operator limitations, and machine design in mind. McCormick and Sanders (1982) propose that important functions and operations should be able to take place in a central location relative to the operator, so, for example, relevant displays should be in front of the operator. Machines which are most frequently used should be conveniently located, machine components (displays and controls) should be grouped according to function, and placed in order of sequence of use. The workplace should take into account the physical dimensions of workers, for example, seats should be designed for comfort.

Work environment and performance

Psychologists have long been interested in whether and how conditions at work affect work behaviour and productivity. Those aspects which have tended to receive most consideration are fairly obvious: noise, heat and illumination. Less obvious are the effects of workspace layout, decor and music on performance. Some physical aspects of the environment are more prevalent in some jobs than others, and are more important to performance than others. In addition, environmental conditions affect different tasks differently.

Illumination

HAWTHORNE
EFFECT

The level of lighting was manipulated in one of the classic series of studies in occupational psychology: those by Mayo at the Hawthorne plant of the Western Electrical Company. The researchers were interested in the connection between illumination and productivity. In their case they discovered the 'HAWTHORNE EFFECT' mentioned at the beginning of the chapter, but subsequent investigation has demonstrated that performance improves with increasing light levels up to a point where it levels off. Where the point is depends on the type of task. For example, the recommended level of lighting for a hospital operating theatre is 20 to 100 times that of a general office environment. Overlighting can produce problems too, such as distracting glare and visual fatigue.

Temperature

Extreme heat, or cold, is perceived as uncomfortable and in some cases debilitating. Temperatures lower than 0, or greater than approximately 32 degrees Celsius have produced decrements in manual and mental performance (Kobrick & Fine 1983). Other studies have shown that temperature and the duration of exposure to temperature increases affect different mental tasks differently (see Hockey 1986 for a review). It is also the case that prolonged changes in the environment lead to acclimatization, hence moderating the effects of temperature (Poulton 1970). Other factors influence the perception of temperature and its effects. Thus increasing humidity leads to considerably increased feelings of discomfort for the same temperature of 26 degrees Celsius (Fanger 1970).

Plate 17.8 An operator with a computerized printing press
Source: Ace Photo library/Positive Images.

Noise

In some occupations high levels of noise are an everyday part of working life. For example, printing presses, automatic looms, machine cutting tools, etc. all generate loud noise. The effects of noise on performance have turned out to be quite complex. For example, in the USA the Environment Protection Agency concluded in 1974 that: noise did not generally impair performance unless it exceeded 90 decibels; that intermittent or unpredictable noise was more disruptive than continuous noise; that high frequency (high-pitched) noise was more disruptive than low-frequency noise; and that noise was more likely to lead to higher work error than lowered rates of performance. Indeed Kerr (1950) showed mean noise level at work was the most potent predictor of accident frequency, although not severity. Since then research, mainly on perceptual and cognitive tasks, has shown that more difficult tasks, those requiring sustained attention, and those which could be done several ways, are more susceptible to noise (Davies & Jones 1985). In addition, noise potentially impairs communication at work, and the ability to use acoustic cues as feedback from machines. In addition to issues of efficiency, noise can also be perceived as uncomfortable, and at high levels can lead to physical damage to the ear.

Decor and music

There is probably a strong belief in industry that a pleasant-looking and sounding work environment has some effect on worker behaviour. Despite this there is not much research to demonstrate that there is a direct effect on performance. However, it is likely that good decor will affect employees' perception of their work environment, hence increase their satisfaction at work and thus have indirect effects on behaviour and performance. Equally a commitment to pleasant working conditions sends a message about the attitude of the company to workers.

Workplace layout can also affect worker behaviour in other ways. For example, the amount of space and its privacy can be perceived to relate to the importance and status of a worker within the organization. Open-plan offices facilitate social interaction and potentially satisfaction, but congested workspace and too much socializing can affect productivity (Canter 1983), and lead to higher staff turnover (Oldham & Fried 1987).

Accidents at work

The consequences of accidents at work are injury to the worker, lost production, disruption to working patterns, and economic and legislative outcomes such as compensation claims. In recent times industrial injury has been at the centre of national policies concerning these issues, and there are various laws governing them. In Britain the Health and Safety Executive (HSE) plays a considerable role in monitoring and enforcing safety standards at work, and in America a similar function is carried out by the Occupational Safety and Health Administration (OSHA). Two main aspects of safety at work concern the behaviour of workers, and the organization and its procedures and standards.

Worker safety behaviour

Early this century a study of accidents in munitions factories in England during the First World War found that the majority of accidents involved relatively few people. This observation gave rise to the idea of 'accident-proneness', that certain people have a disposition to accidents, a concept which has captured the popular imagination. However, subsequent research has tended not to support the idea that there is a stable personality trait of being accident prone; rather, different people go through periods of being more prone (Reason 1990). Generally the highest accident rates are found in young and inexperienced workers. It has been suggested that the reasons behind this observation are that young people are more impulsive, inattentive and have less family responsibility than older workers.

Work groups also influence accidents at work. Groups with experienced and organized leaders were related to fewer accidents (Butler & Jones 1979). Other research has shown that groups with a 'safety climate' had safer work areas. Safety climate is measured by eliciting worker attitudes on issues such as the perceived importance of safety training, management's attitudes to safety, and so on.

Plate 17.9 Safety in the work environment: worker in plastics industry wearing protective clothing
Source: Ace Photo Library/Kevin Phillips.

Organizational safety practices

The procedures and attitudes of an organization to work safety influence the degree of hazard at work. It is no accident that industries with a very good record on safety are those like aviation and chemicals, where safety is seen as of paramount importance, and where there are many safety-orientated regulations governing work practices. Safety programmes are designed to increase safety at work, and to overcome reasons for unsafe behaviour in workers.

Many machinery accidents can be prevented if proper precautions have been taken. The precautions encompass using goggles to protect the eyes, following proper start-up and shut-down procedures, and utilizing safety guards. Workers may not follow safety procedures because they are not aware of them, or they are inconvenient, or they are not part of the workgroup climate.

Safety programmes have tended to concentrate on worker training in safe procedures. Thus employees learn about the procedures and the way to carry them out. However, simply knowing a procedure does not mean a worker will comply with it, thus instituting organizational means to increase safety is also important. One technique which has been demonstrated to be effective uses behaviour modification principles. Haynes et al. (1982) reduced accident rates in bus drivers working in urban transport by 25 per cent using a safety behaviour modification programme. First, safety performance feedback was made public by posting drivers' safety records in the lunchroom. Second, drivers were put into teams that competed against each other's safety record. This meant that the reward contingency related to the group rather than an individual. Finally, winning drivers and teams were given cash and prizes for outstanding safety records. Thus safe behaviour was rewarded. The reward need not be so obvious. Merely posting safety records and publicly recognizing good safety performance has also produced increases in safety.

Human error

Any discussion of safety at work needs to consider not just accidents, but errors which potentially could form the antecedents to industrial calamities such as at Three Mile Island. Here no injury at work, in the sense used in the previous section, results. It is the advent of complex, technological systems, particularly in the nuclear, aviation, chemical and manufacturing industries, which gives impetus to the study of human error, because the consequences of such error can be large-scale indeed, as the incident in 1986 at the Chernobyl nuclear power plant in Russia so emphatically illustrates.

The complexity and efficiency of modern technology in the industries mentioned is handled by computerization and automation. The demand placed on human operators by this technology is largely mental: What do operators understand of the system they control? How does automation affect this understanding, and the cognitive nature of the control task? How much capacity do operators have in dealing with mental workload? What happens when fatigue sets in? Is routine understanding sufficient in an emergency situation? How does stress affect cognitive processing? All these questions are the subject of ongoing research, driven by the need to make hazardous complex systems safe, and technological systems efficient.

Errors cost money, even if they do not result in personal injury to the operator, but at the extreme, errors can cause considerable damage to people and the environment. So far research has shown that people are limited such that their mental capacities can be overloaded. Automating part of the technology can help with this, but introduces its own problems because the job changes from being active to being predominantly passive, where operators monitor equipment rather than control it. The change means factors like sustained attention and boredom become important, with consequent lapses of attention likely to produce error. Understanding routine operations may utilize different skills and cognitive processes to coping with emergency situations, and stress can further alter how the work task is mentally processed (Wickens 1992).

▪ Organizations ▪

The chapter has focused until now on the individual at work, and on their work environment. This last section considers some of those aspects of occupational psychology which relate to the organization as a whole, and which treat the organization as a unit for analysis, rather than the person. Topics included are: organizational structure and function; leadership; and group processes.

Organizational structure and function

Organizations are generally organized around some purpose, and consist of members whose activity is related to the common purpose. The structure of organizations can help or hinder realization of its purpose. The classic managerial functions, planning, organizing, staffing, coordinating and controlling, can all take on a different character depending on the organizational context.

Bureaucracy

One of the earliest analyses of structure, developed by Max Weber, proposed that bureaucratic organization formed an efficient means to achieve an organization's ends. The characteristics of a bureaucracy are: a hierarchical structure; clearly defined roles and responsibilities; a division of labour such that employees carry out the same tasks repeatedly; a strong emphasis on rules and regulations; and written records (Scott et al. 1981). Bureaucracies like to run on routine, and unusual or individual circumstances are difficult for them to deal with. The structure of a bureaucracy can be tall or short, and incorporate a short or large span of control. Tall or short refers to how many levels there are in the hierarchy, and span of control relates to how many people report to each supervisor.

The consequence for workers of bureaucratic structures is that new employees are socialized into the standards and procedures developed by the organization. Thus the structure constrains innovation and individual responsibility, and makes it difficult for the organization to respond to changing demands. However, for organizations whose purpose is routine repetitive work in a stable trading environment, using relatively large numbers of unskilled people, a bureaucratic approach can be efficient.

Social organization

Bureaucratic structures tend to ignore the social aspects of the workplace, and this can be counter-productive. One of the Hawthorne studies mentioned earlier found that workers were ignoring a piecework system in order to keep good social relations. Such observations lead to the development of a view of organizational function emphasizing social aspects of work. Argyris (1957) proposed that workers be seen from a developmental perspective: new employees should be supervised and trained until they had learned their job, when management could then relax control. The autonomy thus gained would lead to a desire to take more responsibility and pride in the job, and hence lead to increased productivity. In short organizations should concentrate on realizing the potential of their employees through training and development. Similar views were put forward by McGregor (1960), who held that people naturally enjoy work and see it as an opportunity for personal growth. Such 'human relations' theorists tended to ignore output, one of the main goals of most organizations. Further, the view that organizations should promote personal development at work depends on the debatable assumption that people always respond well to autonomy and responsibility.

691

Adaptable organization

In contrast to viewing structure or social relations as all-important, the organization can be seen as responding to its environment. Both change over time. Therefore organizations grow, mature and decline. Healthy organizations adapt to changing circumstances, and so should be viewed as a function of the particular environmental demands on them. Demands could be in the form of changing niche markets, legislation on safety or worker rights, and new competitors. Looking at organizations in this way leads to an emphasis on strategic planning, adaptable manufacturing, flexible working and so on. The ability to change relatively quickly, acquire new skills and ways of working, and anticipate change becomes very important. In manufacturing Woodward (1965) analysed around 100 British companies and found that their optimum structure reflected the kind of process they used, which in turn was a function of the market they operated in. Mass production which anticipated demand went hand in hand with small spans of control. In contrast small batch, customized, production, made in response to customer demand, correlated with fewer hierarchical levels and larger spans of control.

Organizational development

Modern technology, and in particular the opportunities created by computer-controlled machinery, has led to a resurgence of interest in how work should be organized around technology. The socio-technical approach proposes that the work system, rather than individual jobs, should be the focus of interest, and hence work groups should form the basis for organizational structure and function. Attributes of work teams encompass self-regulation, multi-skilling of team members, and job variety. According to Galbraith (1973; 1977) team effectiveness is a product of several things, amongst which are: team members perceiving their participation as important and rewarding; the team including members able to implement group decisions; the team containing the necessary knowledge and skill; the productive management of conflict within the team; the possession of good interpersonal skills by team members; and the team leader possessing appropriate leadership abilities that facilitate team decision-making.

Leadership

Leadership is the ability to direct a group to the attainment of goals. At work a leader may be a manager, company chairman, or some other powerful person, but also the leader could be a person with no official status such as a work-group member. Thus management and leadership are usually considered as separate in occupational psychology. Leadership has been studied from three perspectives: the personal characteristics of leaders; leadership behaviour; and the interaction between characteristics and work situations.

Early theories of leadership suggested that specific personality traits such as courage, foresight, intelligence, persuasiveness and charisma, were associated

Plate 17.10 Sir John Harvey Jones, charismatic business leader and entrepreneur
Source: Rex Features.

with effective leaders. The usual way of trying to identify the necessary traits was to examine the background of leaders. That approach of course ignores environmental factors in the emergence of leaders, and the possibility that others with the same traits did not become leaders. Mann (1959) found little evidence for any individual trait being associated with leadership. However, that is probably not the end of the story, since some common characteristics of leaders have been adduced by Bass (1981). They were reported to have high energy levels, good judgement, good communication skills, assertiveness, the ability to cooperate and tactfulness to their followers.

Another tactic adopted by some researchers at Ohio State University was to study leadership behaviour. The behaviours thus observed could be clustered into two dimensions: initiating structure, and consideration. Initiating structure is about tasks and getting the job done efficiently and on time. Consideration is about worker welfare and development. Worker satisfaction has been found to be higher when managers were high on consideration (Morse & Reimer 1956), but the two dimensions have been found not to be consistently related to productivity (Stogdill 1965).

Fiedler (1967) has proposed that leadership is effective when the leader's management style fits with the degree to which the work situation gives control and influence to the leader. Favourable situations might include liking of the leader, having well-defined tasks, and high leader power. Structure-oriented leaders do better in high or low control situations, whereas consideration-oriented leaders do better in moderate control situations. Subsequent research has tended to

Plate 17.11 Nissan
Source: Network/Denis Doran.

lend support to Fiedler's hypothesis, although not all studies have confirmed it (Strube & Garcia 1981). Fiedler went on to suggest that leadership style could not be changed as easily as the organization, and therefore change to the organization could help leaders, for example, by making tasks more defined.

Recently the emphasis has tended towards there being no one best style of leadership. Rodrigues (1988) has suggested that three types of leader are needed for organizations which exist in a dynamic environment. The 'innovator' is characterized by the search for new ideas, boldness, the will to succeed, and the belief that the environment can be controlled and manipulated. This style is likely to be effective when an organization is setting up or renewing. The 'implementor' is typified by the ability to accomplish goals through people, a systematic approach, a willingness to take responsibility for decisions, and the need to control and influence situations. This style is likely to be most effective at the stage where new ideas are consolidated. Finally the 'pacifier' is characterized by the capacity to decentralize decision-making, an ability to pacify important individuals, a desire to use earlier decisions, and the need for a positive social interaction in the workplace. This style is likely to be effective when a stable work environment has been implemented, and people in the organization feel competent to do the job.

Work groups

Work groups can be defined as consisting of two or more people engaged together in meeting a goal or set of goals. The groups can be formal, such as the 'quality circles' common in Japanese industry or the autonomous work groups in European firms, or informal. Within groups individuals can have different roles, and hold role expectations about their responsibilities. Benne and Sheats

Box 17.5   Group Norms

All groups, regardless of roles, have certain rules or 'norms' governing a variety of things like working practices, conduct and dress. Norms can develop through group leaders or dominant members, from group history and past situations (Feldman 1984). Group processes such as conformity help maintain norms. Conflict, on the other hand, can divide a group unless resolved. Group cohesiveness is important for effective group work. Tuckman (1965) identified four main stages in group development: forming, storming, norming and performing. Forming is the initial coming together of group members and the identification of the group's purpose, composition and terms of reference. Storming is the stage at which views are openly expressed about the nature of the tasks and arrangement of the group. This stage can lead to conflict and hostility, but can also give rise to discussion on the way forward. The next stage, norming, is then about establishing agreed procedures and standards. Finally, when the group has been through the first three stages it can concentrate on the attainment of its purpose.

Processes that can affect the decisions taken by any group, not just brain-stormers, are 'groupthink' and 'risky shift'. Groupthink is where, in rare circumstances, critical evaluation of ideas is suspended and decisions are arrived at without proper consideration. Risky shift is where decisions become more extreme than any individual in the group would make, and the tendency noted in initial studies was for riskier decisions. Later research showed groups could also show a cautious shift. Thus group decisions have the propensity to be more extreme *per se* than any one individual member.

(1948) outlined a number of roles under three headings: group task roles; group building and maintenance roles; and self-centred roles.

Group task roles included: initiator/contributor – a person who recommends new ideas about a problem; information giver – a person who contributes relevant information to help with decision-making; elaborator – a person who expands on the points made by others. Examples of group building roles were: encourager; harmonizer; compromiser; follower. Self-centred roles included: aggressor – a person who tries to promote their own status in the group; blocker – a person who attempts to stymie group action; playboy – a person who engages in humour and irrelevant acts to divert the group focus away from the tasks in hand; help-seeker – a person who tries to gain sympathy by expressing insecurity or inadequacy.

A more recent exposition of roles in management teams has been proposed by Belbin (1981). He suggested eight roles useful to have in teams: shaper; resource investigator; monitor–evaluator; completer–finisher; team-worker; plant; chairman; and company worker. The basic idea behind these roles is that an effective team is made up of different roles so the whole is greater than the sum of the parts. See Box 17.5.

The idea of groups at work is that they can be the means for different talents to meet and solve work-related problems. An example is the brain-storming meeting which is designed to facilitate the generation of creative ideas (Osborn 1957). A brain-storming session has a few basic rules, namely that no idea is too wacky, criticism of ideas is not allowed, the more ideas the better, the quality is not important, and members should try to build on others' ideas. Unfortunately subsequent research has tended to show that brain-storming is not any better than individual idea creation (Diehl & Stroebe 1987).

Another example is that of QUALITY CIRCLES, a technique popular in Japan and now the USA. Quality circles are small groups of employees from the same work areas who meet regularly to identify, analyse and solve quality and other work problems. Circle members are trained in quality control, develop communication skills, and learn problem-solving techniques.

Change agents

Organizations can also develop by enlisting the services of outside consultants. Change agents act to develop the organization as a problem-solving system, rather than to solve particular problems, although they may help in that. Thus a typical approach would be to diagnose organizational problems by gathering information from employees, say through a survey. Results from the survey are then fed back to the organization in written and/or verbal form, and used as the basis for planning changes. Once the changes are carried out they can be evaluated through gathering information again.

The survey technique has proved effective if followed by positive action (Bowers & Hauser 1977). Potential benefits from the survey method are an increase in the flow of information from all workers to the management; a feeling that management is taking an interest in workers' problems; and a sharing of attitudes within the organization.

Other organizational development techniques using outside change agents include team-building, and process consultation. Team-building concentrates on bringing groups of workers together to discuss ways to improve their performance. The focus is on team functioning and the attainment of team goals. 'Management by Objectives' was mentioned earlier in connection with performance appraisal. However, the method can be used as a basis for organizational development provided team and organizational goals become part of an individual's goals.

Process consultation (Schein 1969) is aimed at getting the organization to reflect and act upon ways of solving its own problems. Schein proposed several stages where the consultant acts in collaboration with the organization: initial contact; developing the contract which determines the problem, the consultant's role, and expected outcomes; selecting a method and place for change; data gathering and diagnosis of the organization's processes; intervention for change; and finally evaluation of results and disengagement. Schein suggests that successful process consultation results in improved organizational performance by changing some of the values of the organization, and by increasing the interpersonal skills of key managers.

Evaluations of organizational development interventions are difficult. The fact that changes have taken place can be observed, but relating the changes to improvements in organizational performance overall is more difficult. Part of the problem for evaluation is that the unit of analysis is the organization itself. Therefore the organization is like a case study, with attendant problems of comparison with other organizations, generalization, and deciding whether any particular intervention was responsible for changes in organizational performance, or whether some other factor(s) or intervention(s) made the difference.

This chapter has sought to provide a concise introduction to the field of occupational psychology. It is not an exhaustive review but sets out the main issues connected to psychology in the workplace. Occupational psychology is an exciting and developing field of investigation and practice. No doubt as research continues many more issues will be thrown up for discussion and debate.

CHAPTER SUMMARY

1 Occupational psychologists study people in the workplace, the work environment and work organizations. They do so in a socio-political context formed by their access to the workplaces they investigate.

2 The key concerns of occupational psychology are the attitudes, feelings and behaviour of people at work, and their relationship to performance at work. Research into work psychology is based on experimental, correlational and case-study approaches.

3 Personnel psychology is concerned with analysing what jobs people do, how they are selected for jobs, how they are trained, appraised, motivated and rewarded at work.

4 Typical concerns in personnel psychology centre on how effective interviews are for job selection in comparison to pencil and paper ability tests, how best to optimize human learning through training programmes, how to motivate workers, and how to deal with stress at work.

5 Human factors psychology considers, amongst other things, how the work environment affects performance at work, how machines are designed to suit human capability, how accidents arise at work and how accidents can be minimized.

6 Human factors psychology views humans as processors of information and concentrates on the ability of workers to perceive, select, transform, remember and act on relevant task information. The widespread use of computers at work means that much crucial work activity is now mental rather than physical.

7 Organizational psychology focuses on how work organizations function, how work groups should be made up, how organizations are structured, and how organizations develop.

8 Modern organizations are more likely to be in a process of change. Occupational psychologists contribute to the understanding of this process by studying leadership and work groups and by acting as change agents.

9 Chartered Occupational Psychologists in Britain work under the auspices of the British Psychological Society. Chartered Occupational Psychologists are expected to have knowledge in eight main areas: human–machine interaction; design of environments and work health and safety; personnel selection and assessment, including test and exercise design; performance appraisal and career development; counselling and personal development; training (identification of needs, training design, and evaluation); employee relations and motivation; and organizational development.

▓ Further Work ▓

1. What are the main areas of occupational psychology, and how are they researched?
2. What are the main theories of worker motivation?
3. What are the principal effects of the work environment on performance?
4. Explain the process of organizational development, and discuss why it is important.

▓ Further Reading ▓

Anderson, N. and Shackleton, V. (1993) *Successful Selection Interviewing*. Oxford: Blackwell.

> This book takes a practical look at the interview and its use in choosing people for jobs, without neglecting the more theoretical psychological aspects of the selection process.

Cook, M. (1993; 2nd edn) *Personnel Selection and Productivity*. Chichester: Wiley.

> This book covers the broad range of issues connected with personnel selection from a mainly academic angle.

Karasek, R. and Theorell, T. (1990) *Healthy Work: Stress, Productivity, and the Reconstruction of Working Life*. New York: Basic Books.

> An interesting, but involved, consideration of work-related health issues from two leading names in the field.

Patrick, J. (1992) *Training: Research and Practice*. London: Academic Press.

> Patrick provides a comprehensive account of training systems and evaluation, skill and knowledge acquisition in humans.

Robson, C. (1993) *Real World Research*. Oxford: Blackwell.

> A readable, although somewhat long, account of the various approaches to studying people in real-life situations and the issues that need to be considered before carrying out investigations of psychology in the workplace.

Warr, P. (1996; 4th edn) *Psychology at Work*. London: Penguin.

> A selection of topics on issues relevant to the workplace. The topics are drawn from across the range of occupational psychology and provide a good next step into the discipline.

PART 8

Conclusions

CHAPTER 18
Conclusions
Peter Scott and Christopher Spencer

▓ **Diversity** ▓

Psychology is complex.

Beware of any textbook offering a false simplicity.

In this text we have attempted to present you with a flavour of a subject which is challenging and intellectually stimulating because we do not yet know the whole story. In this account we hope to have shown an active field which is itself in development and change. At some point in your study, you should have engaged in a research project to gather new data, to test hypotheses, and to refine the existing models. You too then have become part of this ongoing enterprise. This is why we described psychology at the start of this text as being strongly evidence-based: with each description of a topic we have offered you a range of theories, and tried to show how these have been derived from and then tested against some observations. This evidence may arise from natural events, or from the controlled events that we can occasion in the laboratory.

But, 'Which theory is right?' you might ask, having seen the range of theories, and their supporting evidence. We hope by now that you see that this question is in most cases far too simple. Rather, we should be asking 'How can we combine the aspects of these theories?' on the presumption that they will all offer some insights into the topic in hand. It isn't 'Is X determined by heredity or environment?', but rather seeing how to view these two influences together.

As we have already indicated, psychology's task is to seek models in which such factors interact; rather than, as was done in the past, to ask what were the relative contributions of biological, social and individual factors. Simple allocation to 'nature' and 'nurture' seems now outmoded in psychology.

It is interesting to note that many sciences now recognize that different theories about some phenomenon, with apparently conflicting elements, may actually complement each other. For example, in that most hard-nosed science, physics, where the phenomena are very basic elements of matter, you would think that they would have decided by now if light is a particle or a wave. However, a physicist will tell you that each model for light carries certain advantages in different contexts. The scientific issue moves on from 'Which is right?' to 'Which is useful?' for this difficult question.

But, always, the presumption is that we can develop and test theories using evidence. This evidence may properly derive from a whole range of methods of investigation: you are mercifully encountering psychology now that it has (largely) got over its wish to be more hard-nosed than physics, and now feels (largely) that it can draw on qualitative as well as quantitative data where appropriate. Laboratory-based and 'real-life' studies, observations and computer-based simulations, interviews, subjective interpretations and more objective behaviour descriptions: all have their place in an increasingly eclectic and (we hope) more methodologically tolerant psychology.

Integration

So, if you have got the impression that psychology is made up of many different approaches – each asking a different set of questions and therefore getting different answers – then you have probably got it about right. There is no single framework that all psychologists can agree on for their work; nor is there a liklihood of one arising in the near future. The point is, that it is actually very useful to be able to look at the rich behaviour of humans using a rich theoretical framework.

However, the lack of a single framework for analysis does not mean that the subject is actually fragmented. Think about some of the rich interconnections between the chapters you have read. Let us take just one chapter as an example: chapter 10 on language. One approach to the topic of language was taken in this chapter and pursued in some detail. However, it did not present the whole story – in fact, language research came up in practically every other chapter. While the cognitivist asks about the mental mechanisms of language, the developmental psychologist looks at its development in children and issues like 'parentese'; the social psychologist looks at how we manage our interactions using language; and the psychobiologist looks at how language works in the brain. Language is a major factor in how we define ourselves as individuals; and an important role in our definitions of intelligence. It is likely that you would be hard pressed to find a psychologist who does *not* have some important contribution to make to our understanding of this complex behaviour. Nor is language unique in this: any feature of mind – memory, thinking, learning, etc. – would find that the same was true. Psychology is an integrated subject because its diverse parts all recognize the importance of the others in the whole picture.

The study of contemporary psychology is indeed eclectic. So, now that you have read through the various chapters, it is time to consider if psychology has become eclectic enough. Could it gain from further inputs from other disciplines' approaches? from the understandings of culture that the anthropologist could bring? from the ways of conceptualizing change and continuity that an historian could offer? Perhaps, after reading the chapter on personality theories, you might wish to recommend that the insights of a novelist could be drawn upon!

Glossary

ABDUCTION   in conditional reasoning, the generation of an explanation for an event, taken from a theory of how the world works, the plausibility of which depends in large part on the number and the likelihood of the alternative explanations.

ABSTRACT IDENTIFICATIONS   a category in the analysis of responses to the 'Who Am I?', which includes self-descriptions that are too abstract or general to constitute social identity elements (e.g. a human being).

ACCENTUATION THEORY   one of a variety of social cognition theories, which suggests that when other people's attitudes differ from our own, we tend to exaggerate the difference between them.

ACTION POTENTIAL   the brief, all-or-nothing change in membrane potential that constitutes a single response in a neurone.

ACTOR-OBSERVER DIFFERENCE   in the study of the attribution process, the tendency for actors to attribute their behaviour to the situation and for observers to attribute the actor's behaviour to dispositions.

ACTUALIZING THE SELF   an explanation of individual behaviour as being a striving to fulfil, where self-image is a key filter which can either be in harmony with the organism or in opposition.

ADULT ATTACHMENT INTERVIEW   a type of interview devised to probe adults' memories of their own childhood experiences and relationships with their parents, and from which four basic classifications of parenting styles have been defined.

ADVICE   an ethical obligation on the part of trained psychologists to offer qualified help to participants in an observational study when evidence of mental of physical problems arise in relation to them.

AESTHETICS OF PLACE   in environmental psychology, the physical appearance of particular behavioural settings which affect the behaviour of those living within them.

AFFECT   in environmental psychology, an individual's emotional response to the environment, which is predicted by the naturalness of the place; its upkeep, openness, order; and historical significance.

AFFORDANCES   in environmental psychology, the kinds of activities that a place permits or encourages in those living within them.

AGONIST   a psychoactive drug which when it acts on the synapse between neurones facilitates postsynaptic events.

ALBEDO   *see* SURFACE REFLECTANCE

ALGORITHMIC METHOD   a method for solving problems, which, in contrast to HEURISTICS, will always find a solution, if there is one, but which may be very slow.

ALTRUISM   in human and animal behaviour, the tendency to act in ways that benefit other individuals more than oneself, sometimes even where there is a real cost involved to the giver.

ALZHEIMER'S DISEASE   the most common form of senile dementia, a disease which usually manifests itself in old age, but which can also occur prematurely, and is related to certain, possibly genetic, abnormalities and degeneration in brain tissue.

AMBIGUOUS FIGURE   a kind of VISUAL ILLUSION in which a picture can be seen in two different ways, where the percept usually flips between the two alternative interpretations.

AMNESIA   loss of memory syndrome, characterised by intact LTS and preserved procedural memory and which is caused by damage to one of two specific brain regions, the temporal lobes or the diencephalon.

AMNIOTIC SAC   a kind of water bed inside the female uterus in which the human embryo develops into a fetus and which cushions the embryo, keeping it at a constant temperature.

AMYGDALA an almond-shaped group of cells in the TEMPORAL LOBES of the brain, which is a major part of the limbic system that controls the emotions.

ANALOGICAL MAPPING in problem solving, the use of the solution of another problem as a pattern, by establishing a mapping between the domains from which the problems are drawn – the source (or base) domain – and the target domain.

ANALOGICAL REASONING in the study of intelligence, a form of problem solving involving the comparison of similarities between pairs, often in the form of pictures.

ANALOGICAL STORING in environmental cognition, a method for storing spatial information as an internal spatial representation – i.e. in the head.

ANALYSIS BY SYNTHESIS an extreme form of TOP-DOWN PROCESSING, most often applied to speech perception, in which the listener is thought to make sense of the speech waveform by attempting mentally to produce the same sounds as the speaker.

ANCHORING AND ADJUSTMENT one of three types of HEURISTIC which is based on the idea that people often make estimates, of probabilities among other things, by taking an initial value, or anchor, and adjusting it. *See also* AVAILABILITY, REPRESENTATIVENESS.

ANONYMITY in the study of crowds, the lack of identification of the individual which leads them to act in a less social or responsible way than they otherwise would.

ANTAGONIST a psychoactive drug that acts on the synapse between neurones and blocks the action of another drug

ARCHITECTURE FOR COGNITION (ACT*) a model which provides for a complete framework for the 'Adaptive Control of Thought'. The most recent model, ACT-R (Rational ACT) has a computer implementation that allows experimentation on how people learn to act and think.

AREA 17 the primary visual cortex.

ARTIFICIAL NEURAL NETWORK a means of investigating learning in a way that is more 'brain-like' than traditional, symbolic, approaches, and which has many different possible types, each with different learning rules.

ASCHEMATICS in experiments in self-concept formation, those people who do not possess a self-schema in a

particular domain. *See also* SCHEMATICS.

ASCRIBED CHARACTERISTICS a system for analysing responses to the 'Who Am I?', which outlines 30 categories of responses under eight broad headings referring to social identity elements.

ASSIMILATION-CONTRAST THEORY one of a variety of social cognition theories which suggests that when other people hold attitudes similar to our own we tend to exaggerate the similarity.

ASSOCIATION CORTEX one of several areas in the frontal region of the brain, occupying the temporal, occipital and parietal lobes which receives information from sensory cortical areas as well as other association areas.

ATMOSPHERE HYPOTHESIS in SYLLOGISTIC REASONING, an hypothesis for accounting for errors made when subjects are asked to assess conclusions presented to them, rather than to generate conclusions of their own.

ATTACHMENT BEHAVIOURS a preferential system of approaching and interacting with familiar care givers, also known as PROXIMITY-MAINTAINING BEHAVIOURS, such as crying and clinging, which the infant develops in the first nine months of its life.

ATTACHMENT FIGURE the primary care giver recognized by the infant as part of its behavioural system, with whom it maintains proximity by crying or reaching out, and with whom it feels secure.

ATTACHMENT THEORY an analytical attempt to explain the various factors that bind people to another in emotional terms, primarily that attachment first established in infancy between the baby and its mother or primary care giver, which is seen as forming the later expectation experienced by the adult in their relationships with others.

ATTACHMENT TO PLACES in environmental cognition, the development and maintenance of personal and social well-being through identification with particular places.

ATTENTION TO THE OTHER in the DYAD, the interpretation of the output from the other.

ATTITUDE ACCESSIBILITY MODEL in the evaluation of social attitudes, an approach which stresses the evaluative component of attitudes as a learned association between an entity and its evaluation, which is stored in memory.

ATTRIBUTION OF A DISPOSITION in correspondent inference theory, the second of a two-stage process, when observers determine whether a person has a disposition which gives rise to a particular intention. *See also* ATTRIBUTION OF INTENT.

ATTRIBUTION OF INTENT in correspondent inference theory, the first of a two-stage process, when observers infer the intention of the person performing a particular behaviour. *See also* ATTRIBUTION OF A DISPOSITION

ATTRIBUTION THEORY in the psychology of personality, an explanation of social behaviour by attributing to it the core characteristics of the individual rather than the specifics of the situation they might be in.

ATTRIBUTIONAL PROCESSES in applied psychology, how individuals assign causal meaning to events.

AUDITORY NERVE the nerve that carries information from the ear to the brain.

AUTOMATICITY the property of performance of a skill that makes it no longer depend upon effortful, conscious monitoring, such as learning to drive a car or other cognitive skills like reading or playing chess.

AUTONOMIC NERVOUS SYSTEM a self-governing system within the PERIPHERAL NERVOUS SYSTEM which helps regulate the internal environment of the body, receiving information from and sending commands to the heart, intestines and other organs in order to regulate vital bodily functions.

AUTORECEPTOR a site located on the SYNAPTIC BOUTON from which MONOAMINE TRANSMITTERS are released into the synaptic gap of the brain.

AVAILABILITY one of three types of HEURISTIC, according to which the probability of an event, or of an item having a property, is judged by the ease with which instances can be brought to mind – their availability from memory. *See also* REPRESENTATIVENESS, ANCHORING AND ADJUSTMENT.

AXON a prominent, branched fibre attached to the cell body.

BABBLE the first stage in the infant's progress towards speech production, highlighted by the playful production of universally recognizable single-consonant and vowel-like sounds and repetitive syllable strings.

BACKGROUND FIRING RATE most NEURONES are not 'silent', but respond spontaneously with a background, or resting, rate of ACTION POTENTIALS, even when not directly stimulated.

BASAL GANGLIA a collective name for a set of structures located around the THALAMUS, also known as the putamen and globus pallidus, that are part of the motor control mechanism of the brain.

BASE RATES those rates of occurrence of a phenomenon which need to be taken into account in order to determine the DIAGNOSTICITY of evidence.

BASILAR MEMBRANE the part of the COCHLEA of the inner ear responsible for breaking down incoming sound waveforms into their HARMONIC components.

BEHAVIOUR SETTING in environmental psychology, those aspects of a sociophysical environment with which the individual interacts, such as other people and inanimate objects.

BEHAVIOURAL INTENTION in the explanation of social attitudes, the tendency to act towards the entity in a particular way.

BELIEF in the explanation of social attitudes, the cognitive component of the person's overall evaluation of an entity.

BIAS in the consideration of arguments, an inability to allow all possible arguments about an issue, thus considering mainly or only the arguments on one side of a particular case.

THE BIG FIVE the five major personality dimensions, defined by various theorists, which are now generally applied in research on personality traits.

BINAURAL COMPARISON comparison of the responses in the two ears, which is particularly important in location the direction of sound sources.

BINET-SIMON SCALE in intelligence testing, a system of 30 tests in a scale of increasing difficulty as a way of measuring the child's scholastic performance in comparison with expected levels of performance of other children of the same age.

BINOCULAR DISPARITY the small positional differences in the images formed in the two eyes which arise because they have slightly different viewpoints on the world.

BINOCULAR STEREOPSIS literally 'two-eyed sold vision', this is the process of using BINOCULAR DISPARITY to recover information about the relative distance of objects.

BINOCULARLY-DRIVEN CELL a cell with a RECEPTIVE FIELD in each of the eyes, which will thus respond to appropriate stimulation of either eye.

BIOLOGICAL MOTION the stimulus motion produced by animate things which is most often used to refer to particular moving stimuli, where the movement of a person in represented only by a few lights attached to the major joints.

BIOMEDICAL APPROACH a psychological approach to abnormality which emphasizes both qualitative and quantitative differences in order to ascertain what is underlying a particular symptom or deviation of a diagnostic sign.

BIOPSYCHOSOCIAL MODEL   a theoretical model applied to the diagnosis of physical and mental-health problems.

BIPOLAR CELL   a type of retinal cell that connects RETINAL RECEPTOR cells to RETINAL GANGLION CELLS.

BIPOLAR DEPRESSION   also known as manic depression, a severe form of depression where the sufferer alternates between periods of depression and mania, and during the manic phase is irritable, overactive and shows extreme recklessness.

BIRTH   one of the two points in child development where change is relatively sudden, in this case where the child reaches the outside world after being in the womb for nine months.

BODY-IMAGE   in self-descriptions, a person's perceptions of their own body, which may involve either neutral descriptions relating to height, weight, etc., or evaluative judgements of appearance.

BOTTOM-UP PROCESSING   a type of information processing which is thought to progress from a simple description of the stimulus (e.g. the image) to a more complex description of the external world (i.e. a PERCEPTUAL MODEL).

BRIGHTNESS   the perceived amount of light in a scene, corresponding roughly to the level of physical illumination. *See also* SURFACE LIGHTNESS.

BROCA'S APHASIA   a condition, described by the French surgeon, Paul Broca, where people have slow and stilted speech as a result of a dysfunction in the precentral gyrus responsible for organizing speech output.

BULLYING   persistent aggressive behaviour directed towards a particular victim, particularly children at school, who cannot retaliate effectively.

CANALIZATION   the strongly pre-determined process of pre-natal growth in the womb which gives clear genetic instructions for the ZYGOTE to differentiate into the embryo.

CASE GRAMMAR   a form of semantic grammar which represents the semantic roles of phrases using semantic cases such as agents, objects and instruments.

CASE STUDY   a detailed study of one particular example of a phenomenon which involves in-depth analysis of a particular individual's behaviour.

CENTRAL NERVOUS SYSTEM (CNS)   one of the two major divisions of the body's nervous system, which is comprised of the brain and the spinal cord. *See also* PERIPHERAL NERVOUS SYSTEMS.

CENTRE SUBREGION   one of two concentric, circular regions which make up the RECEPTIVE FIELDS of RETINAL GANGLION CELLS and which are of opposite sign (excitatory or inhibitory) and exhibit LATERAL INHIBITION.

CEREBELLUM   meaning literally 'little brain' the large and richly connected structure at the back of the brain, located under the CEREBRUM, that links with other subcortical structures and with areas of the cerebral cortex to produce finely controlled motor skills – particularly in quick-reaction sports which require rapid movements.

CEREBRO-SPINAL FLUID   a plasma filtrate that is secreted from the capillaries of the ventricles of the brain and other blood vessels and circulates around these and other cavities.

CEREBRUM   the two major hemispheres of the brain, which dominate its external appearance and control all voluntary motor activity and higher mental functions.

CHILD-DIRECTED SPEECH (CDS)   a term, formerly called Motherese, to describe the short, fluent, grammatically correct utterances, with enhanced intonation, by which mothers, other adults and older children help toddlers to learn language.

CISTERNA   a structure which contains the SYNAPTIC VESICLES and from which bits of vesicle membrane are pinched off.

CISTRON   a piece of DNA, often also called a GENE.

CLADISTIC TAXONOMY   a classification scheme applied to primates, which uses the possession of shared, derived features as a way of defining groups.

CLASSICAL CONDITIONING   the way in which an infant, during its development, learns to associate one event with another. The term is derived from procedures first introduced by Pavlov in his experimentation with dogs, in which a Conditional Stimulus (a bell) was paired with an Unconditional Stimulus (salivating) in order to elicit a response (known as the Conditioned Response), in this case that of the dog salivating even when the bell was sounded without food.

CLIENT-CENTRED THERAPY   also known as person centred or Rogerian therapy, a form of therapy which brings the client's personal needs into action, viewing the client as intrinsically good and offering a sense of unconditional acceptance and regard for them.

CO-ACTOR   one of two individuals performing the same task within the same space.

COCHLEA   the main organ of the inner ear, responsible for the initial analysis of sound waveforms.

COCKTAIL PARTY PHENOMENON   the ability to attend to a single conversation in a crowded room; an example of STIMULUS SEGMENTATION.

CODON   a triplet of bases along DNA which build amino acids.

COEFFICIENT OF RELATEDNESS   in sociobiology, the average proportion of genes that are shared between family members.

COGNITIVE-SOCIAL APPROACH TO PERSONALITY   in personality studies, an approach to the study of behaviour which emphasizes the individual's expectations and hypotheses about the social world.

COLOUR CIRCLE   a simple way of illustrating how perceived HUE and SATURATION depend upon the wavelength and spectral composition of a light and which can be used to predict the perceived colour of mixtures of MONOCHROMATIC LIGHT. See also COLOUR SOLID.

COLOUR CONSTANCY   the perceptual phenomenon by which the perceived colour of a surface remains constant despite variations in the spectral composition of the light that it reflects.

COLOUR SOLID   an extension of the COLOUR CIRCLE which adds the dimension of perceived BRIGHTNESS.

COMPARATIVE METHOD   an approach applied in sociobiology, where the distribution of a particular bodily feature among a living species is studied in order to deduce at what point in evolution that feature was first seen.

COMPETENCE   that aspect of a theory which is the abstract knowledge which helps to describe some phenomena, as opposed to the PERFORMANCE THEORY. In language research a competence theory tries to capture generalizations about what language is and what it does.

COMPLEMENTARY COLOUR   a colour that complements any colour evoked by a monochromatic light, such that when the two lights, e.g. red–green, blue–yellow are mixed in equal proportions, the resulting colour is white.

COMPLEMENTARY COLOURED AFTER IMAGE   a phenomenon which occurs when the eye adapts to one colour (e.g. red) and then the gaze is shifted to an achromatic (e.g. grey) region, an after image of the COMPLEMENTARY

COLOUR (e.g. green) is seen for a short time.

COMPLEX CELL   a type of cell in the visual cortex that is orientationally selective and has a relatively large receptive field. See also SIMPLE CELL, HYPERCOMPLEX CELL.

COMPUTER AIDED DESIGN PROGRAMS (CAD)   in ENVIRONMENTAL PROGRAMMING, an interactive way of working with the user on the on-screen design of buildings etc., by trying out a whole range of alternatives.

CONCEPTUAL DEPENDENCY (CD)   a form of case grammar which aims to represent the key semantic concepts in language and to capture how these concepts depend upon each other.

CONCRETE OPERATIONAL STAGE   the period from the ages of seven to eleven years during which children's processing capacity increases and they develop the use of memory encoding and retrieval strategies, becoming more aware of their own capabilities and limitations.

CONDITIONAL REASONING   a form of reasoning that indicates that other types of a particular situation are possible.

CONES   a type of RETINAL RECEPTOR that is active in daylight (PHOTOPIC) conditions. The three different types of cone found in the human retina provide the basis for colour vision. See also ROD.

CONFIDENTIALITY   the protection of the anonymity of a participant in a psychological study through the correct storage and published use of their data.

CONFLICT-RESOLUTION STRATEGY   the expression of HEURISTICS in a uniform way as sets of 'if...then' rules or ways of deciding what to do when the conditions for more than one production are satisfied.

CONFORMITY   the tendency, among young adults in particular, to adopt attitudes, styles of dress and behaviour patterns that are guided by peer pressure and the desire to belong to a group rather than by personal choice.

CONJUNCTION FALLACY   in the REPRESENTATIVE HEURISTIC, an error of judgement where the second of two statements is selected because a person fails to recognize that everything that is both A and B must also be A.

COMPLIANCE   in GROUP MEMBERSHIP, the act of yielding to the will of others within the group.

CONJUNCTION FALLACY   in the method of ANCHORING AND ADJUSTMENT used in HEURISTICS, the error of selecting a second statement without recognizing that everything that is both A and B must also be A.

CONNECTIONISM   in cognitive psychology, the major formal language for the description of sub-symbolic learning.

CONSENSUAL VALIDATION   in group membership, the process by which the group affirms and supports the views of a particular individual.

CONSENT   one of the components of the 'Ethical Principles for Conducting Research with Human Participants' drawn up by the British Psychology Society, which underlines the participant's need to consent to a particular study and be fully informed about the nature of the work.

CONSERVATION TASK   a type of task, described by Jean Piaget, where superficial changes in an object or group of objects do not necessarily alter the properties of those objects.

CONSPECIFIC   in sociobiology, a name for another animal of the same species.

CONSTRUCTIVE PLAY   a stage of play amongst children when they develop skills by using objects in non-pretend ways, such as doing a jigsaw or pouring sand or water from one container into another.

CONTAGION   in the study of crowd behaviour, the spread of feeling or a mood through a crowd which leads them to behave in particular, concerted and often violent ways.

CONTEXT   in encoding specificity experiments, INTRINSIC context refers to various features that are an integral part of a target stimulus, whilst EXTRINSIC context represents those features that are present when the target is encountered.

CONVERGENT EVOLUTION   an increase in similarity between species in response to the same selection pressure brought about by the problems of living in a particular niche.

CONVERSION   in SYLLOGISTIC REASONING the swapping round of the two terms, A and B, which is valid in statements of type I and E and invalid for types A and O.

COORDINATED REFERENCE SYSTEM   in environmental psychology, the system of abstract geometric patterns which children acquire by the end of Piaget's concrete operations stage.

COPING RESOURCES   those resources both within the individual and in the environment around them which enable them to deal with stressful situations.

CORPUS CALLOSUM   a set of nerve fibre tracts visible in the midline SAGITTAL SECTION of the brain and which link its two hemispheres.

CORRESPONDENCE PROBLEM   the problem of deciding which feature of the image in the left eye matches each feature in the right eye image. Correct matches are needed for BINOCULAR STEROPSIS.

CORTICAL PLASTICITY   the ability of the cerebral cortex to change as a function of learning or damage, such as the reacquisition of language function following damage to the language hemisphere.

COUNSELLING PSYCHOLOGIST   a clinical practitioner who specializes in helping and advising adults in troubled and dysfunctional relationships, or who are struggling with social problems such as drug or alcohol addiction through interpersonal procedures such as interviewing and tests.

CRANIAL NERVE   a group of twelve nerves in the PERIPHERAL NERVOUS SYSTEM which are attached directly to the brain and supply the head and neck region of the body.

CREOLE   a PIDGIN language which has become the native tongue of the children growing up in a pidgin speech community.

CROSS-SECTIONAL STUDY   a study of adult behaviour drawn from adults of different ages.

CRYSTALLIZED INTELLIGENCE   one of the two most important general factors which influence performance across many tasks, referring to performance on well-learned and familiar tasks. *See also* FLUID INTELLIGENCE.

CUE   a particular feature of the stimulus that forms the basis for further processing, for example a DEPTH CUE.

CYTOCHROME OXIDASE BLOBS   an anatomical (and possibly functional) feature of the visual cortex revealed by selectively staining with cytochrome oxidase.

DARWINIAN FITNESS   in the theory of evolution, the ability to reproduce successfully and leave descendants, a fact which is dependant upon particular attributes rather than physical health.

DEBRIEFING   a session set up after completion of a psychological study, which explains the exact nature of that study to the subject, where this has not been possible at its commencement and where any use of deception during the experiment is revealed to them.

DECLARATIVE MEMORY   a single form of memory embracing episodic and semantic components.

DECUSSATION   the crossing of nerve fibres from one side of the brain to the other.

DEDUCTIVE REASONING   reasoning from facts that are known or supposed to be true, to other facts that necessarily follow from them.

DEFENCE MECHANISM   in Freudian psychology, a pattern of self-protective reaction employed by the EGO in situations arousing distress or anxiety.

DEFENSIBLE SPACE   in environmental psychology, the individual's personalization of the particular area they inhabit and are familiar with and which they feel safe in.

DEFICIENCY MOTIVES   in self-actualization, those motives which reduce the personal needs lower in the hierarchy, such as reducing hunger and thirst and the need for obtaining security.

DELAYED INHIBITION   the temporal equivalent of LATERAL INHIBITION, where responses are subtracted from a delayed copy of themselves so that unchanging stimuli are filtered out and only temporal changes are transmitted.

DELIBERATE PRACTICE   a form of acquiring a skill under close supervision, in which specific aspects of the skill are trained, as opposed to general play in which there is no such deliberate plan.

DELINQUENCY   a type of reckless behaviour, particularly among adolescents, and sometimes influenced by hormonal changes, which often involves crime, underage drinking and sexual activity, and illegal drug use.

DELTA RULE   a powerful form of learning, also known as gradient descent learning, which suggests that following a particular action, the difference between the planned outcome and the actual outcome (the error) is calculated, and the system adjusted to reduce the error next time.

DELUSIONS   an erroneous belief the defies rational argument and despite all evidence to the contrary; this can also take the form of a psychiatric disorder manifest in conditions such as schizophrenia and paranoia.

DENDRITES   twig-like fibres which are attached to the cell body and which receive inputs to the NEURONE.

DENSITY-INTENSITY EFFECT HYPOTHESIS   in environmental psychology, the correlation between varying levels of social density and the individual's positive and/or negative reaction to them.

DEPENDENT VARIABLE   a feature of a particular phenomenon which varies according to the theory because it depends directly on how a given situation is manipulated.

DEPRESSION   a catch-all term used to describe any of several complex, and sometimes extreme psychological states where the emotions are affected, either by internal factors such as by low spirts and low self-esteem or external factors, such as traumatic events in someone's life.

DEPTH CUE   one of a number of features of the visual stimulus that may be used to recover the relative distance of objects.

DERIVED FEATURE   in sociobiology, a feature whose possession is unique to the group of species descended from the single (originator) population.

DESCRIPTIVE HIERARCHY   the idea that a stimulus is represented internally at several different levels of detail, with simple features like edges at the lower levels being combined into more complex features, like corners, at the higher levels.

DESIGN OUT   in architectural planning, the taking into account of special needs or social factors affecting a particular area or community, such as housing estates, and making them less vulnerable to crime and vandalism by redesigning their layout.

DIAGNOSTICITY   in HEURISTICS, the selection of evidence in order to facilitate choice between hypotheses.

DIARY STUDY   a naturalistic complement to a THINK-ALOUD PROTOCOL in which subjects are asked to make their own record of their behaviour and feelings during a psychological experiment by keeping a log in a diary.

DIRECT PERCEPTION   an approach to vision, sometimes called ECOLOGICAL PERCEPTION in which features of the stimulus are thought to correspond directly to features of the world, without the need for inference or high level knowledge of the world.

DIRECTIONAL SELECTIVITY   a property of many visual neurones in which the neurone responds better to some directions of stimulus motion than to others.

DISPOSITIONS   see TRAITS

DISSONANCE THEORY   in the study of attitude functions, the suggestion that people are motivated to attend to and prefer information that is consistent with their current attitudes rather than information that is inconsistent (i.e. dissonant).

DOCILITY   among humans, the genetical trait of non-reciprocal altruism and acceptance.

DOUBLE OPPONENT CELL   a type of visual cell found, for example, in the LATERAL GENICULATE NUCLEUS, that has a complex receptive field showing inhibition both between different wavelengths and different positions.

DRAMATURGICAL APPROACH   an approach used in the explanation of behaviour in social situations, where social life is seen as a metaphor for stage performance, with individuals selecting the roles and scripts to be played.

DUALISM   the concept, discussed by various philosophers since Descartes, that the mind and the brain (i.e. matter) are dual entities which have separate functions, with the mind exerting an influence on the physical workings of the brain that in turn control the muscles of the body.

DYAD   an encounter between two individuals.

ECHOIC MEMORY   *see* SENSORY STORE

ECOLOGICAL APPROACH   in environmental psychology, the study of BEHAVIOUR SETTINGS in order to predict their effect on particular individuals.

ECOLOGICAL PERCEPTION   *see* DIRECT PERCEPTION

EFFECTS OF CONTENT   in the solving of syllogisms, the effects of prior beliefs and knowledge relating to the basic information presented, which may affect the process of syllogistic reasoning.

EFFORT AFTER MEANING   the amount of effort utilized by witnesses to describe a recent specific event or a particular person's behaviour.

EGO   in Freudian psychology, one of the three fundamental components of the personality; in the baby, the ego develops out of the ID from the age of about 6–8 months as a result of its life experiences, to become the locus of the emotions. *See also* ID, SUPEREGO.

EGO DEVELOPMENT   a collective term for the various stages of life during which a human being acquires and masters those functions necessary to deal with the world at large. The American psychoanalyst, Erik Erikson, has described ego development in terms of eight distinct, psychosocial stages which a human moves through during a lifetime life.

EGOCENTRIC ORIENTATION   in environmental psychology, the child's understanding of its environment only as it relates to self, and which is characteristic of the sensorimotor stage of development.

ELABORATION LIKELIHOOD MODEL OF PERSUASION (ELM)   a theory which tries to account for the contradictory findings in the acceptance of PERSUASIVE COMMUNICATIONS by asserting that acceptance of a message can be achieved by two routes, the CENTRAL and the PERIPHERAL, either of which depends on the extent to which the person thinks about and evaluates the message.

EMBRYO   the implanted fertilized egg which over a period of about six weeks develops into a fetus in the womb of the human female and mammal.

EMPIRICAL EVIDENCE   recorded observations which together form the basis of psychology as a science and which can be inspected and publicly questioned.

EMPTY NEST   a popular term for that time in an adult's life when they have to come to terms with their sense of loss and loneliness when their children grow up and leave home.

ENCODING   the extraction of information from a stimulus in order to form a memory trace.

ENCODING SPECIFICITY PRINCIPLE   a proposition that retrieval is a function of the overlap between a memory trace and the information provided at retrieval, which led to the view that recall and recognition are different aspects of the same process.

ENVELOPE   the overall shape of a waveform.

ENVIRONMENTAL COGNITION   in environmental psychology, the individual's perception of the real world at molar (i.e. comprehensive) rather than molecular level.

ENVIRONMENTAL DETERMINISM   in environmental psychology, those everyday, external aspects of living, such as good or bad housing, which make the occurrence of a certain behaviour more likely.

ENVIRONMENTAL GRAMMAR   the terms of reference acquired by an individual in relation to the spaces and settings around them, from which they develop the appropriate expectancies and hence, the corresponding search strategies.

ENVIRONMENTAL PROGRAMMING   in the design of buildings, the systematic collection of data on user-needs in order to understand better their collective needs.

ENVIRONMENTAL SIMULATIONS   in ENVIRONMENTAL PROGRAMMING, the use of certain communication tools, such as drawings and models, in order to elicit responses from potential users of buildings etc.

EPIDEMIOLOGY   the study of how diseases spread, the effect that they have on the environment and how they are controlled.

EPISODIC MEMORY   a proposed memory system which contains a record of personal events.

EQUILIBRIUM MODE   in the DYAD, the balancing of the level of intimacy through the GAZE PATTERN, which is adjusted according to the distance the two people are away from each other.

ERGONOMICS   the study of the relationship between the individual worker and the demands of their job and their working environment, paying particular attention to the efficiency with which their work is performed.

EVERYDAY REASONING   a form of reasoning that is linked with practical action and is based on people's ability to develop convincing arguments about everyday issues, and which is based on SITUATION MODELLING.

EVIDENCE   *see* EMPIRICAL EVIDENCE

EVOLUTIONARY STABLE STRATEGIES (ESS)   in sociobiology, a strategy for species preservation, in the form of an adaptive behaviour, which can resist invasion by other strategies.

EXPECTANCY–VALUE MODEL   in the explanation of social attitudes, a model devised as a uni-dimensional, or one-component, view of attitudes which provides a useful basis for understanding why different people hold different attitudes towards the same entity.

EXPERIMENTAL AESTHETICS   in cognitive psychology, the examination in detail of the relationship between particular physical and environmental features and people's aesthetic response to them.

EXPLANATORY STYLE   a method adopted in social psychology for examining the idea that people have stable ways of explaining the positive and negative events in their lives and which is often applied to the areas of mental and physical health

EXPLICIT MEMORY   any memory task requiring conscious recollection.

EXTENSION   *see* REFERENCE

EXTROVERSION–INTROVERSION   with NEUROTICISM–NORMALITY, one of two orthogonal dimensions applied in the description of personality, as proposed by the psychologist Hans Eysenck, and used in the statistical analysis of behavioural data, where variations in behaviour are defined between these two opposite, end points.

EYSENCK PERSONALITY INVENTORY (EPI)   a questionnaire devised by the psychologist Hans Eysenck to capture the dimensions of personality in a questionnaire format for use in psychiatric diagnosis, using the EXTROVERSION-INTROVERSION and NEUROTICISM-NORMALITY dimensions. *See also* EPQ.

EYSENCK PERSONALITY QUESTIONNAIRE (EPQ)   a modification of the EYSENCK PERSONALITY INVENTORY, incorporating a third dimension, PSYCHOTICISM to account for more of the variance in data.

FACTOR ANALYSIS   in intelligence testing, a mathematical technique used to identify the underlying factors which could account for the correlations between different tests.

FALSE-BELIEF TASKS   a series of tasks used in the study of THEORY OF MIND which provide a test case for finding out whether children really understand the relationship between beliefs and behaviour.

FALSE CONSENSUS EFFECT   in the study of the attribution process, the tendency to use our own attitudes and behaviour as the basis for deciding consensus for that behaviour, by overestimating the number of people who share our beliefs and habits.

FALSE UNIQUENESS   an aspect of the FALSE CONSENSUS effect, where the subject underestimates the number of people who share their particular skills and abilities.

FALSIFIABLE THEORY   a theory capable of generating hypotheses that show it to be false and which is an essential feature of scientific method.

FALSIFICATION   in experiments with selection tasks, a level of insight into the logical structure of the task demonstrated by the choosing of cards that are falsifying rather than confirming instances.

FAST MAPPING   the process whereby the child learns new nouns and verbs by relating a novel object or action to a novel word via the formation of a new concept in as little as a single experience.

FEATURE DETECTOR   the idea deriving from early neurophysical studies of the visual cortex that an individual cell (specifically a SIMPLE CELL) could signal the presence of an individual line or edge of a specific orientation at a specific position in the image.

FEATURE-TRACKING   the process thought to be used by the LONG RANGE MOTION SYSTEM by which image motion is recovered by tracking a distinct feature of the image from one moment to the next.

FIEDLER'S CONTINGENCY THEORY   in the study and assessment of leadership amongst social groups, a method which takes account of the leader's personal style appropriate to a given situation.

FIELD EXPERIMENT   an experiment that is more naturalistic in content than that performed in a laboratory, in that it is in less danger of distorting the evidence by taking the phenomenon out of its true context.

FINITE STATE MACHINE   a simple theoretical mechanism which shows how each word in a string of words can be related to the next.

FIXED SYSTEM OF REFERENCE   in environmental psychology,

the child's use of known locations — home, friends' houses, shops, school — to provide an understanding of large-scale place.

FLUID INTELLIGENCE   one of the two most important general factors influencing human performance, which relates to a person's capacity to solve new problems and to learn. *See also* CRYSTALLIZED INTELLIGENCE.

FORM STREAM   the neural pathway in the VISUAL CORTEX thought to be concerned primarily with the analysis of the stimulus's spatial structure. *See also* MOTION STREAM.

FORMAL OPERATIONAL THINKING   a term defined by Jean Piaget to describe the stage, arrived at by around age 11 or 12, when children are able to first think in abstract, logical and systematic ways.

FORMAL REASONING   the type of reasoning needed for solving formal problems relating, in particular, to logic and mathematics.

FORMAL SIGN LANGUAGE   a system of gestures, used as a replacement or supplement for spoken language, where each specific gesture has an agreed definition

FORMANT   a discrete band of frequencies forming a distinct feature of many (especially periodic) speech sounds, for example vowel sounds.

FORMANT TRANSITION   the changes over time of the frequencies of the FORMANTS in some speech sounds, for example, voiced stops (/d/, /g/, /b/).

FORMATS   a type of familiar play or care routine within which carers constructively support a child's language development. *See* LANGUAGE ACQUISITION SUPPORT SYSTEM (LASS).

FOURIER SERIES   the spectrum of a periodic waveform, which is composed of discrete HARMONICS. *See also* FOURIER TRANSFORM.

FOURIER TRANSFORM   the spectrum of an aperiodic waveform which can contain all frequencies, rather than discrete HARMONICS. *See also* FOURIER SERIES.

FRAME   in environmental psychology, a locus or set of loci with respect to which spatial position is defined.

FRAMES OF REFERENCE   the developing child's expanding range of geographical experience, labelled as EDOCENTRIC (relating to body-part coordination), ALLOCENTRIC (relating to the immediate world) and GEOCENTRIC (relating to the spatial relationships between places).

FREE ASSOCIATION   in Freudian psychoanalysis, a technique for accessing the patient's subconscious, by encouraging them to relax in a reclining posture and

move freely and spontaneously from thought to thought

FRONTAL LOBE   one of the four major lobes which comprise the CEREBRUM.

FUNDAMENTAL ATTRIBUTION ERROR   in the analysis of how people make attributions, the tendency to overestimate the impact of dispositional factors and to underestimate the impact of situational factors in making attributions.

FUNDAMENTAL FREQUENCY   in perception, the first harmonic of a PERIODIC WAVEFORM, being a pure tone with the same basic frequency as the original waveform.

GANGLIA   a collection of NEURONE CELL bodies in the sympathetic nervous system.

GAZE PATTERN   in the study of channels of communication between individuals, the pattern of looking at the other that can have communicative value.

GENE   a term for the portion of chromosomal material that carries the inherited characters of an individual and which potentially serves as a unit of natural selection.

GENERALIZED CONE   the basic building block of Marr's model of visual object representation, having a cross-section, an axis, and a description of the way that the cross-section changes along the axis.

GENERALIZED OTHER   in self-concept formation, the global view we develop about how we are seen by others.

GENERATION-RECOGNITION   a model of retrieval in which there is a generative phase and a recognition phase and which proposes that recall and recognition are different processes.

GENERATIVE GRAMMAR   a way of thinking about grammar rules where they are seen as generating *all and only* those sentences that are legitimate in the language in question.

GENERATIVITY   one of the polarities of MATURITY, as described by Erik Erikson, where an adult is able to give of him/herself without expectation of personal gain.

GENETIC PREDISPOSITION   those aspects of an individual that may lead them to respond more negatively to an unpleasant event, which are related to events they have experienced in the past.

GEON   the basic building block of Biederman's model of visual object representation, which is a simplified version of a GENERALIZED CONE, having an axis and a cross-section which are defined only in terms of simple dichotomies (straight or curved, symmetrical or asymmetrical).

GESTALT PSYCHOLOGISTS a group of mainly German psychologists, who were most active in the 1920s and interested, among other things, in the way that perception imposes structure upon its stimulus.

GLIAL CELL a cell in the nervous system which provides the chemical support that is essential to maintain neural functioning.

GRADED RECEPTOR POTENTIAL the response of a typical receptor cell involving a change in membrane potential that is proportional to the strength of the stimulus, rather than being an all-or-nothing ACTION POTENTIAL.

GRADUALISM in the study of evolution, the view that most of the time a species exists it will stay exactly the same, with only slow changes occurring.

GREAT APES the larger group of apes – the orangutan, gorilla and two species of chimpanzee – which are the closest animal relatives to man.

GROUP COHESION in the study of groups, the development of friendships and the structuring of the group, which occurs as some individuals take the lead and others tend to follow.

GROUP FACTOR THEORY an approach in the theory of intelligence, which emphasizes the independence of different factors that make up intelligence rather than one important general factor; using factor analysis, the American psychologist Thurstone identified seven separate factors in the performance of intelligence tests.

GROUP MEMBERSHIP acceptance of the individual into a particular social group, which in turn is a powerful influence in the formation of the self.

GROUP SELECTION in sociobiology, the evolution of traits for the good of the species or group, even though they disadvantage the individual.

GROUPTHINK a phenomenon related to decision-making by groups, where errors of judgement arise as a result of an over-emphasis placed on the need for consensus, at the expense of individual critical evaluation procedures.

GROWTH MOTIVES in self actualization, those motives which move a person up to the higher part of a hierarchy, to an achievement of things beyond the satisfaction of essential needs.

GROWTH NEED STRENGTH in the psychology of the workplace, a theory relating to the perception of job meaningfulness, where those low in growth need will not be motivated by increases in job characteristics – such as skill, responsibility, autonomy – whereas those high in growth need will benefit.

GYRI the ridges formed by adjacent clefts or SULCI in the CEREBRUM.

HAIR CELL the auditory receptor cell type, found in the COCHLEA.

HAPLORHINES one of the two great branches of the primate order, comprised of monkeys and apes. *See also* STREPSIRHINES.

HARMONIC the simplest basic sound into which all auditory waveforms can be broken down, consisting of a sinusoid of a specific frequency and amplitude.

HAWTHORNE EFFECT in the psychology of the workplace, the connection between increased productivity and the introduction of new working methods, the argument being that workers respond positively, if only temporarily, to any kind of innovation.

HEBB RULE or HEBBIAN LEARNING a natural form of learning which suggests that 'cells that fire together, wire together' – i.e. if two neurones are active at the same time and they synapse to each other, then the strength of the synapse will be increased.

HEURISTICS a set of experimental, trial-and-error kinds of procedures used for assessing the probabilities of events or of properties that objects might have and for making inferences from those probabilities.

HIGH DENSITY SETTING in the evaluation of personal environment the level of proximity and crowding within buildings such as housing blocks or the locality in which people live, which may have an effect on their psychological well-being.

HIPPOCAMPUS a major structure located within the forebrain and which forms part of the brain's limbic system, playing an important part in emotional behaviour and memory.

HIV an acronym for human immunodeficiency virus, the virus which causes AIDS and which is generally transmitted via sexual activity or drug use.

HOLOPHRASES two-word utterances, such as 'allgone', 'oh-dear', which the child learns as a single word during early speech development.

HOME RANGE in environmental psychology, the particular area through which any animal species will move, on both a daily and seasonal basis, in order to gain the resources it needs.

HOPE that quality of ego functioning, as defined by Erik Erikson, which enables the infant to differentiate between TRUST and MISTRUST and develop a capacity for viewing life with optimism.

HORIZONTAL CELL a type of retinal neurone that collects the responses of many receptor cells and relays them to a BIPOLAR CELL.

HUE the correct term for what is generally called colour. Scientifically, colour is broken down into hue, SATURATION and BRIGHTNESS.

HYPERCOLUMN the complete set of several hundred thousand cells in the primary visual cortex responsible for the preliminary analysis of one small region of the image.

HYPERCOMPLEX CELL a type of cell in the visual cortex, also known as end-stopped cell, that is orientationally selective, having a relatively large receptive field, and which responds best to stimuli that end within its receptive field. *See also* SIMPLE CELL, COMPLEX CELL.

HYPOTHALAMUS a small structure located inside the brain which is important in numerous motivational processes such as hunger, thirst and sex and which also plays a role in controlling emotion, sleep and bodily temperature. In addition, it can exert certain physical and emotional effects by directing the release of hormones from the PITUITARY GLAND.

HYPOTHESIS a set of predictions gathered as the basis of a theory that can themselves be tested with respect to EVIDENCE.

HYPOTHESIS TESTING a procedure for testing the truth or usefulness of a hypothesis, by deducing specific consequences from it and finding out whether those consequences are true.

ICONIC MEMORY *see* SENSORY STORE

ID in Freudian psychology, one of the three fundamental components of the personality; the id is present at birth and is entirely unconscious, and is responsible for the basic sexual and destructive-aggressive instincts. *See also* EGO, SUPER-EGO.

IDEAL SELF in the perception of self, that view of the self which implies 'Me as I would like to be'. *See also* OUGHT SELF, POSSIBLE SELF.

IDENTITY STATUS four categories of reaction in young people to certain questions posed them in a SEMI-STRUCTURED INTERVIEW and which have been defined as 'confusion', 'foreclosure', 'moratorium' and 'achievement'.

IDIOSYNCRASY CREDIT in the study of social influence processes, a pre-existing, powerful role displayed by a 'minority' member of a particular group which can lead the group members to comply unexpectedly with them.

IDIOT SAVANT a child or adult who despite often (but not always) having a mental handicap has an extraordinary ability to perform mental calculations or demonstrate feats of knowledge, in many cases relating to numbers.

IF–THEN PROFILE in trait research, a formulation for analysing data types of behaviour by plotting the conditional if...then's of the particular responses to particular social situations.

ILLOCUTION in SPEECH ACT theory, the intention of the speaker that is actually transmitted to the listener, which can be very different from the LOCUTION itself.

ILLUSORY CORRELATION in reasoning, the relationship between variables that is strongly influenced by real-world knowledge rather than rational thought.

IMAGEABILITY in environmental psychology, the symbolic significance of place related to its distinctiveness of form, its visibility, and patterns of use.

IMMUNOLOGICAL FUNCTIONING in the study of psychological stress, the body's ability to resist infection and illness, a state which can be affected to low moods.

IMPLICIT MEMORY any memory task which tests memory indirectly, e.g. repetition priming.

IMPRESSION REGULATION in the DYAD, the control over the output from oneself to the other.

INCLUSIVE FITNESS in the study of evolution, the theory that inherited traits take account of all effects on relatives as well as the self, being the sum of their effects on the reproduction of the individual itself, plus the effect on the reproduction of all of its relatives, each devalued by the appropriate coefficient of relatedness.

INDEPENDENT VARIABLE a variable that takes some part in the manipulation of a particular situation in scientific experimentation.

INDIRECT PERCEPTION the approach to perception that emphasizes the indirectness of the relationship between the final conscious impression and the initial pattern of stimulation and which suggests that perception is an active process involving sophisticated knowledge*See also* DIRECT PERCEPTION.

INDIVIDUATION the process, generally experienced in the transitional period between early and middle adulthood, whereby an adult becomes more reflective about his/her life and increasingly compassionate, accepting and more loving of self and others.

INDUCTION a non-deductive type of reasoning where, even if a person knows the premises given are true, and knows that they have reasoned as they intended, they cannot be sure that their conclusion will be true, the end result being a HYPOTHESIS.

INFERENTIAL EXPLOSION the point arrived at when the use of rules to reason about a representation become vulnerable and therefore unsustainable.

INFORMATION PROCESSING a way of thinking about perception, usually associated with the INDIRECT APPROACH, that views it as a process of creating and manipulating internal representations.

INHIBITION in social psychology, the restraining effect on the individual of the presence of others when they are performing certain tasks, which stems from their apprehension at being evaluated by the other

INSECURE ATTACHMENT the lack of attachment by an infant to a particular care giver, so that it does not use the attachment figure as a secure base and when distressed will show some ambivalence to or avoidance of that attachment figure. *See also* SECURE ATTACHMENT.

INSIGHT *see* REPRESENTATIONAL UNDERSTANDING

INSTRUMENTAL CONDITIONING an experimental procedure in which reinforcement takes place only after the subject has made the appropriate response and which is used almost interchangeably with the term OPERANT CONDITIONING.

INTEGRATED INTERNAL REPRESENTATION the method applied by a blind child for building up an awareness of a particular area, which is relative to the amount of lifetime freedom it has been allowed to explore space by its parents or carers.

INTELLIGENCE QUOTIENT (IQ) the ratio of intelligence in an individual, calculated by dividing their MENTAL AGE by their chronological age and multiplying by 100.

INTELLIGENCE SCALE a scale devised by Binet and Simon, which was based on already-existing tests of memory, comprehension, vocabulary and reasoning, the selection being based on items which generated good performance from children rated as bright as well as poor performance from children considered less able.

INTENSION *see* SENSE

INTENSITY CUE one of the main sources of information in locating the direction of sound sources. Sounds coming from the left, for example, will be more intense in the left ear than in the right. *See also* TIMING CUE.

INTENTIONAL DECEPTION one of the thorniest of ethical issues in psychological research, deception is used in psychological studies through the use of confederates in order to gauge the response of subjects to wrong answers. The use of deception is usually revealed to the subject in the DEBRIEFING SESSION.

INTERACTIONAL SYNCHRONICITY a stage of development whereby babies over the age of 2 or 3 months develop a readiness for communicative interaction with their carers.

INTERACTIONALIST RESOLUTION in the analysis of personality dimension, the study of behaviour as a product of traits expressed in interaction with social situations.

INTERAURAL DELAY a difference in the time of arrival of a stimulus at the two ears. An important source of information about the direction of a sound source. *See also* TIMING CUE.

INTERGROUP AWARENESS AND HOSTILITY in social psychology, the existence of prejudice and hostility as part of the normal relations within groups.

INTERGROUP COMPARISON in social identity theory, the comparison between one's own group and other groups.

INTROSPECTION the most informal kind of SELF-REPORT, in which a SUBJECT speculates on his/her cognitive states and processes, and which produces data of a highly qualitative nature.

INVARIANT a feature of the stimulus that reliably signals some useful feature of the world and which is usually associated with the DIRECT APPROACH to perception.

JARGON the second stage of speech development in the child after BABBLE, where the child forms syllable sequences which increasingly use the sound combinations, rhythms and intonation patterns of the language it hears.

JOINT ATTENTION the ability of a baby after the age of approximately 5 months to look where another person is looking.

KIN SELECTION in evolution, the use of INCLUSIVE FITNESS to explain apparent cases of ALTRUISM, and which accounts for animal (and perhaps human) behavioural choices.

LABORATORY EXPERIMENT an experiment that, unlike a

FIELD EXPERIMENT is strictly controlled and far from natural. It can however make up for taking the phenomenon out of its context by allowing much more careful control of the different variables involved.

LAMARCKISM the theory, propounded by the French naturalist, Jean Baptiste de Lamarck, that species can alter as a result of individuals gaining characters during their lifetime.

LANGUAGE ACQUISITION SUPPORT SYSTEM (LASS) the conclusion of American psychologist Jerome Bruner that for a child to learn language normally it must have a support system of social interaction based on highly familiar play or care routines which support each next step of its language development.

LATENCY PERIOD a period in human sexual development prior to puberty during which the sexual urges are considered to be in abeyance.

LATERAL GENICULATE NUCLEUS (LGN) part of the visual pathway between the retina and the PRIMARY VISUAL CORTEX.

LATERAL INHIBITION the suppression of the response in one neurone by the responses of other neurones dealing with nearby regions of the stimulus. A property of almost all sensory systems, it serves to filter out uniform stimulation and emphasize spatial changes. *See also* DELAYED INHIBITION.

LAW OF EFFECT the theory, developed by American psychologist E. L. Thorndike, that behaviours that lead to 'good' outcomes are repeated whilst those that lead to 'bad' outcomes are not, and which can form the basis for an evolutionary account of how the organism learns to make appropriate responses in its environment.

LEARNED HELPLESSNESS one of the main theories developed to explain the experience of depressions, derived from experiments in which animals, subjected to inescapable aversive stimulation, became very passive in their responding.

LEARNING DIFFICULTIES the various ways in which children underachieve or perform badly at school, often caused by dyslexia o other difficulties in dealing with reading, writing or solving mathematical problems.

LEAST PREFERRED CO-WORKER (LPC) in FIEDLER'S CONTINGENCY THEORY the identification of a fellow group-member on a scale indicating how far the leader can separate the personal characteristics of this person from the work characteristics.

LEGIBILITY OF PLACES in environmental cognition, the image people develop of places in a form which is easy to comprehend and to remember.

LEVELS OF PROCESSING an alternative to the modal model in which the relation between perception and memory is emphasized.

LEXICAL CATEGORY also known as parts of speech, this is a class of words which appear to share some of the same features.

LIFE CYCLE the various stages of life and development that a person experiences from birth to death, which some psychologists are now emphasising in studies of the life-span development perspective in adults.

LIFE-SPAN DEVELOPMENT PERSPECTIVE *see* LIFE CYCLE

LIGHTNESS CONSTANCY the perceptual phenomenon by which surfaces appear to have the same reflectance despite changes in illumination.

LIGHTNESS CONTRAST the perceptual phenomenon by which the lightness of one region of the image is affected by nearby regions, such as how a given region will look darker when surrounded by a bright region than when surrounded by a light region.

LIKEABILITY in environmental psychology, the qualities accounting for preferences of place and location.

LINGUISTIC DETERMINISM the theoretically 'stronger' version of the SAPIR–WHORF HYPOTHESIS, that language must determine thought, i.e. that what one says causally affects what one thinks. *See also* LINGUISTIC RELATIVITY.

LINGUISTIC RELATIVITY a theoretically 'weak' version of the SAPIR–WHORF HYPOTHESIS that language must influence thought, but which does not take account of the fact that if a language has no word for something, then it cannot be thought about.

LINKAGE in the study of genetics, the link between the genetic basis of characters which results from both genes lying on the same chromosome.

LITERACY SKILLS the acquisition of grammar leading to the ability to read and write.

LOCAL OPTIMALITY in the study of evolution, the optimization by natural selection on a local scale, of animals living within a particular habitat.

LOCUTION in SPEECH ACT theory, the literal speech act, i.e. the utterance itself.

LONG RANGE MOTION SYSTEM one of two systems thought to underpin human motion perception which operates indirectly, by inferring motion from the change in image position of a given feature over time. *See also* FEATURE TRACKING.

LONG-TERM POTENTIATION an increase in postsynaptic potential caused by repeated stimulation of a cell, which is thought to occur in many structures, providing the basis for much of learning and memory, probably in the form of long-term modification of neural pathways.

LONG-TERM STORE (LTS) the permanent store of knowledge which is of infinite capacity and which is often referred to as SECONDARY MEMORY.

LONGITUDINAL STUDY in personality assessment, a study of adult development drawn from research data compiled from the same group of adults at different points in their lives, which are based on material form Q- and R-DATA.

LOOKING-GLASS SELF see REFLECTED APPRAISALS

M-CELL a type of RETINAL GANGLION CELL which typically predominates in the central region of the retina, with a large RECEPTIVE FIELD and a TRANSIENT RESPONSE.

MACHIAVELLIAN INTELLIGENCE in the theory of evolution, the development of an intelligent response to social complexity, where animals living in competitive social groups learn to manipulate, deceive and to cooperate according to the dictates of circumstance.

MATCHING BIAS MODEL in analysis of poor performance in the selection task, a proposal that claims that subjects choose cards in the task in two ways, either by correct logical reasoning, or by looking at items in an abstract fashion.

MATERNAL DEPRIVATION HYPOTHESIS a term defined by the English psychiatrist John Bowlby to describe the critical period of around 6 months to 3 years during which the child needs continuous love and care from one person, the mother or a permanent mother-substitute.

MATURITY the stage in human development when the adult is seen as having achieved certain socially-acceptable levels of sexual, intellectual and emotional fullness. As defined by Erik Erikson, the adult at this stage develops the need to concern him/herself with the development of the next generation, either through parenthood or through the passing on of skills and knowledge to others.

MEDULLA an area of the brain situated below the PONS that contains nuclei that help control body functions like heart beat, respiration and digestion.

MEMORY CUEING HYPOTHESIS an explanation for the effects of content in the selection task, which suggests that familiar concrete content can remind a person of a similar problem that they have encountered in the past.

MENARCHE the onset of menstruation in adolescent girls.

MENTAL AGE in intelligence testing, the mental level at which a person has arrived compared with their actual, chronological age.

MENTAL MODELS THEORY a framework for presenting research in thinking and reasoning based on manipulation of the models of parts of the world that people have in their minds.

MENINGES the three layers of connective tissue that cover the brain and spinal cord.

METABOLIC COSTS in the study of evolution, the expenditure of metabolic energy by brain tissue in order to support intelligence.

METALINGUISTIC AWARENESS the ability to recognize how people use language in its various linguistic forms and how language functions within particular cultures.

METAMEMORY the self-awareness of memory abilities in the young child which leads it to realize more about the need to apply strategies effectively.

METAPHYSICAL MIND in philosophical discussion of neuroscience, a definition of the human mind as being non-physical, i.e. as a separate entity that is not a property of brain function.

MICROGENESIS in environmental psychology, the development of knowledge about a new environmental area based on the skills acquired through ONTOGENESIS.

MIDDLE EAR the part of the ear between the ear drum (part of the outer ear) and the COCHLEA (part of the inner ear) containing three small bones (ossicles) that efficiently transmit vibration of the ear drum to the cochlea for auditory processing.

MIDLIFE CRISIS a popular term for the phenomenon of mental and emotional crisis which many people experience between the ages of 40 and 45 years at the end of early adulthood. This is often reflected in the individual's desire to embark on an affair, leave a relationship or make a dramatic change of career.

MIND READING see THEORY OF MIND

MINIMAP in environmental cognition, the information children store about local routes in their environment.

MINIMAXING in chess, the technique for mechanically choosing by computer a move in a game.

MISMATCHING the way in which a young child will use words wrongly when it does not fully comprehend the adult meaning of them.

MISTRUST *see* TRUST

MODUS PONENS one of the RULES OF INFERENCE, which states that, no matter what statements P and Q stand for, if P is true and if it is also true that if P then Q, Q must be true as well.

MONISTS in philosophical discussion of the nature of the human mind, those who believe that mental and physical behaviour can both be explained in common terms, in opposition to DUALISM, which views mind and matter as being two separate entities.

MONOAMINE TRANSMITTER one of several families of chemicals manufactured by the neurones, such as hormones.

MONOCHROMATIC LIGHT light of a single wavelength.

MORATORIUM a suspension of activity of one kind or another; Erik Erikson has argued that adolescence can be thought of as a period of 'psychosocial moratorium', during which society allows or sanctions young people to try out different beliefs and practices – sexual, religious, political – without undue pressure.

MOTION AFTER EFFECT a temporary after effect produced by adaption to one pattern of motion, in which stationary stimuli appear to have the opposite pattern of motion.

MOTION-SENSING the direct measurement of retinal motion by specialized neurones which is thought to underpin the human SHORT RANGE MOTION SYSTEM.

MOTION STREAM the neural pathway in the visual system thought to be concerned primarily with the analysis of stimulus movement. *See also* FORM STREAM.

MOTIVATION TO COMPLY in attitude functions, the desire to comply with a particular person or group which affects NORMATIVE BELIEFS.

MOVEMENT in theoretical linguistics, where a phrase seems to belong somewhere in a sentence, but can appear somewhere else, such as a topicalization movement.

MULTIPLE-ACT CRITERION in the study of personality, a pooled combination of many behaviours deemed to be related to a particular trait or characteristic.

MULTI-TRAIT PERSONALITY INVENTORY in psychological analysis, a quick overall summary of individuality prepared in a test format, enabling comparisons to be drawn across a whole sample.

MUTATION in the study of evolution, the mechanism of variation which occurs when the genetic code along the DNA molecule in a chromosome is replicated in-

accurately, a process which is not always destructive.

MYELIN a fat-rich substance from which the sheaths enclosing AXONS in the central nervous system are made.

NEED FOR COGNITION in the study of attitude change, the tendency to engage in and enjoy thinking, which makes people more likely to elaborate the arguments contained in a message.

NEURAL HIERARCHY the idea (now unpopular) that a DESCRIPTIVE HIERARCHY of the stimulus can be achieved simply by wiring together cells with progressively more complex properties.

NEURAL NETWORK a type of computer model consisting of many simple units (thought to be roughly equivalent to individual neurones), connected together by excitatory or inhibitory links.

NEURAL TUBE in the early stages of the development of the brain in the embryo, a tubular structure derived from the outer layer of cells of the embryo and from which the brain and spinal cord develop.

NEUROGLIA the 'nerve glue' which holds NEURONES together.

NEUROMODULATOR a chemical that alters the general sensitivity and responsivity of neurones.

NEURONE a nerve cell which conveys and processes information in the nervous system.

NEUROTICISM–NORMALITY *see* extroversion–introversion

NEUROTRANSMITTER a chemical specific to a particular NEURONE which is secreted by it in order to influence and communicate with other nerve cells.

NICHES in the study of ecology, the environmental slot containing all the determinants of survival into which a particular species fits after going through a period of adaptation.

NODE in environmental cognition, a place where routes intersect in the mental images people develop of maps.

NODES OF RANVIER a bare portion of uncoated AXON on the MYELIN SHEATH and which cause nerve impulses to 'jump'.

NON-ACCIDENTAL PROPERTY a property of the image that probably reflects the same property of the world, such as a straight line in an image which is almost (but not quite) certainly produced by a straight edge.

NON-COMMON EFFECTS in the process of determining a dispositional attribution, the number of very specific effects caused by an action.

NON-VERBAL COMMUNICATION a form of communication

without speech developed between babies and their carers, which makes use of faces, voices, body movements and touch, but which adults and the disabled continue to use throughout life to supplement and to support speech or act as its substitute.

NON-VERBAL VOCAL TONE   in channels of communication, the reinforcement of words by gesture.

NORMATIVE BELIEFS   in attitude functions, those beliefs about whether specific others would approve of the person performing the behaviour which determine the SUBJECTIVE NORM component.

NORMATIVE DEVELOPMENT   a typical pattern of development common to many children used as the basis for descriptive work by psychologists.

OBJECT PERMANENCE   the idea posited by Jean Piaget that objects which are no longer visible still continue to exist even though they are out of sight, which although taken for granted by adults requires the forming of a mental representation on the part of the infant.

OBSERVATIONAL APPROACH   a non-experimental case study of human behaviour which involves the keeping of an accurate record of events which can be studied in detail later.

OCCIPITAL LOBE   one of the four cerebral hemispheres which comprise the CEREBRUM.

OCCUPATIONAL PSYCHOLOGY   the study of work in terms of the feelings, attitudes, behaviour and performance of those at work and those factors which influence workers, attitudes and behaviour.

OFF-CENTRE CELL   a type of RETINAL GANGLION CELL with a RECEPTIVE FIELD in which the CENTRE SUB-REGION is an ON-REGION. *See also* ON-CENTRE CELL.

OFF-REGION   a region of the receptive field of a sensory neurone in which an increase in stimulus intensity produces a decrease in response whilst a decrease in stimulus intensity produces an increase in response. *See also* ON-REGION.

OLIGODENDROCYTE   in the central nervous system, a type of GLIAL CELL which produces an insulating sheath around the AXONS of NEURONES.

ON-CENTRE CELL   a type of RETINAL GANGLION CELL with a RECEPTIVE FIELD in which the CENTRE SUB-REGION an ON-REGION. *See also* OFF-CENTRE CELL.

ON-REGION   a region of the RECEPTIVE FIELD of a sensory neurone in which an increase in stimulus intensity produces an increase in response, whilst a decrease in stimulus intensity produces a decrease in response.

See also OFF-REGION.

ONTOGENESIS   in environmental psychology, the development from infancy of cognitive skills for environmental understanding.

OPEN-ENDED INTERVIEW   a face-to-face set of questions posed to a subject in the course of social research.

OPERANT CONDITIONING   the way in which the infant learns new abilities and new information in order to develop, through the positive reinforcement of repeated actions and patterns of behaviour.

OPPONENCY THEORY   the idea that perceived colour depends, in human vision, upon the balance of activity in mechanisms tuned to complementary colours.

OPTIC ARRAY   the complex but structured pattern of light rays that arrives at any given point in the world and which is, in principle, the visual stimulus available to an observer at that point.

OPTIC CHIASM   a junction in front of the HYPOTHALAMUS and the PITUITARY GLAND where about half the nerve fibres from each eye cross to the other side of the brain

OPTIC FLOW   the smooth changes in the OPTIC ARRAY produced as an observer moves about the world.

ORIENTATION SELECTIVITY   a property of many cells in the visual cortex, where the cell responds to stimuli of one orientation better than to stimuli of other orientations.

OUGHT SELF   in the perception of self, the view of the self in terms of 'Me as I think I should or ought to be'. *See also* IDEAL SELF, POSSIBLE SELF.

OVAL WINDOW   the point at which vibrations are transmitted from the middle ear to the COCHLEA.

OVEREXTENSION   a type of error incurred when a child seeks to identify something verbally without comprehending the full adult meaning of the word it is using, such as using the word 'dog' to refer to cats as well as dogs.

P-CELL   a type of RETINAL GANGLION CELL which typically predominates in the central region of the retina, with a small RECEPTIVE FIELD and a SUSTAINED RESPONSE.

PARASYMPATHETIC SYSTEM   one of two separate systems operating in tandem within the AUTONOMIC NERVOUS SYSTEM which generally has a slowing effect on the heartbeat and digestive functions.

PARIETAL LOBE   one of the four cerebral hemispheres which comprise the CEREBRUM.

PARSE TREE   the structure of the phrases captured by linguistic rules (particularly phrase structure grammar rules) which is often illustrated graphically as an inverted tree.

PARTICULATE INHERITANCE   in the study of heredity, the separate inheritance of characteristics independent of each other.

PERCEIVED BEHAVIOURAL CONTROL   in Ajzen's THEORY OF PLANNED BEHAVIOUR , a component which refers to the person's perceptions of how easy or difficult it would be for them to perform the behaviour, and which takes account of past behaviour and situational and resource factors.

PERCEPTION   the awareness in the infant of different tastes and smells which helps it identify care givers such as its own mother.

PERCEPTUAL MODEL   an internal representation of the world, based upon prior knowledge, that can explain the current pattern of physical stimulation.

PERIODIC WAVEFORM   a repetitive waveform consisting of a sequence of identical cycles.

PERIPHERAL NERVOUS SYSTEMS (PNS)   a series of systems, which together with the CENTRAL NERVOUS SYSTEM forms the two major divisions of the body's nervous system. They are located outside the bony core of the skull and spine and are in turn divided into two systems: the SOMATIC and the AUTONOMIC.

PERLOCUTION   in SPEECH ACT theory, the effect of the act beyond the intention of the speaker, i.e. the things that may happen in a listener's head that the speaker cannot predict.

PERSONAL NORMS   in the theory of reasoned action, those determinants of behaviour such as feelings of moral obligation.

PERSONALITY   the set of habitual attitudes and styles of interacting with people and the world around us which the child acquires as part of its development.

PERSUASIVE COMMUNICATIONS   in the theory of attitude change, those messages that attempt to change people's minds despite being different from the participants' initial attitudes.

PHASE CHANGE   in environmental cognition, the boundaries on a map visualised by an individual, such as where land gives way to water.

PHASE LOCKING   the response of auditory neurones in synchrony with the stimulus and which forms the basis of the TIME THEORY OF PITCH PERCEPTION.

PHENOMENOLOGY   in the study of personality, a method of studying conscious, mental experiences in relation to specific events.

PHONEME   a basic 'atomic' speech sound.

PHOTOPIC VISION   daylight vision, mediated primarily by CONES and therefore preserving colour information. *See also* SCOTOPIC VISION.

PHRASAL CATEGORY   lexical categories which can themselves be clumped together, such as Determiner–Adjective–Noun, and are named after the word that is considered to be the most important lexical category – called the head of the phrase – in this case, a Noun Phrase.

PHRASE STRUCTURE GRAMMAR (PSG)   a set of rules which captures how phrasal categories can be combined to produce grammatically correct sentences, the structures of which are usually illustrated graphically as PARSE TREES.

PIDGIN   an invented language with an apparently reduced range of style, grammar and lexicon which is formed when two or more cultures, particularly in a colonial setting, come into contact and have to communicate with a mixture of their native languages.

PINNA   the external, visible part of the outer ear.

PITCH   the auditory correlate of the frequency of a PERIODIC WAVEFORM.

PITUITARY GLAND   an important endocrinal gland located at the base of the brain which secretes a variety of hormones into the bloodstream, including those regulating growth and other bodily functions.

PLACE THEORY OF PITCH PERCEPTION   the idea that the pitch of an auditory stimulus is signalled by the identity of the responding auditory neurones.

PLACELESSNESS   in environmental psychology, the lack of purposeful encounter through transactions with particular environments.

PLACENTA   a special area on the wall of the female uterus to which the UMBILICAL CORD is connected and which supplies blood, oxygen and nutrients from the mother to the developing EMBRYO.

POLARIZATION   1) in the nerve cell, the electrical potential difference across the cell wall which enables it to transmit a signal along itself or to another cell. 2) in social psychology, the phenomenon whereby the effect of group discussion of an issue serves to leave individuals with an expressed view which is slightly more extreme than the one they expressed beforehand.

POLYANDRY   the mating or marriage of one female with two of more males.

POLYGYNY   the mating or marriage of one male with two

or more females.

PONS   an enlarged section towards the top of the brain containing groups of NEURONES that are involved in processes like sleep and arousal, motor control, and pain sensation and control.

POSSIBLE SELF   in the perception of self, that view about what the self might be like in the future. *See also* IDEAL SELF, OUGHT SELF.

POSTURAL ECHO   a channel of communication, often evident in interview situations, where the interviewee will unconsciously shift position as the interviewer does.

POWER LAW OF PRACTICE   the theory which states that performance at a particular skill will improve as a simple 'power' function of the amount of practice one has had at the skill.

PRAGMATIC REASONING SCHEMA   an explanation of the effects of content in the selection task which suggests that people use context-dependent rules of inference, such as a permission schema, to solve problems of this kind.

PREJUDICE   the negative evaluation of another person, based on some general attribute such as sex, race or disability, rather than on their individual personality and worth.

PREOPERATIONAL STAGE   the period of human development between the ages of two and seven, described by Jean Piaget, during which children are not able to perform various cognitive tasks.

PRETEND PLAY   one of the stages of play amongst children, described by Jean Piaget and Sara Smilansky, which children engage in from 15 months onward and which develop from simple acts of 'feeding' dolls into elaborate role-play episodes.

PRIMARY APPRAISAL   one of two appraisal processes applied in the study of physiological stress, when an individual appraises the threat inherent in a situation. *See also* SECONDARY APPRAISAL.

PRIMARY COLOUR   one of a small set of coloured lights which, when added together in different proportions, can produce a wide range of perceivable colours.

PRIMARY MEMORY   *see* SHORT TERM STORE

PRIMARY VISUAL CORTEX   the first stage of visual processing in the visual cortex, also known as the STRIATE CORTEX, AREA 17B and, in primates only, V1.

PRIMATES   a group of mammals, characterized by having flexible hands and feet and highly developed brains, and which includes, humans, apes, lemurs, tarsiers and monkeys.

PRIMITIVE   in biological terms, a term relating to a trait which has manifested itself in the early stages of the evolution of a species.

PRINCIPLE OF COMPOSITIONALITY   a theoretical principle in semantics which indicates that one can combine the basic meanings of all of the words and phrases involved in an utterance to determine the meaning of the whole utterance.

PROBLEM REDUCTION   in PROBLEM SOLVING, a technique using the method of 'divide and conquer' applied to reduce one large problem to several smaller ones.

PROCEDURAL MEMORY   memory that is not open to conscious inspection (e.g. skills).

PROCESS MODEL OF PERSUASION   in the study of attitude change, an account which suggests that the effect of a persuasive communication is determined by a five-stage process of attention, comprehension, yielding, retention and behaviour.

PROCESSING STREAM   a neural pathway thought to be concerned primarily with the analysis of one stimulus attribute, such as FORM STREAM, MOTION STREAM.

PRODUCTION SYSTEMS   in PROBLEM SOLVING applications, a system for solving problems that is built from a set of 'if...then' rules to be applied to a particular situation.

PROPOSITIONAL STORAGE AND RETRIEVAL   in environmental cognition, the process of storing spatial information as a string of instructions for movement along a route.

PROTECTION   the preservation of the participant from any risk of physical or mental harm during the course of a psychological experiment, as well as the ensuring of their privacy during observation.

PROTOCONVERSATIONS   the earliest form of communication between carer and infant based on an exchange of looks, smiles and sounds which engage the baby's attention.

PROXEMICS   in the study of communication, the use of space between individuals in various social or cultural situations, and which conveys varying degrees of intimacy and friendliness.

PROXIMITY-MAINTAINING BEHAVIOURS   *see* ATTACHMENT BEHAVIOURS

PSEUDODIAGNOSTICITY   in HEURISTICS, the idea that people tend to retain an initial (and often favoured) hypothesis or try to confirm rather than disconfirm hypotheses when making decisions about things.

PSYCHODYNAMIC MODEL   a theoretical model applied to

the diagnosis of mental-health and physical problems

PSYCHOMETRIC a term applied in intelligence research to cover those aspects concerned with the design and the use of intelligence tests, and related research which has been based on the results of intelligence tests.

PSYCHOMETRIC TEST a performance or IQ test often used to assess candidates for jobs.

PSYCHOPATHOLOGY in Freudian analysis, a method for gaining insight by analysing the significance of and underlying motivation for the verbal slips made by patients in conversation.

PSYCHOSOMATICS in clinical psychology, the application of psychological research and theories not only to mental health problems but also to physical health problems, by extending the study of clinical problems to primary-care and general hospital settings.

PSYCHOTICISM in the EYSENCK PERONALITY QUESTIONNAIRE, a personality dimension used in the analysis of behavioural data.

PUBERTY a variable period of a year or so during which the child undergoes relatively rapid development, particularly in its sex organs, and in the case of the female, in its ability to reproduce.

PUNCTUATED EQUILIBRIUM in the theory of evolution, a period of brief bursts of rapid change in a species, activated by favourable environmental conditions.

PURE TONE an alternative word for HARMONIC or SINUSOID.

Q-DATA a category of data used in personality assessment, relating to self-ratings gained from questionnaires.

QUALITATIVE METHOD an increasingly popular method applied by psychologists in reaching insights into human experience and behaviour that cannot be gained from the QUANTITATIVE METHOD.

QUALITY CIRCLES a type of work group, popular in Japan and the USA, where small groups of employees from the same work areas meet regularly to identify, analyse and solve quality and other work problems.

QUANTITATIVE METHOD an approach used by psychologists in research studies in order to count quantities and use statistical support in the evaluation of findings.

QUESTIONNAIRE a less personal version of a face-to-face interview, usually intended for a larger collection of subjects but which is nevertheless highly structured in content.

RANDOM DOT STEREOGRAM a visual stimulus consisting of a pair of random dot patterns whose two members are identical, except that a region in one is displaced relative to the other.

R-DATA a category of data used in personality assessment, relating to others' ratings of a target individual.

RECASTING the often instinctive way in which the young child's ungrammatical utterances are put into correct grammatical forms by its mother or carer and which aid in the development of the child's language.

RECEPTIVE FIELD the region of the stimulus that, when stimulated, causes a change in the response of a sensory neurone.

RECIPROCAL ALTRUISM in evolutionary psychology, the occurrence of cases of non-human behaviour that are mutually helpful in the sense that the agent *cannot* gain, or even loses, inclusive fitness as a result of this action.

RECOGNITION BY COMPONENTS a theory of visual object recognition, holding that objects are represented internally as a constellation of GEONS and that the image is segmented into the parts corresponding to geons so that the resulting description can be matched to the appropriate object description.

REDUCTIONIST PSYCHOLOGY a form of psychology which is based upon an examination of phenomena through the study of their individual components; thus, in social psychology, the study of the group through the psychology of the individuals that make up that group.

REFERENCE an extra-linguistic definition of meaning, also known as EXTENSION, where the reference of an expression is what entities or states it points to in the outside world.

REFLECTED APPRAISALS in symbolic interactionism, the way in which others *actually* evaluate us when mediated by how we *believe* others evaluate us, a fact which is strongly related to our self-concepts. Also known as LOOKING-GLASS SELF.

REFLEX a particular pattern of behaviour, such as sucking, triggered by a specific stimulus with which all children are born and which plays a crucial part in the overall development of the child in the months before and after birth.

REINFORCEMENT a term used differently by various theorists to describe how a reinforcer serves to increase the likelihood of a particular behaviour happening again.

REPERTORY GRID   in psychotherapy, a grid method, base on an individual's particular judgements about people in their environment and from which constructs can be constructed to be elaborated on in interview.

REPRESENTATIONAL UNDERSTANDING   also referred to as IN-SIGHT, the capacity to understand how things work and thereby choose or modify objects that meet precise criteria for tool use, in advance of undertaking a task.

REPRESENTATIVENESS   one of three types of HEURISTIC, according to which a person, thing or event will be judged to be a member of a class whose stereotypical members it closely resembles, regardless of other information. *See also* AVAILABILITY, ANCHORING AND ADJUSTMENT.

RETINAL GANGLION CELLS   the output stage of the retina and the first stage of processing at which ACTION POTENTIALS are generated. Retinal ganglion cells have characteristic circular RECEPTIVE FIELDS exhibiting LATERAL INHIBITION.

RETINAL RECEPTOR   the light sensitive cells in the retina where light is converted into a neural response. In human beings this is comprised of a mixture of RODS and CONES.

RETINEX THEORY   a theory of colour vision proposing that the amount of light in the image is first analysed separately at different wavelengths and that the resulting maps of the image are subsequently compared.

RETINOTOPIC MAP   the orderly projection of neurones from the retina so that the spatial structure of the image is preserved at the destination, for example, nearby cells in the PRIMARY VISUAL CORTEX have receptive fields in nearby regions of the image.

RISK FACTOR   the element of risk involved in any exposure to a potentially harmful agent, for example that of the developing fetus to developmental abnormality, through the use by the mother of harmful drugs, cigarettes, alcohol during pregnancy.

RISK-TAKING   a form of conscious human behaviour influenced by a calculation of risk against possible achievement or reward to be gained, which reaches its peak amongst young men during later adolescence.

ROBBER'S CAVE   a term for the study of group behaviour among children, based on the work of Muzafer and Carolyn Sherif, who set up a classic series of natural experiments at summer camps in the 1950s where they identified the strengths and conflicts of a miniature society and set about resolving the conflicts that had been created.

ROD   a type of RETINAL RECEPTOR that is active in dim lighting (SCOTOPIC) conditions. *See also* CONE.

ROLES AND MEMBERSHIPS   in the system for analysing responses to the 'Who Am I?' devised by C. Gordon, those groups that a person has had some choice about joining, as opposed to the ASCRIBED CHARACTERISTICS assigned to them at birth.

ROLES AND SPECIALISMS   in GROUP MEMBERSHIP, the skills manifested by certain members as leaders or experts within the group and whose role is thus more social-than task-related.

ROUGH-AND-TUMBLE PLAY   a type of play amongst children, involving chasing and tackling each other, which most children by the age of 8 are able to discern from aggressive fighting.

RULES OF INFERENCE   a set of theories applied in the study of how people reason, the best known of which is the MODUS PONENS, and which suggests that people encode what they know as sentences with certain formal structures and use a set of mentally encoded rules of inference to see what other sentences can be derived from them.

SAGITTAL SECTION   a sectional cut across the brain made vertically from front to back.

SAPIR–WHORF HYPOTHESIS   an hypothesis associated with Benjamin Whorf and Edward Sapir that there must be an intimate connection between human language and human thinking.   It is often presented in two versions: in which language determines thought (LINGUISTIC DETERMINISM); or in which different languages will encode different thoughts (LINGUISTIC RELATIVITY).

SATURATION   the intensity of a colour, for example, pink and red have the same HUE, but red is more saturated. The most saturated colours are produced by MONOCHROMATIC LIGHT.

SCAFFOLD   the constructive support system provided by mothers and carers in order for the child to progress through the stages of language development. *See* LANGUAGE ACQUISITION SUPPORT SYSTEM (LASS).

SCHEMATICS   in experiments, those people who rate themselves highly in a particular domain and who see that domain as important to them. *See also* ASCHEMATICS.

SCHEME   A consistent pattern of motor behaviour in the

infant which is based on reflexes, such as sucking or grasping.

SCOTOMA   in cases of partial blindness, a neglect or blindness in the retina for a certain part of the visual field.

SCOTOPIC VISION   nighttime vision, mediated primarily by RODS and therefore without colour information. *See also* PHOTOPIC VISION.

SCRIPT   a representation or scenario which captures a sequence of events that usually happen when people meet.

SEARCH FOR CHEATERS   in SOCIAL CONTRACT theory, an instruction to focus on instances of cheating, not just where only one side cheats, but also where both sides can cheat.

SEASONS   a metaphor, applied by Daniel Levinson to his concept and description of the human developmental eras, where life is seen in the familiar, poetic terms of e.g. spring, summer, autumn, winter.

SECONDARY APPRAISAL   in the study of psychological stress, the second of two processes applied by the individual when they appraise their ability to cope with a particular threat. *See also* PRIMARY APPRAISAL.

SECONDARY MEMORY   *see* LONG-TERM STORE

SECURE ATTACHMENT   a pattern of attachment between an infant of one to three years old and a particular care giver who serves as a secure base from which that infant can explore, and when distressed, by whom it is reassured. *See also* INSECURE ATTACHMENT.

SELF-AUTHENTICATION   an attempt to learn the truth about oneself by carrying out limited social experiments.

SELF-CONCEPT   in social-psychological theory, the self as an object of perception.

SELF-CONSISTENCY   the validation of the self by confirming one's beliefs about the self.

SELF-ESTEEM   in the perception of self, the self-concept considered as a whole, taking into account all its various dimensions.

SELF-HANDICAPPING   an aspect of the SELF-SERVING BIAS, which involves making an attribution before one has performed a behaviour.

SELF-IDENTITY   in the theory of reasoned action, a determinant of behaviour that is just as important as attitude in predicting a particular action.

SELF-REPORT   the result of a psychological experiment contributed by a person involved which throws light on the quality of their experience, usually in the form of an interview or survey, a test, introspection, think-aloud protocol, or even a diary study.

SELF-SCHEMAS   in self-concept formation, those elements which reflect areas of enduring importance, investment and concern to us that are likely to be invoked in many different social situations.

SELF-SERVING BIAS   in the study of the attribution process, the tendency to attribute one's success to internal factors and one's failure to external factors, thus avoiding blame for negative events and accepting credit for positive events, which in turn increase our SELF-ESTEEM.

SELF-SOCIALIZATION   the process whereby a child develops a sense of gender identity in the course of sex-role identification, and which is not directly dependent on external reinforcement.

SEMANTIC GRAMMAR   a grammar which seeks to directly deliver the meaning of any sentence, before (or without regard to) its syntax.

SEMANTIC MEMORY   a proposed memory system which contains general knowledge, language, rules and concepts.

SEMISTRUCTURED INTERVIEW   a technique developed by James Marcia which put the ideas of Erik Erikson on adolescent development into a testable form.

SENILE DEMENTIA   *see* ALZHEIMER'S DISEASE

SENSE   also known as INTENSION this is a linguistic definition of meaning, where an expression can be defined by purely linguistic things.

SENSORIMOTOR COMMUNICATION   the baby's early signalling system, which emphasizes the fact that communication in the first year and a half is rooted to vocalizations and gestural actions centred around feeding, dressing, bathing and play.

SENSORIMOTOR STAGE   the developmental period in the infant from birth until 18 months of age, as defined by the Swiss psychologist, Jean Piaget.

SENSORY STORE   the memory store which holds incoming sensory information for a brief period of time. The two most widely investigated are ICONIC MEMORY (vision) and ECHOIC MEMORY (hearing).

SEPARATION ANXIETY TEST   a photographic test devised to measure attachment quality in older children and adolescents and differentiate between those who place value on intimate relationships with others, and those who act in ways likely to elicit rejection.

SEX-ROLE STEREOTYPES   the belief originally found amongst children, including those not yet attending school, about what are most appropriate characteristics for each sex.

SEXUAL DIMORPHISM   a characteristic of species, such as humans, where there are two distinguishable forms of male and female, in which males compete over females and are larger than the female or endowed with more dangerous weaponry.

SHARED DEFINITION OF THE SITUATION   in the DYAD an understanding arrived at by the two individuals involved as to what the nature of their encounter is.

SHARED REFERENCE   the ability of a baby, by the end of its first year, to look at something another person is pointing at.

SHORT RANGE MOTION SYSTEM   one of two systems thought to underpin human motion perception, which operates by directly measuring retinal motion. *See also* LONG RANGE MOTION SYSTEM.

SHORT-TERM STORE (STS)   the limited capacity storage system supporting conscious mental activity, previously known as PRIMARY MEMORY.

SIMPLE AFFIRMATIVE ACTIVE DECLARATIVES (SADD)   a term applied to single, simple expressions that are affirmative and declarative, in that they are making positive declarations about something being true and are presented in an active voice.

SIMPLE CELL   a type of cell in the visual cortex that is orientationally selective and has a relatively small RECEPTIVE FIELD divided into discrete ON and OFF SUB-REGIONS.

SINGLE-ACT TECHNIQUE   in the study of personality, the use of a single behaviour to act as a measure for a generalization of all similar situations.

SINUSOID   alternative word for HARMONIC or PURE TONE.

SITUATION MODELLING   the basis for EVERYDAY REASONING which is thinking about how things are and how things might be in the world; these can lead to errors in everyday reasoning by being biased or incomplete, or both.

SIZE CONSTANCY   in vision, the phenomenon whereby an object appears to have the same size whatever its distance away from the person seeing it.

SOCIAL COMPARISON THEORY   in self-concept formation, the questions of when we make comparisons, what we compare, and why, as well as with whom comparisons are made; this phenomenon is also applied by the individual in social group processes.

SOCIAL CONTRACT   an explanation, used in discussion of the selection task, that specifies that in social exchanges, if one takes a benefit one is expected to pay a cost in return.

SOCIAL DESIRABILITY   in the ATTRIBUTION OF A DISPOSITION the likelihood of a particular action being performed or approved of by most other people in that situation.

SOCIAL FACILITATION   in social psychology, the improvement of a person's performance at a given task when they are joined in the same room by a CO-ACTOR.

SOCIAL IDENTITY THEORY   in social psychology, the method of examining the group in the context of the individual, where membership of that group is perceived as offering identity to its members, particularly in the context of other, possibly competing, groups.

SOCIAL INTERACTION   the communication and relationships between people that influence the shaping of the self.

SOCIAL LEARNING THEORY   the various factors in a child's upbringing which contribute to its difference from the opposite sex. Sex hormones contribute in part to this learning process, which is also enhanced by observation and imitation of same-sex models, thus adding to the child's growing sense of gender identity.

SOCIAL SUPPORT   those positive, supportive features of an individual's environment which enable them to respond to and deal with stressful situations effectively.

SOCIOBIOLOGY   the study of kin selection to account for animal and sometimes human, behavioural choices.

SOCIODRAMATIC PLAY   a stage of elaborate role-play amongst children over the age of 3 or 4, where pretend games are developed around various characters, such as mothers, fathers and babies, which are often influenced by books, TV programmes and films.

SOCIOECOLOGY   the study of how environment influences society in the process of natural selection and which perceives social systems as being flexible and subject to change over evolutionary time-scales.

SOCIOGRAM   a diagrammatic representation of the observation of friendships amongst groups of children.

SOCIOMETRIC STATUS-TYPES   the categorization of children as 'popular', 'controversial', 'rejected', 'neglected' or 'average' during sociometric studies, according to whether they are high or low on positive and negative nominations.

SOCIOMETRY   the study of friendships in groups, particularly of children.

SOMA   the cell body of a NEURONE.

SOMATIC NERVOUS SYSTEM   a system within the PERIPHERAL

NERVOUS SYSTEMS which interacts with the outside world by conveying information from sensory receptors (in skin, muscles and joints) to the CENTRAL NERVOUS SYSTEM and which sends motor signals to muscles and glands.

SOMATOMOTOR SYSTEM the system of sensory messages that passes from the cerebral cortex to the muscles in the periphery.

SOMATOSENSORY SYSTEM the system of receptors in the body that communicates the messages relating to sensation and touch.

SPATIAL GEOMETRY in the ontogeny of environmental cognition as described by Piaget, the child's concept of space constructed on topological principles.

SPECTRAL REFLECTANCE the proportion of each incident stimulus wavelength that a surface reflects.

SPECTRAL SENSITIVITY the pattern of response of a neurone to different stimulus wavelengths.

SPEECH ACTS in semantic theory, an action that confirms the intention of the party involved in it to do the thing uttered. *See also* LOCUTION, ILLOCUTION, PERLOCUTION.

SPIKE *see* ACTION POTENTIALS

STAGNATION the opposite of GENERATIVITY, this is one of the two polarities of the stage of MATURITY, as described by Erik Erikson, when the adult is unable to give to others in an unselfish way and becomes increasingly preoccupied with his/her own concerns.

STATE the different levels of arousal experienced by infants, such as sleeping, waking and crying.

STANFORD–BINET TEST a revision of the BINET-SIMON intelligence test, which provides a scale of ninety items that can be used to test all people, from individuals with LEARNING DIFFICULTIES to superior adults; the test also provides examples of acceptable and unacceptable answers to test items so that scoring can be carried out with precision.

STATE–ACTION TREE in problem solving, the complete set of choices available to a problem solver, set out in a diagrammatic form, showing the possible states of the world, represented together with the actions that lead from one state to another.

STATISTICAL REASONING a form of reasoning applied to arguments that depend on statistics or probability, and which is often important in deciding how to conduct our everyday lives.

STEREOTYPING the imposition, as a result of irrational prejudices, of a set of simplified characteristics upon a racial, social or other person or group, despite evidence to the contrary.

STIMULUS SEGMENTATION the organization of a stimulus into parts that belong together and parts that don't and which is also known as grouping or parsing.

STRANGE SITUATION the procedure used with infants aged 1 to 3 years to measure the relationship between an infant and a particular care giver, which assesses the infant's response to being mildly stressed by being taken from them and left with a stranger.

STREPSIRHINES one of the two great branches of the PRIMATE order, comprised of lemurs and lorises.

STRIATE CORTEX *see* PRIMARY VISUAL CORTEX.

STRUCTURED INTERVIEW a set of face-to-face questions posed to a subject in social research.

SUBJECT the participant in any kind of observational research study.

SUBJECTIVE NORM in the theory of reasoned action, a person's perceptions of social approval for their performing a particular behaviour and which will serve as a predictor of the action taken.

SUGGESTIBILITY in the study of crowd behaviour, the responsiveness of individuals within a crowd to taking part in often violent group activity, as if in a hypnotic trance.

SULCI the clefts in the CEREBRUM.

SUPER-EGO in Freudian psychology, one of the fundamental components of the personality; the super-ego develops in the child from the age of 3–5 years, emerging out of the ego as the seat of the conscience and controlling instinctive desires as a result of the learning of standards of social behaviour from the parent.

SUPERIOR CONFORMITY OF THE SELF in social comparison processes, the belief that everyone within a particular group has that their position is like the others', only a little better.

SURFACE REFLECTANCE the proportion of incident light that a given surface will reflect, rather than absorb, also known as ALBEDO, and which is the physical correlate of perceived LIGHTNESS.

SURROUND SUBREGION one of two concentric, circular regions in which the RECEPTIVE FIELDS of RETINAL GANGLION CELLS are typically arranged.

SURVEY the least structured and least personal form in the interview range of instruments used in social research, which takes the form of a type of questionnaire.

SUSTAINED RESPONSE the type of neural response that continues throughout the presentation of a stimulus.

See also TRANSIENT RESPONSE.

SYLLOGISM   a deductive argument with two premises, each of which must take one of four forms, and which must also take one fo the same four forms as its conclusion.

SYLLOGISTIC REASONING   in psychology, a form of reasoning based on the used of SYLLOGISMS

SYMBOLIC PLAY   *see* PRETEND PLAY

SYMPATHETIC SYSTEM   one of two systems that operate in tandem within the AUTONOMIC NERVOUS SYSTEM and which is activated when the body is in states of distress, increasing the rate of heart beat, releasing adrenalin and inhibiting digestion.

SYNAPTIC BOUTON 148   *see* TERMINAL BOUTON

SYNAPTIC VESICLE   a small spherical packet located within each TERMINAL BOUTON and which contains NEUROTRANSMITTERS.

SYNOMORPHY   in environmental psychology, the fit between the activities that go on within a BEHAVIOUR SETTING and the actual physical arrangements of that setting.

T-DATA   a category of data used in personality assessment, relating to objective tests of behaviour.

TELEGRAMMATIC SPEECH   the way in which the young child under 3 selectively omits grammatical markers such as '-ing', '-ed', and words which carry relatively little information, such as 'the', 'and' and 'is' thus creating an abbreviated style of speech.

TEMPERAMENT   the varying categories of behaviour in young babies which may persist and contribute to the development of PERSONALITY in adulthood.

TEMPORAL LOBE   one of the four cerebral hemispheres that comprise the CEREBRUM.

10-YEAR RULE   a rule of thumb that suggests that in order to become outstanding in any skill – in the top 1% of performers – around ten years' dedicated practice is required.

TERATOGENS   a class of environmental hazards which cause marked abnormalities in the fetus during prenatal development and which are can be caused by the use of harmful drugs or substances, such as thalidomide and cocaine, cigarette smoking and heavy use of alcohol.

TERMINAL BOUTON   a swelling located at the end of an AXON which butts on to the DENDRITE or cell body of other nerve cells.

TEST   the most formal kind of SELF-REPORT, which is nor-

mally highly quantitative in nature with the subject's responses being tightly controlled.

THALAMUS   a structure located at the top of the brain stem in the diencephalon, that is subdivided into several nuclei that act as relays in the transmission of information such as sensation and pain to and from other brain regions.

THEORY   a coherent collection of principles used in the science of psychology to explain phenomena. A substantial proportion of theories in psychology are related to the mechanisms by which things work.

THEORY OF MIND   also known as MIND READING, the process described by some psychologists, and still the subject of considerable debate, whereby children develop hypotheses about other people's emotions, desires and beliefs.

THEORY OF PLANNED BEHAVIOUR   the modification of the theory of reasoned action, in which attempts are made to explain less volitional behaviours through the component of PERCEIVED BEHAVIOURAL CONTROL.

THINK-ALOUD PROTOCOL   a useful source of psychological data which although similar to an INTROSPECTION does not allow for speculation about process and which usually collects behaviour in an experimental or highly controlled setting, by asking people to 'say what is in their mind' as they solve problems.

THOG PROBLEM   a problem devised as part of the SELECTION TASK, involving four geometric figures with different shapes and colours, where the subject has to work through the consequences of each possibility to see how it classifies the other figures in the group.

THREE-TERM SERIES PROBLEM   a kind of deductive reasoning problem, which has two statements about three people or objects that can be ordered according to a relation such as height.

TILT AFTER EFFECT   the temporary visual distortion of perceived orientation following adaptation to an oriented stimulus.

TIMBRE   perceived sound quality, corresponding roughly to the physical shape of each cycle of a periodic sound waveform or, equivalently, to the shape of its FOURIER SPECTRUM.

TIME THEORY OF PITCH PERCEPTION   the idea that perceived pitch depends upon the temporal pattern of activity in the auditory nerve.

TIMING CUE   one of the main sources of information in locating the direction of sound sources. *See also* IN-

TENSITY CUE, INTERAURAL DELAY.

TONOTOPIC MAP the orderly projection of neurones from the COCHLEA so that nearby cells at the destination are tuned to nearby frequencies.

TOP-DOWN PROCESSING a type of information processing in which prior knowledge about the world is thought to influence earlier levels of processing, such as the description of the image.

TOPICALIZATION a feature of all languages, and which is very common in some dialects, in which some phrase, which appears logically to belong buried deep in a sentence, is moved to the front of the sentence for emphasis.

TRAITS those enduring characteristics or DISPOSITIONS of a person which give rise to behaviour and define their particular responses to things.

TRANSFORMATIONAL GRAMMAR the rules governing a proposition by Noam Chomsky that the most basic sentences, essentially SADDs are transformed into more complex sentences by a sequence of one or more transformations.

TRANSIENT RESPONSE the type of neural response that occurs only at the onset or offset of a stimulus. *See also* SUSTAINED RESPONSE.

TRAVELLING WAVE the dynamic distortion of the BASILAR MEMBRANE in the COCHLEA produced by auditory stimuli.

TRICHROMATIC THEORY the idea that perceived colour depends, in human beings, upon three mechanisms, each sensitive to a different range of wavelengths. *See also* OPPONENCY THEORY.

TRUST the polar opposite of MISTRUST, which the young child learns to master as part of the development of ego functioning.

2-4-6 PROBLEM a problem used in the SELECTION TASK, where the subject has to discover the rule governing a sequence of numbers by asking about other sequences of numbers.

TYMPANIC MEMBRANE the ear drum.

UMBILICAL CORD a flexible, tubelike cord which connects the fetus to the PLACENTA and through which blood, nutrients, oxygen and waste products are interchanged between the mother and the foetus.

UNDEREXTENSION a type of error incurred by a child when it is striving to use a word without comprehending its full adult meaning, for example by using the generic term 'dog' to refer to the family dog.*See also* OVEREXTENSION.

UNIPOLAR DEPRESSION one of two types of severe depression, where the person only has depressive symptoms without the manic phase.*See also* BIPOLAR DEPRESSION.

UNIVERSAL GRAMMAR (UG) the theory, suggested by the American linguist Noam Chomsky, that all children possess an in-built faculty for spoken language, a theory which is disputed by others, who consider that children are born only with general learning processes which enable them to learn language amongst other things.

V1 the PRIMARY VISUAL CORTEX of a primate.

VENTRICLE one of four large, tubular cavities in the brain, lying under the cortex, that are a leftover characteristic of the brain's early, embryonic development.

VERBAL CHANNEL in an interview situation, the spoken element, as opposed to the various other non-verbal channels of communication used.

VISUAL ILLUSION a mental distortion of perception, sometimes misleadingly called an optical illusion, where visual stimuli are seen incorrectly.

VOICED STOP a type of PHONEME. Main voiced stops as /b/, /d/ and /g/.

WASON SELECTION TASK an abstract version of the selection task where the subject is shown one face of each of four cards, but not the other face, and has to select those cards that must be turned over to find out if a particular rule is true.

WAVELENGTH in a PERIODIC WAVEFORM, the distance between any point on one cycle and the equivalent point on the next cycle.

WECHSLER ADULT INTELLIGENCE SCALE an intelligence test for adults, designed to compensate for the deficiencies in the STANFORD-BINET TEST, by including additional sub-tests making up two scales – one verbal and one based on performance; both scales can be scored separately to give a verbal or a performance IQ as well as an overall measure of IQ based on a person's score for the whole test.

WERNICKE'S APHASIA a condition, described by German neurologist Carl Wernicke, where an inability to understand what words mean affects a persons ability to produce meaningful utterances.

WISDOM as defined by Erik Erikson, this is the quality that results from the resolution of ego integrity and despair, which is achieved by the adult in old age, when he/she has been able to find a midway between the calm acceptance of a life lived and the fear of impending death.

WITHDRAWAL   one of the 'Ethical Principles for Conducting Research with Human Participants' endorsed by the British Psychology Society in which a subject retains the right to his/her 'data' and is able to withdraw consent at any time and have any data pertaining to them excluded from the study.

WORKING MEMORY   a development of the STS concept, comprising a central executive and two slave systems, the articulatory loop and the visuo-spatial scratch pad.

WORKING SELF-CONCEPT   a temporary structure in memory which is invoked by the requirements of a particular situation and forms the configuration of self-views made salient by ongoing social events.

YOUNG ADULTHOOD   that period of human development, as defined by Erik Erikson, when a person develops the need and capacity for intimacy and the ability to be committed to other people despite loss of attention to their own needs.

ZONE OF PROXIMAL DEVELOPMENT   those aspects of a child's performance, described by the Russian psychologist Lev Vygotsky, where she would not be able to achieve on her own, but only with the support, help and instruction of another person.

ZYGOTE   the fertilized human egg which implants on the wall of the uterus, where it develops into an EMBRYO.

References

Abernethy, B. (1987) Anticipation in sport: A review. *Physical Education Review*, 10, 5–16.

Aboud, F. (1988) *Children and Prejudice*. Oxford: Blackwell.

Abrams, D. and Hogg, M. A. (1993) *Group Motivation: Social Psychological Perspectives*. London: Harvester Wheatsheaf.

Adams, J. S. (1965) In L. Berkowitz (ed.), *Advances in Experimental Social Psychology* 2. New York: Academic Press, 267–99.

Adams, M. J. (1990) *Beginning to Read: Thinking and Learning about Print*. Cambridge, Mass.: MIT Press.

Aiken, L. R. (1991; 7th edn) *Psychological Testing and Assessment*. Boston: Allyn and Bacon.

Ainsworth, M. D. S., Blehar, M. C., Waters, E. and Wall, S. (1978) *Patterns of Attachment: A Psychological Study of the Strange Situation*. Hillsdale, NJ: Lawrence Erlbaum.

Ajzen, I. (1985) From intentions to actions: A theory of planned behavior. In J. Kuhl and J. Beckman (eds), *Action Control: From Cognitions to Behavior*. Heidelberg: Springer.

Ajzen, I. (1991) The theory of planned behavior. *Organizational Behavior and Human Decision Processes*, 50, 1-33.

Ajzen, I. and Fishbein, M. (1977) Attitude–behavior relations: A theoretical analysis and review of empirical research. *Psychological Bulletin*, 84, 888–918.

Ajzen, I. and Madden, T. J. (1986) Prediction of goal directed behavior: Attitudes, intentions and perceived behavioral control. *Journal of Experimental Social Psychology*, 27, 453–74.

Allport, F. W. (1924) *Social Psychology*. Boston: Houghton Mifflin.

Allport, G. W. and Oddbert, H. S. (1936) Trait names: A psycholexical study. *Psychological Monographs*, 47 (Whole No. 2).

Altman, I. (1975) *The Environment and Social Behavior*. Monterey: Brooks/Cole.

Altman, I. and Low, S. M. (1992) *Place Attachment*. New York: Plenum Press.

American Psychiatric Association (1994; 4th edn) *Diagnostic and Statistical Manual of Mental Disorders* (DSM IV). Washington, DC: APA.

Anderson, J. R. (1983) *The Architecture of Cognition*. Cambridge, Mass.: Harvard University Press.

Anderson, J. R. (1995) *Learning and Memory: An Integrated Approach*. New York: John Wiley and Sons Ltd.

Anderson, J. R. and Bower, G. H. (1972) *Human Associative Memory*. Washington, DC: Winston.

Anderson, M. (1992) *Intelligence and Development: A Cognitive Theory*. Oxford: Blackwell.

Andreasen, N. C. (1988) Brain imaging: Applications in psychiatry. *Science*, 239, 1381–8.

Antonovsky, A. (1988) *Unravelling the Mystery of Health*. San Francisco: Jossey-Bass.

Argyle, M. (1971; and subsequent edns) *The Psychology of Interpersonal Behaviour*. Harmondsworth: Penguin.

Argyle, M. (1988) *Bodily Communication*. London: Methuen.

Argyle, M. and Dean, J. (1965) Eye-contact, distance and affiliation. *Sociometry*, 28, 289–304.

Argyris, C. (1957) *Personality and Organization – The Conflict Between System and the Individual*. New York: Harper and Row.

Arnett, J. (1992) Reckless behavior in adolescence: A developmental perspective. *Developmental Review*, 12, 339–73.

Asch, S. (1956) Studies of independence and conformity: A minority of one against a unanimous majority. *Psychological Monographs: General and Applied*, 70, 1–70.

Aslin, R. N. (1981) Development of smooth pursuit in human infants. In D. F. Fisher, R. A. Monty and J. W. Sanders (eds), *Eye Movements: Cognition and Visual Perception*. Hillsdale, NJ: Erlbaum.

Astington, J. W., Harris, P. L. and Olson, D. R. (eds) (1988) *Developing Theories of Mind*. Cambridge:

Cambridge University Press.

Atkinson, R. C. and Shiffrin, R. M. (1968) Human memory: A proposed system and its control processes. In K. W. Spence (ed.), *The Psychology of Learning and Motivation: Advances in Research and Theory Vol. 2*. New York: Academic Press.

Austin, J. L. (1962) *How to Do Things with Words*. New York: Oxford University Press.

Baddeley, A. D. (1966a) Short term memory for word sequences as a function of acoustic, semantic and formal similarity. *Quarterly Journal of Experimental Psychology*, 18, 362–5.

Baddeley, A. D. (1966b) The influence of acoustic and semantic similarity on long-term memory for word sequences. *Quarterly Journal of Experimental Psychology*, 18, 302–9.

Baddeley, A. D. (1976) *The Psychology of Memory*. New York: Basic Books.

Baddeley, A. D. (1978) The trouble with levels: A reexamination of Craik and Lockhart's framework for memory research. *Psychological Review*, 85, 139–52.

Baddeley, A. D. (1986) *Working Memory*. Oxford: Oxford University Press.

Baddeley, A. D. (1992) Working memory. *Science*, 255, 556–9.

Baddeley, A. D. (1997; rev. edn) *Human Memory: Theory and Practice*. Hove: Psychology Press.

Baddeley, A. D. and Hitch, G. (1977) Working memory. In G. A. Bower (ed.), *Recent Advances in Learning and Motivation, Vol 8*. New York: Academic Press.

Baddeley, A. D., Logie, R., Nimmo-Smith, I. and Brereton, N. (1985) Components of fluent reading. *Journal of Memory and Language*, 24, 119–31.

Baddeley, A. D., Thomson, N. and Buchanan, M. (1975) Word length and the structure of short-term memory. *Journal of Verbal Learning and Verbal Behaviour*, 14, 575–89.

Bailey, D. A. and McCullough, R. G. (1990) Bone tissue and physical activity. *Canadian Journal of Sport Science*, 15, 229–39.

Baird, P. A. and Sadovnik, A. D. (1988) Maternal age-specific rates for Down's syndrome: Changes over time. *American Journal of Medical Genetics*, 29, 917–27.

Bakeman, R. and Adamson, L. B. (1982) Co-ordinating attention to people and objects in mother–infant and peer–infant interaction. *Child Development*, 55, 1278–89.

Bales, R. F. (1950) *Interaction Process Analysis*. Cambridge, Mass.: Addison-Wesley.

Baltes, P. B. (1973) Prototypical paradigms and questions in lifespan research on development and aging. *The Gerontologist*, 113, 458–67.

Baltes, P. B. (1987) Theoretical propositions of lifespan developmental psychology: On the dynamics between growth and decline. *Developmental Psychology*, 23, 611–26.

Baltes, P. B. (1993) The aging mind: Potential and limits. *The Gerontologist*, 33, 580–94.

Baltes, P. B. and Schaie, K. W. (1976) On the plasticity of intelligence in adulthood and old age: Where Horn and Donaldson fail. *American Psychologist*, 31, 720–5.

Bandura, A. (1969) Social learning theory of identificatory processes. In D. A. Goslin (ed.), *Handbook of Socialization Theory and Research*. Chicago: Rand McNally, 213–62.

Bandura, A. (1977) Self efficacy: Towards a unifying theory of behavior change. *Psychological Review*, 84, 191–215.

Bandura, A. (1977) *Social Learning Theory*. Englewood Cliffs, NJ: Prentice-Hall.

Bandura, A. (1992) Self-efficacy: Mechanism in human agency. *American Psychologist*, 37, 122–47.

Bannerji, N. and Spencer, C. P. (1986) Strategies for sharing student accomodation. *Architecture and Behaviour*, 3, 123–35.

Bannister, D. (1966) A new theory of personality. In B. Foss (ed.), *New Horizons in Psychology*. Harmondsworth: Penguin.

Barker, R. G. (1968) *Ecological Psychology: Concepts and Methods for Studying the Environment of Human Behavior*. Stanford, Calif.: Stanford University Press.

Barker, R. G. and Gump, P. V. (1964) *Big School, Small School*. Stanford, Calif.: Stanford University Press.

Barker, R. G. and Wright, H. F. (1955) *Midwest and its Children: The Psychological Ecology of an American Town*. New York: Row Peterson.

Barlow, H. B. and Levick, W. R. (1965) The mechanism of directionally selective units in a rabbit's retina. *Journal of Physiology*, 178, 477–504.

Baron-Cohen, S. (1993) From attention–goal psychology to belief–desire psychology: the development of a theory of mind, and its dysfunction. In S. Baron-Cohen, H. Tager-Flusberg and D. Cohen, *Understanding Other Minds: Perspectives from Autism*. Oxford: Oxford University Press, 59–82.

Baron-Cohen, S., Leslie, A. M. and Frith, U. (1985) Does the autistic child have a 'theory of mind'? *Cognition*, 21, 37–46.

Barrett, G. V. (1992) Clarifying construct validity: Definitions, processes, and models. *Human Performance*, 5, 13–58.

Barrett, R. and Robinson, B. (1994) Gay dads. In A. E. Gottfried and A. W. Gottfried (eds), *Redefining Families*. New York: Plenum Press.

Barry, H., III., Bacon, M. K. and Child, I. L. (1957) A cross-cultural survey of some sex differences in socialization. *Journal of Abnormal and Social Psychology*, 55, 327–32.

Bartlett, F. C. (1932) *Remembering*. Cambridge: Cambridge University Press.

Bass, B. M. (1981) *Stogdill's Handbook of Leadership*. New York: Free Press.

Baum, A. and Paulus, P. B. (1987) Crowding. In D. Stokols and I. Altman, *Handbook of Environmental Psychology*. New York: John Wiley.

Baum, A. and Valins, S. (1977) *Architecture and Social Behavior*. Hillsdale, NJ: Erlbaum.

Baydar, N. and Brooks-Gunn, J. (1991) Effects of maternal employment and child-care arrangements on preschoolers' cognitive and behavioral outcomes: Evidence from the children of the *National Longitudinal Survey of Youth. Developmental Psychology*, 27, 932–45.

Beattie, G. and Anderson, I. (1995) Questioning attribution theory: Are Kelley's dimensions spontaneously requested? *Semiotica*, 103, 277–90.

Beck, A. T. (1976) *Cognitive Therapy and Emotional Disorders*. New York: International Universities Press.

Beehr, T. A. and Bhagat, R. S. (eds) (1985) *Human Stress and Cognition in Organizations: An Integrated Perspective*. New York: John Wiley and Sons.

Begg, I. and Denny, J. (1969) Empirical reconciliation of atmosphere and conversion interpretations of syllogistic reasoning. *Journal of Experimental Psychology*, 81, 351–4.

Belbin, R. M. (1981) *Management Teams: Why They Succeed or Fail*. Oxford: Butterworth Heinemann.

Bell , P. A., Fisher, J. D., Baum, A. and Greene, T. E. (1990) *Environmental Psychology*. Fort Worth, Tex.: Holt, Rinehart and Winston.

Belsky, J. (1984) The determinants of parenting: A process model. *Child Development*, 55, 83–96.

Belsky, J. (1988) Infant day care and socioemotional development: The United States. *Journal of Child Psychology and Psychiatry*, 29, 397–406.

Belsky, J. and Steinberg, L. D. (1978) The effects of day care: A critical review. *Child Development*, 49, 929–49.

Bem, D. J. and Funder, D. C. (1978) Predicting more of the people more of the time: Assessing the personality of situations. *Psychological Review*, 85, 485–501.

Benedict, H. E. (1979) Early lexical development: Comprehension and production. *Journal of Child Language*, 6, 183–200.

Benne, K. D. and Sheats, P. (1948) Functional roles of group members. *Journal of Social Issues*, 4, 41–9.

Bentall, R. (1990) *Reconstructing Schizophrenia*. London: Routledge.

Bentler, P. M. and Speckart, G. (1979) Models of attitude–behavior relations. *Psychological Review*, 86, 452–64.

Berlin, B. and Kay, P. (1969) *Basic Colour Terms*. Berkeley: University of California Press.

Berman, K. F., Zec, R. F. and Weinberger, D. R. (1986) Physiological dysfunction in dorsolateral prefrontal cortex in schizophrenia: II. Role of neuroleptic treatment, attention, and mental effort. *Archives of General Psychiatry*, 43, 126–35.

Berndt, T. J. (1979) Developmental changes in conformity to peers and parents. *Developmental Psychology*, 15, 608–16.

Best, D. L., Williams, J. E., Cloud, L. M., Davis, S. W., Robertson, L. S., Edwards, J. R., Giles, H. and Fowles, J. (1977) Development of sex-trait stereotypes among young children in the United States, England and Ireland. *Child Development*, 48, 1375–84.

Beyth-Marom, R. and Fischhoff, B. (1983) Diagnosticity and pseudodiagnosticity. *Journal of Personality and Social Psychology*, 45, 1185–95.

Biederman, I. (1987) Recognition by components: A theory of human image understanding. *Psychological Review*, 94, 115–47.

Bigelow, B. J. and La Gaipa, J. J. (1980) The development of friendship values and choice. In H. C. Foot, A. J. Chapman and J. R. Smith (eds), *Friendship and Social Relations in Children*. Chichester: Wiley, 15–44.

Biglan, A., Metzler, C. W., Wirt, R., Ary, D., Noell, J., French, C. and Hood, D. (1990) Social and behavioral factors associated with high-risk sexual behaviour among adolescents. *Journal of Behavioral Medicine*, 13, 245–61.

Binet, A. and Simon, T. (1905) Méthodes nouvelles pour le diagnostic du niveau intellectuel des anormaux. *L'Année Psychologique*, 11, 191–244.

Birnholz, J. C. and Benacerraf, B. R. (1983) The development of human fetal hearing. *Science*, 222, 516–18.

Birren, J.E. (1969) The concept of functional age. *Human Development*, 12, 214–15.

Birren, J. E., Bueter, R. N., Greenhouse, S. W., Sokoloff, L. and Yarrow, M. R. (eds) (1963) *Human Aging: A Biological and Behavioral Study*. Washington, DC: US Government Printing Office.

Bjorkqvist, K. L., Lagerspetz, K. M. J. and Kaukainen, A. (1992) Do girls manipulate and boys fight? Developmental trends in regard to direct and indirect aggression. *Aggressive Behaviour*, 18, 117–27.

Blades, M. and Spencer, C. P. (1995) The development of children's ability to use spatial representations. In H. W. Reese (ed.), *Advances in Child Development and*

Behavior, 25, 157–99.

Blake, R. R. and Mouton, J. S. (1962) Overevaluation of own group's product in intergroup competition. *Journal of Abnormal Social Psychology*, 64, 237–8.

Blanz, F. and Ghiselli, E. E. (1972) The mixed standard scale: A new rating system. *Personnel Psychology*, 25, 185–99.

Blass, E. M., Ganchrow, J. R. and Steiner, J. E. (1984) Classical conditioning in newborn humans 2 to 48 hours of age. *Infant Behavior and Development*, 7, 223–35.

Block, J. (1971) *Lives Through Time*. Berkeley: Bancroft.

Blumberg, H. H. (1972) Communications and interpersonal evaluations. *Journal of Personality and Social Psychology*, 23, 157–62.

Boesch, C. (1991) Teaching among wild chimpanzees. *Animal Behaviour*, 41, 530–2.

Bonarius, J. C. (1965) Research in the personal construct theory of George A.Kelly: Role construct repertory test and basic theory. In B. A. Maher (ed.), *Progress in Experimental Personality Research*. New York: Academic Press.

Bootzin, R. R. E. and Acocella, J. R. (1988) *Abnormal Psychology: Current Perspectives*. New York: Random House.

Boulton, M. G. (1983) *On Being a Mother: a Study of Women with Pre-school Children*. London: Tavistock.

Bowers, D. G. and Hauser, D. L. (1977) Work group types and intervention effects in organizational development. *Administrative Science Quarterly*, 22, 76–94.

Bowlby, J. (1953) *Child Care and the Growth of Love*. Harmondsworth: Penguin.

Bowlby, J. (1969) *Attachment and Loss*, vol.I: *Attachment*. London: Hogarth Press.

Braddick, O. J. (1974) A short range process in apparent motion. *Vision Research*, 14, 519–27.

Brainerd, C. J. (1983) Working-memory systems and cognitive development. In Brainerd (ed.), *Recent Advances in Cognitive-developmental Theory*. New York: Springer-Verlag.

Brantingham, P. L. and Brantingham, P. J. (1993) Nodes, paths and edge: Considerations on the complexity of crime and the physical environment. *Journal of Environmental Psychology*, 13, 3–29.

Brazelton, T. B., Koslowski, B. and Main, M. (1974) The origins of reciprocity: The early mother–infant interaction. In M. Lewis and L. A. Rosenbloom (eds), *The Effect of the Infant on its Caregiver*. New York: Wiley, 49–76.

Breakwell, G. M. and Fife-Schaw, C. (1992) Sexual activities and preferences in a United Kingdom sample of 16–20-year-olds. *Archives of Sexual Behavior*, 21, 271–93.

Bretherton, I., Beeghly-Smith, M. and McNew, S. (1981) Early person knowledge as expressed in gestural and verbal communication: When do infants acquire a 'theory of mind'? In M. E. Lamb and L. Sherrod (eds), *Infant Social Cognition*. Hillsdale, NJ: Erlbaum, 333–73.

Bretherton, I., Fritz, J., Zahn-Waxler, C. and Ridgeway, D. (1986) Learning to talk about emotions: A functional perspective. *Child Development*, 57, 529–48.

Bretherton, I. and Waters, E. (eds) (1985) Growing points of attachment theory and research. *Monographs of the Society for Research in Child Development*, 50/1–2.

Broca, P. (1861; repr. 1965) Paul Broca on the speech centers. Trans. M. D. Boring. In R. J. Herrnstein and E. G. Boring (eds), *A Source Book in the History of Psychology*. Cambridge, Mass.: Harvard University Press.

Broch, T. C. and Balloun, J. L. (1967) Behavioral receptivity to dissonant information. *Journal of Personality and Social Psychology*, 6, 413–28.

Brooks, L. R. (1968) The suppression of visualization by reading. *Quarterly Journal of Experimental Psychology*, 19, 289–99.

Brown, B. B. and Bentley, D. L. (1993) Residential burglars judge risk: The role of territoriality. *Journal of Environmental Psychology*, 13, 51–62.

Brown, B. B., Mory, M. S. and Kinney, D. (1994) Casting adolescent crowds in a relational perspective; caricature, channnel, and context. In R. Montemayor, G. R. Adams and T. P. Gullotta (eds), *Personal Relationships during Adolescence*. London: Sage.

Brown, G. W. and Harris, T. (1978) *Social Origins of Depression*. London: Tavistock.

Brown, G. W. and Harris, T. (1989) *Life Events and Illness*. New York: Guildford.

Brown, J. D. and Taylor, S. E. (1986) Affect and the processing of personal information: Evidence for mood-related self-schemata. *Journal of Experimental Social Psychology*, 22, 436–52.

Brown, R. (1986) *Social Psychology*. New York: Free Press.

Brown, R. and Fish, D. (1983) The psychological causality implicit in language. *Cognition*, 14, 237–73.

Browne, K. (1989) The naturalistic control of family violence and child abuse. In J. Archer and K. Browne (eds), *Human Aggression: Naturalistic Approaches*. London: Routledge.

Bruner, J. S. (1977) Early social interaction and language development. In H. R. Schaffer (ed.), *Studies in Mother–Child Interaction*. London: Academic Press.

Bruner, J. S. (1981) The social context of language acquisition. *Language and Communication*, 1, 155–78.

Budd, R. J. and Spencer, C. P. (1986) Lay theories of behavioural intention: A source of response bias in the theory of reasoned action. *British Journal of Social Psychology*, 25, 109–17.

Buhler, C. and Massarik, F. (eds) (1968) *The Course of Human Development*. New York: Springer.

Bullough, V. L. (1981) Age at menarche: A misunderstanding. *Science*, 213, 365–6.

Burnstein, E. and Vinokur, A. (1977) Persuasive argumentation and social comparison as determinants of attitude polarization. *Journal of Experimental Social Psychology*, 13, 315–32.

Bushnell, I., Sai, F. and Mullin, J. T. (1989) Neonatal recognition of the mother's face. *British Journal of Developmental Psychology*, 7, 3–15.

Buss, D. M. (1985) Why not measure that trait? *Journal of Personality and Social Psychology*, 48, 934–46.

Buss, D. M. (1994) *The Evolution of Desire*. New York: Basic Books.

Butler, M. C. and Jones, A. P. (1979) Perceived leader behavior, individual characteristics, and injury occurrence in hazardous work environments. *Journal of Applied Psychology*, 64, 299–304.

Butters, N. and Brandt, J. (1985) The continuity hypothesis: The relationship of long-term alcoholism to the Wernicke–Korsakoff Syndrome. In M. Galanter (ed.), *Recent Developments in Alcoholism*, 3, 207–26.

Butterworth, G. (1991) The ontogeny and phylogeny of joint visual attention. In A. Whiten (ed.), *Natural Theories of Mind*. Oxford: Blackwell, 223–32.

Byrd, R. E. (1938) *Alone*. New York: Plenum.

Byrne, R. W. (1993) Do larger brains mean greater intelligence? *Behavioural and Brain Sciences*, 16, 696–7.

Byrne, R. W. (1995) *The Thinking Ape: Evolutionary Origins of Intelligence*. Oxford: Oxford University Press.

Byrne, R. W. (1996) Relating brain size to intelligence in primates. In P. A. Mellars and K. R. Gibson (eds), *Modelling the Early Human Mind*. Cambridge: Macdonald Institute for Archaeological Research.

Byrne, R. W. and Whiten, A. (1988) *Machiavellian Intelligence: Social Expertise and the Evolution of Intellect in Monkeys, Apes and Humans*. Oxford: Clarendon Press.

Byrne, R. W. and Whiten, A. (1991) Computation and mindreading in primate tactical deception. In A. Whiten (ed.), *Natural Theories of Mind*. Oxford: Blackwell.

Byrne, R. W. and Whiten, A. (1992) Cognitive evolution in primates: Evidence from tactical deception. *Man*, 27, 609–27.

Calev, A., Ben-Tzvi, E., Shapira, B., Drexler, H., et al. (1989) Distinct memory impairments following electroconvulsive therapy and imipramine. *Psychological Medicine*, 19, 111–19.

Campbell, A. and Muncer, S. (1994) Sex differences in aggression: Social representation and social roles. *British Journal of Social Psychology*, 33, 233–40.

Campion, J. E. (1972) Work sampling for personnel selection. *Journal of Applied Psychology*, 56, 40–4.

Cannon W. B. (1929) *Bodily Changes in Pain, Hunger, Fear and Rage*. Boston: Bramford.

Canter, D. (1977) *The Psychology of Place*. London: Architectural Press.

Canter, D. (1983) The physical context of work. In D. J. Oborne and M. M. Grunenberg (eds), *The Physical Environment At Work*. Chichester: John Wiley and Sons, 11–38.

Canter, D. (1984) Putting situations in their place. In A. Furnham (ed.), *Social Behavior in Context*. London: Allyn and Bacon.

Canter, D. (ed.) (1990) *Fires and Human Behaviour*. London: David Fulton Publishers.

Canter, D. and Larkin, P. (1993) The environmental range of serial rapists. *Journal of Environmental Psychology*, 13, 63–9.

Carlson, N. R. (1994; 5th edn) *Physiology of Behavior*. Boston: Allyn and Bacon.

Carraher, T. N., Carraher, D. W. and Schliemann, A. D. (1985) Mathematics in the streets and in schools. *British Journal of Developmental Psychology*, 3, 21–9.

Carroll, J. B. (1956) *Language, Thought and Reality: Selected Writings of Benjamin Lee Whorf*. Cambridge, Mass.: MIT Press.

Case, R. (1985) *Intellectual Development: Birth to Adulthood*. Orlando: Academic Press.

Cattell, J. M. (1890) Mental test and measurements. *Mind*, 15, 373–80.

Cattell, R. B. (1940) A culture-free intelligence test. *Journal of Educational Psychology*, 31, 161–79.

Cattell, R. B. (1957) *The Structure of Human Personality*. New York: World Book.

Cattell, R. B. (1965) *The Scientific Analysis of Personality*. Harmondsworth: Penguin.

Ceci, S. J. (1990) *On Intelligence . . . More or Less: A Bioecological Treatise on Intellectual Development*. New Jersey: Prentice-Hall.

Cernoch, J. M. and Porter, R. H. (1985) Recognition of maternal axillary odors by infants. *Child Development*, 56, 1593–8.

Chaiken, S. (1980) Heuristic versus systematic information processing and the use of source versus message cues in persuasion. *Journal of Personality and Social Psychology*, 39, 752–66.

Chamove, A. S., Eysenck, H. J. and Harlow, H. F. (1972) Personality in monkeys: Factor analyses of Rhesus social behaviour. *Quarterly Journal of Experimental Psychology*, 24, 496–504.

Chance, J. E. and Goldstein, A. G. (1976) Recognition of faces and verbal labels. *Bulletin of the Psychonomic Society*, 14, 115–17.

Chapman, L. J. and Chapman, J. P. (1959) Atmosphere effect re-examined. *Journal of Experimental Psychology*, 58, 220–6.

Chapman, L. J. and Chapman, J. P. (1967) Genesis of popular but erroneous diagnostic observations. *Journal of Abnormal Psychology*, 72, 193–204.

Chase, W. G. and Ericsson, K. A. (1981) Skill and working memory. In G. H. Bower (ed.), *The Psychology of Learning and Motivation*. New York: Academic Press.

Chase, W. G. and Simon, H. A. (1973) The mind's eye in chess. In Chase (ed.), *Visual Information Processing*. New York: Academic Press.

Chase, W. G. and Simon, H. A. (1973) Perception in chess. *Cognitive Psychology*, 4, 55–81.

Cheng, P. W. and Holyoak, K. J. (1985) Pragmatic reasoning schemas. *Cognitive Psychology*, 17, 391–416.

Cheng, P. W., Holyoak, K. J., Nisbett, R. E. and Oliver, L. M. (1986) Pragmatic versus syntactic approaches to training deductive reasoning. *Cognitive Psychology*, 18, 293–328.

Cheng, P. W. and Holyoak, K. J. (1989) On the natural selection of reasoning theories. *Cognition*, 33, 285–313.

Cherniss, C. (1980) *Staff Burnout: Job Stress In Human Services*. Beverly Hills: Sage.

Cherry, E. C. (1953) Some experiments on the recognition of speech, with one and with two ears. *Journal of the Acoustical Society of America*, 25, 959–79.

Cheyney, D. L. and Seyfarth, R. M. (1982) How vervet monkeys percieve their grunts: Field playback experiments. *Animal Behaviour*, 30, 739–51.

Cheyney, D. L. and Seyfarth, R. M. (1985) Vervet monkey alarm calls: Manipulation through shared information. *Behaviour*, 94/2, 150–66.

Chi, M. T. H., Feltovich, P. J. and Glaser, R. (1981) Categorization and representation of physics problems by experts and novices. *Cognitive Science*, 5, 121–52.

Chi, M. T. H. (1978) Knowledge structures and memory development. In R. Siegler (ed.), *Children's Thinking: What Develops?* Hillsdale, NJ: Lawrence Erlbaum.

Chmiel, N. and Wall, T. (1994) Fault prevention, job design and the adaptive control of advanced manufacturing technology. *Applied Psychology: An International Review*, 43/4, 455–73.

Chomsky, N. (1959) Review of Skinner's *Verbal Behaviour*. *Language*, 35, 26–58. Reprinted in Fodor and Katz (1964).

Chomsky, N. (1965) *Aspects of the Theory of Syntax*. Cambridge, Mass.: MIT Press.

Chomsky, N. (1986) *Knowledge of Language: Its Nature, Origin and Use*. New York: Praeger.

Chugani, H. T. and Phelps, M. E. (1986) Maturational changes in cerebral function in infants determined by positron emission tomography. *Science*, 231, 840–3.

Clark, A. H., Wyon, S. M. and Richards, M. P. M. (1969) Free-play in nursery school children. *Journal of Child Psychology and Psychiatry*, 10, 205–16.

Clark, D. (1986) A cognitive approach to panic. *Behaviour Research and Therapy*, 4, 461–70.

Clark, H. H. (1969) Linguistic processes in deductive reasoning. *Psychological Review*, 76, 387–404.

Clark, H. H. and Clark, E. V. (1977) *Psychology and Language*. New York: Harcourt Brace Jovanovich.

Clarke-Stewart, K. A. (1991) A home is not a school: The effects of child care on children's development. *Journal of Social Issues*, 47, 105–23.

Clarke-Stewart, A. (1989) Infant day care: Maligned or malignant? *American Psychologist*, 44, 266–73.

Clarkson, M. G., Clifton, R. K., Swain, I. U. and Perris, E. E. (1989) Stimulus duration and repetition rate influence newborns' head orientation toward sound. *Developmental Psychobiology*, 22, 683–705.

Clegg, C. W. (1983) Psychology of employee lateness, absence, and turnover: A methodological critique. *Journal of Applied Psychology*, 68, 88–101.

Codol, J.-P. (1975) On the so-called 'superiority of self' behaviour. *European Journal of Social Psychology*, 5, 457–501.

Cohen, S. and Williamson, G. M. (1991) Stress and Infectious Disease in Humans. *Psychological Bulletin*, 109/1, 5–24.

Cohn, E. G. (1993) The prediction of police calls for service: The influence of weather and temporal variables on rape and domestic violence. *Journal of Environmental Psychology*, 13, 71–84.

Coie, J. D., Dodge, K. A. and Coppotelli, H. (1982) Dimensions and types of social status: A cross-age perspective. *Merrill-Palmer Quarterly*, 18, 557–70.

Coie, J. D. and Dodge, K. A. (1983) Continuities and changes in children's social status: A five-year longitudinal study. *Developmental Psychology*, 29, 261–82.

Coleman, J. C. (1980) *The Nature of Adolescence*. London: Methuen.

Condon, W. S. and Sander, L. W. (1974) Neonate movement is synchronised with adult speech: Interactional participation and language acquisition. *Science*, 183, 99–101.

Conrad, R. (1964) Acoustic confusion in immediate memory. *British Journal of Psychology*, 55, 75–84.

Conrad, R. (1971) The chronology of the development

of covert speech in children. *Developmental Psychology*, 5, 398–405.

Cooley, C. H. (1902) *Human Nature and the Social Order*. New York: Scribners.

Cooper Marcus, C. (1992) Environmental memories . In I. Altman and S. M. Low (eds), *Place Attachment*. New York: Plenum Press.

Cooper Marcus, C. and Sarkissian, W. (1987) *Housing as if People Mattered*. Berkeley: University of California Press.

Cosmides, L. (1989) The logic of social exchange: Has natural selection shaped how humans reason? Studies with the Wason selection task. *Cognition*, 31, 187–276.

Cosmides, L. and Tooby, J. (1992) Cognitive adaptations for social exchange. In J. Barkow, L. Cosmides and J. Tooby (eds), *The Adapted Mind: Evolutionary Psychology and the Generation of Culture*. New York: Oxford University Press.

Costabile, A., Smith, P. K., Matheson, L., Aston, J., Hunter, T. and Boulton, M. (1991) Cross-national comparison of how children distinguish serious and playful fighting. *Developmental Psychology*, 27, 881–7.

Cote, J. E. and Levine, C. (1988) A critical examination of the ego identity status paradigm. *Developmental Review*, 8, 147–84.

Courage, M. L. and Adams, R. J. (1990) Visual acuity assessment from birth to three years using the acuity card procedures: Cross sectional and longitudinal samples. *Optometry and Vision Science*, 67, 713–18.

Cowan, W. M. (1979) The development of the brain. In D. Flanagan (ed.), *The Brain*. New York: D. H. Freeman.

Cox, T. (1988) Psychobiological factors in stress and health. In S. Fisher and J. Reason (eds), *Handbook of Life and Stress, Cognition and Health*. Chichester: John Wiley.

Craik, F. I. M. (1977) 'A level of analysis' view of memory. In P. Pliner, L. Krames and T. M. Allaway (eds), *Communication and Affect, Vol 2, Language and Thought*. New York: Academic Press.

Craik, F. I. M. and Lockhart, R. S. (1972) Levels of processing: A framework for memory research. *Journal of Verbal Learning and Verbal Behaviour*, 11, 671–84.

Craik, F. I. M. and Tulving, E. (1975) Depth of processing and the retention of words in episodic memory. *Journal of Experimental Psychology: General*, 104, 268–94.

Craik, K. (1943) *The Nature of Explanation*. Cambridge: Cambridge University Press.

Crick, F. (1989) The recent excitement about neural networks. *Nature*, 337, 129–32.

Crick, N. R. and Dodge, K. A. (1994) A review and reformulation of social information-processing mechanisms in children's social adjustment. *Psychological Bulletin*, 115, 74–101.

Crittenden, P. (1988) Distorted patterns of relationship in maltreating families: The role of internal representation models. *Journal of Reproductive and Infant Psychology*, 6, 183–99.

Crook, J. H. (1965) The adaptive significance of avian social organisations. *Symposium of the Zoological Society of London*, 18, 181–218.

Crook, J. H. and Gartlan, J. S. (1966) Evolution of primate societies. *Nature* (London), 210, 1200–03.

Crook, J. H. and Osmaston, H. (eds) (1988) *Himalayan Buddhist Villages*. Warminster: Aris and Phillips.

Crossman, E. R. F. W. (1959) A theory of the acquisition of speed-skill. *Ergonomics*, 2, 153–66.

Crow, T., DeLisi, L. E. and Johnstone, E. C. (1989) Concordance by sex in sibling pairs with schizophrenia is paternally inherited. *British Journal of Psychiatry*, 155, 92–7.

Cruttenden, A. (1974) An experiment involving comprehension of intonation in children from 7 to 10. *Journal of Child Language*, 1, 221–31.

Cumming, E. and Henry, W. E. (1961) *Growing Old*. New York: Basic Books.

Cummings, E. M., Iannotti, R. J. and Zahn-Waxler, C. (1989) Aggression between peers in early childhood: Individual continuity and developmental change. *Child Development*, 60, 887–95.

Cunningham, C. C. and Sloper, P. (1976) *Down's Syndrome Infants: A Positive Approach to Parent and Professional Collaboration*. Manchester: Hester Adrian Research Centre, University of Manchester.

Daly, M. and Wilson, M. (1983; 2nd edn) *Sex, Evolution and Behavior*. Belmont, Calif.: Wadsworth.

Daneman, M. and Carpenter, P. A. (1980) Individual differences in working memory and reading. *Journal of Verbal Learning and Verbal Behaviour*, 19, 450–66.

Darwin, C. (1877) A biographical sketch of an infant. *Mind*, 2, 285–94.

Davidson, A. R. and Jaccard, J. J. (1975) Population psychology: A new look at an old problem. *Journal of Personality and Social Psychology*, 31, 1073–82.

Davies, D. R. and Jones, D. M. (1985) Noise and efficiency. In W. Tempest (ed.), *The Noise Handbook*. London: Academic Press.

de Groot, A. D. (1965) *Thought and Choice in Chess*. The Hague: Mouton.

DeCasper, A. and Fifer, W. P. (1980) Of human bonding: Newborns prefer their mother's voice. *Science*, 208, 1174–6.

DeCasper, A. and Spence, M. (1986) Prenatal maternal speech influences newborns' perception of speech sounds. *Infant Behavior and Development*, 9, 133–50.

Diehl, M. and Stroebe, W. (1987) Productivity loss in brainstorming groups: Toward the solution of a riddle. *Journal of Personality and Social Psychology*, 53, 497–509.

Dienstbier, R. (1989) Arousal and physiological toughness: Implications for mental and physical health. *Psychological Review*, 96, 84–100.

Digman, J. M. (1990) Personality Structure: emergence of the five-factor model. *Annual Review of Psychology*, 41, 417–40.

Dittmar, H. (1992) Perceived material wealth and material possessions. *British Journal of Social Psychology*, 31, 379–92.

Dodge, K. A., Pettit, G. S., McClaskey, C. L. and Brown, M. M. (1986) Social competence in children. *Monographs of the Society for Research in Child Development*, 51.

Dodge, K. A., Schlundt, D. C., Shocken, I. and Delugach, J. D. (1983) Social competence and children's sociometric status: The role of peer group entry strategies. *Merrill-Palmer Quarterly*, 29, 309–36.

Doherty, M. E., Mynatt, C. R., Tweney, R. D. and Schiavo, M. D. (1979) Pseudodiagnosticity. *Acta Psychologia*, 43, 111–21.

Dolen, L. S. and Bearison, D. J. (1982) Social interaction and social cognition in aging. *Human Development*, 25, 430–42.

Dollaghan, C. (1985) Child meets word: 'Fast mapping' in preschool children. *Journal of Speech and Hearing Research*, 28, 449–54.

Doms, M. and van Avermat, E. (1982) The conformity effect: A timeless phenomenon. *Bulletin of the British Psychological Society*, 35, 383–5.

Donaldson, M. (1978) *Children's Minds*. London: Fontana.

Drucker, P. F. (1954) *The Practice of Management*. New York: Harper and Row.

Duck, S. W. and Spencer, C. P. (1972) Personal constructs and friendship formation. *Journal of Personality and Social Psychology*, 23, 40–5.

Dunbar, R. I. M. (1992) Neocortex size as a constraint on group size in primates. *Journal of Human Evolution*, 20, 469–93.

Duncker, K. (1945/1935) *On Problem Solving*. Psychological Monographs, 58 (Whole number 270), 1–113 (originally published in German in 1935).

Dunn, J. and Kendrick, C. (1982) *Siblings: Love, Envy and Understanding*. Oxford: Blackwell.

Dunn, J. and Shatz, M. (1989) Becoming a conversationalist despite (or because of) having an older sibling. *Child Development*, 60, 399–410

Duval, T. S., Duval, V. H. and Mulalis, J. (1992) The effects of self focus, discrepancy between self and standard, and outcome expectancy favorability on the tendency to match self to standard or to withdraw. *Journal of Personality and Social Psychology*, 62, 340–8.

Eagly, A. (1987) *Sex Differences in Social Behavior: A Social Role Analysis*. Hillsdale, NJ: Erlbaum.

Ebbinghaus, H. (1885) *Uberdas Gedachtnis*. Leipzig: Dunker.

Edwards, D. and Potter, J. (1992) *Discursive Psychology*. London: Sage.

Egan, D. W. and Greeno, J. G. (1974) Theories of rule induction: Knowledge acquired in concept learning, serial pattern learning, and problem solving. In L. W. Gregg (ed.), *Knowledge and Cognition*. New York: John Wiley and Sons, 43–104.

Eibl-Eibesfeldt, I. (1989) *Human Ethology*. New York: Aldine de Gruyter.

Eich, J. E. (1980) The cue-dependent nature of state-dependent retrieval. *Memory and Cognition*, 8, 157–73.

Eisenberg, J. E. (1981) *The Mammalian Radiations: An Analysis of Trends in Evolution, Adaptation, and Behavior*. Chicago: University of Chicago Press.

Eiser, J. R. and Stroebe, W. (1972) *Categorisation and Social Judgment*. London: Academic Press.

Elkind, D. (1967) Egocentrism in adolescence. *Child Development*, 38, 1025–34.

Ellis, A. (1962) *Reason and Emotion in Psychotherapy*. New York: Lyle Stuart.

Emler, N. and Reicher, S. D. (1995) *A Social Psychology of Adolescent Delinquency*. Oxford: Blackwell.

Ericsson, K. A. (1990) Theoretical issues in the study of exceptional performance. In K. Gilhooly, M. Keane, R. Logie and G. Erdos (eds), *Lines of Thinking: Reflections of the Psychology of Thinking*, Vol. 2. Chichester: John Wiley and Sons, 5–28.

Ericsson, K. A. and Charness, N. (1994) Expert performance: Its structure and acquisition. *American Psychologist*, 49, 725–47.

Ericsson, K. A. and Simon, H. A. (1993) *Protocol Analysis: Verbal Reports as Data*. Cambridge, Mass.: MIT Press.

Erikson, E. (1950) *Childhood and Society*. New York: W. W. Norton.

Erikson, E. (1968) *Identity, Youth and Crisis*. London: Faber.

Evans, G. W. and Lepore, S. J. (1992) Conceptual and analytical issues in crowding research. *Journal of Environmental Psychology*, 12, 163–74.

Evans, J. St B. T. (1989) *Bias in Reasoning: Causes and Con-*

sequences. Hove, East Sussex: Lawrence Erlbaum Associates.

Evans, J. St B. T., Barston, J. and Pollard, P. (1983) On the conflict between logic and belief in syllogistic reasoning. *Memory and Cognition*, 11, 295–306.

Evans, J. St B. T. and Lynch, J. S. (1973) Matching bias in the selection task. *British Journal of Psychology*, 64, 391–7.

Eysenck, H. J. (1967) *The Biological Basis of Personality.* Springfield: Charles C. Thomas.

Eysenck, H. J. (1970) *The Structure of Human Personality.* London: Methuen.

Eysenck, H. J. (ed.) (1961) *Handbook of Abnormal Psychology.* London: Pitman.

Eysenck, H. J. and Kamin L. J. (1981) *Intelligence: The Battle for the Mind.* London: Macmillan.

Eysenck, M. W. (1978) Levels of processing: A critique. *British Journal of Psychology*, 69, 157–69.

Falbo, T. and Polit, D. F. (1986) Quantitative review of the only child literature: Research evidence and theory development. *Psychological Bulletin*, 100, 176–89.

Falk, P. (1994) Lesbian-mother child custody cases. In A. E. Gottfried and A. W. Gottfried (eds), *Redefining Families.* New York: Plenum Press.

Fanger, P. O. (1970) *Thermal Comfort, Analysis, and Applications in Environmental Engineering.* Copenhagen: Danish Technical Press.

Farrell, C. (1978) *My Mother Said.* London: Routledge and Kegan Paul.

Farrington, D. P. (1990) Childhood aggression and adult violence: Early precursors and later-life outcomes. In D. J. Pepler and K. H. Rubin (eds), *The Development and Treatment of Childhood Aggression.* Hillsdale, NJ: Erlbaum, 5–29.

Fawcett, A. J. and Nicolson, R. I. (1996) Impaired performance of children with dyslexia on a range of cerebellar tasks. *Annals of Dyslexia*, in press.

Fawcett, A. J., Nicolson, R. I. and Dean, P. (1996) Impaired performance of children with dyslexia on a range of cerebellar tasks. *Annals of Dyslexia*, 46, 259–83.

Fazio, R. (1987) How do attitudes guide behavior? In R. M. Sorrentino and E. T. Higgins (eds), *The Handbook of Motivation and Cognition: Foundations of Social Behaviour.* New York: Guilford Press.

Fazio, R. (1990) Multiple processes by which attitudes guide behavior: The MODE model as an integrative framework. In L. Berkowitz (ed.), *Advances in Experimental Social Psychology* (vol. 23). Orlando, Fla.: Academic Press.

Fazio, R., Chen, J., McDonel, E. C. and Sherman, S. J.

(1982) Attitude accessibility, attitude–behaviour consistency, and the strength of the object-evalaution association. *Journal of Experimental Social Psychology*, 18, 339–57.

Fazio, R. and Williams, C. J. (1986) Attitude accessibility as a moderator of the attitude perception and attitude–behavior relations: An investigation of the 1984 presidential election. *Journal of Personality and Social Psychology*, 51, 505–14.

Feather, N. T. (1994) Values, national identification and favouritism towards the in-group. *British Journal of Social Psychology*, 33, 467–76.

Fernald, A. and Simon, T. (1984) Expanded intonation contours in mothers' speech to newborns. *Developmental Psychology*, 20, 104–13.

Ferri, E. (1984) *Stepchildren: a National Study.* London: NFER/Nelson.

Festinger, L. (1954) A theory of social comparison processes. *Human Relations*, 7, 117–40.

Festinger, L. (1957) *A Theory of Cognitive Dissonance.* Stanford: Stanford University Press.

Fiedler, F. E. (1967) *A Theory of Leadership Effectiveness.* New York: McGraw-Hill.

Fiedler, F. (1981) Leadership effectiveness. *American Behavioural Scientist*, 24, 619–32.

Fiedler, K. (1982) Causal schemata: Review and critique of research on a popular construct. *Journal of Personality and Social Psychology*, 42, 1001–13.

Fillmore, C. (1968) The case for case. In E. Bach and R. T. Harms (eds), *Universals in Linguistic Theory.* New York: Holt, Rinehart and Winston.

Finkelstein, N. W. and Haskins, R. (1983) Kindergarten children prefer same-color peers. *Child Development*, 54, 502–8.

Fishbein, M. and Ajzen, I. (1974) Attitudes towards objects as predictors of single and multiple behavioral criteria. *Psychological Review*, 81, 59–74.

Fishbein, M. and Ajzen, I. (1975) *Belief, Attitude, Intention and Behavior: An Introduction to Theory and Research.* Reading, Mass.: Addison-Wesley.

Fiske, D. W. (1949) Consistency of the factorial structures of personality ratings from different sources. *Journal of Abnormal and Social Psychology*, 44, 329–44.

Fiske, S. and Taylor, S. (1992; 2nd edn) *Social Cognition.* New York: McGraw-Hill.

Fitts, P. M. and Posner, M. I. (1967) *Human Performance.* Belmont, Calif.: Brooks-Cole.

Flaubert, G. (1981 [1857]) *Madame Bovary.* English trans. H. Hamilton, 1949. Oxford: Oxford University Press.

Flavell, J. H., Beach, D. R. and Chinsky, J. M. (1966) Spontaneous verbal rehearsal in a memory task as a function of age. *Child Development*, 37, 283–99.

Flavell, J. H., Frederichs, A. G. and Hoyt, J. D. (1978) Developmental changes in memorization processes. *Cognitive Psychology*, 1, 324–40.

Foddy, M. and Crundall, I. (1993) A field study of social comparison processes in ability evaluation. *British Journal of Social Psychology*, 32, 287–305.

Fodor, J. and Katz, J. (1964) *The Structure of Language: Readings in the Philosophy of Lanaguage*. Englewood Cliffs, NJ.: Prentice-Hall.

Fouts, R. S. and Mellgren, R. L. (1976) Language, signs and cognition in the chimpanzee. *Sign Language Studies*, 13, 319–46.

Fredericksen, N. (1962) Factors in in-basket performance. *Psychological Monographs*, 76/541.

Freedman, J. L. (1975) *Crowding and Behavior*. New York: Viking Press.

Frey, D. (1986) Recent research on selective exposure to information. In L. Berkowitz (ed.), *Advances in Experimental Social Psychology* (vol. 19). Orlando, Fla.: Academic Press.

Frey, D. and Rosch, M. (1984) Information seeking after decisions: The roles of novelty of information and decision reversibility. *Personality and Social Psychology Bulletin*, 10, 91–8.

Fried, Y. and Ferris, G. R. (1987) The validity of the job characteristics model: A review and meta-analysis. *Personnel Psychology*, 40, 287–322.

Friedman, M. and Rosenman, R. H. (1974) *Type A Behavior and Your Heart*. New York: Alfred A Knopf.

Frodi, A. M., Lamb, M. E., Leavitt, L. A. and Donovan, W. L. (1978) Fathers' and mothers' responses to infant smiles and cries. *Infant Behaviour and Development*, 1, 187–89.

Furnham, A. and Lewis, A. (1986) *The Economic Mind: The Social Psychology of Economic Behaviour*. Brighton: Wheatsheaf.

Galbraith, J. R. (1973) *Designing Complex Organizations*. Reading, Mass.: Addison–Wesley.

Galbraith, J. R. (1977) *Organization Design*. Reading, Mass.: Addison-Wesley.

Galton, F. (1869) *Hereditary Genius: An Inquiry into its Laws and Consequences*. London: Macmillan.

Garcia, J. and Koelling, R. A. (1966) Relation of cue to consequence in relational learning. *Psychonomic Science*, 4, 123–4.

Gardner, B. T. and Gardner, R. A. (1975) Evidence for sentence constituents in the early utterances of child and chimpanzee. *Journal of Experimental Psychology: General*, 104, 244–67.

Gardner, B. T. and Gardner, R. A. (1969) Teaching sign language to a chimpanzee. *Science*, 165, 664–72.

Gardner, H. (1983) *Frames of Mind: The Theory of Multiple Intelligence*. New York: Basic Books.

Gardner, H. (1993) *Multiple Intelligences: The Theory in Practice*. New York: Basic Books.

Garfinkel, H. (1967) *Studies in Ethnomethodology*. Englewood Cliffs, NJ: Prentice-Hall.

Gärling, T. and Evans, G. W. (1991) *Environment Cognition and Action*. Oxford: Oxford University Press.

Gazzaniga, M. S. (1970) *The Bisected Brain*. New York: Appleton-Century-Crofts.

Gentner, D. and Gentner, D. R. (1983) Flowing waters and teeming crowds: Mental models of electricity. In D. Gentner and A. L. Stevens (eds), *Mental Models*. Hillsdale, NJ: Lawrence Erlbaum Associates, 99–129.

Gergen, K. J. (1985) The social constructionist movement in social psychology. *American Psychologist*, 40, 266–73.

Gibson, J. J. (1966) *The Senses Considered as Perceptual Systems*. Boston: Houghton Mifflin.

Gibson, J. J. (1979) *The Ecological Approach to Visual Perception*. Boston: Houghton Mifflin.

Gick, M. L. and Holyoak, K. J. (1980) Analogical problem solving. *Cognitive Psychology*, 12, 306–55.

Gick, M. L. and Holyoak, K. J. (1983) Schema induction and analogical transfer. *Cognitive Psychology*, 15, 1–38.

Gifford, R. (1993) Crime and context: A complex, crucial conundrum. *Journal of Environmental Psychology*, 13, 1–3.

Gigerenzer, G. and Hug, K. (1992) Domain-specific reasoning: Social contracts, cheating and perspective change. *Cognition*, 43, 127–71.

Gil, D. (1970) *Violence against Children*. Cambridge, Mass.: Harvard University Press.

Gilligan, C. (1982) *In a Different Voice*. Cambridge, Mass.: Harvard University Press.

Girotto, V. (1993) Modèles mentaux et raisonnement. In M-F. Ehrlich, H. Tardieu and M. Cavazza (eds), *Les Modèles mentaux: approche cognitive des représentations*. Paris: Masson, 101–19.

Girotto, V. and Legrenzi, P. (1993) Naming the parents of the THOG: Mental representation and reasoning. *Quarterly Journal of Experimental Psychology*, 46A, 701–13.

Glanzer, M. and Cunitz, A. R. (1966) Two storage mechanisms in free recall. *Journal of Verbal Learning and Verbal Behaviour*, 5, 351–60.

Glanzer, M. and Razel, M. (1974) The size of the unit in short-term storage. *Journal of Verbal Learning and Verbal Behaviour*, 13, 114–31.

Glaser, R. and Chi, M. T. H. (1988) Overview. In Chi, Glaser and M. J. Farr (eds), *The Nature of Expertise*. Hillsdale, NJ: Lawrence Erlbaum.

Godden, D. and Baddeley, A. D. (1975) Context-dependent memory in two natural environments: On land and under water. *British Journal of Psychology, 66,* 325–31.

Godden, D. and Baddeley, A. D. (1980) When does context influence recognition memory? *British Journal of Psychology, 71,* 90–104.

Goffman, E. (1959) *The Presentation of Self in Everyday Life.* New York: Doubleday Anchor.

Goldberg, S. (1991) Recent developments in attachment theory. *Canadian Journal of Psychiatry, 36/6,* 393–400.

Goldner, V., Penn, P., Sheinberg, M. and Walker, G. (1990) Love and violence: Gender paradoxes in volatile attachments. *Family Processes, 29/4,* 343-64.

Golledge, R. G., Ruggles, A. J., Pellegrino, J. W. and Gale, N. D. (1993) Integrating route knowledge in an unfamiliar neighbourhood: Along and across route experiments. *Journal of Environmental Psychology, 13,* 293–308.

Golledge, R. G., Smith, T. R., Pellegrino, J. W., Doherty, S. and Marshall, S. P. (1985) A conceptual model and empirical analysis of children's aquisition of spatial information. *Journal of Environmental Psychology, 5,* 125–52.

Goodall, J. (1986) *The Chimpanzees of Gombe: Patterns of Behavior.* Cambridge, Mass.: Harvard University Press.

Goodluck, H. (1991) *Language Acquisition: An Introduction.* Oxford: Blackwell.

Goodwin, D. W., Powell, B., Bremer, D., Hoine, H. and Stern, J. (1969) Alcohol and recall: State-dependent effects. *Science, 163,* 1358–60.

Gordon, C. (1968) Self-conceptions: Configurations of content. In C. Gord0n and K. J. Gergen, *The Self in Social Interaction,* Vol. 1. New York: Academic Press.

Goren, C., Sarty, M. and Wu, P. (1975) Visual following and pattern discrimination of face-like stimuli by newborn infants. Pediatrics, 56, 544–549.

Gould, P. and White, R. (1986) *Mental Maps.* London: Allen and Unwin.

Gould, R. L. (1978) *Transformation: Growth and Change in Adult Life.* New York: Simon and Shuster.

Gould, S. J. (1977) *Ever since Darwin: Reflections in Natural History.* New York: Norton.

Gould, S. J. (1981) *The Mismeasure of Man.* Harmondsworth: Penguin.

Gould, S. J. and Eldredge, N. (1977) Punctuated equilibria: the tempo and mode of evolution reconsidered. *Paleobiology, 3,* 115–51.

Goulet, C., Bard, C. and Fleury, M. (1989) Expertise differences in preparing to return a tennis serve: A visual information processing approach. *Journal of Sport and Exercise Psychology,* 11, 382–98.

Greenberg, J. and Ornstein, S. (1983) High status job title as compensation for underpayment: A test of equity theory. *Journal of Applied Psychology,* 68, 285–97.

Gregory, R. (1972; 2nd edn) *Eye and Brain.* New York: World University Library.

Gregory, R. (1992) *Psychological Testing: History, Principles and Applications.* Boston: Allyn and Bacon.

Grice, H. P. (1975) Logic and conversation. In P. Cole and J. L. Morgan (eds), *Syntax and Semantics,* vol. 3: *Speech Acts.* New York: Academic Press, 225–42.

Griggs, R. A. and Cox, J. R. (1982) The elusive thematic-materials effect in Wason's selection task. *British Journal of Psychology,* 73, 407–20.

Grundy, E. (1994) Live old, live well. *MRC News,* Autumn, 22–5.

Gump, P. V. (1987) School and classroom environments. In D. Stokols and I. Altman (eds), *The Handbook of Environmental Psychology.* New York: John Wiley.

Gustafson, J. E. (1984) A unifying model for the structure of mental abilities. *Intelligence,* 8, 179–203.

Gutteridge, T. G. (1986) Organizational career development systems: The state of the practice. In D. T. Hall and Associates, *Career Development in Organizations.* San Francisco: Jossey-Bass, 50–94.

Hackman, J. R. and Oldham, G. R. (1976) Motivation through the design of work: Test of a theory. *Organizational Behavior and Human Performance,* 16, 250–79.

Hall, E. T. (1966) *The Hidden Dimension.* New York: Doubleday Anchor.

Hamilton, W. D. (1964a) The genetical evolution of social behaviour, I. *Journal of Theoretical Biology,* 7, 1–16.

Hamilton, W. D. (1964b) The genetical evolution of social behaviour, II. *Journal of Theoretical Biology,* 7, 17–52.

Happé, F. (1994) *Autism: An Introduction to Psychological Theory.* London: University College London Press.

Hardyk, C. D. and Petrinovich, L. R. (1970) Subvocal speech and comprehension level as a function of the difficulty level of reading material. *Journal of Verbal Learning and Verbal Behaviour,* 9, 647–52.

Harris, P. (1989) *Children and Emotion: The Development of Psychological Understanding.* Oxford: Blackwell.

Harris, P. (1993) Pretending and planning. In S. Baron-Cohen, H.Tager-Flusberg and D. Cohen (eds), *Understanding Other Minds: Perspectives from Autism.* Oxford: Oxford University Press, 228–46.

Hart, R. A. (1979) *Children's Experience of Place.* New York: Irvington Press.

Hartshorne, H. and May, A. (1928) *Studies in the nature of character, Vol. 1: Studies in Deceit.* New York: Macmillan.

Haynes, R. S., Pine, R. C. and Fitch, H. G. (1982) Reducing accident rates with organizational behavior modification. *Academy of Management Journal*, 25, 407–16.

Hebb, D. O. (1949) *The Organization of Behavior: A Neuropsychological Theory*. New York: Wiley.

Heider, F. (1948) *The Psychology of Interpersonal Relations*. New York: Wiley.

Helmholtz, H. von (1866) *Treatise on Physiological Optics*. Trans. and ed. by J. P. Southall, from the 3rd German edn (1909–11). Rochester, NY: Optical Society of America.

Henchy, T. and Glass, D. C. (1968) Evaluation apprehension and the social facilitation of dominant and subordinate responses. *Journal of Personality and Social Psychology*, 10, 446–54.

Herbert, M. (1988) *Working with Children and their Families*. Leicester: BPS Books.

Hering, E. (1964) *Outlines of a Theory of the Light Sense*. Trans. L. M. Hurvich and D. Jameson. Cambridge, Mass.: Harvard University Press.

Herrick, N. Q. and Maccoby, M. (1975) Humanizing work: A priority goal of the 1970's. In L. E. Davis and A. B. Cherns (eds), *The Quality of Working Life* 1. New York: Free Press, 63–77.

Hertz-Lazarowitz, R., Feitelson, D., Zahavi, S. and Hartup, W. W. (1981) Social interaction and social organisation of Israeli five-to-seven-year olds. *International Journal of Behavioral Development*, 4, 143–55.

Herzberg, F. (1966) *Work and the Nature of Man*. Cleveland, Ohio: World.

Hetherington, E. M. (1989) Coping with family transitions: Winners, losers and survivors. *Child Development*, 60, 1–14.

Hewstone, M. (1989) *Causal Attribution: From Cognitive Processes to Collective Beliefs*. Oxford: Blackwell.

Higgins, E. T. (1987) Self-discrepancy: A theory relating self and affect. *Psychological Review*, 94, 319–40.

Hladik, C. M. (1975) Ecology, diet and social patterning in Old and New World monkeys. In R. H. Tuttle (ed.), *Socioecology and Psychology of Primates*. Paris: Mouton, 3–35.

Hobson. P. (1994) *Autism and the Development of Mind*. Hove: Lawrence Erlbaum Associates.

Hockett, C. F. (1960) The origin of speech. *Scientific American*, 203 (Sept.).

Hockey, G. R. J. (1986) Changes in operator efficiency as a function of environmental stress, fatigue, and circadian rhythms. In K. R. Boff, L. Kaufman and J. P. Thomas (eds), *Handbook of Perception and Human Performance* (vol. II). New York: Wiley.

Hofer, M. A. (1981) *The Roots of Human Behavior*. San Francisco: Freeman.

Hogg, M. A. and Moreland, R. L. (eds) (1993) Social processes in small groups. *British Journal of Social Psychology*, 32, 1–106; 107–90 (two special issues).

Hogg, M. A. and Abrams, D. (1988) *Social Identification*. London: Routledge.

Hollander, E. P. (1964) *Leaders, Groups and Influence*. Oxford: Oxford University Press.

Hood, B. and Willatts, P. (1986) Reaching in the dark to an object's remembered position: Evidence for object permanence in 5-month-old infants. *British Journal of Developmental Psychology*, 4, 57–65.

Horn, J. L. and Cattell, R. B. (1966) Refinement and test of the the theory of fluid and crystallized general intelligences. *Journal of Educational Psychology*, 57, 253–70.

Houk, J. C. and Wise, S. P. (1995) Distributed modular architectures linking basal ganglia, cerebellum and cerebral cortex: Their role in planning and controlling action. *Cerebral Cortex*, 5, 95–110.

Hovland, C. I., Janis, I. L. and Kelley, H. H. (1953) *Communication and Persuasion*. New Haven: Yale University Press.

Howe, M. J. A. (1988) Intelligence as an explanation. *British Journal of Psychology*, 79, 349–60.

Howe, M. J. A. (1990) *Sense and Nonsense about Hothouse Children: A Practical Guide for Parents and Teachers*. Leicester: British Psychological Society Books.

Howe, M. J. A. (1990) Does Intelligence exist? *The Psychologist*, 3, 490–3.

Howe, M. J. A. (1991) *Fragments of Genius: The Strange Feats of Idiots Savants*. London: Routledge.

Howe, M. J. A. and Smith, J. (1988) Calendrical calculating in 'idiots savants': How do they do it? *British Journal of Psychology*, 79, 371–86.

Howell, P. and Darwin, C. J. (1977) Some properties of of auditory memory for rapid format transitions. *Memory and Cognition*, 5.

Hubel, D. H. and Wiesel, T. N. (1959) Receptive fields of single neurons in the the the cat's striate cortex. *Journal of Physiology* (London), 148, 574–91.

Hubel, D. H. and Wiesel, T. N. (1962) Receptive fields, binocular interaction and functional architecture in the cat's visual cortex. *Journal of Physiology*, 160, 106–54.

Hubel, D. H. and Wiesel, T. N. (1979) Brain mechanisms of vision. *Scientific American*, 241/9, 150–68.

Huesmann, L. R., Eron, L. D., Lefkowitz, M. M. and Walder, L. O. (1984) Stability of aggression over time and generations. *Developmental Psychology*, 20, 1120–34.

Hull, C. L. (1943) *Principles of Behavior*. Englewood Cliffs, NJ: Prentice-Hall.

Humphrey, N. K. (1976) The social function of intellect. In P. P. G. Bateson and R. A. Hinde (eds), *Growing Points in Ethology*. Cambridge: Cambridge University Press.

Hunt, E. (1978) Mechanics of verbal ability. *Psychological Review*, 85, 109–30.

Hunt, E. (1980) Intelligence as an information processing concept. *British Journal of Psychology*, 71, 449–74.

Hunt, E., Frost, N. and Lunneborg, C. L. (1973) Individual differences in cognition: A new approach to intelligence. In G. Bower (ed.), *Advances in Learning and Motivation*, vol. 7. New York: Academic Press.

Hunter, I. M. L. (1957) The solving of three-term series problems. *British Journal of Psychology*, 48, 286–98.

Huttenlocher, P. R. (1990) Morphometric study of human cerebral-cortex development. *Neuropsychologia*, 28, 517–27.

Iaffaldano, M. T. and Muchinsky, P. M. (1985) Job satisfaction and job performance: A meta-analysis. *Psychological Bulletin*, 97, 251–73.

Jackson, S. E., Schwab, R. L. and Schuler, R. S. (1986) Toward an understanding of the burnout phenomenon. *Journal of Applied Psychology*, 71, 630–40.

James, W. (1890) *Principles of Psychology*. New York: Holt, Rinehart and Winston.

Jamieson, D. W. and Zanna, M. P. (1989) Need for structure in attitude formation and expression. In A. R. Pratkanis, S. J. Breckler and A.G. Greenwald (eds), *Attitude Structure and Function*. Hillsdale, NJ: Erlbaum.

Janis, I. L. (1972) *Victims of Groupthink*. Boston: Houghton Mifflin.

Jeffries, R., Polson, P. G., Razran, L. and Atwood, M. E. (1977) A process model for missionaries-cannibals and other river crossing problems. *Cognitive Psychology*, 9, 412–20.

Jennings, D. L., Amabile, T. M. and Ross, L. (1982) Informal covariation assessment: Data-based versus theory-based judgments. In D. Kahneman, P. Slovic and A. Tversky (eds), *Judgement under Uncertainty: Heuristics and Biases*. Cambridge: Cambridge University Press, 211–30.

Jersild, A. T. and Markey, F. V. (1935) Conflicts between preschool children. *Child Development Monographs*, 21. Teachers' College, Columbia University.

Johansson, G. (1973) Visual perception of biological motion and a model for its analysis. *Perception & Psychophysics*, 14, 201–11.

Johnson, C. L. (1985) Grandparenting options in divorcing families: An anthropological perspective. In V. L. Bengtson and J. F. Robertson (eds), *Grandparenthood*. Beverly Hills: Sage.

Johnson, M. H. (1990) Cortical maturation and the development of visual attention in early infancy. *Journal of Cognitive Neuroscience*, 2. Repr. in M. H. Johnson (ed.), *Brain Development and Cognition: A Reader*. Oxford: Blackwell, 1993.

Johnson, M. H. (ed.) (1993) *Brain Development and Cognition: A Reader*. Oxford: Blackwell.

Johnson, M. H. and Morton, J. (1991) *Biology and Cognitive Development: the Case for Face Recognition*. Oxford: Blackwell.

Johnson-Laird, P. N. (1983) *Mental Models: Towards a Cognitive Science of Language Inference, and Consciousness*. Cambridge: Cambridge University Press.

Johnson-Laird, P. N. (1993) *Human and Machine Thinking*. Hillsdale, NJ: Lawrence Erlbaum Associates.

Johnson-Laird, P. N. (1994) A model theory of induction. *International Studies in the Philosophy of Science*, 8, 5–29.

Johnson-Laird, P. N. and Byrne, R. (1991) *Deduction*. Hove, East Sussex: Lawrence Erlbaum Associates.

Johnson-Laird, P. N., Legrenzi, P. and Legrenzi, M. S. (1972) Reasoning and a sense of reality. *British Journal of Psychology*, 63, 395–400.

Jolly, A. (1964) Prosimians' manipulation of simple object problems. *Animal Behaviour*, 12, 560–71.

Jolly, A. (1966) Lemur social behaviour and primate intelligence. *Science*, 153, 501–6.

Jones, E. E. and Davis, K. E. (1965) From acts to dispositions: The attribution process in person perception. In L. Berkowitz (ed.), *Advances in Experimental Social Psychology* (vol. 2). New York: Academic Press.

Jones, E. E., Davis, K. E. and Gergen, K. J. (1965) Role playing variations and their informational value for person perception. *Journal of Abnormal and Social Psychology*, 63, 302–10.

Jones, S. E. and Yarborough, A. E. (1985) A naturalistic study of the meanings of touch. *Communication Monographs*, 52, 19–56.

Josselson, R. (1996) *The Space Between Us*. London: Sage.

Jost, J. T. and Banaji, M. R. (1994) The role of stereotyping in system-justification and the production of false consciousness. *British Journal of Social Psychology*, 33, 1–27.

Judd, C. M. and Kulik, J. A. (1980) Schematic effects of social attitudes on information processing and recall. *Journal of Personality and Social Psychology*, 38, 569–78.

Jusczyk, P. W. (1985) The high-amplitude sucking technique as a methodological tool in speech perception research. In G. Gottlieb and N. A. Krasnegor (eds), *Measurement of Audition and Vision During the First Year of Postnatal Life: A Methodological Review*. Norwood, NJ: Ablex.

Kahneman, D. and Tversky, A. (1972) Subjective probability: A judgement of representativeness. *Cognitive Psychology*, 3, 430–54.

Kail, R. (1990; 3rd edn) *The Development of Memory in Children*. New York: Freeman.

Kalma, A. (1992) Gazing in triads: A powerful signal in floor apportionment. *British Journal of Social Psychology*, 31, 21–39.

Kaplan, R. (1983) The role of nature in the urban context. In I. Altman and J. Wohlwill (eds), *Human Behavior and Environment*, vol 6: *Behavior and the Natural Environment*. New York: Plenum Press.

Kaplan, R. and Kaplan, S. (1989) *The Experience of Nature: A Psychological Perspective*. Cambridge: Cambridge University Press.

Karasek, R. A. (1979) Job demands, job decision latitude, and mental strain: Implications for job redesign. *Administrative Science Quarterly*, 24, 285–307.

Kay, P. and Kempton, W. (1984) What is the Sapir–Whorf hypothesis? *American Anthropologist*, 86/1, 65–79.

Kelley, H. H. (1967) Attribution theory in social psychology. In D. Levine (ed.), *Nebraska Symposium on Motivation*. Lincoln, Neb.: University of Nebraska Press.

Kelly, G. (1951) *The Psychology of Personal Constructs*. New York: Norton.

Kelly, G. (1955) *The Psychology of Personal Constructs*. New York: Norton.

Kelso, J. A. S. (1995) *Dynamic Patterns: The Self-organization of Brain and Behavior*. Cambridge, Mass.: MIT Press.

Kelso, S. R. and Brown, T. H. (1986) Differential conditioning of associative synaptic enhancement in hippocampal brain slices. *Science*, 232, 85–7.

Kempe, C. H. (1980) Incest and other forms of sexual abuse. In C. H. Kempe and R. E. Helfer (eds), *The Battered Child*, 3rd edn. Chicago: Chicago University Press.

Kendon, A. (1967) Some functions of gaze direction during social interaction. *Acta Psychologica*, 26, 22–63.

Kendzierski, D. (1990) Exercise self-schemata: cognitive and behavioral correlates. *Health Psychology*, 9, 69–82.

Kerr, W. A. (1950) Accident proneness of factory departments. *Journal of Applied Psychology*, 34, 167–70.

Kety, S. S., Rosenthal, D., Wender, P. H., Schlusinger, F. and Jacobson, B. (1975) Mental illness in the biological and adoptive families of adoptive individuals who have become schizophrenic. In R. R. Fieve, D. Rosenthal and H. Brill (eds), *Genetic Research in Psychiatry*. Baltimore, Md.: John Hopkins University Press.

Kimble, G. A. (1961; 2nd edn) *Hilgard and Marquis' Conditioning and Learning*. Englewood Cliffs, NJ: Prentice-Hall.

Kimura, D. (1993) Sex differences in the brain. *Scientific American*, 267, 80–7.

Kirk, S. A. (1958) *Early Education of the Mentally Retarded*. Urbana: University of Illinois Press.

Kirkwood, T. (1994) The biological basis of aging. *MRC News*, Autumn, 14–17.

Kitzinger, C. (1987) *The Social Construction of Lesbianism*. London: Sage.

Kleinhesselink, R. R. and Edwards, R. E. (1975) Seeking and avoiding belief-discrepant information as a function of its perceived irrefutability. *Journal of Personality and Social Psychology*, 31, 787–90.

Kline, P. (1991) *Intelligence: The Psychometric View*. London: Routledge.

Kobasigawa, A. (1974) Utilization of retrieval cues by children in recall. *Child Development*, 45, 127–34.

Kobrick, J. L. and Fine, B. J. (1983) Climate and human performance. In D. J. Oborne and M. M. Gruneberg (eds), *The Physical Environments at Work*. Chichester: John Wiley and Sons, 69–107.

Kohlberg, L. (1969) Stages and sequence: The cognitive-developmental approach to socialization. In D. A. Goslin (ed.), *Handbook of Socialization Theory and Research*. Chicago: Rand McNally, 347–480.

Köhler, W. (1925) *The Mentality of Apes*. London: Routledge & Kegan Paul.

Kolbasa, S. C., Maddi, S. R. and Kahn (1982) Hardiness and health: A prospective study. *Journal of Personality and Social Psychology*, 42, 168–77.

Koluchova, J. (1972) Severe deprivation in twins: A case study. *Journal of Child Psychology and Psychiatry*, 13, 107–14.

Krahé, B. (1992) *Personality and Social Psychology: Towards a Synthesis*. London: Sage.

Kreutzer, M. A., Leonard, C. and Flavell, J. H. (1975) An interview study of children's knowledge about memory. *Monographs of the Society for research in Child Development*, 40 (serial no. 159), 1–58.

Kubler-Ross, E. (1975) *Death: the Final Stage of Growth*. Englewood Cliffs, NJ: Prentice-Hall.

Kuhn, D., Nash, S. C. and Bruken, L. (1978) Sex role concepts of two-and-three-year-olds. *Child Development*, 49, 445–51.

Kuhn, M. H. and McPartland, T. S. (1954) An empirical investigation of self-attitudes. *American Sociological Review*, 19, 68–76.

Küller, R., and Lindsten, C. (1992) Health and behaviour of children in classrooms with and without windows. *Journal of Environmental Psychology*, 12, 305–18.

Kunda, Z., Fong, G. T. and Sanitioso, R. (1993) Directional questions direct self-conceptions. *Journal of Experimental Social Psychology*, 29, 63–86.

Ladd, G. W. (1983) Social networks of popular, average and rejected children in school settings. *Merrill-Palmer Quarterly*, 29, 283–307.

Lamb, M. E. (1981) The development of father–infant relationships. In M. E. Lamb (ed.), *The Role of the Father in Child Development*, 2nd edn. New York: Wiley.

Lamb, M. E. (1987) Introduction: The emergent American father. In M. E. Lamb (ed.), *The Father's Role: Cross-cultural Perspectives*. New Jersey: Lawrence Erlbaum.

Land, E. H. (1977) The retinex theory of colour vision. *Scientific American*, 237, 108–28.

Landy, F. J. (1976) The validity of the interview in police officer selection. *Journal of Applied Psychology*, 61, 193–8.

Landy, F. J. and Farr, J. L. (1980) *The Measurement of Work Performance*. New York: Academic Press.

Larkin, J. H. (1979) Information processing models and science instruction. In J. Lochhead and J. Clement (eds), *Cognitive Process Instruction*. Philadelphia: Franklin Institute Press, 109–18.

Larkin, J. H. (1983) The role of problem representation in physics. In D. Gentner and A. L. Stevens (eds), *Mental Models*. Hillsdale, NJ: Lawrence Erlbaum Associates, 75–98.

Lashley, K. (1950) In search of the ngram. *Society of Experimental Biology, Symposium 4*, 454–82.

Latané, B. and Darley, J. M. (1970) *The Unresponsive Bystander: Why Doesn't He Help?* New York: Appleton-Century-Crofts.

Latham, G. P., Steele, T. P. and Saari, L. M. (1982) The effects of participation and goal difficulty on performance. *Personnel Psychology*, 35, 677–86.

Lave, J. (1988) *Cognition in Practice*. Cambridge: Cambridge University Press.

Lave, J., Murtaugh, M. and de la Rocha, O. (1984) The dialectic of arithmetic in grocery shopping. In B. Rogoff and J. Lave (eds), *Everyday Cognition: Its Development in Social Context*. Cambridge, Mass.: Harvard University Press, 67–94.

Lazarus R. S. and Folkman S. (1984) *Stress Appraisal and Coping*. New York: Springer.

Le Bon, G. (1908) *The Crowd: A Study of the Popular Mind*. London: Unwin. (Trans. of French original, 1895.)

Leaf, A. (1973) Getting old. *Scientific American*, 229, 44–52.

Lecanuet, J.-P., Granier-Deferre, C., Cohen, H., Le Houezec, R. and Busnel, M.-C. (1989) Fetal responses to acoustic stimulation depend on heart rate variability pattern, stimulus intensity and repetition. *Early Human Development*, 13, 269–83.

Lendrum, S. and Syme, G. (1992) *Gift of Tears*. London: Routledge.

LeVay, S. (1991) A difference in hypothalamic structure between heterosexual and homosexual men. *Science*, 253, 1034–7.

Lever, J. (1978) Sex differences in the complexity of children's play and games. *American Sociological Review*, 43, 471–83.

Levine, J. M. and Murphy, G. (1943) The learning and forgetting of controversial material. *Journal of Abnormal and Social Psychology*, 38, 507–17.

Levinson, D. J. (1978) *The Seasons of a Man's Life*. New York: Knopf.

Levinson, D. J. (1990) A theory of life structure development in adulthood. In C.N. Alexander and E. J. Langer (eds), *Higher States of Human Development*. New York: Oxford University Press.

Lewis, C. (1986) *Becoming a Father*. Milton Keynes: Open University Press.

Lewis, C. and Osborne, A. (1990) Three-year-olds' problems with false belief: Conceptual deficit or linguistic artifact? *Child Development*, 61, 1514–19.

Lewis, K. G. (1980) Children of lesbians: Their point of view. *Social Work*, 25, 198–203.

Light, L. L. and Carter-Sobell, L. (1970) Effects of changed semantic context on recognition memory. *Journal of Verbal Learning and Verbal Behavior*, 9, 1–11.

Light, P., Buckingham, N. and Robbins, A. H. (1979) The conservation task as an interactional setting. *British Journal of Educational Psychology*, 49, 304–10.

Likert, R (1932) A technique for the measurement of attitudes. *Archives of Psychology*, 140, 44–53.

Likert, R. (1967) *The Human Organization*. New York: McGraw-Hill.

Linssen, H. and Hagendoorn, L. (1994) Social and geographical factors in the explanation of the content of European nationality stereotypes. *British Journal of Social Psychology*, 33, 165–82.

Liska, A. E. (1984) A critical examination of the causal structure of the Fishbein/Ajzen attitude–behavior model. *Social Psychology Quarterly*, 47, 61–74.

Locke, J. L. (1993) *The Child's Path to Spoken Language*. Cambridge, Mass.: Harvard University Press.

Locke, J. L., Bekken, K. A., McLinn-Larsen, L. and Wein, D. (1995) Emergent control of manual and vocal-motor activity in relation to the development of speech. *Brain and Language*, 51, 498–508.

Loftus, E. F. and Loftus, G. R. (1980) On the permanence of stored information in the human brain. *American Psychologist*, 35, 409–20.

Lombroso, C. (1911) *Crime: Its Causes and Remedies*. Boston: Little, Brown.

Loo, C. and Ong, P. (1984) Crowding perceptions, attitudes and consequences among the Chinese. *Environment and Behavior*, 16, 55–87.

Luria, A. R. (1966) *Human Brain and Psychological Processes*. New York: Harper and Row.

Lynch, K. (1960) *The Image of the City*. Cambridge: MIT Press.

Maccoby, E. E. and Jacklin, C. N. (1974) *The Psychology of Sex Differences*. Stanford: Stanford University Press.

MacDonald, I. (1989) *Murder in the Playground*. London: Longsight Press.

Macnamara, J. (1972) Cognitive basis of language learning in infants. Psychological Review, 79, 1–13.

Madden, T. J., Ellen, P. S. and Ajzen, I. (1992) A comparison of the theory of planned behavior and reasoned action. *Personality and Social Psychology Bulletin*, 18, 3–9.

Magnusson, D., Stattin, H. and Allen, V. L. (1985) Biological maturation and social development: A longitudinal study of some adjustment processes from mid-adolescence to adulthood. *Journal of Youth and Adolescence*, 14, 267–83.

Magnusson, D. and Törestad, B. (1992) The individual as interactive agent in the environment. In Walsh, W. B., Craik, K. H. and Price, R. H. (eds), *Person–Environment Psychology*. Hillsdale, NJ: Erlbaum.

Main, M. (1991) Metacognitive knowledge, metacognitive monitoring, and singular (coherent) vs. multiple (incoherent) model of attachment: Findings and directions for future research. In C. Murray Parkes, J. Stevenson-Hinde and P. Marris (eds), *Attachment Across the Life Cycle*. London: Routledge, 127–59.

Main, M. and Cassidy, J. (1988) Categories of response to reunion with the parent at age 6: Predictable from infant attachment classifications and stable over a one-month period. *Developmental Psychology*, 24, 415–26.

Main, M. and Goldwyn, R. (1984) Predicting rejection of her infant from mother's representation of her own experience: Implications for the abused–abusing inter-generational cycle. *Child Abuse and Neglect*, 8, 203–17.

Main, M., Kaplan, N. and Cassidy, J. (1985) Security in infancy, childhood, and adulthood: A move to the level of representation. In I. Bretherton and E. Waters (eds), *Growing Points of Attachment Theory and Research*. Monographs of the Society for Research in Child Development, 50, nos 1–2.

Malpass, R. S. and Devine, P. G. (1981) Guided memory in eyewitness identification responses. *Journal of Applied Psychology*, 66, 343–50.

Manktelow, K. I. and Over, D. E. (1990) *Inference and Understanding: A Psychological and Philosophical Perspective*. London: Routledge.

Manktelow, K. I. and Over, D. E. (1991) Social roles and utilities in reasoning with deontic conditionals. *Cognition*, 39, 85–105.

Mann, R. D. (1959) A review of the relationship between personality and performance in small groups. *Psychological Bulletin*, 56, 241–70.

Manstead, A. S. R. and Semin, G. (1980) Social facilitation effects: Mere enhancement of dominant responses? *British Journal of Social and Clinical Psychology*, 19, 119–36.

Marans, R. W. and Stokols, D. (1993) *Environmental Simulation: Research and Policy Issues*. New York: Plenum Press.

Markus, H. (1977) Self-schemata and processing information about the self. *Journal of Personality and Social Psychology*, 35, 63–78.

Markus, H. and Kitayama, S. (1991) Culture and the self: Implications for cognition, emotion and motivation. *Psychological Review*, 98, 224–53.

Markus, H. and Kunda (1986) Stability and malleability of the self-concept. *Journal of Personality and Social Psychology*, 51, 858–66.

Markus, H. and Nurius, P. (1986) Possible selves. *American Psychologist*, 41, 954–69.

Markus, H. and Ruvulo (1992) Possible selves and performance: The power of self-relevant imagery. *Social Cognition*, 10, 95–124.

Markus, H., Smith and Moreland (1985) The role of the self-concept in the perception of others. *Journal of Personality and Social Psychology*, 49, 1494–1512.

Markus, H. and Wurf (1987) The dynamic self-concept: A social psychological perspective. *Annual Review of Psychology*, 38, 299–337.

Marr, D. (1982) *Vision*. San Francisco: Freeman.

Marr, D. and Poggio, T. (1976) Cooperative computation of stereo disparity. *Science*, 194, 283–7.

Marsh, P. , Rosser, E. and Harré, R. (1978) *The Rules of Disorder*. Milton Keynes: Open University Press.

Marshall, M. (1972) Privacy and environment. *Human Ecology*, 1, 93–110.

Martin, R. D. (1981) Relative brain size and basal metabolic rate in terrestrial vertebrates. *Nature*, 293, 56–60.

Maslow, A. H. (1965) *Eupsychian Management*. Homewood, Ill.: Richard D Irwin.

Maslow, A. H. (1968) *Towards a Psychology of Being*. New York: Van Nostrand.

Maslow, A. H. (1970; 2nd edn) *Motivation and Personality*. New York:Harper and Row.

Mason J. W. (1975) A historical view of the stress field.

Journal of Human Stress, 1, 22–36.

Masson, J. M. (1992) *Against Therapy*. London: Picador.

Masur, E. F. (1983) Gestural development, dual-directional signaling, and the transition to words. *Journal of Psycholinguistic Research*, 12, 93–109

Matteson, M. T. and Ivancevich, J. M. (1987) *Controlling Work Stress: Effective Human Resource and Management Strategies*. San Francisco: Jossey-Bass.

Maurer, D. and Barrera, M. (1981) Infants' perception of natural and distorted arrangements of a schematic face. *Child Development*, 52, 196–202.

Maurer, D. and Salapatek, P. (1976) Developmental changes in the scanning of faces by young infants. *Child Development*, 47, 437–50.

Maynard Smith, J. and Price, G. R. (1973) The logic of animal conflict. *Nature*, 246, 15–18.

Mazumdar, S. (1992) How programming can become counterproductive. *Journal of Environmental Psychology*, 12, 65–91.

McArthur, L. A. (1972) The how and what of why: Some determinants and consequences of causal attributions. *Journal of Personality and Social Psychology*, 22, 171–93.

McClelland, D. C. (1975) *Power: The Inner Experience*. New York: Irvington Press.

McClelland, D. C. (1961) *The Achieving Society*. New York: Van Nostrand.

McClelland, D. C. (1980) Motive dispositions: The merits of operant and respondent measures. In L. Wheeler (ed.), *Review of Personality and Social Psychology*, 1. Beverly Hills: Sage Press, 10–41.

McConkey, D. D. (1983; 4th edn) *How to Manage by Results*. New York: AMACOM.

McCormick, E. J., Jeanneret, P. R. and Mecham, R. C. (1972) A study of job characteristics as based on the Position Analysis Questionnaire (PAQ). *Journal of Applied Psychology*, 56, 347–68.

McCormick, E. J. and Sanders, M. S. (1982; 5th edn) *Human Factors in Engineering and Design*. New York: McGraw-Hill.

McDougall, W. (1908) *An Introduction to Social Psychology*. London: Methuen.

McGregor, D. (1960) *The Human Side of Enterprise*. New York: McGraw-Hill.

McGrew, W. C. (1992) *Chimpanzee Material Culture: Implications for Human Evolution*. Cambridge: Cambridge University Press.

McGuire, W. J. (1985; 3rd edn) Attitudes and attitude change. In G. Lindzey and E. Aronson (eds), *Handbook of Social Psychology* (vol. 2). New York: Random House.

McGuire, W. J. and McGuire (1988) Content and process in the experience of self. In L Berkowitz (ed.),

Advances in Experimental Social Psychology (vol. 21). Orlando, Fla.: Academic Press.

McLeod, P. (1987) Visual reaction time and high-speed ball games. *Perception*, 16, 49–59.

McLeod, P. and Jenkins, S. (1991) Timing accuracy and decision time in high-speed ball games. *International Journal of Sport Psychology*, 22, 279–95.

McShane, J. (1991) *Cognitive Development: An Information Processing Approach*. Oxford: Blackwell

Mead, G. H. (1934) *Mind, Self and Society*. Chicago: University of Chicago Press.

Melhuish, E. M., Mooney, A., Martin, S. and Lloyd, E. (1990) Type of childcare at 18 months – I: Differences in interactional experience. *Journal of Child Psychology and Psychiatry*, 31, 849–59.

Meltzoff, A. N. and Moore, M. K. (1977) Imitation of facial and manual gestures by human neonates. *Science*, 198, 75–8.

Meltzoff, A. N. (1988) Infant imitation and memory: Nine-month-olds in immediate and deferred tests. *Child Development*, 59, 217–55.

Meltzoff, A. N. and Moore, M. K. (1983) Newborn infants imitate adult facial gestures. *Child Development*, 54, 702–9.

Menn, L. (1975) Counter-example to 'fronting' as a universal in child language. *Journal of Child Language*, 2, 293–6.

Milgram, S. (1974) *Obedience to Authority*. London: Tavistock.

Miller, E. H., Callander, J. N., Lawhon, S. M. and Sammarco, G. J. (1984) Orthopaedics and the classical ballet dancer. *Contemporary Orthopaedics*, 8, 72–97.

Miller, J. G. (1984) Culture and the development of everyday social explanations. *Journal of Personality and Social Psychology*, 46, 961–78.

Milner, B. (1974) Hemispheric specialization: Scope and limits. In F. O. Schmitt and F. G. Wordern (eds), *The Neurosciences: Third Study Program*. Cambridge, Mass.: MIT Press, 75–89.

Milton, K. (1981) Distribution patterns of tropical plant foods as a stimulus to primate mental development. *American Anthropologist*, 83, 534–48.

Miner, J. B. (1983) The unpaved road from theory: Over the mountains to application. In R. H. Kilmann, K. W. Thomas, D. P. Slevin, R. Nath and S. L. Jerrell (eds), *Producing Useful Knowledge for Organizations*. New York: Praeger, 37–68.

Minsky, M. A. and Papert, S. (1969) *Perceptions*. Cambridge, Mass.: MIT Press.

Mischel, W. (1973) Towards a a cognitive social learning reconceptualization of personality. *Psychological Review*, 80, 252–83.

Mischel, W. (1983) Delay of gratification as process and as person variable in development. In D. Magnussen and V. P. Allen (eds), *Interactions in Human Development*. New York: Academic Press.

Mischel, W. and Shoda, Y. (1995) A cognitive-affective system theory of personality. *Psychological Review*, 102, 246–68.

Moely, B. E., Olson, F. A., Halwes, T. G. and Flavell, J. H. (1969) Production deficiency in young children's clustered recall. *Developmental Psychology*, 1, 26–34.

Moore, R. (1986) *Childhood's Domain*. London: Croom Helm.

Moretti, M. M. and Higgins, E. T. (1987) Relating self-discrepancy to self-esteem: The contribution of discrepancy beyond actual self-ratings. *Journal of Experimental Social Psychology*, 26, 108–23.

Morris, C. D., Bransford, J. D. and Franks, J. J. (1977) Levels of processing versus transfer appropriate processing. *Journal of Verbal Learning and Verbal Behaviour*, 16, 519–33.

Morris, D. C., Marsh, P. and O'Shaugnessey (1979) *Gestures: Their Origins and Distribution*. London: Cape.

Morse, J. and Gergen, K. J. (1970) Social comparison, self-consistency and the concept of self. *Journal of Personality and Social Psychology*, 16, 874–84.

Morse, N. C. and Reimer, E. (1956) The experimental change of a major organizational variable. *Journal of Abnormal Social Psychology*, 51, 120–9.

Moscovici, S. Notes toward a description of social representations. *European Journal of Social Psychology*, 18, 211–50.

Moscovici, S. (1985a) Social influence and conformity. In G. Lindzey and E. Aronsen (eds), *Handbook of Social Psychology*, vol. 2. New York: Random House, 115–50.

Moscovici, S. (1985b) *The Age of the Crowd*. Cambridge: Cambridge University Press.

Moscovici, S. (1996) Just remembering. *British Journal of Social Psychology*, 35, 5–14.

Muchinsky, P. M. and Tuttle, M. L. (1979) Employee turnover: An empirical and methodological assessment. *Journal of Vocational Behavior*, 14, 43–77.

Mueller, E. and Brenner, J. (1977) The origins of social skills and interaction among playgroup toddlers. *Child Development*, 48, 854–61.

Muller, H. (1985) Voice change in human biological development. *Journal of Interdisciplinary History*, 16, 239–53.

Muller, H. (1987) The accelerated development of youth: Beard growth as a biological marker. *Comparative Study of Society and History*, 29, 748–62.

Myers, D. G. and Lamm, H. (1976) The group polariza-tion phenomenon. *Psychological Bulletin*, 74, 297–308.

Nasar, J. L. and Fisher, B. (1993) 'Hot spots' of fear and crime: A multi-method analysis. *Journal of Environmental Psychology*, 13, 187–206.

Nelson, K. E., Denninger, M., Bonvillian, J., Kaplan, B. and Baker, N. (1984) Maternal adjustments and non-adjustments as related to children's linguistic advances and language acquisition theories. In A. Pellegrini and T. Yawkey (eds), *The Development of Oral and Written Language: Readings in Developmental and Applied Linguistics*. Norwood, NJ: Ablex, 31–56.

Nelson, T. O. (1977) Repetition and depth of processing. *Journal of Verbal Learning and Verbal Behavior*, 16, 151–72.

Nemeth, C. (ed.) (1996) Minority influences. *British Journal of Social Psychology*, 35, 1–218 (special issue).

Nemeth, C. (1986) Differential contributions of majority and minority influence. *Psychological Review*, 93, 23–32.

Nettelbeck, T. (1987) Inspection time and intelligence. In P. A. Vernon (ed.), *Speed of Information Processing and Intelligence*. New York: Ablex.

Nettelbeck, T. (1990) Intelligence does exist. *The Psychologist*, 3, 494–7.

Neuchterlein, K. H. and Dawson, M. (1984) An heuristic vulnerability/stress model of schizophrenic episodes. *Schizophrenia Bulletin*, 10, 300–12.

Neugarten, B.L., Havighurst, R.J. and Tobin, S.S. (1968) Personality and patterns of aging. In B. L. Neugarten (ed.), *Middle Age and Aging*. Chicago: Univ. of Chicago Press.

Neugarten, B. L. and Weinstein, K. K. (1964) The changing American grandparent. *Journal of Marriage and the Family*, 26, 199–204.

Newcomb, T. M. (1961) *The Acquaintance Process*. New York: Holt, Rinehart and Winston.

Newell, A. (1990) *Unified Theories of Cognition: The 1987 William James Lectures*. Cambridge, Mass.: Harvard University Press.

Newell, A. and Rosenbloom, P. S. (1981) Mechanisms of skill acquisition and the law of practice. In J. R. Anderson (ed.), *Cognitive Skills and their Acquisition*. Hillsdale, NJ: Lawrence Erlbaum.

Newell, A., Shaw, J. C. and Simon, H. (1957) Empirical explorations with the Logic Theory Machine. *Proceedings of the Western Joint Computer Conference*, 15, 218–39.

Newell, A., Shaw, J. C. and Simon, H. (1963) Chess-playing programs and the problem of complexity. In E.A. Feigenbaum and J. Feldman (eds), *Computers and Thought*. New York: McGraw-Hill, 39–70.

Newell, A. and Simon, H. A. (1972) *Human Problem Solv-*

ing. Englewood Cliffs, NJ: Prentice-Hall.

Newman, O. (1972) *Defensible Space*. New York: Macmillan.

Newstead, S. E. (1990) Conversion in syllogistic reasoning. In K. Gilhooly, M. Keane, R. Logie and G. Erdos (eds), *Lines of Thinking: Reflections of the Psychology of Thinking*, Vol. 1. Chichester: John Wiley and Sons, 73–84.

Newstead, S. E. and Griggs, R. A. (1992) Thinking about THOG: Sources of error in a deductive reasoning problem. *Psychological Research*, 54, 299–305.

Newstead, S. E., Pollard, P., Evans, J. St B. T. and Allen, J. (1992) The source of belief bias effects in syllogistic reasoning. *Cognition*, 45, 257–84.

Newton, I. (1704) *Opticks: Or, a Treatise of the Reflexions, Refractions, Inflexions and Colours of Light*. London: S. Smith & B. Walford.

Nicolson, R. I. and Fawcett, A. J. (1990) Automaticity: A new framework for dyslexia research? *Cognition*, 35, 159–82.

Nicolson, R. I. and Fawcett, A. J. (1996) *The Dyslexia Early Screening Test*. London: The Psychological Corporation.

Nisbett, R. E., Fong, G. T., Lehman, D. R. and Cheng, P. W. (1987) Teaching reasoning. *Science*, 238, 625–31.

Nisbett, R. E., Krantz, D. H., Jepson, C. and Kunda, Z. (1983) The use of statistical heuristics in everyday inductive reasoning. *Psychological Review*, 90, 339–63.

Norman, D. A. (1982) *Learning and Memory*. San Francisco: Freeman.

O'Brien, D. P., Noveck, I. A., Davidson, G. M., Fisch, S. M., Brooke Lea, R. and Freitag, J. (1990) Sources of difficulty in deductive reasoning: The THOG task. *Quarterly Journal of Experimental Psychology*, 42A, 329–51.

Oakhill, J. V. (1984) Inferential and memory skills in children's comprehension of stories. *British Journal of Psychology*, 73, 13–20.

Oakhill, J. V. and Johnson-Laird, P. N. (1985) The effects of belief on the spontaneous production of syllogistic conclusions. *Quarterly Journal of Experimental Psychology*, 37A, 553–69.

Oakhill, J. V., Johnson-Laird, P. N. and Garnham, A. (1989) Believability and syllogistic reasoning. *Cognition*, 31, 117–40.

Oakhill, J. V., Yuill, N. and Parkin, A. J. (1986) On the nature of the difference between skilled and less skilled comprehenders. *British Journal of Psychology*, 54, 31–9.

Oakley, A. (1980) *Women Confined*. Oxford: Martin Robertson.

Ogden, J. A. and Corkin, S. (1991) Memories of HM. In W. C. Abraham, M. C. Corballis, and K. G. White (eds), *Memory Mechanisms: A Tribute to G.V. Goddard*. Hillsdale, NJ: Earlbaum Associates.

Oldham, G. R. and Fried, Y. (1987) Employee reactions to workspace characteristics. *Journal of Applied Psychology*, 72, 75–80.

Olweus, D. (1993) *Bullying At School: What We Know and What We Can do*. Oxford: Blackwell.

Ornstein, P. A., Naus, M. J. and Liberty, C. (1975) Rehearsal and organizational processes in children's memory. *Child Development*, 46, 818–30.

Osborn, A. F. (1957) *Applied Imagination*. New York: Charles Scribner's Sons.

Osgood, C. E., Suci, G. J. and Tannenbaum, G. H. (1957) *The Measurement of Meaning*. Urbana: University of Illinois Press.

Ottosson, T. (1987) Mapreading and wayfinding. *Goteborg Studies in Educational Sciences*, 65 (whole volume).

O'Connor, P. (1992) *Friendships between Women: a Critical Review*. London: The Guilford Press.

Paikoff, R. L. and Brooks-Gunn, J. (1991) Do parent-child relationships change during puberty? *Psychological Bulletin*, 110, 47–66.

Papert, S. (1980) *Mindstorms: Children, Computers and Powerful Ideas*. New York: Basic Books.

Papousek, H. (1967) Conditioning during early postnatal development. In Y. Brackbill and G. G. Thompson (eds), *Behavior in Infancy and Early Childhood*. New York: Free Press.

Parke, R. D. and Tinsley, B. J. (1987) Family interaction in infancy. In J. D. Osofsky (ed.), *Handbook of Infant Development*, 2nd edn. New York: Wiley, 579–641.

Parker, J. G. and Asher, S. R. (1987) Peer relations and later personal adjustment: Are low-accepted children at risk? *Psychological Bulletin*, 102, 357–89.

Parkin, A. J. (1996) *Explorations in Cognitive Neuropsychology*. London: Erlbaum.

Parkin, A. J. (1997; 2nd edn) *Memory and Amnesia*. Oxford: Blackwell.

Parkin, A. J. and Leng, N. R. C. (1993) *Neuropsychology of Amnesic Syndromes*. London: Erlbaum.

Parkin, A. J., Montaldi, D., Leng, N. R. C. and Hunkin, N. (1990) Contextual cueing effects in the remote memory of alcoholic Korsakoff patients. *Quarterly Journal of Experimental Psychology*, 4ZA, 585–96.

Parkin, A. J., Pitchford, J. and Binschaedler, C. (1994) Further characterisation of the executive memory impairment following frontal lobe lesions. *Brain and Cognition*, 26, 23–42.

Parkin, A. J., Yeomans, J. and Bindschaedler, C. (1994) Further characterisation of the memory impairment following frontal lobe lesions. *Brain and Cognition*, 26, 23–42.

Parmelee, A. H., Schulz, H. R. and Disbrow, M. W. (1961) Sleep patterns in the newborn. *Journal of Pediatrics*, 58, 241–50.

Parsons, T. (1951) *The Social System*. New York: Free Press.

Parsons, T. (1959) An approach to psychological theory in terms of the theory of action. In S. Koch (ed.), *Psychology: The Study of a Science*. New York: McGraw-Hill.

Parten, M. B. (1932) Social participation among pre-school children. *Journal of Abnormal and Social Psychology*, 27, 243–69.

Passingham, R. E. (1973) *Brain, Behavior and Evolution*, 7, 337.

Passingham, R. E. (1982) *The Human Primate*. Oxford: W. H. Freeman.

Passini, R. (1984) *Wayfinding in Architecture*. New York: Van Nostrand Rheinhold.

Patterson, G. R., DeBaryshe, B. D. and Ramsey, E. (1989) A developmental perspective on antisocial behavior. *American Psychologist*, 44, 329–35.

Pavlov, I. P. (1927) *Conditioned Reflexes*. Oxford: Oxford University Press.

Paykel, E. S. (1992; 2nd edn) *Handbook of Affective Disorders*. Edinburgh: Churchill Livingstone.

Pelham, B. W. and Swann, W. B. (1989) From self-conceptions to self-worth: On the sources and structure of low self-esteem. *Journal of Personality and Social Psychology*, 57, 672–80.

Pennebaker J. W. (1982) *The Psychology of Physical Symptoms*. New York: Springer.

Perkins, D. N. (1989) Reasoning as it is and could be: An empirical perspective. In D. M. Topping, D. C. Crowell and V. N. Kobayashi (eds), *Thinking Across Cultures: The Third International Conference on Thinking*. Hillsdale, NJ: Lawrence Erlbaum Associates, 175–94.

Perkins, D. N., Farady, M. and Bushey, B. (1991) Everyday reasoning and the roots of intelligence. In J. F. Voss, D. N. Perkins and J. W. Segal (eds), *Informal Reasoning and Education*. Hillsdale, NJ: Lawrence Erlbaum Associates, 83–105.

Perner, J. (1991) *Understanding the Representational Mind*. Cambridge, Mass.: MIT Press.

Perrin, S. and Spencer, C. P. (1981) Independence or conformity in the Asch experiment as a reflection of cultural and situational factors. *British Journal of Social Psychology*, 20, 205–9.

Petty, M. M., McGee, G. W. and Cavender, J. W. (1984) A meta-analysis of the relationships between individual job satisfaction and individual performance. *Academy of Management Review*, 9, 712–21.

Petty, R. and Caccioppo, J. T. (1986) *Communication and Persuasion: Central and Peripheral Routes to Persuasion*. New York: Springer.

Petty, R. and Caccioppo, J. T. (1986) The elaboration-likelihood model of persuasion. In L Berkowitz (ed.), *Advances in Experimental Social Psychology* (vol. 19). Orlando, Fla.: Academic Press.

Petty, R., Wells, G. L. and Caccioppo, J. T. (1976) Distraction can enhance or reduce yielding to propaganda: Thought disruption versus effort justification. *Journal of Personality and Social Psychology*, 34, 874–84.

Pfungst, O. (1911; trans. 1965) *Clever Hans: The Horse of Mr von Osten*. New York: Holt, Rinehart and Winston.

Phoenix, A., Woollett, A. and Lloyd, E. (1991) *Motherhood: Meanings, Practices and Ideologies*. London: Sage.

Piaget, J. (1972) Intellectual evolution from adolescence to adulthood. *Human Development*, 15, 1–12.

Piaget, J. and Inhelder, B. (1951) *La Génèse de l'idée de hasard chez enfant*. Paris: Presses Universitaires de France.

Piaget, J. and Inhelder, B. (1969) *The Psychology of the Child*. London: Routledge and Kegan Paul.

Pick, H. L. and Lockman, J. J. (1981) From frames of reference to spatial representations. In L. S. Liben, A. H. Patterson and N. Newcombe (eds), *Spatial Representation and Behavior across the Life Span*. New York: Academic Press.

Plato (1928 trans.) *The Republic*. New York: Scribner.

Pollack, S. R. (1983) Salience of a communicator's physical attractiveness and persuasion: A heuristic versus systematic processing interpretation. *Social Cognition*, 2, 156–68.

Pollard, P. (1990) Natural selection for the selection task: Limits to social exchange theory. *Cognition*, 36, 195–204.

Popper, K. R. (1934; repr. 1959) *The Logic of Scientific Discovery*. London: Hutchinson.

Porier, G. W. and Lott, A. J. (1967) Galvanic skin responses and prejudice. *Journal of Personality and Social Psychology*, 5, 253–9.

Poulton, E. C. (1970) *Environment and Human Efficiency*. Springfield, Ill.: Charles C. Thomas.

Prechtl, H. F. R. (1984) Continuity and change in early neural development. In Prechtl (ed.), *Continuity and Neural Function From Prenatal to Postnatal Life*. Oxford: Blackwell.

Premack, A. J. and Premack, D. (1972) Teaching language to an ape. *Scientific American*, 227, 92–9.

Pullum, G. K. (1991) *The Great Eskimo Hoax and Other Irreverent Essays on the Study of Language*. Chicago:

University of Chicago Press.

Quirk, R., Greenbaum, S., Leech, G. and Svartvik, J. (1985) *A Comprehensive Grammar of the English Language*. New York: Longman.

Rabbie, J. M. and Horowitz, M. (1969) Arousal of ingroup–outgroup bias by a chance win or loss. *Journal of Personality and Social Psychology*, 13, 269–77.

Radin, N., Oyserman, D. and Benn, R. (1991) Grandfathers, teen mothers and children under two. In P. K. Smith (ed.), *The Psychology of Grandparenthood: An International Perspective*. London: Routledge.

Ramsay, D. S. (1984) Onset of duplicated syllable babbling and unimanual handedness in infants: Evidence for developmental change in hemispheric specialization? *Developmental Psychology*, 20, 64–71.

Reason, J. T. (1990) *Human Error*. Cambridge: Cambridge University Press.

Recazone, G. H., Merzenich, M. M., Jenkins, W. M., Grajski, K. A. and Dinse, H. R. (1992) Topographic reorganization of the hand prepresentation in cortical area 3b of owl monkeys trained in a frequency-discrimination task. *Journal of Neurophysiology*, 67, 1031–56.

Recazone, G. H., Schreiner, C. E. and Merzenich, M. M. (1993) Plasticity in the frequency representation of primary auditory cortex following discrimination training in adult owl monkeys. *Journal of Neuroscience*, 13, 87–104.

Reicher, S. D. (1987) Crowd behaviour as social action. In J. C. Turner, M. A. Hogg, P. J. Oakes, S. D. Reicher and M. S. Wetherell (eds), *Rediscovering the Social Group: A Self-categorization Theory*. Oxford: Blackwell.

Reicher, S. D. and Levine, M. (1994) Deindividuation, power relations between groups and the expression of social identity. *British Journal of Social Psychology*, 33, 145–63.

Relph, E. C. (1976) *Place and Placelessness*. London: Pion Press.

Rescorla, R. A. (1968) Probability of shock in the presence and absence of CS in fear conditioning. *Journal of Comparative and Physiological Psychology*, 66, 1–5.

Rescorla, R. A. and Wagner, A. R. (1972) A theory of Pavlovian conditioning: Variations on the effectiveness of reinforcement and nonreinforcement. In A. H. Black and W. F. Prokasy (eds), *Classical Conditioning II: Current Research and Theory*. New York: Appleton-Century-Crofts, 64–99.

Rich, A. (1980) Compulsory heterosexuality and lesbian existence. *Signs: Women in Culture and Society*, 5, 631–60.

Richards, M. (1994) The international year of the family: Family research. *The Psychologist*, 8, 17–24.

Richardson, K. (1991) *Understanding Intelligence*. Milton Keynes: Open University Press.

Rivers, I. (1996) The victimisation of lesbian, gay and bisexual youths. Paper presented at the Research on Lesbian, Gay and Bisexual Youths: Implications for Developmental Intervention Conference, The Pennsylviania State University, USA, 7–9 June, 1996.

Rivlin, L. G. (1992) A tribute to Harold M. Proshansky (1920–1990). *Journal of Environmental Psychology*, 12, 1–4.

Roberts, J. V. (1985) The attitude–memory relationship after 40 years: A meta-analysis of the literature. *Basic and Applied Social Psychology*, 6, 221–41.

Robertson, I. T. and Downs, S. (1989) Learning and the prediction of performance: Development of trainability testing in the United Kingdom. *Journal of Applied Psychology*, 64, 42–50.

Robinson, S. and Weldon, E. (1993) Feedback seeking in groups: A theoretical perspective. *British Journal of Social Psychology*, 32, 71–86.

Roche, A. F. (ed.) (1979) Secular trends in human growth, maturation, and development. Monographs of the Society for Research in Child Development, 44, nos 3–4, 1–120.

Rodrigues, C. A. (1988) Identifying the right leader for the right situation. *Personnel*, Sept., 43–6.

Rogers, C. R. (1951) *Client-centered Therapy: Its Current Practice, Implications and Theory*. Boston: Houghton Mifflin.

Rogers, C. R. (1960) *Client-Centred Therapy: Its Current practice, Implications and Theory*. Boston: Houghton-Mifflin.

Rogers, C. R. (1974) In retrospect: Forty-six years. *American Psychologist*, 29, 115–23.

Rokeach, M. (1973) *The Nature of Human Values*. New York: Free Press.

Rosch, E. (1974) Linguistic relativity. In A. Silverstein (ed.), *Human Communication: Theoretical Perspectives*. New York: Halstead Press.

Rosenberg, M. J. (1965) *Society and the Adolescent's Self-Image*. Princteon, NJ: Princeton University press.

Rosenberg, M. J. (1979) *The Self-Concept*. New York: Basic Books.

Rosenberg, M. J. and Hovland, C. I. (1960) Cognitive, affective and behavioral components of attitudes. In Hovland and Rosenberg (eds), *Attitude Organization and Change*. New Haven: Yale University Press.

Rosenberg, M. J. and Pearlin, L. (1978) Social class and self-esteem among adults and children. *American Journal of Sociology*, 84, 53–77.

Rosenhan, D. L. and Seligman, M. E. P. (1995) *Abnormal Psychology*. New York: Norton.

Rosenstein, D. and Oster, H. (1988) Differential responses to the four basic tastes in newborns. *Child Development*, 59, 1555–68.

Rosenthal, R., Hall, J. A., DiMatteo, M. R., Rogers, P. and Archer, D, (1979) *Sensitivity to Nonverbal Communication: The PONS Test*. Baltimore: John Hopkins University Press.

Ross, L. D., Amibile, T. M. and Steinmetz, J. L. (1977) Social roles, social control and biases in social perception processes. *Journal of Personality and Social Psychology*, 35, 485–94.

Rossi, A. S. and Rossi, P. H. (1990) *Of Human Bonding*. New York: Aldine de Gruyter.

Rossor, M. (1994) Uncovering the seeds of senile dementia. *MRC News*, Autumn, 29–32.

Ruffwarg, H. P., Muzio, J. N. and Dement, W. C. (1966) Ontogenetic development of the human sleep–dream cycle. *Science*, 153, 604–19.

Rumelhart, D. E. (1989) The architecture of mind: A connectionist approach. In M. I. Posner (ed.), *Foundations of Cognitive Science*. Cambridge, Mass.: MIT Press.

Rumelhart, D. E. and McClelland, J. L. (1986). On learning the past tenses of English verbs. In Rumelhart, McClelland and the PDP Research Group (eds), *Parallel Distributed Processing: Explorations in the Microstructure of Cognition*, vol. 2: *Psychological and Biological Models*. Cambridge, Mass.: MIT Press, 216–71.

Rushton, J. P. (1989) Genetic similarity, human altruism, and group selection. *Behavioral and Brain Sciences*, 12, 503–59.

Rutter, M. (1981; 2nd edn) *Maternal Deprivation Resassessed*. Harmondsworth: Penguin.

Rutter, M., Graham, P., Chadwick, O. and Yule, W. (1976) Adolescent turmoil: Fact ot fiction? *Journal of Child Psychology and Psychiatry*, 17, 35–56.

Ryle, G. (1949) *The Concept of Mind*. London: Hutchinson.

Saariluoma, P. (1991) Aspects of skilled imagery in blindfold chess. *Acta Psychologica*, 77, 65–89.

Sacks, O. (1985) *The Man who Mistook his Wife for a Hat*. London: Duckworth.

Sapir, E. (1921) *Language: An Introduction to the Study of Speech*. New York: Harcourt, Brace and World.

Sarraga, E. (1993) The abuse of children. In R. Dallos and E. McLaughlin (eds), *Social Problems and the Family*. London: Sage.

Scarr, S. and Carter-Saltzman, L. (1982) Genetics and intelligence. In R. J. Sternberg (ed.), *Handbook of Human Intelligence*. Cambridge: Cambridge University Press.

Schacter, D. L. (1987) Implicit memory: History and current status. *Journal of Experimental Psychology: Learning, Memory and Cognition*, 13, 501–18.

Schank, R. C. (1982) *Dynamic Memory*. Cambridge: Cambridge University Press.

Schank, R. C. and Abelson, R. P. (1977) *Scripts, Plans, Goals and Understanding*. Hillsdale, NJ: Lawrence Erlbaum.

Schank, R. C. and Riesbeck, C. K. (1981) *Inside Computer Understanding*. Hillsdale, NJ: Lawrence Erlbaum.

Scheier M. F. and Carver C. S. (1992) Effects of optimism on psychological and physical wellbeing: Theoretical overview and empirical update. *Cognitive Research and Therapy*, 16, 201–28.

Schein, E. H. (1969) *Process Consultation: Its Role in Organization Development*. Reading, Mass.: Addison-Wesley.

Schiff, M., Duyme, M., Dumeret, A., Stewart, J., Tomkiewicz, S. and Feingold, J. (1978) Intellectual status of working-class children adopted into upper-middle-class families. *Science*, 200, 1503–4.

Schildkraut, J. J. and Kety, S. S. (1967) Biogenic amines and emotion. *Science*, 156, 21–30.

Schlenker, B. R. , Weingold, M. F. and Hallam, J. R. (1992) Self-serving attributions in social context: Effects of self-esteem and social pressure. *Journal of Personality and Social Psychology*, 58, 855–63.

Schmitt, N. (1976) Social and situational determinants of interview decisions: Implications for the employment interview. *Personnel Psychology*, 29, 79–101.

Schneider, J. and Locke, E. A. (1971) A critique of Herzberg's incident classification system and a suggested revision. *Organizational Behavior and Human Performance*, 6, 441–57.

Schneider, W. (1987) Connectionism – Is It a Paradigm Shift for Psychology? *Behavior Research Methods, Instruments and Computers*, 19, 73–83.

Schneider, W. and Shiffrin, R. M. (1977) Controlled and automatic human information processing I: Detection, search and attention. *Pyschological Review*, 84, 1–66.

Schofield, M. (1965) *The Sexual Behaviour of Young People*. London: Longmans.

Scott, W. G., Mitchell, T. R. and Birnbaum, P. H. (1981; 4th edn) *Organizational Theory: A Structural and Behavioral Analysis*. Homewood, Ill.: Richard D. Irwin.

Searle, J. R. (1969) *Speech Acts: An Essay in the Philosophy of Language*. Cambridge: Cambridge University Press.

Seligman, M. E. P. (1975) *Helplessness On Depression, Development and Death*. San Francisco: W. H. Freeman.

Selye, H. (1976; 2nd edn) *The Stress of Life*. New York: McGraw-Hill.

Serpell, R. (1977) Estimates of intelligence in a rural community of Eastern Zambia. In F. M. Okatcha (ed.), *Modern Psychology and Cultural Adaption*. Nairobi: Swahili Language Consultants and Publishers.

Shankweiler, D. and Liberman, I. Y. (1976) Exploring the relations between reading and speech. In R. M. Knights and D. K. Bakker (eds), *The Neuropsychology of Learning Disorders: Theoretical Approaches*. Baltimore: University Park Press.

Shayer, M. and Wylam, H. (1978) The distribution of Piagetian stages of thinking in British middle and secondary school children. *British Journal of Educational Psychology*, 48, 62–70.

Shea, J. B. and Morgan, R. L. (1979) Contextual interference effects on the acquisition, retention, and transfer of a motor skill. *Journal of Experimental Psychology: Human Learning and Memory*, 5, 179–87.

Sheeran, P., Abrams, D. and Orbell, S. (1995) Unemployment, self-esteem and psychological distress: A social comparison theory approach. *Basic and Applied Social Psychology*, 17, 65–82.

Sheldon, W. H. (1940) *The Varieties of Human Physique: An Introduction to Constitutional Psychology*. New York: Harper.

Sheppard, B. H., Hartwick, J. and Warshaw, P. R. (1988) The theory of reasoned action: A meta-analysis of past research with recommendations for modifications and future research. *Journal of Consumer Research*, 15, 325–43.

Sherif, M. and Hovland, I. C. (1961) *Social Judgement*. New Haven, Conn.: Yale University Press.

Sherif, M. and Sherif, C. (1953) *Groups in Harmony and Tension*. New York: Harper and Row.

Sherrington, C. (1940) *Man and His Nature*. Cambridge: Cambridge University Press.

Shields, P. J. and Rovee-Collier, C. K. (1992) Long-term memory for context specific category information at six months. *Child Development*, 63, 245–59.

Shiffrin, R. M. and Schneider, W. (1977) Controlled and automatic human information processing II: Perceptual learning, automatic attending and general theory. *Pyschological Review*, 84, 127–90.

Shrauger, J. S. and Schoeneman, T. J. (1979) Symbolic interactionist view of the self: Through the looking glass darkly. *Psychological Bulletin*, 86, 549–73.

Siegal, A. W. and White, S. (1975) The development of spatial representations of large-scale environments. In H. W. Reese (ed.), *Advances in Child Development and Behavior*, vol. 10. New York: Academic Press.

Simon, H. A. (1990) A mechanism for social selection and successful altruism. *Science*, 250, 1665–8.

Skinner, B. F. (1948) *Walden 2*. New York: Macmillan.

Skinner, B. F. (1951) How to teach animals. *Scientific American*, 185, 26–9.

Skinner, B. F. (1957) *Verbal Behaviour*. New York: Appleton-Century-Crofts.

Skinner, B. F. (1971) *Beyond Freedom and Dignity*. New York: Knopf.

Sklar, L. S. and Anisman, H. (1981) Stress and cancer. *Psychological Bulletin*, 89, 369–406.

Skuse, D. (1984) Extreme deprivation in early childhood – II: Theoretical issues and a comparative review. *Journal of Child Psychology and Psychiatry*, 25, 543–72.

Slater, A. M., Mattock, A. and Brown, E. (1990) Newborn infants' responses to retinal and real size. *Journal of Experimental Child Psychology*, 49, 314–22.

Slater, A. M., Morison, V., Somers, M., Mattock, A., Brown, E. and Taylor, D. (1990) Newborn and older infants' perception of partly occluded objects. *Infant Behaviour and Development*, 13, 33–49.

Slobin, D. (1979) *Psycholinguistics*. New York: Prentice Hall.

Small, R., Brown, S. and Lumley, J. (1994) Missing voices: What women say and do about depression after childbirth. *Journal of Reproductive and Infant Psychology*, 12, 89–103.

Smilansky, S. (1968) *The Effects of Sociodramatic Play on Disadvantaged Preschool Children*. New York: Wiley.

Smith, J. A. (1990) Transforming identities: A repertory grid case study of the transition to motherhood. *British Journal of Medical Psychology*, 63, 239–53.

Smith, N. V. (1973) *The Acquisition of Phonology: A Case Study*. Cambridge: Cambridge University Press.

Smith, P. K. (1980) Shared care of young children: Alternative models to monotropism. *Merrill-Palmer Quarterly*, 26, 371–89.

Smith, P. K. (1986) Exploration, play and social development in boys and girls. In D. Hargreaves and A. Colley (eds), *The Psychology of Sex Roles*. London: Harper and Row, 118–41.

Smith, P. K. (1991) Introduction: The nature of grandparenthood. In P. K. Smith (ed.), *The Psychology of Grandparenthood: An International Perspective*. London: Routledge.

Smith, P. K. and Connolly, K. J. (1980) *The Ecology of Pre-School Behaviour*. Cambridge: Cambridge University Press.

Smith, P. K. and Cowie, H. (1991; 2nd edn) *Understanding Children's Development*. Oxford: Blackwell.

Smith, P. K. and Sharp, S. (eds) (1994) *School Bullying: Insights and Perspectives*. London: Routledge.

Smith, S. G. (1994a) The essential qualities of a home. *Journal of Environmental Psychology*, 14, 31–46.

Smith, S. G. (1994b) The psychological construction of home life. *Journal of Environmental Psychology*, 14, 125–36.

Smith, S. M. and Vela, E. (1992) Environmental context-dependent eyewitness recognition. *Applied Cognitive*

Psychology, 6, 125–39.

Snow, C. E. (1986) Conversations with children. In P. Fletcher and M. Garman (eds), *Language Acquisition*, 2nd edn. New York: Cambridge University Press, 363–75.

Snowling, M. (1987) *Dyslexia: A Cognitive Developmental Perspective*. Oxford: Blackwell.

Solomon, S., Greenberg, J. and Pyszcznski, T. (1991) A terror management theory of social behavior: The psychological functions of self-esteem and cultural worldviews. In L. Berkowitz (ed.), *Advances in Experimental Social Psychology* (vol. 24). Orlando, Fla.: Academic Press.

Sommer, R. and Olson, H. (1980) The soft classroom. *Environment and Behaviour*, 13, 412–17.

Sparks, P. and Shepherd, R. (1993) Self-identity and the theory of planned behaviour: Assessing the role of identification with 'green consumerism'. *Social Psychology Quarterly*, 55, 388–99.

Spearman, C. (1904) 'General intelligence' objectively determined and measured. *American Journal of Psychology*, 15, 201–93.

Spearman, C. (1927) *The Abilities of Man*. New York: Macmillan.

Spencer, C. P., Blades, M. and Morsley, K. (1989) *The Child in the Physical Environment*. Chichester: Wiley.

Spencer, C. P. and Budd, R. J. (1985) Exploring the role of personal normative beliefs in the theory of reasoned action: The problem of discriminating between different path models. *European Journal of Social Psychology*, 15, 299–313.

Sperling, G. (1960) The information available in brief visual presentations. *Psychological Monographs: General and Applied*, 74, 1–29.

Sperry, R. W. and Gazzaniga, M. S. (1967) Language following surgical disconnection of the hemispheres. In *Brain Mechanisms Underlying Speech and Language*.

Squire, L. (1992) Memory and the hippocampus: A synthesis from findings with rats, monkeys, and humans. *Psychological Review*, 99, 195–231.

Stammers, R. (1996) Training and the acquisition of knowledge and skill. In P. Warr (ed.), *Psychology at Work*. London: Penguin.

Stanovich, K. E. (1988) Explaining the differences between the dyslexic and the garden-variety poor reader: The phonological-core variable-difference model. *Journal of Learning Disabilities*, 21, 590–612.

Staples, R. and Smith, J. W. (1954) Attitudes of grandmothers and mothers toward child rearing practices. *Child Development*, 25, 91–7.

Steers, R. M. and Porter, L. W. (eds) (1983; 3rd edn) *Motivation and Work Behavior*. New York: McGraw-Hill.

Steinberg, L. (1987) Impact of puberty on family relations: Effects of pubertal status and pubertal timing. *Developmental Psychology*, 23, 451–60.

Sternberg, L. (1988) A triangular theory of love. *Psychological Review*, 93, 119–35.

Sternberg, R. J. (1985) *Beyond IQ: A Triarchic Theory of Human Intelligence*. Cambridge: Cambridge University Press.

Sternberg, R. J., Conway, B. E., Ketron, J. L. and Bernstein, M. (1981) People's conceptions of intelligence. *Journal of Personality and Social Psychology*, 1, 37–55.

Sternberg, R. J. and Rifkin, B. (1979) The development of analogical reasoning processes. *Journal of Experimental Child Psychology*, 27, 195–232.

Sternberg, S. (1966) High speed memory scanning in human memory. *Science*, 153, 652–4.

Stogdill, R. M. (1948) Personal factors associated with leadership. *Journal of Psychology*, 23, 35–71.

Stogdill, R. M. (1965) *Managers, Employees, Organizations*. Columbus: Ohio State University, Bureau of Business Research.

Stokols, D. (1972) A social-psychological model of human crowding phenomena. *Journal of the Institute of American Planners*, 38, 72–83.

Stokols, D. and Altman, I. (eds) (1987) *The Handbook of Environmental Psychology*. New York: John Wiley.

Stoner, J. A. F. (1961) A comparison of individual and group decisions including risk. Masters thesis, Massachusetts Institute of Technology, Boston, Mass.

Strom, R. and Strom, S. (1989) Grandparents and learning. *International Journal of Aging and Human Development*, 29, 163–9.

Strube, M. J. and Garcia, J. E. (1981) A meta-analytic investigation of Fielder's contingency model of leader effectiveness. *Psychological Bulletin*, 90, 307–21.

Stryker, S. (1982) *Symbolic Interactionism: A Social Structural Version*. Menlo Park, Calif.: Benjamin Cummings.

Studdert-Kennedy, M. (1991) Language development from an evolutionary perspective. In N. Krasnegor, D. Rumbaugh, R. Schiefelbusch, and M. Studdert-Kennedy (eds), *Language Acquisition: Biological and Behavioral Determinants*. Hillsdale, NJ: Erlbaum.

Sulser, F. (1982) Antidepressant drug research: Impact of neurobiology and psychobiology. In E. Costa and G. Racagni (eds), *Typical and Atypical Antidepressants*. New York: Raven Press.

Sulser, F. and Sanders-Bush, E. (1989) From neurochemical to molecular pharmacology of antidepressants. In E. Costa (ed.), *Tribute to B. B. Brodie*. New York: Raven Press.

Super, C. M. (1983) Cultural variation in the meaning and uses of children's 'intelligence'. In J. Deregowski, S. Diziurawiec and R. Annis (eds), *Explorations in Cross Cultural Psychology*. Amsterdam: Swets and Zeitlinger.

Suzuki, S. (1981) Discovery of the law of ability and the principle of ability development: Proof that talent is not inborn. In E. Herrman (ed.), *Shinichi Suzuki: The Man and His Philosophy*. Athens, Ohio: Ability Development Associates.

Suzuki, S. and Yamamuro, T. (1985) Fetal movement and fetal presentation. *Early human Development*, 11, 255–63.

Swann, W. B. (1985) The self as architect of social reality. In B. Schlenker (ed.), *The Self and Social Life*. New York: McGraw–Hill.

Sweeney, P. D. and Gruber, K. L. (1984) Selective exposure: Voter information preferences and the Watergate affair. *Journal of Personality and Social Psychology*, 46, 1208–21.

Tajfel, H. (1981) *Human Groups and Social Categories*. Cambridge: Cambridge University Press.

Tajfel, H. (1974) Social identity and intergroup behaviour. *Social Science Information*, 13, 65–93.

Tajfel, H. and Billig, M. (1974) Familiarity and categorization in intergroup relations. *Journal of Experimental Social Psychology*, 10, 159–70.

Takahashi, K. (1990) Are the key assumptions of the 'strange situation' procedure universal? *Human Development*, 33, 23–30.

Takeuchi, A. H. and Hulse, S. H. (1993) Absolute pitch. *Psychological Bulletin*, 113, 345–61.

Taylor, D. M. and Jaggi, V. (1974) Ethnocentrism and causal attribution in a S. Indian context. *Journal of Cross-Cultural Psychology*, 5, 162–71.

Taylor, G. (1993) Challenges from the margins. In J. Clarke (ed.), *A Crisis in Care*. London: Sage.

Templin, M. (1957) *Certain Language Skills in Children: Their Development and Interrelationships*. University of Minnesota Institute of Child Welfare Monograph, 26.

Terrace, H. S. (1980) *Nim*. London: Methuen.

Thelen, E., Fisher, D. M. and Ridley-Johnson, R. (1984) The relationship between physical growth and a newborn reflex. *Infant Behaviour and Development*, 7, 479–93.

Thelen, E. and Smith, L. B. (1994) *A Dynamic Systems Approach to Cognition and Action*. Cambridge, Mass.: MIT Press.

Thomas, A. and Chess, S. (1977) *Temperament and Development*. New York: Brunner-Messel.

Thomas, W. I. and Znaniecki, F. (1918) *The Polish Peasant in Europe and America*. Boston: Badger.

Thompson, R. A., Tinsley, B. R., Scalora, M. J. and Parke, R. D. (1989) Grandparents' visitation rights: Legalizing the ties that bind. *American Psychologist*, 44, 1217–22.

Thorndike, E. L. (1911) *Animal Intelligence*. New York: Macmillan.

Thorpe, W. H. (1963; 2nd edn) *Learning and Instinct in Animals*. Cambridge, Mass.: Harvard University Press.

Thurstone, L. L. (1928) Attitudes can be measured. *American Journal of Sociology*, 33, 529–54.

Thurstone, L. L. (1931) *Multiple Factor Analysis*. Chicago: University of Chicago Press.

Tinsley, B. J. and Parke, R. D. (1984) Grandparents as support and socialization agents. In M. Lewis (ed.), *Beyond the Dyad*. New York: Plenum.

Tognoli, J. (1987) Residential environments. In D. Stokols and I. Altman (eds), *Handbook of Environmental Psychology*. New York: John Wiley and Sons.

Tolman, E. C. (1948) Cognitive maps in rats and men. *Psychological Review*, 55, 189–209.

Torrell, G. and Beil, A. (1985) Parental restriction and children's aquisition of neighbourhood knowledge. In T. Gärling and J. Valsiner (eds), *Children Within Environments*. New York: Plenum.

Torrey, E. F. (1991) A viral-anatomical explanation of schizophrenia. *Schizophrenia Bulletin*, 17, 15–18.

Trafimow, D., Triandis, H. C. and Goto, S. G. (1991) Some tests of the distincthÅn between the private and the collective self. *Journal of Personality and Social Psychology*, 60, 649–55.

Triandis, H. (1989) Self and social behavior in different cultural contexts. *Psychological Review*, 96, 269–89.

Triplett, N. (1898) The dynamogenic factors in pacemaking and competition. *American Journal of Psychology*, 2, 507–33.

Trivers, R. L. (1971) The evolution of reciprocal altruism. *Quarterly Review of Biology*, 46, 35–57.

Tuckman, B. W. (1965) Development sequences in small groups. *Psychological Bulletin*, 63, 384–99.

Tulving, E. (1972) Episodic and semantic memory. In E. Tulving and W. Donaldson (eds), *The Organization of Memory*. New York: Academic Press.

Tulving, E. (1983) *Elements of Episodic Memory*. Oxford: Oxford University Press.

Tulving, E. (1989) Memory, performance, knowledge and experience. *European Journal of Cognitive Psychology*, 1, 3–26.

Tulving, E. and Osler, S. (1968) Effectiveness of retrieval cues in memory for words. *Journal Experimental Psychology*, 77, 593–601.

Tulving, E., Schacter, D. L. and Stark, H. A. (1982)

Priming effects in word-fragment completion are independent of recognition memory. *Journal of Experimental Psychology: Learning, Memory and Cognition*, 8, 336–42.

Tulving, E. and Thomson, D. M. (1973) Encoding specificity and retrieval processes in episodic memory. *Psychological Review*, 80, 353–73.

Tversky, A. and Kahneman, D. (1971) Belief in the law of small numbers. *Psychological Bulletin*, 76, 105–10

Tversky, A. and Kahneman, D. (1974) Judgement under uncertainty: Heuristics and biases. *Science*, 125, 1124–31.

Tversky, A. and Kahneman, D. (1982) Judgements of and by representativeness. In D. Kahneman, P. Slovic and A. Tversky (eds), *Judgement under Uncertainty: Heuristics and Biases*. Cambridge: Cambridge University Press, 84–98.

Tyerman, A. and Spencer, C. P. (1983) A critical test of the Sherifs' Robbers' Cave experiments: Intergroup competition and cooperation between groups of well aquainted individuals. *Small Group Behaviour*, 14, 515–31.

Tyszkowa, M. (1991) The role of grandparents in the development of grandchildren as perceived by adolescents and young adults in Poland. In P. K. Smith (ed.), *The Psychology of Grandparenthood: An International Perspective*. London: Routledge.

Ultan, R. (1969) Some general characteristics of interrogative systems. *Working Papers in Language Universals*, 1, 41–63.

Ungar, S., Blades, M., Morsley, K. and Spencer, C. P. (1994) Can visually impaired children use tactile maps to estimate directions? *Journal of Visual Impairment and Blindness*, 88, 221–33.

Valentine, C. W. (1942) *The Psychology of Early Childhood*. London: Methuen.

Valian, V. (1986) Syntactic categories in the speech of young children. *Developmental Psychology*, 22, 562–79.

Velten, H. (1943) The growth of phonemic and lexical patterns in infant language. *Language*, 19, 281–92.

Verafaellie, M., Bauer, R. M. and Bowers, D. (1991) Autonomic and behavioral evidence of implicit memory in amnesia. *Brain and Cognition*, 15, 10–25.

Vernon, P. E. (1950) *The Structure of Human Abilities*. London: Methuen.

Vidmar, N. and Rokeach, M. (1974) Archie Bunker's bigotry: A study in selective perception and exposure. *Journal of Communications*, 24, 36–47.

Visalberghi, E. and Limongelli, L. (1994) Lack of comprehension of cause–effect relationships in tool-using capuchin monkeys (*Cebus apella*). *Journal of Comparative Psychology*, 103, 5–20.

Visalberghi, E. and Trinca, L. (1987) Tool use in capuchin monkeys: distinguishing between performing and understanding. *Primates*, 30, 511–21.

Voss, J. F., Greene, T. R., Post, T. A. and Penner, B. C. (1983) Problem-solving skill in the social-sciences. *Psychology of Learning and Motivation-Advances In Research and Theory*, 17, 165–213.

Vroom, V. H. (1964) *Work and Motivation*. New York: John Wiley and Sons.

Vygotsky, L. S. (1934; trans. 1962) *Thought and Language*. Cambridge, Mass.: MIT Press.

Vygotsky, L. S. (1978) *Mind in Society*. Cambridge, Mass.: Harvard University Press.

Wagner, D. A. (1978) Memories of Morocco: The influence of age, schooling, and environment on memory. *Cognitive Psychology*, 10, 1–28.

Wagner, U. and Ward, P. L. (1993) Variation of outgroup presence and evaluation of the in-group. *British Journal of Social Psychology*, 32, 241–52.

Waldman, D. A. and Avolio, B. J. (1986) A meta-analysis of age differences in job performance. *Journal of Applied Psychology*, 71, 33–8.

Wallerstein, J. S., Corbin, S. B. and Lewis, J. M. (1988) Children of divorce: A 10-year study. In E. M. Hetherington and J. P. Arasteh (eds), *Impact of Divorce, Single Parenting and Stepparenting on Children*. Hillsdale, NJ: Lawrence Erlbaum.

Walsh, W. B., Craik, K. H. and Price, R. H. (1992) *Person–Environment Psychology*. Hillsdale, NJ: Erlbaum.

Walton, G. E., Bower, N. J. A. and Bower, T. G. R. (1992) Recognition of familiar faces by newborns. *Infant Behaviour and Development*, 15, 265–9.

Wason, P. C. (1960) On the failure to eliminate hypotheses in a conceptual task. *Quarterly Journal of Experimental Psychology*, 12, 129–40.

Wason, P. C. (1966) Reasoning. In B. Foss (ed.), *New Horizons in Psychology*. Harmondsworth: Penguin, 135–51.

Wason, P. C. and Brooks, P. G. (1979) THOG: The anatomy of a problem. *Psychological Research*, 41, 79–90.

Wason, P. C. and Evans, J. St B. T. (1975) Dual processes in reasoning? *Cognition*, 3, 141–54.

Wason, P. C. and Johnson-Laird, P. N. (1972) *Psychology of Reasoning: Structure and Content*. London: Batsford.

Wason, P. C. and Shapiro, D. A. (1971) Natural and contrived experience in a reasoning problem. *Quarterly Journal of Experimental Psychology*, 23, 63–71.

Waterman, A. S. (1988) Identity status theory and Erikson's theory: Communalities and differences. *Developmental Review*, 8, 185–208.

Watson, J. B. (1924) *Behaviourism*. New York: Norton.

Watson, J. B. and Rayner, R. (1920) Conditioned emotional reactions. *Journal of Experimental Psychology*, 3, 1–14.

Watson, O. M. and Graves, T. D. (1966) Quantitative research in proxemic behaviour. *American Anthropologist*, 68, 971–85.

Wechsler, D. (1981) *Manual for the Wechsler Adult Intelligence Scale – Revised*. New York: Psychological Corporation.

Weiman, C. (1977) A study of occupational stressors and the incidence of disease risk. *Journal of Occupational Medicine*, 19, 119–22.

Weizenbaum, J. (1966) ELIZA – a computer program for the study of natural language communication between man and machine. *Communications of the ACM*, 9, 36–45.

Weizenbaum, J. (1976) *Computer Power and Human Reason*. New York: W. H. Freeman.

Wellman, H. M. (1990) *The Child's Theory of Mind*. Cambridge Mass.: Bradford Books.

Wellman, H. M. and Lempers, J. D. (1977) The naturalistic communicative abilities of two-year-olds. *Child Development*, 48, 1052–7.

Werner, E. E. (1991) Grandparent–grandchild relationships amongst US ethnic groups. In P. K. Smith (ed.), *The Psychology of Grandparenthood: An International Perspective*. London: Routledge.

Werner, P. D. and Middlestadt, S. E. (1979) Factors in the use of oral contraceptives by young women. *Journal of Applied Social Psychology*, 9, 537–47.

Wetherell, M. (1987) Social identity. In J. C. Turner, M. A. Hogg, P. J. Oakes, S. D. Reicher and M. S. Wetherell (eds), *Rediscovering the Social Group: A Self-categorization Theory*. Oxford: Blackwell.

Wickens, C. D. (1992; 2nd edn) *Engineering Psychology and Human Performance*. New York: Harper-Collins.

Wicker, A. W. (1969) Attitudes versus actions: The relationship of verbal and overt behavioral responses to attitude objects. *Journal of Social Issues*, 25, 41–7.

Wicker, A. W. (1979) *An Introduction to Ecological Psychology*. Pacific Grove, Calif.: Brooks/Cole.

Wilcox, B. M. (1969) Visual preferences of human infants for representations of the human face. *Journal of Experimental Child Psychology*, 7, 10–20.

Wilkinson, G. S. (1984) Reciprocal food sharing in the vampire bat. *Nature*, 181–4.

Wimmer, H. and Perner, J. (1983) Beliefs about beliefs: Representations and constraining function of wrong beliefs in young children's understanding of deception. *Cognition*, 13, 103–28.

Winch, R. F. (1967) Another look at complementary needs in mate selection. *Journal of Marriage and the Family*, 29, 756–62.

Wingfield, A. (1979) *Human Learning and Memory: An Introduction*. New York: Harper and Row.

Winograd, T. (1985) What does it mean to understand language? In A. M. Aitkenhead and J. M. Slack (eds), *Issues in Cognitive Modelling*. Hillsdale, NJ: Lawrence Erlbaum.

Wissler, C. (1901) The correlation of mental and physical tests. *The Psychological Review, Monograph Supplement*, 3/6.

Wober, M. (1974) Towards an understanding of the Kiganda concept of intelligence. In J. W. Berry and P. Dasen (eds), *Culture and Cognition: Readings in Cross-Cultural Psychology*. London: Methuen.

Wolff, P. H. (1966) The causes, controls and organization of behavior in the neonate. *Psychological Issues*, 5 (Monograph no. 17).

Wong, C. Y., Sommer, R. and Cook, E. J. (1992) The soft classroom seventeen years later. *Journal of Environmental Psychology*, 12, 337–44.

Wood, D. J., Wood, H. A. and Middleton, D. J. (1978) An experimental evaluation of four face-to-face teaching strategies. *International Journal of Behavioral Development*, 1, 131–47.

Woodward, J. (1965) *Industrial Organization: Theory and Practice*. London: Oxford University Press.

Woodworth, R. S. and Sells, S. B. (1935) An atmosphere effect in formal syllogistic reasoning. *Journal of Experimental Psychology*, 18, 451–60.

Wright, J., Binney, V. and Smith, P. K. (1995) Security of attachment in 8- to 12-year-olds: A revised version of the Separation Anxiety Test, its psychometric properties and clinical interpretation. *Journal of Child Psychology and Psychiatry*, 36, 757–74.

Wylie, R. (1979). *The Self-Concept*. Lincoln, Neb.: University of Nebraska Press.

Young, M. (1958) *The Rise of the Meritocracy 1870–2033*. Harmondsworth: Penguin Books.

Young, T. (1948 [1801]) Observations on vision. In W. Dennis (ed.), *Readings in the History of Psychology*. New York: Appleton-Century-Crofts, 96–101.

Zajonc, R. B. (1965) Social facilitation. *Science*, 1429, 269–74.

Zeki, S. (1980) The representation of colours in the visual cortex. *Nature*, 284, 412–18.

Zeskind, P. S. (1980) Adult responses to cries of low and high risk infants. *Infant Behaviour and Development*, 3, 167–78.